Right Word
Wrong Word

Words and structures
confused and misused
by learners of English

L. G. Alexander

Longman

Pearson Education Limited
Edinburgh Gate, Harlow
Essex CM20 2JE, England
and Associated Companies throughout the world.

www.longman-elt.com

First published 1994
Seventh impression 2001
Illustrated by Chris Ryley

British Library Cataloguing in Publication Data
Alexander, L. G.
    Right Word Wrong Word: Words and
    Structures Confused and Misused by
    Learners of English. - (Longman
    English Grammar Series)
    I. Title II. Ryley, Chris
    III. Series
    428.24
    ISBN 0-582-21860-8

Library of Congress Cataloging-in-Publication Data
Alexander, L.G.
    Right word wrong word: words and structures confused and misused
    by learners of English/L. G. Alexander.
        p.   cm.
    Includes bibliographical references and index.
    ISBN 0-582-21860-8
    1. English language--Usage. 2. English language--Errors of usage.
    I. Title.
    PE1460.A48   1993
    428.2'4--dc20   93-11963
                                                         CIP

We have been unable to trace the copyright holder of the text for
Exercise 52 *Everybody, Somebody, Anybody, Nobody* and would
appreciate any information that would enable us to do so.

Set in Times New Roman, TrueType

Printed in Malaysia, PP

ISBN 0 582 21860 8

Acknowledgements

I would express my sincere thanks to the following people who supplied extremely useful data while this work was being developed:

Julia Alexander
Mohamed Eid, Cairo, Egypt
Professor Jacek Fisiak, O.B.E., Adam Mickiewicz University, Poznan, Poland
Cristina Germanis, Verona, Italy
Jürgen Kienzler, Ludwigsburg, Germany
Roy Kingsbury
Professor Hanna Komorowska, University of Warsaw, Poland
Gottfried Kumpf, Vaihingen, Germany
Chris Lynch, Tokyo, Japan
Penelope Parfitt
Professor T. Takenaka, Kagawa University, Japan

Longman English Grammar Series

by L. G. Alexander

Longman English Grammar: a reference grammar for English as a foreign language
Step by Step 1-3: graded grammar exercises (beginners' to pre-intermediate level)
Longman English Grammar Practice: reference and practice (intermediate level)
Longman Advanced Grammar: reference and practice (advanced level)
The Essential English Grammar: a handy reference grammar (all levels)

Contents

Upper Intermediate to Advanced Level

Introduction

About *Right Word Wrong Word*

Little green men

In 1877 the Italian astronomer Giovanni Schiaparelli (1835-1910) observed some markings on the planet Mars which he referred to as *canali*. This was mistranslated into English as *canals*, suggesting man-made structures and the existence of intelligent life on Mars, instead of *channels*, which occur naturally. The idea of *canals* appealed to the imaginations of scientists and novelists alike. The astronomer Percival Lowell used it as the basis for his 'scientific observations', recorded in such works as *Mars and its Canals* (1908). The novelist H.G. Wells was inspired to write his powerful story about the invasion of the earth by Martians, *The War of the Worlds* (1898). In 1938, a simulated newscast of this novel was broadcast, describing the Martian invasion of New Jersey, which reduced millions of listeners to a state of near panic. The idea of Martians was not exploded till 1965 when the US spacecraft Mariner 4 sent back close-up pictures of Mars, which proved conclusively that there were no canals and no little green men!

The story shows how powerfully mother tongue *interference* can affect our understanding of a foreign language, with unpredictable consequences. It also shows how we have to suppress our own language if we want to acquire a foreign language.

What is *Right Word Wrong Word*?

Right Word Wrong Word is a Reference and Practice Book based on common errors in English. It covers items like the following:

- Words often confused, where the student's native language interferes with English (false friends): for example, *benzine/petrol*.
- Word-confusions that exist within English itself: for example, *rob/steal/burgle*.
- Structures in the student's language that interfere with English structures: for example, *it has* compared with *there is/it is*.
- Confusions of structures within English itself: for example, *must/had to*.
- Particular words and structures which are a well-known source of error: for example, *get* and *enjoy*.

Right Word Wrong Word is therefore a comprehensive usage book that provides answers to students' questions that are not easily available from any other source.

Who is the book for?

The book is suitable for students of English as a foreign or second language at intermediate level and above, whether they are preparing for examinations or not. It is also suitable for teachers. It extends the knowledge of non-native teachers by clarifying the meanings and uses of related items; it sensitizes native-speaking teachers by making them aware of mistakes that students really make. For both kinds of teachers, it is a handy reference for dealing with awkward questions on the spot.

The basis of the selection

I have been collecting 'right word wrong word' items since the early 1960s and my collection has grown into a large database. This database was checked against the *Longman Learners' Corpus* (drawn from 70 countries) and then filtered through a representative spread of languages, including Arabic, European (Germanic, Romance, Greek, Slavonic) and Asiatic (Japanese). The words in this collection are the survivors of the original database that followed this investigation and number more than 5,000 items.

A description of the material
The material consists of the following sections:
- A reference section (pages 1-201)
- Test Yourself (pages 203-283)
- Answer Key (pages 284-288)
- Technical Terms (pages 289-290)
- Index (pages 291-308)

How to use *Right Word Wrong Word*

Index
If you are in doubt about the use of a word, look in the index to find it, then go to the reference section. You may have to do this more than once to locate the meaning you are looking for. When you find the word you want, check whether the mistake listed is one you are likely to make yourself and which you must train yourself to suppress.

The reference section
The 'wrong word' is generally listed first, followed by the 'right word'. For example:

> **block • pad**
> – *I've brought this nice new **pad** to take notes*
>   *during the meeting.* (Not *block*)
>   (*pad/writing pad* = sheets of paper held
>   together, used for writing or drawing)
> – *How did the ancient Egyptians cut and move*
>   *such huge stone **blocks**?*
>   (= stone, wood, etc., cut with straight sides)

Some words appear in different places. For example, *mark* has its own entry, but is also listed under *grade/mark/degree*, *note down/mark* and *speck/spot/mark*. The reference section focuses sharply on particular problems of contrast or use. It is not a dictionary and so does not deal with every possible meaning of a particular word.

Technical terms
The terms used in the reference section are briefly explained on pages 289-290.

Test Yourself
Exercises 1-41 are suitable for students of all levels, but especially for intermediate; exercises 42-96 are upper intermediate and advanced. The exercises deal with topics (e.g. *health*), functions (e.g. *doing things for people*) or grammar (e.g. *phrasal verbs*). You may work through the exercises in the order they occur, or pick and choose, according to level.

1. Attempt an exercise, then check your answers in the answer key.
2. Look up any item or items you aren't sure of in the index, which will refer you to the reference section.

Practise using the items you have learned in your own speech and writing.

A

a • an

- *Kirsty's got an M.A. in history.*
  (Not *a M.A. in history*)
- *She's got a Master's degree.*
  (Not *an Master's degree*)
  (*a* + consonant sound; *an* + vowel sound)

a/an • one

- *I need a screwdriver to do this job properly.*
  (Not *one screwdriver*)
- *It was one coffee I ordered, not two.*
  (Not *a coffee*)
  (*a/an* = 'any one', 'it doesn't matter which';
  one, two, etc., when we are counting)

a/an • some

- *Please bring me a glass/an envelope.*
- *I want some glasses/some envelopes.*
- *I want some water.* (Not *a water*)
- *I'd like a coffee please.*
  (*some* = an unspecified number or amount is
  the plural of *a/an* where the reference is to
  quantity; we normally use *a/an* only with
  countable nouns. We also use *a/an* for all
  drinks seen as a complete measure: *a coffee,
  a beer,* but use *some* for fluids of which
  there is more in the tap, bottle, etc.: *some
  water, some wine*)

a/an • (-)

- *Lucy wants to be a doctor.*
  (Not *wants to be doctor*)
- *Kevin wants to be an electrician.*
  (Not *wants to be electrician*)
  (*a/an* + singular countable noun)

ability to

- *I wasn't happy at school until I found I had
  the ability to make people laugh.*
  (Not *ability of/on making*)
  (from *able to*)

able • possible

- *It will be possible to see you on Friday.*
  (Not *It will be able*)
- *I'll be able to see you on Friday.*
  (Not *I'll be possible*)
  (*It* + *possible*; human subject + *able*)

about • around

- *Few people can afford to go on a cruise
  (a)round the world.* (Not *about*)
  ((*a)round* for circular movement)
- *They've built a motorway (a)round London.*
  (= surrounding, encircling)

- *The fax was received at around/about 8 pm.*
  (= approximately; but *approximately* in
  place of *around* and *about* is very formal)
- *The journey took about/around an hour.*
  (Not *an hour about* *an hour around*)
  (preposition + object)

about • on • over

- *Have you read this article on the Antarctic?*
- *There's an article about tourism in today's
  paper.* (preferable to *on*)
  (*on* for serious and specific information;
  about for general interest)
- *Let's agree to differ. Let's not have an
  argument over/about it.* (Not *on*)
  (*over* after *argument, concern, dispute*)

abroad

- *John has gone/is abroad on business.*
  (Not *has gone to abroad/is at abroad*)
  (*abroad* is an adverb, not a noun; *be/live/go
  abroad* are fixed phrases, otherwise we have
  to say *come/return from abroad,* where
  abroad is used as a noun)

absent oneself • absent

- *Where's Jane today? - She's absent. I think
  she's ill.* (Not *She has absented herself.*)
- *The soldier absented himself without leave
  for three weeks and was arrested.*
  (*be absent from* = 'not present'; *absent
  oneself* implies deliberate rule-breaking)

absent • away

- *I'm going on holiday and I'll be away for a
  fortnight.* (preferable to *absent*)
- *How many students were absent from your
  class today?* (Not *away*)
  (*away* = elsewhere; *absent* = not present)

abstracted • absent-minded • distracted

- *Professor Boffin is generally very absent-
  minded.* (Not *abstracted* *distracted*)
  (= not paying attention to present reality)
- *Sorry, I didn't hear what you said. I was
  abstracted for a moment.*
  (= thinking about something else)
- *Sorry, I didn't hear what you said. I was
  distracted by the telephone.*
  (i.e. something claimed my attention)

abuse • insult • swear at • curse

- *The sergeant major abused the soldiers
  unmercifully.*
  (= shouted at them and called them names)
- *Mrs Tomkins insulted the bride's family by
  refusing to attend her son's wedding.*
  (= behaved in a way that caused offence)

- *Traffic wardens rightly ignore motorists who **swear at** them.*
  (= use foul language)
- *Before he died, the religious leader **cursed** all enemies of the faith.*
  (= asked God to do them harm)
- *Don't **curse/swear** under your breath.*

accede to • comply with
- *You'll get into trouble if you don't **comply with** the planning laws.* (Not *accede to*)
  (= obey, go along with)
- *I **acceded to** his request for a reference.* (Not *complied with*)
  (= agreed to, consented to; formal)

accept • agree to/with
- *They invited me to their wedding and I've **agreed to go**.* (Not *accepted to go*)
  (*agree to do* something)
- *She offered me some clothes her children had grown out of and I **accepted** them.*
  (*accept* + object = take what is offered)
- *I don't **accept** your opinion/**agree with** your opinion that we can't control inflation.*
  (*agree with* an opinion)

accept • allow • admit
- *They won't **admit** anyone to the theatre/**allow** anyone into the theatre after the performance has started.* (Not *accept*)
  (= give someone the right to go in)
- *If the performance has started, they just won't **allow you in/admit you**.* (Not *admit you in* *allow you* *accept you*)
  (= let you go in)
- *I applied to join the club, but they won't **accept** me.* (Not *admit* *allow*)
  (= let me join)

accessories • spare parts • reserve • spare tyre
- *My car hasn't been repaired yet because the garage is still waiting for **spare parts**.* (Not *accessories* *reserves*)
  (= essential replacement parts to keep a machine in running order)
- *My new car has a whole lot of **accessories**, including a roof rack.* (Not *reserves*)
  (= additional, but not essential parts)
- *Where is the **spare tyre** kept in this vehicle?* (Not *reserve* *reserve tyre*)
- *Does this motorbike have a **reserve** fuel tank?* (Not *spare*)
  (i.e. which could be used if needed)

accident • incident • episode
- *Someone rammed the back of my car. It was an unfortunate **accident**.* (Not *episode*)
  (= an unplanned happening, often bad)
- *There was an unpleasant **incident** on the train this morning when a drunk attacked one of the passengers.* (Not *episode*)
  (= a single happening, good or bad)
- *That was an **episode/incident** in my life which I'm not proud of.*
  (*episode* = one part of a continuing story)

accidentally • unfortunately
- *I knocked on your door, but **unfortunately** you were out.* (Not *accidentally*)
  (= unluckily)
- *I've **accidentally** dialled the wrong number.*
  (= by chance, by mistake)

accommodation
- *While touring Britain, we found (**some**) excellent **accommodation** in old inns.*
  (note the spelling, not *accomodation* *acommodation*; uncountable: not *an accommodation*; the plural form *accommodations* is AmE only)

accomplish • perform
- *Soldiers must **perform** their duties without asking questions.* (Not *accomplish*)
  (= do a task, a service)
- *Churchill **accomplished** a great deal while he was Prime Minister.* (Not *performed*)
  (= succeeded in doing)

accomplishment • achievement • completion
- *The re-unification of Germany was a great **achievement**.* (preferable to *accomplishment*)
  (= something successfully done)
- *She has many **accomplishments**, including a command of three foreign languages.*
  (= acquired skills)
- *Did the **completion** of the Eurotunnel go according to plan?*
  (Not *achievement* *accomplishment*)
  (= finishing)

accord • behalf • account • part
- *We're acting **on behalf of** our client/**on our client's behalf**.* (Not *accord* *part*)
- *Don't go to all that trouble **on my behalf/on my account**.* (Not *on my accord*)
  (= for me)
- *That was a mistake **on my part**.*
  (= by me)
- *I didn't ask her to do the washing-up. She did it **of her own accord**.* (Not *of/on her*

own behalf* *on her own accord*)
(= without being asked)

according to • by • in my opinion
- *It's 4.30 according to/by the station clock.*
  (= as shown by; both possible when referring to clocks and watches)
- *According to many scientists, the level of the oceans is rising.* (Not **By**)
  (= as stated by other people)
- *In my opinion, scientists take a pessimistic view.* (Not **According to my opinion/To me* *To/After/By my opinion**)

account: on any/no account
- *You mustn't disturb him on any account. On no account must you disturb him.*
  (Not **with no account/in any account**)

account • deposit
- *They won't accept an order for goods without a deposit.*
  (= part payment in advance)
- *I've opened an account with Westland Bank.* (Not **a deposit**)
- *I've just transferred money to my (current) account from my deposit account.*
  (*a bank account* = where money is paid in or out; a *deposit* at a bank or anywhere else is a sum of money held by someone who is not the owner)

accusation
- *I want to know who made this accusation against me.* (Not **did this accusation**)
  (some other nouns that combine with *make*: *an agreement, an announcement, an apology, an application, an appointment, an attempt, a change, a choice, a claim, comments, a criticism, a difference, an effort, an escape, an exception, an experiment, a fortune, a gesture, a habit of something, a law, love, a mistake, a name for oneself, an offer, peace, plans, progress, a proposal, room for someone, a start, a success of something, a suggestion, war, a will, a wish*)

accused: the accused
- *The accused have nothing to say for themselves.*
- *The accused has nothing to say for himself/herself.*
  (*the accused* is used in formal legal contexts to refer to one person or more than one, but we have to say *he's/she's accused*, not **he's/she's an accused* *they're accuseds**)

ache • hurt • pain
- *My head hurts.* (Not **pains**)
  (intransitive use: you feel pain, possibly from injury)
- *I hurt my foot.* (Not **ached* *pained* *hurted**; irregular verb: *hurt - hurt - hurt*)
  (transitive use = injured)
- *My head aches.* (Not **pains**)
  (intransitive; you feel dull, constant pain)
- *It pains me to recall my schooldays.*
  (= makes me feel sad)

acoustics
- *The acoustics in ancient Greek theatres are amazing.* (Not **acoustics is* *acoustic is**)
  (plural form + plural verb for specific references)
- *Acoustics is a branch of physics.*
  (Not **The acoustic is**)
  (plural form + singular verb to refer to the academic subject)

acquire • gain/increase in value
- *Property has gained/increased in value considerably over the last ten years.*
  (Not **acquired (in) value**)
- *As our company is expanding, we've had to acquire more office space.* (Not **gain**)
  (= obtain, e.g. by buying or renting)

across • over • through
- *They're laying a pipeline across Siberia.*
  (Not **over* *through**)
  (*across* = from one side to the other of a surface area)
- *We skated over the frozen lake.*
  (*over* = on or above a surface, not necessarily from one side to the other)
- *Water flows through this pipe.*
- *It was difficult to cut through the forest.*
  (*through* = movement within a solid or enclosing medium)

act • action • deed
- *The situation requires immediate action.*
  (Not **act* *deed**)
  (= doing something, often as a response)
- *I shall always remember her many acts of kindness to me.* (Not **actions* *deeds**)
  (*act of* + noun phrase, not **action**; *act* = specific thing done; *action* = a move to do something; *act/action* are interchangeable after adjectives: *It was a kind act/action.*)
- *Visiting Mrs Hollis in hospital was a good deed that had to be done.* (Not **act/action**)
  (*deed* is only used in a context where an *action* is being judged: *a good/evil deed*)

act • take effect

- *Has the medicine **taken effect** yet?*
  (Not **acted**)
  (= had a specific effect)
- *This drug **acts/takes effect** quickly in the system.*
  (= has a general effect on)
  (Compare: *This drug **acts on/affects** the central nervous system.*)

action • campaign

- *The government is launching a **campaign** against smoking.* (Not **an action**)
  (= a planned series of actions)
- *The government's **action** to control interest rates has been very prompt.*
  (= a move to do something)

actual • news

- *Have you seen the **news report** on malaria?*
  (Not **actual report**)
  (= the one reported in the news)
- *I've read the **actual report** on malaria.*
  (= that report, the real thing)

actual • real • topical • up-to-date

- *Public transport is a highly **topical** issue at present because of the row over the new bypass.* (Not **actual**)
  (i.e it's in the news)
- *The **real/actual** problem is the civil war.*
  (= true, the one we are concerned with)
- *I can't comment before I have read the **actual report**.* (Not **real report**)
  (= the report itself)
- *Magazines in doctors' waiting rooms are never **up-to-date**.* (Not **actual** **topical**)

actualities • the news • current events

- *You should take a daily paper if you want to keep track of **the news/of current events**.*
  (Not **actualities**)
  (= facts that are reported)
- *Before you pass judgement, you should consider the **actualities** of the case.*
  (= the true conditions, circumstances)

actually • at present/for the present • at the moment

- *Frank's been travelling for a month now. **At present/For the present/At the moment**, I have no idea of his whereabouts.*
  (Not **Actually** **To the present**)
  (= now, for the time being)
- *Do you realize that Martin has **actually** been off work for a month now?*
  (= as a matter of fact, really)

adapt (to) • adopt • adjust (to)

- *We have **adopted** the same sort of assembly methods they use in Japan.* (Not **adapted**)
  (= taken and used)
- *We have **adapted** the assembly system they use in Japan to suit our circumstances here.*
  (Not **adopted**)
  (= changed it to suit our needs)
- *I have found it difficult to **adapt to/adjust to** living in the country after living in a large city.* (Not **adjust myself to**; preferable to *adapt myself to*)
  (= become used to)
- *The picture is out of focus. Could you **adjust** it slightly please?* (Not **adapt**)
  (= change it in order to correct it)

addition • bill • account

- *Would you bring me the **bill** please?*
  (Not **addition** **account**)
  (= the account for immediate payment)
- *I've just received a **bill/an account** from my solicitors.* (Not **an addition**)
  (= a formal application for payment)
- *Old-style grocers were good at **addition**.*
  (= adding numbers together)

adieu • goodbye

- *It's time to say **goodbye**.* (Not **adieu**)
- *We bade them **adieu/goodbye** and left.*
  (*bid adieu* is old-fashioned, literary)

admire

- ***I admire** Mozart's music more than anyone else's.* (Not **I'm admiring**)
  (stative use: my admiration is involuntary)
- *Where's Fred? - **He's admiring** your garden.* (Not **He admires**)
  (dynamic use = at this moment he's looking at your garden with admiration)

admire • wonder • admiration

- *I **wonder** why she's left.* (Not **admire**)
  (= I'm puzzled)
- *I **admire** the Pompidou building in Paris.*
  (Not **wonder** **wonder at**)
  (= I look at it with approval/pleasure)
- *Rowland Emmet's creations fill me with **wonder/admiration**.* (Not **admire**)
  (*wonder*, noun = astonishment; *admiration* = strong approval)

admit (to)

- *Sally **admits to using** your computer.*
  (*admit to* = confess)
- *Sally **admits using/that she used** your computer.* (Not **admits to use**)
  (*admit* + object = agree something is true)

- The man **admitted his guilt to the police**.
  (Not *admitted the police his guilt*
  admitted to the police his guilt)

admittance • admission
- What's the **admission**? - £3 a head.
  (Not *admittance*)
  (= the cost of entry)
- You need to be accompanied by a member to
  gain **admission/admittance** to the club.
  (admission = being allowed in; admittance =
  being allowed in by the authorities; note No
  Admission = 'you won't be allowed in' and
  No Admittance = 'the authorities won't allow
  you in'; compare entry/entrance, which don't
  refer to the idea of permission)

adore • worship
- At which church do you **worship**?
  (Not *adore*)
- I **adore** staying in Rome. (Not *worship*)
  (= I really love it)
- As far as Sylvia is concerned, her son is
  perfect. She **adores/worships** him.
  (adore and worship with reference to people
  are usually interchangeable)

advance • progress
- Now that we've mastered this step, we can
  progress to the next one.
  (preferable to advance)
- We began our new course book in May and
  advanced/progressed rapidly.
- **Advance** two squares. (Not *Progress*)
  (both advance and progress mean 'go
  forward', but advance is usually physical/
  concrete, while progress means go forward
  in the sense of 'improve')

advantage: take advantage of
- **Take advantage of** our offer of a 50%
  reduction in package tours.
- If you're having to work every weekend, your
  boss **is taking advantage of** you.
  (take advantage of something = make the
  most of; take advantage of someone = make
  unfair use of; it can also mean 'exploit
  sexually' as in: Doctors are forbidden to
  take advantage of their patients.)

adventure • by chance • incidentally
- We met **by chance/incidentally** at an office
  party. (Not *by adventure*)
  (= without expecting to: by accident)
- I've just opened the back door, which,
  incidentally, was unlocked all night.
  (Not *by chance*)
  (= by the way)

- When we rowed out to sea in our dinghy, we
  didn't expect to have such an **adventure**.
  (= an unusual, dangerous experience)

adventure • experience
- People who have been tortured can't forget
  the terrible **experience**. (Not *adventure*)
  (= what happened to them)
- Jim had many **adventures** in the jungle but
  lived to tell the tale. (Not *experiences*)
  (= unusual, exciting experiences)

advertisement • warning
- I haven't paid my gas bill and have received
  a final **warning**. (Not *advertisement*)
  (i.e. bringing attention to a possible penalty)
- How much does it cost to place a large
  advertisement in the paper?
  (= an announcement that makes it known
  that something is for sale, etc.)

advice • advise • opinion
- She gave me **(some) good advice about** jobs.
  (uncountable noun spelt -ice, pronounced
  /aɪs/; not *an advice* *(some) advices*
  advice for)
- She **advised** me about applying for jobs.
  (verb spelt -ise, pronounced /aɪz/; not
  adviced me)
- Mr Foley **advised me to apply** to your
  company. (preferable to advised me I should;
  and note: He **advised (me) against applying**.
  = He **advised me not to apply**.)
- I **took your advice** and applied for
  promotion. (Not *took your opinion*)
- I don't know whether my essay is good or
  bad and I'd like to have your **opinion**.
  (advice = what you think I should do;
  opinion = what you think about something)

affair • case • liaison
- Even Inspector Wiley couldn't solve the **case**.
  (Not *affair*)
  (= an event or events that the police are
  looking into)
- What I do in my spare time is entirely my
  own **affair**.
  (= a matter that concerns me, my business)
- Their (love) **affair** became known after his
  death. (Not *case*; liaison here would mean
  'improper relationship')
  (= a sexual relationship, outside marriage)
- There's always been a close **liaison** between
  our two organizations. (Not *affair*)
  (= a link, relationship)

affairs • business
— *Business hasn't been doing very well lately.*
  (Not *Affairs haven't**)
  (= work to do with buying and selling)
— *You can keep your nose out of my affairs.*
  (= matters connected with my private or professional life)

affect • (have an) effect (on) • come into/take effect
— *This hay fever is having a serious effect on my work.* (Not *affect**)
  (*effect* is the noun relating to the verb *affect*: *have an effect on* something)
— *This hay fever is seriously affecting my work.* (Not *effecting**)
  (*affect* is the verb relating to the noun *effect*)
— *The new law comes into effect/takes effect next Monday.* (Not *has an effect/affect**)
  (= will be in operation)
— *Mr Court effected numerous changes while running this company.* (Not *affected**)
  (= brought about, *put into effect*)

affection • affectation • infection
— *Ann is much nicer now that she's lost her silly affectations.* (Not *affections**)
  (= unnatural behaviour to impress others)
— *Don't come near me. I'm suffering from a nasty throat infection.* (Not *affection**)
  (= disease caused by germs or virus)
— *His affection for his family is obvious.*
  (= love, deep fondness for)

affirm • maintain
— *Despite the statistics, you still maintain that inflation is falling.* (Not *affirm**)
  (= claim, whether it's true or not)
— *The witness affirmed it was the same man.*
  (i.e. said he/she believed it)

afford: can/can't afford • have the means
— *We can/can't afford an exotic holiday this year.* (Not *We afford/don't afford**)
  (*can/can't afford* is preferable to *have/don't have the means for/the means to buy*)

afloat • floating
— *The raft was afloat/floating on the river.*
— *The pilot quickly spotted the floating raft.*
  (Not *afloat**)
  (we cannot use *afloat* in front of a noun, only after a noun + *be, seem to be*, etc.)

afraid (of) • frightened (of/by)
— *The children were afraid of/frightened of/frightened by the wicked witch.*
— *We did all we could to comfort the frightened children.* (Not *afraid**)

(we cannot use *afraid* in front of a noun, only after a noun + *be, seem to be*, etc.)

after • afterwards • after that • behind
— *Come and see me after work.*
  (Not *afterwards work**)
  (*after* as a preposition + object; *afterwards* is an adverb and cannot govern a noun)
— *We'll discuss the programme after you arrive.* (Not *afterwards you arrive** *after you will arrive** *after that you arrive** *after to arrive**)
  (*after* as a conjunction + present tense)
— *We made the house tidy and our guests arrived soon afterwards/after.*
  (both possible, but *afterwards* is generally preferable; *after* is used as an adverb only after *soon* and *not long*)
— *We had dinner first. After that/Afterwards, we went to a show.* (Not *After, we went to a show** *After from that**)
— *Stand behind me in the queue.*
  (Not *after** *behind of**)
  (*behind* for position)
— *You're after me in the queue.*
  (*after* for next in turn, sequence)

after • in
— *I'll see you in a week.* (Not *after a week**)
  (= within, before the end of)
— *I'll see you in a week's time.*
  (Not *after a week's time**)
— *It's hard to get back to work after a week on holiday!*
  (= at the end of)

after • later
— *I arrived at the party first, and my husband arrived later.* (Not *arrived after** to refer to time, though we could say *arrived after me* to refer to sequence)
  (= at a later time)
— *I can quote the first line of 'To be or not to be', but I don't know what comes after.*
  (Not *later**)
  (*after* as an adverb, for sequence)

afternoon: this afternoon
— *They're arriving this afternoon.*
  (Not *today afternoon**; compare *tomorrow afternoon, yesterday afternoon*; similarly *morning, evening*)

again • back
— *Sue invited us to dinner last month; it's time we invited her back.* (Not *again**)
  (i.e. returned her hospitality; compare *phone someone back* = return their call)

- *We enjoyed having our neighbours to dinner and we must invite them **again**.*
  (= on another occasion; compare *phone someone again*)

age • epoch • era • period • century
- *The whole **period** was marked by important changes in the earth's surface.*
  (*period* is the best word to refer to geotime)
- *Satellite TV brought in an **epoch** of worldwide communication.*
  (an *epoch* is a period of time beginning with an important event)
- *We live in an **age/era** where fast food is the norm.* (Not *epoch*)
- *There's no way of knowing exactly when the **Iron Age** really began.* (Not *Epoch*)
  (*The Iron Age* is a fixed phrase; compare *in the age* of Shakespeare, etc. = at that time)
- *The Industrial Revolution began in the 18th **century**.* (Not *age*)

age • get old
- *Have you noticed how Mrs Briggs **is getting old/is ageing**?* (Not *is olding*; note the spelling of *ageing*, though *aging* is often seen, especially in AmE)

age • old
- *How **old** is he?* (Not *age* *big*)
- *What **age** is he?* (Not *old* *has he*)
  (*How old ... ?* is generally preferable)
- *How **old** are you? - **I'm ten** (years old).*
  (Not *I'm ten years.* *I have ten years.*)
- *How **old** is your car? - **It's ten years old**.*
  (Not *It has ten years.* *It's ten.*)
  (we can't omit *years old* when referring to the age of a thing)

aged • elderly
- *Who will look after us when we're **elderly**?*
  (Not *aged*)
  (= in or near old age)
- *I was approached by **an elderly man** who asked me for directions.* (Not *an elderly*)
  (we cannot use *elderly* on its own to mean 'an elderly person'; *an elderly man* is preferable to *an aged man*, which is literary, and is more complimentary than *an old man*)
- *Monica devotes a lot of her spare time to helping **the aged/the elderly**.*
  (Not *the ageds* *the elderlies*)
  (*the* + adjective for the group as a whole)
- *Constance looks after her **aged** parents.*
  (= very old; *aged* can be used in front of a few nouns: e.g. *my aged parents, an aged aunt, an aged friend of mine*, etc.)

agenda • diary
- *I've made a note of your birthday in my **diary**.* (Not *agenda*)
  (= a book with spaces for days of the year)
- *What's the first item on the **agenda**?*
  (= schedule of business at a meeting)
- *We had to work through three **agendas**!*
  (Not *agenda*)

agent • representative
- *Who's our company's **agent/representative** in Tokyo?*
  (*agent*: usually someone self-employed who works on a commission; *representative*: usually an employee of a company)

ages • years
- *Children are so carefree in their younger **years**, before they start school.* (Not *ages*)
  (= at that time, during those years)
- *A child's basic personality is formed between the **ages** of one and five.*
  (referring to how old children are)

aggravated • annoyed
- *I got really **annoyed/aggravated** by the bad behaviour of Karen's children.*
  (many native speakers don't accept the widespread use of *aggravate* to mean *annoy*)
- *The bad situation was further **aggravated** by the reinforcement of troops at the border.*
  (Not *annoyed*)
  (= made worse)

agitate • shake • move
- *I could feel the earth **move/shake** as the earthquake began.* (Not *agitate*)
  (*move* suggests a single large movement; *shake* = rapid movements from side to side)
- *We got really **agitated** when our daughter didn't return from school at the usual time.*
  (Not *shaken* *moved*)
  (= very anxious, worried)
- *After the break-in, we felt really **shaken**.*
  (i.e. we were in a state of shock)
- ***Shake** the bottle well before you take any of that medicine.* (Not *Agitate* *Move*)

agony • anxiety
- *He's in a state of **anxiety** waiting for the result of his blood test.* (Not *agony*)
  (= fear of what may happen)
- *I've twisted my ankle and I'm **in agony**.*
  (= extreme pain; *in agony* is a fixed phrase)

agree
- *I **agree with** you.*
  (Not *agree to you* *agree you*)

(*agree with* someone: *agree* is not an adjective: not **I am agree with you.**)
- *I **agree to** the proposal.* (Not *agree with*)
  (*agree to* something)
- *Surely we can **agree on** this.*
  (*on* = about)
- *We live in difficult times. - I **agree**.*
  (Not **I'm agreeing.**)
  (stative use in 'declarations')

agreeable • in agreement (with)
- *I'm entirely **in agreement with** your proposal.* (Not *agreeable with*)
- *I enjoy the company of the Robinsons. They're very **agreeable**.*
  (= nice; the opposite is *disagreeable*)
- *I've discussed the idea with her and she agrees/she's **in agreement/agreeable**.*
  (*in agreement* is preferable to *agreeable*)

ahead (of) • in front (of)
- *In most cars, the engine's **in front**.*
  (Not *ahead*)
- *Right up to the end of the race, College Boy was just **ahead of/in front of** Red Fur.*
- *College Boy was **ahead/in front**.*
  (*in front (of)/behind/at the back* for absolute position; compare *ahead (of)/behind* for position relative to others)

aid • help
- *Please **help** me.* (Not *aid*)
  (*aid* as a verb is unusual; *help* is preferable)
- *Do you know anything about **first aid**?*
  (Not *first aids* *first help* *first helps*)
  (*first aid* is a fixed phrase)
- *They heard our cries and came to our **aid/help**.* (nouns)

air • expression
- *The colonel had an odd **expression** on his face as he listened to the news.* (Not *air*)
  (= facial appearance at a specific moment)
- *Colonel Fawcett has the **air** of someone who has travelled widely.* (Not *expression*)
  (= general appearance)

air • tune • melody
- *The main theme of the symphony is based on a well-known **air/tune/melody**.*
  (*an air* often suggests 'an old melody')
- *Hum 'Yesterday' to me. I can't remember the **tune**.* (Not *air* *melody*)
  (*melody* has a narrower meaning than *tune*, suggesting 'a sweet tune')

air • wind • breeze
- *There's a lot of **wind** today.*
  (Not *air* *breeze*)
  (= moving currents of air)
- *I love to walk in a nice sea **breeze**.*
  (= a pleasant, gentle wind)
- *Is it warm enough to sit **out**/to sit **in the open**/to sit **in the open air**?*
  (Not *in the fresh* *in the full air*)
- *Open the window. I need some **fresh air**.*
  (*air* is what we breathe)
- *I want to send this letter **by air**.*
  (Not *with air* **via/per air** *by plane*)

air-conditioning/air-conditioner • air-conditioned
- ***Turn off** the **air-conditioning**/the **air-conditioner**. I'm freezing!*
  (Not **Close the air-condition.**)
- *The whole building is **air-conditioned**/has **air-conditioning**.* (Not *air-condition*)

alarm • alert • alarmed
- *In case of fire, **alert** the hotel guests.*
  (Not *alarm*)
  (= warn them of the danger)
- *Don't **alarm** us with awful tales about the dangers of air travel.*
  (= make us feel anxious)
- *This door activates an **alarm**.*
  (Not **This door is alarmed.**)
- ***We got alarmed** when we found the door wide open.* (Not *We alarmed*)

alight • burning
- *The bonfire was **alight/burning** and could be seen for miles around.*
- *I can smell **burning** rubber.* (Not *alight*)
  (we cannot use *alight* in front of a noun, only after a noun + *be, seem to be,* etc.)

alike • similar • same
- *We've received two **similar offers**.*
  (Not *alike offers* *same offers*)
- *The two offers are **similar/alike**.*
  (= nearly the same; we cannot use *alike* in front of a noun)
- *The houses in this street are all **the same**/are all **similar**.*
- *Yours is **the same as** mine/**similar to** mine.*
  (Not *the same with* *similar with*)
  (*the same* = exactly alike; *similar* = they resemble each other)

alive • living • live
- *Everything that is **alive/living** (that **lives**) needs air and water.* (Not *live*)

- *Are your grandparents still **alive/living**?*
  (Not **Do your grandparents live?** **Are
  they alives/livings?**)
  (= not dead)
- *All **living** creatures need air and water.*
  (Not **alive** **live**)
- *Careful! It's a **live** lobster./That lobster is
  alive.* (Not **living**)
- *After midnight, there's a cabaret show and
  dancing to **live** music.* (Not **alive** **living**)
  (*living* and *alive* both mean 'not dead', but
  we cannot use *alive* in front of a noun; *live*,
  pronounced /laɪv/, can also mean 'happening
  now/active')
- *Careful! That wire is **live**!*
  (Not **alive** **living**)
  (adjective = electrically charged)

all • everyone • everything • every
- ***Everyone** wanted Marilyn's autograph.*
  (Not **All** **Every people** **Every person**
  All (the) people)
  (we rarely use *all* to mean 'all the people',
  preferring *everyone/everybody*)
- ***All/Everything** I have belongs to you.*
  (it's possible, but unusual, to use *all* to mean
  'all the things'; *everything* is the normal
  word; *all things* to mean *everything* occurs
  only in poetic language)
- ***We all agree/All of us** agree.*
  (Not **All we** **All us**)
- *The company entertained **us all/all of us**.*
  (Not **all us**)
- ***Everyone/Every person** over the age of
  eighteen must fill in this form.*
- ***Everything/Every thing** in this flat is up for
  sale.*
  (*every (single) person* and *every (single)
  thing* are emphatic)

all ready • already
- *I tried to get her on the phone, but she'd
  already left.* (Not **all ready** **allready**)
  (i.e before that time)
- *We're **all ready**.* (Not **already**)
  (= all of us are ready)

all right
- *I feel **all right**.* (preferable to *alright*)
  (*alright* is a common alternative spelling,
  sometimes considered to be less correct)

all that • what • all
- *I didn't catch **what** you said.*
  (Not **all what** **all which** **that which**)
- *I didn't catch **all that** you said.*
  (Not **all what** **all which** **which**)
  (= everything, the thing(s) which)

- ***All we want/What we want/All that we want***
  is to prevent waste. (Not **All what/All
  which/That which we want**)

all these things • all this
- *Who's going to pay for **all this**?*
- *Who's going to pay for **all these things**?*
  (preferable to *all these*)
  (*all these* + noun)

all ways • always
- *They **always** win.*
  (Not **all ways** **allways**)
  (position: before a main verb or after *be,
  have, can*, etc.: *She's **always** late.*)
- *We've looked at the problem **all ways**.*
  (= from all sides)

allowance • permission • pocket money
- *The farmer gave us **permission** to camp in
  his field.* (Not **allowance**)
  (i.e. he allowed us to)
- *We receive an **allowance** from the state for
  each of the children.*
  (= a regular payment of money)
- *How much **pocket money** do your children
  get?*
  (generally refers to spending money given
  regularly by parents to their children)

almost • nearly
- *I think there's **almost/nearly** enough food
  here to feed a dozen people.*
- ***Almost all cars/Nearly all cars** use unleaded
  petrol these days.*
- *There's **not nearly** enough food here to feed
  twenty people.* (Not **not almost**)
  (*nearly* and *almost* are only interchangeable
  in the affirmative)

already • still • yet
- *We must hurry. It's **already** 5 o'clock.*
  (*already* = sooner than expected)
- *There's no hurry. It's **still** early.*
  (*still* is often used in the affirmative)
- *There's no hurry. It **isn't** 5 o'clock **yet**.*
  (*yet* is often used in the negative)
- *Has he arrived **yet**?* (Not **still**) - *No, **not
  yet**.* (Not **not still**)
  (*yet* in questions = up to this point in time)
- *Is he **still** angry?* (Not **yet**)
  (*still* in questions, pointing to continuity)
- *He **hasn't** arrived **yet**.*
  (Not **still** in this position)
  (= up to this point in time)
- *He **still hasn't** arrived.*
  (Not **yet** in this position)
  (*still* in negatives, pointing to continuity)

also • thus/so

- *We went by bus and **thus/so** saved the price of a taxi.* (Not *also*)
  (= consequently; *thus* is more emphatic)
- *The bus is cheaper, but **also** slower.*
  (= in addition)

alternate • alternative • possibilities

- *We must choose from several **possibilities**.*
  (preferable to *alternatives*)
  (i.e. a choice between more than two)
- *We must choose between **alternatives**.*
  (noun = choice between two)
- *That's what we should do - unless you have an **alternative** suggestion.* (Not *alternate*)
  (adjective: i.e. a different suggestion)
- *I visit my parents on **alternate** weekends.*
  (adjective: i.e. every second weekend)

altogether • all together

- *Let's sing it again. **All together** now!*
  (Not *Altogether*)
  (= everyone together)
- *As far as I'm concerned, Frank's proposal is **altogether** nonsensical.*
  (adverb of degree = entirely)

am I not • aren't I

- ***Aren't I** invited?* (Not *Amn't I*)
  (the usual negative question form)
- ***Am I not** invited?*
  (a formal negative question: full form)

am/is/are • have/has been

- *I **have been** in Rio since May.* (Not *I am*)
- *I **am** in Rio at the moment.*
- *I **am** in Rio for two weeks.*
  (this could mean 'I am in the middle of spending two weeks in Rio', or 'I will be visiting Rio soon and will stay two weeks.')

amazed • amazing

- *I'm **amazed** at you.* (Not *amazed with*)
- *I was **amazed** by what they told me.*
  (Not *amazing* *amazed with/from*)
  (*-ed* endings describe people)
- *I heard an **amazing** story.* (Not *amazed*)
  (*-ing* endings describe things, events, etc.)
- *Hemingway is an **amazing** writer.*
  (a number of *-ing* endings can also be used to describe people, suggesting the effect they have on others)
  (some other pairs of *-ed/-ing* adjectives are: *alarmed/alarming, amused/amusing, annoyed/annoying, appalled/appalling, astonished/astonishing, bored/boring, confused/confusing, depressed/depressing, distressed/distressing, embarrassed/*

embarrassing, enchanted/enchanting, excited/exciting, exhausted/exhausting, frightened/frightening, horrified/horrifying, interested/interesting, moved/moving, pleased/pleasing, relaxed/relaxing, satisfied/satisfying, shocked/shocking, surprised/surprising, terrified/terrifying, tired/tiring; and note: *delighted/delightful, impressed/impressive,* and *upset/upsetting*)

American

- *I'm **learning/doing** English/American English.* (Not *making American English* *american english*)
  (= the language: proper noun, capital letter)
- *He's/She's **American**.*
  (preferable to *an American*)
  (we generally prefer to use an adjectival complement; the noun form is *an American*)
- *They're **American**.*
  (adjectival form)
- *They're **Americans**.*
  (noun form)
- *I was just speaking to **an American/two Americans**.*
  (their sex is not stated, though a pronoun will often show whether they are male or female)
- ***(The) American people/(The) Americans** are wonderfully hospitable.*
  (= the group as a whole)
  (similarly to refer to people: *African, Chilean, Costa Rican, Cuban, Korean, Latin American, Libyan, Mexican, Paraguayan, Ugandan, Venezuelan, Zimbabwean*)

among/amongst • between

- *There are quite a few talented artists **among/amongst** the people I know.*
  (*among* many; *among* is always preferable to *amongst*)
- *It's hard to choose **between** these two pictures. I like them both.*
  (*between* two)

amount • number

- *A large **number of our students** are American.* (Not *amount*)
- *A large **amount of our time** is taken up with administration.*
  (*amount* + uncountable noun; careless speakers often say e.g. *a large amount of students*)

amuse • occupy

- *Looking after the children **occupies** a great deal of our time.* (Not *amuses*)
  (= uses up)

– My children can **amuse/occupy themselves** for hours without getting bored.
(= spend their time pleasantly)

ancient • old
– You have to remember Mrs Briggs is very **old/a very old lady** now. (Not *ancient*)
– Property developers often have little regard for **old/ancient** buildings.
(*old* in terms of time; *ancient* = old in terms of history as in *the ancient Greeks*)
– Mr Briggs is **an old friend** of mine.
(Not *an ancient friend*)
(= one I've known for a long time)

and • and so
– John can speak French **and so can I**.
(Not *and me too*)
– John speaks French **and so do I**.
(Not *and me too*)
– John brought a present for my sister **and** (*for*) *me (too).*

and • to
– Go **and** buy yourself a paper. (Not *to*)
– Come **and** see the goldfish. (Not *to*)
But: **Try and/to** see my point of view.
(imperatives with *go, come, wait*, etc., are followed by *and* where we might expect *to*; *go buy* is also possible, especially in AmE)

anger • get angry
– Don't **get angry** every time someone asks you a question. (Not *anger (yourself)*)
– Even the smallest things **anger him/make him angry**. (Not *make him to anger*)

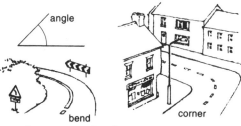

angle

bend

corner

angle • corner • bend
– I'll meet you on the **corner** under the clock, just as we've arranged. (Not *angle*)
– An isosceles triangle contains three **angles**, each of $60°$.
– Be careful when you drive along this road. There are lots of sharp **bends**.
(Not *corners*)

angry with • angry at/about
– People in our town are very **angry at/about** the new parking charges. (Not *angry with*)
(*angry at/about* something)

– It's no good getting **angry with** the waiter because the food is badly cooked.
(*angry with* - sometimes *at* - someone)

anniversary • birthday
– How clever of you to remember my **birthday**! (Not *anniversary*)
(= the date of birth of a person)
– How on earth did you know it is our wedding **anniversary**?
(= the date of an event, such as a wedding)

announcement • advertisement • small ad • commercial
– I saw the **announcement** of his death in the paper. (Not *advertisement*)
(i.e. it was made known in the press)
– Here's an **advertisement/a small ad** for a two-room flat that might interest you.
(classified *advertisements* or *small ads* are placed in newspapers by people buying and selling things; note the spelling with an 'e': not *advertisment*)
– I turn the sound off during TV **commercials**.
(more usual than *advertisements*)
(= advertisements on TV)

annoy • bother • disturb
– There are quite a few unexplained matters in this case that **bother** me. (Not *annoy*)
(= make me uncomfortable)
– Don't **disturb** your father now. He's busy.
(Not *annoy*)
(= interrupt while he's working, etc.)
– If you want to **annoy** Mr Flint, just ring his front doorbell.
(= make him angry)

annoyed (with/at/about)
– I think she's **annoyed with/at** me.
– Passengers are **annoyed at/about** the recent increase in rail fares.
(in broad terms, *annoyed with* someone *about/over* something)
– The lecturer **got annoyed** when he was asked the same question again and again.
(Not *The lecturer annoyed*)

another
– Do you need **another** chair?
(= an additional one, one more)
– Give me **another** cup. This one's cracked.
(Not *an other* *one more*)
(= a different one)

answer (to)
– When can you **give me an answer**?
(Not *make me an answer*)

- Will you please **answer my question**.
  (Not *answer to my question*, though we
  can use *answer* as a noun and say: *That's the*
  answer to *your question*.)
- The police have picked up a boy who
  answers (to) *Rupert's description*.
  (= fits; corresponds with)

antenna • aerial
- I think the TV **aerial** needs adjusting.
  (*antenna*: AmE only; plural: *antennas*)
- How does an ant use its **antennae**?
  (= feelers; the plural is *antennae* when
  antenna is used as a biological term)

antiquity • antique
- It must cost you a fortune insuring all these
  valuable **antiques**. (Not *antiquities*)
  (= furniture and objects made in the past;
  often rare and valuable)
- Much of the work of the great writers of
  antiquity has not survived.
  (= ancient times, especially the Greek and
  Roman classical periods)
- There's an excellent display of **antiquities** in
  the local museum.
  (= items surviving from the distant past)

anxious about
- Jackie's very **anxious about** her exam
  results. (Not *for*)

any
- This isn't just **any** cake.
  (i.e. it's special)
- He'll need **any** help he can get.
  (= all the)
- Give me a plate please. **Any** plate will do.
  (i.e. it doesn't matter which; *any* has special
  uses in addition to its normal use as a
  quantifier)

any one • anyone
- There **wasn't anyone** at the party whom I
  knew. (Not *any one*)
  (= not any person)
- I don't think **any one** of these plants will be
  suitable in a small garden. (Not *anyone*)
  (= one of)

apart • separate
- The two houses are quite **separate**; each
  house has its own **separate** entrance. (Not
  apart; note the spelling, not *seperate*)
  (adjective = different, distinct)
- Jill and Ben **separated** years ago.
  (Not *aparted*)
  (= parted)

- They've **lived apart** for years. (Not *lived
  separate*, but we can say *lived separately*)
  (*apart* = at a distance from each other)

apart from • except for • except (+ object)
- Everyone has helped in some way **apart
  from you/except for you/except you**.
  (Not *apart you* *apart for you*)
  (all three prepositions are possible)
- **Apart from you/Except for you**, everyone
  has helped in some way. (Not *Except you*)
  (we cannot begin a sentence with *except* +
  object; we need *except for/apart from*)

apartment/flat
- We live in a small **apartment/flat**.
  (*flat* is more usual in BrE, *apartment* in
  AmE; note the spelling: not *appartment*
  apartement; in AmE *a flat* is often used to
  mean 'a flat tyre' or a *puncture*)

apology • defence
- The accused had nothing to say in his own
  defence. (Not *apology*)
  (i.e. to protect himself; AmE *defense*)
- Lynn isn't prepared to speak to you unless
  she receives **an apology** for what you said.
  (i.e. unless you say you are sorry)

appear
- **She appears** to be aware of what's going on.
  (Not *She's appearing*)
  (stative use)
- **She's appearing** in 'Showboat'.
  (dynamic use = she is or will be taking part
  in it as a performer)

appear • arise
- Problems should be solved as they **arise**.
  (Not *appear*)
  (= occur)
- You should be able to spot a mistake when it
  appears.
  (= can be seen)

appear • present • show • present myself
- You'll have to **show/present** your passport at
  the frontier. (Not *appear*)
  (*present* = show is very formal)
- Our new washing machine hasn't **presented**
  any problems. (Not *shown* *appeared*)
  (= given)
- I can't **appear** in pyjamas. I must get
  something on. (preferable to *present myself*)
  (= be seen)
- Take great care how you **present yourself** at
  tomorrow's interview. (Not *appear*)
  (= look and behave)

appear • seem

- *You **appear to/seem to** think that nothing matters so long as you get what you want.*
- *It **appears/seems odd** that he hasn't written.* (Not **appears oddly**)
(= it is odd, strange)
- *This **seems** wrong.* (Not **is seeming**)
(stative use only)
- *He **appeared** from nowhere.* (Not **seemed**)
(= arrived within view)

applause • a round of applause

- *When she finished speaking the audience responded with **a round of applause**.* (Not **an applause* *a round of applauses* *applauses**)
- *There **was** loud **applause** at the end of the performance.* (Not **were ... applauses**)
(*applause* is uncountable)

appoint • hire

- *Farms always **hire** additional workers at harvest time.* (Not **appoint**)
(= employ, usually for a short period)
- *They've just **appointed** a new manager at my bank.* (Not **hired**)
(= chosen for a position or job)

appreciate

- ***We appreciate** your help.*
(Not **We are appreciating**)
(stative use: *appreciate* + object = a person recognizes the value of)
- ***Houses are appreciating** in value.*
(dynamic use, intransitive = a thing increases/is increasing in value)
- *We **appreciate having** such good friends at this difficult time.* (Not **to have**)
- *I would **appreciate it** if you could help me.*
(Not **appreciate if you could help**)
(= be grateful)
- *Thank you for your help. **I appreciate it**.*
(Not **I appreciate.**)
(*appreciate* + object after a personal subject)
- *We **appreciate John's/his** offering us a temporary loan.* (Not **John/him**)
- *Her kindness was **appreciated** by everybody.*
(Not **very appreciated**)
(*appreciated* is part of the passive, not an adjective)

approach • come here • go near

- *'**Come here!**' she said.* (Not **Approach!**)
- *If a stranger calls to you from a car, **don't go near** him/keep away from him.*
(the use of *don't* makes *approach* too formal in this context)

- *As we came out of the cinema, a beggar **approached us** asking for money.*
(Not **approached to/from us**)
(= came up to)
(no preposition after *approach*)

approve (of)

- *Most people don't **approve of smoking** these days.* (Not **approve smoking**)
- *Smoking is still allowed in restaurants, but a lot of people don't **approve (of it)**.*
(we always need *of* after *approve* = 'like' if an object follows; compare *approve* = 'give formal consent to', which is transitive: *The Board has to **approve the appointment**.*)

archives • filing system • files

- *You must have my details somewhere in your **filing system/files**.* (Not **archives**)
(= a system used for storing information)
- *A lot of the material in this documentary film was found in the British Museum **archives**.* (Not **archive**, but we can say *It's **archive** material.*)
(= a filing system for documents, etc., of historical importance)

argument/row • quarrel • discussion • dispute

- *Some married couples seem to spend a lot of time **quarrelling/having arguments/having rows**.* (Not **disputing* *discussing**)
(= disagreeing, often with strong feeling; *have a row* is informal)
- *We're **having a** big **discussion about/argument about** the date of the next election.* (Not **making/doing a discussion about/an argument about**)
(*a discussion* = a talk, exchange of information or opinions; *an argument* contains the idea of disagreement)
- *We're having a **dispute** with our neighbours over our property boundaries.*
(= a serious disagreement, often legal)

arise • rise • raise

- *The whole audience **rose** to cheer the soloist.* (Not **arose* *raised**)
(*rise - rose - risen*: intransitive = stand up)
- *If you'd like to ask a question, **raise** your hand.* (Not **rise* *arise**)
(*raise - raised - raised*: transitive = lift up)
- *A serious problem **has arisen** which will take time to solve.* (Not **risen* *raised**)
(*arise - arose - arisen* = come into being)

arm • hand
- *This glove won't fit my* **hand**. (Not **arm**)
  The best basketball players have long **arms**.
  (Not **hands**)

aroma • flavour • taste • scent • perfume
- *What* **flavour** *do you want, strawberry or*
  vanilla? (Not **aroma* *perfume* *taste**)
  (i.e. that has this taste)
- *Few things can beat the* **aroma** *of freshly-*
  ground coffee. (Not **perfume**)
  (= a strong appetizing smell)
- *The room was filled with the* **scent** *of roses.*
  (Not **flavour* *aroma**)
  (= a delicate smell, e.g. of flowers)
- *Dorothy wears too much* **perfume/scent**.
  (Not **aroma**)
  (= manufactured, sweet-smelling liquid;
  perfume is now the commoner noun)
  I love the sharp sour **taste** *of lemon.*
  (= experience of flavour)

arrange • settle • sort out
- *We've* **settled/sorted out** *our differences and*
  there won't be any more arguments.
  (Not **arranged**)
  (i.e. we've come to an agreement)
- *We've* **arranged** *a meeting to settle/sort out*
  our differences.
  (= set up)

arrange • tidy
- *It's time you* **tidied** *your room.*
  (Not **arranged**)
  (= put everything in it in order)
- *I've* **arranged** *these books in alphabetical*
  order. (Not **tidied**)

arrangement(s)
- *I've* **come to/made an arrangement** *to leave*
  early on Fridays.
  (Not **done an arrangement**)
  (= agreed)
- *I've* **made arrangements** *for my holiday next*
  month. (Not **done**)
  (= sorted out how something will be done)

art • skill • technique • craft
- *I don't think I'll ever master the* **art/skill** *of*
  public speaking. (Not **technique**)
  (= a *skill* is the knowledge and ability to do
  something; *art* is the same, but 'higher')
- *Some drivers never master the*
  technique/skill *of reversing into a parking*
  space. (*art* would be a bit overstated here)
  (= specific method)

- *Everyone should be taught a* **craft**.
  (= the knowledge and skill involved in
  making something by hand)

artistic • art
- *A lot of* **art** *treasures were lost in the floods*
  of 1966 in Florence. (Not **artistic**)
  (*art treasures* is a compound noun)
- *I hope my daughter can find work which*
  suits her **artistic** *inclinations.*
  (= concerned with art, literature, etc.)

as • than • else
- *You can wear clothes like that because*
  you're **taller than** *I am.* (Not **as* *else**)
  (comparative + *than*)
- **As** *parents, we're responsible for our*
  children's actions. (Not **Else**)
  (= in the capacity of)
- *We made the injured man comfortable, but*
  there was little **else** *we could do for him.*
  (= more, additionally)

as • when
- *Nina started playing the piano* **when** *she*
  was a child. (Not **as**)
  (*when* + clause of time)
- **As** *Nina is a child, you can't expect her to*
  practise for more than half an hour.
  (*as* + clause of reason)

as if to • as if/as though
- *Henry always looks* **as if/as though** *he's*
  angry. (Not **as if to be* *as though to be**)
- *Eleanor shrugged her shoulders* **as if to** *say*
  she couldn't care less.
  (= in such a manner)

as soon as
- *We'll discuss the matter* **as soon as** *he*
  arrives. (Not **as soon as he will arrive**)
  (*as soon as* as a conjunction + present tense
  form when referring to the future; also: *after,*
  before, directly, immediately, the moment,
  when)

ashamed (of/about)
- *I feel really* **ashamed**. (Not **I ashamed* *I*
  ashamed myself* *I have shame*)
- *I feel really* **ashamed of myself**. *It was my*
  mistake and I'm **ashamed about** *it.*
  (Not **I ashamed for/from myself.* *I*
  ashamed for/from it.*)
  (the verb phrase is *be ashamed of oneself/*
  someone, be ashamed about something)

ask
- *'When does the train arrive?' he* **asked**.
  (direct question with *ask*)

- *I asked my teacher **when I would get** my exam results.* (Not **when would I get**) (indirect question with *ask*)
- *Mr Foley **asked me to** call him today.* (neutral) *He **asked that I call** him later.* (formal) (Not **asked me that I should**)
- ***Guests are asked to vacate** their rooms by 12.00 on the day of departure.* (formal) (Not **It is asked the guests to vacate**)
- *I **asked a question**.* (also: *ask a favour, the price, the time*)

ask for • ask about
- *Mrs Wilmot **asked me about** the children.* (Not **asked me for**) (= enquired after)
- *The school **is asking for** contributions towards a new swimming pool.* (= hopes to receive, is requesting)

asleep • sleeping
- *The children are **asleep/sleeping**.*
- *The cat curled up beside the **sleeping** children.* (Not **asleep**) (we cannot use *asleep* in front of a noun, only after a noun + *be, seem to be*, etc.)

ass • ace
- *What are your cards? - An **ace** and two queens, a jack and a ten.* (Not **ass**)
- *Do you know Aesop's story 'The Miller, his Son, and the **Ass**'?* (*ass* is an old-fashioned word for *donkey*)

ass • pig
- *Morley has appalling manners and always behaves like **a pig**, especially when he's been invited to a party.* (Not **an ass**) (*pig* is an extremely derogatory and offensive description of a person)
- *Alan can be a silly **ass** at times, but he's quite likeable.* (Not **pig**) (*ass, donkey* and *bonehead* are all familiar for 'silly fool', sometimes friendly)

assist in • be present at/attend
- *I **was present at/attended** their wedding.* (Not **assisted at* *attended at**)
- *I'd like to thank everyone who **assisted in** the making of this film.* (= helped; formal)

association • club • organization
- *I used to be a member of the School Film **Club**.* (Not **Association* *Organization**) (a *club* consists of a number of people who enjoy a particular activity)
- *If you buy such an old car, you'd better join the Automobile **Association**.* (Not **Organization**) (an *association* looks after the interests of the people who are its members)
- *As one of the biggest US companies, General Motors is a huge **organization**.* (= a business structure)

assorted • matching
- *We chose a flower-patterned wallpaper with **matching** curtains.* (Not **assorted**) (i.e. curtains which match, that is, have the same or a similar colour and pattern)
- *During the film, the woman beside me opened a big box of **assorted** sweets.* (i.e. different sweets packed together)

assume
- *I **assume**/I'm **assuming** our new assistant can write French as well as speak it.* (stative and dynamic use = believe)
- *While the boss is away, **I'll be assuming** responsibility for her workload.* (dynamic use = having, taking on)

assurance • insurance
- *I've taken out an **insurance** policy.* (Not **assurance**)
- *I'm insured with a big **life insurance/ assurance** company.* (*assurance* is the old term to refer to protection against misfortune)
- *He gave me his **assurance** that the bill would be paid on time.* (Not **insurance**) (= promise)

assure (oneself) • insure (against)
- *Most offices are having to **insure** themselves **against** computer theft.* (Not **assure**) (= pay money to an insurance company to cover theft)
- *Mr Biggs agreed to resign after he had **assured himself** that he'd be compensated.* (*assure oneself* = make certain)

assure (oneself) • make sure • check • verify
- *I've **checked** the tyres and the pressures are OK.* (Not **assured**) (= examined)
- *I went back to **assure myself/check/make sure/verify** that I really had locked the door.* (= make certain)
- *So far there's been no evidence to **verify** the theory that there might be life on Mars.* (= confirm, show it to be true)

asylum • old people's home
- *When she could no longer look after herself, Aunt Alice went to live in an **old people's***

home. (Not *asylum*)
(= accommodation and care for old people)
- *You can't turn away refugees who seek political **asylum**.*
(= protection, shelter)
- *The term 'psychiatric hospital' has now replaced the old-fashioned word **asylum**.*
(= a hospital for mentally-ill people)

at • against • into • to
- *In the bad old days, the border guards had orders to **shoot at** people trying to cross the border illegally.* (Not *against*)
- *The bull **ran** straight **at** me.* (Not *against*)
(i.e. deliberately in that direction)
(*at* can sometimes have the sense of 'against', but cannot be replaced by it; *at* combines with other verbs to suggest 'aggression': e.g. *aim at, shout at, shoot at, stare at, throw at*)
- *We ran **to** our car to escape the rain.*
(*to* = direction towards; compare *shout to, throw to*; no aggression is implied)
- *Who's for the idea or **against** it?* (Not *at*)
(= opposed to)
- *He **drove into** a tree.* (Not *against*)
(i.e. he accidentally crashed into it; *into* combines with other verbs to suggest collision: *bump into, crash into, run into*)

at • in • on (place and time)
Place
- *We waited **at** the door.* (Not *in* *on*)
(*at* a point)
- *There was an unpleasant atmosphere **in** the dentist's waiting room.* (Not *at* *on*)
(*in* an area or volume)
- *Don't leave your dirty laundry **on** the floor.*
(Not *in* *at*)
(*on* a surface)
- *I'll meet you **at/in** the airport.*
(*at* refers to a meeting point; *in* suggests inside the building)
- *He's **at** school/his aunt's house/a wedding.*
(*at* refers to location, for events, addresses, or to mean 'attending')
- *They're **in** Paris/the Mediterranean/the kitchen/hospital.* (Not *at*)
(*in* for towns, large areas, rooms and particular nouns like *bed, hospital*)
Time
- *I'll see you **at** 10.* (Not *in* *on*)
(*at* 10, at lunch, at noon, at Easter, etc.)
- *I'll see you **on** Monday.* (Not *in* *at*)
(*on* Monday, on May 1st, on that day, etc.)
- *I'll see you **in** March.* (Not *on* *at*)
(*in* March, in 2020, in the morning, etc.)

at • to
- *Jim's gone **to** London Airport.* (Not *at*)
(*to*: direction towards)
- *Jim's **at** London Airport.* (Not *to*)
(*at*: destination or position after movement)

at last • in the end • finally
- *It was impossible to guess who had done the murder. **In the end** it turned out to be the cook.* (Not *At last*; preferable to *Finally*)
(= 'when the story ended')
- *We searched everywhere for accommodation and **at last/finally/in the end** a farmer offered us his barn for the night.*
(*at last* = after a long time; *finally* = after effort; *in the end* = 'when the story ended')
- *During the meeting we always have sales reports, production reports, work in progress, and **finally** any other business.*
(Not *in the end* *at last*)
(i.e. as the last thing in a series.)
- *I wonder whether Mallory **finally** got to the summit of Everest/Mallory got to the summit of Everest **in the end**.* (Not *at last*)

at once • immediately • coming
- *'Waiter!' - '**Coming**, sir. I won't be a moment.'* (Not *At once* *Immediately*)
- *When a restaurant is so crowded, you can't expect to be served **at once/immediately**.*
(= without any delay)

ate • eat
- *I **ate** too much last night.* (Not *eat*)
- *I **eat** too much; I'm too fat.* (Not *ate*)
(*eat - ate - eaten*)

athletics
- *The **athletics** (events) **are** nearly over.*
(Not *The athletics is* *The athletic is*)
(plural form + plural verb for specific references)
- ***Athletics is** an important part of physical training.* (Not *The athletic is*)
(plural form + singular verb to refer to *athletics* as a subject to be studied)

attached to • connected with
- *There's nothing coincidental about these events. They're all **connected with** each other.* (Not *attached to*)
(= related to)
- *The lamp is **attached to** the ceiling by means of a hook.* (Not *connected with*)
(= fixed in position, fastened physically)

attack
- *It's criminal to **attack civilian populations** during a war.*

(Not *attack against civilian populations*, though attack used as a noun can be followed by on or against: It's time we launched a serious **attack against/on** this policy.)

attend • visit • wait for • go/come to
- You must **visit** the Louvre. (Not *attend*)
  (= go to, spend time at)
- I'll **wait for you** in the bar. I'll be there at 6.
  (Not *attend you* *attend for you*)
  (i.e. stay in that place till you arrive)
- I'd like to **attend a service** at St Paul's.
  (Not *attend to/at a service*)
  (= go to, be present at an event)
- I'd love to **come/go to** your party.
  (Not *attend* *attend to*)
  (attend is too formal here)

attention (to) • care (for) • caution
- Pippa held the photographs by the edges, with great **care**. (Not *attention*)
  (i.e. very carefully)
- Could I have your **attention** for a moment?
  (Not *care*)
  (= concentration)
- Notice the **attention to/care for** detail in this painting.
- **Caution!** Roadworks! (Not *Attention!*)
  (= warning, danger)

attract • attractive
- Flowers **attract** bees. (Not *are attracting*)
  (stative use = draw)
- The latest model of this sports car **is attracting** a lot of attention.
  (dynamic use = inviting interest)
- It's a very **attractive** car. (Not *attracting*)
  (adjective = good-looking)

audience
- The **audience was/were applauding** wildly.
  (collective noun + singular or plural verb; audience can also be used as a countable noun with a normal plural: audiences are; also: class, club, committee, company, congregation, council, crew, crowd, family, gang, government, group, jury, mob, staff, team, union)

audience • auditorium
- The **auditorium** was packed for the first performance. (Not *audience*)
  (= that part of the theatre in which the audience sits to watch a performance)
- The **audience** packed the auditorium for the first performance.
  (= the people watching the show)

austere • strict • severe
- My old headmaster was very **strict/severe** in applying the school rules. (Not *austere*)
  (= stern in his behaviour)
- My old headmaster was very **austere**.
  (i.e. had a stern appearance, manner)
- There were **severe/strict** penalties for misbehaviour. (Not *austere*)

author/authoress
- Catherine Cookson is the **author** of 'The Black Velvet Gown'. (rather than authoress)
  (author applies to both sexes; similarly manager is preferable to manageress, etc.)

autumn • autumnal
- It was a typical **autumn** day: clear, with a slight frost. (Not *autumnal*)
  (an autumn day = a day in autumn)
- It's theoretically spring, but it's rather **autumnal** today.
  (= like autumn)
  (also: summer/summery, winter/wintry; and note spring/spring-like)

avenue • alley
- The shop is located in an **alley** that runs off Oxford Street. (Not *avenue*)
  (= a very narrow street)
- Brasilia is a modern city with wide tree-lined **avenues**. (Not *alleys*)
- There was a victory march down the Grand **Avenue**. (Not *Alley*)
  (= a wide street in a town or city, often with trees along the sides)

awake
- As soon as Samantha's **awake** she has to start thinking about work.
  (we cannot use awake in front of a noun, only after a noun + be, seem to be, etc.)

B

baby
- Ivy **had a baby** yesterday. (Not *made/did*)

back • backside • behind (nouns)
- Some people need a kick **in/up the backside**/a kick **in/up the behind** before they'll do any work. (Not *in the back*)
  (backside/behind are very informal words for the part of the body which you sit on)
- John has a continual pain **in the back**.
  (the back of the body is the opposite of the front of the body)
- Let me show you the **back** of the house.
  (Not *backside*)

back • backwards • backward

- *I drove my children to school and then drove* **back** *(home).*
  (= returned)
- *I engaged reverse gear and drove* **backwards.**
  (= in that direction; opposite: *forwards*)
- *He left without so much as a* **backward** *glance.* (Not **back** **backwards**)
  (*backward* as an adjective, not *backwards*)

back • behind • at the back (of)

- *We have a nice garden* **behind the house/at the back of the house.** (Not **back the house** **back from the house**)
  (*behind/at the back of*: prepositions + noun object)
- *There's a paved area in front and a garden* **behind/at the back.** (Not **back**)
- *I wish you'd* **put things back** *in their places.* (Not **behind** **at the back**)
  (*put things back* = return them; *behind* and *(at the) back* are adverbs)

backache

- *I have/I've got* **a backache/I've got backache.** (Not **I have my back.**)

bad

- *I know she's annoying, but I don't think she's* **bad/a bad person.** (Not **a bad**)
- *I know they're infuriating, but they're not really* **bad/bad people.** (Not **bads**)
  (never *bad* on its own to mean 'a bad person')
- *We can't ever be sure that* **the bad** *will be punished.* (Not **the bads**)
  (*the* + adjective for the group as a whole)
- *I enjoy the work.* **The bad thing** *is the pay.* (Not **The bad is**)
  (also *the awful/the extraordinary/the interesting/the strange thing is ...*)

bad: go bad

- *Those apples will* **go bad** *if you don't keep them in a cool place.* (Not **bad** **badden**)

bad • badly

- *I play tennis* **badly.** (Not **play bad**)
  (*badly* is an adverb modifying the verb *play*)
- *Business is slow and* **things look bad.**
  (Not **things look badly**)
  (*bad* is an adjective describing *things*; compare *taste/seem/smell/sound* **bad**)

bad at

- *Lots of people claim to be* **bad at** *maths.*
  (Not **bad to** **bad in**)
  (also *awful at, clever at, good at, quick at, slow at*)

badly • very • very much

- *None of us was hurt in the crash, but we were all* **badly** *shaken/upset.*
  (*badly* is preferable to *very/very much* here)
  (= to a serious degree)
- *You* **badly** *need a haircut.*
  (Not **very**: *badly* is preferable to *very much* here; *badly* often combines with *want/need*)

baggage/luggage • a case/suitcase • valise • coffer

- *I'm travelling light. I've got* **a small case/suitcase** *with me and that's all.*
  (Not **a baggage** **a luggage** **coffer**)
- *I've brought* **a lot of baggage/luggage** *and can't manage on my own. I need a porter.*
  (Not **a lot of baggages/a lot of luggages**)
  (*baggage* and *luggage* are uncountable)
- *You don't need more than a small* **valise** *if you're going away for the weekend.*
  (= a small suitcase: old-fashioned, self-conscious/literary)
- *You'd have to be mad these days to keep your money at home in an old* **coffer.**
  (= a strong box: old-fashioned)

bake • cook • roast

- *I'll* **cook** *supper tonight.* (Not **bake**)
  (*cook* is the general verb for 'prepare food by heating')
- *I* **bake** *all our own bread.* (Not **cook**)
  (= bake any made-up dish in the oven, especially one made with flour)
- *It says in the recipe that you* **cook/bake** *it in a hot oven for twenty minutes.*
  (referring to a dish of some kind, not necessarily bread or cakes)
- *I've just had a look in the oven and the beef is* **roasting/cooking** *nicely.* (Not **baking**)
  (*roast* = oven-cook any large piece of meat: *roast chicken*, sometimes with vegetables in the same dish: *roast potatoes*)

balance • scales

- *I don't know what this chicken weighs. Put it on the* **scales.** (Not **balance**)
  (= a weighing machine; always plural in BrE, but singular - *scale* - in AmE)
- *We still use a fine* **balance** *in our laboratory to weigh small amounts of substances.*
  (= a precise weighing instrument)

band • gang

- *I don't approve of that* **gang** *of friends he goes around with.* (Not **band**)
  (= an informal group, especially of young people, who do things together)

- *My son plays in a **band**.* (Not **gang**)
  (= a music group)

band • tape
- *I've still got a lot of music **on tape**.*
  (Not **on bands**)
  (= magnetic tape for recording sound)
- *The security man put a nylon **band** round my case to show that it had been examined.*
  (= a strip of metal, plastic, elastic, etc.)

bank • bench • form
- *Let's sit on this **bench** and watch the world go by.* (Not **bank* *form**)
  (= a long wooden seat, with or without a back, especially out of doors)
- *When I was at school, we sat on hard wooden **forms/benches**.* (Not **banks**)
  (*forms* = long schoolroom seats without a back, now old-fashioned)
- *A river **bank** is a fine place for a picnic, especially on a sunny day.*
  (= the side of a river)

bankrupt: go bankrupt
- *They **went bankrupt**.* (Not **bankrupted**)
  (= were forced by debt to close a business)
- *We're **bankrupt**!* (Not **bankrupted**)
- *The sudden fall in demand for our products **bankrupted us/made us bankrupt**.*

barely
- *They **have barely enough** to live on.*
  (Not **don't have barely enough**)
  (only one negative in any one clause; also *hardly, scarcely*)

barracks • shack • hut • shed
- *Severino's family lived in a **shack** outside Rio.* (Not **a barracks/a shed**)
  (= a rough dwelling of local materials)
- *If you want the foreman, you'll find him in his **hut**.* (Not **barracks/shack/shed**)
  (= a temporary building, often made of wood, e.g. on a building site)
- *We need a **shed** to store our garden tools.*
  (Not **barracks/hut/shack**)
  (= a simple permanent building, often made of wood, and used as a storeroom)
- *The soldiers have been confined to **barracks** the whole weekend.* (Not **barrack**)
  (= military buildings for housing soldiers; with a singular verb when regarded as a single unit: *the barracks is*; with a plural verb when used as a collective: *the barracks are*; also *crossroads, headquarters*)

barred • closed • shut
- *We're going to have to turn off soon. The road ahead is **closed**.* (Not **shut* *barred**, but we can say *barred to traffic*)
  (we use *closed* on its own for roads; we can only use *barred* if we add more information)
- *The shop is all shut up. Look, the windows are **barred**.*
  (= closed with bars)
- *I was sure she was watching me from behind her **closed** window.* (Not **shut**)
  (we don't use *shut* before a noun)
- *Most shops are **closed/shut** on Sundays.*
  (interchangeable)

barrier • fence
- *There's a high **fence** right round the estate.*
  (Not **barrier**)
  (*a fence* is rather like a wall, but made of wood, or wire on wooden or concrete posts)
- *The police have put up a **barrier** to keep people away.* (Not **fence**)
  (= a line of metal, wood or rope, which people may not cross)

barrier • frontier
- *You have to have your passport checked at the **frontier**.* (Not **barrier**)
  (= the division between two countries)
- *They won't let us through the **barrier** until they've checked our luggage.*
  (= a wooden or metal 'arm' used to control the movement of people and vehicles)

base • basis
- *What's your **basis** for making such a decision?* (Not **base**)
  (= basic principle, foundation: pronounced /'beɪsɪs/; plural *bases*, pronounced /'beɪsiːz/)
- *The **base** of the Memorial is engraved with the names of those who died.* (Not **basis**)
  (= the lowest part that supports what is built on it; plural *bases*, pronounced /'beɪsəz/)

basin • swimming pool
- *I'll check the temperature, before I dive into that **(swimming) pool**.* (Not **basin**)
- *Please fill this **basin** with water.*
  (= a deep bowl-shaped object for holding liquids, etc.)

bath • bathe • swim
- *I think I'll **have/take a bath**.* (noun)
  (Not **do/make a bath* *bath myself**)
- *I'm going to **give the baby a bath**.* (noun)
  (Not **do/make the baby a bath**)
  (we can also say *bath the baby*, not **bathe the baby**)

- *I don't think many people **bath** more than once a day.* (verb)
  (= have a bath in a bathtub/in a bath)
- *I can't bear to **bathe** if the sea temperature is under 15°C.* (Not *bath*)
  (*bathe* = have a swim, now becoming old-fashioned; AmE also = have a bath in a tub; also note *to sunbathe*, or *have a sunbathe*)
- *What's she doing? - She's **bathing**.*
  (= having a bath /ˈbɑːθɪŋ/ or a swim /ˈbeɪðɪŋ/: both spelt the same)
- *I'm going down to the beach for a **swim/a bathe**.* (Not *bath*)
- *Let me **bathe** those scratches for you before you put on any ointment.* (Not *bath*)
  (= wash gently, especially a wound)

bazaar • bargain
- *We've **made/struck a bargain** and we're going to keep to it.* (Not *done a bargain* *made/done a bazaar*)
- *How long will you go on **bargaining** for a better price?* (Not *bazaaring*)
  (= negotiating a price)
- *We're having a **bazaar** next Saturday to raise money for the hospital.*
  (= an event where things are sold to raise money for a good cause)
  (*bazaar* can be used only as a noun)

bazaar • market/market place
- *We do the shopping at the **market/market place** every Friday.* (Not *bazaar*)
  (= a place where people buy and sell goods)
- *We're having a **bazaar** next Saturday to raise money for the hospital.*
  (= an event where things are sold to raise money for a good cause)
- *I love visiting **bazaars** when I'm travelling in the Arab World.*
  (= street markets, especially in Eastern countries)

BC • AD
- *Pompey died in 48 **BC**.* (or ***B.C.***)
- *Tiberius died in **AD** 37.* (or ***A.D.***)
  (BC = **B**efore **C**hrist; AD = **A**nno **D**omini, 'in the year of Our Lord'. AD is not usually necessary, except in the early centuries to avoid confusion: *Rome was sacked in **AD 410***; the 11th to the 21st centuries will always be taken to mean *AD*. Note the position of *BC/AD* in dates.)

beam • ray
- *A **ray** of sunshine streamed into the room.* (Not *beam*, but we can say *a sunbeam*)
  (= a thin bar of light, especially sunlight)

- *I was blinded by the **beam** of the car's headlights.* (Not *ray*)
  (= a strong stream of light, often from an artificial source)

bear • bare
- *The table was **bare**.* (Not *bear*)
  (= with nothing on it; pronounced /beəʳ/)
- *Imagine meeting **a bear** in the forest!*
  (= a large animal; pronounced the same way)

bear: can't bear
- *I wish she wouldn't eat so fast. I **can't bear to watch** her.* (i.e. now)
- *I wish she wouldn't eat so fast. I **can't bear watching** her.* (i.e. now or in general)
  (*-ing* or *to* after *bear*)

bear • carry
- *We had to **carry** the baby.* (Not *bear*)
  (= lift and move)
- *I don't think your car suspension will **bear** such a heavy load.*
  (= support the weight of; *bear* in the sense of 'carry' is old-fashioned)

bear • suffer (from) • put up with
- *Isobel **suffered** terrible pain after her operation.* (Not *bore*)
  (= experienced pain)
- *This place is so untidy. I don't know how you can **bear** living/how you **put up with** living in it.* (Not *suffer*)
  (= endure without protest)
- *If you eat so fast, no wonder you **suffer from** stomach-ache.* (Not *suffer of/by*)

beat • hit • bang • strike
- *Jimmy was rude to his mother and she **hit/struck** him.* (Not *beat/banged*)
  (i.e. once; *strike* is more formal than *hit*)
- *You can't teach children by **beating** them.* (Not *hitting/banging/striking*)
  (= hitting repeatedly)
- *If we play music, the people downstairs **bang** (on) the ceiling.* (Not *hit/strike*)
  (= strike sharply; *hit the ceiling* = lose one's temper, is an idiom)
- *I **banged/hit/struck** my head against the low doorway and hurt myself.* (Not *beat*)

beat • win • conquer
- *Tottenham **won** the Cup Final.* (Not *beat*)
  (you **win** something: e.g. a match)
- *What was the result of the Cup Final? - Tottenham **won**.* (Not *beat*)
  (*win* can be used intransitively)
- *Who **won** the war?* (Not *beat/conquered*)
  (= defeated/beat the enemy)

- *Tottenham **beat Liverpool** in the Cup Final.*
  (Not **won Liverpool**)
  (you *beat* someone *in* a match; *beat* someone
  at e.g. tennis)
- *Alexander the Great **conquered** half the
  world before he was 33.* (Not **won/beat**)
  (= took land by force of arms)

beautiful • handsome • good-looking • pretty • attractive
- *Boris is a **handsome/good-looking** young
  man/an **attractive** young man.*
  (Not **beautiful** **pretty** for men)
- *Linda is a **beautiful/handsome/good-
  looking/pretty/attractive** girl.*
  (*beautiful* refers to natural beauty; *handsome*
  refers to healthy-looking characteristics;
  good-looking is general, and not as strong as
  beautiful; *beautiful* and *pretty* are used for
  women and children with attractive looks)

because (of) • as • since • for
- *I expected you to ring **because/since** you
  promised you would.* (Not **for**)
  (we use *because* or *since* to explain what has
  been said; *as* in the above sentence would
  mean 'in keeping with the way')
- ***Because/As/Since** they won't give me a pay
  rise, I'm leaving this company.* (Not **For**)
  (we cannot use *for* to begin a sentence)
- *We rarely go abroad, **for** we can't afford it.*
  (*for* = because; rare in speech)
- *Sam got behind in his schoolwork **because
  of** his illness.* (Not **because**)

become • be
- *I'll say what I think. I won't **be** quiet!*
  (Not **become**)
- *The children **were** quiet.*
  (= a state)
- *The children **became** quiet.*
  (= they had previously been noisy)
- *I won't **be/become** a racing driver. It's too
  dangerous.*

become • have • obtain/get
- *Can I **have** a coffee please?* (Not **become**)
- *I **obtained/got** a couple of seats for
  'Traviata' at Covent Garden.*
  (Not **became**)
- *Remember me if you **become** famous.*
  (i.e. that's what happens to you)

become (of) • happen (to) • what's the matter
- *I haven't been in touch with Melanie for
  years now. I wonder what's **become of/
  happened to** her.* (Not **become her**
  become to her **what she's become**)

(i.e. What's her present situation? What's she
doing now?)
- *Melanie **has become** a company director.*
  (= 'that's what she's turned into')
- *The whole house is shaking. **What's
  happening**?* (Not **What's the matter?**)
  (= What's going on?)
- *You look upset. **What's the matter**?*
  (Not **What's happening?**)
  (= Is there anything wrong?)

bed
- *Joe's **in bed**.* (Not **to bed** **in the bed**)
- *Joe's gone **to bed**.*
  (Not **in bed** **to the bed**)
- *I'll **make** the bed.* (Not **prepare**)
  (*do* is possible when 'making the bed' is
  viewed as one in a series of tasks)

beef • bullock • ox(en)
- *I don't fancy walking across a field full of
  young **bullocks**.* (Not **beefs**)
  (= young bulls, young oxen)
- *You don't often see farmers using **oxen** to
  plough the land.* (Not **beefs** **bullocks**;
  note: *ox - oxen*, not **oxes**)
- *I'll get some **beef** for Sunday lunch.*
  (= meat from a bull or heifer; uncountable)

beef • steak/beefsteak • roast beef
- *I'd like **a steak** please, medium rare.*
  (Not **a beef**; we can usually specify: *fillet
  steak, rump steak* or *sirloin steak*)
  (= a flat piece of beef, often grilled;
  beefsteak means the same as *steak*, but is
  rarely used)
- *We've having **roast beef** on Sunday.*
  (Not **roast beefsteak**)
  (*roast beef* = meat from a bull or heifer,
  cooked in a large piece in an oven)

beefsteak • hamburger/beefburger
- *We haven't got enough time for a sit-down
  meal. Let's have a **hamburger/beefburger**
  somewhere.* (Not **beefsteak**; see above)
  (= minced beef rounds, grilled or fried)

been • being
- *He **is being** difficult again.* (Not **is been**)
- *He **has been** difficult all day.*
  (Not **has being**)
  (*be - being - was - have been; being* is the
  present participle; *been* is the past participle)

before • ago
- *We visited Madeira about **five years ago**.*
  (Not **five years before** **before five years**
  before five years ago)
  (*ago* = back from now)

- *It was a pleasure to visit Madeira, especially as I'd never been there **before**.* (Not **ago**)
(*before* = on a previous occasion)

before • in front of
- *Wait **in front of** that shop.* (Not **before**)
(*in front of*, opposite *behind*, refers to absolute position or place)
- *I'm/I come **before** you in the queue.*
(= ahead of: position relative to others)
- *We'll discuss the matter **before he arrives**.*
(Not **before he will arrive* *before that he arrives**)
(*before* as a conjunction + present tense form when referring to the future)
- *Don't comment on the film **before seeing/ you see** it.* (Not **before to see it**)

before • used to • before that
- *I drive a taxi now. **I used to work** in a restaurant.* (Not **Before, I worked ...**)
- *I worked in a restaurant **before I became** a taxi driver.* (Not **before to become**, though *before becoming* would be all right)
- *I used to drive a taxi. **Before that**, I worked/I used to work in a restaurant.*
(Not **Before from that**)

begin • start
- *I couldn't **start** my car this morning; the battery was flat.* (Not **begin**)
(you *start* a machine or it *starts*)
- *We **began/started working/to work** on the project as soon as we got the commission.*
(*begin* or *start* an activity + *to* or *-ing*)
- *I **began/started** the lesson **by** telling them about Pasteur.* (Not **began/started with**)
*Let's **begin/start with** soup.* (Not **by**)

began • begun
- *Sh! The play **has begun**.* (Not **has began**)
- *It **began** a minute ago.* (Not **begun**)
(*begin - began - begun*)

behaviour
- *How can we deal with **such** bad **behaviour**?*
(Not **such behaviours/such a behaviour**)
(*behaviour* is uncountable)

believe (in) • belief
- *Try to have more **belief** in your own ability.*
(Not **believe**)
(*believe* is the verb; *belief* the noun)
- *I **believe in** God.* (Not **believe to* *belief**)
- *Surely you **believe** there's more to life than just making money.* (Not **are believing**)
(only stative; no progressive form)
- *Are they at home? - I **believe so**.*
(Not **I believe.* *I believe it.**)

belong
- *This farm **belongs** to me and it **belonged** to my father before me.*
(Not **is belonging* *was belonging**)
(only stative; no progressive form; also: *astonish, believe, comprise, concern, consist of, constitute, contain, deserve, desire, detest, differ, disagree, disbelieve, dislike, envy, excel, fancy, fear, matter, merit, need, own, perceive, possess, result from/in, suit, understand, want*)

belong to • own
- *I **own** this vehicle.* (Not **belong**)
(= it's mine)
- *This vehicle **belongs to** me.* (Not **owns me* *owns to me* *It belongs me this vehicle.**)
(= it's mine)

belongings
- *All my **belongings are** in this bag.*
(Not **belonging is* *belongings is**)
(= everything I own; plural noun with no singular form + plural verb)

below • under/underneath • beneath
- *He had a parcel **under** his arm.*
(Not **below* *underneath* *beneath**)
(*under*, opposite *over* = at a lower place than, sometimes touching)
- *The stone hit me **below** the knee.*
(Not **under**)
(*below*, opposite *above*, refers to position)
- *We camped just **below/under** the summit.*
(sometimes interchangeable)
- *We could see him swimming just **below/ under/beneath/underneath** the surface.*
(*beneath* is less common than *under* and *below* and more literary; *underneath* = completely covered by)

bend • curve
- *I always admire the fine **curves** in a Henry Moore sculpture.* (Not **bends**)
- *Drive carefully. The road ahead is full of dangerous **bends/curves**.*
(a *bend* is more pronounced than a *curve* and therefore more dangerous; a *curve* is more rounded and U-shaped than a *bend*; *bend* is the usual word to refer to roads)
- *Look at the map. Do you see this **curve/bend** in the river?*

benefit from
- *We need a long holiday and we hope we'll really **benefit from** it.* (Not **benefit by**)
(i.e. it will do us good; note the spelling of

-ing/-ed forms: *benefiting/benefited*, not
benefitting/benefitted)

benzine • petrol • diesel oil • paraffin • petroleum/oil/crude

– *How much **petrol** (AmE gas/gasoline) does
  your tank hold?* (Not **benzine**)
  (= refined fuel we use in cars)
– *Dry cleaners now use more modern solvents
  than **benzine**.*
– *Diesel engines will only run on **diesel** (oil).*
  (= a heavy fuel used in place of petrol)
– *I have a small heater in my greenhouse that
  runs on **paraffin** (AmE kerosene).*
  (= a petroleum product used in lamps,
  heaters, candle-making, etc.)
– *Saudi Arabia is the world's largest producer
  of **petroleum/oil/crude** (oil).*
  (= the basic mineral from which products
  like *petrol, paraffin*, etc., are derived)

beside • besides

– *There were a lot of people at the party
  besides us.* (Not **beside* *beside of**)
  (= in addition to)
– *She has so much else to do **besides**.*
  (Not **beside**)
  (= additionally; adverb)
– *Come and sit **beside** us.* (Not **besides**)
  (= next to)

best

– *Juan is a world-class tennis player who is
  counted among **the best**.* (Not **the bests**)
  (*the* + adjective for the group as a whole)
– ***Do your best**.* (Not **Make your best/bests.**)

best • favourite ⸰ beloved • dearest

– *I see you're wearing your **favourite** tie.*
  (Not **beloved* *dear* *loved**)
  (= the one you like best)
– *I see you're wearing your **best** tie.*
  (= finest in quality)
– *Elspeth, **beloved/dearest** wife of Paul, 1927-
  1988.* (Not **favourite* *best* *loved**)
  (*dearest* and *beloved* for the person you love
  best, but *beloved* is formal, old-fashioned;
  favourite can also be used for people: *Who
  was your **favourite** teacher at school?*)

bet

– *Try phoning him, but **I bet** you won't find
  him in.* (Not **am betting**)
  (stative use = I'm sure)
– *How much **are you betting** on this horse?*
  (dynamic use = risking money)

better

– *Your car is **better** than mine.*
  (Not **more good**)
– *You play chess **better** than I do.*
  (Not **more good* *more well**)
– *How are you now? - I'm **better**.*
  (i.e. in health)

better • get better

– ***The road gets better** a bit further on.*
  (Not **The road betters**)
– *I've been ill, but **I'm getting better**.*
  (Not **I'm bettering* *I'm getting weller**)
  (= I'm improving in health)
– *Let's try to **better** last year's results.*
  (= improve on)

better • had better

– ***You'd** (= you had) **better** leave now so as not
  to be late for your appointment.*
  (Not **You better* *You would better**)
  (*had* abbreviates to *'d*; omitting *had* or *'d*
  altogether is common but substandard)

better • more • best • most

– *I like tennis **more** than I like football.*
  (preferable to *better*)
– *I like football, but I like tennis **better**.*
  (preferable to *more*)
– *Of all sports, I like tennis **best**.*
  (preferable to *most*)
– *Of all sports, tennis is the **most** enjoyable.*

big • large • great

– *A language always benefits from the work of
  its **great** writers.* (Not **big* *large**)
  (*great*, opposite *minor*, generally refers to
  importance)
– *If he's a Sumo wrestler, you'd expect him to
  be a **big/large** man.* (Not **great**)
  (*big*, opposite *little*, and *large*, opposite
  small, generally refer to relative size)

billet • ticket

– *I've lost my train **ticket**.* (Not **billet**)
– *This fine old house was used as a **billet** for
  soldiers during World War II.*
  (= a place where soldiers live)

billiards

– ***Billiards is** my favourite game.*
  (Not **Billiard is* *Billiards are**)
  (plural in form + singular verb)

biscuit • sponge cake • cookie

– *Mother has made a **sponge cake** for tea.*
  (Not **biscuit**)
– *I always like a **biscuit** (BrE)/**cookie** (AmE)
  with my morning coffee.*

(*cake* = a sweet soft food made with flour, sugar and eggs; *biscuit* = like a cake, but flat, and baked hard and dry)

bitter • sour • plain
- *How long has this yoghurt been in the fridge? It tastes **sour**.* (Not **bitter**)
- *I just couldn't drink strong black coffee without sugar. It's too **bitter**.* (Not **sour**)
  (the opposite of *bitter* and *sour* is *sweet*)
- *I love **plain/bitter** chocolate.*
  (*plain* is more common for *chocolate*; compare *milk chocolate*)

bizarre • odd/strange
- *Mrs Grenville's a bit **odd/strange** sometimes.* (Not **bizarre**)
  (= out of the ordinary; eccentric)
- *Many pop groups seem completely **bizarre** to the older generation.*
  (= strange enough to invite unfavourable comment or give cause for concern)

blame (for) • criticize (for) • show (me) up
- *Try not to **criticize** teenage children for their appearance.* (Not **blame**)
  (= express disapproval of)
- *Don't **blame** me **for** missing the plane. You didn't allow enough time.*
  (= say I'm responsible for something bad)
- *Tim speaks French much better than me. He really **shows me up**.* (Not **blames me**)
  (= makes me feel/look silly)

blind
- *Mr Parkins is **blind/a blind man** and owns a guide dog.* (Not **a blind**)
- *Mr and Mrs Parkins are both **blind/blind people**.* (Not **blinds**)
  (we cannot use *blind* on its own to mean 'a blind person')
- *More money is collected for **the blind** than for any other group of handicapped people.* (Not **the blinds**)
  (*the* + adjective for the group as a whole)
- *For a moment, we were **blinded** by a flash of lightning.* (Not **blind**) ⎵
  (*blind* is also a verb, often passive)

block • hold up
- *We were **held up** on the motorway, in a 20 mile tailback.* (Not **blocked**)
  (= delayed)
- *A lorry has jack-knifed and completely **blocked** the motorway.*
  (= prevented movement along)

block • pad
- *I've brought this nice new **pad** to take notes during the meeting.* (Not **block**)
  (*pad/writing pad* = sheets of paper held together, used for writing or drawing)
- *How did the ancient Egyptians cut and move such huge stone **blocks**?*
  (= stone, wood, etc., cut with straight sides)

blood
- *Mr Griffiths had to have a transfusion because he had lost **a lot of blood**.* (Not **a lot of bloods**)
  (*blood* is uncountable)

blouse   smock   sweater

blouse • smock • sweater
- *Everyone's idea of a painter is a person dressed in a **smock** and standing in front of an easel.* (Not **blouse**)
- *I like to dress casually during the weekend - in a **sweater** and jeans.* (Not **blouse**)
- *Monica wore a pink **blouse** that went very well with her black skirt.*

blow up • burst
- *One of our pipes **burst** after the cold weather and we had some large plumbing and redecorating bills.* (Not **blew up**)
  (= broke open)
- *The mine **blew up** as soon as it was struck by a shell.* (Not **burst**)
  (= exploded: e.g. of a bomb)

boast of/about
- *I wish Ron wouldn't keep **boasting of/about** his success.* (Not **boasting for/with**)

body • silhouette • figure • shape • physique • physic
- *With a **figure/shape** like yours, you can wear any clothes you like.*
  (Not **body* *physique* *silhouette**)
  (*figure* is the most common word to refer to the shape or form of the body)
- *I think I have a healthy mind and **body**.*
  (Not **figure* *physique* *silhouette**)
- *You have to lift weights if you want to build up a **physique** like that!* (Not **physic**)
  (= body-shape; unlike *figure* it refers to strength, fitness and muscles)

- *The man had his back to me and I could see his **silhouette** against the firelight.*
  (= image in outline with a light behind it)
- *Camomile tea is said to be an excellent **physic** for stomach pains.*
  (= medicine: old-fashioned)

bomb • gas cartridge
- *I'll have to fit a new **gas cartridge**. This one's run out.* (Not *bomb*)
  (= a container for butane gas)
- *The police have found an unexploded World War II **bomb** in the playground.*
  (= an explosive device)

border • frontier • boundary
- *That line of trees over there marks the school **boundary**.* (Not *border* *frontier*)
  (= the edge of a piece of land or property)
- *A few years ago it was hard to cross the **border/frontier** from East to West Germany.*
  (= the line where two countries join)

bored: get bored (with)
- *I got **bored** long before the film ended.* (Not *I bored*)
- *I got **bored** (with) waiting for you.* (Not *got bored to wait* *got bored at waiting*)
- *I quickly **get bored** with TV quiz shows.* (Not *get bored of/from*)

boring • annoying
- *I don't know why your brother keeps throwing pebbles at the window. He's extremely **annoying**.* (Not *boring*)
  (i.e. he makes me angry)
- *I don't know why your uncle keeps telling me the same jokes all the time. He's extremely **boring**.*
  (= dull, tedious, uninteresting)

born • borne
- *When were you **born**?*
  (Not *When are you born?*)
- *He was **born** in 1982.* (Not *He born* *He borned* *He has born* *He was borne*)
  (*be born* = come into the world)
- *She has **borne** three children.* (Not *born*)
  (*bear - bore - borne*: = give birth/carry: *She has **borne** three children/She **has borne** a lot of responsibility.*)

borrow (from) • lend (to)
- *Can you **lend** me £20 please? I'll pay/give it back tomorrow.* (Not *borrow me*)
  (*lend* something *to* someone = give money, etc., to be paid back or given back)
- *Can I **borrow** £20 (**from** you) please? I'll pay/give it back tomorrow.* (Not *lend*)

(*borrow* something *from* someone = take money, etc., to be paid back or given back)

both ... and
- ***Both** Meg **and** her husband have gone down with flu.* (Not *And ... and*)

both • the two (of them)
- *The twins are going to meet for the first time. **The two of them** were separated at birth.* (preferable to *Both of them*)
  (*the two of them* = two people or things considered separately)
- *Which of the two would you like? - I'll take **both of them**.* (preferable to *the two of them*; not *the both of them* *both them*)
  (*both* = not only one, but also the other)
- *They **both helped** in the kitchen.*
  (position before a main verb or after *be, have, can*, etc.: *They're **both** late.*)

bouillon • consommé • broth • soup
- *There's nothing like a bowl of **broth** when you're not feeling very well.*
  (= clear soup; *bouillon* and *consommé* also mean 'clear soup', but *bouillon* is mostly used in the term *bouillon cube*, and *consommé* is used on menus and tins; compare *bullion* = gold/silver bars)
- *I only **had** a bowl of **soup** for lunch.*
  (*have* is the usual verb in connexion with soup, not *eat* or *drink*)

box • boxing
- *I don't think I'm the only one who thinks **boxing** is barbaric.* (Not *the box*)
  (= the sport)
- *You've eaten the last chocolate in **the box**!*
  (= a container)

boy • young man • child
- *Charles has just joined our firm. He's a very ambitious **young man**.* (preferably not *boy*, which is patronizing in formal contexts)
- *We've got a girl of 16 and a **boy** of 12.*
- *Flora's chief regret in life was that she was never able to have a **child**.*
  (*child* = a young boy or girl; *boy* = a male child, informally used in place of *son*)

braces • brace
- *Some men think it's stylish to wear **braces** instead of a belt.* (Not *a brace*)
  (*braces/a pair of braces*: no singular)
- *Polly has to wear **a brace** on her teeth to stop them sticking out.* (Not *braces*)
  (= a wire band for straightening teeth)

brain • brains

— *Believe me, that young woman really **has brains/a good brain** and will go far.*
(Not **has brain/has a brain**)
(*brains* = good intelligence is plural in form and takes a plural verb)
— *Nobody understands how **the brain** works.*
(i.e. the organ)

brake • break

— *Take care with that vase. Don't **break** it.*
(Not **brake**)
(*break - broke - broken*)
— *I had to **brake** hard to avoid hitting her.*
(= use the *brakes* of a vehicle to make it slow down or stop; *brake - braked - braked*)

brave • courageous • good • nice

— *Hans is a really **good/nice** man with a pleasant manner. You'll like him.*
(Not **brave/courageous**)
— *Firemen always seem to be naturally **brave/courageous** in the face of danger.*
(= able to ignore fear)

bread • a loaf of bread • a (bread) roll

— *Nip out and get **a loaf of bread/two loaves of bread**, will you?*
(Not **a bread** **two breads**)
— *We've eaten **a lot of bread** today.*
(Not **a lot of breads**)
(*bread* is uncountable)
— *I'll just have a bowl of soup and **a (bread) roll**.* (Not **a small bread**)
(= a small separately-baked piece of bread)

break

— *You've been overworking - why don't you **have a break**.* (Not **make/do a break**)
(= a holiday)

breakdown • nervous breakdown

— *There's nothing worse than **having a breakdown** when you're on a motorway.*
(Not **making/doing a breakdown**)
(*a breakdown* = vehicle failure)
— *Kim was overworked and **had a (nervous) breakdown**.* (Not **made/did a breakdown**)
(= suffered extreme anxiety and stress)

breakfast

— *We've **had breakfast**.* (Not **the breakfast**)
(*take breakfast* is possible, but dated; no articles for meals, except in specific references: *The breakfast today was awful*; also: *dinner, lunch, supper, tea*)

breath • breathe

— ***Breathe** deeply.* (Not **Breath**)
(*breathe* is the verb)
— *Mr Quinn is old and fat and short of **breath**.*
(Not **breathe**)
(*breath* is the noun)

brief • letter

— *We were very pleased to get a **letter** from our children yesterday.* (Not **brief**)
— *As a young barrister, Carol was lucky to be given such an important **brief**.*
(= case)

bright • brightly

— *The sun shone **bright/brightly** all day.*
(*bright* occurs in fixed phrases: *shine/glow bright, look bright* = be bright)
— *She answered all my questions **brightly**.*
(Not **bright**)
(adverb = in a cheerful manner)

bright • shining • shiny

— *He looked very smart in a new suit and **shiny** black shoes.* (Not **shining/bright**)
(= reflecting light)
— *It's a long time since we had a **bright** day.*
(Not **shining/shiny**)
(= full of light)
— *Claudia stands out from the rest like a **shining/bright** star.* (Not **shiny**)
(= producing light)

bring • deliver

— *Old-fashioned grocers who **deliver** goods are pretty rare these days.* (Not **bring**)
(= take to people's houses as a service)
— *We can **deliver/bring** the goods to you this afternoon.*

bring • fetch • take • carry

— *If you're going to the kitchen, would you mind **bringing** me a glass of water please?*
(i.e. you will be there, so bring it here)
— *Please **fetch** me a glass of water.*
(= go from here to another place and bring it back here)
— ***Take** this glass of water to your father.*
(i.e. you are here; carry it there)
— *I had to **carry** the twins all the way home.*
(= lift and move)

British

— *He's/She's **British**.* (Not **a British**)
(adjectival form, = anyone who comes from England, Scotland, Wales or Northern Ireland; *a Briton, two Britons; a Britisher/ two Britishers* is old-fashioned)

- *They're **British**.* (Not **Britishes**)
  (the adjectival form is preferred to the noun form *Britons*)
- ***The British/(The) British people** are wonderfully practical.* (Not **British**; preferable to *The Britons*)
  (= the group as a whole)

broad/breadth • wide/width
- *The fireplace is two metres **wide/in width**.*
  (= in measurement across; *wide* is the usual word in references to measurement)
- *The fireplace is two metres **broad/in breadth**.*
  (= in the distance from one side to the other; in measurement expressions, *broad* suggests 'strikingly/noticeably large')
- *We came to a **wide/broad** fast-flowing river.*
  (*wide* = large in measurement across; *broad* = big and open from one side to the other; note also *a broad grin*, *a broad outline*, in which *broad* = that can be seen openly and easily)

broil • grill • boil
- *How would you like your eggs? - I'd like them **boiled** please.* (Not **broiled**)
  (= cooked in boiling water)
- *I'd like **broiled** (AmE)/**grilled** (BrE) steak please.* (Not **boiled**)
  (= cooked under or over direct heat)

broken • not working • out of order
- *That stupid lift **isn't working/is out of order** again.* (Not **is broken**, though we can say *is/has broken down*)
  (= not functioning)
- *It will be very difficult mending a vase that's **broken** into so many pieces.*

brutal • bestial • beastly
- *Medieval peasants lived in what we would consider **bestial** conditions.*
  (Not **brutal* *beastly**)
  (= revolting, disgusting, 'like beasts')
- *On their release, the hostages said that they had been subjected to **brutal** treatment by their captors.* (Not usually *bestial*)
  (= very cruel, 'like a brute')
- *We had **beastly** weather while we were on holiday.* (Not **brutal* *bestial**)
  (= extremely unpleasant)

buffet • sideboard
- *You'll find the wine glasses in the **sideboard**.*
  (Not **buffet**)
  (= a piece of dining-room furniture for storing plates, glasses, etc.)

- *I'll get a roll at the station **buffet**.* /'bʊfeɪ/
  (= a shop on a train or at a station where food and drink are sold over a counter)
- *We've invited so many people, we're having a **buffet** /'bʊfeɪ/, not a sit-down meal.*
  (= a self-service meal)

bus
- *How did you get here? - **By bus/On the bus**.*
  (Not **With the bus.**)
  (*by bus* is a fixed expression indicating means of transport; *on the bus* can refer to a particular journey; similarly: *bike/bicycle, train, tube, underground*; *by car/in the car*)

business
- *We used to **do business** with them.*
  (Not **make business**)
  (= trade; note the spelling, not **bussiness* *busines**)
- *We **do a lot of business** in the Far East.*
  (Not **do a business/a lot of businesses**)
  (*business* = trade is uncountable)
- *I run **a travel business** in Manchester and another in Glasgow. Two **businesses** are as much as I can manage!*
  (*business* = an organization is countable)
- *I'm **in business** with a partner.*
  (Not **into business**)
  (= I work with)
- *I'm not on holiday. I'm here **on business**.*
  (Not **for business**)
  (= for the purpose of conducting business)

businessman • entrepreneur
- *We need an injection of capital from an **entrepreneur/businessman** who's prepared to take risks.*
  (we describe a *businessman* as an *entrepreneur* when we want to emphasize the risk-taking nature of business)
- *The bar was crowded with tired **businessmen**.* (Not **entrepreneurs**)

bust • burst
- *The balloon **burst**.* (Not **bust**)
- *The door **burst** open.* (Not **bust**)
- *We **bust/busted/burst** the door open.*
  (i.e. we used force)
  (*bust* is often used informally for 'broke/broken': *I've **bust** the iron.*)

busy • occupied • engaged • in use
- *The lavatory's **occupied/engaged/in use** just now. You'll have to wait.* (Not **busy**)
  (i.e. someone is in there)
- *We're all **busy/occupied getting** ready for the wedding.* (Not **busy/occupied to get**)

- *The line's **busy/engaged** at the moment. I'll phone again later.* (Not **occupied**)
  (i.e. someone is phoning)
- *The boss is **busy/engaged** with a client at the moment. You can see him later.*
- *All the chairs were **occupied**.*
  (Not **busy* *engaged* *in use**)

but • yet
- *I have an ingenious **yet/but** simple solution to your problem.*
  (*yet* for emphasis: more formal than *but*)
- *I called **but** you were out.* (Not **yet**)
  (*but* for simple contrast)

butcher • butcher's
- *Where's Vanessa? - She's gone to **the butcher's**.* (Not **the butcher(s)**)
  (= the butcher's shop)
- *Any **butcher** knows that some people will pay high prices for top-quality meat.*

button • knob • key
- *The left-hand **knob** controls the volume.*
  (Not **button* *key**)
  (= a large, round control that turns)
- *To start the machine, you press this **button**.*
  (Not **knob* *key**)
  (= the small object, round or square, that you press to start a machine)
- *Which **key** do I press to quit the program?*
  (Not **button* *knob**)
  (= a square shape on e.g. a computer keyboard which you press down)

buy
- *They **bought us a present**. They **bought a present for us**.* (Not **They bought for us a present.* *Us they bought a present.**)
  (some other verbs that work like this are: *bring, build, choose, cook, cut, do, fetch, find, fix, get, keep, leave, make, order, reserve* and *save*)

by • near • on
- *We live **near** London.* (Not **by**)
  (= a short way from)
- *I sat **by** the phone and waited for it to ring.*
  (= right next to; beside)
- *Our house is right **on/by** the road.*
  (*on* a line: e.g. a road, a river)

by • with
- *He was killed **with** a knife.* (Not **by**)
  (i.e. deliberately)
- *He was killed **by** a falling stone.*
  (Not **with**)
  (i.e. accidentally)

- *You can lock this window **by** moving this catch to the left.* (Not **with**)
  (*by* + *-ing* for actions)

by and by • gradually
- *As the snow fell, the whole landscape **gradually** turned white.* (Not **by and by**)
  (= little by little)
- *We walked for some hours. **By and by**, we came to a tiny cottage in the forest.*
  (= after a time; old-fashioned narrative)

C

cabin • cubicle • (tele)phone box/call box
- *That **cubicle's** free if you want to try on those dresses.* (Not **cabin**)
  (= a small, curtained space where people can change their clothes)
- *I can't phone home yet. Every **(tele)phone box/call box** is occupied.* (Not **cabin**)
  *If we're sailing overnight, it's worth paying the cost of a **cabin**.*
  (= sleeping accommodation on a ship)

cabinet • lavatory • WC • toilet • closet
- *Where's Egon? - He's in the **lavatory/toilet**.*
  (Not **cabinet* *closet* *WC**)
  (*lavatory* is the normal word; *toilet* is a widely-used alternative; *lav* and *loo* (BrE) and *john* (AmE) are common colloquial alternatives; *WC* is old-fashioned)
- *Your crystal glasses look beautiful in that fine old **cabinet**.*
  (= a piece of furniture with drawers and shelves, often used to store valued objects; also *a filing cabinet* or *a medicine cabinet*)
- *There's a built-in **closet** in our bedroom.*
  (AmE for *a cupboard* used to store clothes; *(water) closet* (WC, also written wc) for *lavatory* is no longer in common use, though it is sometimes seen in writing)

café • coffee • cafeteria
- *Let's order **a coffee**, shall we?* (Not **café**)
  (= a cup of coffee)
- *When you're out, please get **some coffee**.*
  (Not **café**)
  (= coffee beans or coffee powder)
- *We had a cheap meal at a **café** (or **cafe**) before going to the theatre.*
  (= a simple restaurant serving light meals, especially BrE)
- *I hate queueing for egg and chips at a motorway **cafeteria**.* (Not **café**)
  (= a self-service restaurant, on a motorway, in a station, college, workplace, etc.)

calculate • estimate • reckon

- *We've **calculated** the cost of a new office and it's more than we can afford.*
  (= worked out accurately)
- *I **reckon/estimate** there must be at least eight hundred names on the list.*
  (= roughly calculate)

calendar • time-table/schedule • diary

- *We're hoping to keep to the **time-table/ schedule** and deliver your order on time.*
  (Not *calendar* *diary*)
  (also note: a *school time-table*)
- *I've made a note of your birthday in my **diary**.* (Not *calendar*)
  (= a book with spaces for days of the year)
- *According to the **calendar**, the 4th is a public holiday.*
  (a *wall* or *desk calendar* = a publication, often decorative, which tells you the date)

call/phone call

- *Excuse me. I just want to **make a (phone) call**.* (Not *do a (phone) call*)
- *Why don't you **give me a (phone) call**?*
  (Not *do/make me a (phone) call*)

call on • appeal to

- *Oxfam constantly **appeals to** us for contributions to its funds.* (Not *calls on*)
  (= makes strong requests)
- *The rebel leader **called on** his men to lay down their arms.*
  (= formally and publicly told them to)

call • shout (at) • cry • cry out • scream

- *You won't get the co-operation of the children if you keep **shouting at** them.*
  (Not *calling (at)* *crying (at)*)
  (*shout* = use a loud voice; *shout at* = speak to someone loudly and aggressively)
- *You'd better go now. I think that's your mother **calling**.*
  (= speaking loudly and clearly so as to be heard at a distance)
- *'Don't do that!' he **cried**.*
  (= raised his voice in brief exclamation)
- *When I told her the news, she **cried**.*
  (= wept, shed tears)
- *When I told her the news, she **cried out/shouted** in pain and anger.*
  (= raised her voice)
- *I could hear someone **screaming** for help in the distance.*
  (= shouting in fear or pain; stronger than *cry out* and *shout*)

camera • room

- *As soon as we arrived at the hotel, we were shown to our **room**.* (Not *camera*)
- *This is the smallest **camera** ever made.*
  (= a device for taking photographs)
- *The court hearing was **in camera**.*
  (= private, in a closed room: legal Latin)

camping • camping site/campsite

- *Is there **a camping site/a campsite** near the beach?* (Not *a camping* *camping*)
  (*camping site* is a countable noun)
- ***Camping** is cheap.* (Not *The camping*)
  (uncountable noun describing the activity)
- *We love to **go camping** in fine weather.*
  (Not *go for camping* *go for to camp*)

can

- *If you'd like to come this way please, Mr Wainwright **can see** you now.*
  (Not *can to see* *cans to see* *cans see*)
- *I **can go** soon.* (Not *I can (that) I go*)
- ***Can you** drive?* (Not *Do you can?*)
  (no *to*-infinitive or third person *-(e)s* ending after *can* and other modals; the negative *can't* is an abbreviation of *cannot*, which is written as one word: not *can not*)

can/could

- ***Can/Could** I use your car tomorrow please?*
  (*could* is more polite, or expresses greater uncertainty; *can* anticipates the answer *yes*)

can • will be able to

- *I'**ll be able to** pass my driving test after I've had a few lessons.* (Not *I can/I will can*)
  (*will be able to* predicts future achievement)
- *I **can see** you tomorrow if you're free.*
  (Not *I will can see*)
  (*can* can refer to the future in the sense of 'be free to'; *will be able to* is also possible here, but emphasizes practicality)

canal • channel

- *The **channel** between Britain and France is one of the world's busiest seaways.*
  (Not *canal*)
  (= a narrow sea passage)
- *In this part of the site you can see how the Romans collected rainwater through a system of **channels**.* (Not *canals*)
  (= open 'pathways' where water can run)
- *The Suez **Canal** is a major source of income for Egypt.* (Not *Channel*)
  (= an artificial waterway system on which boats can sail)

– *I can't get **Channel 4** because of the fog.*
(Not **Canal**)
(= the wavelength of a TV or radio station)

cancel • postpone
– *The match has had to be **cancelled/ postponed** because of the bad weather.*
(*cancelled* = prevented from happening; *postponed* = put to a later date)
– *I **postponed taking** my driving test when I wasn't well.* (Not **postponed to take**)

canopy • settee/sofa
– *Make yourself comfortable on the **settee/sofa** and I'll make us some tea.* (Not **canopy**)
(= a long comfortable seat with a back)
– *The garden is shaded by a **canopy** of leaves.*
(= a roof made of canvas or leaves that gives shade; compare *canapés* = small biscuits, etc., with cheese or meat on top)

can't (be) • can't have (been)
– *Alicia **can't have seen** it because she wasn't there.* (Not **can't see* *mustn't have seen**)
(*can't have* refers to present certainty or deduction about the past)
– *He **can't be** more than 30.*
(*can't (be)* refers to present certainty or deduction about the present)
– *He **can't leave** hospital before Friday.*
(= he isn't allowed to: present or future reference)
– *She **can't be** given the keys to the house till she's eighteen.*
(= it isn't possible: present or future reference)

canteen • restaurant
– *Just before Christmas, the company entertained us at an expensive **restaurant**.*
(Not **canteen**)
– *We have lunch in the school **canteen**.*
(= a self-service restaurant in a school or workplace, similar to a *cafeteria*)

capital
– *I'd like to start a magazine, but I haven't got **the capital**.* (Not **a capital* *capitals**)
(= a necessary sum of money, uncountable)
– *Paris is the **capital** of France.*
(= the centre of government, countable)

car • cart • lorry/truck • coach
– *People were fleeing from the fighting, pulling **carts** piled high with their possessions.* (Not **cars**)
(= vehicles with two or four wheels, drawn by horses or pulled by hand)

– *Never buy anything which they tell you has fallen off the back of a **lorry**.* (Not **car**)
(*lorry* (BrE)/*truck* (AmE) = a large motor vehicle for transporting goods)
– *As there are thirty of us, we've hired a **coach** (BrE)/**bus** (AmE) to take us to the football match.* (Not **car**)
(= a bus for long-distance travelling)
– *There is no speed limit for **cars** on most German motorways.*
(BrE *car/motorcar*; AmE *auto(mobile)*)
– *We're going to travel to Portugal **by car**.*
(Not **with the car**)

card • ticket
– *Book the seats on the phone and collect your **tickets** at the booking office.* (Not **cards**)
(*a ticket* = a piece of paper or card you buy to see a show or to use public transport)
– *If you want to contact me, here's my **card**.*
(= a small rectangular stiffened paper with your name and address printed on it)

cards • a game of cards
– *Let's **play cards/a game of cards**.*
(Not **play card* *play with/at cards**)
– *It's my turn to **play a card**.*
(Not **play card**)
(*cards*, as a game, is plural in form; but you can play a single *card* during a game)

care about/for
– *Angus is only interested in himself and **doesn't care about** anyone else.*
(Not **isn't caring* *isn't caring for**)
(only stative; no progressive form)
– *Who's **caring for** the children while you're both on holiday?*
(= looking after; dynamic use)

careful of/about
– *Since that injury, she has to be very **careful of/about** her back.* (Not **for/with**)

carry • wear • have (on)
– *Did he **have** long hair?*
(Not **Was he wearing**)
(*have* for physical characteristics: *have a scar, blue eyes, a beard, long hair*, etc.)
– *Was he **carrying** a briefcase?/Did he **have** a briefcase?*
(*carry*: i.e. have in his hand)
– *Was she **wearing** a hat?/Did she **have** a hat **on**?*
(*wear* = have something *on*)

cart • chart • map
– *If we're going to Crete, we'd better get an up-to-date **map**.* (Not **cart* *chart**)

(= a printed representation of the geographical features of a country or place)
- *If you're going to sail across the Mediterranean, you'll need a **chart**.* (Not *map* *cart*)
(= a map of the sea, ocean or sky)
- *He started life as a rag-and-bone man, collecting junk with a horse and **cart**.*

cart • menu
- *Let's have a look at the **menu**.* (Not *cart*)
(= the printed or displayed list of dishes at a restaurant; note *à la carte* = dishes from the general menu, not the fixed-price menu)
- *He started life as a rag-and-bone man, collecting junk with a horse and **cart**.*

cartel • card • label • etiquette
- *You can get in touch with me if you want to. Here's my **card**.* (Not *cartel* *etiquette*)
(= a small rectangle of stiff paper with your name and address printed on it)
- *Put a **label** on your suitcase before you check it in.* (Not *a cartel* *an etiquette*)
(= a specially-made card which can be used to identify an object)
- *The major oil companies constantly deny they operate as a **cartel**.*
(= an association of companies working together to control prices)
- *It's **etiquette** to write to thank your host for dinner, but not for lunch.*
(= the correct social procedure)

carton • cardboard
- *If you want to pack those books up, use some **cardboard**.* (Not *carton*)
(= thick stiffened paper)
- *It's more convenient to buy milk in a **carton** than in a bottle.*
(= a container made of cardboard)
- *I need some **cardboard**/a piece of **cardboard**/two pieces of **cardboard** to pack these books up.* (Not *a cardboard* *some cardboards* *two cardboards*)
(*cardboard* is uncountable)

case • cash desk
- *Pay at the **cash desk**.* (Not *case* *cash*)
(= the place in a shop where you can pay)
- *You should take legal action. You have a very good **case**.*
(= legal argument)

case: in case • in case of • in the case of
- *Take this umbrella **in case** it rains/**in case of** rain.* (Not *in the case* *in the case of*)
(= so as to be safe if/as provision against)

- *In the case of the ship's captain, there is no evidence to show he was negligent.*
(= in the matter concerning)

case • situation • occurrence
- *An earthquake in Britain is a rare **occurrence**.* (Not *case*)
(= a happening, event)
- *The waiter brought me the bill and I didn't have enough money. I've never been in such a **situation** before.* (Not *case*)
(= a position)
- *Do you know the date of the last recorded **case/occurrence** of smallpox?*
(= a particular instance)

cash • (in) cash
- *They'll only accept **cash**. Are you carrying any **cash**?* (Not *a cash* *any cashes*)
(*cash* is uncountable)
- *Can I pay **(in) cash**?* (Not *with cash*)

casket • peaked cap
- *In his **peaked cap** and splendid uniform, the railway guard looked like a five star general.* (Not *casket*)
(= a hat with a shade at the front, often part of a uniform)
- *The key was kept in a silver **casket**.*
(= a decorated box, sometimes ceremonial; also a *coffin*, AmE)

casserole

saucepan

casserole • saucepan
- *If you want to heat up some milk, use this **saucepan**.* (Not *casserole*)
- *The only way to serve so many guests was to prepare a large **casserole**.*
(= a dish cooked slowly in a closed pot; also a heavy pot with a lid for use over direct heat or in an oven)

catch
- *I **caught her reading** my diary.* (Not *caught her to read*)

cattle
- *The **cattle** are in the next field.* (Not *The cattle is* *The cattles are*)
(collective noun + plural verb; also: *the*

clergy, the military, the people, the police, vermin)

cause of • reason for
- *What was the **reason for** the delay?* (Not **cause for**) (= the explanation)
- *What was the **cause of** the delay?* (Not **reason of**) (= the thing that made it happen)
- *The **reason** I'm late **is that** I missed the bus.* (Not **the reason ... is because**) (missing the bus is the *cause of/reason for* my lateness)
- *I **have reason to suppose** he may be lying.* (= something makes me think)

cave • cellar • grotto
- *This garden has everything - even a **grotto**!* (Not **cave**) (= a decorative cave, often man-made)
- *It's an old house with a large **cellar**, ideal for storing wine.* (Not **cave**) (= a storeroom below the ground)
- *There's a big **cave** at the bottom of the cliff.* (= a natural opening in the side of a mountain or cliff)

certain of/about
- *I'm not **certain of/about** the facts.* (Not **certain for/from**)

certified • qualified
- *All the applicants we've had for the job are very well **qualified**.* (Not **certified**) (= have proof that they have reached a required standard and have *qualifications*)
- *Anyone who can behave like that ought to be **certified**.* (= officially declared to be insane)
- *Are you the **certified** owner of this vehicle?* (i.e. the one who possesses a certificate)

certify/declare • confirm/assure someone
- *I **confirm** that/I **assure you** that his story is true.* (Not **certify/declare** *confirm you* *assure that**) (*confirm* = say that it is true; *assure you* = promise that it is true)
- *The doctor **certified/declared** that the patient was dead on arrival.* (an official *certifies*; a witness *declares*)

chair • seat
- *You can easily fit three people on to the back **seat** of your car.* (Not **chair**) (= a place to sit, with room for one person or a few people)

- *Won't you **have/take a seat**.* (= sit down)
- *There are five of us, so we'll need another **chair** at the dining table.* (Not **seat**) (= a piece of furniture for one person to sit on)

chaise longue • deckchair
- *Sitting in the sun in a **deckchair** is one of life's rare pleasures.* (Not **chaise longue**) (= a wood-and-canvas seat that folds flat; AmE *beachchair*)
- *I think that **chaise longue** will be perfect for our living room.* (= a long seat with a back rest at one end)

chant • sing
- *It's the same song she **sang** in the Eurovision Song Contest.* (Not **chanted**)
- *When the minister got up to speak, the audience began **chanting**, 'Resign, resign'.* (Not **singing**) (= repeating rhythmically)

charge • be charged • charge with
- *They **charged** us too much for repairs.* (= asked us to pay: *We **were charged** a lot of money*.)
- *The police **charged** him **with** murder.* (= formally accused him: *He **was charged with** murder*.)

charge: in (the) charge of • responsible for
- *Simpson is now **in charge of/responsible for** the whole department.* (= has the responsibility for managing)
- *The department is now in **the charge of** Simpson.* (= in his care)
- *Who was **responsible for** making this decision?* (Not **in charge of** *the responsible for**) (= had the duty, but implying here that the decision was a wrong one)

chase • hunt
- *In most countries you need a special licence to **hunt** wild animals.* (Not **chase**) (= find and kill)
- *Police are still **hunting** the escaped prisoners.* (Not **chasing**) (= trying to catch)
- *I'm tired out after **chasing** the children round the garden.* (Not **hunting**) (= running after, not necessarily implying 'catching')

cheap • cheaply • reasonably-priced/ inexpensive
- *Most business is based on the idea that you buy **cheap/cheaply** and sell dear.*
  (both forms possible after verbs like *buy, find, get, obtain, sell*)
- *Countries with low labour costs can make textiles **cheaply**.* (Not *cheap*)
  (only *-ly* to describe a process)
- *I'm looking for a **reasonably-priced/ inexpensive room**.*
  (preferable to a *cheap room*, which can refer to price and/or appearance)

cheat (out of) • copy • deceive
- *I thought he'd been telling me the truth, but he completely **deceived** me.* (Not *cheated*)
  (= caused me to believe what was false)
- *The exam is carefully supervised, so it's hard to **cheat/copy**.* (Not *deceive*)
  (*cheat* = act dishonestly to get an advantage; *copy* = here, *cheat* by writing what someone else has written)
- *Miranda **cheated** her company **out of** thousands of pounds in false expense claims.* (Not *deceived* *copied*)
  (= dishonestly took from the proper owner)

check • cheque
- *You can pay **by cheque** (BrE)/**by check** (AmE) if you want to.*
  (note pay **by** cheque/check or pay **by** credit card, not *with*)

cheer • applaud
- *The audience **cheered/applauded** loudly at the end of the performance.*
  (*cheer* = shout loudly to show approval: *applaud* = clap the hands to show approval)

chemist • chemist's • pharmacist • pharmacy
- *We both studied at the London School of **Pharmacy**.*
- *My wife is a hospital **pharmacist**.*
- *The **chemist's** (AmE **pharmacy**) is open, but the **chemist** (AmE **pharmacist**) himself isn't back till 2.0.*
  (*chemist's*, BrE = chemist's shop)
- *My brother did a chemistry degree and is now an industrial **chemist**.*
  (= a person who has studied *pharmacy* works in a *chemist's* (BrE) or in a *pharmacy* (AmE) to sell medicines or make up prescriptions; *a drugstore* (AmE) sells medicines, but is also a general shop; a *chemist* = 1) a person who sells medicines or 2) a person who works in the field of chemistry)

chess • a game of chess
- *Let's play **chess/a game of chess**.*
  (Not *a chess*)
  (*chess* is uncountable; also: *football, ping-pong, table-tennis, tennis, volleyball*)

chest • bust • breast
- *Women should have regular checks for cancer of the **breast**.* (Not *chest* *bust*)
  (the words *breast/breasts* are used in connexion with women, but not men)
- *Is that dress only a 34 **bust**? It looks bigger.*
  (= a woman's chest measurement)
- *Grandad had a severe pain in the **chest**.*
  (*the chest* for men and children; the area around and above the breasts for women)

chick • chic/fashionable
- *Princess Diana was wearing an extremely **chic/fashionable** outfit.* (Not *chick*)
  (*chic* /ʃiːk/ = elegant, stylish; *fashionable* is safer to refer to up-to-date clothes, etc.)
- *When will the **chick** hatch out of the egg?*
  (= a baby bird, a chicken)

chief • boss • director • chef
- *Who's the **boss**/(managing) **director** of this company?* (Not *chief* *chef*)
  (= the person in charge of a company; *boss* is generally informal)
- *Norman Schwarzkopf was **chief** of the United Nations forces in the Gulf War.*
  (= the leader of a group of people)
- *If the food is bad, blame the **chef**.*
  (= the cook in a restaurant)

child/children
- *We have two **children**, a boy and a girl.*
  (Not *childs* *childrens*)
  (*children* is an irregular plural; the possessive forms are *child's* and *children's*)

child • baby • infant • toddler • kid
- *I learnt to ride a bicycle when I was a **child/a kid**.* (Not *a baby*)
  (*child* = a young human being; *kid* is very informal for young children and teenagers)
- *Doctors say that a **baby** should be breast-fed if possible.* (preferable to *an infant*)
  (= a very young *child*; *infant* is formal, official)
- *Some of the children at the day-school are just **toddlers**.*
  (= children who have just learnt to walk)

chimney • funnel • fireplace
- *We love to sit in front of the **fireplace** on a cold winter night.* (Not *chimney* *funnel*)

(= the place in a room where you can burn coal or logs to provide heat)
- *It's a hopeless fireplace. The heat goes straight up the **chimney**.* (Not **funnel**)
(= the vertical pipe to carry smoke away from a fire)
- *The Titanic was a large passenger liner with four **funnels**.* (Not **chimneys**)
(*funnel* = a metal pipe to carry gases away from a machine)

china/crockery
- *I think they'd like **some china/crockery** as a wedding present.* (Not **a china/a crockery* *some chinas/some crockeries**)
(= cups, plates, etc.; *china* and *crockery* are uncountable; *China* = name of the country)

chocolate • a bar of chocolate • chocolates
- *Whenever I go cycling, I always take **some chocolate/a bar of chocolate/two bars of chocolate**.* (Not **a chocolate**)
(*chocolate* is uncountable here)
- *Someone has had **a chocolate/four chocolates** out of this box.*
(*chocolate* is countable here and refers to separate sweets in *a box of chocolates*)

choice • choose
- *You have to **make a choice. Choose** carefully!* (Not **Do a choice* *Chose**)
(*choice* is the noun; *choose* is the verb)
- *Which **have** you **chosen**?* (Not **choosen**)
(*choose - chose - have chosen*)

cigar • cigarette
- *I hate the smell of **cigarettes**, but I don't mind the smell of **cigars**.*
(*a cigarette* = finely-chopped tobacco, rolled in a thin tube of white paper; *a cigar* = leaves of tobacco rolled into a fat tube)

cinema
- *What did you do last night? - We went **to the cinema**.* (Not **We went to cinema.* *We went cinema.**)
(*the + cinema*, even for 'any' cinema)

circulate • run
- *At what time in the morning do the buses begin to **run**?* (Not **circulate**)
(i.e. according to their timetable)
- *A clot can be dangerous if it prevents the blood from **circulating** freely.*
(= going round)

circulation • traffic
- *The **traffic** in London is very heavy during rush hour.* (Not **circulation**)
(= vehicles on the road)
- *My feet are always cold because of my bad **circulation**.*
(= the movement of blood round the body)
- *Isn't there **a lot of traffic** this morning!* (Not **a traffic* *a lot of traffics**)
(*traffic* = moving vehicles, is uncountable)

circumstances: in/under no circumstances
- ***In/Under no circumstances should you accept** this offer.* (Not **In/Under no circumstances you should accept ...**)
(inversion after negative adverbs; formal and emphatic. Compare normal word order with a negative verb: *You **shouldn't accept** this offer in/under **any** circumstances.* Some careful speakers prefer *in no/any circumstances* to 'under')

citron • lemon • citrus
- *Grilled fish tastes good with a generous squeeze of **lemon**.* (Not **citron**)
- *This birthday cake contains currants, sultanas and a little **citron** peel.*
(= a yellow thick-skinned fruit related to a lemon)
- ***Citrus fruits** only grow in warm climates.* (e.g. oranges, lemons, limes)

city • town • village
- *Berlin is the capital **city** of Germany.*
- *I don't mind not living near the capital, but I'd hate to live far from a **town**.*
- *Apart from a few houses, we have a shop, a pub and a church in our **village**.*
- *She was born **in Guildford/in the town of Guildford**.* (Not **in the town Guildford**; similarly: *village, city*)
(a *city* is larger than a *town*; a *town* is larger than a *village*. We say *in/from/to/out of town* to refer to our nearest town or city: *I spent the day **in town**.*)

civilization • civilized • developed (country)
- *Germany is a **developed/civilized** country.* (Not **a country with civilization**)
(i.e. it has an advanced social, industrial and political system)
- *A low infant mortality rate is one of the advantages of modern **civilization**.*

civilization • life and institutions
- *A lot of people want to learn English without being interested in British **life and institutions**.* (Not **civilization**)

(note: we do not use *civilization* to mean *way of life*: not *rural civilization*)
- *Western society has developed from the ancient **civilizations** of Greece and Rome.*

claim from • demand from
- *We've had a lot of storm damage and we're **claiming/demanding** compensation **from** our insurance company* (Not *claiming to*)
(*claim* = ask for something you think you have a right to; *demand* = make a strong request for something)

class
- *The children are **in class**.*
(Not *to/at class* *in the class*)
- *I think the **class is/are** fully prepared for the exam.*
(collective noun + singular or plural verb)

classic • classical
- *Darren is one of those people who can't bear **classical** music.* (Not *classic*)
(= serious and lasting)
- *'Between you and I' is a **classic** example of bad grammar.* (Not *classical*)
(= typical, or excellent of its type, as in *a classic mistake, a classic suit*, etc.)

classroom • class • lesson
- *I must hurry. I have a **class/a lesson** at 11.*
(Not *a classroom*)
(spoken by a teacher, this means 'I am taking a class/giving a lesson'; spoken by a student, this means 'I am attending a class/a lesson')
- *The students are waiting for you **in the classroom/in class**.* (Not *in the lesson*)
(*classroom* = place; *in class* = gathered together for a lesson)

clean • cleanly
- *With a single swing of the axe, he cut the log **clean/cleanly** in two.*
(*cleanly* = neatly, in a clean way; *clean* = completely in e.g. *clean forget, clean in two, (get) clean away, (be) clean off his head*)
- *I don't mind how you do the job, as long as you do it **cleanly**.* (Not *clean*)
(= in a clean way)

cleaning
- *Who **does the cleaning** in this household?*
(Not *makes the cleaning*)
(specific reference with *the*)
- *This house needs **a lot of cleaning**.*
(Not *much cleaning*)
- ***Cleaning** takes a long time.*
(Not *The cleaning* *The cleanings*)
(general statement)

clear (of) • clearly
- *Stand **clear of** the doors!* (Not *clearly*)
(*clear (of)* = away (from): move/stand/stay *clear of* someone or something)
- *I want to **make it clear** that I'm not paying this bill.* (Not *make it clearly*)
(i.e. be sure that I am understood)
- *Please write **clearly**.* (Not *clear*)
(*clearly* to describe a deliberate action)

clerk • employee • shop assistant • attendant • official
- *ICI has thousands of **employees**.*
(general term for paid workers)
- *John's just got a job as a **clerk** at the bank.*
(an *employee* who does office work; *pen pusher* is used humorously or dismissively; *scribe* is archaic)
- ***Shop assistants** aren't highly paid.*
(*employees* who serve in a shop; AmE *salesclerks*)
- *Ask an **attendant** when the park closes.*
(Not *shop assistant* *employee* *clerk*)
(*attendants* look after places: e.g. gates, filling stations, parks, museums, swimming-pools)
- *The bank has appointed **officials** to investigate complaints by customers.*
(= people in responsible positions in government departments, banks, etc.)

client • customer • patient • guest
- *During the sales, the department stores are full of **customers**.* (Not *clients* *guests*)
(= people who buy things)
- *Small **clients** demand the same service from their bank as large **clients**.*
(= people who buy services from banks, lawyers, etc.; *customer* can also be used, but it is less formal than *client*)
- *Shall I send in the next **patient**, doctor?*
(Not *customer* *client*)
(= a person who seeks medical services)
- *Parking facilities are available only for hotel **guests**.* (Not *clients* *customers*)
(= people staying at a hotel)

climb up/down
- *Is it harder to climb **up** a mountain, or to climb **down** one?*
(we climb *down* as well as *up*)

climbing
- *We **went climbing** last holidays.* (Not *went for climbing* *went for to climb*)
(also: *camping, fishing, hunting, riding,*

sailing, shopping, sight-seeing, skiing, walking)

clock • watch
– *It's usual to wear a watch on your left wrist, not your right.* (Not **clock**)
– *What an attractive kitchen clock!*
(a *clock* is larger than a *watch*: it hangs on a wall or stands on a surface; a *watch* is worn on the wrist or carried in the pocket)

close (to) • closely
– *Stand close to me.* (Not **closely to**)
(*close (to)* = near (to))
– *I studied her face closely.* (Not **close**)
(*closely* = in detail)

close • turn off
– *Turn off the tap/the light.* (Not **Close**)
(*turn off* for taps and switches)
– *Please close the window/the door.*
(*close* for windows and doors; note *close/draw the curtains*, not **turn off**; *draw the curtains* is ambiguous and can mean either 'open' or 'shut' unless specified: *Draw the curtains back/across.*)

closed/shut • off • out
– *Are the taps/lights off?* (Not **closed/shut**)
– *Are the lights out?* (Not **closed/shut**)
(*taps*, *lights*, *the gas*, *the electricity* can be *on* or *off*; lights can be *on* or *off/out*)
– *Are all the doors and windows closed/shut?* (Not **off** **out**)
(*doors/windows* are *open* or *closed/shut*)

cloth/material • clothe
– *Wipe up the mess with a cloth.*
(Not **a clothe** **a material**)
(*a cloth* = a piece of material for cleaning: countable noun; the plural is *cloths*)
– *There's enough cloth/material there for a skirt.* (Not **clothe**)
(*cloth* and *material* are uncountable)
– *We can't hope to feed and clothe our children if we don't both work.*
(verb = provide clothes for; dress)

clothes • clothing • garment
– *My clothes are getting shabby.*
(Not **My clothe is** **My clothes is**)
(plural noun with no singular form + plural verb)
– *Elisabeth owns a lot of clothes.*
(Not **a clothing/a lot of clothings**)
– *The Red Cross appealed for tents and clothing.*
(*clothing* = uncountable, things that will

clothe people, in a general sense; we can also say *an article of clothing*)
– *This garment must be washed at 40°C.*
(Not **This cloth** **This clothe**)
(we can use *a/this garment* - formal - to refer to a single item of *clothing*)

coach • bus • train • Pullman
– *You can travel very quickly from Alexandria to Cairo by coach* (BrE only)/*by bus* (BrE/AmE). (Not **Pullman**)
(BrE uses *bus* as well as *coach* for long-distance)
– *The best way to see America is by train* (BrE/AmE)/*by Pullman* (AmE).
(a *Pullman* - spelt with a capital *P* - is a specially comfortable railway carriage for long-distance journeys)
– *The railway station is only a ten-minute journey on the bus.* (Not **coach/Pullman**)

coal • charcoal
– *You need more charcoal for that barbecue.*
(Not **coal** **a charcoal/more charcoals**)
– *Coal doesn't burn as cleanly as oil.*
(*coal* = black, stone-like fuel from the earth; *charcoal* = fuel made by burning wood very slowly. Both words are normally uncountable, though *a coal, hot coals* can occur in specific references)

coarse • course
– *I'm doing a French course.* (Not **coarse**)
(= a series of lessons)
– *He wore an old jacket made of coarse cloth.*
(= rough, not smooth)

coast • shore • cost • beach/seaside • sea
– *There is rain over the whole of the west coast of Britain.* (Not **shore** **cost**)
(we use *coast* when we are thinking of a country in terms of a map; take care with the spelling: *coast*, not **cost**)
– *In bad weather a lifeboat is ready to set out from the shore at very short notice.*
(preferable to *coast*)
(we use *shore* to refer to the dry land at the edge of the sea)
– *With the increase in oil prices, the cost of a holiday has risen sharply.*
(= the price)
– *There's nothing the children enjoy more than a day at the beach/at the seaside.*
(Not **on the coast** **at/to the sea**; preferable to *on the shore*)
(= the part of the shore used for pleasure)

- *The **beach** was crowded.*
  (Not **coast* *shore* *seaside**)
  (specific reference to a sandy or pebbly area)
- *There were a lot of people in the **sea**.*
  (= in the water)

coat • jacket
- *I need a **coat** which is warm but light.*
  (= an item of clothing worn over all other clothes to protect from the cold or rain)
- *Those trousers don't match that **jacket**.*
  (= the top part of a suit, or a short coat)

cocktail • cocktail party
- *Are you coming to **the cocktail party** on Friday night?* (Not **the cocktail**)
  (= a party at which alcoholic drinks and light food are served)
- *I've asked the barman to fix me a Manhattan - my favourite **cocktail**.*
  (= a mixed drink, usually alcoholic)

cold: be/get cold, have/catch (a) cold • cool
- ***It** (= the weather) **is cold** today.*
  (Not **It has cold* *It makes cold**)
- *My coffee **is cold**.* (Not **colded**)
  (= not warm)
- ***I'm cold**. I think I'll put on a pullover.*
  (Not **I have cold.* *I cold.**)
  (= I don't feel warm)
- *You'll **get cold** without a coat.*
  (Not **You'll cold* *You'll cool**)
  (= you will feel cold)
- *The Colonel seems rather a **cold** person.*
  (= not friendly, not well-disposed)
- *I **have a cold**./I've **caught (a) cold**.*
  (Not **I have cold.**)
  (*a* with *cold* to refer to the illness)
- *Mind you don't **catch cold/a cold**!*
  (we can sometimes omit *a* after *catch*; *catch cold* = get chilled)
- *You should **cool** the food/**make** the food **cool** before putting it in the fridge.*
  (*cool*, verb = cause to lose heat)

collaborator • colleague
- *May I introduce my **colleague**?*
  (Not **collaborator**)
- *After the war, Lord Haw-Haw was arrested, tried as an enemy **collaborator** and hanged.*
  (= someone who works with the enemy)

collar • collier • necklace
- *This **necklace** looks fabulous, but it's just costume jewellery.* (Not **collar* *collier**)
  (= jewellery for the neck)
- *He was wearing a shirt with a wide **collar**.*
  (Not **collier**)

- *Dogs should be required by law to wear **collars**.* (Not **necklaces* *colliers**)
  (= bands worn by animals round the neck)
- *I was a **collier** before the mines closed.*
  (= a coal miner)

collation • snack
- *After four hours' work, we stopped for a **snack**.* (Not **collation**)
  (= a light meal; *a collation* = a formal light meal is now old-fashioned; note that we don't use *lunch* to mean *snack*)
- *I've been left to deal with the **collation/collating** of these papers on my own.*
  (= putting them in the right order)

collect • pick/gather
- *Professional growers keep apple trees small so that **picking/gathering** the fruit is easy.*
  (Not **collecting**)
  (= take fruit/flowers while they are growing)
- *Once a year I volunteer to **collect** money for cancer research.* (Not **pick* *gather**)
  (= bring together from different sources)

college • colleague
- *I know Mike Seymour very well. He's a **colleague** of mine.* (Not **college**)
  (= someone I work with)
- *What sort of job do you expect to get after three years at **college**?*
  (= an institution of higher learning)

college • university
- *Ann's at York **University**.* (Not **College**)
  (= an institution that awards degrees)
- *Our daughter started **college** last October.*
- *Joe's **at college** for three years to study engineering.* (Not **to college**)
- *Joe's going **to college** next October.*
  (Not **in/at the college* *to the college**)
  (= BrE: any institution of higher learning, not always leading to a degree; in the UK a *university* may consist of different *colleges*; some independent schools use *College* as part of their title: e.g. *Eton College*)

colour
- *His hair is **brown**.*
  (Not **The colour of his hair is brown.**)
  (we don't need to use the noun *colour* - AmE *color* - when naming a colour)

column • line/queue of cars
- *There's been an accident and there's a **line/queue of cars** that stretches back ten miles.* (Not **column**)
- *A **column** of smoke rose from the chimney.*
  (= a solid line)

combination • petticoat/slip • bathing costume

- *That dress would look better with a **petticoat/slip** under it.*
  (Not **combination**, but *combinations* = an old-fashioned item of underwear)
  (*a petticoat/slip* = an underskirt; *slip* is not used in English to mean *pants/knickers*)
- *The **combination** of hydrogen and oxygen produces water.*
  (= putting together)
- *Get your **bathing costume** on and we'll go for a swim.* (Not **slip**)
  (*bathing costume* and *swimming costume* (both sexes), *swimsuit* and *bikini* (women) and *bathing/swimming trunks* (men) are in common use; *bathers* + plural verb is a colloquial alternative for both sexes)

combine • conspiracy • holding

- *The Minister denied that there had been a **conspiracy** to bring down the party leader.* (Not **combine**)
  (= a secret plan involving people acting together to do something wrong)
- *I have a **holding** of 100 shares in BASF.* (Not **combine**)
  (= the ownership of shares in a company)
- *BASF is a large industrial **combine**.*
  (= a group of companies)

come

- *Do you want to **come shopping** with us?* (Not **come for shopping**)
- *Do you want to **come for a walk** with us?*
- ***Come walking** with us in the Lake District.* (Not **Come walk**)
  (i.e. as an outdoor sport, pursuit)
- ***The time has come** to help them.*
  (Not **It's come the time to help them.**)

come from

- *Where **do you come from**?*
  (Not **are you coming from**)
  (only stative in this sense = what is your country of origin?)
- *Which station **is he coming from**?*
  (dynamic use)

comforts • conveniences

- *They live in a cottage without any modern **conveniences**.* (Not **comforts**)
  (*modern conveniences*, commonly 'mod cons' = full services and equipment)
- *Young people are often reluctant to go out into the world and surrender the **comforts** of living at home.* (Not **conveniences**; note the spelling: not **conforts**)
  (= the things that make life easy and comfortable)

comical • comic/comedian

- *Bob Hope is **a natural comic/comedian**. He only has to raise an eyebrow to make you laugh.* (Not **a comical**)
  (nouns = a person who makes you laugh: *a comic actor*; *comics* refers to more than one comic actor: *Laurel and Hardy were a couple of **comics/comedians**.*)
- *We were in this **comic/comical** situation where we couldn't go up or down.*
  (adjectives = funny)

comma • point • (full) stop • dot

- *The front pressures should be **1.8** (**one point eight**).* (Not **one comma eight** **one stop eight** **1,8**)
  (when writing, we mark decimals with stops, not with commas; in speech we call the stop 'point'. We say each number after the *decimal point* separately: 45.987 = *forty-five point nine eight seven*)
- *If you start a sentence with 'However', you should use a **comma** after it.*
- *Always end a sentence with a **(full) stop**.*
- *We always put a **dot** over the letters i and j.* (Not **(full) stop**)
  (= a small round mark)

command • order

- *I didn't **order** a steak. I **ordered** fish.* (Not **command** **commanded**)
  (= asked to be brought)
- *The officer **ordered/commanded the men to return** to barracks.* (Not **ordered the men that they should return**)
  (i.e. he spoke to them directly)
- *The officer **ordered that the soldiers should retreat**.* (Not **commanded**)
  (i.e. he gave the order directly or indirectly)
- *In the Gulf War, General Schwarzkopf **commanded** the United Nations forces.*
  (= was in charge of)

commissionaire • agent

- *Who's the Rank Xerox **agent** in Cairo?* (Not **commissionaire**)
  (= the person who acts for them)
- *Fred works as a **commissionaire** outside a posh hotel and earns a fortune in tips.*
  (= an attendant in a uniform, outside a hotel, cinema, etc.; BrE)

commode • chest of drawers

– *I need a **chest of drawers** in my bedroom as well as a wardrobe.* (Not **commode**)
(= a piece of furniture with drawers to store clothes)
– *The idea of a **commode** in your bedroom would be funny today.*
(= a chair with a built-in chamber pot)

common • vulgar • normal • ordinary

– *I'm not looking for anything fancy, just an **ordinary/normal** kettle.* (Not **common**)
(= simple, not elaborate)
– *I'm just an **ordinary** person.* (Not **vulgar**)
(= not distinguished in any way)
– *In this block we have a **common** responsibility for maintaining the staircase.* (Not **vulgar* *normal* *ordinary**)
(= shared)
– *I wish you wouldn't use such **common/ vulgar** expressions in your speech.*
(= rough, socially unacceptable)

companion • partner

– *I've just started this business with a **partner**.* (Not **companion**)
(= a business associate)
– *I want to travel to the Himalayas and I'm looking for a **companion**.*
(= someone to come with me, to be company for me)

compliment • complement

– *The inspector **paid** our teacher **a compliment** on the way she managed her class.* (Not **did/made* *complement**)
(= expressed appreciation, admiration; the adjective is *complimentary*, as in ***complimentary** remarks*)
– *Mustard is often thought to be the ideal **complement** to beef.* (Not **compliment**)
(i.e. they go very well together; the adjective is *complementary*: *Mustard and beef are **complementary**. Compliment(ary)* and *complement(ary)* are pronounced the same)

compose • arrange

– *You've **arranged** those flowers beautifully!* (Not **composed**)
(fixed phrases: *arrange flowers, make a flower arrangement*: e.g. in a vase)
– *I'll have to be very careful how I **compose** this letter.*
(= 'create' in words or music)

composed of

– *A jury is **composed of** people from all walks of life.* (Not **composed from**)

compost • compote • stewed fruit

– *We had **stewed fruit**/a cold **compote** for dessert.* (Not **compost**)
(*stewed fruit*, uncountable, is the usual term for fruit boiled with sugar and eaten hot or cold; a *compote*, countable, is a less common French loanword for the same thing)
– *We need some **compost** on this rose-bed.*
(= decayed vegetable matter)

concern • concerned with/about • concerning

– *The state of the environment **concerns** everyone on earth.* (Not **is concerning**)
(= matters to; only stative)
– *There's no problem about working overtime **as far as I'm concerned/as far as it concerns me**.*
(= as I'm affected/it affects me)
– *Our boss isn't **concerned with** the day-to-day running of the company.*
(= involved in)
– *I am **concerned about** my health.* (Not **concerned with* *am afraid of* *have fear about**)
(= anxious about, worried about)
– *We still have a great deal to discuss **concerning** pay and conditions.* (Not **concerning about* *concerned about**)
(= about; formal)

concert • concerto

– *The young pianist played a difficult **concerto** by Bartok.* (Not **concert**)
(= a piece for orchestra and solo instrument)
– *The **concert** begins with the overture to 'William Tell'.* (Not **concerto**)
(= a musical performance e.g. by an orchestra)

concurrence • competition • race

– *Quality control is the only way to stay ahead of **the competition**.*
(Not **the concurrence* *the race**)
(= those trying to do better than you)
– *The **competition** for jobs is unbelievable.*
(= rivalry)
– *No **race** is more demanding than the Marathon.* (Not **competition**)
(= a competition in speed)
– *Obviously, we can't do anything about this without Andrew's **concurrence**.*
(= consent)

condemned (to) • convicted (of)

– *He was **convicted of** murder and jailed for life.* (Not **condemned of**)
(= judged to be guilty of a crime)

– *He was found guilty and **condemned to** two years in jail.*
(= given a punishment of)

conduct oneself • behave (oneself)

– *It isn't reasonable to expect young children to **behave (themselves)**, even in a church.* (Not **conduct themselves**)
(= behave well, especially in formal social situations)
– *The trial was an ordeal, but she **conducted herself very well**.* (Not **behaved**)
(we can use *conduct oneself* to mean *behave*, but *conduct oneself* must always be followed by an adverb: *He conducted himself **well**,* not **He conducted himself.**)

conductor • driver/chauffeur • motorist • leader • guide • director

– *The **driver** kindly stopped the bus in the middle of nowhere and let me off.*
(Not **conductor* *chauffeur**)
(= the person driving)
– *Here's the money for when the **conductor** comes to collect fares.* (Not **driver**)
(= the person who collects fares on buses; compare *the inspector* who inspects tickets)
– *Hasn't Douglas done well! He even employs a **chauffeur/driver**!* (Not **conductor**)
(*chauffeur* = a private driver; formal)
– ***Motorists/Drivers** always complain when road taxes are increased.*
(= people who drive cars)
– *He was a popular **leader** of his country.* (Not **conductor**)
– *When we visited the pyramids, we hired a **guide**.* (Not **conductor**)
– *Who's the **conductor** of the London Symphony Orchestra?*
(Not **director** for a musician)
(= the musician who regulates the playing of other musicians e.g. with a baton)
– *Who's the **director** of the LSO?*
(= the person responsible for its business management)

confection • sweet(s)

– *If you eat those **sweets** now, you won't want your dinner.*
(Not **confections**, but compare *confectionery*: uncountable noun = sugary foods)
– *The chef had prepared an extraordinary **confection** for the wedding.*
(= a strange or elaborate sweet dish)

confectioner's • sweet shop • tea shop

– *Bonne Bouche is my favourite **tea shop**.*
(Not **confectioner's/sweet shop**)
(= a shop where you drink tea and/or have something to eat)
– *Mr Hailey runs a small **sweet shop/ confectioner's** near the station.*
(= a shop that sells sweets and chocolates)
– *You can only get chocolates like this at a real **confectioner's**.* (Not **sweet shop**)
(= a specialist sweet maker)

confound • confuse

– *I'm always **confused** by the sort of information you get from public opinion polls.* (Not **confounded**)
(= unable to form a clear view)
– *Chris was **confounded** to meet us socially after he'd been so rude to us in the street.* (Not **confused**)
(= embarrassed, not knowing what to say)

confuse (with) • get confused

– *I **got confused** and turned left by accident.* (Not **I confused* *confused myself**)
– *Don't **confuse** me **with** my twin brother.*
(= mistake me for)

congealed • frozen

– *Quick! I want to get the **frozen** foods home and into the freezer.* (Not **congealed**)
– *Alan kept me on the phone till my dinner was completely **congealed**.*
(= became cold, thick and sticky)

congratulate • felicitate

– *I must **congratulate** you **on** your success.* (Not **congratulate for** or *felicitate*, which is so rare in English as to sound insincere)
(the noun, always plural, is *congratulations* + *on*: ***Congratulations on** your success!*)

connect/join • unite

– *The party leader has successfully managed to **unite** the different elements in his party.* (Not **connect/join**)
(= make them one/whole)
– *You have to **join** these two wires **together/connect** them.* (Not **unite**)
(= put together, attach them to each other)

conscience • conscientious • conscious • consciousness

– *When you're in Paris you can't help being **conscious** of the way the streets are kept clean.* (Not **conscience* *conscientious**)
(= aware)

- A **conscientious** worker is an asset to any company. (Not *conscious* *conscience*) (i.e. who works seriously and with care)
- If your **conscience** tells you it isn't the right thing to do, don't do it. (Not *conscious*) (= your inner sense of right and wrong)
- He fainted and it took him a minute to regain **consciousness**. (Not *conscience*) (= possession of his senses)

conscious • sensible
- Amy's a **sensible** woman and I can rely on her judgement. (Not *conscious*) (i.e. she has good sense and judgement)
- When I first became **conscious**, I didn't remember anything about the accident. (= awake, in possession of my senses)

conservatives • preserves • preservatives
- I never buy cold meats. They're full of **preservatives**. (Not *conservatives*) (= substances that stop food going bad)
- Barbara's larder is absolutely full of **preserves** and pickles. (*preserves* is generic for 'bottled fruit and jam' and is therefore normally plural; it's the occasional singular use that is unusual: Tiptree's Damson **Preserve**)
- People who are **conservatives** with a small 'c' object to any kind of change. (i.e. they want things to stay as they are)

conserve • preserve
- How did people **preserve** food when there were no refrigerators? (Not *conserve*) (= prevent it from going bad)
- There's only enough water for a couple of days, so we must **conserve** what we have. (= make it last as long as possible; *preserve* would suggest 'not use at all')
- We have to **preserve/conserve** the countryside for future generations. (the nouns are *preservation, conservation*)

conserves • tinned/canned food • a tin/a can
- It really isn't healthy to live on **tinned/canned food**. (Not *conserves*) (= food preserved in *tins* or *cans*)
- There isn't much to eat. Let's open a **tin**. (or a can, AmE) (Not *a conserve*)
- It's called 'Mrs Harvey's Old-Fashioned Strawberry **Conserve**'. (= jam; only used on manufacturers' labels)

consider
- Professor Heinz is **considered an expert/considered to be an expert** on molluscs. (Not *considered as an expert*)

- **Considered as** neighbours, the Clarks are reasonable enough. (*as* = in their capacity as)
- I'm seriously **considering leaving** the company. (Not *considering to leave*) (*consider* + *-ing*, not *to*, = think about)
- **I consider** that the matter is now closed. (Not *I'm considering*) (stative use in 'declarations' = believe)

construe • construct
- The town council has allowed a developer to **construct** an office block in front of a 14th century church. (Not *construe*) (= build)
- Clause 8 could be **construed** to mean that we aren't insured against fire. (= analysed and understood)

consult • advise
- A lot of people were **advised** that the bank's finances were sound. (Not *consulted*) (= given advice)
- A lot of people were **consulted** about the bank's finances. (= asked for advice)

consummation • refreshment(s) • consumption
- There's no dining car, but an attendant brings round a trolley of light **refreshments**. (Not *consummations*) (= food and drink)
- The restoration of this castle to its former glory is the **consummation** of a life's work. (= the completion)
- The **consumption** of organically-grown food is on the increase. (= eating)

contemplate
- I couldn't **contemplate changing** my lifestyle. (Not *to change*) (= consider)

content • happy • pleased
- I was **happy/pleased** to hear that your son has got into Cambridge. (Not *content*) (i.e. it gave me pleasure)
- Tania is quite **content/happy** in her present job. (Not *pleased*) (= satisfied)

continent • Europe • the Continent
- Much of the African **continent** is unsuitable for cattle because of tsetse fly. (= a large land mass)

– *The British often refer to* **Europe** *as 'the Continent'.*
(*the Continent = the rest of Europe; BrE*)

continual • continuous

– *The* **continual** *noise of building going on upstairs is driving us mad.*
(= constant, with interruptions)
– *There is nothing more annoying than the* **continuous** *wailing of a burglar alarm.*
(= constant, without interruptions)

contrary: the contrary • on the contrary • in contrast with/to

– *I'm not opposed to what you're trying to do.* **On the contrary,** *I wholly approve.*
(Not *Contrary* *The contrary*)
(= quite the opposite)
– *The situation isn't as you suggest. It's quite* **the contrary.**
(= the opposite)
– **In contrast with/to** *other parts of the country, we've had a lot of rain.*
(Not *On the contrary with*)

contrary • conflicting

– *How can they get on well together when they have such* **conflicting/contrary** *interests?*
(= opposing; *conflicting* is more usual)

control • check • keep a check on • set

– *They're going to* **check** *our passports.*
(Not *control*)
(= examine e.g. money, passports, identification; we can say *We have to go through* **passport control**, using *passport control* as a compound noun)
– **Check** *the tyres before you leave.*
(Not *Control*)
(= examine)
– *It's hard to* **keep a check on** *the number of people coming into the country.*
(Not *control*)
(= monitor, keep a record of; we can use *control* in the above sentence to mean e.g. 'limit the number of')
– *My watch can't be wrong. I* **set** *it by the pips on the radio.* (Not *controlled*)
OPEC no longer **controls** *the price of oil.*
(= has power over)

conveniences • social conventions

– *You can't go through life ignoring the* **social conventions.** (Not *conveniences*)
(= accepted standards of behaviour)
– *Where are the public* **conveniences**?
(= lavatories; BrE)

convenient • comfortable • suitable

– *We'd all like to live in a* **comfortable** *house.*
(i.e one that makes life easy and pleasant; the opposite is *uncomfortable*)
– *Our house is very* **convenient** *for the shops.*
(= near; the opposite is *inconvenient*)
– *What you're wearing isn't* **suitable** *for the occasion.* (Not *convenient*)
(= appropriate; the opposite is *unsuitable*)
– *Yes, Friday will be* **convenient/suitable.**
(both words are possible for dates, appointments, etc.)

convent • monastery

– *The* **monastery** *is famous for a fine liqueur made by the monks.* (Not *convent*)
(a *monastery* is inhabited by *monks*)
– *Some of the nuns from the* **convent** *teach in the local schools.* (Not *monastery*)
(a *convent* is inhabited by *nuns*)

conversation • discussion • dialogue

– *NATO members are to have a* **discussion** *about arms reduction.*
(Not *conversation* *dialogue*)
(= a serious exchange of views on a particular topic)
– *I* **had** *a long* **conversation** *with my mother on the phone last night.*
(Not *dialogue* *made/did a conversation*)
(= an informal talk on all kinds of subjects; the verb *converse (with)* is formal)
– *I find it hard to* **make conversation** *at parties.* (Not *do/have conversation*)
(= keep a flow of talk going)
– *Actors have to learn a lot of* **dialogue.**
(Not *conversation*)
(= written conversation)

convert • persuade • convince

– *You have* **convinced/persuaded** *me that we need a new computer.* (Not *converted*)
(= made me change my views)
– *The salesman* **persuaded** *me to buy a new computer.* (Not *convinced*, which should be followed by *that*)
(= made me take action)
– *Angela is very religious and tries to* **convert** *everyone she meets.*
(= persuade them to become religious)

cook • boil

– *I'm* **boiling** *some water. I want a couple of* **boiled** *eggs.* (Not *cooking* *cooked*)
(*boil* = heat a liquid till it turns to vapour; *boil eggs* = cook eggs in boiling water, so the result is *boiled eggs*)

– It's my turn to **cook** the lunch. (Not *boil*)
(*cook* is the general verb for 'prepare food by heating': *boil water*, but *cook a meal*)

cooker • cook
– My husband is a good **cook**. (Not *cooker*)
(= a person who *cooks* food)
– Is your **cooker** gas or electric?
(= the apparatus on or in which food is cooked, BrE, or *stove*, especially AmE)

cooking
– I do most of **the cooking**.
(Not *make the cooking*)
(some other nouns that combine with *do*: damage, duty, exercise, someone a favour, the flowers, the gardening, someone's hair, someone an injury, the ironing, a job, someone a kindness, the kitchen, etc. (= clean), my nails, someone a service, work)

cop • cup • bowl
– Have a **cup** of coffee. (Not *cop*)
– Use a large **bowl** for the salad. (Not *cup*)
– Look out! There's a traffic **cop**.
(informal for *policeman*)

copies • papers • pages
– They've done the exam. Now we've got to correct the **papers**. (Not *copies* *pages*)
– Do authors get free **copies** of their books?
(a *copy* = one book from an edition)
– How many **pages** are there in an average novel? (Not *papers*)
(= sheets of paper in a book)
– Make ten **copies** of this page for me please.
(= e.g. photocopies)

copy • imitate • mime • mimic
– It was only when I **mimed/imitated** a chicken that the waiter understood what I wanted to order. (Not *copied*)
(*mime* = use actions without language; *imitate* = act like)
– I wish you'd stop **imitating/copying** the way I speak. (Not *miming*)
– You should hear her **mimic** our teacher.
(= copy actions and speech very exactly, possibly so as to make other people laugh; a person who does this is *a mimic*)

cordon • cord • shoelace
– Your **shoelace** is undone. (Not *cordon*)
(= a special string used to fasten shoes)
– You can draw the curtains with this **cord**.
(Not *cordon*)
(= strong string or very thin rope)
– There's been a bomb scare and the police have put a **cordon** round Piccadilly.

(= a ring of e.g. police, or a physical barrier to protect something or to keep people away)

corn • horn
– I sounded my car **horn**. (Not *corn*)
(= a device that makes a warning sound)
– I play the **horn**. (Not *corn*)
(= a wind instrument)
– The USA grows more **corn** than Europe.
(*corn* = the general agricultural term for food grains, e.g. wheat, barley; also the short form for *Indian corn* = maize)

cornice • frame
– I'm going to put this picture in a nice **frame**.
(Not *cornice*)
(= the border round a picture, usually wood)
– It's a beautiful old room with a high ceiling and a decorative **cornice**.
(= an overhang along the top of a wall)

corpse • body • corps
– Looking after your **body** becomes essential as you get older. (Not *corpse* *corps*)
– I tried to get her autograph but couldn't get through the press **corps** /kɔː^r/.
(Not *body* *corpse*)
(= the people representing that group; also the diplomatic corps)
– The police found **a corpse** /kɔːps//a (dead) **body** buried in the garden.

correct • repair
– Please **repair** these shoes. (Not *correct*)
(*repair* = make good something that is worn or broken; *mend*)
– Some computer programs will **correct** your spelling mistakes. (Not *repair*)
(= point out or put right mistakes, especially in speech and writing)

correct • right
– I don't think it's **right** to worry my friends with my own problems. (Not *correct*)
(*right* and *wrong* refer to consideration for others, moral behaviour, etc.)
– Is this the **correct/right** way to address an envelope?
(*correct/right* = without mistakes; the opposite is *wrong*)

correspond with
– The fingerprints on the lock **correspond** exactly **with** the ones on the gun.
(Not *are corresponding with*)
(stative use = match)
– My claim isn't settled yet. **I'm** still **corresponding with** the insurance company.
(dynamic use = exchanging letters)

cost
- *It costs a lot to buy a house.* (Not **It makes**
  is costing; past tense: *cost*, not **costed**)
  (stative use in general statements)
- *This holiday is costing a lot of money.*
  (dynamic use = 'it is actively costing')

cost • price
- *What's the price of this radio please?*
- *What will be the cost of a 10,000 km
  service?* (Not **What will it make**)
  (*price* is preferable when referring to
  particular objects; *cost* is preferable when
  referring to services, jobs to be done, etc.)

costume • suit • habit
- *Very few people can afford to have their
  suits specially made.* (Not **costumes**)
  (*a suit* = matching jacket and trousers or
  jacket and skirt)
- *The dancers looked splendid in their
  national costumes.*
  (Not **suits** and not to be confused with
  customs)
  (a *costume* is a complete set of clothes
  designed to say something about the wearer,
  usually in a theatrical or ceremonial setting)
- *The monks wear a plain brown habit.*
  (= a special robe worn by monks and nuns)

cough
- *You've got a bad cough.* (Not **You've got
  bad cough.**; pronunciation: /kɒf/)

could
- *Looking down from the plane, we could see
  lights on the runway.* (Not **could to see**)
  (no *to*-infinitive after modals like *could*)

could • managed to • was able to
- *I managed to get/was able to get two tickets
  for the Cup Final yesterday.*
  (Not **could get** **could to get**)
  (= *managed to/was able to* for a particular
  event in the past; never *to* after *could*)
- *Andrew could sing like an angel before his
  voice broke.* (Not **managed to sing**)
  (*could* for general ability in the past; *was
  able to* is also possible but less usual)

**couldn't • wasn't able to • was unable to
• didn't manage to**
- *I tried to ring yesterday, but I couldn't get
  through/wasn't able to/was unable to/didn't
  manage to get through to you.*
  (*couldn't*, but not *could*, can be used for
  particular events in the past; see above)

counsel • council
- *The decision to build on this site was taken
  by the town council.* (Not **counsel**)
  (= elected representatives; noun only)
- *The council is/are meeting today.*
  (collective noun + singular/plural verb)
- *'Cruse' is a charity that gives counsel
  to/counsels widowed people.*
  (= *advice*: noun; *advise*: verb)

count
- *In the end what counts is real ability, not
  high marks in exams.* (Not **is counting**)
  (stative use = matters, is important)
- *Don't interrupt him. He's counting the
  children in the group.*
  (dynamic use = finding out the number)

count • measure
- *We'd better measure the room carefully
  before we order a new carpet.*
  (= find the size by *measuring*)
- *Make sure you count your change!*
  (= find the amount of money by *counting*)

couple (of) • pair (of)
- *Mr Lewis and his brother are a funny pair.*
  (Not **couple**)
  (= two people who are especially connected,
  but not by marriage)
- *Mrs and Mrs Soames are a nice old couple.*
  (= two people who are connected, especially
  by marriage; preferable to *pair*)
- *A couple of Americans sat near us.*
  (Not **A pair of Americans**)
  (= two, no relationship implied)
- *Use this pair of scissors.* (Not **couple**)
  (= something made of two matching parts
  joined together; also *pliers*, *tweezers*, etc.)

**coupon • voucher • gift token/discount
certificate**
- *Don't lose your air tickets or hotel vouchers.*
  (Not **coupons**)
  (a *voucher* is a certificate used in place of
  money in exchange for goods or services)
- *We collected all these petrol coupons for the
  Red Cross Fund.* (Not **vouchers**)
  (a *coupon* is a ticket for buying something or
  a service; it is also a ticket which can be
  exchanged for a sum of money or a
  discount)
- *There's a gift token/discount certificate/
  (gift) voucher in every packet of biscuits.*
  (Not **coupon**)
  (= a certificate to be used in place of money,
  offered to customers as a commercial
  incentive by companies)

course • rate of exchange
- *What's today's **rate of exchange** against the dollar?* (Not **course**)
- *We'll find our way out of the wood if we follow the **course** of the river bed.*
  (= the pathway, direction)

court
- *It was the first day of the trial and there were a lot of people **in court**.*
  (Not **to court* *to the court**)
- *He was taken **to court** for failing to pay his taxes.* (Not **in court* *to the court**)

court • (playing) field • playground
- *The footballer was sent off the **(playing) field** for bad behaviour.* (Not **court**)
  (*(playing) field* for *football, rugby,* etc.)
- *It's your turn to supervise the children in the **playground**.* (Not **court**)
  (= an open space for children to play)
- *The Wimbledon tennis final will take place on the centre **court**.*
  (*court* for *badminton, squash, tennis,* etc.)

cover • cover charge
- *In some restaurants **the cover charge**, tax and tips can cost almost as much as the meal.* (Not **the cover**)
  (= the cost of a place setting at a restaurant)
- *It began to rain and we ran for **cover**.*
  (= shelter, protection)

covered with/in
- *Don't sit there! You're **covered with/in** mud!*
  (Not **covered by**)
  (*with* and *in* are generally interchangeable after *covered*)

craft • cunning • power
- *It always amazes me how dictators manage to exercise so much **power**.* (Not **craft**)
- *Odysseus outwitted his opponents with a mixture of **craft** and **cunning**.*
  (*craft* = skill; *cunning* = clever planning)

crash into • collide • bang against
- *The racing car skidded and **crashed into** the barrier.* (Not **crashed with**)
  (= violently ran into, hit)
- *Both cars were on the same side of the road and **collided** violently.*
  (= hit each other)
- *The racing car skidded, **banged against** the barrier and then continued round the track.*
  (*bang against* = 'hit and bounce off' is not as serious as *crash* or *collide*)

cravat • tie
- *They won't let you into the restaurant if you're not wearing a **tie**.* (Not **cravat**)
- *Reg was casually but smartly dressed in an open-necked shirt and a **cravat**.* (Not **tie**)
  (= a wide *tie* worn inside an open-necked shirt, usually by men)

crayon • chalk
- *The teacher drew a map on the backboard in coloured **chalk**.* (Not **crayon**)
- *My teacher asked me to fetch **a piece of chalk/two pieces of chalk**.*
  (Not **a chalk* *two chalks* *some chalks**)
  (*chalk* is uncountable)
- *Annie drew this lovely picture with **crayons**.*
  (= coloured wax pencils; countable)

creak • squeak
- *Cats mew; mice **squeak**.* (Not **creak**)
- *That door is **creaking/squeaking** badly. I'd better oil the hinges.*
  (*squeak* = the sharp high note of e.g. a mouse or metal against metal; *creak* = the slow, cracking noise made by doors, floorboards, etc.; living creatures don't *creak*)

cream • custard
- *My mother always made **custard** from egg yolks, milk and a little sugar.* (Not **cream**)
  (= a sweet sauce made with milk or cream, thickened with egg yolk or starch)
- *There's nothing to beat the taste of strawberries, sugar and **cream**.*
  (= the high-fat part of cow's milk)

credit: with credit • on credit
- *I bought this TV **on credit**.*
  (Not **with credit**)
  (i.e. I'll be paying for it later)
- *The soldier behaved **with credit** in a difficult situation.* (Not **on credit**)
  (= decently, honourably)

creep • crawl
- *Our baby can **crawl**, but he can't walk yet.*
  (Not *creep* in BrE)
  (= move/'walk' on all four limbs)
- *There's a spider **crawling** across the floor!*
  (Not **creeping**)
  (= moving on a surface)
- *We **crept** upstairs so as not to wake grandpa.* (Not **crawled**)
  (= moved quietly so as not to make a noise)

crime
- *I can't understand how anyone can **commit** such **a crime**.*
  (Not **do/make/perform a crime**)

- *There's a lot of **petty/small crime** in our area.* (Not *little crime*)
- *There are a lot of petty/small **crimes** in the workplace.*
(*crime* can be countable or uncountable)

crisps • chips • french fries
- *A lot of people seem to live mainly on burgers and **chips/french fries**.*
(*chips*, BrE, *french fries*, AmE = sticks of potato fried in oil and served hot)
- *A beer and a packet of **crisps/(potato) chips** please.*
(*crisps*, BrE, *(potato) chips*, AmE = very thin fried slices of potato sold in packets)

criterion • criteria
- *What **is the criterion/are the criteria** for judging the competition?*
(= standard/standards; *criterion* is singular; *criteria* is plural)

critic • criticism • critique • review
- *Did you read the excellent **review** of 'Hamlet' in the Sunday paper?*
(Not *critic* *criticism* *critique*)
(= an assessment appearing in the press)
- *I've got one **criticism** to **make**.* (Not *do*)
(= unfavourable comment, spoken or written)
- *Donna wrote a long **critique** on feminism which has been widely quoted.*
(= a careful account of a subject, often in book form and always longer than a *review*)
- *Who's the film **critic** of 'The Times'?*
(= a person who writes reviews: *reviewer*)

cry • weep
- *Mr Clay broke down and **cried/wept** when the police brought him news of the accident.*
(*weep* is always stronger than *cry* to describe the shedding of tears; compare *to sob* = to breathe noisily while weeping)

cultured • cultivated
- *Quality newspapers assume their readers are reasonably **cultivated**.*
(= highly educated; preferable to *cultured*, to describe people)

cure (of) • heal
- *The cut took a week to **heal**.* (Not *cure*)
(*heal* for the mending of cuts, wounds, etc.)
- *Can they **cure** diabetes?* (Not *heal*)
(*cure*, transitive, for disease or illness)
- *What **cured me of** smoking in the end was sheer terror.* (Not *cured me from*)

current • currant
- *Corinth produces some of the world's finest **currants**.* (Not *currents*)
(= dried grapes)
- *Ocean **currents** can be treacherous for swimmers.*
(= movements of water, air, electricity)

current • movement/trend
- *The **movement/trend** towards nationalism is alarming.* (Not *current*)
(= development of opinion)
- *I can't keep up with **current** fashions.*
(= present-day)
- *Ocean **currents** can be very dangerous for swimmers.*
(= movements of water, air, etc.)

cushion • pillow
- *I could never get to sleep at night if I didn't have a nice soft **pillow**.* (Not *cushion*)
(we use *a pillow* on a bed)
- *There were three velvet **cushions** on the sofa.* (Not *pillows*)
(we use *cushions* on sofas, chairs, etc.)

cut • cut out
- *I read this article in the paper this morning and **cut it out** for you.* (Not *cut it*)
(= removed by cutting)
- *Please don't **cut** cardboard with my dressmaking scissors!*

cut • have cut
- *I **had my hair cut**.* (Not *cut my hair*)
(= caused someone to perform this service for me: *had a haircut*)
- *It's not a good idea to **cut your own hair**.*
(= cut it yourself)
(some other verbs that work like this are: *build* a house, *clean* a suit, *coach* a student, *decorate* a building, *deliver* flowers, *develop* a film, *mend* my shoes, *photocopy* a document, *prepare* some food, *press* my trousers, *print* some labels, *repair* my watch, *service* my car, *teach* the children)

cutlery
- *This dishwasher takes **a lot of cutlery**.*
(Not *a lot of cutleries*)
(= knives, forks, spoons, etc.; *cutlery* is uncountable)

D

damage • damages
- *The frost **did a lot of damage** to the crops.*
(Not *a damage* *a lot of damages* *made

a lot of damage*)
(*damage* is uncountable)
- *The pop star claimed that the story had harmed his reputation and he sued the newspaper for* **damages.** (Not **a damage**)
(plural noun = money paid in law for damage caused to reputation or property)

dame • dancing partner • woman • lady
- *I enjoy dancing with Margot. She's my ideal* **dancing partner.** (Not **dame**)
- **Women** *can now serve as fighter pilots in the US Air Force.* (Not **Dames** **Ladies**)
- *Mata seems like a nice old* **lady,** *but she used to be a secret agent.* (Not **dame**)
(*lady* is polite/respectful)
- *Who's that* **dame** *you were with last night?* (old-fashioned, vulgar slang, mainly AmE)

damp • humid • moist • wet
- *You shouldn't wear that shirt if it's still* **damp.** (Not **moist** **humid**)
(= slightly wet, often in an unpleasant way: *damp* walls/clothes, *a damp* building, etc.)
- *I don't mind how hot it is, as long as it isn't* **humid.** (Not **moist**)
(referring to *moisture/humidity* in the air)
- *One good thing about the Scottish climate is that it keeps your skin* **moist.** (Not **damp**)
(= slightly wet in a good way: *moist* cake, *moist* skin, *moist* eyes, etc.)
- *I was caught in the rain and my clothes are completely* **wet.** (Not **damp/moist/humid**)
(the opposite of all these words is *dry*)

damp • wet • fresh
- *Don't sit on that bench. The paint is still* **wet.** (Not **damp**)
(= not dry)
- **Wet Paint.** (Not **Fresh** **Damp**)
- *Don't you like the smell of* **fresh** *paint?* (Not **wet** **damp**)
(= new)
- *You shouldn't wear that shirt if it's still* **damp.** (Not **fresh** **wet**)
(= not quite dry)

dance • dancing • dance hall
- *We* **gave/held a dance** *for our daughter's eighteenth birthday.* (Not **did/made**)
(*dance* is countable = an event)
- *Can I* **have** *the next* **dance?** (Not **do/make**)
(i.e. Can we dance together?)
- **Dancing** *makes you feel good.*
(Not **The dancing** **The dance**)
(*dancing* is uncountable)
- *Let's* **go dancing.**
(Not **go for dancing** **go for a dance**)

- *They won't let you into* **the dance hall** *without a ticket.* (Not **the dancing**)

dare (to)
- *He's on the phone and I* **don't dare (to)** *interrupt him.* (Not **I'm not daring**)
(stative use = haven't the courage to)
- **Are you daring me** *to sound the alarm?*
(*dare* + personal object + *to*, stative or dynamic, = challenge)

darken • get/turn/grow dark
- *It* **gets/grows dark** *early in winter.*
(Not **darkens** **darks**)
- *Blonde hair* **darkens/Blonde hair gets/turns/grows darker** *as a person get older.*

data
- *Most of our* **data is** *stored on computers.*
- *These* **data are** *available in the Proceedings of the Society.*
(*data* is used as an uncountable noun in general contexts, even though it is really the plural of *datum*; it is used as a plural in scientific contexts)

date • appointment
- *I can't stay, I'm afraid. I* **have** *another* **appointment.** (Not **have a date**)
(*have/make an appointment* refers to a pre-arranged meeting with someone not specified, or with a professional person)
- *I* **have a date** *with my girl friend this evening.* (Not **have an appointment**)
(*have/make a date* refers to a pre-arranged meeting for social reasons)
- *What's* **the date** *today? - April 14th.*

day by day • day after day
- **Day after day** *we waited for news from Sally.* (Not **Day with day** **Day by day**)
- *Since her operation, her health has been improving* **day by day.**
(Not **day with day** **day after day**)
(*day by day* = a gradual progression; *day after day* = repeated single actions)

dead
- *The man is* **dead** *and* **a dead man** *feels no pain.* (Not **a dead**)
- *My parents are both* **dead.** (Not **deads**)
(we cannot use *dead* on its own to mean 'a dead person')
- *We owe a debt to* **the dead** *who fought to preserve our freedom.* (Not **the deads**)
(*the* + adjective for the group as a whole; also: *bad, blind, deaf and dumb, disabled, elderly, good, guilty, handicapped, healthy,*

homeless, hungry, innocent, living, old, poor, rich, sick, thirsty, unemployed, young)

deadly • fatal • mortal

- *His injuries were **fatal**. He died before reaching hospital.* (Not **deadly* *mortal**) (= causing or resulting in death; *mortal*, meaning *fatal*, in *mortal injuries*, *a mortal wound*, is literary)
- *You can't buy **deadly** poisons like arsenic at the chemist's.* (Not **fatal* *mortal**) (= likely to cause death)
- *We often behave as if we're going to live for ever, forgetting that we are **mortal**.* (i.e. we have to die)

deaf • deafen

- *Mr Ford is **deaf/a deaf person** so you have to speak slowly and clearly.* (Not **a deaf**)
- *Mr and Mrs Ford are both **deaf**.*
- ***Deaf people** need to be able to see your face when you speak.* (Not **deafs**) (we cannot use *deaf* on its own to mean 'a deaf person/deaf people')
- *People who hear well often make few allowances for **the deaf**.* (Not **the deafs**) (*the* + adjective for the group as a whole)
- ***We were deafened** by the explosion.* (Not **We were deaf**) (*deafen* is a verb, often passive)

dear • dearly

- *We had to pay **dear/dearly** for our mistake.* (both forms are possible after *pay*, but only *dear* after *cost* and *buy*; *dear* is the normal word when the reference is to expense)
- *She loves him **dearly**.* (adverb of manner)
- *I'd **dearly** like to know how you obtained this information.* (Not **dear**) (= very much; *-ly* as an intensifier)

death • dead • died

- *Great artists are often appreciated more after they are **dead**.* (Not **death**)
- *The Picasso Museum opened years after the artist's **death**.* (Not **dead**) (*dead* is the adjective; *death* is the noun)
- *Queen Anne **is dead**.* (Not **is died**)
- *Queen Anne **died** in 1714.* (Not **dead**) (*dead* is an adjective; *died* is the past of *die*)

debt: be indebted to • in debt

- *We can't borrow any more money. We're already **in debt**.* (Not **indebted**) (i.e. we owe money)
- *I'm **indebted to** you for all your help.* (= very grateful)

decade • ten • a set of ten

- *We're expecting about **ten** people for dinner tonight.* (Not **a decade of people**)
- *I've just bought **a set of ten** knives and forks.* (Not **a decade of knives and forks**)
- *The last **decade** of the 19th century came to be known as 'the naughty nineties'.* (= a period of ten years)

decay • rot • spoil • go bad

- *We should use these vegetables before they **spoil/go bad**.* (Not **decay**)
- *It takes a long time for fallen trees to **decay/rot**.* (Not **spoil* *go bad**) (something edible *spoils/goes bad* when it becomes inedible; then it *decays* or *rots*)

decease • disease

- *Poverty and **disease** usually go together.* (Not **decease**) (= illness)
- *A national crisis was caused by the sudden **decease** of the President.* (a formal word for *death*)

deceased

- *They paid their respects to **the deceased**.* (in formal language *the deceased* can be used to refer to one person only or to more than one, but we have to say *He's/She's deceased*, not **He's/She's a deceased.**)

deceive • lie to

- *The witness **lied to/deceived** the court.* (*lie* = say things that aren't true; *deceive* = cause someone to believe what is false)
- *The apparent respectability of the bank **deceived** a lot of investors.* (Not **lied**) (= made them believe something untrue)

decided (on) • determined

- *You have to be very **determined** to sail the Atlantic single-handed.* (Not **decided**) (= strong-willed)
- *I'm retiring soon. I'm quite **decided**.* (i.e. I have made up my mind)
- *I wasn't sure what to study at university and finally **decided on** modern languages.* (Not **decided for* *decided modern languages**)

decision

- *It wasn't easy for me to **come to/make/take** this **decision**.* (Not **do this decision**)

declare • register • report

- *We haven't **registered** the baby's birth yet.* (Not **declared**) (= put into an official record)

- *We must **report** the theft to the police.*
  (Not **declare**)
  (= provide information about)
- *I have to **declare** profits on my tax return.*
  (i.e. make a statement to the authorities of
  information that is otherwise private)

decorate • furnish
- *We're going to **furnish** our flat in
  contemporary style.* (Not **decorate**)
  (= put in furniture)
- *It's cost us a fortune to **decorate** this flat.*
  (= paint or paper the walls/have them
  painted or papered)

decoration • décor
- *Black and white **décor** is not very friendly.*
  (Not **decoration**)
  (= the style of an interior)
- *Can we help with the **decoration** of the
  Christmas tree?* (Not **décor**)
  (= adding things to make it beautiful)

deep/depth
- *How **deep**/What **depth** is this well?*
  (Not **How much deep is/What depth has**)
- *This well **is 20 metres (deep)**.*
  (Not **has depth 20 metres**)

deep • deeply
- *We had to **dig deep** into our pockets to pay
  for our daughter's education.*
  (also: *look deep, run deep, strike deep*)
- *We **deeply** regret the inconvenience we have
  caused you.* (Not **deep**)
  (= very much; *-ly* as an intensifier; *deeply*
  with verbs like *think* and *believe*)

defeat • conquer
- *Alexander the Great **conquered** half the
  world before he was 33.* (Not **defeated**)
  (= took land by force of arms)
- *Alexander **defeated** Darius III at Issus in
  333 BC.* (Not **conquered**)
  (= beat, won a victory over)

defend (against/from) • forbid/prohibit
- *More and more restaurants **forbid/prohibit**
  smoking.* (Not **defend**)
  (*prohibit* = forbid absolutely, especially by
  impersonal authority)
- *I **forbid** you to say a word about this.*
  (Not **defend**, and *prohibit* is unlikely)
- *With the end of the Cold War, we needn't
  spend so much on **defending** ourselves
  (**against/from** attack).*
  (= protecting from attack)

defer (to)
- *We **deferred selling** our house until the
  spring.* (Not **deferred to sell**)
  (= postponed; put off to a later date)
- *I **defer to** your better judgement.*
  (= give way to)

defy • challenge to
- *The defeated champion is **challenging** his
  opponent **to** a return match.* (Not **defying**)
  (= inviting him to compete in)
- *You can't **defy** the law, however unjust you
  think it is.*
  (= refuse to obey)

delay
- *We'll **delay paying** until we receive the
  goods.* (Not **delay to pay**)

delayed • get delayed
- *We **got/were delayed** by a security check.*
  (Not **We delayed**)
- *The Customs **delayed** us by about an hour.*

delicate • fragile • delicious • exquisite
- *This stew is **delicious**.* (Not **delicate**)
  (= very tasty)
- *Ian is a **delicate** boy.* (Not **fragile**)
  (i.e. he is easily made ill)
- *Bill looks very **fragile** after his operation.*
  (= in a weak state of health)
- *Please be careful with those old coffee cups.
  They're rather **delicate/fragile**.*
  (i.e they can be easily broken)
- *Maurice may not be very bright, but he has
  exquisite manners.* (Not **delicate**)
  (= very fine, beautiful; never **peculiar**)

delicatessen • delicacy
- *Some people will pay anything for a **delicacy**
  like truffles.* (Not **delicatessen**)
  (= a rare and expensive thing to eat)
- *Truffles are the sort of thing you can only
  buy at a **delicatessen**.*
  (= a shop that sells food that is ready to eat;
  often high-quality and expensive)

demand
- *The management here **makes** too many
  demands on its staff.* (Not **does demands**)
- *We **demand that they (should) return** the
  money./We **demand the return of** the money.*
  (Not **We demand to return the money.**)

demand • ask (for) • charge
- *If you decide to sell your bike, how much
  will you **ask**?* (Not **demand**)

49

- *If you can't sell your flat, try asking less for it.* (Not *demanding ... for*)
  (*ask (for)* = wish to receive)
- *Sorry. I asked for a single ticket, not a return ticket.* (Not *demanded*)
  (= requested)
- *My dentist charges by the minute, with the aid of a kitchen timer!* (Not *demands*)
  (= applies a rate of payment)
- *She demands an apology before she'll speak to you again.*
  (= insists on receiving)

demand • wonder • request
- *I've just had a request for information about hotels in Scotland.* (Not *demand*)
  (= a polite inquiry)
- *I wonder if we should book in advance.*
  (Not *demand myself*)
- *We've just received a demand for £458 from the Electricity Board.*
  (= a bill)

demonstrate • show
- *Now that you've shown me your machine, can you please demonstrate it.*
  (*shown me* = let me see; *demonstrate* = show how it works)

department • section
- *Which section of the train was involved in the accident?* (Not *department*)
  (= a part of a whole)
- *Which department/section of the Civil Service does your brother work in?*
  (= a division in a large organization)

depend (on)
- *I depend on your support.*
  (Not *depend from*)
- *Now you've taken over your father's business, its success depends on you.*
  (Not *is depending on*)
  (stative use only for *it depends*)
- *Everyone is now depending on you to make this business a success.*
  (dynamic use: 'at the moment of speaking')

dependant • dependent (on)
- *Many poor countries are dependent on foreign aid.* (Not *dependant on*)
  (adjective = cannot survive without)
- *With so many dependants/dependents I need all the work I can get.*
  (noun; *dependant* is BrE; *dependent* is AmE; not used to mean *employees*)

depot • (rubbish) dump
- *The dustmen won't collect this rubbish. We'll have to take it to the dump ourselves.*
  (Not *deposit*; not *depot* unless it's temporary storage)
  (= the end-place for depositing waste)
- *Your goods have arrived from our depot.*
  (= a place where goods are stored)

deprive of
- *She was deprived of the chance to go to university because her parents wanted to keep her at home.* (Not *deprived from*)

descend • come/go/get down • get off
- *The children have climbed to the top of the tree and can't get down!* (Not *descend*)
- *Is this where we get off?* (Not *descend*)
- *We're just beginning to descend and will be landing in fifteen minutes.*
  (we tend to use *descend* mainly to mean 'from a great height')

describe
- *I tried to describe the scene to my parents.*
  (Not *describe my parents the scene*
  describe to my parents the scene)
  (also: *announced their engagement to their friends, confessed his crimes to the court, declared the goods to the Customs, demonstrated his theory to everyone, explained the situation to their friends, mentioned the matter to me, proposed a new date to us, recommended this club to me, repeated the story to me*)

description
- *I didn't really look at him, so I can't give you a description.* (Not *make*)

desert • dessert • deserts
- *The Sahara Desert /ˈdezət/ covers over nine million square kilometres.*
  (= a large sandy area where there isn't much rain and little grows; plural: *deserts* /ˈdezəts/)
- *He got his just deserts /dɪˈzɜːts/ when he was sentenced to 15 years in prison.*
  (always plural = what he deserved; *desert* is also a verb = abandon: *You can't admire a person who deserts his wife and children.*)
- *I don't think I can eat a dessert /dɪˈzɜːt/. I've had too much already.*
  (= a sweet course served at the end of a meal; the plural is *desserts* /dɪˈzɜːts/)

design • drawing
- *Meryl did a lovely drawing of our house when she stayed here.* (Not *design*)
  (= a picture *drawn* in ink or pencil)

- *We've been discussing the **design** of the new house with the architect.* (Not **drawing**)
  (= a plan from which it will be built)

desire • look forward to • want/would like
- *I'm really **looking forward to** the summer holidays.* (Not **am desiring* *desire**)
  (= expecting with pleasure)
- ***We want/We'd like** a room with a view please.* (Not **We desire**)
- *Success has brought her all the material comforts anyone could **desire**.*
  (*desire* expresses a very strong hope or wish and is much more formal than *want/'d like*; it goes with abstract, not concrete, nouns: *desire security*, but not **desire a room**)

desk • office • bureau • study
- *Alan doesn't like anyone to ring him at the **office**.* (Not **desk* *bureau* *study**)
  (= a room or rooms devoted to business)
- *We need another room we can use as a **study**.* (Not **an office**)
  (= a room for academic or domestic reading and writing)
- *The computer takes up half the space on my **desk**.* (Not **bureau**)
  (= a table where you sit and write)
- *The papers you want are in the top drawer of the **bureau**.*
  (= an old-fashioned writing desk with a lid in BrE; a chest of drawers in AmE)
- *Reuters has a news **bureau** in every country in the world.*
  (= an office for collecting and distributing information)

destroy • destruction
- *The hurricane left a trail of **destruction** behind it.* (Not **destroy**)
- *The hurricane **destroyed** everything that lay in its path.* (Not **destructed**)
  (the verb is *destroy*; the noun is *destruction*)

detail • retail
- *We'd all prefer to pay wholesale rather than **retail** prices.* (Not **detail**)
  (i.e. the amount paid by the general public, which is higher than *wholesale*)
- *I studied every **detail** of the contract.*
  (= a small fact)

detailed • in detail • with details
- *You have to complete the form **in detail**.*
  (Not **detailed* *with details**)
  (= thoroughly, including all the small points)

- *I sent them my curriculum vitae **with details** of my previous jobs.*
  (*with details* = including facts)
- *When you've tested the new vehicle, we'd like you to write us a **detailed** report.*
  (= thorough, with all the facts)

deter
- *Do you think the possibility of imprisonment **deters criminals from committing** crimes?* (Not **deters them to commit**)

determine • decide
- ***Decide** what you want.* (Not **Determine**)
  (= make up your mind)
- *You must **determine** the exact nature of the job before you agree to do it.*
  (= find out about)

detest
- *I **detest** unpunctuality.* (Not **I'm detesting**)
  (stative use only; no progressive form)
- *I **detest being** caught in a traffic jam.*
  (Not **detest to be**)
  (*detest* + *-ing*, not **to**)

develop
- Note the spelling and pronunciation:
  - *develop*: /dɪ'veləp/, not **/'dɪveləp/**
  - *developing*, not **developping**:
  /dɪ'veləpɪŋ/, not **/dɪvel'əpɪŋ/**
  - *developed*, not **developped**:
  /dɪ'veləpt/, not **/dɪvel'əpt/**
  - *development*, not **developpment**:
  /dɪ'veləpmənt/, not **/dɪvel'əpmənt/**

devote
- *Mother Teresa **devoted** her life **to helping** the poor.* (Not **devoted ... to help**)
  (the preposition *to* is followed by an *-ing* form or a noun, but not by an infinitive)

die of
- *I don't believe anyone can **die of** a broken heart.* (Not **die from**; present participle: *dying*, not **dieing**; compare *dyeing* = changing the colour of something with *dye*)

differ with • disagree (with) • differ from • differentiate from/between
- *I think smoking should be banned in the workplace. - I'm sorry, **I disagree./I disagree with** you.* (Not **I differ.* *I differ with you.* *I differentiate from you.**)
- *I **disagree with/differ with** John's views about smoking in the workplace.*
  (Not **differ from* *differentiate from**)
  (*differ with* something = *disagree with*)

- *The first version of the poem **differs from** the second.* (Not **differs by**)
  (= is different from)
- *It's almost impossible to **differentiate** one **from** the other/to **differentiate between** them.* (Not **differ from/between them**)
  (= tell the difference, distinguish)

different from • different than • different to • difference

- *Roses are **different from** violets.*
  (Not **different than**)
  (we cannot use *than* after *different* in uncomplicated comparisons)
- *We're planning something **different** this year **than (what)** we did/**from what** we did/**to what** we did last year.*
  (*than* after *different* introduces a clause; *different to what* is an informal alternative; *different to* + noun is widespread - *Roses are different to violets* - though many native speakers don't approve of the use of *to* after *different*)
- *What's the **difference between** them?*
  (Not **What difference do they have?**)
- *It **makes no difference** whether you believe me or not.* (Not **does no difference**)
- *There's a lot of **difference** between the UK and the USA.* (Not **different**)

difficult • fussy

- *Our boss is really **fussy** about details and won't accept poor work.* (Not **difficult**)
  (= hard to please; *particular* is more neutral than *fussy*)
- *You probably don't remember it now, but you were a very **difficult** child.*
  (= hard to manage)
- *I had to give up maths because it **got difficult** (for me)/I **found it difficult**.*
  (Not **it difficulted** **I difficulted myself**)

difficulty (in)

- *Brian's grown a beard and I had **difficulty (in) recognizing** him.*
  (Not **difficulty to recognize**)

digest • (can't) stand

- *Janice asks so many personal questions, I **can't stand** her.* (Not **can't digest**)
  (*stand* = tolerate; the use of *stomach* as a verb would be old-fashioned here)
- *I find cucumber difficult to **digest**.*
  (= process in the stomach; *to stomach* is only figurative)

diminish • cut down (on)

- *It's almost impossible to **cut down (on)** the number of imported cars.* (Not **diminish**)
  (= actively to reduce)
- *The demand for cars is unlikely to **diminish**.*
  (= get less)

dinner • lunch

- *Mr Soames is out for **lunch** at the moment and won't be back till about 2.30.*
- *How many people are we expecting to **dinner** this evening?*
  (In Britain, people who eat *lunch* - a cooked or light meal - in the middle of the day eat *dinner* - the main meal of the day - in the evening. People who eat their main meal in the middle of the day - especially children and people who do manual work - call it *dinner*, and the evening meal, which is at the end of the working day, is called *tea*. *Tea* is sometimes followed later in the evening by another - informal - meal called *supper*)

dinner party

- *We're **giving/having a dinner party** next week.* (preferable to *doing*, not **making**)
- *Carolyn's helping us to **do** (the food for) **the dinner party** because there will be so many people.*

diploma • degree • certificate • licence • qualifications

- *Pat has a **degree** in maths.* (Not **diploma**)
- *I **did/took my degree** at York.* (Not **made**)
- *I did a course in hairdressing and gained a **diploma**.* (Not **degree**)
  (a *diploma* is often a lower qualification than a *degree* and may be awarded for a practical or more specialized skill; a *diploma* can also be used to mean the actual *certificate*)
- *When did you get your driving **licence/ certificate**?* (Not **diploma**)
  (= a document marking official recognition of something: e.g. *a birth/marriage/death certificate*)
- *What **qualifications** do I need to teach English as a Foreign Language?*
  (= proof of having passed essential exams)

direct

- *The doctor **directed me to** stay in bed till I felt better.* (Not **directed that I should**)
  (= told me to)

direct • directly

- *This flight goes **direct/directly** to Cairo.*
  (= without stopping on the way; both forms possible with e.g. *go, phone, write, speak*)

- *She's not in her office at the moment, but she'll be back **directly**.* (Not **direct**)
  (= soon, straightaway)
- *We'll discuss the matter **directly he arrives**.* (Not **directly he will arrive* *directly as he arrives**)
  (*directly* = as soon as: conjunction + present tense when referring to the future)

direct • lead • conduct
- *Who's **leading** the party in the next election?* (Not **directing* *conducting**)
  (*lead* = be in charge of people)
- *Who **directs** party policy?* (Not **conducts**)
  (*direct* = be in charge of a thing, e.g. a policy, a plan, finance)
- *Who **conducts/directs** the London Symphony Orchestra these days?*
  (the *conductor* is in charge of - *conducts* - the musicians in performance; the *director* is in charge of - *directs* - business concerns)

direction • management • administrative offices
- ***The management has/have** agreed to a 5% pay rise at all levels.* (Not **The direction**)
  (= the people who manage; *management* is a collective noun followed by a verb in the singular or plural)
- ***Where are the administrative offices**, please?* (Not **Where is the direction**)
- *The **direction/management** of the company is a matter of concern to shareholders.*
  (*direction* = the way it is going; *management* = governing policy)
- *Which **direction** is north?*
  (= way)

directions • routes
- *We'll have to turn left there, where it says '**all routes/all other routes**'.*
  (Not **all directions/all other directions**)
  (the phrases *all routes* and *all other routes* are used in traffic signs)
- *When the bell rang, the children poured into the playground and ran **in all directions**.*
  (= everywhere)

director • manager • editor • headmaster
- *If you feel so strongly about this article, why don't you write a letter to the **editor**?*
  (Not **director/manager**)
  (= the person who is in charge of the contents of a newspaper or magazine)
- *When I was at school, the **headmaster** always took charge of morning assembly.*
  (Not **director/manager**)
  (= the man in charge of a school, compare

headmistress; the *head*, the *headteacher* or the *principal* often replace *headmaster* and *headmistress*; but we can speak of the *director* of a language school because it's a business; *head of department* = a person in charge of a subject section in a school)
- *Jack is very young to be a bank **manager**/a **manager** of a supermarket.* (Not **director**)
  (= a person who runs part of a business)
- *It has never been my ambition to be a company **director**.* (Not **manager**)
  (= someone in charge of a business)

dirt
- *Wipe your feet! Don't bring **all that dirt** into the house.* (Not **all those dirts**)
  (*dirt* is uncountable)

dirty • dirtily
- *They only won the match because they **played dirty**.* (Not **played dirtily**)
  (*dirty* with verbs like *act, be, talk*)
- *The animals were so **dirtily** kept/kept **in** such a **dirty fashion** that the zoo lost its licence.*

dirty • get dirty
- *I **got dirty** mending that puncture.*
  (Not **I dirtied* *I dirtied myself**)
- *You've already **dirtied** that fresh towel. You've already **made/got it dirty**!*
  (Not **got dirty the towel**)

disappointed in/with • disappointing
- *My results are **disappointing**.*
  (Not **disappointed**)
- *I'm **disappointed in/with** them.*
  (Not **disappointing in them**)
  (*in/with* + person)
- *I'm **disappointed with** their exam results.*
  (*with* + thing)

disc • discus • record • disk • tray
- *I always wanted to be an athlete, but I never imagined I'd end up as a **discus thrower**.*
  (Not **disc thrower**)
- *Since I bought my **compact disc** player, I hardly play **records/LPs** any more.*
  (Not **discs** for 'records'. A *compact disc* is usually referred to as *a CD*; but note *a disc jockey* for someone who plays records on the radio)
- *You should always back your data up on a floppy **disk**.*
  (*disk* is the standard spelling in BrE/AmE to refer to *computer disks*)
- *Put these cups on that **tray**.* (Not **disc**)

discontinue

- *I think the BBC World Service has discontinued broadcasting on this wavelength.* (Not *discontinued to broadcast*; but *continue* takes either *to* or *-ing*)

discotheque • record library/collection

- *The BBC has one of the biggest record libraries/record collections in the world.* (Not *discotheques*; also note *discotheque* is never used to mean 'record shop')
- *Your idea of a holiday seems to be to spend every day on the beach and every night at a discotheque/disco.* (= a place where you can dance to pop records; commonly abbreviated to *disco*)

discount

- *You've bought so much stuff, you should ask them to do you/give you/allow you a discount.* (Not *make you a discount*)

discover • invent • find out

- *Have you any idea who invented the safety pin?* (Not *discovered/found out*) (*invent* = create something that did not exist before; the noun is *inventor*)
- *Captain Cook discovered Antarctica when he was exploring the Eastern Pacific Ocean.* (i.e. found what was already there, but not known about before; the noun is *discoverer*)
- *I'll try and find out the name of the person who invented the safety pin.* (you can *find out* a fact, but not an idea; you can also *find out* by accident: *I found out what had happened.*)

discuss • argue about

- *We discussed politics till late at night.* (Not *discussed about/for politics*) (= talked about it from several points of view, perhaps without disagreement; *discuss* is transitive and is not followed by *about*, though *discussion* is followed by *about*)
- *We argued about politics till late at night.* (*argue* = take up conflicting sides in a discussion, disagree verbally)

dish • plate • course

- *Could you bring me a clean plate please?* (Not usually *dish*) (= a flat thing for serving and eating food; it is always the object, not the food on it)
- *I need a large dish to serve this food from.* (Not *plate*) (= a food container for cooking or serving food; also *dishes* = items used in cooking and serving food: *wash/collect the dishes*)

- *Steak and kidney pie is a traditional English dish.* (Not *plate* *course*) (= one item of prepared food: *a main dish, a side dish, a delicious dish*, etc.)
- *Do you want spaghetti as a starter or as your main course?* (Not *plate*) (a *course* is part of the sequence of a meal: *the first course, the second/the main course, the last course*)

disinfect • sterilize

- *A dentist's instruments need to be constantly sterilized.* (Not *disinfected*) (= made totally free from germs; *sterilize* is for something small enough to be isolated in a *sterilizer*)
- *Your wound has to be disinfected before it can be dressed.* (Not *sterilized*) (= made free from germs locally; you can also *disinfect* a lavatory or a building)

disinterested • uninterested

- *Many teenagers are uninterested in politics.* (Not *disinterested*) (= don't have any interest in)
- *It's good to have your disinterested opinion of my affairs.* (Not *uninterested*) (= free from personal bias) (*disinterested* is often wrongly used in the sense of 'uninterested' by native speakers)

dislike

- *I dislike driving on motorways.* (Not *dislike to drive*; compare *like* + *to* or *-ing*)
- *I dislike driving fast.* (Not *I'm disliking*) (only stative; no progressive form)

dispose of • at one's disposal

- *John has enough money at his disposal to buy the flat without a loan.* (Not *John disposes (of) enough money*) (= available)
- *We disposed of our old hi-fi set when we invested in this new system.* (= got rid of it in some way)

disposition • disposal

- *Waste paper is one of the biggest problems in rubbish disposal.* (Not *disposition*) (= getting rid of)
- *This old house may be charming, but the disposition of the rooms is hardly ideal.* (= the way they are arranged; very formal)
- *He has an easygoing disposition.* (= temperament, character)

dissolve • melt

- *The sun had risen and the ice on the lake was beginning to melt.* (Not *dissolve*)

(= turn from solid to liquid through a change in temperature)
- *Sugar dissolves quickly if it's mixed with hot water.* (Not **melts**)
(= becomes part of the liquid)

district • area • region
- *The Sahara desert covers an enormous area.* (Not **district* *region**)
(= surface measurement; an *area* can be large or small)
- *This district/area of London is mainly residential.* (Not **region**)
(a *district* is an area within a larger whole: *The Lake District of Northern England* ...)
- *The whole of our region/area has been affected by drought.*
(a *region* is a subdivision of a country: *The rock formations of the south-eastern region are made up of shale, chalk and limestone.*)

dive • dip • plunge
- *I dipped my big toe into the water to test the temperature.* (Not **dived**)
(= put into a liquid for a short time)
- *I plunged my head into a bucket of cold water.* (Not **dived my head**)
(= put it all the way in; transitive use)
- *At the start of the race, all the swimmers dived/plunged into the pool at exactly the same moment.* (Not **dipped**)
(*dived* = threw themselves, head first)

diverse • various
- *There were various people at the party whom I'd never met before.* (Not **diverse**)
(= different, a variety of)
- *The peoples of the world are extremely diverse, but we all share a common interest in the survival of the earth.*
(= very different from each other)

divide by/into • part • share
- *We won the lottery and shared the prize money.* (Not **divided* *parted**)
(i.e. we each had some; something can be *shared between* two or *among* many)
- *The crowd parted to let the happy couple go through.* (Not **divided* *shared**)
(= separated itself into two parts)
- *We divided the food into two equal parts.* (Not **parted* *divided to**)
(= separated into amounts; something can be *divided into* two or *between* two)
- *Divide the number by six.* (Not **with/from**)

divine • guess
- *How old am I? Guess! Have/Make a guess!* (Not **Divine!* *Do/Give a guess!**)
(= estimate, decide on instinct)
- *It requires special skill to divine the presence of water under the soil.*
(this use of *divine* = 'sense' is specialized or literary; *divine* occurs mainly as an adjective = godlike: *Caligula wasn't the first madman to believe he was divine.*)

divorce
- *I'm divorced.* (Not **I'm a divorced.**)
- *They're divorced.* (Not **divorceds**)
(we cannot use *divorced* as a noun, but we can say *He's/She's a divorcee, They're divorcees.*)
- *They were/got divorced two years ago.* (preferable to *They divorced*)
- *They divorced each other two years ago.*
- *She's divorcing him/getting divorced from him. He divorced his wife/her.* (Not **They divorced from each other.**)
(*divorce* is often passive: *be/get divorced*; in the active, *divorce* is normally transitive)

do • make
- *What are you doing? - I'm making a cake.*
(*do* = engage in an activity; *make* = create)
(*do* + nouns like *the room, the floor, the clothes* can often mean *clean, sweep, wash,* etc.: *I've done the kitchen*: not **made**)
(*make* combines with nouns like *a difference, friends, enemies, contacts*)

do/does
- *I don't care what I/you/we/they do* /duː/.
- *Does it matter?* /dəz; strong dʌz/, not **/duːz/**

do so • do it
- *Please lay the table. - I've just done so./I've just done it.*
(*do so* = what you just said; *do it* = do that thing; we often use *so* or *it* after *do* to show that an action has been done deliberately, when *do* is used in place of another verb)

doctor (Dr) • Mr
- *Good morning, Dr/Dr. Brown.*
(the title *Dr*, followed by a surname, is always written as an abbreviation, like *Mr*, with or without a full stop; both *doctor* and *Dr* are pronounced 'doctor'; in writing, we use *doctor*, without a capital D, as a form of address: *Good morning, doctor.*)

- *May I introduce **Dr Brown**?* (Not **Mr Dr Brown* *Good morning, Mr Doctor**) (we cannot use *Mr* + another title)
- *I'd like you to meet my surgeon/dentist, **Mr Redpath**.* (Not **Dr**) (surgeons and dentists are 'Mr', not 'Dr')

documentation • literature
- *I'll get some **literature** about Peru from the travel agency.* (Not **documentation**) (= explanatory printed material)
- *I've sent off my passport application with all the necessary **documentation**.* (= relevant papers, e.g. certificates)

dome • cathedral
- *Did you visit St Stephen's **Cathedral** when you were in Vienna?* (Not **Dome**) (= a large and important church)
- *The onion **domes** of the Kremlin may be regarded as a symbol of Moscow.* (= round roofs)

domicile • address • residence
- *What's your new **address**?* (Not **domicile**) (= the place where you live and where you can be reached by letter)
- *We've returned to England after a year's **residence** in the USA.* (Not **domicile**) (= living; very formal)
- *I spend months abroad every year, but my **domicile** is the UK.* (legal term, i.e. where I live and pay tax)

dominate • control
- *We all have to learn to **control** our emotions.* (Not **dominate**) (= manage)
- *Russia has **dominated** her neighbours for hundreds of years.* (= had power over)

dominoes
- ***Dominoes** is an enjoyable game.* (Not **Domino is* *Dominoes are**) (plural form + singular verb)
- *Let's have a game of **dominoes**.* (Not **domino**)
- *One **domino** is/Two **dominoes** are missing.* (= the individual pieces)

don't • not • no • doesn't
- *I asked you **not to forget** to switch the lights off.* (Not **to don't forget**) (*not* goes before a *to*-infinitive)
- ***Don't forget** to switch the lights off.* (Not **No forget* *Not forget**) (negative imperative)
- *I **don't like** broccoli.* (Not **I no like**)

- *He **doesn't like** broccoli.* (Not **He no like* *He not like* *He don't like**)

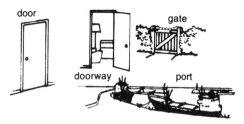

door   gate
doorway   port

door • doorway • gate • port
- *Please don't stand in the **doorway**.* (preferable to *the door*) (= the space where a door opens or closes)
- *Please close the **door**!* (Not **port**)
- *Please shut the **gate**!* (*gates* lead into/out of fields, gardens, etc.)
- *What time did the ship leave **port**?* (= harbour)

dossier • file
- *The letter you're referring to must be somewhere in the **file**.* (Not **dossier**) (= a box or a folder in which we keep information)
- *The police had kept a **dossier** on Blake for years before his arrest.* (= a collection of information, especially on possible criminals or spies)

double • duplicate
- *Don't lose that key: I haven't got a **duplicate**!* (Not **double**) (= an accurate copy, a replica)
- *Who was that woman who made a living as Mrs Thatcher's **double**?* (i.e. who looked almost exactly like her)

doubled • dubbed • lined • folded
- *I'd rather a film had subtitles than a **dubbed** soundtrack.* (Not **doubled**) (i.e. the soundtrack has been changed so you don't hear the voices of the actors on the screen, but those of other actors)
- *This jacket is **lined** with red silk.* (Not **doubled**)
- *I **folded** the tablecloth carefully and put it away.* (Not **doubled**)
- *Fuel prices have **doubled** since last year.* (i.e. they are twice as high)

doubt
- *Mrs West is seriously ill. I have no **doubt about** it.* (Not **doubt for**)
- *You say the situation will improve, but **I doubt it**.* (Not **I'm doubting it* *I doubt**)

(only stative; no progressive form; *doubt* is always transitive)
- *It's hard to make decisions when you're in doubt.* (Not **when you doubt**)
  (the prepositional phrase is obligatory)
- *She must have been delayed. - No doubt.* (Not **Not doubt.**)
  (= without doubt)

douse • shower
- *I showered/had a shower/took a shower and got into some clean clothes.*
  (Not **had a douse* *made/did a shower**)
  (= washed under a spray of water)
- *We doused the fire before it had a chance to spread.* (Not **showered**)
  (= poured water on all of it; *douche* = 'wash internally' is uncommon in modern English)
- *My sister always douses herself in perfume before she goes out.* (Not **showers**)
  (= completely covers with a liquid)

down/up • downstairs/upstairs
- *Where's your father? - He's downstairs/ upstairs.* (Not **He's down/up.**)
  (also note compounds like *the downstairs lavatory, the upstairs bathroom*)
- *The cat has somehow got up on the roof.* (Not **got up the roof**)
  (*get up on/get down from* + noun phrase)
- *The cat is climbing up/down the tree.*
  (*climb up/down* a vertical)
- *In the third round the champion was down on the floor.* (Not **down the floor**)
  (*be/get down on* a low surface)
- *I'm usually up at 6 in the morning.*
  (= opposite of 'in bed')

down • under
- *I wish you wouldn't keep your shoes under the bed.* (Not **down**)
  (position, no movement)
- *I nearly washed my wedding ring down the sink.* (Not **under**)
  (movement in a downward direction)

drake • dragon
- *He disappeared in a puff of smoke, like the dragon in the fairy story.* (Not **drake**)
  (= a mythical animal that breathes fire)
- *How can you tell a duck from a drake?*
  (= a male duck)

drama • tragedy
- *The loss of so many lives in the ferryboat disaster was a real tragedy.* (Not **drama**)
  (= a very sad event)

- *Rescuing everyone from the sinking boat was a real-life drama.*
  (i.e. exciting and interesting, like a play)

dramatic • tragic
- *Tragic accidents occur daily on motorways.*
  (Not **Dramatic* *Tragical**)
  (*comic/comical*, but not *tragic/tragical*)
- *The joyriders gave themselves up after a dramatic chase down the motorway.*
  (= very exciting, as in a play)

draughts
- *Draughts (checkers, AmE) is an enjoyable game.* (Not **Draught is* *Draughts are**)
  (plural form + singular verb; a single piece in the game is called *a draughtsman* or *a draught* in BrE and *a checker* in AmE)

dream
- *I often dream of/about you.*
  (Not **dream myself of/about you**)
  (*dream* is not reflexive)
- *I dreamt of a large empty room.*
  (Not **I dreamt a large empty room.**)
  (*dream of/about*, not *dream* + object)
- *I had a strange dream last night.*
  (Not **I saw a strange dream**)
- *I dreamt/dreamed I was in Alaska.*
  (the past form is spelt *-t* or *-ed*)

dress • costume • clothes • suit
- *The first thing I did when I earned some money was to get myself some decent clothes.* (Not **a/some dress/costume**)
  (*dress/costume* cannot be used as countable nouns for clothes in general)
- *The dancers looked splendid in national costume(s)/dress.* (Not **clothes* *suits**)
  (= theatrical/ceremonial clothes; *dress* and *costume* are uncountable in e.g. *national costume*; we cannot say **He is wearing a national costume/a national dress.**)
- *Must I wear a dress or can I wear jeans?*
  (countable = a woman's garment made of a top like a blouse, with a skirt joined on)
- *Very few people can afford to have their suits specially made.*
  (*a suit* = matching jacket and trousers/skirt)

dress • get dressed • dress up • dress myself
- *I must get up and dress/get dressed.*
  (Not **dress up**)
- *Polly's nearly learned how to dress/dress herself now.*
  (the reflexive use refers to children, invalids, etc., to show conscious effort)
- *Get dressed!* (Not **Dress yourself!**)

- *Is everyone required to **dress up** for this party?* (Not **dress**)
  (= wear special clothes: *I'm going to **dress up** as Napoleon*; or look smarter than usual: *You're all **dressed up**!*)

dressed with • dressed in
- *Why is your aunt **dressed in** black?* (Not **dressed with**)
  (= wearing: *dressed in a black coat*)
- *This salad has been **dressed with** vinegar and oil.* (Not **dressed in**)
  (= mixed/covered with *salad dressing*)

drive • conduct • guide/lead
- *A man in uniform **conducted/led/guided** us past a queue of people straight into the building.* (Not **drove**)
  (*conduct* = officially show the way)
- *Who can **guide/lead** us up the mountain?*
  (*guide* = show the way; *lead* = be in front)
- *When did you learn to **drive** a car?*
  (Not **conduct* *guide/lead**)
- *With the help of two dogs, the shepherd **drove** the sheep down the mountain.*
  (= forced them to go)

drop • fall • let something fall
- *I **fell** and hurt myself.* (Not **dropped**)
  (a person or a thing *falls*; intransitive)
- *The waiter **dropped** a fork.*
  (Not **fell* *It dropped the waiter a fork.**)
  (= let it fall; transitive)
- *Melanie **had a** bad **fall** and hurt herself.*
  (Not **made/did a fall**)
- *Please hold this post in position and don't **let it fall**.* (Not **let it to fall**)
  (= allow it to drop)
- *When we heard shots in the distance, we **dropped** to the ground.*
  (= let ourselves fall; intransitive)

drown • drown oneself • choke • strangle • suffocate
- *She must have swum too far out and **drowned**.* (Not **drowned herself**)
  (the *drowning* was accidental)
- *Her suicide note proves she **drowned herself**.*
  (the *drowning* was deliberate)
- *Something got stuck in my throat and I nearly **choked**!* (Not **strangled**)
  (= was prevented from breathing by something inside the throat)
- *Forensic evidence showed that the murderer had **strangled** the victim.* (Not **choked**)
  (= squeezed the neck till he/she died)

- *Don't let her play with that plastic bag. She might **suffocate**.*
  (= be prevented from breathing by something over the mouth and nose)

drown • get drowned • sink
- *I swam too far out and nearly **drowned/got drowned**.* (Not **sank**)
- *You nearly **drowned me**, holding my head under the water for so long!*
  (= made me drown)
- *Even the biggest ships can **sink**.*
  (= disappear under water)

drug • medicine • narcotics
- *That cough sounds bad. I think you should take this **medicine**.* (Not **drug**)
  (= a substance taken by mouth to cure an illness or disorder)
- *Paracetamol is a much more powerful **drug/medicine** than people realize.*
  (*drug* or *medicine* = a substance designed to treat an illness)
- *The trade in **drugs/narcotics** is almost out of control.*
  (= harmful, addictive substances like heroin)

drunk • drunken
- *Sometimes you talk more sense when you're **drunk** than when you're sober.*
  (Not **drunken**)
  (adjective = have had too much alcohol)
- *How much water have you **drunk**?*
  (Not **drunken**)
  (*drink - drank - drunk*)
- *A **drunk** sat next to me at the bar and asked me to buy him a drink.* (Not **A drunken**)
  (= a person who has had too much alcohol)
- *After the party a lot of people fell into a **drunken** sleep.*
  (adjective used to describe a state or behaviour that is caused by too much alcohol: *a **drunken** sleep, a **drunken** stupor*)

dry up • dry: go/run dry
- *The clothes have **dried**.* (Not **dried up* *gone dry* *run dry* *got dried**)
- *The river **has gone dry/has run dry/has dried up** for lack of rain.* (Not **has dried**)

due to • owing to • because of
- *We **cancelled** the broadcast **owing to/because of** the strike.*
  (Not **due to** after a verb other than *be*)
  (verb + *owing to* or *because of*)
- ***Our delay was due to** the heavy traffic.*
  (Not **Our delay was owing to**)
  (noun + *be* is followed by *due to*)

during • for • along/on • in
- *We were away **for** a week.* (Not **during**)
  (*for* + period, answering *How long?*)
- *It was very hot **during/in the summer**.*
- *He's rung six times **during/in the last hour**.*
- ***Along/On the way** home, we stopped a few
  times to admire the view.* (Not **during**)
  (*during* = within the period named, either
  continuously or occasionally; *along* refers to
  space, not time; *on the way* is a fixed phrase)
- *I didn't learn much **during my teacher-
  training course**.* (Not **in**)
  (*during* cannot be replaced by *in* when we
  refer to an event or activity, rather than a
  period of time)

during • while • during the time (that)
- *Would you water the garden for us **while
  we're away/during the time (that) we're
  away**?* (Not **during we're away**)
  (*while/during the time (that)* + clause)
- *I'll water your garden **during** your absence.*
  (Not **while**)
  (*during* + noun)

dust • cover with dust
- *The fallout from the erupting volcano
  covered everything with dust.*
  (Not **dusted everything**)
- *I've spent the morning **dusting** the furniture.*
  (= removing dust from)
- ***Dust** the baking tin with flour.*
  (= sprinkle with something powdery)

E

each • every
- ***Every child** enjoys Christmas.* (Not **Each**)
  (= all children: *every* + singular verb; *all* +
  plural verb: ***All children** enjoy ...*)
- ***Each child** in the school was questioned.*
  (*each* suggests 'one by one' or 'separately';
  however, we could also say *every child*)
- ***They each have** a share.*
  (Not **They each has**)
  (plural subject + *each* takes a plural verb)
- ***Each of us is** responsible for his/her
  actions.* (Not **Every of us**, but we can say
  ***Every one of us is** ...*)
  (*each of* + plural noun/pronoun + singular
  verb; *each*, not *every*, can also refer to 'two')

each other • one another
- *You and I must try to help **each other**.*
  (*each other* refers to two)
- *We must all help **one another**.*
  (*one another* refers to more than two; in

practice, this distinction is not always
observed)

earache
- *I **have/I've got (an) earache**.*
  (Not **I have my ear.**)

early • soon
- *I found the food strange at first, but I got
  used to it very **soon**.* (Not **early**)
  (= in a short time)
- *Apply **early/soon** for cheap flights.*
  (*early* = before others; *soon* = in the near
  future)
- *Let's catch an **early** train.*
  (adjectival use = one that leaves early)
- ***Early** motorcars were not very comfortable.*
  (adjectival use = at or near the beginning of
  their history)
- *The train arrived **early**.* (Not **earlily**)
  (adverbial use = ahead of time)

earnest • serious • grave
- *I'm quite **serious** about retiring early and
  looking after my garden.* (Not **earnest**)
  (i.e. I'm not joking)
- *Professor Dobbs is always surrounded by
  hordes of **earnest** first year students.*
  (= serious-minded, eager)
- *There's been a **serious** accident at the
  crossroads.* (Not **grave**)
- *The latest news we've had from hospital is
  that her condition is **grave**.*
  (= very serious)

earnings • winnings • profit(s) • gain(s)
- *I put some money on a horse and won. I put
  my **winnings** on another horse and lost.*
  (Not **earnings* *winning* *profits**)
  (= money won by chance, e.g. through
  gambling; plural in form + plural verb)
- *The **earnings** of the company director
  should be in line with company **profit(s)**.*
  (*earnings* = the money you get from
  working; plural in form + plural verb;
  profit/profits = money gained through
  business or trade)
- *You have to set your capital **gain(s)** against
  your capital loss(es).*
  (*gain/gains* = increase in value)

earth • soil • ground • land
- *Clay **soil** is hard to dig.* (Not **earth**)
  (*soil* is a specific reference to the top layer of
  earth in which plants can grow)
- *I use compost for my potted plants, mixed
  with **soil** from the garden.*

- *He threw the ball and it bounced on the* **ground** *just in front of me.* (Not *earth*)
  (= the surface we stand on out of doors)
- *Everything you plant in the* **ground** *grows.*
  (general reference to the surface of the soil)
- *The cellar door was hidden by a layer of* **earth** *and dead leaves brought by the wind.*
  (general reference to *earth* as the substance the ground is made of)
- *People working on* **the land** *are badly paid.*
  (*the land* = ground used for farming; note also that *the land* contrasts with *the sea*)

earth • world • cosmos
- *What kind of* **world** *do we want our children to inherit from us?* (Not *earth* *cosmos*)
  (*world* refers to societies and institutions)
- *The* **earth** *is the only planet in the solar system that supports life.*
  (Not *The world* *The cosmos*)
  (*the earth* refers to the planet)
- *The Antarctic is one of the last natural wildernesses* **on earth/in the world.**
  (Not *in the cosmos*)
  (*on earth* = on this planet; *in the world* = in the sphere we know)
- *Particle physics may provide the key to understanding the origin of the* **cosmos.**
  (= the universe as an ordered system)

ease • facility • convenience • equipment • commodity
- *This house is equipped with every modern* **facility/convenience.**
  (Not *ease* *commodity*)
  (i.e. so that it's easy to run; *facility* is often abstract; *convenience* is often concrete)
- *This gym has a lot of modern* **equipment.**
  (= things necessary for a particular activity)
- *You* **have a** *real* **facility** *for learning languages.* (Not *have an ease*)
  (i.e. you find it easy to do)
- *She learnt French with great* **facility/ease.**
- *Copper is a vital* **commodity** *in industry.*
  (= a (raw) material that is bought and sold)

easy • easily
- *You've been working hard and should* **take it easy** *for a while.* (Not *take it easily*)
  (*easy* = quietly/gently in phrases like *Easy now!, Go easy, Take it easy.*)
- *I finished all the questions* **easily** *in the time allowed.* (Not *easy*)
  (= in an easy fashion: adverb of manner)

easy • light • facile
- *Since my operation, I can only do a little* **light** *housework.* (Not *easy* *facile*)
  (= not heavy, not demanding)
- *Sticking stamps on envelopes is* **easy** *work.*
  (= not difficult)
- *He constantly arrives late for work and I've had enough of his* **facile** *excuses.*
  (= easily produced without thought)

economical • cheap • economic
- *A camping holiday is relatively* **cheap.**
  (Not *economical* *economic*)
  (= not expensive)
- *Our use of the central heating is fairly* **economical.** (Not *cheap*)
  (= careful, cost-conscious, not wasteful)
- *Are electric cars* **economical/cheap** *to run?*
  (both possible when a *to*-infinitive is used, or implied, after them)
- *Europe is more than an* **economic** *community.* (Not *economical*)
  (referring to finance, trade)

economics
- *The* **economics** *of this project* **are** *about right.*
  (Not *The economics is* *The economic is*)
  (= financial aspects; plural form + plural verb for specific references)
- *I've taken my* **Economics** *exam.*
  (Not *Economical exam*)
- **Economics** *is not an exact science.* (Not *(the) economics are* *(the) economic is*)
  (plural form + singular verb to refer to the academic subject)

economies • savings
- *We used all our* **savings** *to make this house comfortable.* (Not *economies* *saving*)
  (= money kept after a sum has been spent; plural form)
- *By* **making economies** *we manage to run a second-hand car.* (Not *making savings*)
  (*make economies* = avoid spending more money than is strictly necessary)

economize • save • spare
- *I* **save** *a little each week.*
  (Not *economize* *spare*)
  (= set money aside and let it collect)
- *We* **economize** *on everything to send our children to private schools.* (Not *save*)
  (= cut back expenditure)
- *I can* **spare** *about £20 a month for luxuries now that I've had an increase in salary.*
  (= have available after essential payments)

edge • end • tip • extreme
- *I pointed to the letter with the **end/tip** of my pencil.* (Not **edge* *extreme**)
  (*end* = the final point; *tip* = a sharp point)
- *Don't go too near the **edge** of the cliff.*
  (Not **end* *tip* *extreme**)
  (= the line where the cliff falls away; compare *a knife edge, the edge of a ruler*)
- *She prodded him with the **tip** of her finger.*
  (Not **end* *edge* *extreme**)
- *You used to have principles, but now you've gone to the other **extreme** and you tolerate anything.* (Not **end* *edge* *tip**)
  (= the furthest limit)

edge • kerb
- *The car swerved sharply and hit the **kerb**.*
  (Not **edge**)
  (= a raised edging, marking the side of a street or road)
- *The car was parked at the **edge** of the road.*
  (= at the side, where the road surface ends)

edit • publish • prepare
- *Shakespeare's collected plays were first **published** in 1623.* (Not **edited**)
  (= printed, distributed and sold)
- *The plays were **edited** by Heminges and Condell.* (Not **prepared**)
  (= prepared for publication)
- *You can't expect me to **prepare** a meal for six people in ten minutes.*
  (= put together)

edition • publication
- *She gave up her job after the **publication** of her first novel.* (Not **edition**)
  (= printing, distribution and sale)
- *Our dictionary has been completely revised and the new **edition** will be out soon.*
  (= version)

editor • publisher
- *Longman was the original **publisher** of 'Roget's Thesaurus'.* (Not **editor**)
  (= a person or company that commissions work from authors and pays for publication)
- *The **editor** of a national newspaper can seriously influence public opinion.*
  (= the person in charge of the contents of e.g. a newspaper)

educate • bring up
- *I was **brought up** to believe in old-fashioned moral values.* (Not **educated**)
  (*bring up* = raise from childhood; *raise*, in this sense, is becoming dated in BrE)

- *The best investment any country can make in its future is to **educate** its children.*
  (= teach them at school, put them in a situation where they learn)

education • good manners
- *An expensive **education** doesn't necessarily provide you with **good manners**.*
  (*education* = schooling; *good manners* = behaviour showing consideration for others)

effect: in effect • in fact/as a matter of fact
- *Your mother phoned while you were out. **In fact/As a matter of fact**, she's left a message for you.* (Not **In effect**)
  (= actually)
- *A work-to-rule is **in effect** a strike.*
  (i.e. that's the reality, even if it doesn't appear to be so)

effective • real/actual
- *Who has **real/actual** power, the government or the civil service?* (Not **effective**)
- *Catalytic converters are reasonably **effective** in reducing harmful emissions from cars.* (Not **effective (of)**)
  (i.e. they produce the intended results)

effectively • really/actually • indeed
- *Penicillin was one of the discoveries that **really/actually** changed the course of modern medicine.*
  (i.e. truly; *effectively* would mean 'had the effect of changing' here)
- *He said he would leave his money to a cats' home and **indeed** he did.* (Not **effectively**)
  (i.e. he really did)
- *Penicillin works **effectively** to destroy bacteria.*
  (i.e. it produces good results)

effort • trial • attempt/try • attempted
- *A judge provides a summary of the evidence at the end of **a trial**.* (Not **an effort**)
  (= a process leading to a judgement)
- *However hard I try, **all my efforts** come to nothing.* (Not **all my trials**)
  (*all my efforts* = the energy I spend; *effort* = use, expenditure of energy)
- *I only passed my driving test after a number of **attempts/tries**.* (Not **efforts* *trials**)
  (= particular acts of trying; nouns related to *try* = attempt are *effort, try, attempt*, not **trial**)
- *He was accused of **attempted murder**.*
  (Not **an attempt of murder**; *attempted* + crime = unsuccessful criminal attempt)

e.g. • i.e.
- *Applications are invited from university graduates, **i.e.** people with a first degree or higher.* (Not **e.g.**)
  (*i.e.* is the abbreviation for *id est*, which is Latin for 'that is', when we want to say what something means)
- *Major financial centres (**e.g.** London, New York, Tokyo) operate 24-hour communications systems.* (Not **f.e.* *i.e.**)
  (*e.g.* is the abbreviation for *exempli gratia*, which is Latin for 'for the sake of example'; we can either write *for example* in full - never abbreviated to **f.e.** - or use *e.g.*; note that we cannot say **by example**)

egoist/egotist • selfish
- *You should bring up children to be generous, not **selfish**.* (Not **egoist**)
  (adjective = concerned only about oneself)
- *Put yourself in his position. Don't be such **an egoist/egotist**.* (Not **a selfish**)
  (an *egoist* is someone who considers the claims of others irrelevant; an *egotist* is someone who behaves in a supremely selfish way; related adjectives are *egoistic* and *egotistic*; we cannot use *selfish* as a noun)

either • neither
- *I haven't seen Joe since last year and I don't want to, **either**.* (Not **neither**)
  (neutral/informal)
  (*either* = as well, in negative sentences)
- *I **neither** saw **nor** heard from Joe.* (formal)
  (*neither ... nor; either ... or*)

elastic • elastic band/rubber band
- *The only way to hold these papers together is with **an elastic band/a rubber band/some elastic**.* (Not **an elastic**)
  (= a circle of thin rubber)
- *The **elastic** on these pants has perished.*
  (= the rubber material that stretches)

elder • older
- *John is **older than** I am.* (Not **elder than**)
  (we cannot use *than* after *elder*)
- *I know both buildings are very old, but which one is (the) **older**?* (Not **elder**)
  (*older*, not **elder**, for things)
- *Who is the **older**/the **elder**?*
  (i.e. of the two people)
- *My **elder/older brother** is a doctor.*
  (we use *elder* in front of a noun with reference to people in a defined group, especially a family)

eldest • oldest
- *Which is **the oldest** inhabited building in Britain?* (Not **the eldest**)
  (*oldest*, not **eldest**, for things)
- *I am the **eldest/oldest** in our family and Jennifer is the youngest.*
  (*eldest* or *oldest* for people in a family)
- *Who's the **oldest** man alive?* (Not **eldest**)
  (we use *eldest* with reference to small groups of people, especially in a family)

elect • choose
- *Which colour did you **choose**?* (Not **elect**)
  (= pick, select; the noun is *choice*: *That was a very good **choice**.*)
- *The government was **elected** with a very small majority.* (Not **chosen**)
  (= chosen by voting; the noun is *election*: *When is the next general **election**?*)

electric • electronic • electrical
- *A modern plane is packed with **electronic/electrical** equipment.* (Not **electric**)
  (*electronic* = equipment controlled by transistors and microchips; *electrical* = to do with *electricity*, very occasionally interchangeable with *electric*: *There's an **electric/electrical** fault.*)
- *If you feel cold, switch on the **electric** fire.* (Not **electronic* *electrical**)
  (*electric* is highly specific: *electric fire, electric shock*, etc.)

electricity • power
- *There's been **a power/an electricity cut**.*
  (*power* is the general word for energy)
- *Many garden machines run on **electricity/electrical power**.* (Not **run on power**)
  (*electricity* for specific reference)
- *A hydroelectric plant generates a lot of **power/electricity**.*

else • other • some more • another
- ***One** of these blouses has buttons; **the other** hasn't.* (Not **One ... the else**)
  (*one ... the other* for alternatives)
- *We need one more helper. Can you find someone/anyone **else**?* (Not **other**)
  (= an additional person)
- *Take this back and exchange it for something **else**.* (Not **other**)
  (= something different)
- *What **else/more** did he say?* (Not **other**)
  (question-word + *else*)
- *If there's some tea left, I'd like **some more**.* (Not **some else* *some other**)
- *I enjoyed that glass of beer. I think I'll have **another**.* (Not **some else* *some other**)

embark • board • launch

- *They're calling our flight number. We have to **board** now.* (Not **embark**)
  (*board* a plane or ship)
- *We **embarked** with the tide.*
  (= began a sea journey)
- *The Hubble telescope was **launched** into space in 1990.* (Not **embarked**)

embarrassed

- *Sarah **gets embarrassed** easily.*
  (Not **She embarrasses**)

embrace • kiss

- *We **embraced** and **kissed** one another for the last time.*
  (*embraced* = put our arms round each other; *kissed* = touched with the lips)

emigrate • migrate • immigrate

- *A lot of people from the countryside are **migrating** to the towns.* (Not **emigrating**)
  (*migrate* refers to the movement of people from one place to another within a country or area: people who do this are *migrants*)
- *Many species of birds **migrate** to warmer climates before the onset of winter.*
  (Not **emigrate* *immigrate**)
  (we never use *emigrate* or *immigrate* for birds and animals; we can refer to e.g. migrating birds as *migrant birds*)
- *Millions of people **emigrated from** Europe **to** the United States at the turn of the 20th century.* (Not **migrated* *immigrated**)
  (*emigrate from* a place = permanently leave your native country; people who do this are *emigrants*)
- *A lot of people **immigrated to** Britain **from** Uganda in the 60s and 70s.*
  (*immigrate to* a place = go to live in a country which is not your native country; people who do this are *immigrants*)

emission • broadcast

- *I first heard the news in a **broadcast** on the BBC World Service.* (Not **an emission**)
  (i.e. what is heard on radio or seen on TV)
- *The **emission** of radioactive material from Chernobyl will have long-term effects.*
  (= a release into the atmosphere)

emphasis

- *We **put** a lot of **emphasis on** good manners in this school.*
  (Not **give ... emphasis to/on**)

empty • blank

- *Every writer feels challenged by a **blank** sheet of paper.* (Not **empty* *shiny**)
  (i.e. it has no writing on it)
- *Your glass is **empty**. Shall I refill it?*
  (i.e. it contains nothing)

end: at the end • in the end

- *We searched everywhere for accommodation and **in the end** someone offered us a barn for the night.* (Not **at the end**)
  (= finally, after effort or difficulty)
- *A lot of people were weeping **at the end** (of the film).* (Not **in the end**)
  (= at the point at which it ended)

end (with) • finish (with)

- *Don't interrupt me. I want to **finish** my essay.* (Not **end**)
  (= complete work on it)
- *I want to **end/finish** my essay **with** a quotation.*
  (= mark the end with)
- *I don't know how to **end** my novel.*
  (i.e. what *ending* to give to it; compare *finish my novel* = complete it)
- *I've **finished with** him.* (Not **ended with**)
  (i.e. the relationship is over)
- *Have you **finished with** that computer?*
  (Not **ended with**)
  (= stopped using it)

endure

- *I can't **endure waiting** in traffic jams.*
  (Not **endure to wait**)
  (= tolerate, put up with)

energetic • effective • vigorous

- *Paracetamol is extremely **effective** as a cure for headaches.* (Not **energetic**)
  (i.e. it brings good results)
- *Your children are so **energetic**!*
  (= full of energy)
- *He agreed with a **vigorous** nod of the head.*
  (Not **energetic**; *vigorous* = strong)

enervate • get on (my) nerves

- *The noise from that disco opposite really **gets on my nerves**.* (Not **enervates me**)
- *When the weather is hot and humid like this I feel completely **enervated**.*
  (= without mental and physical strength)

enervating • annoying • get on (my) nerves

- *That noise outside the window is extremely **annoying**.* (Not **enervating**)
  (= irritating)
- *I find this hot weather extremely **enervating**.*
  (i.e. it deprives me of my energy, tiring)

– *I can't stand Wilfrid. He really **gets on my
nerves**.* (Not **He's enervating.**)
(= makes me feel annoyed, irritated)

engaged • get engaged (to)
– *Jack and Jill **got engaged** last week.* (Not
they engaged *engaged themselves*)
– *Di's **got engaged to** a lawyer and they'll
marry in June.* (Not **got engaged with**)
– *We've **engaged** a builder to fix our roof.*
(= arranged to employ)

engage(d) in • involved in
– *It's none of your business. You shouldn't **get
involved in** his affairs.* (Not **engaged in**)
(= become concerned with)
– *Don't respond if he tries to **engage** you **in**
conversation.* (Not **involve you in**)
(= make you take part in)

engine/motor • machine • machinery
– *This **machine** not only washes clothes but
dries them as well.* (Not **engine**)
(a *machine* stands alone)
– *A car like this needs a powerful
engine/motor.* (Not **machine**)
(an *engine/motor* drives something else)
– *How often should you equip a factory with
new **machinery**/with new **machines**?*
(= machines in general)
– *The **motor** of my sewing/washing machine
is faulty.* (Not **engine* *machine**)
(a small *machine* is driven by a *motor*, not
an *engine*; a *motor* is usually powered by
electricity; an *engine* is usually powered by
oil or steam)

engineer • mechanic • technician
– *Can I have a word with the **mechanic** who
serviced my car?* (Not **engineer**)
(a *mechanic* maintains and repairs
mechanical equipment with moving parts)
– *It is every **engineer's** dream to design a
machine that will use water as fuel.*
(Not **mechanic's**)
(an *engineer* designs and builds machines,
engines, bridges, roads, etc.)
– *The computer system in the stock exchange
was installed by skilled **technicians**.*
(Not **engineers* *mechanics**)
(*technicians* install and maintain scientific
and electronic equipment)

English
– *I'm **learning/doing** English.*
(Not **english* *making English**)
(= the language: proper noun, capital letter)

– *He's/She's **English**.* (Not **an English**)
(adjectival form; the noun forms are *an
Englishman, an Englishwoman*)
– *They're **English**.* (Not **Englishes**)
(adjectival form)
*They're **Englishmen/Englishwomen**.*
(noun forms)
– ***The English/(The) English people** are
wonderfully practical.*
(Not **English* *Englishes**; we can say
Englishmen or *Englishwomen* in general
statements)
(= the group as a whole)
(also: *French, Dutch, Irish, Welsh*; compare
Scottish or *Scots/a Scot/a Scotsman-
Scotswoman*; *Scotch* is for Scottish products
like *whisky*)

enjoy
– *I **enjoy skiing** in winter.*
(Not **enjoy to ski* *enjoy the ski**)
– *I **enjoyed** my stay in the USA **very much**.*
(Not **I enjoyed very much my stay.**
enjoyed with my stay; *I **really enjoyed** my
stay* is a colloquial alternative)
– *I **enjoyed myself** during the holidays.*
(Not **I enjoyed during the holidays.**)

enjoy • amuse • entertain • please
– *Uncle Bill **amuses/entertains** the children
for hours at a time.* (Not **enjoys**)
(*amuse someone* = make someone smile or
laugh; *entertain someone* = pleasantly
occupy their attention and interest)
– *We often **entertain** friends at weekends.*
(Not **amuse* *enjoy**)
(= provide them with food and drink)
– *We're really **enjoying your party**.*
(Not **enjoying with your party**)
– *We're really **enjoying ourselves**.*
(*enjoy* is transitive: not **We're really
enjoying.* *We're pleasing ourselves.**)
(= having a good time)
– *When he's in this kind of mood, I can't do
anything to **please** him.* (Not **enjoy**)
(= give him pleasure)
– *There's nothing organized for this afternoon.
We're free to **please ourselves**.*
(= provide our own entertainment; do what
we like)

enjoy • have a good time
– *We're just off to the party. - Great! **Have a
good time/Enjoy yourselves!*** (Not **Enjoy!**)
(*Enjoy!* = e.g. Have a good time! is
increasingly heard, especially in AmE, but is
not generally acceptable; *enjoy* is transitive

and is followed by a reflexive pronoun: *enjoy yourself*, or an object: *enjoy your dinner*)

enlarged • stretched
- *My pullover has **stretched** in the wash.*
  (Not *enlarged*)
  (= got bigger; intransitive)
- *You should have these photos **enlarged**.*
  (= made bigger)

enough
- ***I'm old enough** to know what I'm doing.*
  (Not **I'm enough old**)
  (adjective + *enough*: adverb of degree)
- *We haven't got **enough time/chairs**.*
  (Not *enough of*)
  (*enough* + noun to refer to quantity)

enough • fairly • rather • quite
- *The water is **fairly** warm.* (Not *enough*)
  (*fairly* = less than the highest degree)
- *The water is **warm enough** to swim in.*
  (*enough* follows an adjective or adverb to suggest 'for some purpose')
- *What's the water like? - It's **rather warm**.*
  (*rather* = inclined to be; it often suggests 'surprisingly')
- *What's the water like? - It's **quite warm**.*
  (Not *enough warm*)
  (= reasonably)

enough • too
- *He's strong. He can lift it.*
  → *He's **strong enough to** lift it./He **isn't too weak to** lift it.*
  (= he has the strength to)
- *He's weak. He can't lift it.*
  → *He's **too weak to** lift it./He **isn't strong enough to** lift it.*
  (= he hasn't the strength to)
- *Is this pear **soft enough for me to eat**?*
  (Not *for me to eat it*)
- *This pear is **too hard for anyone to eat**.*
  (Not **for anyone to eat it**)

enter • come in • hullo
- *Someone knocks at the door and the response is **Come in!** (preferably not Enter!)*
- *You answer the phone and might say **Hullo!***
  (Not **Enter!** **Say!** **Speak to me!**)
  (alternative spelling: *Hello*)

enter into • enter • get into
- *We all stood up when the President **entered the room**.* (Not **entered into the room**)
  (*enter*, transitive = go into)
- *We've **entered into an agreement** not to supply goods direct to the customer.*

(Not **entered an agreement**)
(*enter into an agreement/a contract* = sign)
- *Guess what! I've **got into** university!*
  (Not *entered* *entered into*)
  (= managed to gain admission to: the use of *get* + preposition: *get in(to), out of*, etc., often suggests 'go with difficulty')

entertainment • entertaining • amusement
- *The company spends a lot of money on **entertaining** overseas guests.*
  (*the entertainment/entertaining of* is dated)
  (= showing hospitality by taking guests to restaurants, theatres, etc.)
- *To everyone's great **entertainment/ amusement**, Roland arrived as Santa Claus in a red robe and a white beard.*
  (this gave them pleasure/made them laugh)
- *Let's go to a film - I'll check the **entertainments** column in the paper to see what's on.* (Not *amusements*)
  (any show or performance provided for an audience is *entertainment*)

entire • (the) whole • all
- *He told me **the whole truth**.*
  (Not *the entire truth* *all the truth*)
  (*the whole* combines with e.g. *story, truth*)
- *I've lost nearly **all my hair**.*
  (Not *my whole hair* *my entire hair*)
  (*all my/the* combines with some plural countable nouns, e.g. *plants, flowers*, and some uncountable nouns, e.g. *hair, money*)
- *I've wanted to visit Petra **all my life/my whole life/my entire life**.*
  (*all my/the, my/the whole* or *my/the entire* mainly with singular countable nouns)
- ***Whole/Entire forests** in North Africa were destroyed during Roman times.* (Not *All*)
  (*whole* = complete; *entire* = with nothing excluded)
- ***All passengers** must report to Airport Security 60 minutes before departure.*
  (= every single one of them)

entrance • entry • entrance hall
- *We were refused **entry** to Tibet because we didn't have a visa.* (preferable to *entrance*)
- *Which is the main **entrance** to the building?*
  (Not *entry*)
- *I had lost my key, so I gained **entry/ entrance** through the kitchen window.*
  (= the opportunity for entering)
- *As you turn left, there's a sign that says **No Entry/No Entrance**.*
  (*entry* refers to the opening or opportunity to

go in; *entrance* refers to the act of going in, or to the place, ticket, etc., for going in)
— *The house has a large entrance hall.* (= the space beyond the front door)

entrée • first course/starter
— *They served avocado as a first course/ starter, then the entrée was roast beef.* (in English, but not in French, *entrée* means the main course in a formal banquet)

entrust to/with
— *Many people had entrusted their life savings to the Bank of Credit and Commerce.* (Not *had entrusted the bank their savings* *had entrusted to the bank their savings*)
— *Many people had entrusted the bank with their savings.*

envy • jealousy
— *Jealousy can be very destructive in a marriage.* (Not *Envy*) (*jealousy* is the desire to have absolute possession of someone or something)
— *Their jet-setting lifestyle causes envy/ jealousy among their neighbours.* (*envy* is the desire to have the same good fortune as someone else)

equal • (all) the same
— *I don't mind if we stay at home. It's all the same to me.* (Not *equal*) (i.e. it makes no difference)
— *Giving your children equal treatment is different from treating them both the same.*
— *Divide it into two equal parts.* (Not *same*)

equal • level • flat • even
— *Is the floor quite level/flat?* (Not *equal*) (i.e. a horizontal that is straight enough to form a 90° angle with a vertical)
— *The surface of this desk isn't very even.* (Not *equal*) (= smooth, flat, not bumpy)
— *Make sure the legs of the table are all equal in length.* (= the same in measurement or value)

equally
— *Our secretary is leaving next month. I hope we can find someone equally capable to replace her.* (Not *equally as capable*)

equipment
— *Our local gym is full of all the latest equipment.* (Not *equipments*) (*equipment* is uncountable)

escape from • escape
— *They somehow managed to escape capture.* (Not *escape from capture*) (= narrowly avoid)
— *They somehow managed to escape being captured by the border guards.* (Not *escape from being* *escape to be*) (*escape* = avoid is not followed by *from*)
— *There's been a mass breakout and several dangerous men have escaped from prison.* (*escape from* = run away)

especially • specially
— *I've had this area specially designed as a herb garden.* (Not *especially*) (*specially* = for a particular purpose)
— *I wanted to speak to you especially/ specially.* (Not *Especially/Specially, I wanted to speak to you.*) (*especially* = 'in particular', stresses *you*; *specially* = 'in a special manner', stresses *speak*; we rarely begin a sentence with *Especially* or *Specially*)
— *I think you'll find this article specially/ especially interesting.* (= more than usually: both words are often used in the same way; it's best to prefer *special* to *especial* as an adjective: *John's my special friend* = my particular friend)

essence • petrol • perfume
— *All new cars run on unleaded petrol* (AmE *gasoline*). (Not *essence*)
— *This perfume is made from plant essence.* (*perfume* = manufactured sweet-smelling liquid; *essence* = oil extracted from plants)
— *Mrs Hopkins always sees the essence of any argument straight away.* (= the main point)

estimate • value • esteem/respect • evaluate
— *Jim Fox is highly esteemed/respected/ valued in our village.* (Not *estimated*) (*esteem/respect/admire* and sometimes *value* a person)
— *The cost of repair has been estimated at £790.* (Not *valued/esteemed/evaluated*) (= roughly calculated)
— *I got my jewellery valued for insurance.* (Not *estimated* *esteemed* *evaluated*) (= given a price, e.g. by a *valuer*)
— *Examinations are not the only way of evaluating a student's ability.* (= judging the quality of)
— *I estimate they made more than a million.* (= judge: stative use in declarations)

- When **you're estimating** how much wallpaper to buy, it's safest to add an extra roll.
  (= making a rough calculation: dynamic use,
  i.e. at this moment)

etc.

- Accommodation, food, **etc.**, is provided for
  the trip, but bring your own pocket money.
  (Not *e.c.t.* *ect* *and etc.*)
  (etc. is the abbreviation for et cetera, which
  is Latin for 'and the rest')

ethics

- **The ethics** of the situation **are** self-evident.
  (Not *The ethics is* *The ethic is*)
  (plural form + plural verb for specific
  references)
- **Ethics is** part of our course in philosophy.
  (Not *(the) ethic is* *(the) ethics are*)
  (plural form + singular verb to refer to the
  academic subject)

evade • avoid • escape from

- **Avoiding** payment of tax is quite legal.
  (i.e. managing your financial affairs so as
  not to pay tax)
- **Evading** payment of tax is quite illegal.
  (= slipping out of a duty or obligation)
- After he **escaped from** prison, he fled to
  Brazil. (Not *evaded*)
  (= run away from a place or person)
- We **avoid travelling** at the height of the
  tourist season. (Not *avoid to travel*)
  (= try not to travel)

evasion • flight • avoidance

- The **flight** of capital is a basic problem in
  third world economies. (Not *evasion*)
  (= disappearance into other countries, or
  exchange into other currencies)
- The **evasion** of taxes is the basis of the black
  economy.
  (= illegal non-payment)
- The **avoidance** of taxes is perfectly legal and
  every citizen's right.
  (= legal non-payment)

even • still

- Mr Wilks is not only working at the age of
  95; he's **even** running a company.
  (i.e. this is one of the many things he does;
  surprisingly)
- Though he's 95, Mr Wilks **still** plays bowls.
  (= continues to)

evening • afternoon • noon/midday

- I'm out to lunch, then I've got meetings all
  afternoon. (Not *evening*)

(= that part of the day that begins at noon
and ends at about 6)
- The best time to phone is around 7 in the
  evening. (Not *afternoon*)
  (= that part of the day that begins at around 5
  and continues till you go to bed)
- I like to get most of my work done before
  noon/midday. (Not *afternoon*)
  (= 12 o'clock in the middle of the day)

event • fact

- It's a **fact** that world oil resources won't last
  indefinitely. (Not *an event*)
  (i.e. it is true and can be proved)
- The first day of the winter term is a major
  event in the school year. (Not *fact*)
  (= something that happens)

eventual • possible • final

- Brake failure is a **possible** reason for the
  accident. (Not *eventual*)
  (i.e. it could be)
- Over-borrowing led to the **eventual** collapse
  of the company.
  (i.e. in the course of time)
- Hitler's **final** act was to commit suicide.
  (Not *eventual*)
  (= last)

eventually • possibly/perhaps • finally

- If there hasn't been much traffic, they've
  possibly/perhaps reached home already.
  (Not *eventually*)
- Pneumonia **eventually** led to his death.
  (i.e. it was the end of a continuing process)
- So you've **finally** decided to get married.
  (Not *eventually*)
  (= at last, after a long period of time or after
  a series of difficulties)

ever • always

- If you **ever** need any help, just let me know.
  (Not *always*)
  (= at any time)
- You can **always** tell when a person has been
  crying. (Not *ever*)
  (i.e. every time)
- You said you'd love me **always/for ever**.
  (for always is possible, but not usual)
  (always = continuously; for ever refers to
  future time)
- We are **ever/always** hopeful we might win
  something in the national lottery.
  (ever + adjective = always)

ever • never
- *I have **never** been to Beijing.*
  (Not **have ever**)
  (*never* + affirmative verb = 'not ever')
- *I **haven't ever** been to Beijing.*
  (Not **haven't never* *have ever**)
  (*ever* with a negative verb = *never*)
- ***Have** you **ever/never** been to Beijing?*
  (*ever*: normal question; *never*: asking for
  confirmation, or expressing surprise)

every day • everyday • all day
- *Going to work in the morning is just part of
  everyday life.* (Not **every day**)
  (*everyday* is an adjective)
- *I run five miles **every day**.* (Not **everyday**)
  (*every day* is an adverb of frequency)
- *I work hard **all day** and I just want to watch
  TV in the evening.*
  (= the whole day)

every one • everyone
- ***Everyone** wants success.* (Not **Every one**)
  (*everyone* = all the people, indefinite
  pronoun)
- ***Every one** of their children did well at
  school.* (Not **Everyone**)
  (= all of them)

everyone/everybody
- ***Everyone/Everybody** knows what **he has** to
  do, **doesn't he**?*
  (*everyone/everybody* + singular pronoun is
  formally correct)
- ***Everyone/Everybody** knows what **they have**
  to do, **don't they**?*
  (*they* + plural form verb is often used in
  place of 'he or she'; but note *everyone/
  everybody* + singular verb)

evidence • proof
- *The video is **proof** that he broke into the
  bank.* (Not **evidence**)
  (i.e. it shows the truth, beyond doubt)
- *The video film was part of the **evidence** used
  in the case.*
  (= the information used in a court)
- *We need **more evidence** than this to bring a
  case against her.* (Not **more evidences**)
  (= information needed in a court of law;
  evidence is uncountable)

evidently • of course
- *Are you going to finish what's on your
  plate? - **Of course**!* (Not **Evidently!**)
- *Maxwell isn't going to retire after all.
  Evidently, he can't afford to, just yet.*
  (= it seems, apparently)

evil • bad
- *Don't set a **bad** example.* (Not **evil**)
  (= negative, not good)
- *According to the Bible, the love of money is
  the root of all **evil**.* (Not **bad**)
  (*evil* is a noun here)
- *I can name quite a few political leaders in
  the 20th century who were really **evil**.*
  (*evil* = wicked, much stronger than *bad*)

evoke • refer to/mention
- *Professor Kranz **referred to/mentioned** one
  or two topics he would be dealing with
  during the course.* (Not **evoked**)
- *Someone, I forget who, **mentioned** your
  name **to** me recently.* (Not **referred ... to**)
  (*refer to* will not always replace *mention* =
  'bring into a conversation')
- *Even the mention of Marion's name **evoked**
  memories of a bitter family quarrel.*
  (= called to mind)

exam
- *I'm **sitting (for)/taking/doing/having** my
  final **exam** next Friday.* (Not **giving/making
  an exam**; we can also say *I couldn't **do** the
  exam paper*, not **make**; note *pass an exam*
  = be successful in an exam: the opposite is
  fail (in) an exam, not **stay in my exams**)
- *The **exam** starts at 9.* (Not **examine**)
  (*exam* is the abbreviation of *examination*;
  exams, the abbreviation of *examinations*)

**examine • interrogate/question • interview
• ask**
- *Did you **ask** him? Did he give you any
  reasons?* (Not **examine**)
  (*ask* a question/questions)
- *It's normal practice to **interrogate/question**
  prisoners of war.*
  (= ask a large number of questions,
  especially of prisoners, police suspects, etc.)
- *A lot of people are **questioning** the global
  warming theory.*
  (= expressing doubts about)
- *Who **interviewed** you when you got the job?*
  (= asked questions about your abilities and
  experience)
- *David Frost often **interviews** important
  people on TV.*
  (= asks about their opinions, ideas, etc.)
- *A doctor **examined** him but could find
  nothing the matter with him.*
  (= looked at his body, gave him a *medical
  examination*)
- *The police **examined** the marks on the lock.*
  (= looked at them with great care)

example

- *Who can **give** me **an example** of a modal verb?* (Not **show/make/do me an example**)
- *You should **set an example** to the others, not behave worse than they do!* (Not **give**)
  (= show others how to behave)

example • copy • specimen • sample

- *Authors get very few free **copies** of their own books.* (Not **examples**)
  (a *copy* = one book, of many in an edition)
- *Patients always have to provide **a specimen/ a sample** of their blood before an operation.* (Not **an example**)
  (= a small amount for analysis)
- *What do you think of this scent? It was a free **sample**.* (Not **specimen* *example**)
  (= a small amount so you can try it)
- *The fall of Rome in AD 410 is an **example** of how even the greatest empires decay.*
  (i.e. it illustrates the point)

except • besides

- *I have other cookery books **besides** these.* (Not **except* *except for**)
  (= in addition to)
- *I have no other/haven't any other cookery books **except/except for/besides** these.*
  (i.e. these are the only ones I have)

exceptional • extraordinary • strange/ peculiar

- *I can't explain her **extraordinary/strange/ peculiar** behaviour.* (Not **exceptional**)
  (= unusual, surprising and/or displeasing)
- *Watkins is a man of **extraordinary/ exceptional** abililty.*
  (*extraordinary* = unusual;
  exceptional = outstanding, possibly unique)

exchange • change

- *Can I **change** some traveller's cheques in the hotel?* (Not **exchange**)
- *Some shops will always **exchange** unsuitable goods.* (Not **change**)
  (*change* = alter from an existing state: *change money, clothes, a job, one's mind*; *exchange* = give one thing and receive another: *exchange ideas, glances, gossip*)

excited • get excited

- *We **got excited** when we thought we had won the lottery.* (Not **We excited**)
- *The open window **excited** the attention of the police.*

exciting • sexy • erotic

- *Clothes that make one person look **sexy** can make another look quite plain.*

(Not **exciting* *erotic**)
(= sexually attractive)
- *I don't want to hear about your **erotic** fantasies.* (Not **sexy**)
  (= concerned with sexual feelings)
- *There are some **exciting** items in the current fashion show.*
  (= likely to arouse interest; *exciting* on its own doesn't refer to sex: we have to say *sexually exciting*)

excursion

- *Sally **went on a** school **excursion** to Calais last weekend.* (Not **went for an excursion**)
  (*excursion* for formally organized outings)

excuse

- *Please **excuse** /ik'skjuːz/ **his/him interrupting** all the time.* (Not **excuse him to interrupt/that he interrupted**)
  (the possessive *my, your, his, her*, etc., is preferred to *him, me*, etc., after the verb *excuse*, though both forms are used)
- *She **made an excuse** /ik'skjuːs/ and left.* (Not **did an excuse**)

excuse (oneself) (for) • apologize (for)/make an apology

- *I've **apologized for/made an apology for** my rudeness.* (Not **excused myself for**)
  (= said I'm sorry)
- *I really can't **excuse myself for** the way I behaved towards you last night.*
  (= provide acceptable reasons)
- *I just can't **excuse** such behaviour.*
  (= find a justification for, forgive)

excuse me • pardon (me) • (I'm) sorry • forgive me

- ***Sorry/I'm sorry** I'm late!* (Not **Excuse me* *Pardon (me)* *Forgive me**)
  (= 'I apologize')
- ***Excuse me** (for)/**Sorry for**/**Pardon me** (for)/ **Forgive me** (for) interrupting - you're wanted on the phone.*
- *How's Ann? - **Sorry?/Pardon?** What was that?* (Not **Forgive me?**; *Excuse me?* is AmE only, not BrE)
  (= 'I didn't hear what you said')
- ***Excuse me**, can I get past, please?*
  (Not **Pardon me* *Sorry* *Forgive me**)
- *You're standing on my foot. - **Sorry!/I beg your pardon!*** (Not **Excuse/Forgive me!**)
  (*Sorry!* is recommended; *Pardon!* and *Pardon me!* as apologies should be avoided)
- *Please **forgive me** for my awful behaviour last night. I don't know what got into me!*

(forgive me = asking for forgiveness for words/deeds that have offended: formal)
- **Pardon my asking**, but didn't I meet you in Budapest a couple of years ago? (Not *Pardon that I ask* *Pardon me to ask*)

execute
- All the orders received by a mail-order company should be promptly **executed**. (*execute* a thing = carry it out)
- The terrorists were **executed** by hanging. (*execute* a person = kill officially; the noun for both meanings is *execution*)

exercise
- How often do you **take exercise**? (Not *make/do exercise*) (i.e. in general, to improve your physical condition; uncountable)
- I'm **doing exercises** to strengthen my leg muscles. (Not *taking/making exercises*) (i.e. particular exercises; countable)

exercise • practise • drill • train (in)
- You play the piano so well! How often do you **practise**? (Not *exercise* *drill* *train* or in BrE *practice*)
- The soldiers had been **drilled** for a month before the parade. (Not *exercised* *practised* *trained*) (= given repetitive exercises)
- These men have been **trained in** unarmed combat. (Not *exercised in* *drilled in* *practised in*) (= taught)
- You need to be very patient when you **train** dogs. (Not *drill* *practise*) (= teach them to perform tasks; but note: Linda **goes out training** most days, i.e. practises as an athlete)
- If you own a dog, you need to **exercise** it every day. (Not *train* *practise* *drill*) (i.e. take it for walks to maintain good condition: *give it exercise*)

exhausted: get exhausted
- **We got exhausted** walking round the museum. (Not *We exhausted*)

exhibition/show • display • exposition
- We admired the **display** of spring fashions in the department store windows. (Not *exhibition* *exposition*) (= an arrangement of items in a special way so that people can see them)
- Have you seen the **exhibition/show** of Impressionist paintings at the Royal Academy? (Not *display* *exposition*)

(= a public showing of works of art, etc.; *show* is less formal than *exhibition*: *a flower show, a car show,* etc.)
- Stephen Hawking's 'A Brief History of Time' is a good **exposition** of the subject. (= a presentation and explanation, especially of difficult ideas)

exodus • exit
- In case of fire, please use the emergency **exit**. (Not *exodus*) (= the way out of a hotel, cinema, etc.)
- High rents have led to the **exodus** of ordinary people from inner cities. (= a mass departure)

expect
- **I expect** you've heard about the resignation of the chairman. (Not *I'm expecting*) (stative use in 'declarations')
- **I expect/I'm expecting** to hear from you. (= looking forward to; stative or dynamic)
- John should have reached home by now. - **I expect so**. (Not *I expect (it).*) (*expect* + *so* in affirmative responses)

experience • experiment
- A scientific **experiment** is valuable only if it can be repeated. (Not *experience*) (= a test designed to find something out)
- They want someone with **a lot of** scientific **experience** for this job. (= knowledge and practice; uncountable)
- I had a strange **experience** the other day. (i.e. something happened to me; countable)

expert • specialist
- My doctor has arranged for me to see an eye **specialist**. (Not *an expert*) (= a qualified person with detailed knowledge about a subject, often medical)
- I think you should have this picture valued by **an expert/a specialist**. (= someone with particular knowledge)

explain
- They **explained the situation to their friends**. (Not *explained their friends the situation* *explained to their friends the situation*)
- Please **explain (to me) why** you did this. (Not *explain me why*)
- Let me **explain**. Let me **explain it to you**. (Not *Let me explain you/explain you it.*)
- How can you **explain (their) knowing** in advance that the shares would rise? (Not *explain them to know/knowing*; the noun is *explanation*, not *explication*)

export/import • exportation/importation
- *Once computers were truly portable, the old restrictions on the **export/exportation** of high technology became unworkable.*
- *Countries are always tempted to create tariff barriers to restrict the **import/importation** of foreign goods.*
  (*exportation/importation* are legalistic and formal; *import/export* are preferable)
- ***Exports** have again been lower than **imports**.* (Not **exportations/importations**)
  (only *exports/imports* in the plural to refer to goods)

expose • display • exhibit/show
- *I'd like a pen like the one **displayed/shown** in the window.* (Not **exposed* *exhibited**)
  (= on view, especially for sale)
- *The gallery **exhibits/displays/shows** work by unknown artists.* (Not **exposes**)
  (= has on view, especially to be admired)
- *Curtains are bound to fade if they're **exposed to** sunlight.*
  (= not protected from)

exposed (to) • put at risk
- *The amount we have borrowed **puts** us **at risk**.* (Not **exposes us**)
- *We **are** now **exposed to** the possibility of takeover.* (Not **are put at risk to**)
  (= unprotected from, in danger of)

extension • spread
- *There is often danger of a **spread** of cholera in Latin America.* (Not **an extension**)
  (= an expansion to cover an area)
- *The **extension** of our knowledge of the behaviour of genes has been considerable.*
  (= enlargement)

exterior • abroad • foreign
- *Our neighbours are on holiday **abroad** at the moment.* (Not **in the exterior**)
  (= in another country)
- *Who's the Minister for **Foreign** Affairs?* (Not **Exterior* *Abroad**)
- *The **exterior** of my house needs painting.*
  (= the outside surface)

exterior • outside • outer
- *An **outside** (or external) staircase is essential in case of fire.* (Not **exterior**)
- *The **exterior/outside** of our house needs a good coat of paint.*
  (= the outside surface)
- *Do you think there's life in **outer** space?* (Not **exterior* *outside**)
  (= on the outside, at a distance; compare *You*

*dial 071 for **inner/central** London and 081 for **outer** London.*)

extra • best/finest quality • fine • choice
- *Their carpets are **the best** available/**the finest quality**.* (Not **extra**)
- *We could do with an **extra** room.*
  (= additional)
  (*extra* is also an intensifier in e.g. *extra-special, extra-large*)
- *Spain produces some **best quality/choice** fruit and vegetables.*
  (we often use *best quality/choice* for food)
- *The Savoy Grill is a very **fine** restaurant.* (Not **best quality/choice**)
  (= excellent)

extravagant • wasteful • eccentric
- *It's **wasteful** to leave these lights on when you're not in the room.* (Not **extravagant**)
  (= careless with a valuable resource)
- *We've been **extravagant** in buying things for the children.* (Not **wasteful**)
  (i.e. we have spent too much money)
- *Do you think the critics have been (too) **extravagant** in their praise of this film?*
  (i.e. beyond what is normal and necessary)
- *Amy's habits got more and more **eccentric** as she grew older.* (Not **extravagant**)
  (= odd, peculiar)

F

fabric • factory
- *The new **factory** will provide employment for over 2000 people.* (Not **fabric**)
  (= a place where goods are made in large quantities)
- *I prefer cotton to man-made **fabric(s)**.*
  (= cloth)

fabrication • manufacture
- *Low interest rates benefit the **manufacture** of industrial goods.* (Not **fabrication**)
  (= making things in a factory)
- *This story is a complete **fabrication**.*
  (= an invention, deliberately untrue)

face
- *I really **can't face meeting** people this morning.* (Not **can't face to meet**)
- *Our country **faces** so many problems.*
- *We **are faced with/are facing** so many problems.* (Not **We face with**; *with* only in the passive)

face • figure

- *Mao Zedong was one of the greatest figures in modern China.* (Not **faces**)
  (= well-known people)
- *Mervyn came into the room with a big smile on his face.*

face • grimace

- *I wish you wouldn't pull faces/make faces/make grimaces/grimace when you're offered the same food twice.*
  (= shape your mouth to show your disgust)
- *You should teach your children not to pull/make faces at strangers.* (Not **grimace**)
  (= make funny facial expressions)

faction • party

- *There are three major political parties in Britain.* (Not **factions**)
- *Every political party contains factions.*
  (*a party* is a major political organization; *a faction* is a group within a larger organization)

fair • blonde

- *He's fallen in love with a beautiful blonde.*
  (Not **a fair**)
  (*a blonde* = a woman with yellow-coloured hair)
- *You'll recognize him/her easily because he/she has long fair/blonde hair.*
  (*fair/blonde* are adjectives here)
- *People with fair skin get sunburnt easily.*
  (Not **blonde**)
  (= pale in colour)

fair • fairly

- *The important thing is to play fair.*
  (*fair* is more common than *fairly* after *play*)
- *Share the sweets fairly.* (Not **fair**)
  (*-ly* to describe a deliberate action after verbs like *distribute, share, treat*)

fall • bump into

- *I bumped into her by accident because I wasn't paying attention.* (Not **fell on her**)
- *I fell on the escalator and hurt my knee.*
  (i.e. while I was on the escalator; a person or thing *falls*)

false • artificial • processed

- *Some artifical limbs are computer controlled.* (Not **false**)
  (i.e. not the real thing)
- *Perhaps false teeth will be rare in the next generation.* (Not **artificial teeth**)
  (*false* = meant to deceive)
- *Avoid all processed foods.* (Not **artificial**)
  (compare the opposite: *natural foods*)

false • fake(d) • forged • imitation

- *Some fake/imitation jewellery looks better than the real thing.* (Not **false* *forged**)
  (*fake/imitation jewellery, fur,* etc.: a cheaper copy of something expensive)
- *They were caught while trying to pass faked/forged £20 notes.* (Not **false**)
- *Weapons are often smuggled into a country on false/faked/forged documents.*
  (*fake/a fake* = 'not the real thing'; *faked/forged* = copied and used for criminal deception; *false* = which deceive)

false • wrong

- *You've got the wrong number.* (Not **false**)
- *That's wrong! I never agreed to sign the contract.* (Not **false**)
  (*wrong* = incorrect)
- *He gave the police a false/wrong address and a false/wrong telephone number.*
  (*false* = deliberately misleading)

fame • rumour • reputation • character

- *There's a rumour that all cars with dirty exhausts will be banned.* (Not **a fame**)
  (= information that is passed around, but which may not be true)
- *Famous people should try not to take their fame too seriously.*
  (uncountable = being known to a very large number of people and generally admired)
- *Mr Wilkins has an excellent reputation as a dentist.* (Not **a fame* *a character**)
  (*reputation*, mainly countable, can be good or bad, referring to what others think of you)
- *When Meg applied for her job, I acted as referee and vouched for her character.*
  (i.e. the qualities that make up her personality)

familiar (with) • family • well-known

- *John West is an old family friend.*
  (Not **familiar friend**)
  (= a friend of the family; *family* as a noun modifier; there is an adjective *familial*, used in sociology, etc.)
- *Charles Norton is a well-known local author.* (Not **familiar**)
- *I've never met Charles Norton, but I'm familiar with his work.*
  (i.e. it is known to me/I know it)
- *Your face is familiar.*
  (= 'I've seen it before'; *familiar* is an adjective; the noun is *familiarity*)

family
- *My family is/are abroad at the moment.* (collective noun + singular/plural verb)
- *Address the card to Mr and Mrs J. Wilson and family.* (Not *Family Wilson*)

famine • starvation
- *They died of starvation.* (Not *famine*) (*starvation* = a fatal lack of food)
- *Famine affects many parts of the world.* (*famine* = a period of food shortage affecting whole populations)

fancy
- *It's a fine day and I fancy driving down to the coast.* (Not *fancy to drive*) (= I'd like to drive)
- *Do you fancy a drive to the coast?* (Not *Are you fancying*) (only stative; no progressive form)

fantasize (about) • imagine • fancy
- *Imagine a desert island with a long sandy beach!* (Not *Fantasize* *Fancy*) (= think of, form a picture in your mind)
- *I wish you'd stop fantasizing about becoming a famous rock star!* (Not *imagining* *fancying*) (= daydreaming, thinking the impossible)
- *Imagine/Fancy inheriting so much money!* (*Fancy ...!* = 'imagine' is used especially to express surprise)

fantastic • imaginary • imaginative • imaginable
- *'Lord of the Flies' is about life on an imaginary desert island.* (Not *fantastic*)
- *George is an imaginative little boy. He has an imaginary friend called Charlie. George is the most delightful child imaginable.* (*imaginative* = possessing imagination; *imaginary* = which doesn't exist, or which exists only in story; *imaginable* = which you can imagine)
- *A Caribbean holiday would be fantastic!* (= wonderful, perhaps very unlikely)
- *What a fantastic thing to say!* (= hard to believe because it's too wonderful or too awful)

fantasy • imagination • originality
- *Characters like Hamlet were the product of Shakespeare's imagination.* (Not *fantasy*) (= power to make the imagined seem real)
- *Stravinsky's 'Rite of Spring' is a work of great originality.* (Not *fantasy*) (i.e. new, different, unlike anything else)

- *People used to think that building a tunnel from England to France was just a fantasy.* (= a dream that could never be realized)

far from • (away) from • a long way (from)
- *I live twenty miles (away) from here.* (Not *twenty miles far from/far away from*) (*miles*, etc. + *(away) from* = distance from)
- *Cambridge isn't far (away) from London.* (Not *isn't away from*)
- *Wick is a long way (away) from London.* (*far* referring to distance is unusual in affirmative sentences: *It's a long way* is preferred, not *It's far away*; also: *It's a long way away, It's not far away*; *away* often combines with *far* (*far away*), *a long way* (*a long way away*) and *from* (*away from*) to show distance)

far-sighted • long-sighted
- *They say that as you get older you become long-sighted.* (Not *far-sighted*) (i.e. you need glasses to see things that are close up; the opposite is *short-sighted*)
- *Few politicians are far-sighted enough to make wise decisions.* (Not *long-sighted*) (= capable of seeing into the future; the opposite is *short-sighted*)

farce • practical joke • slapstick
- *In most countries April 1st is the traditional day for practical jokes.* (Not *farces*) (= physical tricks played on people to make them feel uncomfortable or embarrassed)
- *Charlie Chaplin's films are full of slapstick.* (Not *farce/farces* *practical tricks*) (= deliberately foolish acting)
- *The French dramatist Feydeau wrote some wonderful farces.* (= plays with ridiculous situations)

farther • further
- *We learnt, further, that he wasn't a qualified doctor.* (Not *farther*) (= in addition)
- *I drove ten miles farther/further than necessary.* (both possible to refer to distance)

fast
- *I like to drive really fast.* (Not *fastly*) (*fast = quickly* is both adjective: *a fast driver* and adverb: *he drives fast*; there is no *-ly* form; the noun is *speed*; note that *fastness*, literary, = a safe place, as in *an island fastness*)

fat • fatten • get fat • thick
- *Don't eat so many biscuits. You'll **get fat**.* (Not **You'll fat.* *You'll fatten.**) (= become fat)
- *What's the best feed for **fattening pigs**?* (transitive = making them fat; generally applied to animals, but we can say *fatten someone up*: *We'll soon **fatten** you **up**.*)
- *Oliver Hardy was **fat/a fat man**.* (Not **thick/a thick man**) (*fat* mainly refers to people and animals and in a few cases to things: *a fat dictionary*)
- *He hit me with a **thick** ruler.* (Not **fat**) (*thick* mainly refers to things; used informally to refer to people, *thick* means 'stupid': *He's **thick/a thickhead**.*)

fault • blame for • accuse of
- *I don't **blame** you **for** what happened.* (Not **fault* *accuse**) (i.e. see you as the cause of something bad)
- *The workmanship is superb. You can't **fault** it.* (Not **blame* *accuse**) (= find anything wrong with)
- *After the fire, they **accused** the night watchman **of** negligence.* (Not **for**) (= said he was guilty)
- *He was **accused of** negligence.* (Not **with**)

fault • mistake • defect
- *This letter's full of spelling **mistakes**.* (Not **faults* *defects**)
- *I'm sorry we're late. It's my **fault**. I made a **mistake** with the train times.* (*It's my fault* = I am to blame)
- *Lack of punctuality is one of Magnus's **faults/defects**.* (Not **mistakes**)
- *The computer won't come on. There's a **fault** somewhere.* (Not **defect**, though we could say *It's defective.*)
- *This chair is well made apart from this small **defect/fault**.* (Not **mistake**) (= imperfection; something not quite right)

favour • charm • grace • sake • charming
- *Of course I agreed to help her. Who could resist such **charm**?* (Not **favour* *grace**) (= pleasant, attractive qualities)
- *Would you mind if I asked you a **favour**?* (= an act of kindness)
- *Your sister has the **grace** of a ballerina.* (= lightness of movement)
- *They both endured a bad marriage for years for the **sake** of the children.* (Not **favour**) (i.e. for the good of the children)
- *What a lovely child! **How charming**!* (Not **What grace!**)

fear • afraid (of)
- *Many children **are afraid of** the dark.* (Not **are afraid the dark* *afraid from* *have fear of**; *fear the dark* is literary, archaic)
- *I'm not **afraid** of the dark.* (Not **I not afraid* *I do not afraid**)
- *We're **afraid**/We **fear** that many lives have been lost in the crash.* (= we feel concern)
- *It is **feared** that many lives have been lost.* (Not **It is afraid**)
- *I'm **afraid** we won't be free next Saturday.* (Not **I have fear**) (= I'm sorry; *I fear* is formal and literary)

feast • banquet
- *The President gave a **banquet** in honour of the returning astronauts.* (Not **feast**) (= a very large meal in terms of social importance and number of guests)
- *It wasn't just a dinner - it was a real **feast**.* (= a very large meal in terms of the quantity of food; *banquet* has replaced *feast* to mean 'a formal dinner')

feast day • festival • holiday • party • festivity
- *The banks are shut tomorrow. It's a **holiday**.* (Not **feast/festival**)
- *Christmas day is an important **feast day/festival** in the Christian calendar.* (= a day that is holy)
- *There's going to be a big **party** tonight to celebrate the end of the year.* (Not **feast**)
- *The New Year is a time for general **festivity**.* (= celebration)

fed up (with)
- *I got **fed up (with)** waiting for you.* (Not **fed up to wait* *fed up from waiting**) (*fed up of* is often heard, but is not universally accepted)

feed • eat • nourish
- *When is it time to **eat**?* (Not **feed**)
- *Have you ever watched lions **feed**?* (people *eat*; animals *feed* or *eat*)
- *All those sweets and biscuits are hardly enough to **nourish** the child.* (Not **feed**) (= help grow and flourish: you can be *fed* without being *nourished*)
- *The plants have been **fed** with compost. It certainly seems to have **nourished** them.*

feel
- *I **feel**/I'm **feeling** cold.* (Not **feel myself**) (stative or dynamic use depending on the speaker's viewpoint; *feel* is followed by an adjective here: not **feel coldly**)

- *I feel at home here.* (Not *I feel as at home*
I feel myself at home)
- *I could feel myself getting angry.*
(= sense; reflexive *feel* + *-ing*)
- *It feels cold today.*
(referring to the weather: its effect on you)
- *Feel the radiator.*
(i.e. touch)
- *It feels cold.*
(i.e. when you touch it)
- *You can feel his heart beat/beating.*
(Not *feel his heart to beat*)

feel like
- *I feel like going for a walk.*
(Not *feel like to go* *feel as if to go*)

feet • foot
- *Dig a six-foot hole.* (Not *six-feet*)
- *He's a six-foot man.* (Not *six-feet*)
- *Jim is six foot/feet tall.*
- *It's ten feet away (from us).* (Not *foot*)
- *Did you walk all that way on foot?*
(Not *with the feet* *by foot* *by feet*)

fell • felt
- *The tree fell with a loud crash.* (Not *felt*)
(past tense of the irregular verb *fall*:
fall - fell - fallen)
- *We'll have to fell this tree.*
(= cut it down: present form of the regular
verb *fell*: *fell - felled - felled*)
- *I felt tired and went to bed.* (Not *fell*)
(irregular verb: *feel - felt - felt*)

female • feminine • womanly
- *Some men just can't resist feminine charm.*
(Not *female*, which is patronizing)
(opposite *masculine*, relating to behaviour;
the noun is *femininity*)
- *'-ess' in 'waitress' is a feminine ending.*
(Not *female*)
(*feminine* refers to grammatical gender)
- *How can you tell whether an insect is male
or female?* (Not *feminine*)
(opposite *male*, relating to sex; note *a female*
is used as a noun for animals, not people)
- *There's certainly no female equality where
top jobs are concerned.* (Not *feminine*)
- *I was expecting a bit of womanly sympathy,
not a bucket of cold water!*
(= like a woman, relating to *womanhood*)
(in general terms, *feminine* refers to sexual
attractiveness, *female* is biological and
womanly is social, referring to the
sometimes idealized qualities of a woman)

fever • temperature
- *'I have a temperature of 39.3,'* he said.
(Not *a fever of 39.3* *39.3 temperature*)
- *I had a high temperature.* (Not *did/made*)
(*temperature* is countable and is used for
specific reference)
- *If you have a fever/fever, you should drink a
lot of water.*
(countable/uncountable: general reference)

few • a few • little • a little
- *Mona has had very few opportunities to
practise her English.* (Not *a very few*)
(*few* is negative, suggesting 'hardly any at all'
and is often used after *very* with countable
nouns in the plural)
- *I'd like to ask a few questions.*
(*a few* is positive, suggesting 'some, a small
number')
- *He has very little hope of winning this race.*
(Not *a very little*)
(*little* is negative, suggesting 'hardly any at
all', and is often used after *very* with
uncountable nouns)
- *I'd like a little time to think about it please.*
(*a little* is positive, suggesting 'some, a small
quantity')

fewer • less • lesser • smaller
- *Less oil was produced this year than last.*
(Not *fewer oil* *lesser oil* *less of oil*)
(*less* + uncountable noun)
- *That's one thing less to worry about.*
(Not *one less thing*)
- *Fewer and fewer people can afford to go
abroad for their holidays.*
(*fewer* + plural countable noun; *less* + plural
countable is often used colloquially: *less
people, less newspapers*, but is avoided by
careful speakers and writers)
- *Jonson is a lesser dramatist than
Shakespeare.* (Not *less*)
(*lesser* = 'smaller', opposite *greater*, is not a
true comparative and we cannot use *than*
immediately after it: not *I have lesser than
you*; *lesser* occurs in fixed phrases, e.g. *to a
lesser degree, the lesser of two evils*)
- *The USA is smaller in size than Russia.*
(Not *less* *lesser*)

fight
- *John and his wife are always having fights.*
(Not *making/doing fights*)

figure • illustration
- *This book about gardening is full of
wonderful illustrations.* (Not *figures*)
(= pictures, designs, diagrams)

- *A Doric column (**figure** 7 above) tapers gradually upwards from the base.*
  (= a picture, often numbered, to illustrate a particular point in a text)

figure(s) • number(s) • price(s) • sum(s)
- *The **numbers** of the houses on this side of the street are even.* (Not *figures*)
- *I'm no good at **figures/sums**.*
  (Not *numbers*)
  (= arithmetic)
- *A Japanese collector has paid an astonishing **figure/price/sum** for a van Gogh painting.* (Not *number*)

fill • full • get full (up)
- *I got **full** (**up**) eating all those crisps.*
  (Not *I filled* *I fulled* *I got filled*)
- *I can't eat any more. **I'm full** (**up**).*
  (= I've eaten enough)
- *Don't **fill yourself** (**up**) with crisps just before dinner!*
- *Have you **filled** the bucket with water? Is it **full**?* (Not *full up*)
  (note: *It's **full up*** = filled to the brim)

finally • after all
- *So you didn't have to pay a parking fine **after all**!* (Not *finally*)
  (i.e. in spite of what you thought)
- *We've **finally** decided to go away for the New Year.* (Not *after all*)
  (= after a process of e.g. hesitation)

find
- *We **found him sleeping** under a tree.*
  (Not *found him to sleep*)
- *I **find/I'm finding** that it's hard to keep a family on a single wage.*
  (stative or dynamic depending on the emphasis you wish to give)

find • find out
- *What we have to do now is **find/find out** why the accident happened.*
  (= discover information; *find* and *find out* can often be interchangeable when they mean 'seek and discover information')
- *I'm sure I've already paid this bill, but I can't **find** the receipt.* (Not *find out*)
  (= discover what might be lost; *find out* cannot be used with concrete nouns)
- *I **find** (that) three hours is long enough.*
  (Not *find out*)
  (i.e. that's my opinion based on experience)

fine
- *It's **fine** today.* (Not *It makes fine*)
  (= the weather is fine)

- *How are you today? - **I'm fine**.*
  (= I'm in good health)

fine • finely
- *We'll be lucky to catch the train; we've **cut it very fine**.* (Not *finely*)
  (*fine* after e.g. *cut it*, *suit someone*, and *is/seems/looks*)
- *Gold threads were woven **finely** into the cloth.* (Not *fine*)
  (= delicately; note *finely* in compounds: *finely-balanced, finely-made*, etc.)

finish • end
- *And that was **the end** of the story.*
  (Not *the finish*)
- *We walked over to where we could see **the finish** of the race.*
  (*the end* = the way it ended; *the finish* = the distinct end-point)
- *I read the book from **start to finish/from beginning to end** without a single pause.*
- *When are you going to **finish writing** your article?* (Not *finish to write*)
- *I **finished work** at 6.* (Not *finished from*)

fire • light • set fire to
- *We'll never know if the building was burnt down by accident or if **someone set fire to** it.*
  (Not *it lit* *it fired*)
  (= made it burn by starting a fire)
- *It's cold today. Shall I **light a fire**?*
  (Not *set fire* *fire*)
  (*light a fire, a candle*, etc. = make it burn: *light - lit - lit*; but not *light a light* for *turn on a light*)
- *The officer gave the command '**Fire!**'*
  (= shoot with a gun)

firm • firmly
- *I tried to get her to change her mind, but she **stayed firm**.* (Not *stayed firmly*)
  (*firm* after verbs with a meaning related to *be*, e.g. *hold, stand, stay*)
- *We agreed on a price and shook hands **firmly**.* (Not *firm*)
  (-*ly* to describe a deliberate action)

firm • signature • trademark
- *Write your **signature** here.* (Not *firm*)
  (= your name as you usually write it)
- *The oil company Shell uses a shell as its **trademark**.* (Not *firm*)
  (= a legally protected name or symbol used to identify a product)
- *My ambition is to run my own **firm**.*
  (= a business company)

first • second • third • fourth
- *I was born **on the first/the second/the third/the fourth of May**.* (Not **the first May**)
- *I was born **on May the first/the second**, etc.* (AmE *on May first/second*, etc.)
(ordinal numbers require *the* when they are spoken or written out in full, but not when they are written in abbreviation:
1st May = 'the first of May'
May 2nd = 'May the second')

first(ly) • at first • at the beginning • in the beginning
- *I didn't ring the bell because **at first** I thought there was no one in.*
(Not **first(ly)** **at/in the beginning**)
(*at first* refers to a point of time)
- *I couldn't follow the film because I wasn't there **at the beginning**.* (Not **at first**)
(i.e. at the opening of the story; we can also say *from the beginning, at the start*)
- *The earth formed 4,500 billion years ago. **In the beginning/At first** there was no life.*
(Not **Firstly**)
(= in the period during which it began: note the spelling, not **begining**)
- ***First** you turn the computer on, then you load the program.* (Not **At first** **Firstly**)
(*first* referring to a sequence of actions)
- *In the first place/**First(ly)** I don't know what you mean, and in the second place/**second(ly)**, I don't want to.*
(*first* or *firstly, second* or *secondly* when we are giving a list of reasons, etc.)
- *Safety always **comes first**.* (Not **firstly**)
(*first* is the normal adverb after *be, come, go,* etc.; the opposite is *last,* which is also used after these verbs)

first aid • ambulance
- *There's been an accident - ring for **an ambulance**.* (Not **the first aid**)
(= a special vehicle which takes someone sick or injured to hospital)
- *We gave the injured **first aid** before the ambulance arrived.*
(= simple medical treatment)

first time
- ***It's the first time I've** ever **been to** America.* (Not **It's my first time to be to/in**)
- ***The first time** I went to America, I was only 18 years old.* (Not **In the first time**)
- *She's marrying **for the first time**, but he's been married before.* (Not **the first time**)

fish • fishes
- *We had **fish** for lunch.* (Not **fishes**)
- *It's hard to clean these **fish/fishes** with sharp spines without hurting yourself.*
(*fish* is both singular and plural; *fishes* are fish seen individually)

fit • fitting
- *When can you **have a fitting/come for a fitting**?* (Not **have a fit** **come for a fit**)
(e.g. at a tailor's or dressmaker's)
- *That coat's **a good fit**.* (Not **a fitting**)
(i.e. it's the right size)
- *I think Miss Saunders will **have a fit** if she comes in while you're doing that.*
(= be very angry; compare *have a fit* referring to a condition like epilepsy: *an epileptic fit*)

fit • suit • match
- *Pastel colours **suit me**.* (Not **fit** **match**)
(= they are right for me/look good on me)
- *That jacket really **fits you** at the shoulders.* (Not **suits/matches you** **is fitting you**)
(stative use = is the right size for you)
- *What are you doing? - **I'm fitting** a new lock to the back door.*
(dynamic use = putting into place)
- *That lamp **matches the curtains**.* (Not **matches/is matching with** **fits** **suits**)
(= has the same colours/pattern as)

five • fifteen • fifty
- *I'm **fifteen** tomorrow.* (Not **fiveteen**)
- *I retired when I was **fifty**.* (Not **fivety**)
- *I can't remember when I was **five**.*

flannel • vest • waistcoat
- *I wear a **vest** in winter.* (Not **a flannel**)
(= a garment worn under a shirt or blouse)
- *He was wearing grey **flannel** trousers.*
(= cloth made of woven wool; uncountable)
- *Wipe your face with **a flannel**.*
(BrE = a piece of cloth for washing yourself)
- *Harry carries an old-fashioned pocket-watch in his **waistcoat** pocket.* (Not **vest**)
(= a piece of clothing without sleeves and with buttons down the front, often worn under a jacket as part of a suit)

flat • flatly
- *He fell **flat** on his face.* (Not **fell flatly**)
(*flat* after e.g. *fall, lie, spread*)
- *Joan **flatly refused** to lend me her car.*
(= completely, with verbs like *refuse, deny*)

flesh • meat
- *We eat **meat** twice a week.* (Not **flesh**)
(= the soft parts of animals used as food)

– *Some horror films make your flesh creep.*
(we generally use *flesh* in connexion with human beings rather than animals)

flew/flown • flow/flowed

– *We flew to Los Angeles on a charter flight.*
We've flown thousands of miles this year.
(Not *We've flied* *We've flowed*)
(irregular verb: *fly - flew - flown*)
– *Originally, the river flowed several miles north of this point.* (Not *flew*)
– *The river has broken its banks and has flowed into the fields.* (Not *flown*)
(regular verb: *flow - flowed - flowed*)

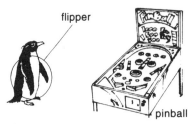

flipper

pinball

flipper • pinball

– *Just think of the hours you've wasted playing pinball!* (Not *flipper*)
(= a game in which players try to prevent a ball from reaching the end of a *pin-table*)
– *Penguins have wings like flippers.*

flirt • flirtation

– *I don't think they had an affair. It was just a mild flirtation.* (Not *flirt*)
(i.e. showing sexual interest)
– *Joan used to flirt with all the boys when she was young.* (Not *make/do flirt*)
(= try to attract sexual interest)

flock • herd

– *The dog was guarding a herd of cattle.*
(Not *flock*)
– *There was a flock of geese/sheep in the field above the farm.* (Not *herd*)
(a *flock* of birds, sheep; a *herd* of cattle, goats, elephants, etc.)

folk • people • popular

– *All the people here have done their best to make this a happy occasion.*
(preferably not *the folk*)
(*people* is the usual word to describe men, women and children together; *folk* is patronizing after *the, these, those*)
– *The people of Britain will be voting on May 14th.* (Not *folk*)
(= the mass of the population)
– *Most folk/people round here have cars.*
(*folk* used like an indefinite *they*)

– *There's a Christmas party every year for the old folk/people.*
(*folk* can combine with particular words: *the old folk, country folk, village folk,* etc.)
– *You can always hear a lot of popular music/ songs on radio request programmes.*
(*popular* means 'liked/enjoyed by a lot of people'; not *of the people*)
– *Some composers like Bartok made use of folk songs/music.*
(= traditional, coming from ordinary country people)

follow • watch • attend

– *I'm watching the match.* (Not *following*)
(= looking attentively at what's going on)
– *Have you ever seen a cat watch/follow a bird's every movement?*
(*follow* in the sense of 'watch' is highly specific: 'follow with one's eyes')
– *The dog followed me all the way home.*
(= came behind me along the same route)
– *When I miss the beginning of a TV serial, I can never follow the story.*
(i.e. 'with the mind' = understand)
– *I've attended English classes for six months now.* (Not *followed*)
(= been going to)

fond of

– *I'm fond of eating.* (Not *fond to eat*)

food • foods

– *What a lot of food! How many people are coming?* (Not *a lot of foods*)
(*food* is normally uncountable)
– *I love the variety of foods on display at a delicatessen.*
(= different kinds of *food(s)*)

fool • foolish

– *Norman is very foolish.* (Not *fool*)
– *Norman is a fool.* (Not *a foolish*)
(*foolish* is an adjective; *a fool* is the noun)

foolishly

– *Dennis foolishly locked himself out.*
(i.e. it was foolish of him to do this)
– *Dennis behaved foolishly at the party.*
(i.e. in a foolish manner)
(the meaning of *foolishly* changes according to whether it is before or after the verb)

foot • leg

– *Many runners have long legs.* (Not *feet*)
(*leg* = the part of the body above the foot)
– *Careful! You're treading on my foot.*
(*foot* = the part of the body below the leg)

footstep • pace • step
- *I was about ten **paces** behind Jill.*
  (Not **steps* *footsteps**)
  (*pace* = the length of a step)
- *Sh! I think I can hear **footsteps** downstairs.*
  (Not **paces* *steps**)
  (*footsteps* for what you hear)
- ***Take a step/a pace** towards me.*
  (Not **Take a footstep* *Make/Do a step**)
  (= put one foot in front of you and bring the
  other foot alongside it)
- *Can you **do this step/do these steps**?*
  (Not **make this step/these steps**)
  (= dance to this pattern)

for • about
- *Who told you **about** this?* (Not **for**)
  (*about* = concerning)
- *How much did you pay **for** this?*
  (*for* = in exchange for)

for • to
- *I've come here **to learn**.* (Not **for learn**
  for to learn *for learning*)
  (*to*-infinitive to express purpose)
- *This manual is very useful **for learning** how
  to type.* (Not **to learn**)
  (*for* + *-ing* = for the purpose of; *for* + *-ing*
  and the *to*-infinitive are not generally
  interchangeable)
- ***Shut** the door please.* (Not **To shut**)
  (the *to*-infinitive is not used as an
  imperative)

forbid • prohibit • No + -ing
- *My doctor **forbade** me **to smoke**.*
  (Not **forbade/prohibited me that I should
  smoke* *forbade me from smoking**)
- ***No Parking, No Smoking, No Waiting**, etc.*
  (Not **It is forbidden/It is prohibited the
  parking**; public notices use *No ... -ing* (*No
  Parking*). *It is forbidden to park* and *Parking
  is forbidden* are correct, but unidiomatic; we
  use *prohibit* in legal notices only: *The sale of
  liquor to persons under 18 is **prohibited**.*)

force • strength • power
- *You need a great deal of **strength** to become
  a weight lifter.* (Not **force* *power**)
  (= the quality of being physically strong)
- *The door was opened **by force**.*
  (Not **with force* *with strength**)
  (= the use of great physical strength)
- *The **force/strength** of the wind was so great
  that roofs were blown off houses.*
  (= amount of power)
- *No politician should forget that in this
  country, political **power** belongs to the*

electorate. (Not **force* *strength**)
(= control, influence)
- *Jackie has great **strength**. She's at her best
  in a crisis.* (Not **strengths**)
  (uncountable use)
- *The support of my family during this difficult
  time has been a great **strength**.*
  (countable use)

forceful • strong • powerful
- *A **strong/powerful** leader needs the support
  of the people.* (Not **forceful**)
  (non-physical reference)
- *You have to be **strong** to become a weight
  lifter.* (Not **forceful* *powerful**)
  (physical reference)
- *The barrister made a **powerful/forceful/
  strong** plea to the jury.*
  (i.e. in an attempt to influence)

forces • powers
- *The division of Europe was decided by the
  great **powers** after 1945.*
  (= the nations with the greatest influence)
- *The end of the cold war has led to a
  reduction in the armed **forces**.*
  (= the army, the navy, the air force)

forget
- *I have a dental appointment next week, but **I
  forget** when exactly.* (Not **I'm forgetting**)
  (mainly stative use)
- *Dont **forget to meet** Bob on the 4 o'clock
  train.* (Not **forget meeting**)
  (referring to a future action)
- *I met you in Prague. Have you **forgotten
  meeting** me?* (Not **forgotten to meet**)
  (referring to the past)

forget • leave
- *It's no good telling the teacher you've **left**
  your books at home.* (Not **have forgotten**)
- *It's no good telling the teacher you've
  forgotten (to bring) your books.*

forgive (for)
- ***Forgive** my interrupting you. **Forgive me
  for interrupting** you.* (Not **Forgive me to
  interrupt you/that I interrupt you**)
- *I **forgive** him **for** what he did to me.*
  (Not **forgive him what he did**)
  (*forgive* someone *for* something)

form • class • grade
- *Which **form/grade** (AmE) are you in at
  school?*
  (i.e. level by age)

– *There are fifteen students in our English class*. (Not **grade* *form**)
(i.e. group of pupils/students)

form • make up
– *This rug has been **made up** from different bits of cloth.* (Not **formed**)
(= deliberately put together)
– *These valleys **were formed** by glaciers at the end of the Ice Age.* (Not **were made up**)
(i.e. took shape as the result of a process)

form • mould • overall(s)
– *If you want to make some shortbread, you can use this **mould**.* (Not **form**)
(= a container used to give shape to things, especially foods and plastic or metal objects)
– *If you want to do some painting, put on **an overall** first.*
(= a protective tunic, from shoulders to knee; compare: *(a pair of) overalls* = an all-in-one trouser suit worn by e.g. mechanics, to protect their clothes)
– *The chef has sculpted the ice cream in the **form** of a swan.*
(= shape)

formidable • terrific • tremendous • fantastic • marvellous • super
– *What was the play like? - **Terrific! Tremendous! Fantastic! Marvellous! Super!*** (Not **Formidable!**)
– *Our new headmistress has a **formidable** reputation for discipline.*
(= very great, causing fear)

formula • prescription
– *You need a **prescription** from a doctor for antibiotics.* (Not **formula**)
(= an order for medicine made by a doctor)
– *How do you make up the baby's **formula**?*
(= (milky) drink, especially AmE)
– *The chemical **formula** for water is H_2O.*
(= the symbol)

fortune • luck • chance/by chance
– *I've been feeding this fruit machine with coins but I haven't had much **luck** yet.*
(Not **fortune* *chance**)
– *I heard the news **by chance**.*
(Not **by luck* *by fortune**)
(= accidentally)
– *I guessed the right answer **by pure chance/luck**.* (Not **fortune**)
(*chance* = accident; *luck* = 'good accident')
– *Some children have the good **fortune/luck** to be born into happy families.*
(we could also say *are lucky/fortunate to*)

founded • found
– *I **found** the address you wanted.*
(Not **founded**)
(past of the irregular verb *find - found - found*)
– *My grandfather **founded** the family business in 1900.*
(= established; past of the regular verb *found - founded - founded*)

fountain • spring • source
– *I know a place in the woods where you can drink from a wonderful **spring**.*
(Not **fountain* *source**)
(= a place where fresh water comes out of the ground)
– *The **source** of the Nile is no longer a mystery.* (Not **spring* *fountain**)
(= the place where a river begins)
– *Have you seen the Trevi **Fountain** in Rome?*
(= a man-made structure to display the movement of water)

four • forty
– *I'm **forty** next birthday.* (Not **fourty**)
(spelling: 4 = *four*; 40 = *forty*)

fowl • chicken • hen • poultry
– *I'd like roast **chicken**.* (Not **fowl* *hen**)
*I must go out and feed the **hens**.*
(*chicken* is served as a meal; *hen* is the live bird; *chickens* or *chicks* are baby live birds)
– *Raina eats fish and **fowl/poultry**, but she won't touch red meat.*
– *Frozen **poultry** is very reasonably priced at the moment.* (Not **fowl**)
(*fowl/poultry*: general words for birds like hens and ducks; *fowl* is what you shoot or eat; *poultry* is what you keep, buy or sell)

frank • honest
– *You can trust Maggie with your key. She's completely **honest**.* (Not **frank**)
(i.e. she doesn't steal, cheat or lie)
– *If you'd like my **frank/honest** opinion, that colour doesn't suit you at all.*
(*frank* and *honest* are sometimes used in the same way to mean *truthful*)

frantic
– *Sylvia is **frantic getting** everything ready for the wedding.* (Not **frantic to get**)

free • freely
– *Children under five years old **travel free**.*
(Not **travel freely**)
(*free* = without payment)

- *The cage door was open and the lion **had gone free**.* (Not **had gone freely**)
  (i.e. was not under control)
- *It's wonderful to be able to travel **freely** in Eastern Europe.*
  (= without restriction)

free • single
- *I enjoy being **single**.* (Not **free**)
  (= unmarried)
- *I'm **free** on Friday evening.*
  (i.e. I haven't got any engagements)

freezing
- *I'm **freezing** this celery so we can use it during the winter.*
  (*to freeze something* = keep it at a very low temperature to preserve it)
- *Shut that window! I'm **freezing**!*
  (= I feel very cold; or *It's **freezing*** = the weather is cold)

fresh • cool
- *At this time of year it's **too cool** to sit outside.* (Not **fresh**)
  (= not warm enough, chilly)
- *I love walking in the **fresh** air.* (Not **cool**)
  (= clean and pure)
- *After such a hot day, I'm glad it's lovely and **cool** this evening.*
  (= pleasantly cold)
- *It's nice and **fresh** outside today.*
  (= pleasantly airy, not stuffy)
- *Store in a **cool** place.* (Not **fresh**)
  (= suitably cold)

fresh • impertinent
- *If it's not an **impertinent** question, how old are you?* (Not **fresh**)
  (= rude, not showing respect)
- *Rita's really annoyed with her boss because he was/he got a bit **fresh** with her.*
  (i.e. he sexually harassed her)

friendly
- *He always greets me **in a friendly way**.* (Not **greets me friendly/greets me friendlily**)
  (*friendly* is an adjective: *She gave me a **friendly** greeting*; the adverb is expressed by a phrase; also: *brotherly, cowardly, fatherly, lively, lovely, motherly, sisterly*)

frighten • startle • scare
- *Sorry! I didn't mean to **startle** you.*
  (Not **frighten**)
  (= make you jump; take you by surprise)
- *Don't **frighten/scare** the children with your silly stories!*
  (= make them feel fear)

- *A lot of young children love running round **scaring** the pigeons.* (Not **startling** and preferable to *frightening*)
  (= causing sudden alarm)

frightened
- *We got **frightened** when we heard the gunfire.* (Not **We frightened**)

from • by • of
- *I was stopped **by** the police.* (Not **from**)
  (*by* in passive constructions)
- *What did you learn **from** him?* (Not **by**)
- *Have you read this novel **by** Hardy?*
  (Not **of* *from**)
- *Tess is a character in one **of** Hardy's novels.*
  (Not **from**)

from now • from now on
- *From now on **I'll** do my best not to complain.* (Not **From now**)
  (= from this time and into the future)
- *The show begins (in) ten minutes **from now**.*
  (= counting from this moment)

fruit • fruits
- *I eat **a lot of fruit**.* (Not **a lot of fruits**)
  (*fruit* is normally uncountable)
- *We import many different tropical **fruits**.*
  (= different kinds of *fruit(s)*)

fuel • fuels
- *The cost of **fuel** varies a lot.*
  (*fuel* is normally uncountable)
- *Fossil **fuels** cause pollution.*
  (= different kinds of *fuel(s)*)

full • complete
- *The new hotel is now **complete/completed**.*
  (= finished)
- *The hotel is **full**.* (Not **complete**)
  (i.e. there are no more vacancies)
- *Have you got a **full/complete** set of cutlery?*
  (i.e. with nothing missing)

full • in full • fully
- *She struck him **full** in the face.* (Not **fully**)
  (= directly: *full in the face, the chest*, etc.)
- *Please write out your name and address **in full**.* (Not **fully**)
- *I **fully** understand why he retired so early.*
  (*fully* as an adverb = 'entirely')

full of • filled with
- *I just love cakes **filled with** cream.*
  (Not **full of* *full with**)
  (= that have had cream put into them)
- *This essay is **full of** spelling mistakes.*
  (Not **full with/from* *filled with**)
  (i.e. it contains a lot of them)

- *The room was **full of** people.*
  (i.e. it contained; if we say *The room **filled with** people*, we mean 'people came in until the room was full')

fumigated • smoked • fumed
- *Would you like some **smoked** salmon?*
  (Not **fumigated* *fumed**)
  (= that has been cured over smoke)
- *We had to have our flat **fumigated** to get rid of ants.* (Not **smoked* *fumed**)
  (= treated with chemical smoke to kill germs, insects, etc.)
- *A moment ago you **fumed** at the waiter and now you're fuming at me!*
  (= expressed anger)

fun • enjoy
- *We **had fun**/We **enjoyed ourselves** at the party.* (Not **We enjoyed at the party.**)
  (we *enjoy ourselves* or we *enjoy something*)
- ***Have fun!*** (Not **Make/Do fun!**)
  (= Enjoy yourself/yourselves!)
- *Don't **make fun of** him.*
  (= ridicule)

fun • enjoyment • pleasure (to/of)
- *Our hosts provided everything imaginable for our **enjoyment/pleasure**.* (Not **fun**)
  (i.e. to make us feel happy)
- *You should have come to the party last night. It was **fun**.*
  (Not **enjoyment* *pleasure**)
  (i.e. it was enjoyable)
- *We had **a lot of fun**.* (Not **a lot of funs**)
  (*fun* is uncountable)
- *It's a pleasure **to be** here.* (Not **of being**)
- *There's nothing to compare with the pleasure **of being** with you.* (Not **to be**)

function • liturgy • duty
- *The **liturgy** in the Eastern Church is rather long.* (Not **function**)
  (= order of prayers in a church)
- *It's my **duty** to check all applications for visas.* (preferable to *function*)
- *The **function** of the apostrophe is to show possession.* (Not **liturgy**)
  (i.e. that is what it's for)

function • work • run (on) • go
- *My watch **won't go/won't work**.*
- *My watch **doesn't work/isn't working** all of a sudden.* (Not **function(ing)* *run(ning)**)
  (*function* = 'work' is sometimes awkward in the negative)
- *The car's **going/functioning/running** very well at the moment.*

(*going* is preferable to *working* for cars and machines like fridges and computers)
- *This lap-top computer **runs on** ordinary batteries.* (preferable to *works, functions*)
- *My watch **is fast/slow**.*
  (*is fast/slow* = shows the wrong time now; compare: *My watch **gains/loses time**,* preferable to *goes fast/slow*, to refer to a permanent condition)

funny
- *I thought there was something **funny** about the parcel, so I phoned the police.*
  (= peculiar)
- *I don't find Jim's jokes very **funny**.*
  (= amusing)

furnace • oven
- *Put the pie in a hot **oven**.* (Not **furnace**)
  (= a box for cooking e.g. bread, meat)
- *All this scrap iron will be melted down in a **furnace** and recycled.*
  (= a device in a factory where metals, etc., are heated to very high temperatures)

furnish • supply (with) • provide
- *Who **supplies** you **with** fresh vegetables?*
  (Not **furnishes* *supplies you fresh vegetables**)
  (= fulfils a need, preferable to *provides*; the nouns are *supply* and *provision*)
- *Our parents **provided** us **with** everything we needed while we were growing up.*
  (Not **supplied* *provided us everything**; preferable to *furnished*: old-fashioned)
  (= made sure we had)
- *My mother **furnished** this room.*
  (*furnish* = supply with *furniture*)

furniture • a piece of furniture
- *That sideboard is **a** very nice **piece of furniture**.* (Not **a nice furniture**)
- *We need some **furniture** for our flat.*
  (Not **some furnitures**)
  (*furniture* is uncountable)

future: in future • in the future
- *I'm still a student, but **in the future** I want to work abroad.* (Not **in future**)
  (referring to what might happen)
- ***In future**, never post letters without checking them first.* (Not **In the future**)
  (= from now on: often used in warnings/ promises: ***In future** I'll be more careful.*)

G

gain • win • earn • profit • benefit
- *Try to save as you **earn**.* (Not **gain**, etc.)
  (= get money by working)
- *It's no good hoping you'll **win** a lottery.*
  (Not **earn* *gain**, etc.)
  (= get money by chance)
- *Who would imagine that a house could **gain**
  so much in a year?* (Not **win**, etc.)
  (= increase in value)
- *Alan's certainly **profited/gained/benefited**
  from his year in the USA.*
  (i.e. it has done him good - not necessarily
  financially)
- *Everybody **benefits/profits/gains** in a
  healthy economy.*
  (= experiences good, not necessarily
  financially)

gallon • braid
- *He's only a ticket collector, but he looks like
  a general with **all that gold braid**.*
  (Not **all those gallons**)
  (= woven gold thread to show rank)
- *How many litres are there in a **gallon**?*
  (= a measure of liquid)

game
- *We **had** a good **game**.* (Not **did/made**)

garage/service station • filling station
- *We're low on fuel and I'll have to pull in at
  the next **filling station**.*
  (more accurate than *garage*)
- *My car's at the **garage/service station** at the
  moment for its 50,000 km service.*
  (properly speaking a *garage* is the place
  where a car is kept, serviced or repaired)

gather
- *I **gather** he's ill.* (Not **I'm gathering**)
  (stative use = understand)
- ***We're gathering** information from people
  who travel regularly on British Airways.*
  (stative or dynamic use = collecting)

gather • pick • pick up
- *I dropped my spoon and bent down **to pick it
  up**.* (Not **to gather it* *to pick it**)
  (= lift something up from a surface,
  especially if it has fallen)
- *I'll **pick you up** at the station.*
  (Not **pick/gather you**)
- *The children are out in the field **gathering/
  picking** wild flowers.* (Not **picking up**)
  (*pick* is the normal verb to describe the act of
  collecting flowers or fruit while they're
  growing; *gather* is more literary)

- *It's taken me a lifetime to **gather** all these
  books.* (Not **pick* *pick up**)
  (= collect)

gaze (at) • stare (at) • gape (at)
- *It's rude to **stare at** strangers.*
  (Not **gaze at**; preferable to *gape at*)
  (= look at hard with the eyes wide open)
- *We all continued **gazing at** the sky after the
  sun had gone down.*
  (= looking steadily at, e.g. *gaze into space*)
- *They **gaped at** me as if I'd just come back
  from the dead.*
  (= looked at with mouth and eyes open in
  astonishment)

gender • sex
- *Which women truly speak for the female
  sex?* (preferable to *female gender*, though
  some people say *gender* because they want
  to avoid using the correct word *sex*)
- *In many languages nouns are classed by
  gender, so they may be masculine, feminine
  or neuter.* (Not **sex**)
  (*gender* is a grammatical term)

genial • gifted
- *Antonia is a **gifted** writer.* (Not **genial**)
  (= of great ability, talented)
- *John's a pleasant, **genial** sort of man.*
  (= cheerful and friendly)

genie • genius
- *It took a **genius** /'dʒiːnɪəs/ like Einstein to
  propose the Theory of Relativity.*
  (Not **a genie* *a genius person**)
  (= a person of rare, exceptional ability)
- *Aladdin rubbed the lamp and the **genie**
  /'dʒiːnɪ/ appeared.*
  (= a spirit in Arab fairy stories)

gentle • kind (of/to) • polite • genteel
- *It was very **kind of** the Robinsons to offer to
  put us up for the night.* (Not **gentle of**)
- *She's **kind to** everyone.* (Not **kind with**)
- *My mother had a **gentle** way of getting us to
  do what she wanted.*
  (= pleasant, calm, not rough)
- *Your son is very **polite**.*
  (i.e. he has good manners, not **kind**
  gentle in this sense)
- *She probably comes from rather a **genteel**
  sort of family.* (Not **gentle* *polite**)
  (= with superior manners, breeding)

German
- *I'm **learning/doing** German.*
  (Not **making German* *german**)
  (= the language: proper noun, capital letter)

- *He's/She's **German**.*
  (preferable to *a German*)
  (we generally prefer to use an adjectival
  complement; the noun form is *a German*)
- *They're **German**.*
  (adjectival form)
- *They're **Germans**.*
  (noun form)
- *I was just speaking to **a German/two
  Germans**.*
  (their sex is not stated, though a pronoun
  will often show whether they are male or
  female)
- *(The) **Germans**/(The) **German people** are
  wonderfully efficient.*
  (= the group as a whole)
  (similarly to refer to people: *Cypriot, Greek,
  Iraqi, Israeli, Kuwaiti, Omani, Pakistani,
  Qatari, Saudi, Thai*)

gesture • shake hands
- *We **shook hands** and said goodbye.*
  (Not **gestured**)
  (= took each other by the right hand)
- *She brushed him away with an angry
  gesture.*
  (= a movement of the hands, head, etc.)

get
- *I **got** a letter from her yesterday.*
  (= received)
- *Where did you **get** that idea?*
  (= obtain)
- *Where did you **get** that lovely jacket?*
  (= buy)
- *Which train did you **get**?*
  (= catch)
- *I'm **getting** fed up with the weather.*
  (= becoming)
- ***Get** him to tell you what happened.*
  (= persuade)
- *I **got in** through the window.*
  (= went, but with difficulty)

get rid of
- *How do you **get rid of** an old refrigerator
  you no longer want?* (Not **get rid from**)
  (= dispose of)

girl • young woman
- *Lorraine has just joined our firm. She's a
  very ambitious **young woman**.* (preferably
  not *girl*, which often sounds patronizing)
- *We've got a **girl** of 16 and a boy of 12.*

giro • short walk/turn
- *I'm going to take **a short walk/turn** round
  the block.* (Not **a giro**)

- *You can pay this bill by **giro**.*
  (= a system used by banks and post offices)

give
- *They **gave us some advice**. They **gave some
  advice to us**.* (Not **They gave to us some
  advice.* *To us they gave some advice.**)
  (also: *bring, grant, hand, lend, offer, owe,
  pass, pay, post, promise, read, sell, send,
  serve, show, sing, take, teach, tell, throw* and
  write)

glad/happy
- *I'm **glad/happy** you've done so well.*
  (*glad* = delighted, very pleased indeed;
  happy = feeling contented and relaxed)
- *John's **a happy man**.* (Not **a glad man**)
  (we don't usually put *glad* before a noun)
- *I was **glad/happy about** my exam results.*
  (Not **glad/happy for**, but we can say
  happy with, not **glad with**)
- *We were so pleased to hear about your
  engagement; we're very **glad/happy for** you.*
  (i.e. on your behalf)
- *I've finished my essay, but I'm not very
  happy with it.* (Not **glad with**)
  (= satisfied with)
- *Take a coat with you. You'll be **glad of** it if it
  rains.* (Not **glad for**)

glance • glimpse
- *I caught a **glimpse** of him as he walked past
  my window.* (Not **caught a glance**)
  (i.e. I saw him briefly)
- *Would you mind **glancing at/having a
  glance** at my essay before I hand it in?*
  (Not **glimpsing* *having a glimpse**)
  (= looking at briefly, having a quick look)

glass   jar   vessels

glass • jar • vessel
- *I can't open this **jar**.* (Not **glass**)
  (= a container, usually made of glass, for e.g.
  jam: *a jar of jam, a jam jar*)
- *I'd love a **glass** of water.*
- *I haven't got a single **vessel** big enough for
  all these olives.*
  (a general term for a storage container, often
  in the kitchen; rather old-fashioned)

glasses
- *It would be useful to have two **pairs of
  glasses**.* (Not *two glasses*)
  (= pairs of spectacles: *a pair/two pairs of
  glasses*, plural form only)
- *He filled two **glasses** with water and brought
  them to us.*
  (i.e. so that we could drink)

glassy • glass
- *Put the roses in a **glass** vase.* (Not *glassy*)
  (= one made of *glass*; *glass* can be a noun
  modifier: *a glass ornament, a glass bowl*)
- *She gave me a **glassy** stare.*
  (= 'like glass', without expression)

go
- *Do you want to **go shopping** with them?*
  (Not *go for shopping*)
- *Do you want to **go for a walk** with them?*
  (Not *go walk*; *go walking* is often used for
  trekking: *We **went walking** in the Alps.*)
- *Dogs **go bow-wow** and cats **go miaow-
  miaow**.* (Not *do/make bow-wow*, etc.)
- *The stamp should **go** in the top right-hand
  corner of the envelope.* (Not *come*)
- *You should let the most senior people **go**
  into the room **first**.* (Not *come first*)
  (= proceed; we use *come first* for
  competitive activities and listing priorities:
  *The children's education **comes first**.*)

go on
- ***Go on ringing** the doorbell until someone
  answers.* (Not *go on to ring*)
  (= continue)
- *After approving the agenda, we **went on to
  discuss** finance.* (Not *to discussing*)
  (= proceeded)

God • the gods
- *Do you believe **in God**?*
  (Not *in the God* *in god* *in the god*)
  (proper noun: capital *G* and no article)
- *Did the Romans really believe in **the gods**?*
  (common noun: small *g*, specific reference
  to particular *gods*, therefore *the*)

golden • gold
- *When Mr Pennyweather retired, they gave
  him a **gold** watch.* (Not *golden*)
  (= one made of *gold*; *gold* can be a noun
  modifier: *a gold ring, a gold bracelet*)
- *As the sun set, the sky became **golden**.*
  (= 'like gold', but not normally for people:
  *She's a **wonderful** woman*, not *golden*)

good
- *Jenny's very **good at** Art.* (Not *good in*)

- *Exercise **does** you **good**.* (Not *makes*)
  (i.e. it is good for you)
- *It **does no good** to worry.* (Not *makes*)
- *It's **no good worrying**.* (Not *to worry*)

good • nice
- *What's Janice like? - She's very **nice**.*
  (Not *good*)
  (i.e. she has a nice character)
- *Lizzie has been very **good**.*
  (= well-behaved, when referring to children;
  in an adult reference, this would mean 'has
  done good/kind things')
- *I don't believe anybody can be entirely **good**
  or entirely **bad**.* (Not *a good* *a bad*)
- ***The good** die young.* (Not *The goods*)
  (*the* + adjective for the group as a whole)
- *Teaching is hard work, but **the good thing** is
  you get long holidays.*
  (Not *the good is*)

good • well
- *John played **well**.* (Not *good*)
  (adverb of manner, modifying *played*)
- *John looks **well**.*
  (adjective = in good health; *well* normally
  comes after *be, feel*, etc.; however, it is used
  in front of nouns in phrases like *He's not a
  well man or **Well Woman's** Clinic*)
- *John looks **good** in a suit.*
  (refers to clothes, etc., not physical features)
- *That pie looks **good**.* (Not *well*)
  (adjective = has a pleasant appearance)

goods
- *All the **goods** in this shop **are** marked down.*
  (Not *the good is* *the goods is*)
  (= articles for sale; plural noun with no
  singular form + plural verb)

gossip
- *There was **a lot of gossip** after the
  Arkwrights suddenly left the neighbourhood.*
  (Not *a gossip* *a lot of gossips*)
  (*gossip* = inaccurate conversation about
  other people's lives, uncountable; *a gossip*,
  countable, is a person who *gossips, has a
  gossip*, or *has a gossipy conversation*)

got/gotten
- *I've **gotten** myself a new briefcase.* (AmE)
- *I've **got** myself a new briefcase.* (BrE)
  (*get - got - have got/gotten*)

got • had (causative)
- *I **had my window repaired** after the storm.*
  (causative = I paid someone to do it for me)
- *I finally **got my window repaired** after the
  storm.*

(*got* is stronger than *had* and suggests special effort: the use of *got* is ambiguous here, suggesting I succeeded in doing it myself, or that I got someone else to do the job)

got • was/were (passives)
- *I was asked to work overtime last week because there was so much to do.*
  (preferable to *I got asked*)
  (*be* + past participle for normal passives)
- *I got dressed as fast as I could.* (Not *was*)
  (*get* + past participle when we do something for ourselves)
- *We got/were delayed in the heavy traffic.*
  (*get* for things that are beyond our control; *be* for normal passives)

government
- *The government has/have resigned.*
  (collective noun + singular/plural verb; note the spelling, not *goverment*)

grade • mark • degree • rank
- *How many marks did you get for your essay?* (Not *grades* *degrees*)
  (a piece of written work is *marked* and may be given *a mark* or *marks* out of e.g. 100)
- *Marcella got good grades/marks in all subjects.* (Not *degrees*)
  (*grades* is common in AmE)
- *I've passed Grade 6 in my music exams.* (Not *rank*)
  (= level, on a scale of ability)
- *It's five degrees below zero outside.* (Not *grades* *marks*)
  (*degrees* measure temperature: Celsius or Fahrenheit)
- *She left university with a good degree.* (Not *mark* *grade*)
  (= a university qualification)
- *What rank was your father when he was in the army?* (Not *grade* *degree*)
  (= an official position on a scale)

grand • big/large • tall • great/important
- *That house may be big/large, but it's not terribly grand.* (Not *grand*)
  (*big*, opposite *little*; *large*, opposite *small*, generally refer to relative size)
- *Mike suddenly grew so tall that his clothes were too small for him.* (Not *grand*)
  (*tall*, opposite *short*, refers to people)
- *Will this tree grow too tall for our garden?* (Not *grand*)
  (*tall*, opposite *small*, for buildings, trees)
- *Great/Important writers always influence the language they write in.*
  (Not *grand* *big/large/tall* *gross*)

(*great*, opposite *minor*, generally refers to importance)
- *A lot of people think Buckingham Palace isn't very grand.* (Not *great*)
  (= impressive)

grass • grasses • herb
- *I've just mowed the lawn, so don't get grass on your shoes.* (Not *grasses* *herb*)
  (*grass* is normally uncountable)
- *This lawn is made up of a mixture of different grasses.*
  (= different kinds of *grass(es)*)
- *Herbs like parsley aren't hard to grow.*
  (= aromatic plants)

grass • grease • oil
- *It's about time you greased the axle of that old wheelbarrow.* (Not *grassed*)
  (= add *grease*, a thick, oily product which is used for lubrication, but doesn't flow)
- *That lock needs oiling.* (Not *grassing*)
  (= the addition of *oil*, a petroleum product which flows and is used for lubrication)
- *The police arrested the whole gang after somebody grassed on them.*
  (= informed the police; very informal)

gratified • obliged (to) • grateful (to)
- *We're very grateful/obliged to you for all the help you've given us.* (Not *gratified*)
  (i.e. we feel indebted)
- *Grandpa was extremely gratified by the fuss everybody made on his 80th birthday.*
  (i.e. he felt satisfied, he appreciated it)
- *You are obliged by law to send your children to school.* (Not *grateful*)
  (i.e. it is required)

grease • fat • oil
- *What sort of fat do you use in cooking?* (Not *grease*)
  (*fat* is the general word for edible fats, e.g. butter, margarine, meat dripping, seed oil)
- *We use (olive) oil for most things.*
  (= vegetable fat that pours)
- *I've been working on my car and I've got grease all over my hands.* (Not *fat*)
  (= a thick petroleum product)
- *Grease/Oil the baking dish first.*
  (= wipe it with edible fat)
- *Please oil these door hinges.* (Not *grease*)
  (= add lubricating fluid)

greasy • fatty • oily
- *I'm not looking forward to washing up all those greasy plates.* (Not *fatty* *oily*)
  (= covered with cold, solid *fat*)

- *I must wash my hands. They're very greasy/oily*. (Not **fatty**)
  (= covered with *fat* or *oil*)
- *You should avoid greasy/fatty/oily foods*.
  (= containing *fat*; *greasy* = sticky fat that doesn't flow; *oily* = containing liquid fat from seeds, or liquid petroleum product)

green: get/go/turn green
- *Trees go/turn green in spring*. (Not **green**)
- *The lawn has got/gone/turned so green with all this rain*. (Not **has greened**)
- *She put this stuff on her hair and it's gone/turned green*. (Not **greened* *got green**)

grey
- *I think I'm going grey.*
  (Not **I'm greying**; alternative spelling: *gray*, especially in AmE)

grilled • toasted • roast • roasted
- *The bread's a bit stale and will taste better toasted*. (Not **grilled* *roast(ed)**)
  (*toast* = put bread close to strong direct heat until it is brown on the outside)
- *How would you like your steak? Grilled?*
  (Not **Toasted?* *Roast?* *Roasted?**)
  (*grill* = cook under or over direct heat)
- *I'd like some roast beef please.*
  (Not **roasted**)
  (we use *roast* as a noun modifier in *roast beef, roast chicken, roast potatoes*, etc., to describe meat/potatoes cooked in an oven)
- *The meat has been roasted in a hot oven.*
  (Not **roast**)

grippe • flu
- *Angela's in bed with flu*. (Not **grippe**)
  (*grippe* = flu - *influenza* - has never been really anglicized)
- *Angela had (the) flu*. (Not **a flu* *some flu**; not **did/made (the) flu**)
  (*the* is possible with *flu*, especially when referring to an epidemic)

gross • fat • large
- *He's got rather fat lately*. (Not **gross**)
  George has got a large collection of Antarctic stamps. (Not **gross**)
- *He's fat, but I wouldn't say he's gross.*
  (= unattractively fat; compare *grossly* = unacceptably, as in *grossly rude*)

ground floor • first floor
- *I've pressed the button for the ground floor/first floor*. (Not **bottom floor**)
  (*ground floor* in BrE is *first floor* in AmE; *first floor* in BrE is *second floor* in AmE; we can say *top floor* and contrast it with *bottom floor* to refer to the lowest level in a building)
- *We're on the ground floor/on the first floor*, etc. (Not **to* *in**, but we can say: *We've arrived at the ground floor*.)

grow • grow up • get/grow tall • bring up
- *What do you want to do when you're grown up?* (Not **when you're grown**)
  (*grown up* = no longer a child)
- *Ann's grown up a lot since I last saw her.*
  (= become more mature)
- *How tall you've got! How you've grown!*
  (Not **You've talled!**)
  (= increased in height)
- *A big city is not the ideal place to bring up children*. (Not **grow**)
  (= raise from childhood)

guard (against) • look after • keep • watch (over) • wake
- *Who looks after/keeps the shop when you're on holiday?* (Not **guards* *watches**)
  (= minds, takes care of)
- *I've had an inoculation to guard against flu.*
  (Not **to guard (myself) from**)
- *Will you look after/watch (over) the baby for a minute while I answer the door?*
  (Not *guard* for people, except e.g. prisoners)
- *A small dog can guard a very large house.*
  (Not **wake**)
  (= protect)
- *Our baby always wakes at dawn.*

guard • keeper • warden • guardian
- *Let's ask a keeper when the zoo closes.*
  (Not **guard* *warden* *guardian**)
  (= a person who looks after a park or zoo; also note *shopkeeper, goalkeeper*)
- *The warden at the old people's home is very strict about visiting hours.*
  (= a person in charge of e.g. an old people's home, a hall of residence)
- *This form must be signed by a parent or guardian.*
  (= a person who acts in place of a parent)
- *In most European countries, border guards are a thing of the past.*
  (*guard* often applies to a soldier, a prison officer, a railway worker)

guilty (of) • valuable • valid
- *Your passport is no longer valid.*
  (Not **guilty* *valuable**)
  (i.e. it carries no authority)
- *Their house is full of valuable antiques.*
  (= worth a lot of money)

- *The jury found her **guilty of** murder.*
  (Not **guilty for/with**)

gum • rubber • eraser • tyre
- *You can remove those pencil marks with **a rubber/an eraser**.* (Not **a gum**)
  (*a rubber* BrE/*an eraser* AmE = a piece of rubber for removing pencil marks; in informal AmE, *a rubber* is used to mean *a condom* = contraceptive sheath)
- *Some trees produce a lot of **gum**.*
  (= a sticky substance, *resin*)
- *This front **tyre** (AmE **tire**) has worn very unevenly.* (Not **rubber**)
  (= the band of rubber filled with air that fits round the wheel of a car, bicycle, etc.; *a tyre* is an object; *rubber* is a substance)

gymnasium • grammar school
- *I attended the local **grammar school** before I went to university.* (Not **gymnasium**)
- *When did you **leave (grammar) school**?*
  (Not **finish the gymnasium**)
- *Athletes spend a lot of time working out in the **gymnasium/gym**.*
  (= a large room with special equipment for training the body)

gymnastics • exercise
- *I try to keep fit by **taking exercise** regularly.*
  (Not **doing gymnastics**)
- ***Gymnastics is** part of our physical training course.* (Not **The gymnastics are** **The gymnastic is**)
  (= the art of training the body by special exercises with bars, ropes, etc.; plural form + singular verb to refer to the subject as taught and practised)
- *Don't **do gymnastics** on the furniture, dear.*
  (Not **do gymnastic**)
  (= behave as if you were in a *gymnasium*)

H

habit • custom • (the) customs
- *Sending birthday cards is not a very old **custom**.* (Not **habit**)
  (= a traditional social or religious activity often repeated every year)
- *Overeating can easily become a bad **habit**.*
  (= something you do often)
- *Do I declare this camera at **(the) customs**?*
  (= the place where travellers declare goods when entering a country)

had (= 'd) • would (= 'd)
- *If **I'd** (= **had**) known you were coming, **I'd** (= **would**) have baked a cake.*
  (Not **If I had've**)

hairdresser • hairdresser's
- *Where's Vanessa? She's gone to the **hairdresser's**.* (Not **the hairdresser(s)**)
  (= the hairdresser's shop)
- *It isn't easy to find a good **hairdresser**.*
  (*hairdresser's* and *hairdresser* are both commonly used to refer to the care of men's hair, not only women's, and have virtually replaced *barber's* and *barber*)

hairs • hair
- *Long **hair is** very difficult to look after.*
  (Not **The long hairs are**)
  (*hair* = all the *hairs* on the head; uncountable)
- *Can you remember the shock of finding your first grey **hair/hairs**?*
  (= a single strand or single strands of *hair*; countable)

half
- *I'd like **half a kilo** of cherries please.*
  (Not **a/one half kilo** **half kilo**)
- *What's the time? - It's **half past six**/It's **half six**.* (= 6.30, not '5.30')

hall • lobby • foyer
- *I'll meet you in the hotel **lobby/foyer** at 5.15.*
  (preferable to *hall*)
  (= the space at the entrance of a hotel or public building; *foyer* for cinemas/theatres)
- *It's an attractive house with a large entrance **hall**.*
  (= the space behind the front door of a private house)

halt • hold • keep
- *How long do you intend to **hold/keep** our passports?* (Not **halt**)
  (= have and not give back)
- *The smallest accident can bring all the traffic on the motorway to a **halt**.*
  (= a stop; note also its special use as a verb: **'Halt!'** the guard cried.)

hand: at/by/in/on/to hand
- *She fainted on the bus, but fortunately there was a doctor **at/on hand**.* (Not **to hand**)
  (*at hand* = nearby; *on hand* = available)
- *This letter was delivered for you **by hand**.*
  (Not **with hand** **with the hands**)
- *I always keep a few tins of sardines **in hand**.*
  (Not **to hand**)
  (= in my stores)

- *Your application is **in hand**.*
  (= it is being dealt with)
- *I'll give you the address. Have you got a pen **to hand**?* (Not *in hand*)
  (= ready)

handle • business
- *What was a small shop has grown into a very big book **business**.* (Not *handle*)
- *We **handle** a lot of business.*
  (= deal with)

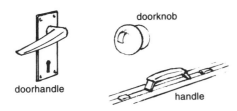

doorknob

doorhandle

handle

handle • doorknob
- *Try turning the **doorknob**/moving the **(door) handle**.*
  (*doorknob* when it's round; *(door) handle* when it's straight)
- *The **handle** of my suitcase has come loose.*
  (= the part we use for lifting/carrying)

hanged • hung
- *It always rains when **I've hung** the washing on the line.* (Not **I've hanged**)
  (*hang - hung - hung*: irregular verb: *to hang something*, e.g. a picture)
- *In the 19th century, people were **hanged** for minor crimes.*
  (*hang - hanged - hanged*: regular verb: *to hang someone*, e.g. a murderer)

happen • occur • take place
- *Exams always **took place** at the end of the summer term.* (Not *happened* *occurred*)
- *All these things **happened/occurred/took place** long before you were born.*
  (things may *take place* by arrangement; *happen* and *occur* refer to unplanned events)
- *A strange thing **happened**.*
  (Not **It/There happened a strange thing.**)
- ***What's happened?*** (Not **What's occurred?** **What's taken place?** **What happen?**)
  (*happen* is more general than *occur*, so is the only verb possible in questions about unspecified events)
- ***He happens** to be at home/**It happens** that he's at home at the moment.*
  (Not *He is happening* *It is happening*)
  (i.e. 'by chance'; stative use)

- *The sun rises every day. **It happens** every day. **It's happening** at this moment.*
  (= occurs/is occurring: stative or dynamic)

hard • cruel • tough
- *It's **cruel** to make a horse pull such a heavy load.* (Not *hard*)
  (a *cruel* person, *cruel* behaviour = causing pain and suffering)
- *Jack may be a **hard** man, but he's also fair.*
  (= severe, but not necessarily *cruel*)
- *You have to be very **tough** to join the parachute regiment.* (Not *hard* *cruel*)
  (= strong; able to tolerate hardship)

hard • harden • get/go hard
- *The cement **has got hard/has gone hard/has hardened**.* (Not *has hard* *has harded*)
- *You need to add resin **to harden** that glue/**make** that glue **hard**.* (Not **to hard that glue** **to get hard that glue**)
- *He's **hard**./He's **a hard man**.*
  (Not **He's a hard.**)

hard • hardly
- *I'll pass if I work **hard**.* (Not *hardly*)
  (*hard* is both adjective: *a hard worker* and adverb: *he works hard*)
- *He's so old now, he **hardly** works at all.*
  (= almost not)

hardly
- ***Hardly had he got** into the car when he began moaning.* (Not **Hardly he had got**)
  (inversion after negative adverbs; formal and emphatic. Compare normal word order: *He **had hardly finished** speaking when ... .*
  Also: ***On no account/On no condition must you** disturb him, **Little did he know** his fate, **No sooner had he finished** speaking ...., **Not only did we arrive** late, **but** we missed our next flight as well, **Rarely have I seen** so many tourists, **Seldom have we received** so many complaints.*)

hardly • hardly any • hardly ever
- *The boy is eight years old and he **can hardly read**!* (Not **can't hardly read**)
- *John's **got hardly any** friends.*
  (Not **hasn't got hardly any friends**)
- *We **hardly ever go** to the cinema these days.*
  (Not *hardly never go*)
  (*hardly*, negative adverb = almost not; we usually have only one negative in a sentence)

harm • hurt
- *I banged my arm against the door and **hurt** myself. My arm **hurts**.*

(Not *harmed* *harms* *hurted*)
(hurt = cause/produce physical pain)
- *Comments like that really* **hurt**.
  (= cause mental pain)
- *There's no end to the number of things that can* **harm** *your health*. (Not *hurt*)
  (= do damage to)
- *Fertilizers have* **done** *a lot of* **harm** *to the soil*. (Not *made harm* *have done bad*)
  (= have had a bad effect on)
- *It's a silly question, but* **there's no harm in asking**. (Not *there's no harm to ask*)
- **It does no harm** *to ask*.
  (Not *It does no bad* *It doesn't do bad*)

hate
- *I* **hate to disturb** *you when you're busy*.
  (= e.g. I'm sorry, but I am about to do so)
- *I* **hate disturbing** *you when you're busy*.
  (in general)
- *I* **hate** *queueing*. (Not *I'm hating*)
  (stative use: the feeling is involuntary)
- *He has to travel miles to get to work and* **he hates/he's hating** *it*.
  (stative or dynamic use depending on the speaker's viewpoint)
- *I'd* **hate you to think** *that I lied to you*.
  (Not *hate you should think*)

have
- *What sort of car* **do you have**? - *I* **have** *a Ford*. (Not *are you having* *I'm having*)
  (stative use of *have* = possess, own)
- *Don't talk to your father while* **he's having** *a shave. He'll cut himself*. (Not *he has*)
  (dynamic use of *have* = take, enjoy, etc.)
- *I must get a ticket. I* **don't have one**.
  (Not *I don't have.*)
- *I must draw some money. I* **don't have any**.
  (Not *I don't have.*)
  (*have* is always transitive)

have • have got
- *I* **have** *a headache. I've* **got** *a headache*.
- **Do you have** *a headache?* **Have you got** *a headache?* (Avoid *Have you a headache?*)
- *I* **don't have** *a headache. I* **haven't got** *a headache*. (Avoid *I haven't a headache*.)
  (*have* and *have got* = possess; generally questions and negatives are formed *Do you have? I don't have* in AmE and *Have you got? I haven't got* in BrE)

have been (painting) • have (painted)
- *I've* **painted** *this room*.
  (i.e. I've finished the job)
- *I've* **been painting** *this room*.
  (i.e. I haven't finished the job: the

progressive form emphasizes that an action has been in progress throughout a period up to the present)

have been • went
- *I* **went** *to the supermarket* **yesterday**.
  (Not *have been ... yesterday*)
  (simple past tense with time reference)
- *I've* **been** *to the supermarket*.
  (present perfect of *be* without a time reference or with *just, already,* etc.)

have gone • have been
- *Ah! You're back! Where* **have you been**? - *I've* **been** *to London*. (Not *I've gone*)
  (i.e. visited and come back)
- *Where* **has John gone**? - *He's gone* *to London*.
  (i.e. he is there or on his way there now)

have to • must • don't have to • needn't • mustn't
- *You* **have to/must slow down** *here*.
  (*must* and *have to* are often used in the same way in the affirmative to express necessity)
- *I* **don't have to/needn't get up** *early when I'm on holiday*. (Not *mustn't get up*)
  (*don't have to* and *needn't* are often used in the same way to express lack of necessity)
- *You* **mustn't park** *on the yellow lines*.
  (prohibition)

hazard • danger
- *All modern vehicles are fitted with* **hazard** *warning lights*. (Not *danger*)
  (*hazard* = 'risk' combines with particular words, e.g. *a health hazard, a fire hazard*)
- *In a situation like that you don't think of the* **danger**. (Not *hazard*)
- **Danger!** *Keep Out!* (Not *Hazard!*)
  (*danger* is the usual noun to express a possibility of harm)

headache
- *I* **have/I've got** *a headache*.
  (Not *I have headache./I've got headache.* *I have my head.*; compare *My head hurts/aches* as a result of injury)
- *I* **got** *an awful* **headache/I had** *an awful* **headache** *last night*. (Not *did/made*)

healthy • good for • hygienic • sanitary
- *Fruit is* **good for** *you*. (Not *healthy for*)
- *It's important to keep fit and* **healthy**.
  (= in good health)
- *See for yourself the* **hygienic** *conditions in our kitchens*. (Not *healthy* *sanitary*)
  (= germ-free)

– The health inspector closed the restaurant down because it didn't meet **sanitary** requirements. (Not *hygienic* *healthy*)
(= to do with cleanliness, hygiene)

heap • a lot of • pile
– I've got **a lot of/a heap of/a pile of** old newspapers to send for recycling.
(a lot of = a large quantity; pile = a quantity of things placed one on top of another; heap = an untidy pile)

hear
– **I hear** very well. (Not *I'm hearing*)
(stative use: natural ability; also I **can hear** very well.)
– **I hear** you've been promoted.
(Not *I'm hearing*)
(stative use = I have been told)
– **I hear/I'm hearing** much better with this new hearing aid.
(stative or dynamic use depending on the speaker's emphasis: natural ability)
– **We've been hearing** all sorts of strange reports about you.
(dynamic use = have been told)
– Did you **hear him leave/leaving**?
(Not *hear him to leave*)
(bare infinitive = the whole action, or -ing = part of the action after hear someone)
– I **heard** what you said. (Not *heared*)
(spelling of past tense)

hear • listen to
– **I hear** music in the distance.
(stative use: the experience is involuntary; the noun is hearing, as in I have good **hearing** = the ability to hear)
– I often **listen to** music.
(stative use of dynamic verb: habit)
– What are you doing? - **I'm listening to** this CD. (Not *I'm hearing* *listening this*)
(dynamic use = giving my attention)
– I **listen to/hear** the 9 o'clock news every evening without fail.
(both verbs are possible to refer to something habitual and deliberate)
– We **heard** some wonderful music at last night's concert. (Not *listened to*)
(hear a live musical performance)
– **Listen to him sing/singing!**
(Not *Listen to him to sing!* *Listen him!*)

hear • listen • obey
– I advised him to travel overland, but he wouldn't **listen**. (Not *hear* *obey*)
(= take something seriously, pay attention)

– If only that dog would **obey**!
(obey = do what you're told to do)
– You can expect to get into trouble if you don't **obey the law**. (Not *obey to the law*)
(obey + direct object: no preposition)
– I won't stand this behaviour any longer. Do you **hear** (me)? (Not *listen to* *obey*, though we could say Are you listening?)
(= hear with attention)

hear about/of
– Have you ever **heard of** a composer called Webern? (Not *heard for* *heard about*)
(hear of = have knowledge of)
– Have you **heard about** the new copyright law? (Not *heard for* *heard of*)
(hear about = receive information)

heaven(s) • sky
– The fighter plane left a great trail of smoke across **the sky**. (Not *the heaven(s)*)
(= what we see above us from the earth)
– You will get your reward in **heaven**.
(= the place where good people are supposed to go after they die)
– **The heavens** opened and the landscape vanished behind a curtain of rain.
(Not *The heaven* *Heaven*)
(the heavens is literary for the sky. Compare the exclamations Heavens! Heavens above!)

heavy
– Your case **will get** very **heavy** if you put so much into it. (Not *will heavy*)

help
– Who **helped you (to) do** your homework?
(help + infinitive with or without to)
– I **can't help worrying**.
(Not *can't help to worry*)
(can't help + -ing = can't avoid)
– Tina needs **a lot of help** with maths.
(Not *a help* *a lot of helps*)
(the noun help is uncountable)

heritage • inheritance
– This property will be part of your **inheritance**. (Not *heritage*)
(= money or possessions passed on when someone dies)
– These ancient buildings are an important part of our national **heritage**.
(= customs, traditions, historical monuments, etc., passed on from one generation to the next)

hers
– Which coat is **hers**? (Not *her's*)
(no apostrophe with a possessive pronoun)

*John's a friend **of hers**. (Not *of her's* *of her*; also: his, ours, yours, theirs)*

he's • his

— *John's lost **his** watch. (Not *he's* *hes*)*
(*his* is the possessive relating to *he*)
— *John says **he's** hungry. (Not *his*)*
— *John says **he's** done his homework.*
(*he's* is short for 'he is' or 'he has')

hide • hide (myself)

— *He used to **hide letters** in his drawer.*
(*hide* used transitively)
— *He **was hiding** behind the door and the children found him.*
(*hide* used intransitively)
— *Penny **hid (herself)** in the bathroom cupboard and someone locked her in.*
(optional reflexive for a deliberate act)

high • highly

— *If you can **jump** that **high**, you'll qualify for the Olympic team! (Not *jump highly*)*
(*high* is both an adjective: *the high jump* and an adverb: *jump high, aim high*)
— *Few dancers are **highly** paid. (Not *high*)*
(= to a great degree)

high school • college

— *I went to **college** after leaving school.*
(Not *(the) high school*)
(= an institution of higher learning for students of 16+)
— *After **high school**, I went to college.*
(= a secondary school for children of 11+; especially AmE for children of 15+)

hill • mountain

— *Everest is the highest **mountain** in the world. (Not *hill*)*
— *Let's cycle to the top of the **hill**.*
(a *hill* is lower than a *mountain*, but *hill* can also be a general term: *high hills;* the highest hills in a region or country are sometimes called *mountains*)

hinder • prevent (from)

— *The climbers hadn't gone far when a heavy fall of snow **hindered** their progress.*
(= made it difficult, but didn't stop it)
— *The strikers **prevented workers from entering/prevented them entering** the factory. (Not *prevented them to enter*)*
(= stopped, didn't allow to; *prevent* + *-ing; from* is usually optional after *prevent*)

hire • let (to) • rent (from)

— *We've **rented** a villa in the south of France for the summer. (Not *let* *hired*)*

(*rent* = buy the use of e.g. a house for a continuous period, usually for more than one payment)
— *We've **let** our house **to some Americans for the summer**. They're **renting** it **from us**.*
(*let to* someone; *rent from* someone)
— *I want to **hire/rent** a car. (Not *let*)*
(*hire*, AmE *rent* = make a single payment for the use of e.g. a vehicle for a period)
— *This house is **to let**. (Not *for rent*)*
(= available for renting)
— *This vehicle is **for hire**.*
(Not *to let* *for rent* *to hire*)
(= available for hiring)

his • her

— ***John** phones **his mother** every Sunday.*
(= his own mother)
— ***John** phoned **her mother** this morning.*
(= someone else's mother; the 'someone else' is female)
— ***Ann** phones **her father** every Sunday.*
(= her own father)
— ***Ann** phoned **his father** this morning.*
(= someone else's father; the 'someone else' is male)
(the possessive adjectives *his, her*, etc., refer to the possessor, not the thing possessed)

historic • historical

— *The falsification of **historical** records is common practice in totalitarian regimes.*
(Not *historic*)
(= relating to the study of history)
— *Pulling down the Berlin Wall will be remembered as one of the **historic** events of the late 20th century.*
(= important in history)

history • story

— *Climb into bed and I'll read you a bedtime **story**. (Not *history*)*
— *We often know little about the **history** of our own times.*
(a *story* is an account, often fictional, of what happened in someone's experience; *history* is a factual account of past public or universal events or 'the study of history')

hold • catch • keep • take

— *We don't want him in our team. He can't even **catch** a ball. (Not *hold*)*
(= take hold of a moving object)
— *We can only hope the police will **catch** this thief. (Not *keep/hold/take*)*
(*catch* somebody *stealing*)

- *Please **hold** the baby till I get the pram.*
  (Not *catch*)
  (= support, carry)
- *I don't want the book back. You can **keep** it.*
  (= have as your own; possess)
- *If you like it, **take** it.*
  (= remove it and have as yours)
- *This jug **holds** two litres.* (Not *is holding*)
  (= contains, stative use)
- *Where's my bag? - **You're holding** it!*
  (= you have it in your hands; dynamic use)

hollow • empty • vacant
- *The fridge is almost **empty**.*
  (Not *hollow* *vacant*)
  (= with nothing in it)
- *That house has been **empty/vacant** for a long time.* (Not *hollow*)
  (vacant = not occupied)
- *The Customs men found the drugs in a **hollow** space under the seat of the car.*
  (= not solid, an empty space inside something, e.g. a hollow wall)

home
- *Where's John? - He's at **home**/He's **home**.*
  (Not *He's to home.*)
- *Where have you been? - I've been (at) **home**.* (Not *I've been to home.*)
- *Where did John go? - He **went home**./ **Home**.* (Not *went to home*)
- *She **left home** at 8.* (Not *left from home*)
- *What did you do on Sunday? - I **stayed (at) home**.* (Not *I stayed to home.*)
- *We **arrived home** late.*
  (Not *arrived to/in/at home*)
- *Where have you come from? - I've come **from home**.* (Not *from the home*)
- *I'm going **to the home**/I was **at the home** of a friend/at a friend's **home**.*
  (specific reference with *the: house* is also possible here)

home • house
- *They live in a large **house**.* (Not *home*)
- *When I'm abroad, my thoughts are never far from **home**.* (Not *(the) house* *the home*)
  (*house* generally refers to the building; a *house* or *flat* becomes *home* when you refer to it as the place you live in)
- *Isn't your father abroad at the moment? - No, he's **(at) home**.*
  (Not *house* *at house* *to house*)
  (= e.g. not away)
- *Where's your father? - He must be somewhere **in the house**.* (Not *at home*)
  (= inside the building)

homework • housework
- *Who **does the housework** when you're both at work?* (Not *homework* *the houseworks* *makes the housework*)
  (= cleaning, etc.; uncountable)
- *I had to tell my teacher I hadn't **done my homework**.*
  (Not *made my homework* *homeworks*)
  (= work set by teachers for students to do at home; uncountable)

honestly • sincerely
- *I **sincerely** hope they return safely soon.*
  (Not *honestly*)
- *I **honestly** think you've made a mistake.*
  (Not *sincerely*)
- *Angela **sincerely/honestly** believes she's doing the best for her children.*
  (*sincerely* refers to 'true feelings'; *honestly* means 'without cheating or lying')

honour • credit
- *Your children have done brilliantly and **are a real credit to** you.* (Not *an honour to*)
- *You should **give credit** where it's due.*
  (*be a credit to* = bring honour, glory; *give credit* = acknowledge, show respect)
- *It was a great **honour** to be invited to such a party.* (Not *credit*)
  (i.e. it made us feel pleased and proud)
- *Your concern for your friend **is to your credit**.* (Not *in your honour*)
  (*be to someone's credit* = bring respect)
- *When our boss retired, the company gave a party **in his honour**.* (Not *to his credit*)
  (*in (his) honour* = as a mark of respect)

hope
- *We **hope/are hoping** business will recover next year.*
  (stative or dynamic depending on the emphasis you wish to give)
- *Will he phone you when he arrives? - I **hope so**.* (Not *I hope.* *I hope it.*)
- *Will you be too late? - I **hope not**.*
  (Not *I hope no.* *I don't hope so.*)
- *I **hope (that) she'll recover/she recovers** soon.* (Not *hope her to recover*)
- *I **hope to** get into university./I **hope that** I'll get into university.*
  (*to* or *that* after hope when the subject is the same)

hospitality
- *We were shown wonderful **hospitality** wherever we went.*
  (Not *a hospitality* *hospitalities*)

(i.e. we were welcomed; *hospitality* is
uncountable)

host • guest

- *We have a **guest** from Nigeria who is staying
  with us.* (Not *host*)
  (= a person who is invited)
- *Our **host** welcomed us with a glass of hot
  spicy wine.*
  (= a person who invites; the feminine form
  hostess is sometimes avoided)

hot

- ***It*** *(= the weather) **is hot** today.* (Not **It has
  hot** **It makes hot/heat** **Is hot today.**)
- *Drink your coffee while it's **hot**.*
- ***I'm hot.*** *I think I'll take off my coat.*
  (Not **I have hot.** **I hot.**)
  (= I don't feel cool)
- ***You're hot.*** *I think you've got a temperature.*
  (= you have a high body temperature)

hot • heat • warm • heated • get hot

- ***I got hot*** *working in the sun.*
  (Not *I hot* *I hottened* *I heated*;
  preferable to *I got warm*)
- *It's **warm** enough to sit out of doors today.*
  (preferable to *hot*; *warm/warmth* is less
  intense than *hot/heat*)
- *I've **heated** the soup for you.*
  (Not *hotted* *hottened*)
  (= made it hot)
- *We had a **heated** discussion about farm
  subsidies.* (Not *hot*)
- *The **heat** is fantastic today.* (Not *The hot*)
  (*heat* is the noun; *hot* is the adjective)

hound • dog

- *What's your **dog** called?* (Not *hound*)
- *If I were a fox, I wouldn't want to be chased
  by a pack of **hounds**.*
  (= hunting dogs)

hour • time • o'clock

- *What **time** do you want to get up tomorrow?*
  (Not *hour* **o'clock**)
  (*What time is it?*; *tell the time*, etc.)
- *We have to put the clocks back an **hour**
  tomorrow.*
  (= a period of 60 minutes)
- *I'll see you at 11 **o'clock**.* (Not *hour*)
- *It's **five past 10**.* (Not **five past 10 o'clock**)
  (*o'clock* only with exact hours)
- *It's **fourteen minutes past 10**.*
  (Not *fourteen past 10*)
  (*minutes to/past* the hour when the reference
  isn't to *fives*, *tens* or *quarters*)

house

- *What a beautiful **house**!* (noun: pronounced
  /haʊs/)
- *What beautiful **houses**!* (noun: pronounced
  /'haʊzɪz/
- *How are we going to **house** the refugees?*
  (verb: pronounced /haʊz/)
- *House*, like *Family*, is not used as a form of
  address: *Mr and Mrs Wilson and family* =
  everyone in the Wilson family, not **House
  Wilson** *Family Wilson*

housemaid • homemade

- *There's nothing like the smell of fresh,
  homemade cakes.*
  (Not *housemaid* *housemade*)
- *My great-grandmother was a **housemaid** in
  a large country house.*
  (= a female servant, now old-fashioned)

how • as

- *Please do it **as** I tell you.* (Not *how*)
  (= in the way)
- *Please tell me **how** to do it.*
  (= which way)
- *This steak is cooked just **how/as** I like it.*
  (= the way)

how • as if • like

- *It seems **as if** he heard the news before we
  did.* (Not *It seems how* *It seems like*)
  (*seem*, etc. + *as if* in clauses of manner)
- *I don't **know how** he heard the news before
  we did.* (Not *know as if* *know like*)
  (indirect question with *how*)
- *Yesterday's meeting was just **like** the first
  one, a complete waste of time.* (Not *as if*)
  (*like* + noun in direct comparisons)

how • what

- ***What*** *do you call this?* (Not *How*)
- ***How*** *do you know this?* (Not *What*)
  (= in what way)
- ***What*** *do you think of him?* (Not *How*)
  (= what's your opinion)
- ***How*** *do you make things like that?*
  (= in what way)
- ***How*** *do you like it?*
  (i.e. 'tell me')

how • what ... like

- *What's your new boss **like**?/**How's** your new
  boss?* (Not **How ... like?**)
  (refers to appearance, character, but *How's
  your new boss?* can also refer to health)
- *What was the film **like**?/**How** was the film?*
  (Not **How ... like?**)
  (i.e. 'tell me')

- *We won't really know **what** the room will look like/how the room will look until it's decorated.* (Not **how it will look like**)

How are you? • How do you do?
- *This is Mr Simms. - **How do you do?*** (Not **How are you?**)
(*How do you do?* in formal introductions; the response is also *How do you do?*, not **Very well, thank you.**)
- *I haven't seen you for ages! **How are you? Are you well?*** (Not **How do you do?**)
(*How are you?* when asking about health)

how long (ago) • for how long/how long for
- ***How long** have you been waiting?*
(Not **How long ago**)
(*how long* to refer to a period of time)
- ***How long ago** did you arrive? - A couple of hours ago.*
(*how long ago* to refer to a point of time in the past)
- ***How long** is your dining table?*
(= what length?)
- *I visited Gibraltar once. - **For how long/ How long for?***
(= for what period of time?; *for* is compulsory with *how long* here)
- *I visited Gibraltar once. - **How long ago?***
(= when?; *ago* is compulsory after *how long* here)

how much • how many
- ***How many names** are there on the list?*
(Not **How much names**)
(*how many* + plural countable noun)
- ***How much bread** did you buy?* (Not **How many bread(s)* How much breads**)
(*how much* + uncountable noun)
- ***How much** is it? **How much** does it cost?*
(Not **How many ... ?* *What costs?**)

how much time • how long
- ***How long** have you lived here? - I've lived here for ten years.* (Not **How much time**)
(*How long* to refer to long periods of time)
- ***How much time/How long** did you spend on your homework? - A couple of hours.*
(we can use either *How much time* or *How long* to refer to short periods of time)

humane • human
- *Using language is the essence of being **human**.* (Not **humane**)
(= a member of the human race; the opposite is *inhuman* = 'cruel', as in *the **inhuman** treatment of prisoners*)

- *Can there really be **humane** ways of rearing animals cheaply for food?* (Not **human**)
(= showing consideration, kindness; the opposite is *inhumane* = 'not showing human kindness', as in *the **inhumane** treatment of animals*)

humidity • moisture • condensation • damp/dampness
- *There was **a dampness**, just short of actual rain, in the air.* (Not **a damp/a humidity**)
(*dampness* is a local, not a general state)
- *If you close up that chimney, you'll have a problem with **damp**.*
(Not **dampness* *humidity* *moisture**)
(= slight general wetness, usually undesirable; uncountable)
- *The ground was too **damp** to sit on.*
(= just slightly wet)
(*damp* is primarily an adjective)
- *I like the heat if there isn't too much **humidity**.* (Not **moisture* *dampness**)
(= water vapour in the air)
- *How can you prevent **condensation** forming on the windows in the kitchen?*
(Not **humidity* *dampness**)
(= steam turning to water on a cold surface)
- *The soil is so sandy that it won't hold any **moisture**.*
(= dispersed water)

hundred: a hundred and one
- *I've got **a hundred and one** things to do this morning.* (Not **a hundred one**)
(also *a thousand and one*, *a million and one*, *a billion and one*)

hundreds • hundred • hundred per cent
- *How many people were present? - About **a/one hundred**.* (Not **About hundred.**)
(*a* or *one hundred*)
- *How many people were at the meeting? - About **two hundred**.* (Not **two hundreds**)
- *The company has laid off **two hundred workers**.* (Not **two hundreds workers* *two hundreds of workers**)
(*hundred* is singular after numbers)
- *How many people were there? - **Hundreds!***
(normal plural)
- ***Hundreds of** people went to the funeral.*
(plural form + *of*)
(also *billions/billion*, *dozens/dozen*, *millions/million*, *thousands/thousand*)
- *It's a **hundred per cent** certain that our flight will be delayed.* (Not **hundred of hundred* *hundred by hundred**)

hunger • hungry

- *Is there anything to eat?* **I'm hungry**.
  (Not *I have hunger.* *I hunger.*)
- *Take some sandwiches with you. You* **might get hungry**. (Not *might hunger*)
- **Hunger** *makes him irritable.*
- **A hungry person** *is generally a bad-tempered one.* (Not *A hungry*)
  (we cannot use *hungry* on its own to mean 'a hungry person')
- *We must do all we can to feed* **the hungry**.
  (Not *the hungries*)
  (*the* + adjective: the group as a whole)
- *He* **hungers after** *money and fame.*
  (= longs for)

hurried • hurry • in a hurry

- *I'm* **in a hurry**. (Not *hurried* *I hurry.*)
  (= I can't wait, I can't take too long)
- *We'd better* **hurry**. (Not *hurry ourselves*)
  (= move, act fast)
- *I won't put up with careless,* **hurried** *work.*
  (= carried out too quickly)

hymn • anthem • psalm

- *Few people know more than the first verse of the national* **anthem**.
  (Not *hymn* *psalm*)
  (= a ceremonial song)
- *A carol is a special* **hymn** *for Christmas or Easter.* (Not *anthem* *psalm*)
  (= a song of praise)
- *The church choir sang a* **psalm** *at the end of the service.*
  (= a setting to music of words from the *Book of Psalms* in the Bible)

I

ice • a cube of ice

- *Would you get* **some ice** *from the fridge please?* (Not *an ice*)
- **One cube (of ice)** *or two?/***One ice cube** *or two?*
  (*ice* = frozen water, uncountable)
- *A day at the zoo is expensive. Even* **an ice** *(cream) costs/***a couple of ices** *cost a fortune.*
  (*ice* = ice cream is countable)

icon • image • picture

- *I have an* **image**/*a* **picture** *in my mind of a cottage by the sea.* (Not *an icon*)
  (= a mental picture)
- *I can take beautiful* **pictures** *with this camera.* (Not *images* *icons*)

- *Some Byzantine churches contain old and valuable* **icons**. (Not *images* *pictures*)
  (= paintings of holy people)
- *Twiggy was the style* **icon** *for the swinging sixties.*
  (= an image for others to imitate)

idea

- *I've* **had an idea**. (Not *It came to me an idea*, but we can say *An idea came to me.*)
- *Who had the* **idea of inviting** *him to our party?* (Not *idea to invite*)
- *Whose* **idea** *was it* **that we should invite** *him?/Whose* **idea** *was it* **to invite** *him to our party?* (Not *idea ... of inviting*)

idiomatic • proverbial

- *'A stitch in time saves nine' is a* **proverbial** *saying* (or *a proverb*). (Not *idiomatic*)
- *In 'We laughed till we were in stitches', 'in stitches' is an* **idiomatic** *expression* (or *an idiom*) *to describe uncontrollable laughter.*
  (a *proverb* is a traditional, 'wise' saying; an *idiom* is a group of words which taken together mean something different from their literal sense)

idle • lazy

- *Kim's too* **idle/lazy** *to get a proper job.*
- *Everyone's on strike and the machines are* **idle**. (Not *lazy*)
  (*lazy* or *idle* to describe people who are unwilling to work; *idle* for machines, etc. = 'not in use')

if

- **If you look** *out of the window,* **you'll see** *it's raining hard.* (Not *If you will look*)
  (*if* + present + *will*)
- **If you asked** *him a question, I'm sure* **he'd answer** *it.* (Not *If you would ask*)
  (*if* + past + *would*)
- **If you had asked** *him a question,* **he would have answered** *it.* (Not *If you would ask* *If you had've asked*)
  (*if* + past perfect + *would have*)
- *Shall I hold the door open for you? - Yes,* **if you will/if you would**.
  (*if* + *will/would* to show willingness)

if • whether

- **Whether** *he likes it or not, I'm going.*
  (Not *If*)
- *The question* **is not when but whether** *he will sign the contract.* (Not *if*)
- *It depends* **on whether** *he'll sign the contract.* (Not *on if*)
  I don't know **whether to** *disturb him or not.*

(Not *if to*)
(= whether I should ...)
(we use *whether*, not *if*, to begin a sentence, after *be*, after prepositions and in front of *to*)
- **Ask** him **whether/if** he'd like to join us. (*whether* or *if* after verbs like *ask* and a few adjectives like *(not) certain, (not) sure*)

ignorant (of) • badly brought up
- It's not her fault she behaves like that. She's **badly brought up**. (Not *She's ignorant.*)
(= wrongly raised from childhood)
- Some pupils are almost completely **ignorant** when they leave school.
(i.e. they leave school knowing nothing)
*I'm completely **ignorant of** the law.*
(= lacking knowledge of)

ignore • neglect
- Heavy drinking is one reason why some people **neglect** themselves. (Not *ignore*)
(= fail to care for)
- I won't accept any responsibility if you choose to **ignore** my advice. (Not *neglect*)
(= pay no attention to; *ignore* never means 'not know')

ill (with) • sick (of/with)
- I'm sorry, I didn't know you'd been **ill** in hospital. (Not *sick* in BrE)
(= not in good health)
- She **fell/became/got ill** at the end of last year. (Not *She illed/sicked*)
- Jimmy's just **been sick**. (Not *'s been ill*)
(= has vomited; *was/is being/will be/has been sick* = vomit)
- I think I'll go home. I'm feeling **sick/ill**.
(after verbs like *look* and *seem*, *sick* = *ill* to mean 'not in good health', but *feel/feeling sick* suggests 'about to vomit')
- Maurice is **a sick man**. (Not *an ill man*)
(= not in good health; *an ill (man)* is heard, but not universally accepted)
- Maurice is **ill with** flu. (Not *ill of*)
- I'm **sick of** asking you to tidy up your room.
(= fed up with, often expressed as *sick and tired of*)
- I was **sick with** fright.
(i.e. with that feeling)

imagine
- **I imagine** you'd like to rest after your long journey. (Not *I'm imagining*)
(stative use = I think)
- I thought I heard something, but perhaps I **was imagining** it.
(dynamic use = forming mental images)

- Life must be hard for her now. - **I imagine so**. (Not *I imagine.* *I imagine it.*)
(= that's what I think)
- **Imagine being** stranded in Paris without any money! (Not *Imagine to be*)
- **Imagine him/his not knowing** the answer to such a simple question!
(some native speakers would approve only of a possessive adjective like *his*)

imitate • forge
- It looks as though someone has tried to **forge** your signature. (Not *imitate*)
(= copy for serious criminal deception)
- However hard I try to **imitate** my teacher's accent, I'll never speak like a native.
(= copy)

immaterial (to) • indifferent (to) • it doesn't matter (to me) • don't worry
- When Mandy gets depressed she becomes completely **indifferent to** her children.
(= uncaring, pays no attention to)
- It is **indifferent to me/immaterial to me/It doesn't matter (to me)** what you do.
(i.e. I'm not interested/I don't care)
- **It doesn't matter to me** whether you complain to the management or not. (Not *I'm indifferent* *It's indifferent whether*)
- I didn't get any fresh milk while I was out. - **It doesn't matter**. (Not *Don't worry.*)
- **Don't worry!** Everything will be all right! (Not *It doesn't matter!*)

immobile • property/real estate
- **Property** (**Real estate** AmE) is not always a good investment. (Not *(the) immobile*)
- A lot of British people are looking for (**a**) **property/for properties** in France. (Not *a real estate* *an immobile* *immobiles*)
(*property* = land, buildings, or land and buildings may be countable or uncountable; *real estate* cannot be plural, though we can say *a piece of real estate*)
- Keep the patient completely **immobile**.
(adjective = without movement)

important • considerable
- Health insurance costs a **considerable** sum of money these days. (Not *important*)
(= large and noticeable)
- It's the city council's job to preserve **important** buildings. (Not *considerable*)
(i.e. buildings of value)

impose (on) • be essential/vital • impress • manage

- *It is essential/vital (for us) to control the spread of malaria.* (Not *It imposes (us)*)
- *Our new headmaster has the kind of authority which impresses everyone he meets.* (Not *imposes on*)
  (= commands respect/admiration)
- *She knows how to manage a class of unruly children.* (Not *impose herself on*)
- *In some countries, traffic police can impose instant fines on motorists.*
  (= place by force)
- *We mustn't impose (ourselves) on them without warning.*
  (= take advantage of)

imposition • tax

- *Tax on drink and tobacco should go up for health reasons.* (Not *Imposition*)
- *Expecting teachers to mind children in the playground is an unfair imposition on them.*
  (= burden)

impotent (to) • incapable (of)

- *Eric has proved himself to be quite incapable of making important decisions.* (Not *impotent* *incapable to make*)
  (= without the ability to make; the opposite is *capable of* + *-ing*, not *capable to*)
- *People living under dictatorships feel quite impotent to do anything.*
  (= unable to, without power to)
- *A man who is impotent should seek medical advice.* (Not *incapable*)
  (= not able to function sexually)

impress (with/by)

- *Steve's skill as a salesman impresses everyone.* (Not *is impressing*)
  (mainly stative use)
- *I'm impressed by your grasp of the politics of the Middle East.*
  (*impress* is often used in the passive)
- *I was very impressed with/by him.*
  (Not *impressed from*)

impress • affect • touch

- *The sad case of the kidnapped child affected/touched us all.* (Not *impressed*)
  (*affected* = influenced our mood or behaviour; *touched* = made us feel pity)
- *No one could fail to be affected/impressed by Olivier's performance as Othello.*
  (*affected* = moved emotionally; *impressed* = filled with admiration)

impression (of)

- *How can I make a good impression at job interviews?* (Not *do an impression*)
- *That comedian does a very good impression of the prime minister.* (Not *makes*)
  (= copies, to make people laugh)
- *I'll go home with a good impression of Britain.* (Not *impression about*)

impression • feeling/sense

- *I read the exam questions with a feeling/sense of panic.* (Not *an impression*)
- *Do professors like to give the impression they're absent-minded?* (Not *do/make*)
  (i.e. create that image)

impression • printing

- *Desktop publishing has made it easy for us to undertake the printing of our own catalogues.* (Not *impression*)
- *Charlotte's novel is a runaway success and is now in its 14th impression/printing.*
  (i.e. it has been printed 14 times)

in • into

- *We're flying into Heathrow, not Gatwick.* (Not *are flying in*)
  (movement verb + *into* shows movement from one place to another)
- *Please phone me when you're in Heathrow.* (Not *into*)
  (*in* shows position, destination after movement)
- *We walked into the park.*
  (i.e. we were outside it and we entered it)
- *We walked in the park.*
  (i.e. we were already inside it)
- *He put his hand in/into his pocket.*
  (both prepositions are possible after a few movement verbs like *drop, fall* and *put*)

in • to

- *John's gone to Paris.* (Not *at*)
  (i.e. he's there or on his way there)
- *John's in Paris at the moment.* (Not *to*)
  (*in* an area: destination after movement)

in all cases • in any event • in all respects

- *I don't know whether it's a formal reception. In any event, I'd better put a suit on.*
  (Not *In all cases*)
  (= whatever happens, whether it's going to be formal or not)
- *Many young girls do better in school than young boys in all respects/in every respect.*
  (Not *in all cases*)
  (= in every way)

- *In a recent survey, doctors found that **in all cases** patients respond better to treatment if it is explained to them.*
  (= in every instance)

include • enclose • comprehend
- *We **enclose** our account for your attention.*
  (Not **include**)
  (= put in the same envelope with a letter)
- ***Does the bill include** a tip?*
  (Not **Is the bill including* *Does the bill enclose* *Does the bill comprehend**)
  (stative use = 'does the bill contain?')
- ***We're including** you in our team.*
  (dynamic use = making you part of)
  *It was clear from the expression on his face that he couldn't **comprehend** a thing.*
  (= understand, usually negative; formal)

indeed • really • (not) at all
- *I'm sorry I didn't answer the phone. I **really** didn't hear it ring.* (Not **indeed**)
- *Ann wants to stay for a week. **Indeed**, she intends to arrive tonight.* (Not **Really**)
  (= in fact, as a matter of fact)
- *Thank you **very much indeed**.* (Not **Thank you indeed* *Thank you really**)
  (*indeed* usually intensifies *very much*)
- *Your mother isn**'t at all** well.*
  (*at all* for emphasis in the negative)

independent of
- *I became quite **independent of** my parents in my teens.* (Not **independent from**)

index (of/to) • forefinger/index finger • indication
- *The finger you point with is called your **forefinger/index finger**.* (Not **index**)
- *There's no **indication** of a possible change in the weather.* (Not **index**)
  (= sign)
- *The price of a hamburger is a good **index of/to** the cost of living.*
  (= a pointer to something on a scale of measurement)

indisposed • ill • not disposed to
- *How long has Martha been **ill**?*
  (preferable to *indisposed*)
- *Mr Potts is **indisposed**, I'm afraid, and will have to postpone his lunch with you.*
  (*ill* is the normal word for 'unwell'; *indisposed* = 'unwell' in a vague way)
- *You may be right, but I'm **not disposed to** argue with you.*
  (= not willing to)

indoors • inside
- *It was nice and warm **inside the building**.*
  (Not **inside of/indoors the building**)
  (*inside* is a preposition + object here)
- *It was nice and warm **inside/indoors**.*
  (adverbs = in a building: the opposites are *outside, out of doors*)
- *The **inside** of the box was beautifully lined.*
  (noun)

industrious • industrial
- *Japan is an **industrial** nation.*
  (Not **industrious**)
  (i.e. with highly developed industries)
- *The Japanese people are very **industrious**.*
  (Not **industrial**)
  (= hardworking)

industry • company • business • firm
- *Glaxo is a very big **company/firm**.*
  (Not **industry**)
- *Our **company/firm** has offices all over the world.* (Not **industry* *business**)
  (*company* and *firm* are specific)
- *A **business** like publishing is labour-intensive.*
  (Not **industry* *company* *firm**)
  (*business* = any kind of activity that is designed to make money)
- *An **industry** like ship-building needs huge capital investment.*
  (*industry* generally refers to manufacture)
- *Boeing make airplanes and they know **their business**.*
  (possessive + *business* = what they are about)
- *Pharmaceuticals is **big business/a major industry** worldwide.*
  (i.e. it involves big money)
- ***Mind your own business!***
  (Not **Mind your business!**)
  (fixed phrase = don't interfere with things that don't concern you)

infamous/notorious • not famous • famous
- *He's well-known as a singer in this country but is **not famous** worldwide.*
  (Not **is infamous**)
  (= not well-known to a lot of people)
- *Al Capone was an **infamous/a notorious** gangster.*
  (= well-known with a bad reputation; the opposite of *famous* is *unknown*, not *infamous*)
- *Charles Dickens is the most **famous** novelist in English literature.* (Not **notorious**)
  (= well-known, with a good reputation)

infer • imply

- From what you say in your letter, we can only **infer** that you won't be meeting our agreed delivery dates. (Not *imply*)
  (= conclude)
- What you say **implies** that you can't meet the agreed delivery date. (Not *infers*)
  (= suggests)

inflammable • flammable

- You should switch off your engine. Petrol is highly **inflammable**/highly **flammable**.
  (i.e. it catches fire and burns easily: it is combustible)
  (inflammable and flammable are not opposites, but mean the same; precise and technical uses prefer flammable to inflammable. Opposites are uninflammable, non-inflammable and non-flammable)

influence on

- Teachers **have/exert** a lot of **influence on** young people. (Not *influence with*)
  (have or exert influence are preferable to exercise influence)

inform (about/of)

- Who **informed you about/of** this?
  (Not *informed you for*)
- We wish to **inform passengers** that flight departures may be delayed.
- **Passengers are informed** that flight departures may be delayed.
  (Not *Are informed the passengers*)
  (very formal)

information • a piece of information • news

- Here's **an** interesting **piece of information**.
  (Not *an information*)
- There was **some** interesting **information** about air fares on the **news** this evening.
  (information and news are uncountable)
- Who **gave** you that **information**?/Where did you **get** that **information**?
  (give/get information, not *take*)
- Do you ever listen to the local **news**?
  (Not *information* *informations*)

ingenious • ingenuous

- You'd have to be completely **ingenuous** to believe a story like that. (Not *ingenious*)
  (= simple, easily-deceived)
- The **ingenious** Thomas Edison patented hundreds of inventions. (Not *ingenuous*)
  (= clever and inventive)

inhabit • live (in/on) • dwell (on) • occupy

- How many people **live in** this house?
  (live in a house is the normal phrase)
- How many people **live on/inhabit** this planet? (Not *dwell on*)
  (inhabit is formal)
- We have a farm and **live on** what we produce. (Not *live from* *live with*)
  (= e.g. eat, clothe ourselves)
- Once upon a time, in a far-off land, there **dwelt** a handsome prince.
  (dwell = 'live' is archaic)
- I know you've lost a lot of money, but I wish you wouldn't **dwell on** the subject.
  (= keep talking about)
- Two people can't **occupy** such a big house.
  (= fill)

injection

- My dentist had to **give me an injection** so I wouldn't feel any pain. (Not *do/make*)

ink

- Please write **in ink**. (Not *with ink*)
  (also: in pencil)

inn • pub • guesthouse • bed and breakfast • boarding house • board and lodging/bed and board • pension

- The Crown and Cushion is an **inn** as well as a **pub**. (Not *a guesthouse*)
  (pub is an abbreviation of 'public house'; a pub serves drinks; an inn is a pub with beds available for travellers to stop overnight)
- In the high season most **guesthouses** display the sign 'No Vacancies'. (Not *pensions*)
  (a guesthouse in Britain is usually a private house which has turned itself into a small 'family hotel' business; unlike an inn, it doesn't cater for non-residents)
- Can you recommend a good **bed and breakfast** round here?
  (= a guesthouse which offers a bed for the night with breakfast in the morning)
- Some old people prefer to live permanently in a **boarding house**.
  (= a guesthouse, not a hotel, that provides meals; it doesn't cater for non-residents and residents tend to stay for long periods)
- It's £100 a week for **board and lodging/bed and board**. (Not *pension*)
  (board refers to the provision of meals)
- My **pension** /'penʃən/ is enough to live on.
  (= money paid during retirement; pension is understood as a French word by English speakers to refer to a guesthouse: We stayed at a small **pension** /'pɑnsjɔ̃/ in the Alps.)

inquiry • enquiry

- Police are **making inquiries** relating to forged banknotes. (Not *doing inquiries*)

- *The bank has had a lot of **enquiries** about its new savings scheme.*
  (*an inquiry* = an investigation; *an enquiry* = a request for information)

inscribe • enrol • register • put one's name down
- *Gerald has **enrolled** in a creative writing course this year.* (Not **inscribed**)
  (= put his name down for a school, etc.; the noun is *enrolment*)
- *You're obliged by law to **register** the birth of a child.* (Not **inscribe* *enrol**)
  (= put on an official record; the noun is *registration*)
- *You have to be rich to **put your son's name down** for a fee-paying school the moment he's born.* (Not **inscribe him* *enrol him* *register him**)
  (= apply for deferred membership)
- *When I retired the company gave me a gold watch with my name **inscribed** on the back.*
  (= written formally, 'specially engraved', e.g. on stone or metal; the noun is *inscription*)

insensible (of) • insensitive (to) • unconscious • senseless
- *You have to be completely **insensitive to** your neighbours to play loud music in the middle of the night.* (Not **insensible to**)
  (= having no consideration for; the opposite is *sensitive*)
- *Jenny went on talking, **insensible of** the effect she was having.* (Not **insensitive to**)
  (= unaware of, not able to feel; the opposite of *insensible* is not *sensible*, but *conscious*)
- *Someone fainted on the train today and was **unconscious/senseless** for several minutes.*
  (= without awareness of the world, not *conscious*, without *sense*)
- *His actions seem quite **senseless**.*
  (= without meaning, foolish)

insist on/that
- *I **insist on speaking** to the manager.*
  (Not **insist to speak**; the noun is *insistence on*, not **insistence to**)
- *My wife **insists that I (should) have** a general checkup.* (Not **insists me to have**)

instant • moment
- *Please wait a **moment**.* (Not **an instant**)
- *For an **instant**/a **moment** the sky was lit up by a shooting star.*
  (*instant* and *moment* are generally only used in the same way when they refer to an extremely brief period of time)

instantly • momentarily
- *I only caught a glimpse of her **momentarily**.*
  (Not **instantly**)
  (BrE = for a moment; AmE = at any moment: *We'll be arriving **momentarily**.*)
- *When you phone her she answers **instantly**.*
  (Not **momentarily**)
  (= immediately)

instead of
- ***Instead of shouting**, you should have kept your temper.* (Not **Instead of to shout**)

instructions • directions
- *We lost our way and had to ask a policeman for **directions**.* (Not **instructions**)
  (usually *directions* for route-finding)
- *We'd better read the **instructions** before trying to install the machine.*
  (*instructions* for information on how to do something)

instruments

tools

instrument • tool
- *We need some basic **tools** like a hammer and a screwdriver.* (Not **instruments**)
- *A dentist's **instruments** need to be constantly sterilized.*
  (*tools* for manufacture and general handiwork; *instruments* for precise scientific and technical processes)

insult • heart attack • offence • injury
- *Mr Trent died after a serious **heart attack**.*
  (Not **heart insult* *heart injury**)
- *The news **gave him/caused him a heart attack**.* (Not **attacked his heart**)
  (we use the word *attack* to describe sudden illness: *an attack of malaria*, etc.)
- *Drawing graffiti on tombstones is an **insult** to the dead.* (Not **injury* *offence**)
  (i.e. it shows lack of respect)
- *His insensitive remarks **caused** a lot of **offence**.* (Not **caused ... injury/insult**)
  (*cause offence* = hurt someone's feelings)
- *Factory workers are insured against **injury**.*
  (= physical hurt)

insult • offend
- *They haven't answered my invitation and I feel a bit **offended**.* (Not *insulted*)
  (i.e. I have hurt feelings)
- *You shouldn't **insult** the waiter just because you don't like the food.* (Not *offend*)
  (= speak or act rudely towards)

intensive • intense
- *I banged my elbow on the door-handle and felt **intense** pain.* (Not *intensive*)
  (= very great)
- *The drug was developed after years of **intensive/intense** research.*
  (*intensive* = highly concentrated)

interested in/to
- *I got **interested in** stamp collecting when I was a boy.* (Not *I interested*)
- *I'm very **interested in** first editions of 20th century poetry.* (Not **interested for/with**)
- *I'm **interested in** emigrating to Canada.* (Not **interested to emigrate**)
  (i.e. I might do this)
- *I'm **interested in** hearing your opinion.* (i.e. it is of interest at any time)
- *I'm **interested to** hear your opinion.* (present and future reference)

interesting condition • expecting a baby/pregnant
- *Mrs Wilson is **expecting a baby/pregnant**.* (Not **in an interesting condition**)
  (*be in an interesting condition* = pregnant, is archaic)

interior • inland • inner
- *How much does it cost to send this parcel **inland**?* (Not *to the interior*)
  (= within the same country; *inland* is often used administratively for post, tax, etc.)
- *We travelled **inland** for several days.*
  (= away from the coast, towards the middle; *inland* is an adverb here)
- *Colonel Fawcett disappeared on an ill-fated expedition into the **interior**.*
  (= the inside of a large country, away from the coast; *interior* is a noun here)
- *The novel is more than a good story: it has a deep **inner** meaning.* (Not *interior*)
  (i.e. 'not superficial')
- *Can you recommend an **interior** decorator?*
  (*an interior decorator* = someone who will paint the inside or *interior* of a house)

interrupter • light switch
- *This faulty **light switch** should be replaced.* (Not *interrupter*)

('interrupter' = a person or device that interrupts barely exists in English)

interview
- *I **went for/had an interview** for a job yesterday.* (Not **did/made an interview**)

intrigue • plot
- *The characters in the play may be banal, but the **plot** is gripping.* (Not *intrigue*)
- *The downfall of the president was the result of **intrigue** among the senior ministers.*
  (= secret conspiracy; *plotting*)

introduce
- *Marion **introduced Tom to her friends**.*
- *Marion **introduced her friends to Tom**.*
  (Not **Marion introduced Tom her friends.** **Marion introduced to Tom her friends.**)
  (*present* = introduce is old-fashioned or theatrical)
- *I wonder when tomatoes **were introduced** into Europe.*
  (= made available for the first time)

invalid • war-wounded
- ***The war-wounded/Those wounded in the war** receive state pensions for the rest of their lives.* (Not *The invalids*)
  (*the war-wounded* is rare; we generally use *the disabled* or *disabled ex-servicemen* to refer to men wounded in battle)
- *Gordon has been **an invalid** since his accident, six years ago.*
  (= someone ill, temporarily or chronically)

involuntary • unwilling
- *I've never seen so many **unwilling** helpers!* (Not *involuntary*)
  (i.e. who don't want to help)
- *As he approached me, I made an **involuntary** gesture.* (Not *unwilling*)
  (i.e. I had no control over it)

involve
- *The job **involves** a knowledge of physics.* (Not *is involving*)
  (stative use = requires)
- *She's trying to raise money for the homeless and she**'s involving** everyone she knows.*
  (dynamic use = making them participate)
- *I don't want to accept the invitation if **it involves driving** across London.* (Not **it involves to drive**)

is • it is
- ***It's** hot today.* (Not **Is hot today.**)
  (*it is* an 'empty subject'; the subject in an

English sentence must be expressed or
strongly implied)

island • Iceland
- *Iceland has a high level of volcanic activity.*
  (Not *Island*)
- *Iceland is a very large island.*
  (= a piece of land surrounded by sea)

isn't it?
- *The play begins tomorrow, doesn't it?*
  (Not *isn't it?*)
- *The play is a great success, isn't it?*
  (we don't use the tag *isn't it?* as a general
  question to suggest *isn't that so?*, but only
  after *is*; *eh?* as a general tag is very informal
  in spoken English)

isolate • insulate
- *This electric wire isn't sufficiently well
  insulated for outdoor use.* (Not *isolated*)
  (= closed in, so that heat, sound, electricity
  cannot escape; the noun is *insulation*)
- *Have scientists isolated the virus that causes
  legionnaire's disease?* (Not *insulated*)
  (= separated completely in order to study;
  the noun is *isolation*)

issue • publish
- *When was your book published?*
  (Not *issued*)
  (= printed, distributed and sold)
- *These leaflets on healthy diet have been
  issued by the Ministry of Health.*
  (= officially made available)
- *When was your passport issued?*
  (Not *published*)
  (= officially made available, delivered)

it • so
- *Has the mail arrived? - I think so.*
  (Not *I think.* *I think it.*)
  (*so* after *believe, hope, think,* etc.)
- *I don't say he's a crook, but I think it.*
  (Not *I think so*)
  (= 'I think this, but I don't say it')

it/they • this/that/these/those
- *Is this/that yours? - Yes, it is.*
  (Not *Yes, this/that is.* *Yes is.*)
- *This/That suit is expensive, isn't it?*
  (Not *isn't this/that?* *is no?* *is not?*)
- *Are these/those yours? - Yes, they are.*
  (Not *Yes, these/those are.* *Yes are.*)
  (*it* and *they* replace *this/these,* etc., in short
  responses)

Italian
- *I'm learning/doing Italian.*
  (Not *making Italian* *italian*)
  (= the language: proper noun, capital letter)
- *He's/She's Italian.* (preferable to *an Italian*)
  (we generally prefer to use an adjectival
  complement; the noun form is *an Italian*)
- *They're Italian.*
  (adjectival form)
- *They're Italians.*
  (noun form)
- *I was just speaking to an Italian/two
  Italians.*
  (their sex is not stated, though a pronoun will
  often show whether they are male or female)
- *(The) Italians/(The) Italian people are
  wonderfully creative.*
  (= the group as a whole)
  (similarly to refer to people: *Algerian,
  Argentinian, Asian, Australian, Austrian,
  Belgian, Brazilian, Bulgarian, Canadian,
  Colombian, Egyptian, German, Hungarian,
  Indonesian, Iranian, Nigerian, Norwegian,
  Russian, Saudi Arabian, Scandinavian,
  Syrian, Tanzanian, Tunisian*)

its • it's
- *Look at the time. It's/It is later than you
  think.* (Not *Its*)
- *It's/It has taken longer to finish these letters
  than I thought.* (Not *Its*)
  (*it's* is short for 'it is' or 'it has'; *has* shortens
  to *'s* only when it is an auxiliary verb)
- *My pen's lost its top.* (Not *it's*)
  (*its* is the possessive adjective related to *it*)

J

jam • sweet(s)
- *Sweets ruin children's teeth.* (Not *Jams*)
  (*sweets* = toffees, chocolates, etc., made of
  sugar; AmE *candy/candies*)
- *There's a nice sweet to follow.* (Not *jam*)
  (BrE = *dessert*; also *pudding,* or informal
  afters; *sweet* is short for 'a sweet course',
  served at the end of a meal)
- *Put some jam on that bread.* (Not *sweet*)
  (= sugar and fruit boiled together: *apricot
  jam, plum jam, strawberry jam,* etc.,
  normally uncountable)
- *Baxters do a good range of jams.*
  (= different kinds of *jam(s)*)

Japanese
- *I'm learning/doing Japanese.*
  (Not *making Japanese* *japanese*)
  (= the language: proper noun, capital letter)

- *He's/She's **Japanese**.*
  (preferable to *a Japanese*)
  (we generally prefer to use an adjectival
  complement; the noun form is *a Japanese
  person*)
- *They're **Japanese**.* (Not **Japaneses**)
  (adjectival form)
- *I've been corresponding with **a Japanese
  man/a Japanese woman**.*
  (preferable to *a Japanese*)
- *I was just speaking to **two Japanese
  men/two Japanese women**.* (Not **two
  Japaneses**, preferably not *two Japanese*)
- ***The Japanese** are/**The Japanese people** are
  wonderfully inventive and hardworking.*
  (Not **Japanese* *Japaneses**)
  (= the group as a whole)
  (similarly to refer to people: *Burmese,
  Chinese, Lebanese, Maltese, Portuguese,
  Sudanese, Swiss, Taiwanese*)

jealous of
- *I think my little boy is **jealous of his
  younger sister**.* (Not **jealous his sister**)

jewellery • a piece of jewellery
- *That ring your mother gave you is **a fine
  piece of jewellery**.* (Not **a jewellery**,
  though we can refer to pieces of *jewellery* by
  name: *a necklace, a bracelet,* etc.; a *jewel* is
  a small valuable stone like a diamond or a
  sapphire; plural: *jewels*)
- *You shouldn't keep **so much jewellery** in the
  house.* (Not **so many jewelleries**)
  (*jewellery*, AmE *jewelry*, is uncountable)

job
- *Thank you for your report. You've **done an
  excellent job**.* (Not **made a job**)
  (*a job* = a piece of work)
- *I always have **a lot of jobs to do** on Saturday
  mornings.* (Not **jobs to make**)
  (= tasks to perform)
- *He **made a good job** of it.*
  (i.e. he did it well)
- *He **made rather a job** of it.*
  (i.e. he did it with some difficulty)

join • become a member of
- *How many countries can **join the European
  Community**?* (Not **join with/to**)
- *I **became a member of/joined** the golf club.*
  (*become a member of/join a club, join the
  army,* etc.)
- *I used a strong glue to **join** all these broken
  pieces together.*
  (= bring together)

joke • trick
- *Can you do card **tricks**?* (Not **jokes**)
  (= actions that seem like 'magic')
- *I must tell you a funny **joke** I heard at the
  office this morning.* (Not **trick**)
  (= a funny story)
- *He's always **playing** silly **jokes/tricks** on
  people.* (Not **making/doing jokes/tricks**)
  (*play jokes/tricks* = perform actions which
  are meant to be amusing; note *make jokes* =
  tell funny stories)

journal • newspaper/paper • diary
- *Which **newspaper/paper** do you prefer: The
  Times or The Independent?* (Not **journal**)
  (a *newspaper*, often called a *paper*, comes
  out every weekday and/or on Sundays)
- *Our library subscribes to several important
  journals like The Economist.*
  (*journals* are serious magazines that often
  specialize in one topic and are published
  weekly, monthly, quarterly or yearly)
- *Are you free tomorrow? - I'll just look in my
  diary.* (Not **journal**)
  (= a day-by-day record of appointments)
- *I kept a **journal/diary** during my trip across
  South East Asia.*
  (= a daily record of events; *journal* is
  literary)

journey • trip • voyage • travel • travels
- *We're taking a weekend **trip** to Moscow.*
  (Not **journey* *voyage* *travel**)
  (a *trip* is temporary, an interruption of the
  normal condition of being in one place)
- *I'm just back from a **business trip**.*
  (*business* combines with *trip*; a *business trip*
  is temporary, but not necessarily short)
- *It's a really long **journey** travelling by car
  from coast to coast across the USA.*
  (Not **voyage* *travel**; a *trip* is possible)
  (a *journey* refers to the act of travelling,
  especially long distance overland; it contains
  no reference to an end point)
- *I can remember the time when the **voyage/
  journey/trip** from England to Australia took
  over six weeks.* (Not **travel(s)**)
  (we use *voyage* for long trips by sea)
- *I always prefer to **travel** by air if I can.*
  (*travel* is used mainly as a verb, not a noun)
- *We're specialists in student **travel**.*
  (*travel* as an abstract uncountable noun)
- *I suppose you'll be writing about your
  travels when you return home.*
  (*travels* as a general collective for
  unspecified trips; sometimes literary)

- *I'm not prepared to **go on/make** such a long **journey/trip/voyage** at my age.* (Not *do*)
- ***Have a** good **journey/trip!*** (Not **Make/Do a good journey/trip!**)
- *We've **been on a** long **journey/trip**.* (Not **have been for a journey/trip**)

joy • happiness
- *Human beings are obsessed with the pursuit of **happiness**.* (Not *joy*)
(**happiness** when we are referring to a general state of mind)
- *I've had my share of **happiness/joy** as well as sorrow.* (Not *happinesses*)
(**happiness** is not normally countable: *a lot of happiness, a great deal of happiness; joy* = delight in something specific, can be countable: *a joy; joys and sorrows,* or uncountable: *to our great joy*)

joyful • happy
- *According to the philosopher Solon, no man is **happy** until he dies.* (Not *joyful*)
(**happy** to refer to the abstract ideal of *happiness*)
- *The air was filled with the **joyful/happy** voices of children.*
(either word here, though *joyful* is more intense and elevated than *happy*)

judge • criticize
- *Don't **criticize** him: he's doing his best.* (= comment on negatively)
- *It's not for me to **judge** your behaviour.* (= decide whether it is good or bad)

judge • think of
- ***What do you think of** A.S. Byatt's latest novel?* (Not *How do you judge*)
(= what is your opinion of)
- *It's going to be hard to **judge** which novel should win the Booker Prize this year.* (= give a decision on/about)

just
- *It was **just** a wrong number.* (= only)
- *It's **just** five o'clock.* (= exactly)
- *The exhibition is **just** wonderful.* (= absolutely)
- *This letter has **just** arrived for you.* (= a very short time ago)

just • fair • exact
- *Everyone will be pleased with his will. He was always a **fair** man.* (Not *just*)

- *I think the jury came to a **just/fair** decision.* (*fair* = 'without prejudice' is general; *just* refers to *justice* and is often legal)
- *You've taken more than your share and that's not **fair**.* (Not *exact* *just*)
(*fair* = proper, correct; we say *It's/That's not fair* to protest about lack of 'fair play')
- *I can't find the **exact** word to describe my feelings.* (Not *just*)

just • just now/right now
- *He's **just** phoned. He phoned **just now**.* (Not **He('s) just now phoned.**)
(i.e. a moment ago)
- *Mr Wilkins can't speak to you at the moment. He's busy **just now/right now**.* (= at the moment)

justice • the legal system
- *The French **legal system** is based on the Napoleonic Code.* (Not *justice*)
- *It's only right that terrorists should be pursued and brought to **justice**.*
(*the legal system* = the courts and how they operate; *justice* = the process of the law)

justly • exactly
- *I'll expect a call from you at **exactly** five o'clock.* (Not *justly*)
(= precisely)
- *It's always hard to deal **justly** with a conflict between two people.* (= fairly)
- *He behaved badly and was **justly** punished.* (= rightly, in line with justice)

K

keen to • keen on/like
- *I'm **keen on**/I **like** cycling.* (Not **It likes me the cycling.** **keen to cycling/cycle**)
- *I can't drive yet, but I'm **keen to learn**.*
(*keen on* + *-ing* = be enthusiastic about an activity; *keen to do* = want to do in the future)

keep
- *Don't throw that newspaper article away. I want to **keep** it.* (= have for some time; not lose)
- *You **keep saying** I'm clumsy.* (Not **You're keeping**)
(*keep* + *-ing*: stative use = continue)
- ***Keep (on) trying**.* (Not *Keep to try*)
(*on* further emphasizes continuity)

kernel • pip • stone

- *I grew this tree from an apple **pip**.*
  (Not **kernel**)
  (= a small, soft seed found in e.g. apples and
  oranges)
- *Stuff the lamb with rice and pine **kernels**.*
  (*a kernel* = the inside of a nutshell, often
  edible: a *nut*)
- *I cracked a tooth on a cherry **stone**.*
  (cherries, peaches, olives have *stones*)

kick

- *They **kicked him** while he was on the
  ground.* (Not **gave him kicks**)
  (*kicked him* = once or more than once)
- *Someone **gave him a kick/kicked him** while
  he was on the ground.*
  (i.e. once)

killed • get killed

- *Their son **got/was killed** in a road accident
  when he was only 18.* (Not **killed**)
- *Dogs that **kill** sheep can be shot on sight.*

kind of/sort of

- *I enjoy **this kind/sort of film**.*
- *I enjoy **films of this kind/of this sort**.*
- *I enjoy **these kinds/sorts of films**.*
- *I enjoy **all kinds/sorts of films**.*
  (Not **this kind/all kind* (or *sort*) *of films**,
  though it is often heard; we avoid *kinds of/
  sorts of* + singular countable: **I use all kinds
  of/sorts of pencil** for *I use all kinds of/sorts
  of pencils*, but we can say *kinds of/sorts of* +
  uncountable: *They sell **all kinds of/sorts of
  cloth**. Not **all kind/sort cloth**)

kindly

- *Dennis **kindly invited** us to lunch yesterday.*
  (i.e. it was kind of him to do this)
- *I greeted her and she **smiled kindly**.*
  (= smiled in a kind manner; the meaning of
  kindly changes according to whether it
  comes before or after a verb)
- *She gave me a **kindly** smile.*
  (adjective = friendly)

kitchen • cuisine • cooking • cookery

- *They do French regional **cuisine/cooking/
  cookery** at this bistro.* (Not **kitchen**)
  (= a style of cooking; *cuisine* suggests a
  grand style; *cooking* and *cookery* are the
  normal words; both are uncountable)
- *I've just been on a **cookery** course.*
  (Not **cooking**)
  (*cookery* to refer to 'the art of cooking')

- *We're having a new **kitchen** fitted.*
  (= the place in a house or restaurant where
  the cooking is done)

knickers

- *How much is **this pair of knickers**?*
- *How much **are these knickers**?*
  (Not **is this knicker**)
  (plural form only except in compounds like
  knicker elastic; also: *bathing trunks, jeans,
  panties, (under)pants, pyjamas* (BrE)/
  pajamas (AmE), *shorts, tights, trousers*;
  similarly: *binoculars, glasses, pliers,
  scissors, spectacles, tweezers*)

knock at • hit

- *He fell backwards and his head **hit** the door.*
  (Not **knocked (at)**)
  (= struck, perhaps painfully)
- *Someone's **knocking at the door**.* (Not **is
  knocking the door* *knocking to the door**)
  (i.e. so that someone will answer)

know (about/how to) • recognize
• acknowledge • identify

- *You **didn't recognize** me because I've grown
  a beard.* (Not **didn't know* *didn't
  acknowledge* *weren't recognizing**)
  (stative use = identify by seeing)
- *The insurance company is now **recognizing**
  that our claim is justifiable.*
  (dynamic use = acknowledging)
- *You **don't know** me. I've just moved into the
  house next door.* (Not **aren't knowing**)
- *Do you **know about** this?* (Not **know for**)
- *Do you **know how to change** a wheel on a
  car?* (Not **Do you know to change**)
  (stative use only = have information about)
- *I **acknowledge** the truth of what you say.*
  (= admit to recognizing)
- *The police asked us to **identify** the dead
  woman.*
  (= recognize and say who she was)

L

laborious • hardworking

- *Being busy is not the same as being
  hardworking.* (Not **laborious**)
  (i.e. working hard)
- *Collating all these pages is extremely slow
  and **laborious** work.*
  (i.e. it needs a lot of slow and tedious work)

labourer • workman

- *Our electrician is an extremely good
  workman.* (Not **labourer**)

(= a man who does physical work involving skill)
- *You can always earn money as a **labourer** on a building site.* (preferable to *workman*)
(= a person who does physical work that needs real strength)

lack
- *There's **a lack of** trained engineers at the moment.* (Not **a lack from**)
(= a shortage of)
- ***We lack** trained staff at the moment.* (Not **It lacks us* *We lack from/of**)
(= we are short of)

lack • lacquer
- *The surface of the table has been treated with hard **lacquer**.* (Not **lack**)
(= paint/varnish that dries to a hard shiny surface)
- *There's a complete **lack** of demand for houses at the moment.*
(= absence)

steps/stepladder

stairs/staircase

ladder

rung

ladder • steps/stepladder • stairs/staircase • rung
- *The **stairs** lead/The **staircase** leads to the attic.* (Not **ladder* *steps**)
- *I need a **ladder** to get onto the roof.*
- *You need a small **stepladder**/a pair of **steps** to reach the top of those cupboards.*
- *Mind the **step(s)**!*
- *Hold the ladder and put your right foot on the first **rung**.* (preferable to *step*)

laid • lain • lied (past participles)
- *She's **lain** on the beach all morning and she's terribly sunburnt.* (Not **laid* *lied**)
(*lie - lay - have **lain** = be in a flat position)
- *I've **laid** your clothes on the bed and you can put them away.* (Not **lain* *lied**)
(*lay - laid - have **laid** = put down)
- *Why should I believe you this time? You've **lied** to me before.* (Not **laid* *lain**)
(regular: *lie - lied - have **lied** = tell lies)

lamp • light • flash of lightning • flashlight
- *There was a roll of thunder and a sudden **flash of lightning**.* (Not **lamp* *light**)
(*lightning*, uncountable = a light in the sky caused by electricity)
- *Where did you get that beautiful table **lamp/light**?*
(= a device, often decorative and movable, which gives light)
- *There's a **light** at the end of the tunnel.*
(= any source of light)
- *If you're going to be walking home late, take a **flashlight** (AmE; **torch** BrE) with you.* (Not **lamp**)

land • country • countryside
- *Both my grandfathers worked **on the land**.*
(*on the land* = in farming)
- *Many Londoners would rather live in **the country**.* (Not **the countryside* *the land**)
(*the country* = the area away from large towns or cities: *the country*, not *the countryside*, is the opposite of *a town* or *city*; *country* also means *nation* as in *my native country*; note the pronunciation /ˈkʌntri/, not **/ˈkaʊntri/**)
- *Motorways have led to the destruction of a great deal of the **countryside**.*
- *There's **a lot of** beautiful **countryside** not far from Manchester.* (Not **a countryside* *a lot of countrysides**)
(*countryside* = country scenery is uncountable)

lard • bacon
- *It's fairly unusual these days to have **bacon** and eggs for breakfast.* (Not **lard**)
(= salted, sometimes smoked, pork belly and back, usually sliced thinly and fried)
- *Most people cook with vegetable oil these days rather than butter or **lard**.*
(= clarified pork fat used for cooking)

large • wide/broad • generous
- *We can't thank you enough for your **generous** hospitality.* (Not **large**)
(= open-handed, freely-given)
- *'Unter den Linden' is a **broad/wide** avenue in Berlin.* (Not **large**)
(i.e. referring to distance from side to side)
- *A **large** house is expensive to heat.*
(= big in scale in relation to others)

largely • greatly
- *The original motorway has been **greatly** widened and improved.* (Not **largely**)
- *The managing director was **largely** responsible for the collapse of the company.*

107

(Not *greatly*)
(= mainly, to a high degree)

last • latest
- *Have you read Forsythe's **latest** book?*
  (= most recent)
- *Have you read Graham Greene's **last** book?*
  (= final, the last one he ever wrote)

last • the last
- *I saw her **last** Monday.* (Not *the last*)
  (no *the* in front of *last* in point of time references)
- *Who was **the last** Roman Emperor?*
  (= the final; as opposed to *the first, the second,* etc.)
- *When was **the last** time you saw her?*
  (= the most recent or final; note that *the last* can be ambiguous)

last/least: at last • at least
- *After days of anxiety, **at last** we learnt the climbers were safe.*
  (= after a long period of time)
- *There isn't much news about the missing climbers, but **at least** we know they're safe.*
  (i.e. that's an advantage in a bad situation)

lastly • last • last of all
- *We arrived **last/last of all**.* (Not *lastly*)
  (we use *last*, not *lastly*, after the verb: *He mentioned that **last**. He came in **last**.*)
- *And **last (of all)/lastly**, I want to thank all my supporters.* (Not *lastly of all*)
  (*lastly* is possible when we are listing a sequence beginning with *first(ly)*; *last* is sometimes possible)

late • lately
- *The train arrived **late**.* (Not *lately*)
  (*late* is an adverb meaning 'not on time')
- *I sat up to watch the **late** show.*
  (*late* as an adjective normally goes after the verb, usually *be*: *I was late*, but can precede some nouns referring to events, not people: *a late appointment, a late night*)
- *My **late** uncle left me some money.*
  (i.e. he died recently)
- *We haven't seen you **lately**.*
  (= recently)

laugh • laugh at
- *You're very kind to **laugh** when I tell a joke.*
- *You always kindly **laugh at** my jokes.*
  (Not *laugh with*)
  (= laugh to express amusement)
- *If you go round saying things like that, everyone will **laugh at** you.*
  (= treat you as if you were foolish)

laughter • laugh
- *Suddenly, I heard a loud **laugh** behind me.*
  (Not *a laughter*)
- *I could hear **a lot of laughter** and shouting from next door.* (Not *a lot of laughters*)
- *I could hear **a lot of laughs** and shouts from next door.*
  (*laughter* is uncountable, and we generally prefer it to *laughs*)
- *We all **had a** good **laugh** at the school reunion dinner.* (Not *had a laughter*)
  (*have a (good) laugh* is a fixed phrase)

lavatory • washbasin • sink
- *I've put some fresh soap by the **washbasin**.*
  (Not *lavatory*)
  (a *washbasin* is usually found in a bathroom)
- *There are a lot of dirty dishes in the **sink**.*
  (Not *washbasin*)
  (a *sink* is usually found in a kitchen)
- *The **lavatory**'s occupied at the moment.*
  (= 'toilet' in BrE, though *lavatory* can mean 'washbasin' in AmE)

lay • laid • lied (past tense)
- *We were so tired after last night's party, we **lay** in bed all morning.* (Not *laid* *lied*)
  (*lie - lay - have lain* = be in a flat position)
- *I **laid** your clothes on the bed so you can put them away.* (Not *layed*)
  (*lay - laid - have laid* = put down; compare normal spelling of vowel + *-y*: *play - played - played*)
  (the past form *lay* = was in a flat position, is the same as the present form *lay* = put down)
- *I know Peter **lied** when he said he'd put the cheque in the post.*
  (*lie - lied - lied* = tell lies)

lay • lie (present form/imperative)
- *Are you going to **lie** in bed all morning?*
  (Not *lay*)
  (*lie - lay - have lain* = be in a flat position)
- *Please **lay** the book open on the coffee table.*
  (Not *lie*)
  (*lay - laid - have laid* = put down)
  (the present or imperative form *lay* = put down, is the same as the past form *lay* = was in a flat position)
- *I wish Peter wouldn't **lie** so much.*
  (*lie - lied - lied* = tell lies)

laying • lying (present participles)
- *Are you going to spend the whole morning **lying** in bed?* (Not *laying* *lieing*)
  (*lie/lying - lay - have lain* = be in a flat position)

- *I'm **laying** your clothes on the bed so you can put them away.* (Not **lying**)
(***lay/laying** - laid - have laid* = put down)
- *Peter says he put the cheque in the post, but I'm sure he**'s lying**.* (Not **laying**)
(***lie/lying** - lied - lied* = tell lies)

lead/led
- *The bushman **led** us to a spot in the desert where there was water.* (Not **lead**)
(*lead* /liːd/ - *led* /led/ - *led* /led/)

leaden • lead
- ***Lead*** /led/ *pipes are a real health hazard.* (Not **leaden**)
(= made of *lead*; *lead* can be a noun modifier: *lead piping*, a *lead roof*)
- *It was a bleak day with **a leaden** sky.* (= 'like lead')

learn (how) to • teach (how) to • learn to • learn about
- *Who **taught** you **(how) to** knit?* (Not **learned you (how) to**)
- *I **learnt (how) to** knit when I was eight.* (*teach/learn (how) to* for skill; the person who gives the knowledge, skill, etc., *teaches*; the person who acquires the knowledge, skill, etc., *learns*)
- *We soon **learnt to** do as we were told in Mr Spinks' class.* (Not **learnt how to**)
(*learn to* for 'learn from experience')
- *I want to **learn about** life in other countries.* (Not **learn for**)

learner • teacher
- *I once worked as a **teacher** in an infants' school.*
(i.e. I taught infants)
- *A good teacher should also be a good **learner**.*
(= someone who *learns*)

leave: on leave • holiday: on holiday
- *Our neighbours have just **gone** (away) **on holiday**.* (Not **for holiday* *for holidays* *they are in holidays* *they are on leave**)
- *Vince is **on leave** from the navy.*
- *When are you going to **have/take a holiday**?* (Not **do/make**)
(you are *on holiday* when you don't go to work; you are *on leave* when you have permission to leave a place where you hold an appointment, especially in the armed services: *on leave* is short for *on leave of absence*)

leave • leave for
- *We **left** London at 9.* (Not usually *left from*)

- *When does the train **leave for** Glasgow?*
(*leave a place* = depart from it; *leave for a place* = start a journey towards it)

leave • let/allow
- *I want to help in the kitchen, but they **won't let me**/they **won't allow me to**.*
(Not **won't leave me* *won't allow me**)
- *We don't **let our children watch TV/allow our children to watch TV** after 8 o'clock.*
(Not **let/allow to our children**)
(= permit; *allow someone to* is more formal than *let someone* + bare infinitive)
- *Promise you'll never **leave** me.*
(= go away from, abandon)

leave • let go (of)
- *The dog's got hold of one of your slippers and he won't **let it go/let go of it**.*
(Not **leave it**, though *leave go of it*, not **leave it go**, is possible informally)
(*let go (of)* = release something held)
- *The dog's **left** your paper by the front door.* (= put)
- *I **left them arguing** among themselves.*
(Not **left them to argue**)
(i.e. they were arguing when I left them)

lecture • reading material/matter
- *Have we got enough **reading material/ matter** for the journey?* (Not **lecture**)
- *Some people think a **lecture** must have been good if they couldn't understand it.*
(= a long talk on a particular subject)
- *Professor Newton **gave** us **a** wonderful **lecture**.* (Not **did/made a lecture**)

less (good) • better • more
- *My pen looks rather like yours, but it's **less good** (than yours).*
(= not as good as; implying they are both good; *worse than* implies they are both bad)
- *My pen looks a bit like yours, but yours is **better** (than mine).* (Not **more good**)
(we can use *less* + one-syllable adjectives, but *more* + one-syllable adjectives is unusual)
- *Yours is **more expensive** than mine.*
(*more* + longer adjectives)

lesson
- *Many teachers of English **give** private **lessons**.* (Not **do/make lessons**)
- *Kay's **having** driving **lessons**.*
(Not **doing/making lessons**)

let('s)
- ***Let's take** a taxi.* (Not **Let's to take**)
(imperative *Let's* for suggestions)

- *Let's not waste* any more time.
  (Not *Let's no waste* *Let's don't*)
  (*Let's not* or *Don't let's* for negatives)
- *Let him speak*. (Not *Let him to speak*)
  (*let* = allow + bare infinitive)
- *They didn't let us speak*. (Not *let's*)
  (*let us* = allow us is not abbreviated to *let's*)

lexicon • dictionary
- *What's a 'gnu'? - I don't know. Look it up in the dictionary*. (Not *lexicon*)
- *The Greek-English Lexicon by Liddell and Scott has never been surpassed.*
  (*dictionary* is the modern word; *lexicon* is old-fashioned and used mainly with reference to ancient languages, especially Greek, Latin, Arabic and Hebrew)

liberate • discharge (from)
- *I was discharged from the army in 1984.*
  (Not *liberated from*)
  (= officially allowed to leave)
- *When was Crete liberated following its occupation in World War II?*
  (Not *discharged*)
  (= set free; we use *liberate* for places rather than people)

liberty • freedom
- *I never feel such freedom as when I'm climbing mountains.* (Not *liberty*)
- *Oppressed peoples have no choice but to fight for their liberty/freedom.*
  (*freedom* is personal and often physical and psychological; *liberty* is often collective, social or institutional)

librarian • bookseller
- *It's hard for small booksellers to survive these days.* (Not *librarians*)
  (*booksellers* sell books in *bookshops*)
- *She's head librarian at our local library.*
  (*librarians* work in public or specialized *libraries* where people can borrow books)

library • bookshop • bookcase
- *I must buy a new bookcase to store all these books.* (Not *library* *bookshop*)
  (= furniture with shelves for storing books)
- *You can buy all the best-selling titles at our local bookshop.* (Not *library*)
- *I've been collecting books for years and I now have a large library.* (Not *bookcase*)
  (= a collection of books)
- *Borrow the book from your local library.*

licence • license
- *Is your car licensed?* (Not *licenced*)
  (i.e. is its use officially allowed?)

- *You can't drive round without a licence.*
  (in BrE *licence* is the noun and *license* the verb; in AmE *license* is both noun and verb)

lid/top • cap/top • cover
- *What did I do with the cap/top of my pen?*
  (Not *lid* *cover*)
- *I can't get the lid/cap/top off this jar.*
  (*a top* is the removable upper part of something - a box, a tin, a jar, a pen, etc.; *a cap* fits closely over the end of e.g. a pen; the general term for the thing we use to close any container is *a lid*)
- *I protect my keyboard with a cover when I'm not using it.* (Not *lid* *cap* *top*)
  (*a cover* is a layer of e.g. cloth, plastic, metal, etc., that completely hides or protects what is inside)
- *I like the cover of this book.*
  (= the outer front of a book which may be hard or soft; a removable paper cover is a *dust jacket* or *dust wrapper*)

life • live
- *We live in London.* (Not *life*)
- *I prefer life in the country.* (Not *live*)
  (*life*, noun, plural *lives*; *live* is the verb)
- *Life is difficult.* (Not *The life*)
  (no article in general statements)

life • living
- *I earned a living as a cook.* (Not *life*)
  (the phrase is *earn a living*)
- *What do you do for a living?* (Not *make*)
  (i.e. as an occupation, to earn money)
- *How does he make a living?* (Not *do*)
  (= earn money to live)
- *You seem to have a comfortable life.*
  (Not *living*)
  (i.e. style of living)

life's aim • aim in life
- *What's your aim in life?*
  (Not *life's aim* *aim of your life*)
  (= your purpose in life)
- *His life's aim is to be Prime Minister.*
  (= his one and only ambition)

lighten • lighter • get lighter
- *The evenings are getting lighter.* (Not *lightening* *lightening themselves*)
- *Take something out of your case to make it lighter/to lighten it.*
- *Joe has lightened his hair/made his hair lighter.*
  (i.e. in colour)

like

- *John **likes** fast cars.* (Not **is liking**)
  (stative use)
- *John's got a job in a supermarket, but he **isn't liking** it very much.*
  (dynamic use = enjoying)
- *Do you **like** London? - Yes, **I do**./Yes, I like it.* (Not **Yes, I like.**)
- *Would you **like** a day in London? - Yes, **I would**./Yes **I'd like it/that**.* (Not **I'd like.**)
  (*like* is always transitive)
- *I'd **like a coffee** please.*
  (Not **I like a coffee**)
- *Do you **like to** watch TV? - Yes, **I do**./ Yes, I **like to**.* (Not **Yes, I like.**)
- *Would you **like to** watch TV? - Yes, **I would**./Yes, **I'd like to**.* (Not **I'd like.**)
- *I **like watching** TV/**to watch** TV.*
  (*to* or *-ing* after *like*)
- *I'd **like you to** help me.*
  (Not **I'd like that you (should) help me.**)
- *I **like/I'm fond of** football.* (Not **It likes me the football.** **Football likes me.**)

like • as • as if • such as

- *Please do **as** I say.* (Not **like I say**)
- *She's behaving **as if** she's mad.* (Not **like**)
  (*as* and *as if* are conjunctions; *like* is heard, especially in AmE, but is not universally accepted)
- *There's no one **like** you.* (Not **as you**)
  (= to compare with)
- *He acts **like** a king.* (Not **like king**)
  (= in the same way as a king)
  (*like* is a preposition + object; *like* + countable noun: *like a king*; *like* + uncountable noun: *like lightning*)
- *He's acting **as** headmaster.*
  (= taking the place of the headmaster)
- ***As** your lawyer, I wouldn't advise it.*
  (Not **Like your lawyer**)
  (*as*: preposition = in the capacity of)
- *Junk food **such as/like** fizzy drinks and hamburgers have invaded the whole world.*
  (Not **Junk food as fizzy drinks**)
  (*such as* or *like* when giving examples)

lime • file

- *I've broken one of my fingernails. Can I borrow your **file**?* (Not **lime**)
  (= a tool with a rough surface for smoothing things)
- *Guess what I paid for a fresh **lime**!*
  (= a green fruit like a lemon)

limit • limitation

- *These rules are a severe **limitation** on our freedom.* (Not **limit**)
  (= a restriction, and note compounds like *speed limit*, *time limit* = restriction)
- *This word processor is quite good, but it has its **limitations**.*
  (i.e. it does a limited number of things)
- *I won't put up with any more nonsense. That's the **limit**.* (Not **limitation**)
  (= the extreme, the end)
- *I've worked to the **limit** of my ability.*
  (Not **limitation**)
  (i.e. to the best I'm capable of, the end)

linen • linens • white goods

- ***Linen** is a very acceptable wedding present.*
  (Not **A linen is** **Linens are**)
  (*linen*, i.e. sheets, etc., is normally uncountable)
- *They're having a sale of household **linen(s)**.*
  (= different kinds of *linen(s)*)
- *They're having a sale of **white goods**.*
  (jargon for refrigerators, cookers, etc.)

linguistics

- ***Linguistics is** a relatively new academic subject.* (Not **(the) linguistics are** **(the) linguistic is**)
  (plural form + singular verb to refer to the academic subject)

liquidation • clearance sale

- *That department store is closing down and they're having a big **clearance sale**.*
  (Not **liquidation**)
  (i.e. selling goods cheaply to clear them)
- *The company is bankrupt and is **going into liquidation**.*
  (= to be sold to meet debts)

literati • literate

- *Annual book prizes are well attended by the **literati**.* (Not **literate**)
  (= people interested in literature; formal)
- *What percentage of the population is **literate**?*
  (= able to read and write)

little • small • short • young

- *Our flat is very **small**. It's a **small** flat.*
  (Not **little**)
- *He likes to work in a **little** corner of his own.*
  (Not **small**)
  (*small* is the normal word for indicating small size, and means 'in relation to other similar things or people'; *little* describes absolute size as it strikes an observer. *Little*

can also imply 'charming': *a little box*, or 'defenceless': *a little child*; we can say *smaller*, *smallest*, but the forms *littler*, *littlest* are rare)
- *They specialize in clothes for **short** people.* (Not *small/little*) (= not tall)
- *Surely she's still too **young** to be given the key to the door.* (Not *little/small*) (= not old)

live • leave
- *What time do you **leave**?* /liːv/ (Not *live*)
- *Where do you **live**?* /lɪv/ (spelling and pronunciation; and note: *He **left** the room. He **lived** in Rome.*)

lively • animated
- *When I raised the subject of payment he became extremely **animated**.* (Not *lively*) (= very excited at that moment)
- *Anita is a **lively** sort of person.* (= generally full of life)

lively • unruly
- *Class 2 is very **unruly** and hard for a teacher to manage.* (Not *lively*) (= badly behaved)
- *The children in that class are very **lively** and it's a pleasure to teach them.* (= full of life)

load/unload • charge/discharge
- *I'll have to **charge** my battery before I can start my car.* (Not *load*)
- *Don't forget your car lights, or you'll **discharge** the battery.* (Not *unload*) (*charge/discharge* = store/run down power in a battery)
- *Help me **load/unload** the luggage.* (Not *charge/discharge*) (= put/remove luggage, etc., into/from a vehicle)
- *If you want to take a picture, you'll have to **load** the camera.* (Not *charge*) (= put in a film)

logical • reasonable • sensible
- *The kind of pay rise you're asking for simply isn't **reasonable**.* (Not *logical* *sensible*) (= just or fair)
- *With **sensible/reasonable** investment, your money will grow.* (Not *logical*) (*sensible* = sound; *reasonable* = well-considered or quite good)
- *It's easy to be persuaded by such a **sensible/logical/reasonable** argument.* (*sensible* = making sense; *logical* =

following the rules of logic; *reasonable* = just or fair)

loneliness • lonely • solitude
- *It's easy to feel **lonely** in London.* (preferable to *loneliness*)
- *I often like to spend time in the **solitude** of my own room.* (Not *loneliness*) (= the state of being alone)
- *The old often suffer from **loneliness** as their friends die off.* (Not *lonely* *solitude*) (= a feeling of unhappiness from being without company)

lonely • lone • alone
- *Mrs Cartwright lives **alone**.* (Not *lonely*) (= without others; we cannot use *alone* in front of a noun)
- *I don't think she's **lonely**. I'm sure she isn't a **lonely** woman.* (Not *alone*) (= sad because of being alone)
- *A **lone** rider disappeared into the sunset.* (Not *an alone rider* *a lonely rider*) (= not accompanied; *lone* is relatively rare and always used in front of a noun)

long • during
- *It rained (all) **during** the night.* (Not *long the night*) (*during* = within the period named, either continuously or occasionally)
- *It rained **all night long**.* (Not *all during night* *all night during*) (= within a period, without stopping)

long/length
- *How **long**/What **length** is this room?* (Not *How much long is/How much length has*)
- *This room **is three and a half metres (long)**.* (Not *has length three and a half metres*)

long: (for) long • (for) a long time • much
- *Jill came round this morning, but she didn't **stay long**.* (Not *much* to indicate time) (= she wasn't here long, a long time)
- *We haven't seen you **for a long time**.* (Not *for long* *for much time* *a long time*)
- *I'm going out, but I won't be **long**.* (Not *for long* *for much*)
- *Sally called yesterday, but she didn't wait **(for) long**.* (Not *for a long time/for much*) (*long* often refers to how much time something takes; *for long* refers to how much time something continues. Use *(for) a long time* in affirmatives: *Sally **stayed** (for) a long time*, and use *(for) long* in negatives and questions: *Sally **didn't stay** (for) long*.)

- *You didn't sell your car **for much**, did you?*
  (= for a lot of money)
- *We haven't seen George **much** lately.*
  (refers to opportunity, not time)

look • look after
- *Please **look after the children** while we're out.* (Not *look the children*)
- ***Look!** The plane's coming in to land!*

look (at) • see • watch
- *I **see** very well without glasses.*
  (Not *look* *watch* *I'm seeing*)
  (stative use: the action is involuntary)
- *I'll **be seeing** you tomorrow.*
  (dynamic use: *see* = meet, etc.)
- *We **saw** a good film at the Rex last night.*
  (*see* a film or play at a cinema or theatre)
- *How long have you been **watching** the match?* (Not *seeing* *looking at*)
- *Do you have to **watch me eat/eating** my supper?* (Not *watch me to eat*)
  (bare infinitive = the whole action, or *-ing* = part of the action after *watch someone*)
  (we deliberately *watch* an action that continues over a period of time)
- ***Look at this card** that John's just sent.*
  (Not *Watch* *See* *Look this card*)
  (we *look at* something deliberately and with attention, e.g. a picture, an object)
- *You **look** well./You're **looking** well.*
  (= appear: stative or dynamic depending on the emphasis you want; *look* is followed by an adjective here: *It **looks** bad*, not *badly*)
- ***Have/Take a look** at this.* (Not *Throw*)

look (here) • look at this
- ***Look at this!*** (Not *Look here!*)
  (*look here* does not mean 'look in this direction')
- ***Look (here)**, let's get this straight.*
  (*look (here)* often expresses impatience and draws attention to what you're about to say)

look forward to
- *I **look forward to seeing** you during the weekend.* (Not *look forward to see* *look forwards to seeing* *look forward seeing*)
  (*to* functions as a preposition + *-ing* here, not as part of the infinitive)

loose • lose • loosen
- *Try not to **lose** your ticket.* (Not *loose*)
  (verb: *lose - lost - lost*)
- *The handle on this suitcase is very **loose**/has come **loose**.* (Not *lose*)
  (*loose*, adjective = not firm; compare *loose*

morals and *buy/sell* (e.g.) *potatoes loose*: i.e. not packaged)
- *I feel very hot. I think I'll **loosen** my tie.*
  (verb: *loosen - loosened - loosened* = make less tight)

loss
- *Our firm **made a big loss** last year.*
  (Not *did a loss*; note that *loss* is the noun from the verb *lose*)
- *We didn't know what to do. We were **at a loss**.* (Not *We were lost*)
  (= uncertain)

lot: a lot/lots • a lot of/lots of
- *I've got **a lot of work/lots of work** today.*
  (Not *a lot/lots work* *a lots of work*)
- *How much work have you got today? - **A lot./Lots.*** (Not *A lot of./Lots of.*)
  (*a lot* or *lots* on their own, or *a lot of/lots of* + countable or uncountable noun; *lots (of)* is informal)

loud • aloud • loudly • strong
- *When I told them the story, they all **laughed aloud/loudly**.* (Not *laughed loud/strong*)
  (*aloud*, or *out loud* = so you can hear; *loudly* = not quietly, making a big noise)
- *I could hear **loud** music coming from upstairs.* (Not *aloud* *loudly* *strong*)
  (*loud* is an adjective)
- *Don't **talk** so **loud/loudly**.* (Not *aloud*)
  (we can use *loud* as an adverb with a few verbs like *talk* and *play (music)*)
- *There was a very **strong** wind/**strong** smell.*
  (Not *loud*)
  (= powerful)

love
- *John **loves** fast cars.* (Not *is loving*)
  (stative use)
- *John's at university and **he's loving** every minute of it.*
  (dynamic use = enjoying)
- *Do you **like** London? - Yes, **I do**./Yes, **I love it**.* (Not *Yes, I love.*)
- *Wouldn't you **love** a day in London? - Yes, **I would**./Yes, **I'd love it**.* (Not *I'd love.*)
  (*love* is always transitive)
- *Do you **like to** watch TV? - Yes, **I do**./Yes, **I love to**.* (Not *Yes, I love.*)
- *Would you **like to** watch TV? - Yes, **I would**./Yes, **I'd love to**.* (Not *I'd love.*)
- *I **love watching** TV/**to watch** TV.*
  (*to* or *-ing* after *love*)
- *I'd **love you to see** our new flat.*
  (Not *I'd love that you (should) see*)

- *I love/I'm fond of football.*
  (Not **It loves me the football.**)
- ***Make love**, not war.* (Not *Do love*)

lovely • loving • lovable
- *She's lucky to have such **loving** children.*
  (i.e. they love her and/or each other)
- *She's lucky to have such **lovely** children.*
  (i.e. they're beautiful, wonderful)
- *She's lucky to have such **lovable** children.*
  (i.e. it's easy to love them)

lower/higher • inferior/superior (to)
- *There's no reason for you to feel **inferior/**
  superior.* (Not **lower/higher**)
  (i.e. in status)
- *This year's exam results are **inferior**
  to/superior to last year's.*
- *The number of passes was **lower/higher** this
  year.*
  (*lower/higher* refer to level; *inferior/*
  superior refer to quality, though we can refer
  to *high* and *low quality*)

low • lowly
- *We flew **low** over the sea.* (Not *lowly*)
  (*low* is an adjective or adverb: *a low*
  building/fly low; *low paid workers*)
- *William began in a **lowly** position at the
  bank, but rose to the top.* (Not *low*)
  (*lowly* is only an adjective = low in rank or
  status, 'humble'; rather old-fashioned)

luckily • by chance
- *I heard the news **by chance**.* (Not *luckily*)
  (= accidentally, without expecting to)
- *I was in a crash on the motorway, but
  luckily I wasn't hurt.*
  (Not *by chance* *by luck*)
  (= fortunately)

lucky • happy
- *A merry Christmas and a **happy** New Year!*
  (Not *lucky* *good*)
- *You have to be very **lucky** to win the pools.*
  (= fortunate)
- *Aren't you **lucky**! **Lucky** you! You **lucky**
  girl! I'm the **lucky** one!*
  (Not **Aren't you a lucky!**, etc.)
  (we cannot use *lucky* as a noun)

lust • desire
- *I have no **desire** to spend every evening
  watching television.* (Not *lust*)
- *I sometimes wonder whether Jake knows the
  difference between love and **lust**.*
  (= strong sexual desire; also used
  metaphorically: *lust for power*)

luxurious • luxury • de luxe
- *The company paid all our expenses
  including our accommodation at **luxury**
  hotels.*
  (Not *luxurious* *de luxe* *luxus*)
- *The **luxury/de luxe** model of this car has
  air-conditioning.* (Not *luxurious*)
  (*de luxe model*: e.g. to describe products
  such as cars)
- *Who wouldn't like to lead a life of **luxury**?*
  (Not *a luxury life* *a luxurious life*)
  (i.e. in great comfort, very expensively)
- *The furnishings are extremely **luxurious**.*
  (Not *luxury* *de luxe*)
  (= very grand, expensive)

M

macaroni
- *Have **some macaroni**.* (Not *macaronis*)
- ***This macaroni** is overcooked.*
  (Not *These macaronis* *These macaroni*)
  (*macaroni* is uncountable; also: *spaghetti*)

machine • camera • apparatus
- *Would you mind taking a photo of me with
  my **camera**?* (Not *machine* *apparatus*
  photographic machine/apparatus)
  (we don't use *machine* or *apparatus* in place
  of the word *camera*)
- *This **machine** not only washes clothes but
  dries them as well.* (Not *engine*)
  (a *machine* stands alone)
- *Divers must check their own breathing
  apparatus.*
  (= equipment for a special purpose)

machinery • a piece of machinery
- *This is a wonderful **piece of machinery**.*
  (Not *a machinery*)
- *They're installing **a lot of** new **machinery** at
  our factory.* (Not **a lot of machineries**)
  (*machinery* is uncountable)

madden • mad • get mad • go mad
- *I'll **go mad** if I have to live in this house on
  my own.* (Not **I'll mad** **I'll madden**)
  (= become insane)
- *Don't **get mad** at me just because I'm ten
  minutes late!* (Not **go mad at/with**)
  (= become angry with)
- *It's her unpunctuality that **maddens**
  me/drives me mad/makes me mad.*
  (= makes me cross; irritates me)

made of/out of • made from • made with
- *Beer is **made from** hops and other
  ingredients.* (Not **made of/out of**)

(*made from* when the ingredients aren't immediately obvious)
- *Our new garden gate is **made of/out of** wrought iron.* (Not *made from*)
(*made of/out of* when we can recognize the material)
- *This cake is **made with** fresh cream.*
(*made with* = using; compare *filled with* = 'containing')

madness • craze
- *The latest teenage **craze** is having your nose pierced.* (Not *madness*)
(= fashion)
- *It would be **madness** to tax bread.*
(= a very foolish action)

magazine • shop • store • boutique • department store • storeroom
- *You can buy anything in our village **shop**.* (Not *magazine/boutique*; not *store* in BrE)
- *The company aims to have a **store** in every important town in Europe.*
(preferable to *shop* if the reference is to a *department store* or *chain store*)
(= a large shop)
- *You'd pay the earth for a skirt like that if you bought it at a **boutique**.* (Not *shop*)
(= a small specialized fashion shop)
- *London has wonderful **department stores**.* (Not *magazines* *departments*)
(= very large shops)
- *We don't have your size on display. I'll look in the **storeroom**.* (Not *magazine*)
- *My favourite **magazine** is Woman's Weekly.*
(= a periodical, published weekly/monthly)

magical • magic
- *The wicked witch put a **magic** spell on the beautiful princess.* (Not *magical*)
(i.e. by the use of secret powers)
- *On stage, the prima ballerina seems to dissolve in the mist. The effect is **magical**.*
(= like magic)

majority • most
- *Now that I've retired, I spend **most of** my time looking after the garden.*
(Not *the majority of* *the most of*)
- *In Britain **the majority is/are** in favour of longer prison sentences.*
(*the majority*, without *of*, takes a singular or plural verb, otherwise we have to say *the majority of people are*; *the majority* means 'more than half' and should not be used to replace *most*; we cannot use *majority* to refer to an uncountable quantity like *time*)

make • cause
- *What **caused** the damage?* (Not *made*)
(*cause* + noun = bring about)
- *What **made her faint/caused her to faint**?* (Not *made her to faint*)
(*make* + object + bare infinitive, or *cause* + object + *to* = be the cause of)
- *He **was made to change** his mind.* (Not *was made change his mind*)
(*make* = compel + a bare infinitive in the active; + a *to*-infinitive in the passive)

make as if • pretend
- *How many people **pretend** to be out of work in order to draw unemployment benefit?* (Not *make as if* *make that*)
- *He **made as if** to leave but then changed his mind.* (Not *pretended*)
(= appeared to be about to)

male • masculine • manly • mannish
- *I'll get my brother to use his **masculine** charm.* (Not *male*)
(opposite *feminine*, relating to behaviour; the noun is *masculinity*)
- *'He' is the **masculine** third person subject pronoun.* (Not *male*)
(referring to grammatical gender)
- *How can you tell whether an insect is **male** or female?* (not *masculine*)
(opposite *female*, relating to sex; note *a male* is used as a noun for animals, not people; also note the abstract noun *maleness* = the essence of being male)
- *Being able to act like Superman is just a **male** fantasy.* (Not *masculine*)
- *Tom has a firm handshake and a fine, **manly** way of greeting people.*
(= like a man, relating to manhood)
- *Women's clothes in the 80's were rather **mannish**, both in colour and outline.*
(in general terms, *masculine* refers to sexual attractiveness, *male* is biological and *manly* is social, referring to the sometimes idealized qualities of a man; *mannish* = imitating a man: not complimentary)

man/husband • woman/wife
- *You must meet my **husband/wife**.* (Not *man/woman*)
(= the man/woman I'm married to)
(*man* = husband occurs in a few old-fashioned fixed phrases, e.g. *man and wife*; *man/woman* = 'male/female companion' occurs in limited contexts: *Who's the new **man/woman** in your life?*)

man/woman • men/women

– *Where are the **men's/women's** toilets please?* (Not **man's/woman's* *mens/womens* *mens'/womens'**)
(*men/women*: irregular plural; the possessive forms are *man's/woman's*, singular, and *men's/women's*, plural)

mania • passion

– *I have a **passion** for jazz.* (Not **mania**)
(a *passion* for something is generally within the bounds of normality or sanity)
– *Gregory has a **mania** about his health.* (Not **passion**)
(= more concern than is normal or sane)

manic • maniac(al) • fanatical

– *He's **fanatical** about cleanliness.* (Not **manic* *maniacal**)
(= obsessed)
– *Her **manic** commitment to work keeps her at the office for up to twelve hours a day.* (= unreasonably enthusiastic)
– *I worked like **a maniac** to get the job finished on time.*
(i.e. with extreme energy; *maniac* is a noun)
– *The film's main characteristic is a note of desperate **maniacal** violence.*
(= demented)

manifestation • demonstration

– *There's a **demonstration** about homelessness in Hyde Park today.* (Not **manifestation**)
(= a public meeting in which people 'demonstrate' their feelings about a cause; often abbreviated informally to *demo*)
– *The number of people out of work is **a clear manifestation/demonstration** of the extent of the recession.*
(*a manifestation* = a sign; *a demonstration* = a piece of evidence, display)

march • walk

– *Shall we **walk** or go by bus?* (Not **march**)
– *During the ceremony, the soldiers **marched** past the tomb of the Unknown Soldier.*
(*march* = walk in step like a soldier)

marine • navy

– *Join **the navy** and see the sea.* (Not **the marine**)
– *He was in the **marines** in World War II.*
(the *Marine* Corps, AmE, or the Royal *Marines*, BrE)
– ***Marine** life is threatened by pollution.*
(*marine* = of the sea)

mark

– *My teacher **gave me a** very good **mark** for my essay.* (Not **put a mark**)
– *I **got a** good **mark** for my essay.* (Not **took a mark**)

marmalade • jam

– *I love **jam** made from fresh strawberries.* (Not **marmalade**)
(= sugar and fruit boiled together: *apricot jam, plum jam, strawberry jam*, etc., made from all kinds of fruit except citrus fruit: *bread and jam* is associated with *tea-time*)
– *What sort of **marmalade** is that? - Oh, the usual. Seville orange.* (Not **orange jam**)
(= sugar and citrus fruit and peel boiled together; *toast and marmalade* is associated with *breakfast-time*)

maroon • chestnut

– *English **chestnuts** are smaller than those the French use for marrons glacés.*
(Not **maroons**; we tend to call the French sweets *marrons glacés*, rather than 'crystallized chestnuts', though we do speak of *crystallized fruits*)
– ***Maroon** doesn't suit you.*
(= a wine-red colour)

marque • make • brand • mark

– *What **make** is your car?*
(Not **marque* *brand* *mark**)
(i.e. What company is the maker?: a *make* of car, watch, computer, dishwasher; compare: *What **type** of car is it? - A hatchback.*)
– *What **brand** of soap do you use?*
(Not **marque** and preferable to *make*)
(i.e. What name does it carry?: a *brand* of soap, toothpaste, washing powder; such products have a *brand name*)
– *Jaguar is now owned by Ford, so this famous **marque** has been saved.*
(= an expensive car from a particular manufacturer; the word *marque* is not in everyday use)
– *My teacher gave me a good **mark** for my essay.* (Not **marque**)

marriage • wedding

– *We had a quiet **wedding**.* (Not **marriage**)
– *What is the secret of a happy **marriage**?*
(*wedding* refers to the ceremony marking the event; *marriage* refers to the state of being married; we can also use *marriage ceremony* in particular contexts: *The **marriage ceremony** took place in a small country church.*)

marry

- *I married in 1980.*
- *I married my wife in 1980.*
  (Not **I married to/with my wife**)
  (*marry* with or without an object)
- *They married their daughter (off) to a professor. They married her off.*
  (*marry* someone *to* someone/*marry off* = find a husband/wife for: old-fashioned in some cultures)
- *I got married in 1980. I got married to John in 1980.* (Not **got married with**)
  (= I married John)
- *I'm married. I'm married to Tom's sister.*
  (Not **I'm married with**)
  (i.e. I married Tom's sister)

martyr • witness • testimony

- *You saw what happened. You were a witness.* (Not **martyr**)
- *Executing terrorists is a sure way of turning them into martyrs.*
  (= people who are put to death for their beliefs and therefore become heroic)
- *The witness's testimony convinced the jury.*
  (= what a witness says, in speech or writing)

mass • bunch • bouquet

- *A bunch of roses costs £10.* (Not **mass**)
  (= a number of things tied together)
- *There was a mass of people queueing for tickets.* (Not **bunch**)
  (= a lot: *mass* for people, things, etc.)
- *I sent a bouquet/a bunch of flowers to say 'thank you'.* (Not **bouquet of flowers**)
  (*bouquet* is more formal; *bunch* is also used for *grapes/bananas*: *a bunch of grapes*)

massage

- *I've had a relaxing massage.*
  (Not **made/done a massage**)
  (and note *give someone a massage*, not **make/do**)

master • Mr

- *You should address the letter to Mr John Smith.* (Not **Master* *Mister**)
  (the written form of address to an adult male; we never write *Mister* in full)
- *Address the letter to Master John Smith.*
  (the written form of address to a young boy, not abbreviated: becoming old-fashioned; these days we generally use the boy's name with no title: *John Smith*)

mathematics/Math(s)

- *Mathematics is a compulsory subject at school.* (Not **(the) mathematics are* *(the)*

mathematic is*)
  (plural form + singular verb)
- *Maths is/Math is a compulsory subject.*
  (*mathematics* is commonly abbreviated to *maths* in BrE and *math* in AmE)
- *I'm doing/taking Math(s) as one of my main subjects.* (Not **making Math(s)**)
  (the name of a subject is often spelt with a capital letter)

matter

- *You've made a spelling mistake in this letter, but it doesn't matter.*
  (Not **it isn't mattering**)
  (stative use only; no progressive form)
- *Are you all right? What's the matter?*
  (Not **What have you?**, etc.)
- *I forgot to post your letter! - It doesn't matter.* (Not **No matter.**)
- *No matter/It doesn't matter where you go, you can't escape from yourself.*
  (*No matter* + question-word introduces a complete sentence: *No matter what I say, you interrupt.*)

matured • mature • ripe/ripen • soften

- *I don't think they're mature enough to get married.* (Not **matured**)
  (= grown up; opposite: *immature*)
- *This cheese isn't mature/hasn't matured.*
  (= developed to its best point, especially for products like cheese and wine)
- *These pears aren't quite ripe, but they will ripen/soften in a few days.* (Not **mature**)
  (*ripe* = ready to be eaten, mainly of fruit)

may/might

- *She may/might arrive early.*
  (Not **mays/mights (to) arrive**)
  (= it's possible; *might* expresses greater uncertainty than *may*)
- *If you had read my letter, you might have avoided this mess.* (Not **may**)
- *May I/Might I make a phone call?*
  (= I'd like permission to; *might* is more polite than *may*, but less commonly used)
- *She said she might be late.*
  (*might* is only a 'past form' in indirect speech)

may be • maybe

- *Maybe I'll ring next week.* (Not **May be**)
  (= perhaps; *maybe* is an adverb)
- *Let's book seats now: it may be our last chance to hear her sing.* (Not **maybe**)
  (= perhaps it is: *may* + *be*)

me • mine
- *Ron is **a friend of mine**.*
  (Not **a friend of me** **a friend of my**)
  (we use a double genitive in this kind of
  construction; similarly *a friend of his/hers/
  ours/yours/theirs*, not **a friend of him/her/
  our/your/their**; we use *'s* after names: *a
  friend of John's*, not **of John**)
- *What must you think **of me**!*
  (object pronoun after a preposition)

meagre • lean • thin • skinny
- *She's **lean** and fit.* (Not **meagre**)
  (= healthily and attractively thin)
- *I wish I weren't so **skinny**.*
  (Not **lean** **meagre**)
  (= thin/underweight in an unattractive way)
- ***Lean** meat is best.* (Not **Meagre**)
  (= without fat)
- *I'd like a **thin** slice of bread please.*
  (Not **lean** **meagre**)
  (= cut thin)
- *Some restaurants serve **meagre** portions.*
  (= small, ungenerous)

meal
- *Let's **have a meal**.*
  (Not **have meal** **take a meal**)
  (= eat)

mean • think
- *I **think** that museums should be free of
  charge.* (Not **I mean**)
  (= that's what I think, that's my opinion)
- *I would have met you at the station. **I mean**,
  you didn't tell me when you'd be arriving.*
  (= that's what I'm trying to say, that's my
  meaning; we often use *I mean* when we want
  to explain something)

meaning • intention • opinion
- *I don't think that's a good decision. What's
  your **opinion**?* (Not **meaning**)
  (= 'what do you think?')
- *It's never been my **intention** to retire early.*
  (Not **meaning**)
  (= plan)
- *What is the **meaning** of 'meagre' in English?*
  (i.e. what sense does it have?)

means
- *We've tried every means possible to rescue
  them. **One means is** still to be tried.*
  (Not **One mean is** **One means are**)
- ***All means** to rescue her **were** tried.*
  (Not **All means was** **All mean was**)
  (= way(s) to an end)

(*means* + singular or plural verb depending
on the word in front of it)
- *Miss Lovelace is a woman **of means**.*
  (Not **with means** **of mean** **of goods**)
  (*of means* = rich)
- *Her **means are** considerable.* (Not **goods**)
  (= wealth and possessions)
  (plural in form + plural verb)
- *May I wait here? - **By all means**.*
  (fixed phrase = certainly)

means • contacts • relations
- *I've got some useful **contacts** in the building
  trade.* (Not **means** **relations**)
  (= people you know who might be useful)
- *We may be rivals in business, but we have
  excellent **relations**.* (Not **contacts**)
  (= dealings, ways of co-operating)
- *We haven't the **means** to go abroad much.*
  (= money)

measles
- ***Measles is** a dangerous disease.*
  (Not **The measle(s)** **Measles are**)
  (no article; plural in form + singular verb;
  similarly: *diabetes, mumps*)

measure
- *This desk **measures** 125 by 60 cms.*
  (Not **is measuring** **makes**)
  (stative use)
- *What are you doing? - **I'm measuring** this
  room.*
  (dynamic use)

meat • meats
- *You shouldn't eat **so much meat**.*
  (Not **so many meats**)
  (*meat* is normally uncountable)
- *You shouldn't use the same knife to cut
  cooked and uncoooked **meats**.*
  (= different varieties of *meat(s)*)

mechanics
- ***The mechanics** of a camera **are** a mystery.*
  (Not **The mechanics is** **The mechanic is**)
  (plural form + plural verb for specific
  references = the way it works)
- ***Mechanics is** a branch of physics.*
  (Not **The mechanics is** **The mechanic is**)
  (plural form + singular verb to refer to the
  academic subject)

media • medium
- *The **media** here **is/are** under the control of
  the government.*
- *News is shown round the globe instantly
  through the **medium** of television.*
  (*media* is the plural of *medium*; *media* can be

used with a singular or plural verb to refer to radio, TV and the press as a group)

medicine
- *Don't forget to take your **medicine**.*
(= a substance to cure an illness; note *take* or *swallow medicine*, rather than *drink*)
- *How long do you have to study **medicine** before you can qualify as a doctor?*
(= the study of disease)

medicine • remedy (for) • cure (for)
- *This herbal mixture is a well-tried **remedy** for the common cold.*
- *A century ago it seemed unlikely that we would find a **cure** for TB.* (Not *remedy*)
- *Aspirin is probably the most useful **medicine** known to man.*
(*remedy* = a specific method of treating something, often traditional; *cure* = something that eradicates a problem entirely; *medicine* = a substance with which to treat illness)

meet • met
- *I'd like to **meet** your mother. I've never **met** her before.*
(*meet - met - met*)

meeting • appointment • rendezvous
- *What time is your **appointment** with the dentist?* (Not *meeting* *rendezvous*)
(= a meeting for professional services)
- *I'm afraid I can't put you through to Mr Grey at the moment. He's at/in a **meeting**.*
(i.e. having a discussion with other people)
- *The directors had a secret **rendezvous** before the formal meeting took place.*
(= a meeting, often secret or in strange circumstances)

meeting • conference • lecture
- *I can't disturb him now. He's **in a meeting/in conference**.*
(= at a private gathering of people where business is discussed)
- *If you're serious about your subject, you mustn't ignore international **conferences**.*
(= formal meetings on a particular subject, often attended by large numbers of people)
- *The Prime Minister will address a **meeting** in Cambridge tonight.* (Not *conference*)
(= a public gathering of people at which there may be a speaker or speakers)
- *When are we **having our** next **meeting**?*
(Not *doing/making a meeting*)

- *Professor Hawkins gave us an interesting **lecture** on termites.* (Not *conference*)
(= a talk, usually by an expert)

member • limb
- *How long does it take for a broken **limb** to mend?* (Not *member*)
(= an arm or a leg)
- *Are you a **member** of the local golf club?*
(= part of)
- *This involves every **member of our family**.*
(Not *family member*)

memoir(s) • memory
- *My **memory** is not as good as it used to be.*
(Not *memoir is/memoirs are*)
(= the ability to remember)
- *He wrote **his memoirs**/They wrote **their memoirs**.*
(= a written account of one's own life experiences; *a memoir*, singular, is an account of a person by someone who knew him/her)

menu • dish of the day
- *What's the **dish of the day**?* (Not *menu*)
(= a particular dish at a restaurant prepared for a particular day of the week)
- *What's on the **menu**?*
(= a list of dishes at a restaurant)

merchant • trader • dealer • tradesman
- *If you have any problems with your car, you should get in touch with your **dealer**.*
(Not *merchant* *trader* *tradesman*)
(*a dealer* = a product specialist who buys at source and sells to the public: *a car dealer, an antique dealer, an art dealer,* etc.)
- *Mr Hill works as a **trader/dealer** in commodities in the City of London.*
(Not *merchant* *tradesman*)
- *Ask your timber **merchant** about fencing.*
(*a merchant* = someone who sells common or ordinary items, such as tea or coffee; *merchant* often combines with the name of the commodity: *a wine merchant, a timber merchant,* etc.; *merchant* = businessman is now old-fashioned: *Once upon a time, a rich **merchant** wanted to find a bride ...*)
- *Value Added Tax has made life difficult for the small **tradesman**.*
(= a shopkeeper)

merit • deserve • be worth
- *It must be hard to decide each year who **merits/deserves** the Nobel Peace Prize.*
(Not *is worth* *worths*)

(*merits* = ought to receive; *deserves* = has earned)
- *I don't think she **deserves** the prize.* (Not **merits* *worths**) (a person *deserves* reward or punishment)
- *This proposal **merits/is worth** your consideration.* (preferable to *deserves*) (something *merits* or *doesn't merit* attention, consideration, etc.)
- *I wouldn't pay so much for a meal. It **isn't worth** it.* (Not **doesn't merit/deserve**) (= doesn't have that value)
- *I wouldn't throw that bike away. **It's certainly worth repairing**.* (Not **It worths to repair.* *It's worth to repair.**) (i.e. it's valuable enough to repair; *worth* is an adjective, not a verb, and is used after *be*)

merry • happy
- *We were all very **happy**.* (= pleased)
- *We were all rather **merry**.* (= cheerful as the result of alcohol, BrE)
- ***Happy/Merry** Christmas!* (we can often use *merry* and *happy* in the same way in certain fixed phrases: *a merry/ happy party,* etc.)

mess
- *I **made a mess** of my exam.* (Not **did**) (= failed to do it properly)
- *Make some jam if you want to, but don't **make** a mess in the kitchen.* (Not **do**) (= make it dirty and untidy)
- *The dog has **done/made a mess** on the doorstep.* (*done/made a mess* = defecated; *made a mess* = e.g. covered with muddy pawmarks: not **done**)

microbe • germ • bug
- *Don't let the baby put that in his mouth! It's full of **germs**.* (Not **microbes* *bugs**)
- *Pasteur's work established the link between **microbes** and disease.* (*germ* is the informal word; *bug* can mean insect, but means *germ* or *virus* in phrases like *pick up a bug, go down with a bug; microbe* is general for 'miniscule life form')

middle • average • on average
- *What's the **average** life expectancy for males in Japan?* (Not **middle* *on average**) (an *average* is calculated arithmetically)
- *This advertising campaign is aimed at people with a **middle** income.* (= in the middle; *middle* is a noun modifier)

- *On **average**, we get 28 cms of rain a year.* (Not **In average**)

middle • centre
- *What's the distance from the **centre** of the circle to the perimeter?* (Not **middle**)
- *I was held up for hours in the **middle** of a traffic jam.* (Not **centre**)
- *Let's take the next photo with you and Jill in the **middle/centre*** (AmE *center*). (*middle* and *centre* are often used in the same way, but the *centre* is an exact point and the *middle* is the central area)

Middle Ages/medieval times • middle years/middle-aged
- *I only caught a glimpse of him, but I would say he was a person in his **middle years**/he was **middle-aged**.* (Not **a middle-aged**) (= aged between 40 and about 60; *middle-aged* is an adjective)
- *The **middle-aged** often bear heavy responsibilities.* (Not **the middle-ageds**) (*the* + adjective for the group as a whole)
- *Life in the **Middle Ages**/in **medieval times** must have been short and brutish.* (= between about 1000 and about 1400 AD in Europe)

middle of the night • midnight
- *The bar closes at **midnight**.* (Not **in midnight* *in the middle of the night**)
- *I couldn't get to sleep, so I watched TV in the **middle of the night**.* (= between midnight and morning)

might • could
- *As we came in to land, we **could see** the lights on the runway.* (Not **might see**) (*could* for ability with verbs of perception)
- *We'd better wait. She **might/could arrive** at any moment.* (*could* or *might* for degrees of possibility; *might* expresses less certainty)
- ***Could I/Might I use** your phone?* (*could* or *might* for permission; *might* is more polite, but less common)

miles/kilometres
- *How many **miles/kilometres** an hour were you **doing**?* (Not **making**)
- *How many **miles/kilometres** to the gallon/ litre do you **do**?* (Not **make**)

military
- *The **military have** surrounded the building.* (Not **The military has* *The militaries have**)

(collective noun + plural verb; *soldiers* is usually preferred to *the military* as a noun)

milk • a carton of/a bottle of/a litre of milk
– *Please get me **a carton of milk/two cartons of milk** while you're out.* (Not *a milk* *two milks*, though *two milks* is possible when ordering something to drink)
– *We don't use **much milk** now the children are grown up.* (Not *a lot of milks*) (*milk* is uncountable)

mince • mincemeat • minced beef/steak
– *These tomatoes have been stuffed with rice and **mince/minced beef/minced steak** (BrE)/**mincemeat** (AmE).* (= ground meat; *minced meat* is rare, perhaps because *mince*, the most common term in BrE, always refers to beef, and if you mean any other kind, you say what it is: *minced lamb, minced pork,* etc.)
– ***Mince pies** are eaten at Christmas in Britain. They're made of pastry stuffed with **mincemeat**.* (Not *stuffed with mince*) (= a sweet spiced mixture of raisins and citrus peel, nowadays without any meat)

mind
– ***Mind** the step!* (= be careful of)
– *Can you **mind** the baby this evening?* (= take care of)
– *Would you **mind waiting** a moment?* (Not *mind to wait*) (= object to waiting)
– *I hope you won't **mind my asking**, but how old are you?* (preferable to *mind me asking*)
– ***To my mind**, that's no way to spend a holiday.* (Not *In my mind*) (= in my opinion)

mine • my
– ***My car's** a Ford.* (Not *Mine car*) (*my* is a possessive adjective, so we use it in front of a noun)
– *This car here is **mine**.* (Not *my*) (*mine* is a possessive pronoun, so we use it on its own)

minority
– *Only a **minority is/are** against the proposal.* (*a/the minority* - without *of* - takes a singular or plural verb, otherwise we have to say *a/the minority **of people** are*; note that *a minority* means less than half of a number and cannot be used with uncountable quantities like *time*)

minute • just a minute
– *Do hurry up! - **Just a minute!*** (Not *Minute!* *A minute!*) (avoid *One minute!* unless you are a person in authority and/or e.g. giving orders)
– *Wait for me here. I'll only be **a minute/I'll be with you in a minute**.*
– *I'll tell him **the minute he arrives**.* (Not *the minute he will arrive*)

miracle
– *I'll do my best, but don't expect me to **do/work/perform a miracle**!* (Not *make*)

miscarriage • misdelivery • abortion
– *This letter isn't for us. It's a **misdelivery/wrong delivery**.* (Not *miscarriage*) (i.e. delivered to the wrong place)
– *Mrs Watson was rushed to hospital, but unfortunately she **had a miscarriage/lost the baby**.* (Not *had a misdelivery*) (= accidentally gave birth too early)
– ***Abortion** raises difficult moral questions.* (= the deliberate ending of pregnancy)

miser • miserly • mean/stingy
– *It makes no sense to be **mean/stingy** with your money when you're alive and then leave a fortune to your heirs.* (Not *miser*) (= ungenerous; *miserly* is literary)
– *The old **miser** preferred to leave all his money to a dogs' home than to his children.* (a *miser* is a *mean* or *stingy* person who hates giving anything and likes to hoard money and possessions)

miserable/wretched • poor
– *Mother Teresa devoted her life to **the poor**.* (= those without money; *poor* and *miserable* occurs as a fixed phrase in e.g. *She lived to a **poor and miserable** old age.*)
– *I've had a cold for three weeks and I'm feeling **miserable/wretched**.* (Not *poor*) (= very unhappy)

misery • poverty
– ***Poverty** is the greatest source of **misery**.* (*poverty* = lack of money; *misery* = unhappiness)
– *The air traffic controllers' strike made our flight home (an) absolute **misery**.* (= a state of pain, unhappiness, discomfort)

Miss/Ms
– *Good morning, **Miss/Ms Jackson**.* (*Miss* is followed by a surname; on its own, it is sometimes used by schoolchildren: *Please Miss!* From one adult to another, e.g. a customer, *Ma'am* or *Madam* is more

socially acceptable than *Miss*: *Can I help you **Ma'am/Madam**?* rather than *Miss*; *Ms* /mɪz, məz/ + surname refers both to married and unmarried women and is more common in writing than speech)

miss • lose • fail

- *I've **lost** my pen.* (Not **missed**)
  (i.e. I can't *find* it)
- *We **lost** a lot of time.* (Not **missed**)
  (= wasted)
- *Hurry or you'll **miss** the train.* (Not **lose**)
  (i.e. you won't be able to *catch* it)
- *I **missed** that film on TV.* (Not **lost**)
  (i.e. failed to take the opportunity to see)
- *I **missed** my English lesson.* (Not **lost**)
  (= failed to attend)
- *The Greens left the district last year and we really **miss** them.* (Not **lose**)
  (i.e. we wish they were here)
- *I just **missed** cutting myself.*
  (Not **failed cutting* *missed to cut**)
  (i.e. I nearly did)
- *I dialled your number for an hour, but I **failed to** get through.* (Not **missed to**)
  (i.e. I didn't succeed in getting through)

missing • lost

- *When he left the country, I knew the money I'd lent him was **lost** forever.*
  (= gone forever, not recoverable)
- *After he left the firm, we found that a lot of important documents were **missing**.*
  (= not there, not where they should be)

mist • fog

- *A light **mist** descended on the mountain.*
- *There's a lot of **fog** today. We often **have fog** in winter.* (Not **It (often) makes**)
  (*mist* is low cloud or very fine rain; *fog* is a thick mixture of moisture and air pollution)

mistake • error • wrong number

- *You've **made** quite a few **mistakes/errors** in this essay.* (Not **done mistakes/errors**)
- *I dialled the wrong number **by mistake/in error**.* (Not **from/in mistake* *by error**)
  (*error* is more formal than *mistake*)
- *Sorry! **Wrong number**!* (Not **Mistake!* *You've made a mistake!**)

mock • make fun (of)

- *On my first day at school, the big boys **made fun of** my spectacles.* (Not **mocked**)
  (= ridiculed, laughed unkindly at)
- *Lydia always **mocks** my attempts to speak French, but at least I'm willing to try.*
  (= disagreeably refuses to take seriously)

mode • in/out of fashion • old-fashioned

- *Wide lapels are the latest **fashion/are in fashion**.* (Not **mode* *in mode**)
- *I thought short skirts had gone **out of fashion**.* (Not **out of mode**)
- *Our **mode of life** had to change when the baby was born.* (Not **fashion of life**)
  (= way of life)
- *There was a time when flared trousers were all **the mode/the latest mode**.*
  (*mode* = fashion is rare and is limited to a few fixed phrases)
- *The word 'topping' to mean 'marvellous' is now **old-fashioned**.* (Not **out of fashion**)
  (*old-fashioned* is more permanent than *out of fashion*)

modest • humble

- *After a **humble/modest** start in life, John achieved great success.*
  (= low)
- *He's too **modest** to mention it, but he won a medal for bravery.* (Not **humble**)
  (= shy, not boastful)
  (*humble* usually describes someone's situation, but not people themselves: *a humble background*; *modest* describes people and their behaviour: *a modest person/manner*; and things that are not showy: *modest qualifications, modest demands*)

molest • derange • disturb • perturb

- *Don't **disturb** him while he's busy.*
  (Not **molest* *derange* *perturb**)
  (= interrupt)
- *Sometimes I think you're quite **deranged**.*
  (= mad)
- *Men who **molest** children must be sick.*
  (= harm, harass or sexually attack)
- *I couldn't help feeling **perturbed** when I saw a policeman at the door.*
  (= rather anxious)

molten • melted

- *Brush the pancake with **melted** butter.*
  (Not **molten**)
- *The **molten** metal flows into these moulds.*
  (Not **melted**)
  (*molten* only for substances that *melt* at very high temperatures like *metal, rock, lava*)

moment • just a moment • the moment

- *Do hurry up! - **Just a moment**!*
  (Not **Moment!* *A moment!**)
  (avoid *One moment!* unless you are a person in authority and/or e.g. giving orders)
- *Wait for me here. I'll only be **a moment**.*

- We'll discuss the matter **the moment he arrives**. (Not *the moment he will arrive* *the moment as he arrives*)
(*the moment* as a conjunction + present tense form when referring to the future)

money • note/coin • cash • (small) change
- I've got **a note/a coin** in my pocket. (Not *a money*)
- Are you carrying **any money/any cash**? (Not *any moneys*, but we can say *any notes*, *any coins*, or *any cash*, uncountable, which refers to coins and/or notes)
- You can **make/earn** a lot of **money** in the used-car trade. (Not *do/gain/win money*)
(*money* is uncountable, though a plural exists in legal English in e.g. *The moneys/monies are in various accounts round the world.*)
- Have you got **(small) change** for a twenty pound note? (Not *(small) money*)
- Keep the **change**! (Not *money*)
(= money that is given back to you when you have paid more than something costs)

montage • assembly
- This table is sold as a kit; the customer does the **assembly**. (Not *montage*)
(= putting it together)
- There's a wonderful **montage** by Matisse called 'Melancholy of the King'.
(= a picture made from pieces that have been cut out and pasted on a surface)

monument • memorial • the sights
- Every November there's a ceremony at the War **Memorial**. (Not *War Monument*)
- There are many **monuments** to Queen Victoria. (Not *memorials*)
(a *monument* is a notable building or statue; a *memorial* is an object - often a monument - created in memory of some person or event: e.g. *a war memorial*)
- I'd love to show you **the sights** of London. (Not *the monuments* *the memorials*)
(= famous buildings, etc., which are particularly interesting to tourists)
- Now I'm in Bangkok I want to **do/see the sights**. (Not *make the sights*)

moody • brave/courageous (of)
- It was very **brave/courageous of** her to risk her own life for the baby.
(Not *moody of* *courageous from*)
(= not showing fear)
- The trouble with Jake is he's so **moody**.
(i.e. his feelings affect his behaviour, so that he is *in a good mood* or *in a bad mood*)

moral • morale • ethic(al)
- How can we raise the **morale** in our company? (Not *moral* *ethic*)
(= spirit, confidence)
- Whatever happened to the old work **ethic**? (Not *moral* *morale*)
(an *ethic* is a system of moral behaviour; the *work ethic* = the belief in hard work)
- Any society has to live by a set of **moral/ethical** principles.
(= based on the idea of right and wrong)

most • the most • mostly
- This is **the most reliable** car I've ever owned. (Not *This is most reliable car*)
(superlative: *the most* + adjective of more than two syllables)
- **Most doctors** don't smoke.
(Not *The most doctors* *Most of doctors*)
- **Most wine** is imported.
(Not *The most wine* *Most of wine*)
(no *the* when *most* means 'the greatest number of' or 'the greatest amount of')
- This car is **most reliable**.
(no *the* when *most* = very)
- My work isn't very varied. It's **mostly** office-work. (Not *most* *the most*)
(= mainly)

most of • most
- **Most people** lead unadventurous lives.
(Not *The most people* *Most of people*)
(*most* + noun for general references)
- **Most of the people I meet** lead unadventurous lives.
(*most of* + *the* for specific references)

most times • most of the time
- You're lucky to find him in. He's out **most of the time**.
(Not *most times* *most of the times*)
- Who's won the World Cup **most times**?
(= on the greatest number of occasions)

move
- It's time for us to **make a move**. (Not *do*)
(*make a move* has two meanings: 'begin to leave' and 'act on a decision'; and note *It's your move* in games like chess)

movement • motion • traffic • business
- The **traffic** in London is very heavy during rush hour. (Not *movement* *motion*)
- Shopkeepers say there isn't much **business** at the moment. (Not *movement* *motion*)
- The **movement/motion** of the ship has made me feel quite seasick.
(= changing position)

Mr • Sir

- *Can I help you, **Sir**?* (Not **Mr**)
  (*Sir* is the form of address to a man whose
  name you don't know, e.g. a customer. It is
  used instead of *Mr* + surname from a junior
  to a senior person: e.g. in organizations and
  schools. In AmE *Sir* is commonly used to
  address a male stranger or acquaintance. We
  can begin a letter to a man we don't know
  with *Dear Sir*, not **Dear Mr**. In BrE, *Sir* +
  first name may be used to address a titled
  man. We can say *Sir John* or *Sir John Smith*,
  but not **Sir Smith**)
- *Good morning, **Mr Smith**.* (Not **Good
  morning, Mr.** **Good morning, Mr John.**)
  (*Mr* is the written form of *Mister*; we use it
  in front of a *surname*, but never in front of a
  first name. A full stop after *Mr* to mark an
  abbreviation is optional; the modern
  tendency is to leave it out)

Mrs • Madam • lady

- *Can I help you, **Madam**?*
  (Not **Mrs** **lady**)
  (*Madam* is the form of address to a woman
  whose name you don't know, e.g. a
  customer. In AmE *Ma'am* is often used to
  address a female stranger or acquaintance.
  We can begin a letter to a woman we don't
  know with *Dear Madam*, not **Dear
  Mrs/Dear Lady**. In BrE, *Lady + first name*
  (*Lady Ann*) or + *surname* (*Lady de Vere*) is
  used to address a titled woman)
- *Good morning, **Mrs Smith**.* (Not **Good
  morning, Mrs.** **Good morning, lady.**
  Good morning, Mrs Ann.)
  (*Mrs + name* is the form we use to address a
  married woman; we use it in front of a
  surname, but not in front of a *first name*)
- ***Mrs Wilkins** is a very nice **lady**.*
  (*lady* is a polite/respectful way of referring
  to a woman)

much/price

- ***How much** is this tie?* (preferable to *What
  price is ...?*; not **What price has?** **How
  many is/has?** **What it makes?**)
- *It's 24 dollars.* (Not **It has 24 dollars.** **It
  has price 24 dollars.**)

much • far • a lot • very (intensifiers)

- *A mountain bike is **much/far/a lot** better
  than an ordinary one.* (Not **very better**)
  (*much/far/a lot* + comparative, or we can say
  very much + comparative: *very much better,
  very much faster*)

- *How was the concert? - **Very good**.* (Not
  Much good. **Far good.** **A lot good.**)
- *This battery isn't **much good/isn't very
  good**.* (Not **far good** **a lot good**)
- *I don't **much like** fish. I don't like fish
  much/a lot. I don't like fish **very much**.*
  (*not much/not a lot* with *like* and *enjoy*)
- *I **much/far prefer** swimming to cycling.*
  (Not **I a lot prefer** **I very prefer**)
  (*much/far* with *prefer*)

much • many • a lot of/lots of (quantity)

- *He hasn't **much money**.*
  (Not **many money**)
  (*not much* + uncountable; avoid *much* +
  affirmative: not **He has much money.**)
- *He hasn't **many books**.* (Not **much books**)
  (*not many* + plural countable; avoid *many* +
  affirmative, especially with concrete nouns,
  not **He has many books.**)
- *He **has a lot of** money. He **has a lot of**
  books.* (or *lots of money/books* informally)
  (*a lot of* + uncountable or plural countable,
  mainly in the affirmative)

much more • (very) much

- *I feel **(very) much** better.*
  (Not **much more better**)
  (= better than I was; *(very) much* with
  comparatives)
- *We need **much more** time.*
  (= more than we have; *much more* +
  uncountable noun)

mud

- *Please don't bring **any mud** into the house.*
  (Not **any muds**)
  (*mud* is uncountable)

music • musician

- *Fidel is a fine **musician**.* (Not **music**)
  (= a performer, composer, etc.)
- *I like **that music**.* (Not **those musics**)
  (*music* is uncountable)

must

- *She **must leave** early tomorrow.* (Not **must
  to leave** **musts to leave** **musts leave**)
  (no *to*-infinitive or third person *-(e)s* ending
  after *must* and other modal verbs)
- ***Must you** leave now?* (Not **Do you must?**)

must • had to

- *Our son was very ill last night and we **had
  to call** the doctor.* (Not **must call** **musted
  call** **musted to call**)
  (*must* has no past form and we use *had to* to
  express 'inescapable obligation' in the past)

– *My lawyer **said** he **must/had to** warn me not to answer any questions.*
(we can use *must* or *had to* as past forms in indirect speech)

must • have to
– *We **have to** complete these tax returns before the end of the month.*
(*have to* is often preferable to *must* when we refer to an 'external authority')
– *You really **must** come and see us some time.*
(*must* is always preferable to *have to* for 'pressing invitations')

must • should/ought to
– *I'm sure your mother's worried. You **should** phone/ought to phone** her.*
(*should* and *ought to* when we give advice)
– *We **must leave** by 3 to avoid the rush hour.*
(Not **should leave/ought to leave**)
(*must* for 'inescapable obligation')

must • will have to
– *I **will have to** phone* them/**must phone** them tomorrow morning.* (Not **will must phone** **will must to phone**)
(we use *must* or *will have to* to refer to future obligation; *must* has no future form)

must have • had to • should have/ought to have
– *I didn't know you'd been so ill. You **should have told/ought to have told** me.*
(Not **must have told** **had to tell**)
(i.e. it was your duty to do this, but you didn't do it)
– *James could see I wasn't well, so I **had to tell** him about it.* (Not **must have told**)
(*had to* for 'inescapable obligation' in the past: I *did* tell him about it)
– *Here's a note from Colin. He **must have called** while we were out.*
(Not **had to call**)
(*must have* + past participle for deduction)

mustn't • shouldn't (worry)/oughtn't to (worry)
– *You **shouldn't worry**./You **oughtn't to worry**.*
(Not **shouldn't to worry** **oughtn't worry**)
(i.e. in my opinion, it is not advisable to; *mustn't worry* is also possible and would simply be stronger)
– *That sign means we **mustn't turn** left.*
(Not **shouldn't** **oughtn't to** **mustn't to** **haven't to**)
(*mustn't* for a strong prohibition imposed by some outside authority)

mustn't (be) • can't (be)
– *I know he looks older, but he **can't be** more than 30.* (Not **mustn't be** **mustn't to be**)
(*can't (be)* is the negative of *must (be)* to express certainty or deduction. Compare: *He **must be** more than 30.*)
– *In future, he **mustn't be** so careless.*
(*mustn't (be)* expresses negative obligation)

mutton • lamb • sheep
– *There was a flock of **sheep** grazing on the hillside.* (Not **mutton(s)** **sheeps**)
(*sheep* - singular and plural form - is the name of the live animal)
– *We're having roast **lamb/mutton** for Sunday lunch.* (Not **sheep**)
(*lamb/mutton* is meat from *sheep*; *lamb* is meat from an animal less than two years old; *mutton* is from an animal of two years or more. These days, *mutton* is rare and expensive. *Lamb* is also used to describe a young live animal: *young lambs in spring*)

my/your, etc. • the
– *The boys were fighting and one of them punched the other **in the teeth**.*
(Not **in his teeth**)
(we often use *the* after prepositions to refer to parts of the body, hair or clothing: *pull someone by the hair, by the sleeve*)
– *I'm cleaning **my teeth**.* (Not **the teeth**)
(normal use of a possessive adjective)

myself • by myself
– *I live **by myself**.*
(= alone)
– *I did all the work **(by) myself**.*
(= without help)
(and for other reflexive pronouns: *yourself, himself, herself, itself, ourselves, yourselves, themselves*)

N

name • call
– ***What's he called?/What's his name?***
(Not **How's he called/named?** **What's he named?**)
– *What's this **called** in Greek?* (Not **named**)
– ***What do you call it?*** (Not **How do you call/name it?** **What do you name it?**)
(*call* for `What name do you use?')
– ***What's your name?***
(Not **What/How do you call yourself?**)
– *They **named/called** him John.*
– *He **was named/called** after his father.*
(*name* or *call* = give a name to people)

nap
- *Don't disturb your mother now. She's **having/taking a nap**.* (Not **doing/making**)

nation • country
- *Haiti is a poor **country**.* (Not **nation**)
  *In 1901 the British **nation** mourned the death of Queen Victoria.* (Not **country**)
- *The President will speak to the **country/nation** this evening.*
  (*country* refers to the area within national borders; *nation* refers to the people who live there; sometimes either word will do)

natives • locals
- *If you're travelling in Wales, you'll find that the **locals** are very friendly.* (Not **natives**)
  (= the people who live there; very informal)
- *The original settlers carried on a brisk trade with the **natives**.*
  (= the original people)
  (*natives* = 'tribal people' is offensive in most modern contexts. The reference is usually joking: *If you want to find a good pub in London, ask one of the **natives**.*)

natural • physical
- *Boxers take a lot of **physical** punishment.* (Not **natural**)
  (= of the body)
- *It's quite **natural** for a boy's voice to break when he's about 14.* (Not **physical**)
  (i.e. to be expected, a process of *nature*)

nauseous • sick
- *Stop the car! I feel **sick**!*
  (AmE also *feel nauseous*)
  (= 'I'm going to vomit'; note also *airsick, carsick, seasick* and *travelsick*)
- *Most women feel **nauseous** in the third month of pregnancy.*
  (= wanting to vomit; *nausea* and *nauseous* are technical medical terms)

nearly • near (to) • close (to)
- *We sheltered in a cave **close to/near** the top of the mountain.* (Not **close the mountain**)
  (*near* and *close to* as prepositions)
- *We were **near to/close to** exhaustion.*
  (*near to* has limited uses, suggesting 'approaching')
- *That dog is vicious. Don't go **near/close**!*
  (Not **nearly** **closely**)
  (*near/close* can be used adverbially)
- *I'm **nearly** ready.*
  (= almost)
  (*nearly* is an adverb of degree)

neat • net • clean • clear
- *The packet contains 60 grams **net**. The **net weight** is 60 grams.*
  (Not **neat/clean/clear weight**)
- *What's the **net tax/profit**?*
  (Not **neat/clean/clear profit**)
  (*net* can combine with *weight, tax, profit*: *net weight* = the actual weight, without packaging; *a net/clear profit* = actual, after all expenses, etc.)
- *We **made a net/clear profit** of £200.*
  (Not **did a clear profit** **neat** **clean**)
  (to *make* or *show* a *clear/net profit/gain*)
- *I've just vacuumed your office, so it's nice and **clean**.* (Not **neat**)
  (= not dirty)
- *My desk is **neat** and tidy.*
  (i.e. everything is well arranged)
- *My desk is **clear**.*
  (= without work that needs attention)
- *I was able to drive to London quickly because the roads were **clear**.* (Not **clean**)
  (= without traffic)

necessary • have to
- *I **have to** go to the doctor's tomorrow.*
  (we normally use *have to* or *must* to express inescapable obligation; *it's/it was/it will be necessary to* are possible, but less common)

necessitate
- *Increasing competition **necessitates** (our) cutting costs.* (Not **to cut**)
  (i.e. we have to cut costs)

need • emergency
- *Dial 999 in **an emergency**.* (Not **a need**)
  (= an unexpected, dangerous event)
- *There was **a great need** for food and tents after the earthquake.* (Not **an emergency**)
  (= a requirement)

need • need to
- *He **needs to leave** now if he's going to get that plane.* (Not **He need/needs leave**)
  (in affirmative sentences, we use the full verb *need to*. *Need* as a modal - that is without the use of *to* after it - occurs mainly in the negative: *We **needn't leave** now*, or with negative adverbs: *I **need hardly tell** you how important this is.*)
- *Need **I say** what a relief it is?*
  (Not **Need I to say**)
- *Do we **need to** carry any money with us?*
  (Not **Do we need carry**)
  (question forms of *need* and *need to*)

need • take
- *It takes an hour by bus.* (Not **It needs**)
  (= 'that's how long the journey lasts')
- *We need an hour to get to the airport.*
  (= 'that's how long we require')
- *This clock needs fixing.* (Not **needs to fix**)

needn't • don't need to
- *We needn't leave yet. We don't need to leave yet.* (Not **needn't to leave**)
  (we use either *needn't* + bare infinitive, or *don't need to*; they have the same meaning: 'we have a choice')

needn't have • didn't have to • didn't need to • shouldn't have • oughtn't to have
The following three sentences mean 'I went there, but it was unnecessary'; after *didn't* in the second and third examples, *have* and *need* are stressed in speech:
- *I needn't have gone to the office yesterday.*
- *I didn't have to go to the office yesterday.*
- *I didn't need to go to the office yesterday.*
The following two sentences mean 'I knew it was unnecessary and I didn't go'; *have* and *need* are unstressed in speech:
- *I didn't have to go to the office yesterday.*
- *I didn't need to go to the office yesterday.*
Shouldn't have and *oughtn't to have* suggest criticism of an action:
- *I shouldn't have paid/I oughtn't to have paid the plumber in advance.*
  (= but I did pay him)

neither • nor • neither ... nor
- *Neither of us is/are working today.*
  (a plural verb is usual in everyday speech, though a singular verb is formally correct)
- *I don't like crowds. - Neither/Nor do I.*
  (Not **Neither and me./Nor and me.**)
- *There isn't any danger. Neither/Nor is there any cause for concern.*
  (Not **Neither/Nor there is any cause ...**)
  (inversion after negative adverbs; formal and emphatic. Compare normal word order with a negative verb: *There isn't (any) cause for concern, either.*)
- *Neither my parents nor my sister is red-haired.* (Not **neither ... or**; the verb generally agrees with the nearest noun)

nerves • nerve • annoyed
- *You've got a nerve asking for a loan when you still owe me £20!*
  (Not **have nerves** **have nerve**)
- *Loud rock music really gets on my nerves.*
  (= irritates me)

- *I have/get awful nerves before exams.*
  (= become anxious, not 'angry')
- *She's annoyed with me.* (Not **has nerves**)

nervous (of) • tense • irritable • irritated
- *Our teacher is so irritable you can hardly ask her a question.* (Not **nervous**)
  (= easily annoyed, often in a bad mood)
- *Our teacher was extremely irritated this morning.* (Not **nervous**)
- *Muhammad is an extremely tense and ambitious young man.* (Not **nervous**)
  (= highly-strung)
- *I feel very nervous/tense before exams.*
  (= anxious, worried)
- *Old Mrs Willis is very nervous of strangers.*
  (Not **nervous with**)
  (= afraid of someone or something)

never
- *I can never read a map and drive a car at the same time.* (Not **can't never**)
  (only one negative in any one clause)
- *Never have so many died for so few.*
  (Not **Never so many have died ...**)
  (inversion after negative adverbs; formal and emphatic; also: *never again, never before* and *at no time*. Compare normal word order: *So many have never died ...*)

new • young
- *I want to have children while I am still young/a young woman.* (Not **new**)
  (= *young* in years; opposite: *old*)
- *Our new secretary is highly-trained.*
  (= newly employed; compare: *Our old secretary was very efficient* = former)
- *Our new car has a catalytic converter.*
  (= recently made or bought; opposite: *old*)

news • a piece of news
- *I have a piece of news that will interest you.*
  (Not **a new** **a news**)
- *The news on TV is always depressing.*
  (Not **The news are**)
  (*news* is plural in form + singular verb)
- *Who gave you the news?*
  (*give someone the news* = fixed phrase)
- *Who's going to break the news to her?*
  (*break the news* = 'give bad news')

next • the next • nearest
- *I'll see you next Monday.*
  (Not **the next Monday**)
  (no *the* in front of *next* in ordinary time references)
- *The next Monday is a holiday.*
  (i.e. that particular one)

- **On the next morning**, *we decided to check out of our hotel.* (Not *On next morning*)
(*the next* after prepositions)
- *Who's* **next** *in the queue?*
(*next* without a noun following it: not a particular reference)
- *Who's* **the next** *(person) in the queue?*
(*the next* (+ noun): particular reference)
- *Where's our* **nearest** *library?* (Not *next*)
(= closest)

next to • next door (to)
- *Who lives* **next door**? (Not *next*)
(when buildings are *beside* each other they are said to be *next door to* each other)
- *The Blairs are our* **next-door** *neighbours.*
(i.e. the people who live next door)
- *There's a field* **next to our house**. (Not *next door to our house* *next our house*)
(= immediately beside)
- *There's a shop* **next to our house/next door to our house**.

nice (to)
- *Try to be* **nice to** *them.* (Not *nice with*)

night: last night
- *They arrived* **last night**. (preferably not *yesterday night* which is old-fashioned/regional; compare *tonight, tomorrow night*)

night: the night • by night/at night/during the night
- *We* **travelled at night/during the night** *to avoid the traffic.* (Not *travelled the night*)
- *We travelled* **by night** *to avoid the blistering heat of the day.*
(*by night* is literary)
- *I'm not sure when it happened: it must have been* **the night** *you came to dinner.*
(i.e. that particular one)

night • evening • tonight
- *They've invited us to drinks* **in the evening** *on Monday/***tonight**. (Not *at night*)
- *New York looks wonderful* **at night**.
(= during the night)
- **Good evening!** *How nice to see you!*
- **Good night!** *Thank you for a lovely evening!*
(*Good evening* is a greeting on arrival; *Good night* is a greeting on departure)

nightclub • cabaret • casino
- *After dinner, we spent a few hours at a* **nightclub**.
(= a place where people go for night-time music and dancing)
- *A nightclub can make a lot of money if it provides a decent* **cabaret**.
(= a show, e.g. comedy, singing, dancing, for a nightclub audience)
- *Only a fool would expect to make easy money at a* **casino**.
(= a place where people play games of chance for money)

nightmare
- *I* **had a** *terrible* **nightmare** *last night.* (Not *I saw a nightmare* *I dreamed a nightmare*)

no • not
- *Who's going to clear up the table? -* **Not me!**
(Not *No me!/Me no!* *No I!/I no!*)
(*Not me* is standard and *Not I* is low frequency, and/or used by people who think it's 'more correct')
- *See you on Monday. - (No),* **not Monday**, *Tuesday.* (Not *no Monday/Monday no*)
(*not* cancels what has just been said)
- *I have* **not** *seen her lately.* (Not *no*)
- *I don't like broccoli.*
(Not *I no like* *I like not* *I not like*)

no • not any
- *I* **can't get any** *news.* (Not *can't get no*)
- *I* **can get no** *news.* (Not *can get any*)
(only one negative in any one clause)

no • not any • none
- *Is there any milk? - No, there's* **none**./*There* **isn't any**. (Not *There's no.* *There's not any.* *There's no any*)
- *Are there any sweets? - No,* **there are none**./***There aren't any**. (Not *No, there are no/no any.* *There are not any.*)
(*none* is a pronoun, so it stands on its own; *any* can also be used as a pronoun and stand on its own; *no* is followed by a noun)
- *There's* **no milk**./*There* **isn't any milk**.
(Not *There's none milk.*)

no one • none
- *She kept* **none** *of his letters.* (Not *no one*)
(= not one)
- *It's* **no one** *you know.* (Not *none*)
(= not any one, not any person)
- **None** *of my friends* **has/have** *been invited to the party.*
(a plural verb is usual after a plural noun in everyday speech, though a singular verb is formally correct after *none*)

no one/nobody • not anyone/anybody
- *There* **was no one/nobody** *at the party whom I knew.* (Not *There wasn't no one/nobody*)
- *There* **wasn't anyone/anybody** *at the party whom I knew.*
(only one negative in any one clause)

no sooner ... than • hardly/scarcely ... when

- *Liz had **no sooner** left the room **than** they began to gossip about her.* (Not **when**) (*no sooner ... than*)
- *Mr Lee had **hardly/scarcely** begun his talk **when** he was interrupted.* (Not **than**) (*hardly/scarcely ... when*)

noble (of) • polite

- *It always pays to be **polite**.* (Not **noble**) (= having/showing good manners; the opposite is *impolite*, not **unpolite**)
- *A lot of nonentities claim **noble** birth.* (i.e. descent from the aristocracy, or *nobility*)
- *It was very **noble of** you to stand in for me when I was away.* (Not **noble from**) (= self-sacrificing)

nod   shake   wink

nod • shake • wink

- *I asked him if he wanted to join us and he **nodded**/he **shook his head**.* (*nod* = say yes, head movement down and up; *shake your head* = say no, head movement from side to side)
- *You **winked**, so I knew you were joking.* (= shut one eye to give a signal)

noise • noises

- *Don't **make a/so much noise**. The baby's asleep.* (Not **do a noise** **make noises**) (= create a disturbance)
- ***Noise** is a kind of pollution.* (Not **The noise**) (*noise* used as an abstract noun: no article in general statements)
- *Jimmy put his hand over his mouth and started **making** funny **noises**.* (Not **doing**) (= making sounds; *noise* = 'disturbance' may be countable or uncountable; *noises* can be used to mean separate sounds)

nominate • name

- *We **named** her Sylvia after my wife's mother.* (Not **nominated**) (= gave her a name)
- *Who's been **nominated** as the next president of the United Nations?* (Not **named**) (= named for an official position)

nonsense • a piece of/a bit of nonsense

- *The article wasn't meant to be taken seriously. It was just **a piece of/a bit of nonsense**.* (Not **a nonsense**) (= something of no importance, a trifle)
- *The whole idea is just **a lot of nonsense/a nonsense**.* (Not **a lot of nonsenses**) (*a nonsense* = a stupidity)
- *I've had enough of Pauline's **nonsenses**.* (*nonsense* is nearly always uncountable, but does have countable uses which are very condemnatory)

nostalgic • homesick • miss • long for • long to

- *I had to come home because I was feeling **homesick**.* (Not **nostalgic**)
- *I **missed/longed for** my home town when I lived abroad.* (Not **I was nostalgic for**)
- *I **long to visit** the place I was born in.* (Not **am nostalgic to see** **long for visiting**) (*long* = want very much, have a strong desire, feel *longing* for)
- *There are so many sights and sounds that evoke in us **nostalgic** memories.* (= affectionate feelings about the past)

not • do not/does not/did not

- *I **don't speak** Basque. He **doesn't speak** Basque. She **didn't speak** Basque.* (Not **I speak not** **I not speak** **don't speaks** **doesn't speaks** **didn't spoke**, etc.)
- *He asked me **why I didn't like it**.* (Not **why I not liked it** **why I no liked it**) (we use *do/does/did* to form the negative with verbs other than *be, can*, etc.)

not a • no

- *He's **not a** lawyer./He **isn't a** lawyer.* (Not **He's not no lawyer./He isn't no lawyer.**)
- *He's **no** lawyer.* (*He's not a lawyer* is a statement of fact; *He's no lawyer* = he lacks the qualities that would make him one. Compare: *He's **no** genius* = He's not at all clever)

not any more • no longer/not any longer

- *Hurry up! I **can't wait any more/any longer**.* (Not **can't wait no more/no longer** **anymore** **nomore**) (only one negative in any one clause)
- *It's a situation we can't ignore **any longer**. It's a situation we can **no longer** ignore. It's a situation we can ignore **no longer**.* (*any longer* is normal in the end-position; *no longer* is normal in mid-position, but is very emphatic or formal in the end-position)

not many/not much • no

- *How many people will be coming to your party? - **Not many**.* (Not **No many.**)
- *How much water does this pot plant need? - **Not much**.* (Not **No much.**)

not to/not -ing • Don't ...

- *We soon learnt **not to ask** too many questions.* (Not **to not ask* *to don't ask**)
- *Tell them **not to make** a noise.* (Not **to not make* *to don't make**) (*not* goes before a *to*-infinitive)
- *I must apologize **for not having** written.* (Not **for having not written**) (*not* goes before the *-ing* form)
- ***Don't eat** that!* (Not **No eat* *Not eat**) (*Don't* introduces a negative imperative)

notable • remarkable

- *Meeting you again was a **remarkable** coincidence.* (Not **notable**)
- *Owen was a **notable/remarkable** athlete.* (*notable* = excellent; *remarkable* = unusual; both can mean 'worth noting')

note (down) • mark

- *Has he **marked** our work yet?* (Not **noted**) (= corrected)
- *Her absence was **noted**.* (Not **marked**) (= seen and remembered)
- *The policeman carefully **noted (down)** what the witness told him.* (Not **marked**) (*noted* = 'made a mental note'; *noted down* = wrote)
- *Who made these **marks** on the desk?* (Not **notes**) (= e.g. scratches)
- *Josephine always gets high **marks** for her essays.* (Not **notes**) (= grades)
- *I can lend you my **notes**.* (Not **marks**) (= written records of e.g. lectures)

nothing • not anything

- *They **didn't teach me anything** at school.* (Not **didn't teach me nothing**)
- *They **taught me nothing** at school.* (only one negative in any one clause)

notice

- *You **never notice** what's going on around you.* (Not **aren't ever noticing**) (stative use)
- *Did you **notice him leave/leaving**?* (Not **notice him to leave**) (bare infinitive = the whole action, or *-ing* = part of the action after *notice someone*)

notice • observe • remark

- *'You're looking very well!' she **remarked/observed**.* (Not **noticed**) (= said; both words are formal and often used as reporting verbs)
- *I've **noticed/observed** that there are more butterflies this year.* (Not **remarked**) (= seen; *notice* is casual/involuntary; *observe* is formal/deliberate; *remark* = see is archaic)

notice • placard • sign • cartel

- *A man appeared with a **placard** that said 'Repent!'.* (Not **notice* *cartel**) (= a large notice which may be carried)
- *I know there's a meeting, because someone pinned a **notice** about it on our notice board.* (Not **placard* *sign* *cartel**) (= a written announcement)
- *We can't turn left. There's a No Entry **sign**.* (Not **notice* *placard* *cartel**) (= a notice providing directions, especially road signs and street signs)
- *The major oil companies constantly deny they operate as a **cartel**.* (= an association of companies working together to control prices)

novel • short story • set book

- *'Jane Eyre' is our **set book** for next year's English exam.* (Not **novel**) (= a book that is required reading for an examination)
- *James Joyce's 'The Dead' is the best **short story** in this collection.* (Not **novel**) (= a work of fiction of any length, but not as long as a novel; the term *novella* = a 'long short story' exists but is little used)
- *Kingsley Amis's 'Lucky Jim' is one of the most successful first **novels** ever written.* (= a full-length work of fiction)

nowhere • not anywhere

- *I've looked everywhere for my glasses but I **can't find them anywhere**.* (Not **can't find them nowhere**)
- *I've looked everywhere for my glasses and **can find them nowhere**.* (emphasis on *nowhere*) (only one negative in any one clause)

nuisance • pest • trouble

- *People who take things from my desk and never return them are a real **nuisance/pest**.* (Not **a trouble**) (referring to people who annoy; *pest* is even less complimentary than *nuisance*; both words describe people: note *They are a **nuisance**; nuisances* usually refers to

specific individuals: *I hope these two young nuisances haven't tired you out.*)
- *Constant roadworks everywhere are a nuisance.* (Not *pest*)
(*nuisance* can also describe things, events)
- *Restaurants should be visited regularly by pest control officers.* (Not *nuisance*)
(*pests* are animals like mice, insects like cockroaches, that can e.g. carry disease)
- *This letter from the tax inspector means one thing only: trouble!*
(= a source of worry, anxiety)

number
- *Our village only numbers about 150 people.* (Not *is numbering*)
(stative use = that is the total)
- *I'm numbering the pages of my manuscript.*
(dynamic use = giving a number to)

nurse • nanny
- *As they both work, they employ a nanny to look after the baby.* (Not *nurse*)
(*nurse*, as in *children's nurse* = nanny, is old-fashioned)
- *My sister has just qualified as a nurse and got a job at our local hospital.*
(= a person, usually a woman, who takes care of the sick; and note *male nurse*)

nursery • kindergarten/nursery school • day nursery
- *How old should children be before they can go to kindergarten/(a) nursery school?* (Not *nursery* *baby school*)
(= a school for children aged 3-6)
- *Many working mothers need the services of a day nursery.* (Not *kindergarten*)
(= a place for children of pre-school age; compare a *crèche* which is for babies)
- *Good manners should be learnt/taught in the nursery.*
(= when you are very young)
(*nursery* is mainly used metaphorically; the meaning a 'special room for young children in a private house' is old-fashioned)

nylon • carrier bag
- *Is that carrier bag strong enough for all those things?* (Not *nylon*)
- *Nobody wears nylon shirts these days.*
(= made of nylon)

O

object to
- *A lot of people object to smoking in public places.* (Not *object to/against smoke*)

(*to* functions as a preposition + *-ing* here, not as part of the infinitive)

observe
- *A good novelist observes everything and misses nothing.* (Not *is observing*)
(stative use describing someone who is always *observant*)
- *The police have been observing the building for some time now.*
(dynamic use = actively watching; keeping under observation)
- *I observed him climb/climbing the wall and enter/entering the garden.*
(bare infinitive = the whole action, or *-ing* = part of the action after *observe someone*)

occasion • bargain/good buy • second-hand • opportunity
- *I bought this suit in the sales. It was a real bargain/a good buy.* (Not *an occasion*)
(i.e. it cost less than its true value)
- *I didn't buy this new. It was second-hand.* (Not *an occasion*)
(= previously owned by someone else)
- *You mustn't miss 'The Wizard of Oz' on TV tonight. It's a wonderful opportunity to see it again.* (Not *occasion*)
- *Our son's wedding was a really memorable occasion.*
(= an event)

occasionally • very occasionally
- *We go to the theatre occasionally.*
- *We only go to the theatre very occasionally.*
(*occasionally* = sometimes; *very occasionally* = rarely)

occupation • profession • job
- *I'm applying for a job in a bank.*
(Not *an occupation* *a profession*)
(*job* is the normal word to describe what someone does for a living; it cannot always be replaced by *occupation*)
- *This form asks for details about your age, occupation/job, etc.* (Not *profession*)
(*occupation* is the formal word for *job* and is used in limited contexts like form-filling)
- *After studying law, I entered the legal profession.* (Not *job* *occupation*)
(high-status work that requires special training and education: law and medicine are *professions*; lawyers and doctors are *professional* people)

of • by

- *It's a piece **by** Mozart*. (Not **of**)
  (= composed by)
  (compare *written by, painted by, made by*)
- *The event is described in **a letter of Mozart's***. (Not **a letter of Mozart* *a letter of Mozarts'* *a letter by Mozart**)
  (= one of Mozart's letters: double genitive)

of • off

- *My car is **off** the road just now*. (Not **of**)
  (i.e. not on the road, not being used)
- *Turn the light **off***. (Not **of**)
- *London is north **of** Paris*. (Not **off**)
  (direction)

of • 's/s' (apostrophe s, s apostrophe)

's and s' normally only for people and some time references
- *Where's my **mother's** handbag?*
  (Not **the handbag of my mother**)
  (*'s*: possession by a person in the singular)
- *We have redesigned the **girls'** uniforms*.
  (Not **the uniforms of the girls**)
  (apostrophe (') added to the plural of personal nouns)
- *Amy fancies **an actress's** career/the career **of an actress***. (Not **actress' career**)
  (*'s* added to singular nouns ending in *s*)
- *Where shall I put the **children's** toys?*
  (Not **childrens'* *the toys of the children**)
  (*'s* added to irregular plurals like *men, women* and *children*)
- *Have you seen **John's** new car?*
  (Not **the new car of John**)
  (add *'s* to a name to show possession)
- *Have you seen **Doris's** new car?*
  (Not **the new car of Doris* *Doris' car**)
  (add *'s* to a name to show possession, even if the name already ends in *s*: first names like *Charles* and *Doris*; surnames like *Jones* and *Watts*)
- *It was **a week's** work*.
  (rather than 'the work of a week')
  (*'s/s'* for some time references and fixed phrases like *the earth's surface*)

compound nouns or of for non-living things
- *Have you seen **the car key**?* (Not **the car's key**; preferable to *the key of the car*)
- *We land at **Luton Airport***. (Not **Luton's Airport* *the Airport of Luton**)
  (we don't normally use *'s* and *s'* for non-living things; where possible, we prefer to use a compound noun rather than a construction with *of*: *the table-leg*, rather than *the leg of the table*)

- *The cost **of living** is too high*.
  (Not **The living's cost* *The living cost**, though we can use the plural *living costs*)
  (if we cannot form a compound, we use *of*)
- *John is **a friend of my father's/of yours***.
  (Not **a friend of my father/of you**, but we can say *my father's friend, your friend*)
  (*of* and *'s* together in 'double genitives')

of course/indeed/naturally

- *Is it hot outside? - **Yes, it is**, etc.*
  (Not **Of course!* *Indeed!**)
  (we normally use a verb in short answers. *Of course!, Naturally!* and *Indeed!* are so emphatic that they can sound rude)
- ***Naturally**, I found it difficult at first*.
  (preferable to *Of course*, which is often over-used to introduce a remark)
- *You will be home this evening, won't you? - **Of course***.
  (i.e. it goes without saying)

offer: on offer • offered

- *No alcohol was **offered** at the party*.
  (Not **on offer**)
  (i.e. for people to accept)
- *They've got 22-inch colour TVs **on offer** for £250 at Randall's*. (Not **offered**)
  (= for sale, especially cheaply)

office • agency

- *Our company can't afford the services of a big advertising **agency***. (Not **office**)
  (an *agency* provides a service, e.g. *a travel agency, an employment agency*)
- *Reuters is a big news agency with **offices** all over the world*.
  (= rooms/buildings where work is done)

officer

office worker

officer • office worker

- *Since we computerized our firm, we employ fewer **office workers***. (Not **officers**)
  (= people who work in offices)
- *An army **officer** expects to be saluted*.
  (= a person in the armed forces, police force, etc., in a position of authority)

officious • obliging • unofficial
- *They say he's retiring, but the news is still* **unofficial**. (Not **officious* *obliging**)
  (= not formally announced, not *official*)
- *The waiters in that restaurant are always so helpful and* **obliging**. (Not **officious**)
  (= willing to help)
- *I'm sure my visa renewal is being held up by some* **officious** *clerk*.
  (= over-zealous in applying the rules; *officious* suggests the abuse of power by minor officials; very uncomplimentary)

offspring
- *Her one* **offspring isn't** *like her at all*.
- *Her* **offspring are** *all terribly like her*.
  (Not **offsprings**)
  (*offspring* is followed by a singular verb to refer to one and a plural verb to refer to more than one, but we cannot say **an offspring**; however, *child/son/daughter/children* are nearly always preferable to refer to humans)

often • several times
- *She rang* **several times** *today*. (Not **often**)
- *We* **often** *sleep late on Sundays*.
  (*several times* for repeated actions; *often* for habit)

old • olden
- **In the old days/In olden times** *this was a prosperous town*. (Not **In old time**)
  (*in the old days* and *in olden times* are fixed phrases; *olden* refers to a remote time in the past, and is not much used these days)

once • one time • at once
- **One time** *in a million, someone will praise your work*. (Not **Once**)
- *The phone rang just* **once**. (Not **one time**)
- *I wish you'd do as I tell you* **for once**.
  (Not **for one time**)
  (= on this one occasion, 'for a change')
- *The postman calls* **once a day**.
  (Not **one time a day**)
  (*once, twice, three times*, etc.)
- *Let's try* **once more/one time more/one more time**.
- *Please answer the phone* **at once**.
  (= immediately)

one • it
- *Did* **that letter** *from America arrive? - Yes,* **it** *came this morning*. (Not **one**)
  (specific reference: *that letter → it*)
- *Did* **a letter** *arrive for me? - Yes,* **one** *arrived this morning*. (Not **it**)
  (non-specific reference: *a letter → one*)

- *What do you think of* **this cake**? - **I like it**.
  (Not **I like.* *I like one.**)
  (*like* is transitive and must have an object: specific reference here, therefore *it*)
- *Would you like* **a biscuit**? - *Yes,* **I'd like one**.
  (Not **I'd like.* *I'd like it.**)
  (*like* is transitive and must have an object: non-specific reference here, therefore *one*)

one • ones
- *Which packet do you want? -* **The large one**.
  (preferable to *The large./The large packet.*)
  (*one* replaces a singular countable noun that has just been mentioned)
- *Which soap packets did you buy?-* **The large ones**. (Not **The larges.**; preferable to *The large./The large packets.*)
  (*ones* replaces a plural countable that has just been mentioned: we never use an adjective as a noun form, so we have to say *I want* **the red ones**, not **the reds**, etc.)
- *Don't use powdered milk. Use* **this fresh (milk)**. (Not **this fresh one**)
  (*one/ones* cannot replace an uncountable)

one/ones: the one • that which • the ones • those which
- *Have you seen* **this dictionary**? - **Is it the one** *that has just been published?*
  (preferable to *Is it that which ... ?*)
- *Have you seen* **these dictionaries**? - **Are they the ones** *that have just been published?*
  (preferable to *Are they those which ... ?*; *that which* and *those which* are very formal)

one's
- **One's** *confidence is easily shaken*.
  (possessive of *one*, formal for 'everyone's' and answering the question *Whose?*)
- *When* **one's** *young,* **one's** *always being asked to parties*.
  (*one is* = a person is, answering the question *Who's/Who is?*)

only
- *It's the* **only one** *(that) I like*.
  (Not **It's the only (that) I like.**)

only then
- *I heard an ambulance in the distance.* **Only then did I realize** *there'd been an accident*.
  (Not **Only then I realized**)
  (= it was not until that moment that ...)
  (inversion after negative adverbs; formal and emphatic. Compare normal word order: *I* **realized** *only then there'd been an accident*; other combinations with *only* work in the

same way: *Only after, Only if, Only by, Only later, Only when, Only with,* etc.)

open: in the open • out of doors • outside
- *A large crowd had gathered **outside the building**.* (Not **out of doors the building** **outside of the building**)
  (*outside* is a preposition here)
- *It's a fine day. Let's sit **in the open/out of doors/outside**.*
  (adverbs = outside a building: the opposites are *inside, indoors*)

open • on • alight
- *Is the **tap on**/the **light on**?*
  (Not **open** **alight**)
  (*taps, lights, the gas, the electricity* can be *on* or *off*)
- *Are all the **doors and windows open**?*
  (Not **on**)
  (*doors/windows* are *open* or *closed/shut*)
- *By the time the firefighters arrived, the building was well and truly **alight**.*
  (= burning)

open • turn on
- ***Turn on** the tap/the light.* (Not **Open**)
  (*turn on* for *taps* and *switches*)
- *Please **open** the **window/the door**.*
  (*open* for *windows* and *doors*; note *open/draw* the *curtains*, not **turn on**)

opened • open
- *When we got home, we found that all the windows were **open**.* (Not **opened**)
  (= not closed: that's how we found them)
  (*opened* is not the adjectival equivalent of *closed* or *shut*: *All the windows were* **closed/shut**.)
- *When we got home, we found that all the windows had been **opened**.*
  (= someone *had opened* them; *opened* here is a past participle)

opportunity of/to • chance of/to
- *Book now, or you won't have **a chance of getting** seats.* (Not **an opportunity of**)
  (= 'a hope')
- *A holiday in the Alps would give us the* ***chance/opportunity to get*** *fit.*
- *Our holiday gave us a **chance/an opportunity of getting** fit.*
  (*to* or *of* + *-ing* after *chance/opportunity*)
- *You never **miss an opportunity to miss** an opportunity.* (Not **lose an opportunity**)

oppose • be opposed to
- *We **are opposed to**/We **oppose** the plan to build a motorway in this beautiful area.*

(Not **We are oppose(d) the plan** **We oppose to the plan**)

opposite (of/to)
- *They're building a supermarket **opposite**.* (*opposite* as an adverb)
- *We have **opposite points of view**.* (*opposite* as an adjective before a noun)
- *He's the **opposite of/to** what I'd imagined.* (*opposite* as a noun, or in place of a noun, followed by *of* or *to*)
- *The **house opposite** is up for sale.* (Not **the opposite house**) (*opposite* as an adjective after a noun for physical position)
- *There's a bank **opposite my office**.* (Not **opposite from** **opposite of**) (*opposite* as a preposition; *to* is possible after *opposite*, but unnecessary)

organism • body • the system • constitution • organization
- *There's a limit to the amount of abuse the human **body** can take.* (Not **organism**)
- *Too much sugar is simply bad for **the system**.* (Not **the organism**) (= the way the body works)
- *You need a terrific **constitution** to be able to walk 40 miles in a day.* (Not **body** **system** **organism**) (= the condition of the body; we can refer to *a weak/strong constitution*)
- *Plankton is made up of billions of tiny **organisms**.* (Not **organizations**) (= living creatures)
- *As one of the biggest Japanese companies, Toyota is a huge **organization**.* (= a group of people with a shared purpose)

organize • arrange
- *We've **arranged to meet** next Friday.* (Not **organized to meet**) (= planned and agreed)
- *We've **arranged/organized** a surprise party for Uncle Matthew's eightieth birthday.* (= done everything that is necessary to ensure that it is a success: *arrange/organize* + direct object)

orientate/orient (towards) • adapt (to)
- *Since we were taken over, we have had to **adapt** (ourselves) **to** a new style of management.* (preferable to *orientate to*) (= learn how to deal with)
- *A lot of our business is **orientated** (BrE)/ **oriented** (AmE) **towards** the US market.* (= directed towards)

original • model

- *Swedish welfare systems are **a model** of social concern.* (Not **an original**)
  (= a perfect example)
- *The design of the Pompidou building in Paris is completely **original**.* (Not **model**)
  (= unlike anything else)
- *The **original** of Botticelli's 'Primavera' is in the Uffizi Gallery.* (Not **model**)
  (i.e. it's not a copy)

other • next

- *It was too wet to go climbing last weekend, so we've put it off till **next** weekend.*
  (Not **the next* *the other**)
- *We went climbing **the other day**, but the weather was awful.*
  (= a few days ago)

other • others • another

- *We're a long way ahead; let's wait for **the other people/the others** to catch up with us.*
  (Not **the others people* *others**)
  (= the rest of the people)
- *There must be **another way** of solving the problem.* (Not **other way**)
  (= a different way)
- *There must be **other ways** of solving the problem.* (Not **others ways**)
  (= some different ways)

out of • outside • out

- *We ran **out of the** burning **building** and **into** the courtyard.*
  (Not **out the building* *out from the building**; *out the building* is heard, especially in AmE, but is not universally acceptable)
  (i.e. we were *in/inside* it and we went *out of* it; *out of* is the opposite of *into* and we use it with movement verbs like *go* and *walk*)
- *Mr Rayne is **out of the office** at the moment. He is **out**.* (Not **out the office**)
  (i.e. he is not here; the opposite is *in*; *out of* is a preposition and *out* is an adverb)
- *Wait **outside my office**. Wait **outside**.* (Not **out of my office* *outside of my office**)
  (i.e. be immediately outside: *outside* can be a preposition or an adverb; as a preposition it shows location, not direction)
- *When are we going to paint **the outside of** the house/paint **the outside**?*
  (*outside* can be a noun)

over • above • on top of

- *Keep the blankets **over you**.*
  (Not **above you* *on top of you**)

(*over*, opposite *under* = covering and sometimes touching)
- *There was no room in the locker **above** my seat.* (preferable to *over*; not **on top of**)
  (*above*, opposite *below* = at a higher level, not touching)
- *My bedroom is **over/above the kitchen**.*
  (Not **on top of the kitchen**)
  (both prepositions can be used to mean 'vertically at a higher level')
- *Details are given in the paragraph **above**/the **above** paragraph.* (Not **over**)
  (a convention in writing)
- *Details are given **over**. See **over**.*
  (= on the next page; formal written style)
- *Don't put anything **on top of the TV** please.*
  (Not **over the TV* *above the TV**)
  (*on top of*, preposition = touching; compare *I was standing **on/at the top** of the mountain*, where *top* is a noun)

overdone

- *The meat is **overdone**.* (Not **too cooked**)
  (i.e. it has been cooked too much; we often use *over* as a prefix to suggest 'too much': *The pear is **overripe**. The bill is **overdue**.* Some native speakers, especially AmE, are using *overly* as an intensifier in e.g. *We shouldn't be **overly concerned*** instead of *We shouldn't be **over-concerned/too concerned***; *overly* should be avoided)

overhear • misunderstand • fail to hear

- *It's important not to **misunderstand** what I'm telling you.* (Not **overhear**)
  (= understand wrongly, which could lead to a *misunderstanding* = a cause for disagreement, complaint)
- *I couldn't help **overhearing** what you just said.* (Not **misunderstanding**)
  (= hearing by accident, or without the speaker's knowledge)
- *I'm sorry. I **failed to hear** what you said.*
  (= didn't hear)

overlook • look over • oversee

- *Would you like to **look over** the house?*
  (Not **overlook* *oversee**)
  (= look round, have a view of)
- *I've been through your list carefully and I hope I haven't **overlooked** anything.*
  (Not **looked over* *overseen**)
  (= failed to notice)
- *All his work needs to be **overseen**.*
  (= watched to make sure it's done properly)
- *My room **overlooks/looks over** the garden.*
  (= has a view of)

overtake • take over

– When does the new management **take over**? (Not *overtake*)
(= take charge; when one company buys another it *makes a takeover*)
– Allow plenty of room if you want to **overtake** a cyclist. (Not *take over* *surpass*)
(= pass e.g. in a vehicle)

P

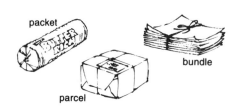

packet

bundle

parcel

packet • parcel • bundle

– I know this **parcel** is large, but can I send it airmail please? (Not *packet* *bundle*)
(*parcel*, BrE, *package*, AmE = a wrapped item or items to be posted; but note that *a packet* can mean 'a small parcel')
– Is a large **packet** of biscuits cheaper than two small ones? (Not *parcel*)
(= a container: *a packet of cigarettes*, etc.)
– We put out a **bundle** of papers for collection every week. (Not *packet* *parcel*)
(= papers, clothes, etc., tied or held together)

pacify • calm (someone) down

– I'm in such a state, I just can't **calm down**. (Not *I can't pacify* *I can't calm*)
(= become less tense, relax)
– I had to pick up the baby to **pacify him/calm him down**/help him **calm down**. (= cause to become quiet)
– The shareholders are so angry, there's nothing the chairman can say to **pacify** them. (Not *calm them down*)
(= 'meet their complaints')

pain

– I need to see the dentist at once. **I'm in** awful **pain**. (Not *I pain.*)
– She's sleeping better now that she's **out of pain**. (Not *doesn't pain*)
(= feels/doesn't feel physical pain)
– I **had** such **a pain** (in the stomach) after eating oysters! (Not *made a pain* *had an ache* *had a hurt*)
(= felt physical pain)

painful • difficult

– I find it **difficult** to understand that kind of behaviour. (Not *painful* *I have pain to*)
(= not easy)
– My leg is still pretty **painful** after the accident. (Not *difficult*)
(i.e. it causes me to feel pain)
– It was a **difficult/painful** decision. (both possible with words like *decision* and *situation*)

panties/pants

– How much **is this pair of panties/pants**?
– How much **are these panties/pants**? (Not *is this panty/is this pant*)
(*panties* or *pants*: underwear for women; *pants*: underwear for men; *pants*, not *panties*, is also informal for *trousers* for both sexes; plural form only)

papa • the Pope

– **The Pope** received a big welcome in Mexico City. (Not *The Papa*)
– Do you think your **papa** will be prepared to lend us his car for the evening? (= father, old-fashioned or precious)

paper • a piece/sheet of paper

– Do you need **a piece/sheet of paper/some pieces/sheets of paper/some paper**? (Not *a paper* *some papers*)
(*paper* in this sense is uncountable; *sheet* is more precise than *piece*; compare *a paper* = a newspaper; *a paper* is also a piece of writing such as an essay; *the papers* = the newspapers; *papers* = documents)

parents • relatives/relations • relationship (with) • relevant

– I have a few **relatives/relations** in Australia. (Not *parents*)
(= members of my family who are *related*, but not usually my mother or father)
– Eric's **relationship with** his boss has always been difficult. (Not *relations* *relatives* *relationship to*)
(referring to how they get on together)
– Eric has good **relations** with everyone. (= understanding and communication)
– I don't know what their **relationship** is. (e.g. of a couple: referring to how they feel about each other)
– My **parents** are over eighty but still in excellent health. (= mother and father)
– These statistics are out of date, so they're not **relevant**. (Not *have no relationship*)
(= related to the subject)

parking • parking space • car park
- *It was ages before I found **a parking space/any parking**.* (Not *a parking**)
  (= a place or some space to leave a vehicle; *parking* is uncountable)
- *There's a large **car park** attached to the supermarket.* (Not *parking**)
  (= an open space or building in which many vehicles may be left)
- ***Parking** is expensive in central London.*
  (Not *The parking**)

part • depart
- *The train **departs** at 4.15.* (Not *parts**)
  (*depart* is more formal than *leave*)
- *I'm afraid the time has come for us to **part**!*
  (= be separated, not be together)

part • place
- *Florence - that's the **place** where I'd like to live!* (Not *part**)
- *That **part** of Italy round Siena is out of this world.* (Not *place**)
  (= an area: *part* of a country)
- *Which **part of/place in** the brain controls speech?* (Not *place of* *part in**)

part • share
- *I think you've had more than your fair **share** of this champagne.* (Not *part**)
- *The design department is in a different **part** of the building.* (Not *share**)
  (= an area lying within a larger area)

part • side
- ***Are** you on my **side** or his?* (Not *part**)
  (*to be on someone's side* = to support)
- *You're always **taking his side/part**.*
  (*to take someone's side/part* = to support)
- ***For my part**, I agree with everything you say.* (Not *For my side/From my side**)
  (= speaking for myself)

participate (in)/take part (in) • share
- *We **share** your sorrow.* (Not *participate (in)* *take part (in)**, though *share in your sorrow* would be possible)
  (i.e. we join with you; *partake of*, not *in*, is old-fashioned and should be avoided)
- *We all **participated in/took part in** raising money for children in need.* (Not *shared**)
  (= co-operated with others)

particular • private
- *I'd like to learn English, but I can't afford **private lessons**.* (Not *particular lessons**)
  (= lessons given to one person)

- *I have a **particular** reason for asking you for your telephone number.*
  (= special)

party
- *We're **giving/having a party** on Friday.*
  (Not *doing/making a party**)

pass (by/from) • cross
- ***Cross** the road carefully.* (Not *Pass**)
  (= go across)
- *Would you mind posting this? You'll **pass** a letterbox on your way to the station.*
  (= go past)
- *I **pass (by)** your house every morning on my way to work.* (Not *pass from**)
  (*by* = close to)
- *Many traditions are **passed from** one generation to another.*
  (= transferred)
- ***A month has passed/It's a month** since I left home.* (Not *It's passed a month**)

pass • happen
- *I can't remember what **happened** just before the crash.* (Not *passed**)
  (*pass* and *come to pass* = 'happen' are archaic)
- *Your sister **passed** me in her sports car, driving at great speed.*
  (= overtook or went past)

pass (through) • sieve • filter
- *The flour's a bit lumpy. I think you should **sieve** it before using it.* (Not *pass* *filter**)
  (= put through *a sieve*, i.e. a fine net on a frame for use in the kitchen)
- *I think you should **pass** the flour **through** a sieve before using it.*
  (*pass* something *through* something, also *pass a thread through a needle*)
- *We always **filter** our water before drinking it.* (Not *pass* *sieve**)
  (*pass through a filter*, i.e. pass through a device that removes solids or impurities from liquids; note *pass water*, which is often euphemistic for the formal verb *urinate*)

pass the time • spend the time
- *I won't be in touch with you while I'm in Berlin. I have to **spend the time** visiting customers.* (Not *pass the time**)
  (*spend time* = use time constructively)
- *It was a very long flight, but we **passed/spent the time** playing pocket chess.*
  (*pass time* = make pleasurable use of time)

passion (for) • affection (for)
- *My **affection for** my old friends has not lessened over the years.* (Not *passion for*) (= a liking for, a lasting love for)
- *King Edward VIII gave up the throne because of his **passion for** the woman he loved.* (Not *affection for*) (= a very strong sexual attraction to)

past • last
- *The first iron ships were built in the **last** century.* (Not *past*) (= previous)
- *We have seen unbelievable advances in technology in the **past** century.* (= the one we are in now)

past • passed
- *You walked **past** me/You **passed** me without even noticing me!* (both words are pronounced in the same way: /pɑːst/, but *passed* is the past tense of the verb *pass*; *past* is a preposition: *He walked **past** me* or an adverb: *He walked **past**.*)

pathetic • passive • operating loss
- *Railways have suffered a huge **operating loss** recently.* (Not *pathetic* *passive*) (= a failure to break even or make a profit)
- *The accounting procedures of this company are **pathetic**.* (Not *passive*) (= hopeless, pitiable: for things or people)
- *The chairman was forced to resign because of his **passive** style of management.* (= not active, allowing things to happen)

pathos • passion • suffering
- *Millions of pounds are needed to relieve the **suffering** of people in famine areas.* (Not *pathos* *passion*) (= pain and distress)
- *There are many moments in Shakespeare's play 'King Lear' which are full of **pathos**.* (= a quality that makes us feel grief/pity)
- *There's no end to my **passion** for travelling.* (Not *pathos*) (= a strong attraction to)

patience
- *You have **such patience**!* (Not *such a patience*) (*patience* is uncountable)

patron • owner • manager • boss
- *The **owner/manager/boss** of a company is responsible for the welfare of all the employees.* (Not *patron*)
- *I want to see the **manager**.* (Not *patron*) (*manager* = the person who *manages*/is in charge of a business, but isn't necessarily the *owner*; *boss* = a person with overall responsibility who may employ a *manager* or *managers*)
- *He will always be remembered as a philanthropist and **patron** of the arts.* (= a supporter, especially with money)

patron • pattern
- *If you can read a paper **pattern**, you can make your own clothes.* (Not *patron*) (a *dress pattern* is usually made from paper and shows the shape of a garment)
- ***Patrons** are requested to park at the rear.* (= customers at pubs and hotels; formal)

pause • stop
- *The rain has **stopped**.* (Not *paused*) (= finally ended)
- *I think it's time we **paused** for a break.* (= stopped for a short period)

pay • pay for
- *How much did you **pay for that dress**? What did you **pay for it**?* (Not *pay that dress* *pay it*) (*pay for* a product or a service)
- *How much did you **pay the plumber**?* (Not **pay for the plumber**, though *pay to the plumber* would be possible)
- *How much did you **pay for the repair**?* (Not *pay the repair*)
- *Let me **pay you for the repair**.* (Not **pay you the repair**) (*pay* someone *for* something, but *pay for* an item or a service; *pay* money *to* someone)
- *I **paid** the bill.* (Not *paid for* *payed*) (*pay* a bill; *pay - paid - paid*; compare normal spelling of vowel + *-y*: *played*)
- *I **paid more** for this dress than I intended.* (Not **I paid more expensive**, though we can say *pay dear(ly)* = suffer for a mistake. Compare: *He **paid a lot** for that car* and *He **paid dear(ly)** for his mistake.*)

peasant • country
- *We find **country life** rather quiet after living in town.* (Not *peasant life*) (*country*, noun modifier = not in the town)
- ***Peasant life** must have been hard in the fourteenth century.* (*peasant*, noun modifier = the life of *peasants*) (*peasants* live by growing food in traditional ways for themselves and local markets: ***Peasant farmers** find it hard to compete with big, industrialized farms.*)

pensioner • boarder

- *Both their children are **boarders**.*
  (= at a *boarding school*, where they receive accommodation and meals)
- *Both my parents are **pensioners**.*
  (i.e. they no longer work, but receive a regular payment of money: a *pension*)

people • peoples

- ***People are** having a difficult time in some of the new democracies.*
  (Not **The people is* *The peoples are**)
  (collective noun + plural verb)
- *The English-speaking **people/peoples** share a common language.*
  (*people* = all the men, women and children; *peoples* = nations)

people • person • persons

- *Vera seems a nice **person**.* (Not **people**)
  (= an individual, a human being)
- *Our neighbours are very nice **people**.*
  (Not **persons* *peoples**)
  (*people* is the plural of *person* to refer to human beings in general)
- *The police keep a list of missing **persons**.*
  (we use *persons* in legal references)

per • for

- *I slept **for hours**.* (Not **per hours**)
- *The rate is calculated on a **per hour** basis.*
  (formal, official for 'by the hour'; hotel tariffs quote *per person per night*)

perceive

- *I **don't perceive** any improvement in the economy.* (Not **I'm not perceiving**)
  (= notice, formal; stative use only; no progressive form)
- *I could just **perceive** the outline of someone **approaching**.* (Not **to approach**)
  (= begin to see, become aware of)

permanent • perm

- *She's just **had a perm**.* (Not **done/made a perm* *done/made a permanent**)
  (*a perm* = putting curls into straight hair has replaced *permanent wave*)
- *This is now my **permanent** address.*
  (adjective = lasting a long time)

permission • permit • licence • leave

- *You can't fish wherever you like. You need a **permit**.* (Not **licence**)
  (= official written permission; *permit* combines with other words, e.g. *a building permit, a residence permit*)
- *You can't get a driving **licence** till you're 17.* (Not **permit* *permission**)
  (= official written permission; *licence* combines with other words, e.g. *a driving licence, a dog licence*)
- *Andrew drove his mother's car without her **permission**.* (Not **permit* *licence**)
  (= agreement, consent; *permission* is always uncountable)
- *How much annual **leave** do you get when you're in the army?* (Not **permission**)
  (= holidays, especially in the army, etc.)
- *I wish you wouldn't borrow my things without **permission**.* (preferable to *leave*)
  (= my letting you)

person • character

- *How many **characters** are there in the play?* (Not **persons**)
  (= the people in a play or story; the Latin phrase *dramatis personae* is archaic)
- *Are you the **person** who left a message on the answerphone?* (Not **character**)
  (= someone)

personal • personnel

- *Who's the **personnel** manager in this company?* (Not **personal**)
  (*personnel* = all the people who work for a company, hence *personnel manager*)
- *My letter was answered by her **personal** assistant.* (Not **personnel**)
  (*personal* refers to one person)
- *It's a **personal** matter which I don't want to discuss.* (Not **personnel**)
  (= private)

personally • in person

- *The President didn't attend the funeral **in person/personally** but was represented by the Vice-President.*
- *I wasn't **personally** involved in the row.*
  (Not **in person**)
  (= directly; *in person* and *personally* are generally interchangeable: we use *personally* before an adjective or after e.g. *be*, and *in person* after an ordinary verb)

perspective • prospect • view

- *It's a job with very good **prospects**.*
  (Not **perspectives* *views**)
  (= outlook, future possibilities)
- *There's an excellent **view** from my window.*
  (Not **perspective**; *prospect* is old-fashioned)
- *It took centuries for artists to master **perspective**.*
  (= the technique in drawing which shows distance and depth)

persuasion • conviction
- His religious **convictions** don't allow him to eat meat. (Not *persuasions*)
- **Persuasion** by argument is the basis of democracy. (Not *Conviction*)
  (= making others accept your arguments)
- People of your **persuasions**/with your **convictions** usually vote conservative.
  (persuasion(s) = belief(s) is very formal)

pest • plague
- **The plague** wiped out millions of people in the Middle Ages. (Not *The pest*)
  (= the infectious disease bubonic plague)
- A **plague of** locusts is sweeping across central Africa. (Not *A pest of*)
  (= an uncontrollable mass of e.g. insects)
- Restaurants should be visited regularly by **pest** control officers. (Not *plague*)
  (pests = animals like mice, insects like cockroaches, that can e.g. carry disease)

phenomenon • phenomena
- You can see extraordinary natural **phenomena** in Iceland like hot springs and lava flows. (Not *phenomenons*)
- A solar flare is a **phenomenon** which can be seen during an eclipse of the sun.
  (Not *a phenomena*)
  (= an unusual event, etc.; (a) phenomenon is singular; phenomena is plural)

philology • literature
- If you're fond of poetry and drama, it's hardly surprising you want to study **literature** at university. (Not *philology*)
- The brothers Grimm made important contributions to the study of **philology** in the nineteenth century.
  (= the development of language, old-fashioned and now replaced by linguistics)

phonetics
- I'm sure the **phonetics are** wrong here.
  (Not *phonetics is* *phonetic is*)
  (plural form + plural verb for phonetics, colloquial for 'phonetic symbols')
- **Phonetics is** an important part of our linguistics course. (Not *(the) phonetics are* *(the) phonetic is*)
  (plural form + singular verb to refer to the academic subject)

photograph • photographer • photography
- I'd love to work as a **photographer**.
  (Not *photograph*)
- I'm very interested in **photography**.
  (Not *photograph*)
- Who took the wedding **photo(graph)s**?
  (a photographer takes a photo(graph) with a camera; photography is the art of taking and producing photographs)

physician • physicist • doctor • medicine
- Albert Einstein is the **physicist** who gave us the Theory of Relativity. (Not *physician*)
- Albert Schweitzer worked in Africa for years as a **physician/doctor**. (Not *medicine*)
  (physician is old-fashioned for doctor; we say a doctor practises medicine; compare medicine man = tribal doctor)
- It's hard to keep up with the advances that have been made in modern **medicine**.
  (= the study of disease and its treatment)

physics
- You could argue that **physics is** more important than any other subject.
  (Not *(the) physics are* *(the) physic is*)
  (plural form + singular verb to refer to the academic subject)

pick • peck • sting • bite • prick • pinch
- I offered the parrot something to eat and it **pecked** my hand. (Not *picked* *stung* *pricked* *pinched*, preferably not bit)
  (a bird pecks food, etc.)
- I was **stung** by a wasp while I was down at the beach. (Not *picked* *pecked* *pricked* *pinched*, preferably not bitten)
  (wasps and bees sting)
- Ow! I've been **bitten** by a mosquito! (Not *picked* *pecked* *pricked* *pinched*)
  (insects, etc., bite to draw blood, or sting to defend themselves)
- I've **pricked** myself with a needle. (Not *pecked* *stung* *pinched* *picked*)
  (= punctured the skin with a sharp point)
- Stop **pinching** me or I'll hit you!
  (Not *pecking* *stinging* *pricking*)
  (= holding flesh between thumb and forefinger)
- I wish you'd stop **picking** your nose.
  (= putting a (fore)finger up a nostril)

pick • pick up • pick out • cut
- I've **picked up** a bad cold. (Not *picked*)
  (= caught)
- The children are out in the field **picking** wild flowers. (Not *picking up* *cutting*)
  (= gathering; we pick flowers and fruit; but flowers from a florist are cut flowers)
- She peeled an apple and **cut** it in two.
- All these ties are so nice, I don't know which one to **pick**. (Not *pick up*)
  (= choose)

– *Look at these photos and see if you can **pick out** my mother.* (Not **pick* *pick up**)
(= distinguish from the rest)

pick-up • record player • gramophone
– *We hardly ever use our **record player** now that we've got a CD player.* (Not **pick-up**; gramophone is now old-fashioned)
– *My record player has a **pick-up** with a sapphire stylus.*
(= the 'arm' and the 'needle' (*stylus*) of a record player)

picnic
– *We're going **on/for a picnic** tomorrow.*
(go *on* = join an organized event; go *for* = for that purpose)
– *This is a good place to **have a picnic**.*
(Not **do/make a picnic**)
(also note the *-ing* form: *I enjoy **picnicking**,* not **picnicing**; and the regular past form: *They **picnicked** by the side of the road.*)

piece/bit
– *I ate **a piece of/a bit of chocolate**.*
(Not **a piece chocolate* *a bit chocolate**)
– *This cake is nice. Have **a piece/a bit**.*
(*a piece of/a bit of* a whole; *a piece* or *a bit* as nouns on their own; *a bit (of)* is informal)
– *I feel **a bit** tired today.*
(*a bit* as an adverb of degree)

piece • each
– *The lemons are 20p **each**.* (Not **the piece**)
– *I cut the cake and gave her **a piece**.*

piece • work
– *He collects **works of art**.* (Not **pieces**)
– *This Moore sculpture is **a late work/piece**.*
(we can use *a piece* on its own to mean *a work of art*, but we cannot say **a piece of art**)
– *This is a fine **piece of music/a fine work/a fine piece**.* (Not **a work of music**)
(we can use *work* on its own to describe a piece of music)

pig • pork • hog
– *We're having roast **pork** for Sunday lunch.*
(Not **pig* *hog**)
(= meat from a pig, uncountable)
– ***Pigs** (AmE Hogs) are intelligent animals.*
(Not **Porks**)
(*pig* is a general name for the male and female animal; more precise terms are *boar* for a breeding male; *hog* for a castrated male for the table; and *sow* for a female; we use *pig* in compound nouns to refer to leather: e.g. *pigskin* gloves)

pin   safety pin   needle

pin • safety pin • needle
– *Babies' nappies that need **safety pins** are now old-fashioned.* (Not **pins* *needles**)
(= a *pin* bent so that it closes on itself, covering the sharp point)
– *I've marked the line of the hem with **pins**.*
(Not **needles**)
(= long thin needles with a rounded head)
– *You need a special **needle** to sew through leather.* (Not **pin**)
(= a thin metal pin with a hole at one end to take thread; used for sewing)

pipe • tube • inner tube
– *Water passes through this glass **tube** and into the flask below.* (Not **pipe**)
(a *tube*, generally made of metal, glass, rubber or plastic, is short enough for an observer to see both ends)
– *Hot water is distributed through the house by these copper **pipes**.* (Not **tubes**)
(a *pipe* is a long tube through which water or gas can flow)
– *Most tyres are **tube**less these days, but they can be fitted with **inner tubes** if you require them.* (Not **pipes**)
(= rubber 'pipes' containing air and used inside tyres on bicycles, cars, etc.)

piquant • hot
– *You'll spoil the natural flavour of this dish if you put **hot** sauce on it.* (Not **piquant**)
(*hot* is more usual than *piquant* to refer to spicy sauce, etc.)
– *It was a **piquant** situation when I interviewed my former boss for a job.*
(= interesting, intriguing, amusing)

pistol • gun
– *You don't argue with someone who's armed with a **pistol/gun**.*
(*pistol* specifically refers to a revolver; *gun* is the general word for all kinds of guns)

pity • sorrow • pain
– *One always feels (a) particular **sorrow** at the death of a child.* (Not **pity* *pain**)
(= a feeling of great sadness)

– *Pity is not enough. What the refugees need is food and medicine.* (Not **Sorrow**)
(= sympathy for someone's misfortune)
– *Pain and suffering are part of the human condition.* (Not **Pity**)
(= physical or mental distress)

pity • take pity on

– *I took pity on the poor beggar and gave him some money.* (Not **took pity for/with**)
(*take pity on* = feel sorry and try to help; *have pity on* = be merciful is only used in old stories)
– *You say you pity the homeless, but what are you doing about them?*
(*pity* refers to feeling and is not necessarily followed by action)

place • job • position/post

– *It isn't easy to get a job these days.*
(Not **place**, preferable to *position*, which is old-fashioned in this sense)
(*a job* can mean employment in general)
– *We're looking for someone with the right experience for the position of general manager.* (Not **place**, preferable to *job*)
(one *applies* for a *post*; an employer *fills* a *position* or a *post*: both words apply to 'white-collar' appointments)
– *Nick got a place at university when he was seventeen.* (Not **position**)
(i.e. one place out of a number of places; *a position* is the only one)
– *I've just finished getting all the seats in place/position for this afternoon's meeting.*
(= where they should be)

place • room/space

– *There's not enough room/space in my office for a two-metre desk.* (Not **place**)
(*room* and *space* refer to physical area here; but note *make room for somebody or something*, not **make space**)
– *I think this is the best place for this picture.*
(= location, position)
– *My room is only just large enough for a bed.*
(Not **place** **space**)
(= e.g. a bedroom)
– *How long will Voyager be travelling in space?* (Not **place** **room**)
(= beyond the earth's atmosphere)

place • seat • ticket

– *I managed to get a seat/ticket for tomorrow's match.* (Not **place**)
– *Have a seat.* (Not **place**)

– *Someone's sitting in my place/seat.*
(*my place* = where I should be sitting, e.g. on a plane, in a theatre, at a table)

place • square

– *Which is the biggest square in London? - Trafalgar Square, I think.* (Not **Place**)
(= an open space in a town or village; the word *circus* = 'large, round open area' is sometimes used with a similar meaning: *Piccadilly Circus, Oxford Circus*)
– *London is a very large place.*
(= a particular area, e.g. a town, a part of the country, etc.)

plane

– *I don't really enjoy travelling by plane.*
(Not **with the plane**)

plaque • plate • record • number plate

– *Do you have any of the original Beatles records?* (Not **plaques** **plates**)
(i.e. which can be played on a record player)
– *My car needs new number plates.*
(Not **plaques**)
(= the plates, front and rear, on a vehicle which show its registration number)
– *A blue plaque on a London house means that someone famous once lived there.*
(= a plate, often decorative/commemorative)
– *Plaque is the major cause of gum disease.*
(= a substance that forms on the teeth)
– *Could you bring me a clean plate please?*
(= a flat dish on which food is served)

play • game • match

– *Thousands of people packed the stadium to see the game/match.* (Not **play**)
(= a contest between competing teams, e.g. football, or individuals, e.g. tennis)
– *We've just had a very good game of chess/a very good chess game/chess match.*
(Not **a play** **a match of**)
– *Which is your favourite Shakespeare play?*
(= a drama written for the stage or TV)

play with • play for

– *Which team did Lineker play for?*
(Not **play with**)
(= 'belong to')
– *I have to make time to play with my children.*
(i.e. together with)

please • ask • beg

– *I begged/asked the traffic-cop not to book me for speeding and he just laughed.* (Not **begged to/asked to + object** **pleased**)
(*beg* = make a strong plea; *ask* is neutral)

- *'Oh, Joy! Andrew **asked me** to tell you he'd be late.'* (Not **pleased me**)
- *Vincent **begged me to** consider the matter carefully.* (Not **begged that I should**)
- *It **pleases me** to say you've got the job.*
  (= gives me pleasure; formal; the verb *please* never means 'ask')

please • thank you/thanks
- *- Let me hold the door open for you!*
  *- **Thank you/Thanks.***
  - (That's OK.)
  (in normal exchanges there is often no response to *Thank you*: not **Please**; a response only needs to be given where the favour has been something important. Informal responses are e.g. *That's OK, That's all right*; more formal responses are e.g. *Not at all, Don't mention it, It's a pleasure*. Not **It's nothing.**)
- *'**Please** tell Joy I'll be late.' Andrew said.*
  (*please* for polite requests)

pleased with
- *We're very **pleased with** the quality of his work.* (Not **pleased from/of**)

plenty (of) • a lot (of)
- *We've got **plenty of time** before the train leaves.* (Not **plenty time**)
- *How much time have we got before the train leaves? - **Plenty/A lot**.*
  (Not **Plenty of.** **A lot of.**)
- *We've got **plenty of time/a lot of time** before the train leaves.*
  (*plenty* or *a lot* on their own, or *plenty of/a lot of* + countable or uncountable noun)
- *We **haven't got a lot of** time before the train leaves.* (Not **haven't got plenty of**)
  (the use of *plenty of* in negative statements is uncommon)

poetry • poem
- *Let me read you **a poem** from this anthology.* (Not **a poetry**)
- *Let me read you **some poetry/poems** from this anthology.* (Not **some poetries**)
  (*poetry* is uncountable)

point: there's no point
- *There's **no point (in) trying** to mend this shirt. It's too old.* (Not **to try**)

point • stitch
- *Bother! I've dropped a **stitch**.* (Not **point**)
  (*stitches* for sewing and knitting)
- *Who won? - I did by two **points**.*
  (*points* for scoring in ball games)

police • policeman
- *A **policeman** waved us down just as we came off the motorway.* (Not **A police**)
- *The **police are** getting a big pay rise.*
  (Not **The police is** **The polices are**)
  (collective noun + plural verb)

policy • politics
- *Harry's **politics are** slightly left of centre.*
  (Not **politics is** **politic is**)
  (= political opinions; plural form + plural verb for specific references)
- *Politics is one of the most important aspects of the study of history.*
  (Not **(the) politics are** **(the) politic is**)
  (plural form + singular verb to refer to the academic subject)
- *This sort of thing won't do. It's a matter of **policy**.* (Not **politics**)
  (= the official line, organizing principle)

polish • shine
- *Your shoes have a nice **shine**.* (Not **polish**)
  (i.e. they reflect light)
- *I'm going to give my shoes a good **polish**.*
  (= clean, using *shoe polish* or *shoe cream*)
- *How often do you **polish/shine** your shoes?*

pollution
- *Pollution is killing many of Europe's lakes and rivers.* (Not **Pollutions are**)
  (*pollution* is uncountable)

pool • pond • lake
- *He's sailing on the **lake**.* (Not **pool/pond**)
  (= a large area of water with land all round)
- *There are some lovely **ponds** with swans in the middle of the park.* (Not **pools**)
  (a *pond* is a small, usually man-made area of water for the use of animals or as a garden ornament)
- *Come for a swim in the **pool**.*
  (a *pool* is a natural occurrence, e.g. a *rock pool*, unless it is a *swimming pool*)
- *Your wet coat has made a **pool** of water on the kitchen floor.* (Not **pond** **lake**)
  (= a small amount of liquid, a *puddle*)

poor
- *She was rich when she was young, but she died **poor/a poor woman**.* (Not **a poor**)
- *The Robinsons are **poor/poor people**.*
  (Not **poors**)
- *You **poor thing**! The **poor girl**!*
  (Not **You poor!** **The poor!**)
  (= unfortunate; we do not use *poor* on its own to mean 'a poor person')

- *The poor need help.* (Not *The poors*)
  (*the* + adjective for the group as a whole; the
  noun is *poverty*, not *poorness*)
- *The rich got richer and the poor got poorer.*
  (Not *they poored*)

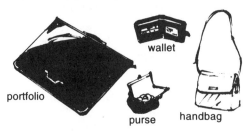

portfolio

wallet

purse

handbag

portfolio • wallet • purse • handbag
- *I'm sure I put the note in my wallet* (AmE
  pocketbook). (Not *portfolio*)
- *My purse is bulging with pennies.*
  (Not *portfolio*)
- *Don't forget your handbag* (AmE *purse*).
- *I need a portfolio for all these drawings.*
  (= a large flat case for storing/carrying e.g.
  drawings; an *investment portfolio* is a
  collection of business shares)

positive • favourable
- *Reviews of Anita Brookner's latest novel
  have been extremely favourable/positive.*
  (*favourable* = expressing approval; *positive*
  = not negative)
- *I'm positive I posted those letters.*
  (= sure)

possibility (of)
- *There's no possibility of arriving on time.*
  (Not *possibility to arrive*)
  (only *of* + *-ing* after *possibility*)

possibly • perhaps
- *Don't worry. Perhaps you'll get a letter
  tomorrow.* (preferable to *possibly*)
- *I could possibly have put the letter in the
  rubbish bin by mistake.*
- *Possibly you're right, but I hate to think so.*
  (*perhaps* = 'I'm not sure', especially when
  we're offering an explanation; *possibly* = 'it's
  possible', 'it might be so')

post: by post • in the post
- *How long will this parcel take to get there
  by post?* (Not *with the post* *in the post*)
- *Your cheque's in the post/been sent by post.*
  (*in the post* = on its way *by post*)

pot
- *There's some stew in the pot.*
  (i.e. *cooking pot* = a saucepan)

- *This lovely pot was a wedding present.*
  (= a clay or ceramic dish, bowl, teapot, etc.)
- *That plant needs a bigger pot.*
  (= a flowerpot, clay, plastic or ceramic)

practicable • practical • practised
- *Anne is so calm and practical. She does
  everything well.*
  (Not *practicable* *practised*)
  (= sensible, competent)
- *I'm not at all practical. I can't even use a
  hammer.* (Not *practicable* *practised*)
  (= good at making or repairing things)
- *It's an excellent teaching course with plenty
  of opportunity for practical experience.*
  (Not *practicable* *practised*)
  (i.e. actually doing things)
- *It just isn't practicable/practical to go back
  to work as soon as you've had a baby.*
  (Not *practised*)
  (= capable of being done/sensible)
- *You'll be OK. Mrs Wilbur is an extremely
  practised* (AmE *practiced*) *osteopath.*
  (i.e. she has had a lot of practice)

practise • practice
- *Your tennis will improve with practice.*
- *I practise* (AmE also *practice*) *yoga daily.*
- *I practise* (AmE also *practice*) *lifting
  weights every day.* (Not *practise to lift*)
  (*practice* is the noun; *practise* is the verb:
  especially in BrE)

prayer(s)
- *Say a prayer for me.* (Not *Tell* *Make*)
  (*say one's prayers*)

precious • valuable • invaluable
- *His help was most valuable./His help was
  invaluable.* (Not *precious*)
  (= e.g. practical and useful)
- *I lost some precious/valuable jewellery.*
  (*precious* = special or loved; *valuable* =
  worth a lot of money or useful: *valuable
  advice. Invaluable* is not the opposite of
  valuable, but means 'extremely useful')

precise • accurate • punctual • exact
- *I haven't yet found a tyre pressure gauge
  that is wholly accurate.*
  (Not *precise* *exact* *punctual*; the
  opposite is *inaccurate*)
  (*accurate* = telling the truth, for watches,
  instruments, etc., especially after a verb)
- *The witness gave us an accurate/precise
  account of what she had seen.*
  (*accurate* = true; *precise* = careful/exact)

- *Your interview is at 4.30 and make sure you're **punctual**.* (Not *exact* *accurate*)
  (= on time; opposite: *unpunctual*)
- *I can't think of the **exact/precise** word to describe my feelings.*
  (Not *accurate* *punctual*)
  (the opposites are *inexact, imprecise*)
- *This is an **accurate/exact** copy of the original painting.*
  (= true and precise)

prefer

- *Which one **do you prefer**?*
  (Not *are you preferring* *do you like*)
  (stative use only; no progressive form)
- *I **prefer waiting/to wait** here.*
  (very little difference in meaning: *I prefer waiting* = I'm waiting: I prefer doing that; *I prefer to wait* = so I'll wait)
- *I **prefer swimming to cycling./I prefer swimming rather than cycling**.*
  (Not *I prefer ... than* *I prefer ... from*)
- *I **prefer to swim rather than (to) cycle**.*
  (Not *I prefer to swim to cycle.*)
  (*rather than* after *prefer* + *to*)
- *Would you **prefer fish**? - Yes, **I'd prefer that**.* (Not *I'd prefer.*)
  (*prefer* is transitive)
- *Would you **prefer to wait**? - Yes, **I'd prefer to**.* (Not *I'd prefer.*)

premium • prize/award

- *John has won lots of **prizes/awards** for his film.* (Not *premiums*)
  (*prize* and *award* are often used in the same way; a *prize* is often an object; an *award* is recognition and often money as well; note *to award a prize*, not *award with*)
- *Insurance **premiums** go up every year.*
  (= charges)
- *Good managers are **at a premium**.*
  (= hard to obtain)

preoccupied • worried • upset

- *We were very **worried/upset** when you didn't telephone us.* (Not *preoccupied*)
  (if you are *worried*, you keep thinking about a problem; if you are *upset* you are unhappy because something bad has happened)
- *I've been so **preoccupied with** moving house, I've neglected nearly everything else.*
  (= absorbed, busy with one thing; a person who is *preoccupied* may also be *worried*, but not necessarily)

prescription • recipe • receipt

- *There's a very nice **recipe** for moussaka in today's paper.* (Not *prescription*

receipt, which is archaic)
  (= a set of instructions for cooking)
- *You need a **prescription** from a doctor for antibiotics.* (Not *recipe* *receipt*)
  (= a written order for medicine by a doctor)
- *We can't accept returned goods without a **receipt**.* (Not *prescription* *recipe*)
  (= a written proof of purchase)

present • presents

- *Roy, please make a list of **those present** at the meeting.* (Not *the presents*)
  (= the people who were there)
- *They've got some lovely wedding **presents**.*
  (= gifts; singular: *present*)

presently • at present/just now • soon

- *We have no news about it **at present/just now**.* (*presently* = 'now' in AmE only)
- *Just give me a moment. I'll be with you **presently**.* (Not *at present/just now*)
  (= soon, in a moment; becoming dated)
- *I'll **soon** know the result of my test.*
  (= in the near future, but not necessarily in the immediate future, like *presently*)
- ***At present** we're staying with our son.*
  (= currently)

preservative • condom • prophylactic • contraceptive

- *People can limit the spread of AIDS if they use **condoms**.*
  (Not *preservatives* *prophylactics*; note the brand name *durex* = a condom/condoms is in common use in BrE and does not mean *sellotape*, as it does in Australian English, or AmE *scotch tape* = clear sticky tape)
- *If you want to avoid flu this winter, a flu jab is the only **prophylactic**.*
  (= something that prevents disease; the terms *prophylactic* and *protective* to mean condom are old-fashioned or affected)
- *Food manufacturers are required by law to state which **preservatives** they use.*
  (= substances that make food last)
- *The condom is one of many forms of **contraceptive**.* (Not *prophylactic*)
  (*contraceptives* = birth control devices)

press • squeeze

- ***Squeeze** this lemon please.* (Not *Press*)
- *This is the time of the year when the wine-growers **press** their grapes.*
  (*squeeze* by hand; *press* by machine as in a wine-press)
- *She **pressed/squeezed** my hand warmly.*
  (= 'grasped my hand firmly when we shook hands')

press/push • ring
- I'll **ring** the bell/the front door bell again. (Not *press*)
- Can you **press/push** that button for me please? It will **ring** a bell upstairs. (*ring* a bell; but *press/push* a button)
- Why don't you **ring** them? (Not *press*) (= phone)

pretty • prettily
- Reg **is sitting pretty** now his aunt's died. (*be sitting pretty* = be well off)
- The little girl smiled **prettily** at the camera. (-*ly* to describe an action)

prevent (from) • avoid
- **Avoid travelling** during the rush hour. (Not *Prevent/Avoid from travelling/to travel*)
- I can't **prevent you (from)/prevent your going** if you want to. (Not *avoid*)

priceless • valueless • worthless
- This isn't a Rembrandt. It's **valueless/worthless**. (Not *priceless*) (= without any value)
- Rembrandt's 'Night Watch' is **priceless**. (= 'beyond price', too *valuable* to be measured)

principle • principal
- The first violin is the **principal** musician in an orchestra. (Not *principle*) (adjective = chief, leading)
- Miss Hargreaves has just been appointed **principal** of the college. (Not *principle*) (noun = Head)
- A good **principle** is not to borrow money you can't repay. (Not *principal*) (= a basic rule; *principle* is never an adjective)

print • type • stamp
- I'll **print** those letters for you. (i.e. on a printer)
- I'll **type** those letters for you. (i.e. on a keyboard)
- Have they **stamped** your passport? (= marked it with a rubber stamp)

probable (that) • probably • likely (to)
- **It's likely to** rain/**It's likely that it will** rain tomorrow. (Not *It's probable to*)
- **It's probable that** it will rain tomorrow. (*probable + that*, not *to*)
- **It will probably** rain soon. (Not *likely*)
- **She's likely to** arrive any day now. (Not *She's probable/likely that she will*) (Not *probable* with a personal subject)

- **She'll probably** arrive any day now.

problem
- My son's **having a problem (in) finding** work. (Not *having a problem to find*)
- It's **a problem to find/finding** work. (the *to*-infinitive is possible after *be + a problem*)

proceed • advance • precede
- **Advance** two squares. (Not *Proceed*) (= move forward in a board game)
- We were **proceeding** towards Rome when the accident happened. (Not *advancing*) (= going forward; formal/legal)
- We had to cut down the undergrowth before we could **advance/proceed** any further. (similar meanings here)
- The contents list in a book should **precede** the preface. (Not *proceed* *advance*) (= go before)

process • trial
- The **trial** lasted a week. (Not *process*) (= a trial in a court of law)
- The **process** of the law is slow and painful. (Not *trial*) (= all the stages, the procedure)
- Learning Japanese was a slow **process**. (= a sequence of actions)

product • products • produce • production
- We grow most of our own **produce** in the garden. (Not *product* *products*) (uncountable noun = fruit, vegetables, etc.)
- This Olivetti computer is an Italian **product**. (Not *produce*) (countable noun = an item made for sale)
- There is no end to the demand for consumer **products**. (Not *produce*) (= usually things that are made for sale)
- We export all we **produce**. (Not *product*) (verb = grow or make; *product* is a noun)
- We'll earn more if we increase **production**. (Not *produce*) (= the amount we produce)

professor • teacher
- Mr Jones was a **teacher** of History before he became a headmaster. (Not *professor*) (a *teacher* teaches in a school)
- He was **Professor** of Physics and head of his university department at the age of 26. (a *professor*, BrE, has the highest position in a university department, or AmE, teaches at a university; we do not address a teacher as *Mr Teacher*: we address a man as *Mr* + surname or as *Sir*, and a woman as *Miss/Mrs*

+ surname; we address a professor, male or female, as *Professor* + surname, not **Mr/Mrs Professor**)

profile • tread
– *What's the minimum **tread** which the law allows on tyres?* (Not **profile**)
(= the depth of pattern on a tyre; but we can say *low/high profile tyres* to refer to the general shape of tyres viewed from the side)
– *I've got a photo of you here **in profile**.*
(= seen from the side)
– *There's a **profile** of the new Minister of Education in today's paper.*
(= an account, outline description)

profit
– *Stores haven't **made** as much **profit** as usual this year.* (Not **done ... profit**)
– *We sold our car **at a profit**.*
(Not **with a profit**)

programme • channel
– *Which **channel** is it on? - It's on **Channel 2**.* (Not **2nd Programme**, etc.)
(= a TV channel)
– *Which TV **programme** do you like best? - I like 'Neighbours'.* (Not **channel**)

programme • syllabus • curriculum • program
– *There's a new **syllabus** for next year's Certificate in Advanced English.* (Not **programme** **curriculum**)
(a *syllabus* is set in one subject either by a school or by an examination board)
– *Art isn't on our school **curriculum**.*
(a school *curriculum* is the general programme in all subjects)
– *What's your **programme** for today?*
(= a sequence of planned activities)
– *This concert **programme** (BrE)/**program** (AmE) is very expensive.*
(= information booklet)
– *Have you seen Microsoft's new wordprocessing **program**?* (AmE and BrE)
(= computer program)

progress
– *Kevin has **made** great **progress** since he joined our class.* (Not **a progress** **progresses** **done progress**)
(*progress* is uncountable)

progressive • gradual
– *Some people say there's been a **gradual/progressive** decline in reading standards in the past ten years.*

(*progressive* = continuous, steady; *gradual* = little by little)
– *Some people say that reading standards have declined because of **progressive** teaching methods.* (Not **gradual**)
(= 'modern', reflecting new thinking)

promise
– *If you've **made a promise** you should keep it.* (Not **done a promise**)
– ***Promise to be** back before midnight.*
– ***Promise me to be** back before midnight.* (Not **Promise to me**)
– ***Promise (me) (that)** you will be back before midnight.*
(*promise (me)* + *to* or *that*)

pronounce • say • call
– *What do you **call** this in English?*
(Not **What do you say** **How do you say**)
(naming things)
– *How do you **say** 'Merci' in English?*
(= 'What is the correct equivalent?')
– *How do you **pronounce/say** 'cough'?*
(= 'What is the correct *pronunciation*?')

pronunciation • accent
– *He spoke fluent English with a strong German **accent**.* (Not **pronunciation**)
(*accent* refers to the way we speak a language, which can show our origin)
– *The **pronunciation** of the word 'ship' is quite different from 'sheep'.* (Not **accent**; note spelling: not **pronounciation**)
(= the way we say particular words)

proof (of) • receipt
– *We can't accept returned goods without a **receipt**.* (Not **proof**)
(= the written statement you receive when you pay a bill)
– *Do you have **proof of** purchase?* (Not **for**)
– *We suspect he's been stealing, but we haven't enough **proof**.*
(= something that shows what is true)

proper • own
– *I'd love to have **my own room/a room of my own**.* (Not **my proper room** **mine own room** **an own room**)
(= solely for my use; *own* after *my*, *your*, etc., emphasizes the idea of possession)
– *Don't use my comb. Use **your own**.*
(Not **your own one** **your proper one**)
– *I translated the poem into Italian **on my own/by myself**.* (Not **by my own**)
(= alone, unaided)

- *What matters is who you are, not what you **own**. (Not *are owning*)*
  (stative use only)
- *It took me ages to learn the **proper** way to use chopsticks.*
  (= correct)

propose • suggest • offer
- *I **suggest** (that) this is the right time.*
  (Not *propose*)
  (*suggest* = put forward an idea)
- *I **propose/suggest** (that) we act immediately.*
  (Not *I propose/suggest us to act*)
  (*propose* = put forward a plan; *suggest* = put forward an idea)
- *I **suggested/proposed** a figure of £5,000.*
  (= put it up as an idea/a plan)
- *I **offered** a sum of £5,000.*
  (= named it as a sum for acceptance or refusal)

prospect • prospectus • brochure
- *I've sent for a **prospectus** about language courses. (Not *prospect* *brochure*)*
  (= a document published by schools and companies describing their activities)
- *I've sent for a **brochure** about skiing holidays. (Not *prospectus* *prospect*)*
  (= a document that advertises and provides information about holidays, hotels, etc.)
- *Is there any **prospect** they'll ever find a cure for the common cold?*
  (= future possibility)

protest • complain • object
- *We all **complained/protested/objected** when the boss suggested we should work Sundays.*
  (*complain* = express dissatisfaction; *protest* = express dissatisfaction very strongly; *object* = be against)
- *Whenever we go on holiday, Eric **complains about** the food. (Not *complains for/of*)*
  (*complain about* something, but *complain of* pain/illness: *He's **complaining of** earache.*)
- *No one believed me when I **protested** I was innocent. (Not *complained* *objected*)*
  (= claimed loudly)

protocol • application • sheet of (exam) paper
- *You have to send three copies of this **application** to the council. (Not *protocol*)*
- *Can I have another **sheet of paper** please? (Not *protocol*)*
  (e.g. while taking an exam)
- *What's the **protocol** for registering complaints between governments?*
  (= the rules of correct diplomatic procedure; *protocol* literally means 'the first sheet of

paper' in e.g. a volume, but it is not used in English to refer to official or legal paperwork, exams, etc.)

proud of • (take) pride in
- *He's so **proud of** his sons. (Not *for/with*)*
- *He **takes pride in** his sons. (Not *for/of*)*

prove
- *This receipt **proves** that I bought these goods here. (Not *is proving*)*
  (stative use = shows)
- *We've been trying to sell our house, but **it's proving** very difficult.*
  (dynamic use = showing itself to be)
- *Am I expected to **prove my ability to you**? (Not *prove you my ability* *prove to you my ability*)*

prove • test • try • try on • experiment
- *We **test** aerodynamic vehicles in these tunnels. (Not *prove* *try (on)*)*
  (= give tests to measure performance)
- ***Try** this jam I've just made. (Not *Prove* *Test* *Try on* *Experiment*)*
  (= taste)
- *This coat's too tight. Can I **try on** the larger size please? (Not *experiment* *prove*)*
  (= put it on to see if it fits, etc.)
- *Many people object on moral grounds to **experimenting** on live animals.*
  (= conducting tests)
- *This video film **proves** he was a thief.*
  (= shows, is evidence that)

prune • plum • damask • damson
- *Don't those fresh ripe **plums** look gorgeous! (Not *prunes* *damasks*)*
  (*plums* are fresh fruit)
- *You will need to soak those **prunes** in water before you cook them.*
  (*prunes* are dried *plums*)
- *You don't see **damask** tablecloths on dining tables very often these days.*
  (= thick cloth, usually white, with a woven pattern of the same colour)
- *Do you like **damson** jam?*
  (= a small dark purple plum for cooking)

public: the public • audience
- *Two unknown comedians told jokes to warm up **the audience** before the star of the show appeared. (Not *the public* *the publics*)*
  (= the people watching a show, e.g. a play, a film; or attending a concert)
- *The new art gallery has generally pleased **the public**. (Not *the publics*)*

– *The public is/are* flocking to the show.
(Not *The publics is* *The publics are*)
(*the public* = people in general is followed
by a singular or plural verb)

publicity • advertising • propaganda
– *There's a lot of clever advertising on TV.*
(Not *publicity* *propaganda*)
(= making something known in order to sell
it)
– *The royal divorce received a lot of publicity.*
(Not *advertising* *propaganda*)
(= making something known to the public)
– *Propaganda against the enemy is an
important weapon in time of war.*
(= information, usually political and often
false)

publicly • in public
– *I hate changing into my bathing costume in
public.* (Not *publicly*)
(i.e. where other people can see me)
– *The date of the wedding hasn't yet been
announced publicly.* (Not *in public*)
(= for everyone to know; note the spelling:
not *publically*)

pudding • caramel custard • flan • blancmange
– *Caramel custard made with fresh eggs is
lovely.* (Not *Pudding*)
(= a baked dessert made with eggs, cream
and burnt sugar)
– *Can you give me the recipe for this (fruit)
flan?* (Not *pudding*)
(= an open case of cake or pastry
filled/topped with e.g. fruit)
– *I used to hate blancmange when I was a
child.* (Not *pudding*)
(= a dessert made from cornflour, sugar and
milk)
– *What's for pudding?*
(the general term for any kind of dessert)
– *Treacle pudding is a rare luxury!*
(*pudding* is also used to describe any dish,
sweet or savoury, that is steamed in a basin,
e.g. *Christmas pudding, steak and kidney
pudding, steamed pudding*)

pupil • student • scholar
– *You expect university students to have
radical political views.* (Not *pupils*)
– *Do the pupils in this school have to wear
uniforms?* (preferable to *students*)
(a *student* has left school and studies at an
institution of higher learning; a *pupil* is at
school; but we can also use *pupil* to describe

an adult studying under someone famous:
Beethoven had been Haydn's pupil.)
– *Scholars are still trying to interpret the
Dead Sea Scrolls.*
(= people who have made a special study of
a subject; *scholar* to describe a child at
school is now old-fashioned)

puree • mashed potato(es)/mash
– *We're having sausages and mashed
potato(es)/mash for supper.* (Not *puree*)
(*mash*: informal BrE for *mashed potato(es)*)
– *The baby loves apple puree.*/'pjʊəreɪ/
(= mashed fruit, or vegetables other than
potatoes)

purpose: on purpose • purposely
– *I had avoided going by car on purpose.*
– *I had purposely avoided going by car.*
(both *on purpose* and *purposely* mean
'deliberately'; the difference is one of
position. We also use *purpose* in front of a
past participle to mean 'for that purpose':
purpose-built, purpose-designed)

put • keep
– *Most people believe that the safest place to
keep/put their money is in a bank.*
– *I never put money on horses.* (Not *keep*)
(*keep* = hold; *put* = place, used here in the
sense of 'bet')

put • prepare • lay
– *Please lay* (or *set*) *the table.*
(Not *put* *prepare*)
(*lay the table* is a fixed phrase)
– *Please put/lay these things on the table.*
(= place)
– *I'll prepare the vegetables.*
(i.e. get them ready for cooking or eating)

put • put in/add
– *Put in/Add the salt.* (Not *Put the salt.*)
– *Where did I put my glasses?*
(= place)

put on • wear • dressed in • have on • get dressed • dress
– *He left home dressed in/wearing his best
suit.* (Not *putting on* *getting dressed*)
– *John had his best suit on this morning.*
(*wear/be dressed in/have on* = actually have
the clothes on your body)
– *Wait a minute! I'm just putting on my coat/
putting my coat on.* (Not *wearing*
dressing in/getting dressed in/having on)
(= in the act of getting into clothes)

- *Hang on a minute! I'm just **getting dressed**.*
  (*get dressed* is the general phrase to describe the act of putting on your clothes)
- *How do people **dress** in Saudi Arabia?*
  (Not **wear**)

puzzle • game • riddle
- *Some children hate parties where they have to play competitive **games**.* (Not **puzzles**)
- *The airline provides toys and books of **puzzles** to keep children happy.*
  (Not **games* *riddles**)
- *What's the answer to this **riddle**?*
  (Not **puzzle**)
  (= a difficult or amusing question)
  (you *play* a game, *solve* a puzzle or *answer* a riddle)

Q

quarrel • argue • fight
- *Let's not **argue** about who's going to pay the bill.* (preferable to *quarrel/fight*)
- *Some families seem to spend a lot of time **quarrelling/arguing/fighting**.*
  (you can *argue* without feeling angry; *quarrelling* always implies anger; *fighting* suggests anger: verbal and/or physical)
- *They **had** a terrible **quarrel/fight/argument**.*
  (Not **did a quarrel**, etc.)

question
- *Can I **ask a question**?* (Not **do/make**)
- *Can I **put a question to** the panel?*
  (*put a question to* someone, not **put someone a question**)
- *The exam paper was very difficult. I couldn't **answer/couldn't do** all **the questions**.*
  (Not **make the questions**)

question • matter • affair • problem
- *The quarrel was over, and the whole **affair/matter** was soon forgotten.* (Not **question**)
  (i.e. the whole business/what had happened)
- *How we make this decision is a crucial **matter/question**.* (Not **affair**)
  (= something that needs to be decided)
- *What's **the matter**? Is something **the matter**?*
  (Not **Do you have a problem?**)
- *Is something **the matter**? - Yes, **the problem** is I'm away next week.* (Not **the matter is**)

quick • quickly
- *Come **quick/quickly**. There's been an accident.*
  (*quick* for sudden actions that are over in a flash: *jump in quick, shut it quick*)

- *We must **move quickly**.* (Not **move quick**)
  (only *-ly* to mean 'rapidly/in a quick way')

quiet • peaceful • calm
- *The sea was very **calm/quiet** this morning.*
  (Not **peaceful**)
  (*calm* = not moving; *quiet* = not noisy)
- *Nobody panicked; everyone stayed **calm** and obeyed the police.* (Not **quiet* *peaceful**)
  (= steady, not alarmed)
- *The house is very **quiet/peaceful** now that the school holidays are over.* (Not **calm**)
  (*quiet* = not noisy; *peaceful* = untroubled, not used for someone's state of mind)

quiet • quietly
- *The children **went** very **quiet** when the show began.* (Not **went quietly**)
  (*quiet* is an adjective; we often use *go* meaning *become* + adjective; compare *Sit quiet* for a moment = be quiet)
- *Now children, **go quietly** to your classes. No talking on the way.* (Not **go quiet**)
  (*quietly* is an adverb of manner)

quiet • quite
- *I'm **quite** happy at my new school.*
  (Not **quiet**)
- *Please be **quiet**.* (Not **quite**)
  (commonly confused pronunciation and spelling for *quiet* and *quite*)

quietly • gradually • slowly
- *Go upstairs **quietly**.*
  (Not **slowly** or **slowly slowly**)
  (= without making a noise)
- *We introduced the changes **gradually**.*
  (Not **slowly** or **slowly slowly**)
  (= little by little)
- *I'm walking **slowly** because I'm tired.*
  (= not fast)

quite
- *Professor Hogg's lecture was **quite good**, but not up to his usual standard.*
  (*quite* = less than the highest degree)
  (*quite* + gradable words like *good, pretty*, etc.; the meaning depends on stress: a falling tone on the word after *quite* means 'less than the highest degree'; a rising tone means 'more than expected')
- *This sauce is **quite perfect**.*
- *Your stamina is **quite amazing**!*
  (*quite* + ungradable words like *dead, unique, lost*, etc., or 'strong' words like *amazing, astonishing* = completely)

R

race • breed
- *The chihuahua is a very unusual **breed** of dog.* (Not **race**)
  (*breed* for animals and plants = type)
- *Who can say what the future will be for the whole of the human **race**?* (Not **breed**)
  (*the human race* for the whole of humanity)
- *Good **race** relations are essential in mixed societies.* (Not **breed**)
  (= relating to different human *races*)

raise • rise (nouns)
- *There's been a big **rise** in car thefts in our area.* (Not **raise**)
- *I've put in for a **rise*** (BrE)/***raise*** (AmE).
  (= an increase in salary)
- *I've had a **pay rise**.* (Not **pay raise**)

raise • rise • rouse • arouse (present)
- *What time does the sun **rise**?*
  (Not **raise* *rouse**)
  (= come up)
- *We **rise** at 6 a.m.* (Not **raise* *rouse**)
  (*rise* = get up is unusual and rather formal)
  (*rise - rose - have risen* is intransitive)
- *Will those who agree with me please **raise** their hands?* (Not **rise* *rouse**)
  (= put them up)
- *Increased Sales Tax will **raise** prices.*
  (Not **rise* *rouse**)
  (= make them go up)
  (*raise - raised - raised* is transitive)
- *If we're going to set out so early, you'll have to **rouse** us all at 6 in the morning.*
  (Not **raise* *rise* *arouse**)
  (= thoroughly disturb, make us get up)
- *We don't want to **arouse** their suspicions that we might be interested in buying their business.* (Not **rouse* *raise* *rise**)
  (*arouse* means 'waken', 'excite'; it often combines with abstract nouns: *arouse concern, interest, suspicion*, etc.)

raised • risen (past participles)
- *You're still in bed and the sun has already **risen**!* (Not **raised**)
  (*rise - rose - have **risen*** is intransitive)
- *Increased Sales Tax has **raised** prices all round.* (Not **risen**)
  (*raise - raised - **raised*** is transitive)

raised • rose (past tense)
- *We stood on the cliff and watched as the sun **rose** in all its glory.* (Not **raised**)
  (*rise - **rose** - have risen* is intransitive)

- *When the management **raised** ticket prices, attendance dropped.* (Not **rised* *rose**)
  (*raise - **raised** - raised* is transitive)

raisins/currants/sultanas • grapes
- *When I was a student, I worked picking **grapes** in the south of France.*
  (Not **raisins/currants/sultanas**)
- *A Christmas cake is full of nuts, **raisins**, **currants** and **sultanas**.*
  (= dried grapes; *raisins* is the general word for dried grapes, *currants* are small dried grapes and *sultanas* are larger than *currants*)

rang/rung • ring/ringed
- *I've **rung** the bell.* (Not **I've rang**)
- *The bell **rang** a moment ago.* (Not **rung**)
  (*ring - rang - rung*; irregular verb)
- *I've **ringed** some advertisements that might interest you.* (Not **I've rung**)
  (*ring - ringed - ringed*, regular verb, = put a circle round)

rare • scarce • unusual
- *Fresh vegetables are **scarce** because of the drought.* (Not **rare**)
  (= hard to obtain)
- *The preservation of **rare** species of birds and animals concerns us all.* (Not **scarce**)
  (= extremely uncommon)
- *Snow is extremely **unusual/rare** at this time of the year.* (Not **scarce**)
  (= uncommon)

rate • instalment
- *We bought the car **on instalments**.*
  (Not **by rate**)
  (= by separate payments over a period; alternative spelling: *installments*)
- *What's the **rate** of interest if I pay by instalments?*
  (= charge on a scale)

rather/sooner
- *I'd **rather/sooner work** on the land **than work** in a factory.* (Not **rather/sooner to work ... than to work**)
  (bare infinitive after *would rather/sooner* and *than*)

reach • arrive at/in • come
- *What time did you **arrive in London**?*
- *What time did you **reach London**?* (Not **reach to/in London* *arrive to* *rich**)
  (*reach*, which is not followed by a preposition, = *arrive* after a journey; *arrive + at* a point or *in* an area, depending on your viewpoint: *I arrived at/in Rome*; *arrive* may be used on its own: *When did you **arrive**?*)

- *When you **reach my age**, you'll be an expert.*
  (Not **reach to**; preferable to *arrive at*)
  (*reach* for contexts other than journeys)
- *Can you get that book down for me please? I can't **reach it/reach**.* (Not **arrive at it**)
  (= succeed in touching it)
- *Waiter! - **I'm coming**!* (Not **I'm arriving!**)

read (about)
- *Your essay **reads** well.* (Not **is reading**)
  (stative use: i.e. it is good to read)
- *I'm **reading** your essay.*
  (dynamic use)
- *Have you **read about** the floods in Texas?*
  (Not **read for**)
- *I **read** /riːd/ the papers every day.*
- *Have you **read** /red/ this morning's paper?*
  (Not **/riːd/**)
  (pronunciation of present and past forms)

read • study
- *I'm **reading/studying** History at university.*
  (specialized use of *read* = study a subject for a degree; we can also *do* a subject: i.e. formally study it, e.g. *do Art, do English, do History*, etc.)
- *I'm **studying** Shakespeare's 'Hamlet'.*
  (= reading carefully, e.g. to prepare for an exam)
- *I'm **reading** Shakespeare's 'Hamlet'.*
  (but not necessarily *studying* it)

ready • get ready
- *I'm **getting ready** for tonight's party.*
  (Not **I'm readying** **I'm readying myself**)
- *While the equipment was loaded, the team **readied themselves** for departure.*
  (= made preparations for something difficult; *get ready* is more usual than *ready oneself*)

ready • ready-to-wear
- *There's a huge choice of **ready-to-wear clothing** in this store.*
  (Not **ready clothing** **ready clothes**)
- *Dinner is **ready**.*

real • genuine • true
- *Is this Rembrandt **genuine**?* (Not **real**)
  (= not a fake)
- *Are ghosts **real**?* (Not **genuine** **true**)
  (= actually existing, not imaginary)
- *It's a **real/genuine** Rembrandt.* (Not **true**)
  (*real* and *genuine* are interchangeable in front of a noun)
- *She told me a **true** story. Her story proved to be **true/genuine**.* (Not **real**)
  (= not false, not made up)

- *Our journey across the desert was a **real** nightmare.* (preferable to *true*)
  (*real* as an intensifier = complete)

realize • understand • bring about
- *I don't think I **understand** the meaning of the sentence.* (Not **realize**)
  (= comprehend)
- *I wandered into the wrong cloakroom without **realizing** it.* (Not **understanding**)
  (= becoming aware of)
- *Everybody **realizes/understands** how vital it is to have clean drinking water.*
  (sometimes interchangeable)
- *A long cold winter could **bring about** a rise in energy prices.* (Not **realize**)
  (= cause)
- *I hope you **realize** that you're making a big mistake.* (Not **are realizing**)
  (stative use = understand)
- *After years of experience and training, Chris is now **realizing** his potential.*
  (dynamic use = getting the value of)

recall
- *I don't expect you **recall meeting** me in Vienna some years ago.* (Not **to meet**)

receive • admit
- *Normally, universities won't **admit** students aged under 18.* (Not **receive**)
- *You need a large room if you're going to **receive** so many guests.*
  (*receive* = have as visitors; *admit* = let in)
  *Paul will never **admit** it, but he's been keen on you for years.* (Not **receive**)
  (= acknowledge)

receive • take • get • obtain
- *He told me to **take/get** the keys from his pocket.* (Not **receive** **obtain**)
  (= remove)
- *Nick **took** the kids to school this morning.*
  (Not **received** **got** **obtained**)
- *When did you **receive/get** that letter?*
  (Not **take** **obtain**)
  (i.e. which has been sent to you)
- *Where did they **get/obtain** this information?*
  (i.e. they took active steps to get hold of it; *receive* would suggest it was sent to them; *take (from)* would suggest 'remove')

reckoning • bill • account
- *The **bill/account** for car repairs came to over £500.* (Not **reckoning**: archaic)
  (= a formal application for payment)

- *You can pay by credit card if you have an* **account** *with us.* (Not **reckoning**)
  (= a credit account e.g. held in a store)
- *On my* **reckoning,** *the bill for repairs will run to more than £500.* (Not **account**)
  (= calculation)
- *Do you believe there'll be a* **day of reckoning***?*
  (*a/the day of reckoning*: Biblical fixed phrase = a/the day when everybody gets what he/she deserves)

reclaim • claim • advertise • complain
- *The new product has been widely* **advertised** *on TV.* (Not **reclaimed**)
  (= made known in order to be sold; the noun is *an advertisement*, not **a reclaim**)
- *Don't* **complain** *to the waiter when it's the cook's fault.* (Not **reclaim**)
- *You can* **reclaim/claim** *expenses from the company if you have to go by taxi.*
  (= ask for the return of; the noun is *reclaim* as in *Put in a* **reclaim/a claim** *for expenses*. The noun *reclamation* is often associated with *land*, as in *land reclamation* = making waste land fit for use)

recommend • introduce • advise
- *Let me* **introduce** *you to our guests.*
  (= present, enable you to meet)
- *Who* **introduced** *you to this club?*
  (= made you aware of it/made it aware of you, brought you in as a member)
- *Who* **recommended** *this club to you?*
  (i.e. praised, suggesting you join it)
- *Who* **recommended** *you for admission to this club?*
  (= suggested you, said you were suitable)
- *Who* **recommended/advised** *you* **to** *see an eye specialist?*
- *Who* **recommended/advised that** *you (should) see an eye specialist?*
  (Not **recommended/advised you that**)
  (*recommend someone* = speak well of; *recommend someone to do something* = advise)

recommend • register
- *Is the letter* **registered***?*
  (Not **recommended**)
  (= sent by registered post)
- *A long holiday is* **recommended***.*
  (= advised)

redden • go/turn red
- *She* **went red/turned red** *with embarrassment when I spoke to her.*
  (preferable to *She reddened*)

- *Keep the tomatoes in a warm place until they* **redden/go red/turn red***.*

reduced to
- *Many pensioners are* **reduced to spending** *their savings.* (Not **reduced to spend**)
  (*to* functions as a preposition + *-ing* here, not as part of the infinitive)

refinery • distillery
- *Would you like to look round a whisky* **distillery** *in Scotland?* (Not **refinery**)
  (= a place where alcohol is made pure, *distilled*)
- *There's a huge oil* **refinery** *in the Thames Estuary.* (Not **distillery**)
  (= a place where e.g. petroleum is *refined*)

refuse • deny
- *The secretary* **denies** *all* **knowledge** *of the missing letter.* (Not **refuses knowledge**)
  (= does not accept as a fact: *deny an accusation, an allegation, knowledge*, etc.)
- *I offered to pay him for his help but he* **refused** *(payment).* (Not **denied**)
  (= didn't accept an offer; *refused to accept*)
- *All those not holding valid tickets will be* **refused/denied entry***.*
  (= not be given *entry, permission*, etc.)
- *The accused strongly* **denies stealing** *food from supermarkets.* (Not **denies to steal**)

regard • look at/on
- *Just* **look at** *those children picking apples!* (Not **regard** **look on**)
  (i.e. use your eyes actively)
- *I don't* **regard** *a degree/***look on** *a degree as a meal ticket for life.* (preferable to *look at*)
  (= consider)

regard as
- *I* **regard** *her* **as** *the best person for the job.*
  (Not **am regarding**)
  (= consider)
- *The management* **regard/are regarding** *the strike* **as** *a challenge to their authority.*
  (= consider/are considering)
  (stative or dynamic depending on the speaker's viewpoint)

regime • system • diet
- *We've just introduced a completely new filing* **system** *in our office.* (Not **regime**)
  (= a way of doing things)
- *I keep to a strict* **regime** *by going to bed early and getting up early.* (Not **system**)
  (= a disciplined routine)
- *It was economic factors that brought an end to the Communist* **regime/system***.*

(*regime* = a style of government; *system* = a way of doing things)
- *I'm watching what I eat because I'm on a diet.* (Not **doing/making a diet/a regime** **I'm in diet**)
- *My doctor advised me to go on a diet.* (Not **do/make a diet/a regime**)

register (of) • index (to) • address book
- *This cookery book would be more use with a proper index at the back.* (Not **register**)
  (= an alphabetical list of topics showing which pages they are on; plural: *indexes*)
- *Is the Dow Jones the best index to US share prices?* (Not **register of**)
  (= an indicator; plural *indices*)
- *We keep a register of everyone who has stayed at our hotel.* (Not **an index of**)
  (= an official list, especially of names)
- *My address book contains names of people who've moved.* (Not **index** **register**)

regret
- *We regret to inform you that your account is overdrawn.* (Not **regret informing**)
  (*regret* + *to* = feel sorry can refer to the present or the future)
- *I now regret leaving my job and becoming self-employed.* (Not **regret to leave**)
  (*regret* + *-ing* refers to finished actions in the present or past)

reign (over) • govern
- *The same party has governed this country for nearly 14 years.* (Not **reigned**)
  (= directed the affairs of)
- *Queen Victoria reigned over Britain for most of the nineteenth century.*
  (*reign* = 'wear the crown': only kings and queens *reign*; governments *rule* or *govern*)

rejuvenate • restore
- *A nice cold beer will restore us.* (Not **rejuvenate**)
  (= bring back to a state of well-being)
- *She looks quite rejuvenated since she left that awful job.*
  (= made young again; formal)

related to
- *His name's Presley, but I don't think he's related to Elvis.* (Not **related with**)
  (= has family connexions with)

relax • rest
- *I had a nice long rest during my holiday and feel quite refreshed.* (Not **relax**)
- *You look tired. Why don't you have/take a little rest?* (Not **make/do a rest**)

(*rest*, noun, is usually physical though it can also refer to the mind)
- *You must try to relax and enjoy yourself.* (Not **relax yourself**)
  (= allow yourself not to worry; we use *relax* only as a verb: the noun, *relaxation*, can be physical and/or mental)

relief • rendering
- *The rendering on the front of the house is cracked.* (Not **relief**)
  (= cement-based paint for outside walls)
- *This design looks very effective in relief.*
  (= with parts of it sticking up/out from the surface)
- *It was a relief to land safely after such a rough journey.*
  (= a feeling of comfort following anxiety)

rely on
- *We're relying on you to get us out of this mess.* (Not **relying from/to**)

remarks • observations • notes
- *The standing stones at Carnac were probably used for astronomical observations.* (Not **remarks** **notes**)
  (= what is seen in a scientific context)
- *The designer's observations on our plan deserve careful consideration.*
  (= comments based on an objective view)
- *Rita has a reputation for making rude remarks about people.*
  (= spoken comments)
- *Did you take any notes during the lecture?*
  (= information or comments in writing)

remember
- *Remember to post the letters.*
  (= don't forget to post)
- *I remembered to post the letters.*
  (= I didn't forget to post)
- *I remember(ed) posting the letters.*
  (= I posted them and I remember the action)
- *Remember me to your parents.*
  (Not **Remember me your parents.**)
  (or it would be more usual to say: *Give my regards to your parents.*)

remembrance • memory • souvenir • memento
- *My memory is unreliable now I'm older.*
  (Not **remembrance** **souvenir**)
  (= the ability to call to mind)
- *The only memory I have of my grandmother is of a smiling old lady in a rocking chair.*
  (Not **souvenir**)
  (= what I remember)

- *This ring is the only **remembrance** I have of my grandmother.*
  (Not *memory*, preferable to *souvenir*)
  (now old-fashioned = a token which makes me remember a person)
- *I bought this **souvenir** of the Colosseum when I was in Rome.* (Not *memento*)
  (= an object which reminds you of an occasion or place, usually sold to tourists)
- *I've kept this photo as a **memento** of the house I used to live in.* (Not *souvenir*)
  (= a small object which reminds you of an experience or a person)
- *This monument was erected **in remembrance/ memory of** those who died in battle.*
  (= to make people remember)

remind • remember • reminisce
- *I **remember** my first day at school as if it were yesterday.* (Not *remind* *reminisce*)
  (= can bring to mind)
- *The smell of cabbage **reminds me of/makes me remember** school.* (Not **remembers me school** **reminds me school**)
- ***Remind me** to post that letter.*
  (Not *Remember me*)
- *Old people like to **reminisce about** the past.*
  (Not *remind*)
  (= remember and talk about)

rent • income
- *Most writers earn their real **income** from ordinary jobs.* (Not *rent*)
  (*income* = money earned or paid as a pension: 'money coming in')
- *The **rent** takes more than half of my income.*
  (= the money paid for a place to live)

reparations • repairs
- *The roof needed a lot of **repairs** after last year's storms.* (Not *reparations*)
  (= fixing, making good)
- *The cost of war **reparations** can be a great burden to a country.*
  (= money paid as compensation for damage or wrongdoing)

repeat (oneself) • recur
- *We're going through a recession. It's the kind of situation that **recurs** from time to time.* (Not *repeats*, though *repeats itself* would be possible)
  (= comes back and happens again; intransitive)
- *History often **repeats itself**.*
  (Not *recurs* *repeats*)
- *I wish you wouldn't keep **repeating yourself**.*
  (Not *recurring*)

(= saying the same thing again; *repeat* is transitive or reflexive)

repeat • rehearse
- *We're **rehearsing** our play all next week.*
  (Not *repeating*)
  (= practising so as to get it right)
- *They're **repeating** that wonderful TV play.*
  (= showing again: *a repeat performance*)

repetition • revision
- *Have you done your **revision** for the exams?*
  (Not *repetition*)
  (= studying the same material again to prepare for an exam)
- ***Repetition** is the only way to learn a poem by heart.* (Not *Revision*)
  (= doing, saying the same thing over and over again)

report
- *Someone has **reported seeing** the car the police are looking for.* (Not *to see*)
- *I **reported the accident to the police**.*
  (Not **reported the police the accident** **reported to the police the accident**)
- *Our correspondent has just sent in **a report on** events in Algeria.* (Not *a report for*)
- *I'd like you to check the accounts and **make/do a report** for me.*

report • reference • certificate
- *My former employer gave me a very good **reference**.* (Not *report* *certificate*)
  (= written information about character and ability)
- *Did your teacher give you a good **report** (AmE **report card**) last term?*
  (Not *reference* *certificate*)
  (= written information about progress in school)
- *Please bring the top copy of your **certificate** to the interview.* (Not *diploma*)
  (= an official document that records official recognition of something: exam success, birth, marriage, death, etc.)

reportage • report
- *Our Tokyo correspondent has sent us the following **report**.* (Not *a reportage*)
  (countable noun = written or spoken account)
- *Good **reportage**/A good **piece of reportage** makes you feel as if you can see events as they happen.* (Not *A reportage*)
  (uncountable noun = the 'product' of the act of reporting)

republic • democracy

- *A **democracy** is ruled by freely elected representatives.* (Not **republic**)
  (= a country with a freely elected government; adjective: *democratic*)
- *Britain is a democracy, but not a **republic**.*
  (= a country whose head of state isn't a king or a queen; adjective: *republican*)

request

- *Learning to **make a** polite **request** is important in a foreign language.* (Not **do**)
- ***Passengers are requested to remain seated** until the aircraft comes to a complete stop.* (formal) (Not **It is requested the passengers to remain seated**)

require

- *Universities **require** a lot more money for research.* (Not **are requiring**)
  (stative use only = need; formal)
- ***Candidates are required to present themselves** fifteen minutes before the examination begins.* (formal)
  (Not **It is required the candidates to present themselves**)

rescue (from) • save (from)

- *There's no doubt that seat belts **save** lives in traffic accidents.* (Not **rescue**)
  (*save a life* = keep from destruction)
- *The helicopter has now **rescued** most of the passengers.* (preferable to *saved*)
  (*rescue a person/people* = remove from danger)
- *He dived into the river and **rescued/saved** the child **from** drowning.*

research

- *Scientists are **carrying out/doing** a lot of **research** into Carbon 60.* (Not **making**)
  (*research* = serious study)

resemble

- *Paul **resembles** his father.*
  (Not **is resembling** **resembles to**)
  (stative use only; no progressive form)

resent

- *I have a feeling Sandra **resents taking** orders from me.* (Not **resents to take**)

reserve • save

- *I've **saved** some of last night's supper for you.* (Not **reserved**)
  (= kept from being thrown away or used by someone else)

- *Would you **save** this seat for me for ten minutes please?* (Not **reserve**)
  (= keep from being taken)
- *We've **reserved** two seats for tomorrow's concert.* (Not **saved**)
  (= booked in advance; *made reservations*)

reserved/taken • occupied

- *All the seats in the front row are **occupied**.* (i.e. people are sitting in them)
- *All the seats in the front row are **reserved/ taken**.*
  (*reserved* = booked; *taken* = not available)

resign oneself (to)

- *We have to **resign ourselves to accepting** traffic delays.* (Not **resign ... to accept**)
  (*to* functions as a preposition + *-ing* here, not as part of the infinitive)

resist

- *We've all **resisted putting** in longer hours for less money.* (Not **resisted to put**)

resort to

- *We've **resorted to walking** to work to save money.* (Not **resorted to walk**)
  (*to* functions as a preposition + *-ing* here, not as part of the infinitive)

respond to • reply to • answer

- *I **answered** her card/**replied to** her card.*
  (Not **answered to/replied her card**)
  (= provided an answer to; *answer* and *reply to* are neutral in meaning)
- *Have you decided how to **respond to their letter** yet?* (Not **respond their letter**)
  (*respond* suggests 'react suitably')
- *My aunt has been in hospital for a week, but she's **responding to treatment**.*
  (Not **answering/replying to treatment**)
  (= reacting favourably)

rest • leftovers • remains (of) • remainder

- *They make the **leftovers** into soup and call it minestrone.* (Not **rests** **remainders**, preferable to *remains* when we don't say what is 'left over')
  (= food that hasn't been eaten at a meal)
- *What am I going to do with the **remains of** last night's meal?* (Not **rests** **remainders**; preferable to *leftovers*)
  (*remains* = 'what is left of a meal' is too general to be used without *of* + noun: *the remains of the meal*)
- *Bach's **remains** have been moved to Leipzig.* (Not **leftovers** **rests** **remainders**)
  (= what is left of a dead body; but note also *ancient remains* = ruins of old buildings)

- *I only need half of that pastry. What on earth can I do with **the remainder/the rest**?* (uncountable = what is extra)

rest • remain • stay

- *Nothing **remains/stays** the same for ever.* (Not **rests**)
(= continues to be)
- *My in-laws are **staying** with us for a few days.* (Not **resting* *remaining**)
*Let's **rest** for a bit before finishing the climb.* (Not **remain* *stay**)
(= pause for a break in order to recover)

rest • (small/loose) change

- *Sorry to give you a £50 note. I haven't got any **change**.* (Not **rest* *rests**)
(= notes of smaller value; coins)
- *I want **(small/loose) change** for this note.* (= coins)
- *If you have to pay with a £50 note, make sure you count your **change**.* (Not **rest(s)**)
(= the money you get back)
- *I spent **the rest** of my savings on a car.* (= what was left)

resume • summarize

- *Can you **summarize** the argument in a couple of paragraphs?* (Not **resume**)
(= give a brief account of; the noun is summary: *I'll write a **summary** of my lecture*; the word *résumé* exists, but tends to be confined to contexts of academic or business jargon)
- *We stopped in Tangiers for a couple of nights before we **resumed** our journey.* (= continued after a break; the noun is resumption: *The peace-keeping force has prevented the **resumption** of hostilities*.)

retire (from) • withdraw (from)

- *Sanchez **withdrew from** the race at the last minute.* (Not **retired**)
(= did not take part in)
- *Sanchez **retired/withdrew from** the race after the fourth lap.*
(= was taking part in, then left)
- *Sanchez has **retired from** rally driving.* (Not **withdrawn from**)
(i.e. given it up completely)
- *Father enjoys life now that he has **retired**.* (= stopped working and taken his pension)

revenge oneself on ... for • avenge

- *Hamlet had to **avenge** his father's murder.* (Not **revenge**)
- *Hamlet had to **revenge himself on** his father's murderer/**revenge himself for** the death of his father.* (Not **avenge**)
(both words mean 'punish the person who has done you wrong'; you *avenge* an action or *take revenge on* someone *for* an action)

revise • review • audit • overhaul

- *The government is **reviewing** its policy on immigration.*
(= reconsidering, looking again at)
- *The government is **revising** its policy on immigration.*
(= making changes to)
- *Our office is closed for a day while our accounts are being **audited**.* (Not **revised* *reviewed* *overhauled**)
(= officially checked)
- *My car's been **overhauled** and is in good working order.* (Not **revised* *reviewed**)
(= examined and repaired)

rhythm • rate • pace

- *I don't know how you can work **at such a rate/pace**!* (Not **with such a rhythm**)
(= at such a speed)
- *I don't know how you can walk at such a **pace/rate**!* (Not **rhythm**)
(*pace* = length of step; *rate* = speed)
- *I wish you'd dance to the **rhythm**!*
(= a regular beat, especially in music)

ribbon • tape • strip

- *The **tape** is rather worn and the sound quality is bad.* (Not **ribbon**)
(= magnetic *tape* used in a *tape recorder*)
- *You should put some insulating **tape** round those bare wires.* (Not **ribbon**)
(= narrow material, often sticky on one side)
- *I finished wrapping the gift and tied it up with a big red **ribbon**.* (Not **tape**)
(= a strip of material for tying things and/or decorating them; in general, *(a) ribbon* is decorative and/or soft and floppy; *tape* is stronger/thicker: functional/non-decorative)
- *You really need to replace the **ribbon** on that printer of yours.* (Not **tape**)
(= a strip of material soaked with ink)
- *Don't throw away that **strip** of paper! I'm using it as a bookmark.*
(= a long thin piece of e.g. paper, material)

rich

- *Frances came from a poor family, but died **rich/a rich woman**.* (Not **a rich**)
- *They may not be millionaires, but **they're very rich/rich people**.* (Not **they're riches**)
(we cannot use *rich* on its own to mean 'a rich person'; *riches* used as a noun to mean 'wealth' is now old-fashioned)

- It's hard to tax **the rich** without taxing the poor as well.
(*the* + adjective for the group as a whole)
- They **got rich** by buying cheap and selling dear. (Not *They riched*)
(compare *enrich* (not *rich*) for 'add something valuable': Children **enrich** your life, even if they make you poorer financially, not *rich your life*)

ride
- Let's **go for/go on** a ride. (Not *do/make*)
- I've just **had a long ride** on my bike.
(Not *made/done a ride*)
- I **rode** here on my bike. (Not *drove*)
(*ride* e.g. a horse or a bicycle)

right (about/for)
- **You're right**! The museums are shut on Mondays. (Not *You have right/reason!*)
- You were **right about** the increase in rail fares. (Not *right for*)
(*about* = concerning)
- I don't think he's **right for** the job.
(*for* = in relation to)
- You **did right** to refuse any money for your advice. (Not *made right*)
(= acted in a proper way)

right • rightly
- You're not **thinking right** about this.
(Not *thinking rightly*)
(a few verbs related to being, seeming and behaving combine with *right*, adjective, rather than *rightly*, adverb: *answer right, feel right, do right*)
- John informed us, **rightly**, that the 8.27 to Brighton had been cancelled. (Not *right*)
(adverbial use = correctly)
- I don't think you acted **right/rightly** there.
(both forms possible after *act*)

ring • telephone • phone/call
- Please **give me a ring/call**.
(Not *do/make me a ring/call* *give me a telephone/a phone*, but we can say *make a (phone) call* in e.g. Excuse me a moment. I've got to **make a call/a phone call**.)
- Please **ring (me)/call (me)/telephone (me)/phone (me)** when you get home.
(*telephone* is more formal than *phone*; *call* is mainly AmE; *ring* is not used in AmE)

risk
- We'd better take a taxi. We can't **risk missing** the plane. (Not *risk to miss*)

rob • steal • burgle
- The man who **stole** my handbag took my address book as well. (Not *robbed*)
- I lost my address book when that man **robbed me of my bag/stole my bag from me**.
(Not *stole me of my bag*)
(*steal* something *from* someone or *from* somewhere; *rob* someone *of* something)
- Gangs have been **robbing** passengers on overnight trains. (Not *stealing*)
- You paid far too much for this souvenir. I think you were **robbed**. (Not *stolen*)
(i.e. 'overcharged')
- **Robbing** banks can hardly be described as a profession. (Not *Stealing* *Burgling*)
- Our house was **burgled** while we were away on holiday. (Not *robbed* *stolen*)
(people or banks/institutions are *robbed*; things are *stolen* (*from* people or places); property is *burgled* or *broken into*; people may be *kidnapped*)

robber • burglar • thief/theft
- The **robbers** went into the bank and demanded money at gunpoint.
- Some **burglars** got into the house at night and stole all our wedding presents.
- There's a **thief** in our office. There have been **thefts** of money from people's bags.
(*thief* is the general word for a person who *steals*, i.e. takes things that belong to someone else and who is guilty of *theft*. A *robber* is a thief who deals directly with his/her victim and is guilty of *robbery*. A *burglar* (also called a *housebreaker*) is a thief who breaks into the victim's home in order to steal and is guilty of *burglary* or *housebreaking*. Other specialist terms are *pickpocket* and *shoplifter*. Someone who 'steals people' is a *kidnapper*)

robe • dress • dressing gown • bathrobe
- I need a new **dress** for the dance tomorrow.
(Not *robe* *dressing gown*)
(= a woman's garment made of a top like a blouse, with a skirt joined on)
- I think she goes round the house all day in a **dressing gown** (AmE *robe*).
(= a long loose garment like a coat worn indoors over pyjamas or a nightdress)
- I always like to dry out in a **bathrobe** after taking a bath. (preferable to *robe*)
(= a coat-shaped garment, often made of towelling, for wearing after a bath)
- The students had to wear **robes** at the degree-giving ceremony.

(= long loose coats worn on ceremonial, historical or theatrical occasions)

rock • stone

- *The demonstrators threw **stones** at the police* (AmE *stones* or *rocks*; countable = small pieces of *stone* and *rock*)
- *The old church is full of beautiful **stone** sculptures.* (Not **rock**)
  (*stone*, uncountable: material for statues, steps, walls, etc.)
- *The flood water had left mud and **stones** all over the fields.*
  (= pieces of stone, small enough for someone to move or handle)
- ***Rocks** had fallen from above, making the roads impassable.* (preferable to *stones*)
  (= pieces of rock too big to move easily)
- *The tunnel goes through solid **rock**.*
  (uncountable = material the earth is made of)

roll (up) • wrap (up)

- *Shall I **wrap** it **(up)** for you?* (Not **roll it**)
  (= make a parcel)
- *This barrel is too heavy to lift. We'll have to **roll it**.* (Not **roll it up**)
  (= move by turning it over and over)
- *We'll have to **roll up** the carpet.*
  (i.e. so that it forms a tube)

romance • roman • novel • fiction • soap opera

- *Kingsley Amis's 'Lucky Jim' is one of the most successful first **novels** ever written.* (Not **romance** **roman**)
  (= a full-length work of fiction)
- *Georgette Heyer's **historical romances** are read all over the world.*
  (= novels of love and adventure set in the past. We use *romance* to mean *novel* when it is preceded by e.g. *historical*. We use *romance* mainly to describe a love affair: *It was the end of a beautiful **romance**.*)
- *Penguin Books publish a lot of **fiction**.*
  (*fiction*, uncountable, is the general term for written works of the imagination; the opposite is *non-fiction* = factual works)
- *The commentary is set in **roman** and the examples are set in italics.*
  (= a style of print)
- *It's easy to become addicted to Brazilian **soap operas/soaps**.* (Not **novellas**)
  (= television or radio programmes, in serial form, about particular people and their daily lives: e.g. *Neighbours, Dallas*)

rooms to let • bed and breakfast

- *We've already passed several **bed and breakfast** signs.* (Not **rooms to let** **rooms** **rooms free**)
  (referring to rooms let for a single night or for short periods; signs displayed say *Bed and Breakfast, B&B* or *(No) Vacancies*, especially BrE)
- *Try the house at the end of the street. I know they have **rooms to let/they let rooms**.*
  (= rooms which are let for long periods)

rough • roughly

- *We travelled light and **slept rough**.*
  (Not **slept roughly**)
  (*rough* is an adjective and gives the verbs it is used after the sense of *be*: *look rough, play rough, talk rough*)
- *I've sketched it **roughly**.* (Not **rough**)
  (adverbial use = with bare essentials only)
- *He spoke **roughly** to the child.*
  (Not **rough**)
  (= in a rough manner: *-ly* for a deliberate action)

round • around

- *The shop you're looking for is **round/ around** the corner.*
- *Quick! He's just disappeared **round the corner**.* (Not **round off/from**; preferable to *disappeared around*)
  (*round* and *around* = circular movement, can be used in the same way, but *round* is often preferable with verbs of movement)

route • road • way

- *There was so much traffic, it was impossible to cross the **road**.* (Not **route** **way**)
  (a *road* is a flat surface that carries traffic)
- *Let's go this **way**.* (Not **road** **route**)
  (= direction)
- *There's lots of traffic **on the road(s)** today.*
  (literally, 'on the road')
- *We're late. I'll ring to say we're **on the way**.* (Not **on the road** **in the way**)
  (= heading in a particular direction)
- *Can you move this suitcase please? It's **in the way/in my way**.* (Not **on the/my way**)
  (= blocking my path)
- *Which is the quickest **way/route** into the town centre?* (preferable to *road*; we can say *This is a **fast road***, to mean that traffic moves along it at speed)
  (a *route* connects two points; we also use *route* when referring to maps; *(the) way* = direction, or connecting series of directions)

routine • red tape
- *Getting a visa for some places involves a lot of red tape.* (Not *routine*)
(= official paper work; informal)
- *William kept to the same routine all his life.*
(= a habitual way of doing things)

row • line/queue • tail • turn
- *There's a long line/queue of people waiting for the bus.* (Not *row* *tail*)
(= people, cars, etc., waiting for their turn; we can speak of *the tail-end of a queue*)
- *We'd better join the queue for tickets.*
(Not *row* *tail*; *line* is possible in AmE) (*a line* is a physical description; *a queue* includes the idea of turn-taking)
- *I wish that car would either pass me or get off my tail.* (Not *queue*)
(*on my tail* = too close behind me)
- *You can see me in this old school photo, standing in the back row.* (Not *line*)
(= a neat line of people, buildings, etc.; *in a row* = side by side)
- *My neighbour and I collect our children from school in turns and it's my turn tomorrow.* (Not *in rows* *my row*)
(= 'alternately' ... 'I'm next')
- *Stop pulling the cat's tail, Susie.*

rubbish/garbage
- *Where shall I throw this rubbish/garbage?*
(Not *these rubbishes/garbages*)
(= waste material; usually *rubbish* in BrE and *garbage* in AmE; both are uncountable)

rude • rough
- *When I phoned he answered me in a very rough voice.*
(= either uneven in sound, or not gentle, but not necessarily impolite)
- *I shouldn't tangle with those boys. They're a pretty rough lot.*
(= wild, perhaps violent)
- *You can complain without being rude!*
(= impolite)

rules
- *Who makes the rules here?* (Not *does*)
- *According to the rules of our club, each member may bring one guest only.*
(Not *With the rules*)

run • drive so fast/too fast • walk so fast
- *I'm not surprised he's had an accident. He always drives so fast/too fast.* (Not *runs*)
- *Don't walk so fast. I can't keep up.*
(Not *Don't run so fast*)

- *There's the bus. We'll have to run!*
(= move quickly on foot)

run • run on
- *Who runs this company?*
(= manages, is in charge of)
- *This engine runs on diesel.*
(Not *runs with/runs by*)
(= functions using)

S

sack • (school)bag
- *You often see very small children carrying very large (school)bags.* (Not *sacks*)
(*schoolbag* = a bag made of e.g. leather, canvas, for carrying books and often worn over the shoulders; also called a *satchel*)
- *Let me help you with that bag.*
(e.g. *a shopping bag, a handbag,* etc.)
- *I couldn't possibly lift that sack of potatoes.*
(= a very large bag for coal, potatoes, etc.)

sacred • holy • saint
- *You pretend to be so holy, but you're as bad as the rest of us.* (Not *sacred*)
(= good according to the rules of religion)
- *These lands are considered sacred by the Australian Aboriginals.* (preferable to *holy*)
(= spiritually important, viewed with reverence: *a sacred memory,* etc.)
- *St. (= Saint) Christopher is the patron saint of travellers.* (Not *Holy* *Sacred*)
(= a title formally given in some Christian churches to holy people of the past)

sad (about) • sorry (for) • sorrowful • unhappy
- *We are very sad about your news and hope things are going better for you.* (Not *sad for* *sorry for* *sorrowful about*)
(= unhappy about)
- *We were sad/sorry to hear that he had died.*
(Not *sorrowful* *sorry for hearing*)
(i.e. we felt sorrow)
(*sad* expresses a more personal regret; *sorry* expresses formal or proper sympathy)
- *I'm sorry for disturbing/I'm sorry to disturb you.* (Not *I'm sad for/to*)
(= I apologize for)
- *Why are you looking so sorrowful/sad?*
(Not *sorry*)
(i.e. with a sad expression on your face)
- *Lizzie had an unhappy childhood because her parents died when she was a baby.*
(preferable to *sad*)

(*unhappiness* is more long-lasting; *sadness* is more temporary)

safety • security • insurance
- *The cost of car **insurance** keeps going up and up.* (Not *safety* *security*)
(= money you pay to a company so that you can be compensated after an accident)
- *We've fitted window locks for our own **safety/security**.* (Not *insurance*)
(i.e. in order to feel safe, secure)
- *Fasten your **safety/seat** belts.*
(Not *security* *insurance*)
- *We have installed a **security** system in our house.* (Not *safety* *insurance*)
(*safety* = personal freedom from physical harm; *security* = prevention of loss or damage)

salad • lettuce • greens
- *All the **lettuces** in my garden are going to seed.* (Not *salads* *greens*)
- *You need **lettuce** to make a green **salad**.*
(*lettuce*, countable or uncountable = a vegetable with green leaves; *salad* = a mixture of fresh, usually raw, vegetables)
- *Small children often dislike **greens**.*
(= boiled, green leafy vegetables of the cabbage family)

sale: on sale • for sale • to sell
- *Did you see the sign outside the house that said **for sale**?* (Not *on sale* *to sell*)
- *Everything you can see in this shop is **for sale/on sale**.* (Not *to sell*)
(*for sale* may refer to a single item or a number of items; *on sale* refers to goods which are displayed)
- *We've got all these cars **to sell** by Friday.*
(Not *for sale* *on sale*)
(= which are to be sold)

salmon
- *I'll have **that salmon/those salmon** please.*
(Not *those salmons*)
(*salmon* has the same singular and plural forms; it can also be uncountable: *I'd like **some salmon** please.*)

salon • saloon • living room/drawing room • hall • living
- *Let's go and sit in the **living room/drawing room**.* (Not *salon* *saloon* *living*)
- *The meeting will be held in the main **hall**.*
(Not *salon* *saloon*)
- *They've just opened a new **hairdressing salon** in the High Street.* (Not *saloon*)
(= business; also *beauty salon*)

- *The cowboys were drinking in the **saloon**.*
(= a bar, especially in a 'Western')
- *It's not much of a job, but it's a **living**.*
(= a way of earning money)

salute

greet

welcome

wave

salute • greet • welcome • wave (to)
- *When we arrived, the whole family turned up to **greet us/welcome us**.* (Not *salute*)
(*greet* = generally show pleasure at meeting someone e.g. by shaking hands; *welcome* = show pleasure e.g. by shaking hands, when someone arrives at a place)
- *She **waved to** us from the boat.*
(Not *saluted*)
(= raised and moved her hand, as a greeting or to say goodbye, etc.)
- *The sentry **saluted** the officer.*
(= gave a military greeting)

same
- *Our TV is **the same as** yours.*
(Not *the same with* *the same like*)
- *I've lost my job. It's **the same with** Alex.*
(i.e. Alex has, too)
- *This cup is cracked. What's that one like? - It's **the same**.* (singular)
- *Those two dresses **are the same**.* (plural)

sane • healthy
- *A sensible diet is essential for keeping **healthy**.* (Not *sane*)
(= in good physical shape; not often ill)
- *I don't know how you've managed to bring up six children and still remain **sane**.*
(= not mad; opposite *insane*)

satisfied with
- *Do you think they're **satisfied with** my work?*
(Not *satisfied from/of*)

sauce • gravy • juice • (salad) dressing
- *My mother used to make a rich **gravy** to serve with roast beef.* (Not *sauce* *juice*)
(= a sauce made from the juices of roast meat)
- *The cauliflower was served with a nice white **sauce**.* (Not *gravy*)

(= a sweet or savoury liquid that adds flavour to prepared food, e.g. *bechamel sauce, tomato sauce, chocolate sauce*)
- *Would you like any of the **juice** with your fruit salad?* (Not **sauce**)
(= liquid that comes from fruit as a result of cutting, cooking or pressing)
- *Would you like some of this **dressing** on your salad?* (Not **juice**)
(= a liquid, often oil and vinegar, added to food, e.g. salad, just before serving)

saucy • with sauce
- *Do you want your fish plain or **with sauce**?* (Not **saucy**)
- *Don't be so **saucy**!*
(= cheeky, impolite)
- *He told a lot of rather **saucy** jokes.*
(= amusingly full of sexual innuendo)

saw • sawed
- *I **saw** Meg yesterday.* (Not **sawed**)
(*see - saw - seen*)
- *I **sawed** the plank in two.*
(= cut with a saw)
(*saw - sawed - sawed*: especially AmE; *sawn*: especially BrE)

say
- *What did you **say**?* /seɪ/
- *I didn't hear what you **said**.* /sed/ not **/seɪd/**
(pronunciation of present and past forms)
- *It **says** here that the next bus is due at 11.18.* (Not **It's saying**)
(stative use)
- *She's **saying**/She **says** that you can't book a room in advance without paying a deposit.*
(dynamic or stative use depending on the viewpoint of the speaker)
- *Who **says** so? - I **say** so!*
(Not **Who says it? - I say it!* *I say!**)
- *Say what you like to the doctor.*
(Not **Say the doctor what you like.* *Say to the doctor what you like.**)
- *Please do this for my sake and **don't say no (to me)**.* (Not **don't say me no**)

say • tell
- *'You haven't got much time,' he **said**/he **said to me**.* (Not **he told* *he said me**)
(*say* on its own, or followed directly by *to me*, etc.)
- *'We must hurry,' he **told me**.* (Not **he told* *he told to me* *he said me**)
(we always use a personal direct object after *tell: tell somebody*, not **tell to somebody**, not *tell* on its own)

- *He **said that**/**told me that** he's retiring.*
(the same rules apply in indirect speech)
- *It **is said that** there is plenty of oil off our coast.* (Not **It is told that**)
- *There **is said to be** plenty of oil off our coast.* (Not **There is told to be/to exist**)
- *Mandy **is said to be** some kind of secret agent.* (Not **Mandy is told to be**)
(*said* = believed)
- *Who **says** so?* (Not **tells so/tells it**)
(also *say a few words, say goodnight, say no more, say nothing, say your prayers, say something*)
- *I **told** you so!* (Not **said you so/said you it**)
(also: *tell the difference, tell a lie, tell a story, tell the time, tell the truth*)

scaffold • scaffolding
- *When are they going to take down **that scaffold**?* (Not **those scaffolds**)
- *When are they going to take away **all that scaffolding**?* (Not **all those scaffoldings**)
(*scaffolding* and *scaffold* = poles round a building during construction or repair)
- *Public execution on the **scaffold** was common until the last century.*
(= a specially-built platform on which people were hanged or beheaded)

scald • burn
- *I've **burnt** the toast.* (Not **scalded**)
- *I **burnt myself** on the toaster.* (Not **scalded myself**)
- *He spilt some boiling milk and **scalded himself**.* (Not **burnt himself**)
(*burn* = destroy or hurt by dry heat; *scald* = hurt by hot liquid or steam)

scale • ladder
- *I'll hold the **ladder** while you climb up.* (Not **scale**)
- *What was the strength of the earthquake on the Richter **scale**?*
(= measure)

scarf • shawl • veil
- *My wife covered her head with a **shawl**/**scarf** before entering the church.*
(*shawl* = a cloth worn by women over the shoulders; *scarf* = a cloth worn round the head or neck by men or women)
- *She attended the funeral dressed in black and with a heavy **veil**.*
(= thin material covering the face, worn by women, usually for religious reasons)

scene • scenery • view

- *The **scenery** round Mistras is magnificent.*
  (Not *scene* *sceneries* *view*)
  (= view of the countryside; uncountable)
- *They don't use a lot of **scenery** in modern productions of Shakespeare.*
  (Not *sceneries*)
  (= painted backgrounds, etc., used on stage)
- *The **view** from our window is lovely.*
  (Not *spectacle* *scenery*)
  (= what can be seen from a particular place)
- *They had a terrific argument in public. It wasn't a pleasant **scene**.*
  (= thing to see)

scene • screen • stage

- *The nurse put a **screen** round my bed to give me some privacy.* (Not *scene*)
- *There's nothing like watching a film on a large cinema **screen**.*
  (large flat area on which a film is projected)
- *The opening **scene** of the play is set in a street in Venice.* (Not *screen*)
  (= a division in a play or film)
- *At the end of the play the entire cast is on the **stage**.* (Not *scene*)
  (= the area where a play is performed)

scheme • diagram

- *For homework, draw a **diagram** of the human eye.* (Not *scheme*)
  (= a detailed drawing)
- *I've just started a new teaching **scheme**.*
  (= a plan, system)

scholastic • fussy/pedantic

- *Lawyers have to be **fussy/pedantic** about the small print in contracts.* (Not *scholastic*)
- *The school is better known for its sporting excellence than its **scholastic** achievements.*
  (= academic)

school

- *I was sent **to school** when I was five.*
  (Not *at (the) school* *to the school*)
- *I was **at school** for ten years.*
  (Not *to (the) school*)
  (i.e. in order to learn; also: *church, hospital, prison, university*. We use an article when referring to the 'building': *There's a meeting at **the school** this evening.*)

science • knowledge

- *Who would discourage the pursuit of **knowledge**?* (Not *knowledges*)
- *Here's **a piece of knowledge** that will interest you.* (Not *a knowledge*)
  (= what can be known, either through formal learning or experience; uncountable)
- *New developments in **science** have always depended on advances in the equipment for observation and measurement.*
  (= pure knowledge based on observation and testing)

scientist • man of letters

- *T.S. Eliot was a great poet, and a famous **man of letters**.* (Not *scientist*)
  (= a person concerned with books and literature; formal)
- *Albert Einstein was not only a distinguished **scientist**, but a considerable violinist.*
  (= a person concerned with a branch of science, such as physics or chemistry)

scratch • scrape

- *It might be better to soak that burnt pan than to **scrape** it.* (Not *scratch*)
  (i.e. remove burnt-on food with a knife; *scrape* = draw one thing over the surface of another; its meaning is often extended with adverbs: *scrape away, scrape out*, etc.)
- *Some people can't resist **scratching** their initials on monuments.* (Not *scraping*)
  (= marking; *scratch* = drag something sharp across a surface to make a mark or line)
- *The cat's **scratched** me!* (Not *scraped*)
  (= made marks in my skin with its claws)

sea

- *It's rather uncommon for young boys to run away **to sea** these days.* (Not *at (the) sea*)
- *Round-the-world yachtsmen expect to be **at sea** for many months.* (Not *to (the) sea*)
  (= sailing)

search • search for/seek

- *The whole village has been **searching for/seeking the missing boy**.*
  (Not *searching the missing boy*)
- *The security guards are **searching each passenger**.* (Not *seaching for* *seeking*)
  (*search for/seek* (formal) = look for someone or something that is lost: *search for your wallet*; *search someone* = carefully examine clothes and possessions; *seach something* = go through carefully: *search your pockets*)

secret • mystery • mystic

- *It's a **mystery** how the Nazca Lines in Peru were formed.* (Not *secret* *mystic*)
- *Teresa of Avila, the Spanish saint and **mystic**, died in 1582.*
  (= a person who seeks the truth through prayer and meditation)

- *The **secret** files of former regimes have now become public.* (Not **mystic* *mysterious**)
- *James Bond is a **secret** agent.*
  (Not **mystic**)
  (= hidden, not revealed)

see
- *I **see** very well without glasses.*
  (Not **I'm seeing**)
  (stative use: my ability is involuntary)
- *I **see** what you mean.* (Not **I'm seeing**)
  (stative use = understand)
- ***I'm seeing** Meg on Thursday.*
  (dynamic use = meeting)
- *I **see** Meg on Thursdays.*
  (stative use = meet, a regular arrangement)
- *Did you **see** him leave/leaving?*
  (Not **see him to leave**)
  (bare infinitive = the whole action, or *-ing* = part of the action after *see someone*)
- *I **saw** him (being) taken away.*
  (Not **saw him to be taken**)

see • see about
- *We'll **see that** tomorrow.*
  (i.e. with our eyes)
- *We'll **see about that** tomorrow.*
  (= consider, deal with)

see again • look at again
- *I think we should **look at her application again**.* (Not **see again her application**)
  (= reconsider it)
- *I want to **see** that film **again**.*
  (= watch once more)

sense (of)
- *Give up smoking. You know it **makes sense**.*
  (Not **does sense**)
  (= it's the logical thing to do)
- *I can't **make sense of** these figures.*
  (= understand)

sensible • sensitive • sore
- *Amy is very **sensitive**. She wouldn't want to hurt anyone.* (Not **sensible**)
  (= quick to feel distress for oneself or for others, opposite: *insensitive* = unfeeling)
- *This seismograph is an extremely **sensitive** instrument.* (Not **sensible**)
  (i.e. it can make exact measurements)
- *I'm sure Amy will make the right decision. She's a **sensible** woman.* (Not **sensitive**)
  (i.e. she has good sense and judgement)
- *The broken skin round my knee is still **sensitive/sore**.* (Not **sensible**)
  (= quick to feel pain/actively painful)

sensuous • sensual
- *Casanova devoted his life to the pursuit of **sensual** pleasure.* (Not **sensuous**)
  (= physical, especially sexual; the noun is *sensuality*)
- *No artist has matched Georgia O'Keeffe's **sensuous** paintings of flowers.*
  (Not **sensual**)
  (= that generally gives pleasure to the senses; the noun is *sensuousness*)

sentence • proposal • verdict
- *They still haven't reacted to our **proposal** to ban overtime.* (Not **sentence* *verdict**)
- *The arms smugglers received a heavy **sentence**.* (Not **verdict**)
  (= punishment by a court)
- *The **verdict** of the jury was 'Not Guilty'.*
  (Not **sentence**)
  (= a decision based on facts)

sentiment(s) • feeling(s)
- *People often have strong **feelings** about capital punishment.* (Not **sentiments**)
  (*feelings* come from the capacity to *feel* love, hate, anger, etc.)
- *Public **sentiment/feeling** is against major changes in the Health Service.*
  (*sentiment* = attitude of mind)
- *Your views on 'political correctness' exactly echo my own **sentiments/feelings**.*

sentimental • emotional • emotive
- *Some people get very **emotional** when they listen to music and are moved to tears.*
  (Not **emotive**)
  (i.e. they have or show strong feelings)
- *Some people get very **sentimental** when they recall their childhood years.* (Not **emotive**)
  (i.e. they indulge emotions that may not be very deep or sincere)
- *Abortion is an extremely **emotive** topic.*
  (Not **emotional* *sentimental**)
  (= arousing strong feelings)

series • in series • in order
- *The **series** runs from 1 to 10.* (Not **serie**)
  (*series* as a singular noun)
- *There **are** several **series** of books which help young children to develop reading skills.*
  (more than one *series*)
- *Lottie arranged the pebbles **in order** of size.*
  (Not **in series**)
- *The coins have been arranged **in series**.*
  (Not **in serie**)
  (*in series* = one following another in a numerical order or sequence)

– *The publications are a **series**.*
  (i.e. they form a related whole)

serious • trustworthy

– *Nursing is a job in which you have to be completely **trustworthy**.* (Not **serious**)
  (= dependable, can be trusted, respectable)
– *Tony is an ambitious young man, perhaps a bit **serious** for his age.*
  (= without humour)
  (*serious* is more commonly applied to situations, etc., than to people: *serious difficulties, a serious matter,* etc.)

serve

– ***Are you being served?***
  (Not **Do they serve you?**)
  (= receiving attention, e.g. in a shop; other fixed phrases: *Yes, please? Can I help you?*)

service • attention

– *Your case will receive **attention** as soon as possible.* (Not **service**)
  (i.e. it will be dealt with)
– *The **service** on some airways has improved enormously.* (Not **attention**)
  (i.e. as received by customers)

service • tip

– *London taxi drivers always expect a **tip**.*
  (Not **service**)
  (= a small sum of money in addition to e.g. a fare or a restaurant bill)
– *Does the bill include **service/a service charge**?* (preferable to *a tip*)
  (a formal way of referring to *a tip*)

several • a lot of

– ***A lot of** public **money** is spent on services.*
  (Not **Several ... money**)
  (*a lot of* + uncountable noun)
– ***A lot of students/Several students** are applying for grants.*
  (*a lot of/several* + plural countable)
  (*a lot of* = much/many, an unspecified number; *several* = a limited number of)

sewed/sewn • sowed/sown

– *Have you **sowed/sown** any lettuce this year?*
  (Not **sewed/sewn**)
  (*sow - sowed - sowed/sown* = put seeds to grow)
– *I've **sewed/sewn** your button on.*
  (Not **sowed/sown**)
  (*sew - sewed - sewed/sewn* = join with needle and thread)
  (both pronounced in the same way)

sewing

– *I've got a lot of **sewing** to **do**.* (Not **make**)
– ***There's** a lot of **sewing** to be done.*
  (Not **There are a lot of sewings**)
  (*sewing* is uncountable)

shade • shadow

– *I can see your **shadow** against the wall.*
  (Not **shade**)
  (countable = a dark shape made by blocking the light)
– *It's very hot in the sun. Come and sit in the **shade**.* (Not **shadow**)
  (uncountable = an area protected from sunlight)
  (every object *casts a shadow*, not **shade**)

shampooing • shampoo

– *I'm **having a shampoo** and cut.* (Not **doing/making a shampoo/a shampooing**)
  (i.e. at a hairdresser's; compare: *I'm **washing my hair**,* i.e. at home)
– *Who says constant **shampooing** is bad for the hair?* (Not **shampoo**)
  (= the act of *shampooing*)

shape • form

– *With such a small majority, how are they going to **form** a government?* (Not **shape**)
  (= put together)
  (we *form* a government, opinions, etc.)
– *What are the issues which will **shape** our defence policy?*
  (= e.g. influence our decisions; we *shape* our ideas, our attitudes, etc.)

sharp • sharply

– *You'd better **look sharp**. The boss is coming.*
  (Not **look sharply**)
  (usually a command = watch out, be careful)
  (*sharp*, adjective = alert, exact, after the verbs *be, seem, feel,* etc.; also *sound sharp/ sound flat* in music that is 'off pitch'; also directions: *turn sharp right/turn sharp left,* not **sharply**)
– *I was **woken sharply** by the sound of breaking glass.* (Not **woken sharp**)
  (adverbial use = in a sharp manner)

shave

– *I've just **had a shave**.* (Not **done/made**)
  *I must get up and **shave/get shaved**.*
  (it would not be 'wrong' to say *shave myself*, but it would be unusual)
– ***Get shaved!*** (Not **Shave yourself!**)
– *You've actually managed to **shave/shave yourself** without cutting your head off!*
  (the reflexive use shows conscious effort)

sheep
- *Can you see **that sheep/those sheep** just beyond the trees?* (Not *those sheeps*)
  (same singular and plural form; also *deer, salmon*)

shelf • shelves • shelve
- *I'm putting up a **shelf**/some **shelves**.*
  (noun: singular and plural forms)
- *We'll have to **shelve** this idea for the time being.* (Not *shelf*)
  (verb = put on one side, 'put on the shelf')

sherry • cherry brandy
- *This **sherry/cherry brandy** is rather sweet.*
  (*sherry* is a strong wine made in the region of Jerez, Spain; *cherry brandy* is a strong alcoholic drink made from *cherries*)

she's
- *Sally says **she's** hungry.*
- *Sally says **she's done** her homework.*
  (*she's* is short for 'she is' or 'she has')

shine • glow
- *We were welcomed into a warm room with a **glowing** fire.* (Not *shining*)
  (= giving out heat/light without flames)
- *The beautiful parquet floors **shone**.* (Not *glowed*)
  (= reflected light; also 'give out light', as in the sun **shines**)

ship • boat • liner
- *I wouldn't go out in a small **boat** in rough weather.* (Not *ship*)
  (a *boat* can be large or small; only *boats* are used on rivers and are relatively small)
- *How many **ships** are there in our merchant fleet?* (Not *liners*; preferable to *boats*)
  (*ships* are large and carry people, etc., at sea)
- *It's fun to cross the Atlantic **by ship/by boat/by (ocean) liner**.*
  (a *liner* is a large passenger ship)

shock • crash
- *The passengers were thrown forward in the **crash**.* (Not *shock*)
  (= an accident, collision in a vehicle)
- *A lot of passengers who were in the crash are still suffering from **shock**.*
  (= emotional and physical stress)

shock • get/have a shock/give someone a shock
- *I **got/had** a real **shock** when I entered the house.* (Not *I shocked* *I shocked myself*)
  (= experienced stress because of something unexpected)

- *What I saw **gave me a shock**.* (Not **did/made me a shock**)
  (= gave me an unpleasant surprise)
- *The violent crime **shocked** even **the police**.*
  (= gave them an unpleasant surprise; transitive verb)

shocking • dirty stories
- *Lionel embarrassed everybody by telling a **dirty story**/several **dirty stories**.* (Not *a shocking* *shockings*)
  (= rude anecdotes; *shocking* is not a noun)
- *Parts of this film are quite **shocking**.*
  (adjective = morally or socially offensive)

shopping
- *Did you **go shopping** this morning?* (Not *go for shopping* *go for shop*, but *go to the shops* is commonly used)
- *Who **does the shopping** in this household?* (Not *makes shopping*)
- *We did **a lot of shopping** this morning.* (Not **a lot of shoppings**)
- ***Shopping** takes a lot of time.* (Not *The shopping* *The shoppings*)

short
- *I'm too **short** to reach that shelf.*
  (= not tall)
- *Are **short** skirts in fashion?*
- *I'm often away for **short** periods.*
- *The station is a **short** walk from here.*
  (= not long)

short • brief
- *I won't give you a long speech. I promise you I will be **brief**.* (Not *short*)
  (= short in time or tedium; not long)
- *The Minister wasn't prepared to comment, but she read a **short/brief** statement.*
  (*short* = in length; *brief* = in time; note: *I'll be brief*, not **I'll be short.**)

short • shortly
- *He began to tell us the story and then **stopped short**.*
  (= suddenly)
  (we use *short*, not *shortly*, to mean 'just before the end': *cut someone short* = interrupt; *run short of something* = come nearly to the end of a supply; *stop short* = stop before the intended place or moment)
- *I'll be with you **shortly**.* (Not *short*)
  (adverbial use = soon, in a short time)

shortly • in brief • in short
- *This is the news **in brief**.* (Not *shortly* *in short*)
  (= in a few words)

– *It will take them years to recover from this defeat in the elections.* **In short**, *it's a catastrophe.* (Not **Shortly* *In brief**)
(= 'without going into details')
– *Mr Perkins will be with you* **shortly**.
(= in a short time, soon)

should • ought to
– *She* **should leave** *early tomorrow.*
(Not **should to leave* *shoulds to leave* *shoulds leave**)
(no *to*-infinitive or third person *-(e)s* ending after *should* and other modal verbs)
– *She* **ought to leave** *early tomorrow.*
(*should* and *ought to* have the same meaning; *should* is never followed by *to*, while *ought* is always followed by *to*)

show (up) • appear
– *John didn't* **show up/appear** *till the party was over.*
(= arrive)
– *I've been crying, but I hope it* **doesn't show**.
(Not **show up* *appear**)
(= isn't visible)

show • point to • point at • point out
– *All these coats look the same to me.* **Point to** *the one that belongs to you.* (Not **Show (to) the one**, but we can say *Show me the one*)
– *It's rude to* **point at** *people.*
(Not **point to* *show (to)**)
(*pointing* involves the use of the index finger: *at* after a verb often suggests aggression: *aim at, stare at, throw at,* etc.)
– *You'll pass a signpost* **pointing to** *Sutton.*
(Not **pointing at* *showing (to)**)
(*point to* for direction)
– **Point out** *the road we're looking for on the map.* (preferable to *point at/to*)
(*point out (to)* = identify: **Point her out to me please.**)
– *I'll* **show you** *my car.* (Not **point you to**)
(= let you see it in detail, take you over it)

shrink • gather
– *The sleeves have been* **gathered** *at the wrist.*
(Not **shrunk**)
(= made narrower with a row of stitches drawn up to make little pleats)
– *My pullover has* **shrunk** *in the wash.*
(Not **gathered**)
(= become smaller through washing; *shrink* is not reflexive: not **It has shrunk itself.**)

shut • lock
– *Please make sure the door is* **shut/locked**.
(*shut* = closed; *locked* = secured with a key)

shy (of) • embarrassed • ashamed (of/about) • shameful
– *Doris spent two years in gaol and feels* **ashamed of/about** *her past.*
(Not **embarrassed/shy/shameful of/about**)
(= unhappy about having done something disgraceful)
– *I think he must be* **ashamed of** *his brother because he always avoids mentioning him.*
(Not **shy/embarrassed/shameful of**)
(= not proud of)
– *I can't excuse such* **shameful** *behaviour.*
(Not **ashamed* *shy* *embarrassed**)
(= disgraceful, making one lose the respect of others)
– *Katy feels* **shy** *at parties/is* **shy of** *strangers.*
(Not **ashamed/shameful (of)**)
(*shy* = lacking in confidence)
– *I felt so* **embarrassed** *when I spilt coffee on their beautiful carpet.*
(Not **shy* *ashamed* *shameful**)
(= very uncomfortable)

sickly • poorly
– *I think I'll go home. I'm feeling* **poorly**.
(Not **sickly**)
(= unwell; *poorly* can be used after *be*, etc., to refer to people)
– *Amanda is a* **sickly** *child.* (Not **poorly**)
(= prone to sickness; often becoming ill; *sickly* can be used before a noun or after *be*)
– *That plant looks* **sickly**. (Not **poorly**)
(= not very healthy)

side • hand
– *I know working in London is expensive.* **On the other hand**, *you do get a London allowance.* (Not **On the other side* *From the other end**)
(= from another point of view)
– *On the one side we have Ray James, and* **on the other side** *we have Joe Molloy.*
(= opposing, e.g. in a contest, match)

sideways • at the side
– *There's an entrance to the building* **at the side**. (Not **sideways**)
(i.e. at the side of the building)
– *The corridor was so narrow, we had to move along it* **sideways**.
(= facing the wall, not facing forwards)

sight • view • spectacle • uproar • vision
– *There's an excellent* **view** *from our bedroom window.* (Not **sight* *spectacle**)
(= what can be seen from a particular place)
– *Thousands of tulips all flowering at the same time are a wonderful* **sight**.

167

(Not *view* and preferably not *spectacle*)
(= something specific that is or can be seen:
an event, an activity, a notable item)

- There was **(an) uproar** in Parliament when
the Minister resigned. (Not *a spectacle*)
(= (a) loud noise made by a lot of excited
people)
- The parade on the Queen's birthday was a
magnificent **spectacle/sight**. (Not *view*)
(*spectacle* = a public display)
- You're lucky you have excellent **vision/sight**.
(= the ability to see)

sign • signal

- I'll wait by the Exit **sign**. (Not *signal*)
(= a notice)
- She's taking a little food. It must be a **sign**
that she's getting better. (Not *signal*)
(= something that shows)
- I **signalled/gave a signal** before overtaking.
(= an action to warn or show intentions)

signify • mean

- 'Meagre' doesn't **mean** 'thin' in English.
(Not *isn't meaning* *doesn't signify*)
(stative use = have the meaning of)
- He shouldn't phone her. I **mean** it wouldn't
be right. (Not *I'm meaning*)
(i.e. that's what I imply)
- She hasn't phoned him yet, but I know **she's
meaning** to.
(dynamic use = intending to)
- I overslept, which **meant taking** a taxi.
(Not *meant to take*)
(i.e. that was the consequence)
- What does a ring round the moon **signify**?
(= 'what is it a sign of?'; *mean* is also
possible)

silken • silky • silk

- I bought this lovely **silk** scarf in the airport
shop. (Not *silken* *silky*)
(= made of *silk*; *silk* can be a noun modifier:
a silk tie, a silk handkerchief)
- This is the conditioner that leaves your hair
soft and **silky**. (Not *silk* *silken*)
(= 'feeling like silk')
- She addressed us in a **silken/silky** voice.
(= 'as smooth as silk')

silly

- Don't be **silly/a silly fool**!
- Those two are just **silly/silly fools**.
(exceptionally, we can use a silly/sillies, = a
silly fool/silly fools, as nouns in a familiar or
affectionate way: He's such **a silly**! They're
just a couple of **sillies**!)

- I wish you wouldn't **speak in a silly way**.
(Not *speak silly/sillily*)
(*silly* is an adjective and the adverb must be
expressed by a phrase)

silvery • silver

- A Georgian **silver** teapot would be very
valuable these days. (Not *silvery*)
(= made of *silver*; *silver* can be a noun
modifier: a silver bracelet, a silver pen)
- We danced by the **silvery** light of the moon.
(= 'like silver')

simple • plain • ordinary (people)

- I was rather **plain** as a child.
(= not good looking, not attractive)
- Jane is an **ordinary** girl. (Not *simple*)
(*plain* describes facial appearance and is
usually applied to females; it is not applied
to people in the sense of *ordinary* = not
exceptional, approachable. Compare: Let me
make myself **plain** = clear)
- John is rather **simple**. (Not *plain*)
(= a bit retarded, *simple-minded*: not
condemnatory)
- Mrs Tibbs is a **simple** soul. (Not *plain*)
(= uncomplicated, innocent)

simple • plain • ordinary (things)

- I like **plain** cooking best.
(Not *simple* *ordinary*)
(= not fancy)
- I've prepared a **simple** meal for this evening.
(Not *plain* *ordinary*)
(= not elaborate)
- The solution is quite **simple/plain**.
(*simple* = easy; *plain* = obvious)
- We live in an **ordinary** house.
(Not *simple* *plain*)
(= not grand, not exceptional)

simple • stupid • dull • dim

- Sometimes I think you're really **stupid/a
really stupid** boy. (Not *simple*)
(= boneheaded, foolish; *stupid* is very
uncomplimentary and offensive)
- All work and no play makes Jack a **dull** boy.
(Not *simple* *stupid*)
(= boring)
- Jack's good at games, but a bit **dim** at
schoolwork. (Not *simple* *stupid*)
(= slow to learn)
- Mrs Tibbs is a **simple** soul.
(Not *stupid* *dull*)
(= uncomplicated, innocent)

since

- *Tom hasn't been home **since** he was a boy.*
  (= from the time; *since* as a conjunction in time clauses)
- ***Since** there was very little support, the strike was not successful.*
  (= because; *since* as a conjunction in clauses of reason)
- *I saw Fiona in May and I haven't seen her **since**.*
  (= from that time; *since* as an adverb of duration)
- *I haven't seen Tim **since January**.*
  (= from that time; *since* as a preposition)

since • for

- *I haven't seen Tim **for six months**.*
  (Not **since six months**)
  (*for* + period of time)
- *I haven't seen Tim **since January**.*
  (Not **for/from January**)
  (*since* + time reference)

since • from

- *The tourist season runs **from** June **to/till** October.* (Not **since ... to/till**)
- *We're open **from** 9 o'clock.* (Not **since**)
  (i.e. from 9 onwards)
- *We've been open **since/from** 9 o'clock.*
  (i.e. from that time up till now)
- *I've been interested in flying **since** I was a boy.* (Not **from** as a conjunction)
  (= from the time when)

single • only • own

- *This is **the only** phone in the village.*
  (Not **the single**)
  (= the only one)
- *There is **a single** phone in the village.*
  (Not **an only** **an own**)
  (= only one)
- *I'd like **a single room** please.*
  (Not **an only room** **an own room**)
  (= a room for one person)
- *I have **my own room/a room of my own**.*
  (Not **an own room**)
  (i.e. solely for my use)

single • ordinary

- *I'd like a **single**/an **ordinary** ticket please.*
  (*single* = one-way; *ordinary* = not first-class, or 'not special')

sink to

- *I hear you've **sunk to borrowing** money from strangers.* (Not **sunk to borrow**)
  (*to* functions as a preposition + *-ing* here, not as part of the infinitive)

sister • nurse

- *I'm a **nurse** at the local hospital.* (Not *sister*, unless referring to particular status as a senior *nurse* in charge of a hospital ward)
- *Can you help me get out of bed please, **Sister/Sister Jones/Nurse**?*
  (the use of *nurse* or *sister* sometimes depends on seniority; *nurse* is always used on its own; *Sister* or *Sister* + surname in hospitals: *Sister Jones*; *Sister* + first name in religious orders: *Sister Mary*)

sit (down) • take a seat

- *Please **sit down/take a seat**.*
  (Not **sit yourself** **sit you** **sit**)
  (*sit* is not normally reflexive. We would only say e.g. **Sit yourself down** and tell me about it if we wanted to be emphatic)
- *My dog instantly obeys the command '**Sit!**'*
  (Not **Sit down!**)
  (The command *Sit!* is given to animals)

sit on • sit at

- *When I went into the classroom, all the pupils were **sitting at/sitting on** their desks.*
  (*sitting at their desks* and ready for work; *sitting on their desks* = on top of them; compare *Who **sits on** the committee?*)

situation • condition(s) • position • state

- *I phoned to ask how she was and they told me her **condition** is unchanged.*
  (Not **situation** **position** **state**)
  (= state of health)
- *My bicycle's in a terrible **condition/state**.*
  (Not **situation** **position**)
  (= state of repair)
- *Tina is attending an interview this morning and she'**s in a real state**.* (Not **condition**)
  (*to be in a state* = be very anxious, upset)
- *I didn't have enough money to pay my restaurant bill. I've never been in such a **situation/position** before.* (Not **condition**)
  (i.e. faced with a problem)
- *What's our exact **position** on the map?*
  (Not **situation** **condition**)
  (= location)
- ***Conditions** for investment are/**The situation** for investment is very bad at present.*
  (*conditions* = matters which affect daily life; *the situation*: i.e. in general)

skin • complexion • flesh • leather • hide

- *I've such a bad **skin/complexion**, I'm always coming out in spots.*
  (*skin* and *complexion* are interchangeable as countable nouns when they refer to

colouring and quality of facial skin: *a fair/dark/fresh*, etc., *skin/complexion*)
- *I got so sunburnt that my **skin** peeled.* (uncountable = the covering of the body; *skin* can be countable as in e.g. *an animal skin, animal skins*; *a hide* can also refer to a whole animal skin)
- *I've cut myself, but it isn't serious. It's just a **flesh** wound.* (Not **leather* *hide**) (*flesh* is below the skin, not part of it)
- *Shoes made of real **leather** have become so expensive.* (preferable to *hide*) (= treated animal skin used to make shoes, handbags, coats, etc.; compare *fur* = animal skin covered with hair)
- *This sofa is made from real **hide/leather**.* (the standard term is *leather*; *hide* refers to large areas of leather from large animals, e.g. *cowhide*, but note *pigskin*, not **pig hide**)

skin • rind • peel • shell
- *The **rind** of Parmesan cheese is like rock.* (Not **skin* *peel**) (= the inedible, often hard, outer layer of food such as cheese or a thick-skinned fruit)
- *It's not very funny to slip on a banana **skin**.* (Not **rind* *peel**) (= the soft, often thin, outer layer of a fruit, which may be edible or inedible)
- *The top of the mountain is littered with orange **peel** and rubbish.* (Not **peels**) (= the outer layer removed - *peeled* - from a fruit or vegetable before it is eaten; uncountable)
- *My hands are black because I've been **shelling** fresh walnuts.* (Not **peeling**) (a *shell* is the outer covering of nuts and shellfish)

sleep • bed
- *I'm **going to bed**.* (Not **I'm going to sleep.* *I'm going for sleep.* *I'll fall to sleep.**) (= e.g. in order to sleep)
- *It took me a long time to **go to sleep**.* (Not **go asleep**) (= *fall asleep* after you go to bed)
- *I've just **had a** long **sleep**.* (Not **done/made a sleep**)

sleep • get sleepy
- *I **get sleepy** watching TV.* (Not **I sleepy**)
- *I often **sleep** through long films.*

slow/fast
- *This clock **is slow/fast**.* (Not **goes slow/fast**) (i.e. it's behind/ahead of the right time)

- *My old car **goes slow** uphill and **goes fast** downhill.* (i.e. that's how it travels)

slow • gradual
- *He is showing **slow/gradual** improvement.* (*slow* = not fast; *gradual* = little by little)

slow • slowly
- *This train's **going** terribly **slow/slowly**.* (*go slow* = be slow; *go slowly* = travel in a slow fashion)
- *Eat your food **slowly**!* (Not **slow**) (only *-ly* to describe a deliberate action)

small • narrow
- *The road is too **narrow** for two cars to pass.* (Not **small**) (= not wide)
- *Hay Court is a **small** street near St. Paul's.* (= not large)

smell (of)
- *This fish **smells bad**.* (Not **is smelling* *smells badly**; *smell* functions like *be*, so we use an adjective after it: *bad*; not an adverb: *badly*; this use is always stative)
- *What are you doing? - **I'm smelling** the fish to see if it's all right.* (Not **I smell**) (dynamic use)
- *You **smell of** soap. The desk **smells of** varnish.* (Not **smell(s) from/with**) (i.e. you have/it has that smell)
- *I **smell/can smell** something **burning**.* (Not **smell (something) to burn**)
- *I love to **smell** the trees **give off** that scent of resin.* (Not **smell ... to give off**)

smile
- *She **gave me** a big **smile**.* (Not **made/did me a big smile* *gave to me a big smile**)
- *She **smiled at** me.* (Not **She smiled me.**)

smoke
- *The kitchen is full of **smoke**.* (Not **smokes**) (*smoke* is uncountable)

smoking • dinner jacket
- *I've been invited to a black-tie affair so I'll have to borrow your **dinner jacket** (AmE tuxedo).* (Not **smoking**) (*smoking jacket*, as worn by men in the nineteenth century, is archaic)
- ***Smoking** among teenagers is increasing.* (= the smoking of tobacco)

snob/snobbish • elegant/smart/chic
- *Princess Diana was wearing an extremely **elegant/smart/chic** outfit.* (Not **snob**) (= beautiful/stylish)

– *You have to be a real **snob/really snobbish** to believe that membership of this club makes you socially superior.*
(i.e. you are claiming social superiority; a *snob* is a person who is *snobbish* and is affected by *snobbery*, not *snobbism*)

so (have you) • so (you have)!

– *I've got a rash on my arm. - **So you have!***
(Not **So have you!**, though *So have I!* = 'I have too' would be possible)
(*So you have!* echoes the statement previously made, confirming what is said; compare *So it is!*, *So you were!*, etc.)
– *I've got a rash on my arm and **so have you**.*
(Not *so you have*)
(= you have too; *so* + inversion when one statement is 'added' to another)

so • such (a/an) • like this/like that

– *Dance to the music **like this/like that**.*
(Not *like so*)
(= in this way, in that way)
– *I'd love to live in **a house like this/that**.*
(Not *such a house* **such kind of house**)
– *There was **such a large choice**!* (Not *so large choice* **a so/a such large choice**)
– *We had **such trouble/such difficulties**!*
(Not *so trouble* *so difficulties* **such kind of trouble** **such kind of difficulties**)
(*such a/an* + countable noun, or *such* + uncountable noun or plural countable)
– *The choice was **so large**!/There was **so large a choice**!* (Not **such large (a choice)**)
(*so* + adjective, not noun)
– *We had **so much** trouble/**so many** difficulties!* (Not **such much/many**)

so • this • that

– *It was about **so/this/that** big.*
(actually indicating with a gesture)
– *Look at that hot air balloon! It's **so big**!*
(Not *this big*)
(= exclaiming that it is very big; *It's **that big**!* is an informal alternative to *It's so big!*)

so • very

– *I'm afraid your essay **wasn't very** good.*
(a polite way of saying it was bad, with *not very*)
– *Your work **hasn't been so** good lately.*
(compared e.g. with earlier work)

so-and-so • so-so

– *Our hotel was only **so-so**.* (Not *so-and-so*)
(= neither very good nor very bad)

– *The new office manager is **a real so-and-so**.*
('something you cannot say because it's a rude word' = unpleasant)

so as not to/in order not to • not to

– *I went to France **not to study** French, **but to study** architecture.*
(Not **so as not to/in order not to**)
(*not to ... but to* to refer to alternatives)
– *I shut the door quietly **so as not to/in order not to wake** the baby.*
(Not *to not wake* *for to not wake* **to don't wake**; preferable to *not to wake*)
(*so as not to* and *in order not to* refer to 'negative purpose')

so that/in order that

– *We arrived early **so that/in order that we might get** good seats.* (Not *for to get*)

soap • a bar of soap

– *I bought **some soap/a bar of soap/two bars of soap**.* (Not *a soap* *two soaps*)
(*soap* is uncountable)

social • sociable

– *Ron has always been a **sociable** sort of person.* (Not *social*)
(i.e. he enjoys the company of other people)
– *Ron has always had an active **social** life.*
(Not *sociable*)
(i.e. in society, e.g. going out with friends)

society • community

– *Rising unemployment in the area is bad for the whole **community**.*
(= the people who live in a particular area)
– *In a civilized **society**, everyone should have access to health care and education.*
(= the way people live together)

soft • low

– *What a lovely **soft** pillow!*
(= not hard)
– *Does the sound of **soft/low** music in the background make people work better?*
(= not loud: *low* as the opposite of *loud*)
– *The stool is too **low** for him and he can't reach the table.*
(= not high: *low* as the opposite of *high*)

soft • soften • get/go soft

– *Put the biscuits in a tin or **they'll go/get soft**.*
(Not **they'll soft** **they'll soften**)
– *Use some of this cream **to soften your hands/to make your hands soft**.* (Not **to soft your hands** **to get soft your hands**)

soft • tender

– *I hope the meat is **tender**.* (Not *soft*)
  (*tender* is the word we apply to meat and the opposite is *tough*, not *hard*)
– *This **soft** mattress is bad for my back.*
  (Not *tender*)
  (opposite *hard/firm*)

solicitors • prostitutes

– *Is there a law against **prostitutes** soliciting passers-by?*
  (*prostitutes* might *solicit* = offer sex for money: *soliciting*, but they aren't *solicitors*)
– *The matter is with our **solicitors**.*
  (BrE *lawyers*, AmE *lawyers* or *attorneys*; *solicitors advise*, but don't *solicit*)

solid • massive • thick

– *The old dining room in the castle used to contain a **massive** table which could seat 100 people.* (Not *solid*)
  (= very large and solidly-built)
– *This table is made of **solid** oak.*
  (Not *massive*)
  (i.e. it's all oak, right the way through)
– *The table top is a **thick** piece of solid wood.*
  (*thick* refers to measurement)

solution to

– *The ozone layer is depleting and there's no easy **solution to** this problem.* (Not *for*)

some • any

– *Are there **any** letters for me this morning?*
  (*any* is usual in questions, but *some* is possible when we are expecting the answer *Yes*, e.g. *Have you got **some** news for me?*)
– ***There aren't any letters** for you this morning.* (Not **There aren't some letters**)
  (*any* in negative statements)
– ***There are some letters** for you this morning.* (Not **There are any letters**)
  (*some* in affirmative statements)

some/any • one

– *Would you **like some/any** sandwiches/cake?*
  *- Yes, I'd **like some** please.* (Not **I'd like.**)
  *- No, I don't **want any**, thank you.*
  (*some/any* after a transitive verb to replace *any/some* + noun)
– *Would you **like a** sandwich?*
  *- Yes, I'd **like one** please.* (Not **I'd like.**)
  *- No, I don't **want one**, thank you.*
  (*one* replaces *a/an* + noun after a transitive verb)

some • (-)

– *(-) **Women** are fighting for their rights.*
  (= all women in general)

– *Some women are fighting for their rights.*
  (and others aren't)

some time/sometime • some times • sometimes

– *My son calls in **sometimes** on his way to work.* (Not *sometime* *some times*)
  (= now and again)
– *There are **some times** when I feel very depressed.* (Not *sometime* *sometimes*)
  (= particular occasions)
– *You must visit us **some time/sometime**.*
  (Not *sometimes*)
  (= on some occasion, not specified)

someone/somebody • anyone/anybody

– *Is there **anyone/anybody** in?*
  (*anyone/anybody* is usual in questions, but *someone/somebody* is possible when we are expecting the answer *Yes*, e.g. *Is **somebody** meeting you at the station?*)
– ***There isn't anyone/anybody** in.*
  (Not **There isn't someone/somebody**)
  (*anyone/anybody* in negative statements)
– ***There's someone/somebody** waiting to see you.* (Not **There's anyone/anybody**)
  (*someone/somebody* in affirmative statements)

something • anything

– *Is there **anything** we can do?*
  (*anything* is usual in questions, but *something* is possible when we are expecting the answer *Yes*, e.g. *Can I get you **something to eat**?*)
– ***There isn't anything** we can do.*
  (Not **There isn't something**)
  (*anything* in negative statements)
– ***There's something** I want to tell you.*
  (Not **There's anything**)
  (*something* in affirmative statements)
– *Don't just sit there. **Do something**. Haven't you got **anything to do**?* (Not *make*)
  (= occupy your time, take action)
– *Emma **made something** for your birthday.*
  (= created)
– *Alexander Calder, the sculptor, could **make anything** out of bits of wire.* (Not *do*)
  (= create)

somewhere • anywhere

– *Is there **anywhere** we can park?*
  (*anywhere* is usual in questions, but *somewhere* is possible when we are expecting the answer *Yes*, e.g. *Is there **somewhere** I can leave my coat?*)

- *There isn't anywhere we can park.*
(Not *There isn't somewhere*)
(*anywhere* in negative statements)
- *I know somewhere we can park.*
(Not *I know anywhere*)
(*somewhere* in affirmative statements)

sorry to/for
- *I'm sorry to interrupt you, but there's a telephone call for you.*
(i.e. but I'm going to interrupt you)
- *I didn't mean to barge in. I'm sorry for interrupting you.*
(i.e. I have interrupted you)

sorts/sort • goods • appliance
- *We stock electrical goods and hi-fi.*
(Not *sorts*)
(= articles for sale; plural noun with no singular form + plural verb)
- *What sorts of radios/sort of radio do you want to see?*
(Not *sort of radios* *sorts of radio*)
(= kinds, varieties)
- *I'm looking for an electrical appliance for crushing ice.* (Not *sort*)
- *John is a very good sort.* (Not *type*)
(= type of person)

sound
- *A day in the country sounds (like) a nice idea.* (Not *is sounding*)
- *That sounds interesting.*
(Not *sounds interestingly*)
(stative use only = it is interesting)
- *You sound/You're sounding more and more like your father.*
(stative or dynamic use depending on the speaker's viewpoint)

sour
- *The milk has gone/turned sour.*
(Not *has soured*)
- *I've added too much lemon juice to the soup and made it sour.* (Not *soured it*)
- *Their relationship soured/turned sour/went sour long before they split up.*
(*sour* as a verb = become acid)

Spanish
- *I'm learning/doing Spanish.*
(Not *making Spanish* *spanish*)
(= the language: proper noun, capital letter)
- *He's/She's Spanish.* (Not *a Spanish*)
(adjectival form)
- *They're Spanish.* (Not *Spanishes*)
(adjectival form)

- *I've been corresponding with a Spaniard.*
(Not *a Spanish*)
(this is usually understood as 'a Spanish man'; otherwise we have to say *I've been corresponding with a Spanish woman*.)
- *I was just speaking to two Spaniards.*
(this suggests 'two Spanish men'; otherwise we have to say *I was just speaking to two Spanish women*.)
- *The Spanish/(The) Spanish people are increasingly successful and prosperous.*
(Not *Spanish* and preferably not *(The) Spaniards*)
(= the group as a whole)
(also: *Arabic/an Arab/(the) Arabs, Danish/a Dane/(the) Danes* or *the Danish, Finnish/a Finn/(the) Finns* or *the Finnish, Philippine/a Filipino/(the) Filipinos, Polish/a Pole/(the) Poles, Swedish/a Swede/(the) Swedes* or *the Swedish, Turkish/a Turk/(the) Turks*)

spare
- *You can sleep in the spare room.*
(= not in use; compare *spare tyre*)
- *Have you got a spare moment/a moment to spare?*
(= free; compare *spare time*)
- *Where can I get spare parts for this engine?*
(= essential replacement parts to keep a machine in running order)

speak • talk
- *We spent the whole night talking.*
(Not *speaking*)
- *The lecturer took up the entire hour speaking and didn't answer any questions.*
(preferable to *talking*)
(*talk* suggests conversation; *speak* suggests a single person saying something: *I want to talk to you* = have a conversation with you; *I want to speak to you* = tell you something - perhaps serious or unpleasant; also: *speak a language*; you ask to *speak to* someone on the phone)
- *I wish you wouldn't speak/talk like that in front of your mother!*
(interchangeable)

speak of/on/about
- *She spoke of/about her childhood at some length.* (Not *spoke for* *spoke on*)
(= told us about)
- *She spoke on/about childhood and the problems of growing up.* (Not *spoke for*)
(= gave a lecture about: *speak, lecture, write on* or *about* a topic)

speak to
- I'll **speak to** (AmE *speak with*) **my lawyer** about this. (Not *speak my lawyer*)

species
- **This species** of butterfly **is** very rare. (Not *specie*) (*species* as a singular noun)
- Seven **species** of poisonous snake **are** to be found on the peninsula. (more than one *species*)

speck • spot • mark
- There's **a spot/mark** on your tie. (Not *a speck* on its own) (= a small stain)
- I've got **a spot** on my nose. (Not *a speck* *a mark*) (= a small infection in the skin)
- There's **a speck of dust** in my eye. (Not *a spot of dust* *a mark of dust*) (= a tiny amount of; *a speck* is usually followed by *of*: a speck of dust/dirt/soot)

spectator • audience • viewers
- The **audience** applauded the soloist. (Not *the spectators*) (= people watching a show, e.g. a play, a film, or attending a concert)
- How many **viewers** watch the European contest? (Not *spectators*) (= people watching TV)
- The **spectators** jumped back as the racing car hit the barrier. (Not *audience*) (= people watching an outdoor event, usually sporting; such events are often referred to as *spectator sports*)

speech • talk • chat
- The minister **gave/made a speech** about social welfare. (Not *did a speech*)
- I'm going to **give a talk** about wildlife at our local museum. (Not *do/make a talk*) (a *speech* is formal and generally given on big occasions; a *talk* is informal and generally given on small occasions)
- Frank always speaks through his teeth, so his **speech** isn't very clear. (Not *talk*) (= the way he speaks)
- We **had** a nice **chat/talk**. (Not *speech* *made/did a chat/talk*) (= an informal conversation)

spend • offer/buy
- He **offered/bought** me a beer. (Not *spent*)
- I can't **spend** any more money on this car. (*spend* time, money)

spirit/soul • ghost
- What's the matter? You look as if you've seen a **ghost**! (Not *spirit* *soul*) (= the imagined form of a dead person)
- God rest his **spirit/soul**! (= that part of a human being which is thought by many to survive death; no 'form' is imagined)

spirit • spirits • alcohol
- Slivovitz is a fiery **spirit**. (Not *alcohol*) (= a strong alcoholic drink)
- What steps can be taken to curb the consumption of **spirits/alcohol**? (= strong alcoholic drinks; *spirits* generally means distilled drinks like *gin, whisky* and *vodka*; *alcohol* can mean any alcoholic drink)
- This beer contains only 2% **alcohol**. (Not *spirit* *spirits*)
- The champion defended her tennis title with a lot of **spirit**. (Not *spirits*) (= determination)
- Everyone at the party was in high **spirits**. (Not *spirit*) (= mood: *high* or *low spirits*)

spiritual • intellectual • witty
- Terry is an extremely **witty** speaker.
- He gave a **witty** answer to my question. (Not *spiritual* *intellectual*) (= clever, funny, full of *wit*)
- People who consider themselves to be **intellectuals** often arouse a lot of suspicion. (Not *spiritual* *witty*) (= thinkers)
- Can psychiatrists really attend to our **spiritual** needs? (= of the spirit)

spit • kebab • grill • skewer • barbecue
- I had a **kebab** and a salad. (Not *spit*) (= small pieces of meat grilled on a skewer)
- Meat has to be turned frequently on a **spit/grill** if you want it to be properly cooked. (a *spit* = a long metal rod; a *grill* = a metal shelf on which food is cooked by heat from above or below)
- 'Teriyake' is little pieces of meat cooked on a **skewer**. (a *skewer* = a small metal or wooden stick pushed through food to hold it while it is cooked)
- Let's take the **barbecue** to the beach today.
- We're having a **barbecue** on Sunday. (a *barbecue* is: 1) the apparatus for cooking food, especially meat, over an open fire;

2) the occasion when food is cooked in this manner: *a barbecue party*)

sport/sports
- *We **do/play** a lot of **sport/sports** at this school.* (Not **make sport/sports**)

sportive • sporting • sporty • fond of sport • sport
- *Both my boys are extremely **sporty/fond of sport**.* (Not *sportive* *sporting* *sports*)
- *It's very **sporting** of you to give him another chance to play in our team.*
  (Not *sportive* *sporty*)
  (= generous, decent)
- ***Sportive** dolphins are wonderfully entertaining.*
  (= playful in the manner of animals or children; *sportive* is fairly rare)
- *John/Jane is a really good **sport**.*
  (= a person who is fair-minded and has a generous nature, not to be confused with *sportsman/sportswoman* = a person who plays or enjoys sporting activities)

sprang • sprung
- *The soldiers **sprang/sprung** to attention when their commanding officer appeared.*
  (*sprang* is the usual form, but *sprung* occurs)
- *I think we've **sprung** a leak.*
  (Not *have sprang*)
  (only *sprung* as a past participle: *spring - sprang/sprung - **sprung***)

stadium • stage • floor
- *Both parties have now reached a delicate **stage** in their negotiations.* (Not *stadium*)
  (= point)
- *My flat is on the seventh **floor**.* (Not *stage*)
- *At the end of the play the entire cast is on the **stage**.* (Not *stadium*)
  (= the area where a play is performed)
- *Maracana is one of the biggest football **stadiums/stadia** in the world.*
  (= a sports field with seats round it)

stand (for)
- *What do the initials IBM **stand for**?*
  (Not **are they standing for**)
  (stative use = represent)
- *Don't tell me **you're standing** for Parliament!*
  (dynamic use = putting your name forward so as to be elected)
- *I **can't stand hearing** the same tune played over and over.* (Not **can't stand to hear**)
  (= can't bear/tolerate, hate)

stark • strong
- *You have to be really **strong** to work in the furniture removals business.* (Not *stark*)
  (= have physical strength)
- *I need some **strong** coffee.* (Not *stark*)
  (i.e. made with a lot of coffee)
- *The waiting room was **starkly** furnished/cold and **stark**.*
  (= bare, severe; *stark* describes places and effects)

start
- *It's time we **made a start**.* (Not *did*)
- *I **started working/work** when I was sixteen.*
  (*working* is a participle; *work* is a noun)
- *The machine has to warm up before it **starts to work**.*
  (*start to work*: i.e. begin to function on a particular occasion; *start working*: i.e. in general)
- *How can we **start him working**?*
  (Not **start him to work**)

state • county • province • land
- *Some countries, like Britain, are divided into **counties**; others, like America, are divided into **states**; and others, like Spain, are divided into **provinces**.* (Not *lands*)
- *Once, in a **land** far away across the sea, lived a beautiful princess.*
  (= country: literary; note that *department* in English refers only to parts of an organization, not a geographical area: *I work in the design **department**.*)
- *Most former colonies are now independent **states**.*
  (= countries with their own political organizations)

stationary • stationery
- *Godwins are suppliers of office **stationery**.*
  (Not *stationary*)
  (= writing materials, especially paper)
- *The traffic was **stationary** because of a security alert.* (Not *stationery*)
  (= not moving)

statistic • statistics
- *What **are** the **statistics** for school leavers looking for work?*
  (Not *is the statistic* **are the statistic**)
  (plural form + plural verb for specific references)
- ***Statistics** is an inexact science.*
  (Not **(the) statistics are** **(the) statistic is**)
  (plural form + singular verb to refer to the academic subject)

- *Here's **a statistic** that will interest you.*
  (= a single figure in a set of statistics)

steely • steel
- ***Steel** cutlery will last for ever.* (Not **steely**)
  (= made of *steel*; *steel* can be a noun modifier: *a steel pan, a steel drum*)
- *I could see he was determined by the **steely** look in his eye.*
  (= hard, 'like steel')

steer • drive • pilot • fly
- *It's quite possible to **drive** from Geneva to London in a day.* (Not **steer** **pilot**)
- *She **steered** the car skilfully into a tiny parking space.* (preferable to *drove*)
- *The captain **steered** his ship into the harbour.* (Not **drove**, though *piloted* would be possible)
  (*drive* = be in control of e.g. a vehicle; *steer* = make a vehicle go in a particular direction: you *steer* a car while *driving* it by moving the *steering wheel*)
- *It's hard to imagine that anyone could **pilot/ fly** some of the old planes you see in museums.* (Not **drive** **steer**)
  (*pilot* a plane; compare *pilot* = guide a ship e.g. through a canal)

still • stile • style
- *He may not be very clever, but he has a lot of **style**!* (Not **still** **stile**)
  (= 'elegance', 'poise')
- *George Orwell is regarded as a master of (prose) **style**.* (Not **still** **stile**)
  (= way of writing)
- *Please help me over this **stile**.*
  (= a specially-constructed step over a wall or fence)
- *A two-year-old can't keep **still** for long!*
  (= unmoving)

stir • mix • beat • dissolve
- *With the pan off the heat, add the beaten eggs to the milk and **mix** them well.*
  (= work them together till they combine)
- *Heat the mixture gently, and **stir** it occasionally.* (Not **mix**)
  (= move it around with a spoon)
- ***Beat** the sugar and the egg-yolks together.*
  (= mix vigorously with a fork or mechanical beater)
- ***Dissolve** the sugar in a cup of water.*
  (= mix a solid into a liquid until they become one substance)

stockings • tights • socks
- *I bought my father a pair of **socks** for his birthday.* (Not **stockings** **tights**)
  (*socks* are short; they are worn more by men and children than by women)
- *I bought my mother a pair of **stockings/ tights** for her birthday.*
  (*stockings* and *tights* are worn by women; *tights*, AmE *pantyhose*, are made in one piece, combining *pants* and *stockings*)

stomach-ache
- *I have/I've got (a) **stomach-ache**.*
  (Not **I have/I've got my stomach.**)
- *I had (a) **stomach-ache** last night.*
  (Not **did/made (a) stomach-ache**)

stony • stone
- *They don't build fine **stone** walls like this nowadays!* (Not **stony**)
  (= made of *stone*; *stone* can be a noun modifier: *a stone step, a stone tablet*)
- *The ground is too **stony** to grow crops.*
  (= with a lot of stones)
- *My jokes were met with **stony** silence!*
  (= 'like stone': i.e. hard, unfriendly)

stop
- *We **made** a couple of **stops** on our way here.*
  (Not **did ... stops**)
- *I've **stopped buying** newspapers.*
  (Not **stopped to buy**)
- *On the way to the station, I **stopped to buy** a paper.* (Not **stopped buying**)
  (= stopped in order to buy)
- *How can we **stop him complaining**?*
  (Not **stop him to complain**)

stop • hitch/hitchhike
- *We **hitched lifts/hitchhiked** right across Europe.*
  (Not **We did (auto)stop** **We stopped**)
- ***Hitching/Hitchhiking** is the only way to travel if you're broke.* (Not **The stop**)
  (= getting a driver of a vehicle to stop and take you the whole or part of your journey)

story • storey
- *My office is on the tenth **storey**.*
  (*story* only in AmE)
  (= a floor, or level in a building; plural: *storeys*)
- *Read me a **story**, Mum.* (Not **storey**)
  (plural: *stories*)

straight
- *I've got such a bad headache, I can't see **straight**.* (Not **straightly**)
  (= in a straight line; *straight* is both

adjective and adverb: a *straight line, think straight,* etc.; there is no *-ly* form)

strange • curious • foreign

– *I'm* **curious** *to know why they suddenly left the district.* (Not **strange**)
  (= eager to know, having *curiosity, curious about* something)
– *We should try to cut down on* **foreign** *imports.* (Not **strange* *curious**)
  (= from abroad)
– *There are many* **curious/strange** *phenomena in physics that still can't be explained.*
  (= unusual, odd)

strangeness • curiosity

– **Curiosity** *killed the cat.* (Not **Strangeness**)
  (= wanting to know)
– *It took me a while to get used to the* **strangeness** *of my new school.*
  (= the unfamiliar quality)

stranger • foreigner • alien • guest

– *I've lived in France for years, but I still speak French like a* **foreigner**.
  (Not **stranger* *guest* *alien**)
  (= one who is not a native)
– **Aliens** *have to apply for work permits, as well as residence permits.*
  (preferable to *Foreigners*)
  (*alien* is formal for a foreigner living long-term in another country)
– *We're expecting* **guests** *for supper.*
  (Not **strangers* *foreigners* *aliens**)
  (= people who have been invited)
– *Given half the chance, she'd tell her life story to a complete* **stranger**.
  (= a person who is unknown to her)

street • road

– *Is this the* **road** *to Damascus?* (Not **street**)
– *A water pipe had burst and there was a hole in the* **road**. (Not **street**)
– *Our house is in this* **street**.
  (a *road* is a flat surface that carries traffic; a *street* is a place consisting of a road with buildings along the sides)

streetwalker • pedestrian • walker

– *You can't drive in this street: it's for* **pedestrians** *only.*
  (Not **streetwalkers* *walkers**)
– *On the way here, I was approached by a woman who must have been a* **streetwalker**.
  (euphemistic, old-fashioned for *prostitute*)
– *The mountain paths are used by* **walkers**.
  (= people who walk for pleasure, especially in the countryside)

strengthen • strong • get/grow stronger

– *I* **got/grew stronger** *again after my illness by taking regular exercise.*
  (Not **I strengthened* *I stronged**)
– *Exercise* **made me strong** *again after my illness.* (preferably not *strengthened me*)
– *We'll have to put a beam in to* **strengthen** *that wall/**make** that wall **strong**.*
  (Not **strong that wall**)

stretch • spread • extend

– *Daphne emptied her handbag and* **spread** *the contents on her desk.*
  (= opened out horizontally)
– *He* **spread** *his arms wide.*
  (i.e. opened them out)
– *This butter is still too cold to* **spread**.
  (Not **stretch* *extend**)
  (= make into a flat layer: *spread with butter*)
– *I'm going for a walk to* **stretch** *my legs.*
  (Not **extend**)
– *He* **extended** *his hand warmly.*
  (Not **stretched**)
– **Stretch/Extend** *your arms as far as they will go.* (Not **Spread**)
  (*stretch* = pull out, making bigger/longer; *extend* = open out in a line)

strike

– *The workers* **are striking/are on strike**.
  (Not **are doing/making strike**)

strong • heavy • hard

– **Heavy smoking** *and* **hard/heavy drinking** *are the shortest route to an early grave.*
  (Not **strong smoking/drinking**)
– *It's been* **a hard winter**.
  (Not **a heavy/strong winter**)
  (Compare: *This case is* **heavy**!/*What a* **heavy** *case!* = in weight)
– *Whisky is a* **strong** *drink.*
  (note also *weak/strong tea, mild/strong coffee, weak/thin/strong beer*)
– *These mints are extra* **strong**.
  (i.e. in effect or flavour)

strong • strongly

– *Grandma's over 90 and still* **going strong**.
  (Not **going strongly**)
  (*going strong* is a fixed expression = be healthy)
– *I* **strongly** *support high taxes on tobacco.*
  (adverbial use = to a high degree)

strophe • verse

– *How many* **verses** *are there in the national anthem?* (Not **strophes**)
  (*a verse* = a set of lines of poetry; *a strophe*

= a verse is a technical term in descriptions of classical poetry)

stuck • get stuck
- *During the power-cut we got stuck in the lift for over an hour.* (Not *we stuck*)
  (= were unable to move)
- *I stuck the broken pieces of that vase together with quick-drying glue.*

stuff • substance • fabric • material • matter
- *It took a lot of fabric/material to make these curtains.* (Not *stuff* - archaic in this sense - or *substance* *matter*)
  (= cloth)
- *I prefer natural fabrics/materials like cotton to synthetics like polyester.*
  (Not *stuffs* *substances* *matters*)
  (= types of cloth)
- *They use some awful waxy stuff/substance on lemons to stop them going bad.*
  (preferable to *matter*)
- *We had to sell so much of our stuff when we moved to a smaller house.*
  (Not *matter* *material* *substance*)
  (*stuff* is uncountable; we use it informally to refer to things in general, possessions, etc.)
- *Sub-atomic particles form the building matter of the universe.*
  (= the material from which it is made)

stuffed (with) • filled (with) • filling
- *This cake is filled with lemon cream/has a lemon cream filling.* (Not *stuffed with*)
  (fabricated or man-made food e.g. *chocolate* is *filled* or contains *filling*)
- *The tomatoes have been stuffed with rice, mince and parsley.* (Not *filled with*)
- *We're having stuffed tomatoes tonight.*
  (Not *filled*, which isn't used before a noun)
  (natural foods like meat, fish or vegetables are *stuffed*; the noun is *stuffing*)

stupidity
- *The environment is the constant victim of our stupidity.* (Not *stupidities*)
  (*stupidity* is generally uncountable)

succeed in
- *Power in a democracy depends on how well you succeed in persuading people to vote for you.* (Not *succeed to persuade*; the noun is *success* + *in* + *-ing*; the adjective is *successful* + *in* + *-ing*)

suck • lick
- *I wish you wouldn't lick your ice cream in such a noisy fashion!* (Not *suck*)

(you move the tongue across a surface when you lick: *lick a stamp*)
- *I wish you wouldn't suck your ice lolly in such a noisy fashion!*
  (you draw something into the mouth when you *suck*, or you hold it in the mouth: *suck a sweet*)

suds
- *You've used too much washing powder: the machine is full of suds.* (Not *sud*)
  (plural noun with no singular form + plural verb)

suffer • allow • bear • support
- *The hospital won't allow visitors during the morning.* (Not *suffer* *support*)
- *Please turn that music down. I can't bear it.* (Not *suffer* *support*)
- *I can't bear to see children suffer.*
  (= experience pain; *suffer* in the sense of 'allow' is now archaic)
- *I can't afford to be out of work. I have a family to support.*
  (= provide money for)

sugar
- *One spoonful of sugar in your tea, or two?*
  (Not *a sugar*, though *two sugars* is often heard in informal speech)
  (*sugar* is uncountable)

suggest
- *Who suggested that idea to you?*
  (Not *suggested you that idea* *suggested to you that idea*)
- *To save time, I suggest we meet/I suggest we should meet/I suggest meeting at the restaurant.* (Not *suggest to meet* *suggest we to meet* *suggest we meeting*)

suggestive • inspiring • imaginative • suggested
- *The orchestra gave us an inspiring/imaginative performance of Tchaikovsky's 6th.* (Not *suggestive*)
  (*inspiring* = that raised our spirits, gave us *inspiration*; *imaginative* = that showed use of the *imagination*)
- *The suggested menu/the menu suggested seemed too elaborate.* (Not *suggestive*)
  (= which has been suggested)
- *Making suggestive comments is a kind of sexual harassment.*
  (= full of sexual innuendo)

suite • suit

- *Why is grey always the favourite colour for a business **suit**?* /suːt/ (Not *suite*)
  (= a *suit* of clothes)
- *We've just bought a new three-piece **suite*** /swiːt/ *for the living room.* (Not *suit*)
  (= matching armchairs and settee)
- *I wonder what it costs to spend a night in the Presidential **Suite**?* /swiːt/
  (= a set of rooms in a hotel)

sunk • sunken

- *The **sunken** wreck of a ship blocked the entrance to the harbour.* (Not *sunk*)
  (adjective = which has *sunk*, lying under the surface)
- *How many ships **have sunk** in the Bermuda Triangle?* (Not *have sunken* *have sank*)
  (sink - sank - sunk)

supplement • complete • complement

- *I never **completed** my degree course because I ran out of money.*
  (Not *supplemented* *complemented*)
  (= finished)
- *I **supplemented** my student grant by doing part-time work.*
  (Not *completed* *complemented*)
  (= added to)
- *You should **complement** your study of language with the study of literature.*
  (Not *supplement*)
  (= make complete by combining things that go together)

support • endure • put up with/stand

- *We **endured** dreadful anxiety when one of the plane's engines failed.*
  (Not *supported* *put up with/stood*)
  (= suffered)
- *However do you **put up with/stand** those awful neighbours of yours?* (Not *support*)
- *That stool won't **support** your weight.*
  (= hold up)
- *You need a high income these days to **support** a large family.*
  (= provide for)

suppose • supposed to be

- *I **suppose/am supposing** the journey won't take more than a couple of hours.*
  (stative or dynamic depending on the emphasis you wish to give)
- *Will he phone when he arrives? - I **suppose so.*** (Not *I suppose.* *I suppose it.*)
- *It won't matter much if we're late. - I **suppose not./I don't suppose so.***
  (Not *I suppose no.*)

- *He is **supposed to be** at work today.*
  (Not *It is supposed him to be at work*)
  (= 'people think he is at work' or 'it is his duty to be at work')
- *The train's **supposed to arrive** at 9.14.*
  (Not *It is supposed the train to arrive*)
  (= 'but perhaps it won't arrive')

sure • safe • secure

- *The survivors have been rescued and are all **safe**.* (Not *sure* *secure*)
- *Do you think it's **safe** to keep cash in this drawer?* (Not *sure* *secure*)
  (= out of danger: Is it likely to be stolen?)
- *Lock up and make sure all the windows are **secure**.* (Not *sure* *safe*)
  (= protected from danger, so that no one can break in)
- *We've fitted window locks because we want to feel **safe/secure**.* (Not *sure*)
- *I feel **sure** you'll recognize her when you see her.* (Not *safe* *secure*)
  (= positive)

sure (of) • surely • certainly • certain

- *I **sure** (AmE)/**certainly** am late.*
  (Not *surely*)
  (*sure* as an adverb in AmE)
- ***Surely** you can ride a bike!/You can **surely** ride a bike!* (Not *certainly*)
  (i.e. Is it possible that you can't?)
- *I don't know how far it is to Edinburgh, but it's **certainly** a long way.*
  (= 'there's no doubt')
- *I'm **certainly** not suggesting you did it on purpose.* (Not *surely*)
  (= 'it is certain')
- *Ask your father. He's **sure/certain** to know.*
- *Could I make a phone call? - **Certainly**.*
  (BrE)/**Certainly** or **Surely**. (AmE)
- *You should be **sure of** your facts before you open your mouth.* (Not *sure for/from*)

surgery • consulting room • office • operating theatre

- *I'm afraid the doctor can't take a call at the moment. He's busy in his **surgery/consulting room** (BrE)/**office** (AmE).*
  (= a place where patients visit doctors and dentists for treatment)
- *Mrs Williams was rushed to the **operating theatre** for immediate **surgery**.*
  (*surgery* is cutting performed by a *surgeon*; the *operating theatre* is where this takes place; not *the operations room*, which is the control room for the police, etc.)

surprise/surprising • surprised at
– We'll **give her a** nice **surprise** on her birthday. (Not *do/make her a nice suprise* *give to her a nice surprise*)
– It **surprises me** that/It's **a surprise to me** that/It's **surprising** that they can't sell their flat. (Not *I surprise* *Is surprising me* *It does/makes me a surprise*)
– I was very **surprised at** the news. (Not *surprised with* *surprised from*)

susceptible to • impressionable
– Seventeen is an extremely **impressionable** age. (Not *susceptible*)
– Teenagers are very **impressionable** and **susceptible to** advertisements for smoking. (*impressionable* = easily impressed; *susceptible to* something = easily influenced by something)

suspect of
– They **suspect** him **of** fiddling his expense accounts. (Not *suspect him for/to*)

suspicious (of) • suspected (of) • suspicious-looking
– A lot of people are **suspected of** smuggling drugs. (Not *suspicious*) (i.e. someone *suspects* them, is *suspicious*)
– If travellers look nervous, customs officers get **suspicious**. (Not *suspected*) (= believe something might be wrong, etc.)
– Customs officers are **suspicious of** nervous-looking travellers. (Not *suspected of*)
– You get a lot of **suspicious**-*looking* characters in this bar. (i.e. they look as if they might be guilty of something, up to no good)
– Don't leave your luggage unattended. It looks **suspicious**. (Not *suspected*) (i.e. so people suspect something is wrong)

sweep • wipe • brush
– **Wipe** your nose/the table! (Not *Sweep*) (i.e. with a handkerchief, a cloth, etc.)
– **Sweep** the floor/the room. (i.e. with a broom)
– Let me **brush** your coat. (Not *sweep*) I'm going to **brush** my teeth. (i.e. with a brush)

sweet • fresh
– It's always more difficult to swim in **fresh** water than in sea water. (Not *sweet*)
– How do you like your Turkish coffee? - **Sweet**, please. (= with a lot of sugar)

swim/swimming
– I've just **had** a lovely **swim**. (Not *done/made a swim*)
– We **went for a swim**. We **went swimming**. (Not *went for swim* *went for swimming*)

swim • float
– First we teach you how to **float** and then we teach you how to **swim**. (*float* = remain on the surface of water without sinking; *swim* = move through water using your arms and legs)
– I **swam** ten lengths today. (Not *swum*)
– I've **swum** ten lengths. (Not *have swam*) (*swim - swam - swum*)

sympathetic • nice/friendly/likeable
– What's your impression of Kitty's fiancé? - He's very **nice/friendly/likeable**. (Not *sympathetic*)
– The police aren't always **sympathetic** when they are asked to sort out a family quarrel. (= kind and understanding)

sympathize (with) • like/love
– He **likes/loves** Lucy too much to criticize her. (Not *sympathizes*)
– I'm sorry you caught my cold. I really **sympathize (with you)**! (= feel sorry)

sympathy • love
– It seemed like the **love** of a lifetime and that it would last forever! (Not *sympathy*)
– Those children need a lot more than **sympathy** now that they've lost their mother. (= feelings of sorrow)

syndicate • co-operative • trade union
– The **trade** (AmE **labor**) **unions** are calling for safety improvements. (Not *syndicates*) (= organizations which protect the interests of workers who are members)
– The wine growers have now formed a **syndicate/co-operative** to market their wine. (Not *trade union*) (= an association concerned with business; only a *syndicate* is concerned with examinations, etc.)

synthesis • composition
– The concert began with an early **composition** by Mozart. (Not *synthesis*) (= a piece of music)
– The extension to the National Gallery in London is a **synthesis** of different architectural styles. (technical = bringing together)

T

tableau • picture
- *I'll hang these **pictures**.* (Not **tableaus**)
- *This picture shows a **tableau** of the whole family, taken on Grandmother's birthday.* (= a formally arranged scene)

tachometer/rev-counter • speedometer • mileometer/odometer
- *How fast are we going according to your **speedometer**?* (Not **tachometer**)
  (= an instrument which shows how fast a vehicle is travelling; informally *the speedo*)
- *Only sporty vehicles are fitted with **tachometers/rev-counters**.*
  (= instruments that show how fast an engine turns by measuring 'revs' = *revolutions*)
- *How many miles does it show on the **mileometer** (BrE)/**odometer**(AmE)/on the **clock**?* (informal)
  (*a mileometer/an odometer* measures distance; compare a *trip counter* which is used in vehicles to measure short distances)

take • buy
- *Where did you **buy** that car?* (Not **take**)
- *Who **took** my umbrella?*
  (= removed)

take • catch
- *I've **caught** an awful cold.* (Not **taken**)
  (*catch* a cold)
- *The chimney **caught fire**.* (Not **took fire**)
  (*catch* fire)
- *Which train did you **take/catch**?*
  (*take* or *catch* a train)

take care (of/with) • pay attention • be careful • care for
- *I wish you'd **pay attention** when I'm speaking to you!* (Not **take care* *be careful* *care for/of me* *give attention**)
  (= listen)
- *Do **take care/be careful** on the way home.* (Not **pay attention* *care for* *be care**)
  (= avoid danger)
- *Do **be careful with/take care with** that tray. You nearly dropped it!*
  (Not **pay attention* *care for/of**)
  (= be attentive)
- *Who **takes care of/cares for** this garden?* (Not **pays attention to* *is careful of**)
  (= looks after, attends to)
- *It's precisely because she **cares for** her family so much that she goes out to work.*
  (= loves, is concerned about)

take from • take by
- *You'd better **take her by** the hand when you cross the road.* (Not **take her from**)
- *Will that pigeon **take** food **from** your hand?*

take it easy • go easy (on)
- *I've decided to **go easy on** chocolate so I don't get fat.* (Not **take it easy with**)
  (= not have too much)
- *I've been working too hard and I'll have to **go easy/take it easy** for a while.*
  (= not make too great an effort)

take off • put off • take out • put out
- *Would you please **put off/out** all the lights before you go to bed?* (Not **take off**)
  (*put off* and *put out* are the opposite of *put on*; compare *turn off* and *turn out* which are the opposite of *turn on*)
- ***Take off** your coat.* (Not **Put off/out**)
  (*take off*, opposite of *put on* = get into)
- *I've **put off** the meeting till next week.*
  (= postponed)
- *I'll **take** the dog **out** today.*
  (i.e. for a walk)
- *Don't forget to **put out** the cat.*
  (= let out of the building)

take place • take part (in) • sit down
- *How many of you are **taking part in** the play?* (Not **taking place**)
  (= participating in)
- *All these events **took place** before you were born.* (Not **took part* *had place**)
  (= happened)
- *Do **sit down**.* (Not **take place**)

tall • high
- *New York is full of **tall** buildings.*
  (Not **high**)
- *The **highest** mountains in the world are in the Himalayas.* (preferable to *tallest*)
- *The redwood is a **tall** tree.* (Not **high**)
- *The tree hasn't grown very **tall** yet.*
  (i.e. in relation to what one expects of it)
- *That shelf is too **high** to reach.* (Not **tall**)
  (we use *tall* to describe things we can see from top to bottom and that are big vertically, and often narrow, compared with others of the same type: *a tall man, a tall tree, a tall building*; we use *high* to mean 'reaching a point above the normal level': *a high mountain, a high wall, a high fence*)
- *It's hard to find suitable ready-made clothes if you're very **tall**.* (Not **high**)
  (*tall* for people)

- *These prices are too **high**.* (Not *tall*)
  (*high* prices, *high* rents, *high* costs, etc.)

tall/height • high
- ***How tall is** Roy?* (Not *What height* **How
  much tall is** **How much height has**)
- ***Roy is six foot/feet tall. Roy is six foot/feet.***
  (Not **has (height) six foot/feet**)
- ***How tall/What height/How high is** the
  church steeple?* (Not **How much tall/high
  is** **How much height has**)
- ***It's 200 metres (high)**.*
  (preferable to *200 metres tall*)

tank • reservoir • cistern
- *There's been so little rain that the **reservoir**
  is very low.* (Not *tank* *cistern*)
  (= an artificial lake which holds the public
  water supply)
- *We use this **tank** for storing rainwater.*
  (Not *reservoir* *cistern*)
- *What does it cost to fill your **tank**?*
  (Not *reservoir*)
  (= the petrol tank in a vehicle)
- *What's that noise? - It's just the **cistern**
  filling.* (Not *tank* *reservoir*)
  (= a closed container for water, especially
  for a lavatory)

tapestry • wallpaper • carpet • moquette
- *The Smiths have had their house decorated
  with very fancy **wallpaper**.* (Not *tapestry*)
  (usually uncountable = decorative paper for
  covering, or *papering*, walls)
- *The whole flat is fitted with (a) wall-to-wall
  carpet.* (Not *tapestry*)
  (countable or uncountable = woven material
  for covering, or *carpeting*, floors)
- *It's a **tapestry** of a medieval hunting scene.*
  (countable = a woven - or sometimes sewn -
  picture for hanging on a wall)
- *The sofa was upholstered in red **moquette**.*
  (= a kind of textured cloth; old-fashioned)

tariff • charge(s) • tax • price-list • fee
- *The hotel/bar/restaurant **tariff** is very high.*
  (*tariff* = charges in catering)
- *I had to pay a £10 **tariff** on this at Customs.*
  (= a fixed charge per item)
- *Can you send me an up-to-date **price-list**?*
  (Not *tariff*)
- *These **charges** include the cost of materials.*
  (= the list of costs on a bill)
- *Imported goods carry a high **tax/tariff**.*
  (*tax* is the general word for money collected
  by governments; *a tariff* is a tax on goods
  that are imported or exported)

- *If you want a consultation with a medical
  specialist, you can expect to pay a high **fee**.*
  (Not *charge* *tariff*)
  (= the sum due for consulting a professional
  person)

tart • cream cake • gateau • flan • pastry
• pasta
- *You'll get fat if you eat so many **cream
  cakes/pastries**.* (Not *pastas*)
- *I'd like a slice of **gateau** with my coffee.*
- *I've made a nice fruit **tart** for tea.*
- *Would you like a slice of this **flan**?*
  (a *cream cake* is a cake with a fresh cream
  filling; a *gateau* is a large fancy cake served
  in slices; *pastries* is a general term for small
  bakery items; a *tart* is an open *pastry* case
  filled with fruit or jam; a *flan* is an open case
  of cooked *pastry* filled with fruit, etc., and
  served in slices)
- *There's nothing to beat fresh **pasta** served
  with tomato sauce.* (Not *pastry*)
  (*pasta* = any type of macaroni, spaghetti,
  etc.; *pastry*, uncountable = flour-based
  casing for other foods: *I'm making **some
  pastry** for this pie.*)

taste (of/like)
- *This egg **tastes bad**.* (Not *is tasting* **tastes
  badly**; *taste* functions like *be*, so we use an
  adjective after it, e.g. *bad*; not an adverb,
  e.g. *badly*; this use is always stative)
- *What are you doing? - **I'm tasting** the soup.*
  (Not *I taste*)
  (dynamic use)
- *This soup **tastes of** mushrooms.*
  (i.e. it has that flavour)
- *I can't describe it. It **tastes like** mushrooms.*
  (i.e. it has a flavour that is similar)

taste • try • probe
- *You really must **try** to overcome your
  shyness.* (Not *taste* *probe*)
- *You could at least **taste/try** my onion pie
  before making rude remarks.* (Not *probe*)
  (= eat a little to see if you like it)
- *Reporters have been round here again today
  probing for information.*
  (= searching, trying to dig out)

tasty/delicious • (in good) taste • tasteful
• pretty
- *You **have** excellent **taste**.*
  (Not **You are tasty/tasteful.**)
  (i.e. you have good judgement in matters of
  style, etc.)

- *The whole flat is in very good taste.*
  (Not *is very tasty* *has very good taste*)
  (= shows good judgement in matters of style)
- *Diana turned up in a tasteful, high-necked gown with long sleeves.* (Not *tasty*)
  (= in good taste, appropriate: usually before a noun; the adverb is *tastefully*, as in *tastefully furnished/decorated*, etc.)
- *They do tasty/delicious food at low prices.*
  (= appetizing, nice to eat)
- *Moira is a pretty woman.* (Not *tasty*)
  (= attractive to look at)

technique • technician/specialist • technology
- *Our computers were installed by skilled technicians/specialists.* (Not *techniques*)
  (*technicians* install and maintain scientific and electronic equipment; *specialists* is the general word for people who do skilled and specialized work)
- *Watch me. This is an excellent technique for relaxing the neck muscles.*
  (countable = a method)
- *Tanya's violin teacher wants her to alter her bowing technique.*
  (uncountable = a way of doing something)
- *Modern technology has made it possible for astronomers to probe deep space.*
  (Not *technique*; there is no word *technic(s)* in English)
  (= the practical application of scientific knowledge)

teeth • teethe
- *Have you done your teeth?*
  (Not *tooths* *made your teeth*)
  (= cleaned; irregular plural of *tooth*)
- *Babies often suffer discomfort when they teethe/are teething.* (Not *teeth*)
  (verb = grow *teeth*)

temper • mood
- *You seem to be in a very good mood this morning.* (Not *temper*)
  (*mood* = a person's general state of mind, feelings, which can be good or bad)
- *Don't ask your father for money just now. He's in a very bad mood/temper.*
  (*a bad mood* = not feeling cheerful; *a bad temper* = feeling angry; a *bad-tempered* person is one who is often angry)
- *Sometimes I lose my temper/find it hard to keep my temper.* (Not *mood*)
  (*lose my temper* = become angry; *keep my temper* = not let myself become angry)

- *You can't speak to him at the moment. He's in a temper/in a mood.*
  (= angry/depressed)

temperament • liveliness/spirit
- *Don't discourage him. The boy has such liveliness and spirit.* (Not *temperament*)
  (= vivacity, 'he's full of life')
- *How you speak and behave is a matter of temperament.*
  (= a person's basic nature/character, which can be lively or quiet/withdrawn)

temple • church
- *We got married in a registry office, not in a church.* (Not *temple*)
  (= a building for Christian worship)
- *The temple was dedicated to Zeus.*
  (= a place where the gods are worshipped: *a pagan temple*, though we can also speak of a *Hindu temple* or a *Mormon temple*)

tempt • attempt
- *Do what you can. You don't have to attempt the impossible.* (Not *tempt*)
  (= try to achieve)
- *I've stopped smoking, so please don't tempt me to have a cigarette.* (Not *attempt*)
  (= invite/encourage me to do something unwise)

tend
- *I'm afraid Maggie tends to lose her temper rather easily.* (Not *is tending*)
  (stative use = is inclined to)
- *George is tending his roses in the garden.*
  (dynamic use = looking after)

term • end • terminus/terminal • bus stop • station
- *I read this novel right to the end without putting it down!* (Not *term*)
- *My insurance policy is near its term.*
  (*term* = end, has specialized/limited uses and refers to a fixed or agreed period of time; note also that a pregnant woman may be *near her term* when her baby is due)
- *I'd like to get off at the next (bus-)stop.*
  (Not *term/terminus/terminal* or *station* for buses)
- *I'd like to get off at the next stop/station.*
  (Not *term* *terminus* *terminal*)
  (*stop* or *station* for trains)
- *Is it easy to get a taxi from the railway terminus/terminal?* (Not *term*)
  (*terminus/terminal* are interchangeable to describe the end of the line for railways and

buses: *Victoria Bus Terminal*; we use only *terminal* for planes: *the air terminal*)

terrace • balcony • penthouse • roof
– *The **balconies** for each flat have been fitted with railings.* (Not **terraces**)
(a *balcony* is a platform built on to the outside of a building above ground level, acting as an extension of the indoor space; compare *veranda(h)* = an open area with a floor and roof built on to a house at ground level)
– *The **penthouse** is easily the most expensive flat in this block.* (Not **terrace**)
(= a flat or house on the top of a building, often with excellent views)
– *It's not easy to keep a flat **roof** free of leaks.*
– *Our living room opens on to a wide **terrace**.*
(= a flat paved area, often at ground level)

terrible • terrific • frightening/terrifying • frightful
– *There's been a **terrific** demand for cheap flights to the USA.* (Not **terrible**)
(= very large)
– *We've had a **terrific** holiday.*
(informal = wonderful)
– *We've had a **terrible/frightful** holiday.*
(informal = very bad)
– *I witnessed a **terrible/frightful** accident.*
(*terrible* = very severe; *frightful* = 'shocking')
– *Some of the videos young people watch these days are quite **frightening/terrifying**.*
(Not **terrific** **terrible**)
(= causing fear, making people feel *frightened* or *terrified*)

testament • will
– *A lot of people die without having made a **will**.* (Not **testament**)
(= a legal document showing how you want to distribute your money and possessions after death; note *(my) last will and testament*: a fixed legal phrase)
– *This memorial is a **testament** to the courage of those who died for their country.*
(i.e. it provides a public declaration)

than
– *Come for a walk. It's better **than staying** at home.* (Not **than to stay** **than stay**)

than • from
– *Gerda is **from** Berlin.* (Not **than**)
(*from* shows origin)
– *Gerda knows better **than** you.* (Not **from**)
(*than* in comparisons)

thank • thanks
– *I've changed the engine oil for you. - **Thank you./Thanks**.* (Not **Thank./Thanks you.**)
(the plural form *Thanks*, in place of *Thank you*, is informal)
– ***Thank God** we're home!* (Not **Thanks God** **Thanks to God** **Thank to God**)
(= let us thank God)

thank you • no thank you/no thanks
– *Would you like some more potatoes? - **No thank you/No thanks**. I've had enough.* (Not **Thank you.**)
(*No thank you* for polite refusals, or informally, *No thanks*)
– *Have some more potatoes. - **Thank you**. I'd love some.*
(*Thank you* for polite acceptance)

that • what • that which
– *I've forgotten **what** you told me.* (Not **that** **that which**)
– *I forgot **that** it was your birthday.*
– *We'll only pay for **what** we've received.* (preferable to *that which*)

that • who • whom • which
– *He's the man **who/that lives** next door.* (Not **who/that he lives** **whom lives**)
(*who/that* as subjects for people, male or female)
– *This is the photo **which/that shows** my house.* (Not **which/that it shows**)
– *This is the cat **which/that caught** the mouse.* (Not **which/that it caught**)
(*which/that* as subjects for things and animals)
– *He's the man **who/whom/that** I met in Paris.* (Not **He's the man that I met him**)
(*who/whom/that* as objects for people, male or female; we often use *who* in place of *whom*, but usually omit the relative: *He's the man I met in Paris.*)
– *This is the photo **that/which** I took.* (Not **This is the photo that/which I took it.**)
(*that/which* as objects for things and animals; we usually omit the relative: *This is the photo I took.*)

the • on
– *I'll see you **(on) Friday**.* (Not **the Friday**)
– *We had a card from her **(on) the Friday** after she got back.* (Not **(on) Friday**)
(*on* + days of the week, often omitted informally; *the* for specific reference)

the • per • a/an
– *It's £3 **a kilo/per kilo**.* (preferable to *the*)

- *We were doing 40km **an/per hour**.*
  (Not *the hour*)
- *Take this twice **a/per day**.* (Not *the day*)
  (*a/an* for one unit of measurement; *per* =
  'each' is emphatic and formal)
- *Eggs are sold **by the dozen**.* (Not **a/per**)
- *Our car does 30 miles **to the gallon**.*
  (preferable to *a/per*)
  (*the* in prepositional phrases)

the • (-)
- *(-) **Museums** are closed on Mondays.*
  (Not *The museums*)
  (no article with plural countable nouns in
  general statements)
- ***The museums you want to visit** are shut on
  Mondays.* (Not **Museums you want to ...**)
  (*the* for specific reference)
- *(-) **Water** is precious.* (Not *The water*)
  (no article with uncountable nouns in
  general statements)
- ***The water we drink** comes from the river.*
  (Not *Water we drink*)
  (*the* for specific reference)
- ***Korea** is becoming a major industrial
  nation.* (Not *The Korea*)
  (most place names have no article)

their • there • they're
- *I live **there**.* (Not *their* **they're**)
  (= in/at that place)
- *I love Westerns. **They're** so entertaining.*
  (Not *Their* *There*)
  (= they are)
- *The Smiths are careful with **their** money.*
  (= which belongs to them)
  (*their*, *there* and *they're* are all pronounced
  in exactly the same way)

theme • subject • topic
- *What was the **subject/topic** of last night's
  lecture?* (preferable to *theme*)
- *The **theme** of this year's conference is 'Ends
  and Means'.* (preferable to *subject/topic*)
  (*subject* and *topic* are specific, referring to
  subject matter; *theme* refers to the main idea,
  the broad issues)
- *Which **subjects** are you **doing/taking** for
  your exams?* (Not *lessons* *making*)

then: from then on
- *I started exercising and **from then on** I
  began to feel fitter.* (Not *from then*)

then • last
- ***The last** Minister of Education introduced
  some important reforms.*

- *In the 80s, Mrs Thatcher, **the then** Prime
  Minister, rejected a proposal to privatize the
  Royal Mail.*
  (*the last* = the previous; *the then* + noun =
  the one at that time)

there is/there are, etc. • it is • they are • it has • there exists • it exists
- ***There's** a letter for you.* (Not *Has* *It has*
  It is **Is a letter for you**)
- ***It's** from Gerald.* (Not *Is*)
  (= the letter already referred to)
- ***There are** a couple of lemons in the fridge.*
  (Not *It has* *Has* *Are*)
- ***They are** rather dried-up.*
  (= the lemons already referred to)
  (*there is/are* establishes existence; personal
  pronouns like *it* and *they* give details)
- ***There were** a lot of people at the match.*
  (Not **Had a lot of people**)
- ***There's** the bus!*
  (i.e. I've just seen it; compare *Here's your
  passport*: offering or indicating)
- *You'll recognize my coat. **It has** a wide
  velvet collar.* (Not *There is*)
- *Somewhere in the universe **there exists** a
  planet which supports life.* (Not *it has*)
- *You can visit the Parthenon. **It still exists**
  after all these centuries.*
  (we use the verb *exist* to refer to *existence*
  and not in everyday reference, where *there
  is*, etc., is preferred)

these days/nowadays • at this time
- *I generally go and collect him from the
  station **at this time** (of the day).*
- *Children grow up quickly **nowadays/these
  days**.* (Not *in these days* *at this time*)

thick • thickly
- ***Cut** the slices **thick/thickly**.*
  (both forms possible with verbs like *cut, lie,
  spread*)
- *Holland is **thickly** populated.* (Not *thick*)
  (= 'very much'; *-ly* as an intensifier)

thin • get/wear thin
- *Hasn't he **got thin**!* (Not *thinned*)
- *My pyjamas have **got/worn** really **thin**.*
  (Not *have thinned*)
- *I'm going to **thin this paint** with some
  turpentine.* (Not **get this paint thin**)
  (transitive = make thin/dilute, usually with
  reference to liquids)

thin • thinly

- *Cut the slices **thin/thinly**.*
  (both forms possible with verbs like *cut, lie, spread*)
- *Iceland is **thinly** populated.* (Not **thin**)
  (= 'not very much'; *-ly* as an intensifier)

thing

- ***The thing is**, if you miss the last collection, your letter won't arrive till Monday.*
  (Not **It is that which* *The fact is**)
- *The **good thing** is ... The **bad thing** is ... The **first/last thing** is ... The **best/worst thing** is ... The **nicest thing** is ...*
  (we usually need to supply *thing* because we don't normally use adjectives on their own in place of nouns)

think

- ***I think** I've won.* (Not **I'm thinking**)
  (stative use = believe)
- *What are you doing? - **I'm thinking**.*
  (dynamic use = using my brain)
- *Does she agree with us? - **I think so**.*
  (Not **I think.* *I think it.**)
- *Has the postman been? - **I don't think so**.*
  (Not **I think no** and preferable to *I think not*, which is becoming old-fashioned)

think of • think about

- ***Think of** a person you know. **Think of** a number.* (Not **Think a person/a number**)
  (= bring one to mind)
- *I've been **thinking about** you/**thinking about** the lovely holiday we had last year.*
  (*think about* = 'turn something round' in the mind)
- *I'm **thinking of moving** south.*
  (Not **thinking to move**)
  (*think of* = consider: 'perhaps I will')

thirst (for) • thirsty

- *Is there anything to drink? **I'm thirsty**.*
  (Not **I have thirst.* *I thirst.**)
- *Take a flask of tea with you. You might **get thirsty**.* (Not **might thirst**)
- ***Thirst** is your worst enemy in the desert.*
- *A **thirsty person** is generally a bad-tempered one.* (Not **A thirsty**)
  (we cannot use *thirsty* on its own to mean 'a thirsty person')
- *The rescue team took food and water to **the hungry** and **the thirsty**.*
  (Not **the hungries* *the thirsties**)
  (= the group as a whole)
- *The children **thirst for/have a thirst for/are thirsty for** knowledge.*
  (= long for)

this country • that country

- *I'd hate to live in **that country**. It never stops raining.* (Not **this country**)
  (= a country, not your own, already referred to)
- *In **this country**, we generally have elections every five years.*
  (= here, the country we live in)

this night • tonight

- *See you **tonight**.* (*this morning/afternoon/ evening*, but not **this night**)
- *I was born on **this night** fifty years ago.*

this/that/these/those

- *I found **this** wallet. I found **this**.*
  (*this* can stand on its own to refer to a thing)
- *I know **this** girl.* (Not **I know this.**)
  (*this* cannot stand on its own to refer to a person, but we say *Who's this?/Who's that?* to identify a person when e.g. pointing at a picture; otherwise it is socially undesirable)
- *What are **these/those**?*
  (*these/those* on their own to refer to things)
- *Who are **these/those people**?*
  (Not **Who are these/those?**)
  (we have to say *Who are these/those people/ men/women?*, etc., to identify people)

three • thirteen

- *I'll be **thirteen** soon.* (Not **threeteen**)
  (spelling: 3 = *three*; 13 = *thirteen*)

throat • neck: sore throat/neck

- *My throat hurts. I've got **a sore throat**.*
- *My neck hurts. I've got **a sore neck**.*
  (the *throat* is 'internal' and begins at the back of the mouth; *a sore throat* is generally caused by an infection; the *neck* joins the head and shoulders)

throw down • knock down

- *He was **knocked down** by a car.*
  (Not **thrown down**)
  (= struck)
- *You **knocked** my sandcastle **down**.*
  (= destroyed)
- *The baby picked up his rattle, then **threw it down**.*
  (i.e. to the ground)

throw to • throw at • throw away/out • drop

- *Don't **throw** stones **at** the dog.* (Not **to**)
  (i.e. in order to harm it)
- ***Throw** the ball **to** the dog.*
  (i.e. for the dog to catch/fetch it)
  (*at* for 'aggression'; *to* for destination)

– *Shall I* **throw** *this old newspaper* ***away/out****?*
(Not **Shall I throw it?**)
(= get rid of)
– ***Drop it!/Throw it away!*** *It's dirty!*
(Not **Throw it!**)

thunder and lightning

– *I'm scared of* **thunder and lightning***.*
(Not **thunders and lightnings**)
(*thunder* and *lightning* are uncountable; note spelling: *lightning,* not 'lightening', which is part of the verb *lighten* = grow lighter)

tight • tightly

– *A lot of people are just* **sitting tight** *and refusing to pay the new tax.* (Not **tightly**)
(we use *tight,* not *tightly* = securely in place/ unmoving, after verbs like *bind, fasten, hold, tie;* and intransitive verbs like *sit* and *sleep.* Compare: *Screw the lid on* **tight** = securely in place; *Screw the lid on* **tightly** = in a tight manner: *-ly* for a deliberate action)
– *The string was* **tightly knotted***.*
(Not **tight knotted**)

tighten • tight • get tight

– *These shoes* **have got** *very* **tight***.*
(Not **have tightened* *have tighted**)
– *Hang on a moment. I need to* **tighten** *my* **shoelaces***/make my shoelaces* **tighter***/fasten my shoelaces* **tight***.* (Not **get them tight**)

till • to • as far as

– *We walked* **as far as the river/to the river***.*
(Not **till the river**)
(*to/as far as* for direction)
– *It's ten* **to** *four.* (Not **till**)
(*to* and *past* when telling the time)
– *We're open* **from 9 to/till 5***.*
(*from ... to/till*)
– *We're open* **till/until** *five.* (Not **to**)
– *We had to wait* **till Wednesday** *before we got an answer.* (Not **to Wednesday**)
(*till/until* for 'up to a point of time')

timber

– *That looks like a nice* **piece of timber***.*
(Not **a timber**)
– *There was* **a lot of timber** *stacked in the yard.* (Not **a lot of timbers**)
(*timber* is normally uncountable)

time: on time • in time

– *If you set this digital alarm clock for 6.58, it will wake you exactly* **on time***.*
– *I got an earlier train to be sure I would be* **in time** *for my interview.*
(*on time* = exactly at a stated time; *in time* = ahead of a stated time)

time: that time • at that time

– *Grandma was born in 1900.* **At that time** *few houses had electricity.* (Not **That time**)
(= at that period; also: *in those times*)
– *Careful when you're kicking that ball. You nearly hit me* **that time***.*
(= on that occasion)

time • weather • climate

– *What bad/good* **weather** *we've been having!*
(Not **time* *What a weather/climate!**)
(*weather* is generally uncountable; a plural form exists in the fixed phrase *I go out* **in all weathers***.*)
– *Do you think the* **climate** *of the world is really warming up?*
(*weather* is day to day, *climate* is general)
– *You were away for a long* **time***!*

timid • shy • fearful

– *I sometimes feel terribly* **shy** *when I'm meeting strangers.* (preferable to *timid*)
– *I keep my money in the bank. I'm too* **timid/fearful** *to take risks.* (Not **shy**)
(*shy* = socially unconfident; *timid* = lacking courage; *fearful* = filled with fear)

tired (of)

– *I get* **tired waiting** *around in airports.*
(Not **tired of waiting* *tired to wait**)
(= while I am waiting: participle phrase)
– *I'm* **tired of clearing up** *after you.* (Not **tired to clear* *tired from clearing**)
(normal use of gerund after a preposition)

tired • tire • get tired • tire yourself

– ***I've got tired/I'm tired*** *of telling you to keep your room tidy.* (Not **tired myself** and preferable to *I've tired*)
– *You're doing too much. You'll* **tire yourself** *(out).* (Not **You'll get tired.* *You'll tire.**)
(= become exhausted)
– *I always try to keep to a diet when I start one, but I soon* **tire** *(of it).*
(*tire* often refers to failure to keep something going)
– *Don't bother me now. I'm* **tired***.*
(adjective)

tiredness • fatigue

– *After the long march the soldiers were suffering from* **fatigue***.* (Not **tiredness**)
(= accumulated need for rest, *exhaustion*)
. – *I had been up all night with the baby and felt stupid with* **tiredness***.*
(= the natural need for rest)

to • towards

– *Take two steps **towards** me.* (Not **to**)
(***towards***, to emphasize direction, without describing the whole movement)
– *Does this bus go **to** York?* (Not **towards**)
(***to*** for general direction)

toast • toasted sandwich

– *I ate **a slice of toast**.* (Not **a toast**)
– *We ate **some toast**.* (Not **some toasts**)
(= grilled slices of bread; uncountable)
– *They do snacks like **toasted sandwiches** and salads.* (Not **toasts**)

today • present

– ***The present generation** of young people has had more opportunities than ours.*
(Not **The today generation**)
– ***The young people of today/Today's young people** enjoy many advantages.*

today • this

– *Your aunt is arriving **this morning**.*
(Not **today morning/afternoon/evening**)
– *Your aunt is arriving **today**.*

toilet • clothes • dressing table

– *Daphne has a lot of **clothes**.*
(Not **a lot of toilet(s)**, though *a large wardrobe* = clothes, is possible)
– *Use the mirror on my **dressing table**.*
(Not **toilet**)
(= a table in a bedroom, used for dressing, putting on make-up, etc.)
– *Could you direct me to the **toilet** please?*
(= lavatory)

tomb • grave

– *The dead soldiers were buried in **graves** near the battlefield.* (Not **tombs**)
(*a grave* = the ground in which a dead person is buried)
– *No one achieves immortality with an expensive **tomb**.* (Not **grave**)
(= a decorative or imposing stone container for a dead body, above ground)

tomorrow

– *I'll see you **tomorrow at noon**.*
(Not **tomorrow the noon**)
– *I'll see you **tomorrow morning/ afternoon/evening/night**.*
(Not **tomorrow the morning**, etc. **at/on tomorrow morning**, etc.)

tongue • language

– *He speaks four **languages**.* (Not **tongues**)
(*tongue* = 'language' is literary: *He spoke in a strange **tongue***, or exists only in a few fixed phrases, like *mother tongue*)
– *The doctor asked me to stick out my **tongue**.*
(= the organ inside the mouth)

too • also • as well • not either

– *I like John and I like his wife, **too/as well**.*
(preferable to *also*)
– *I play squash and I **also** play tennis.*
(Not **too* *as well**)
(*also* refers to the verb that follows: 'squash is not the only game I play'. Compare: *I, **too**, play tennis*, where *too* refers to the subject *I*)
– *I don't play squash and I don't play tennis **either**.* (Not **too* *also* *as well**)
(*not ... either* in negative sentences)

too • very

– *I arrived **very** late at the airport and just caught my plane.* (Not **too late**)
– *I arrived **too** late at the airport and missed my plane.* (preferable to *very*)
(*very* is the normal intensifier; *too* suggests 'more than is necessary or desirable', so we cannot say e.g. **I was too happy when I heard your news.**)

too much • very much • a lot

– *John likes football **very much/a lot** and plays in a team.* (Not **too much**)
(= as much as is necessary/desirable)
– *John likes football **too much** and is neglecting his schoolwork.*
(= more than is necessary/desirable)
– *I paid **a lot/too much** for this car.*
(Not **very much**)
(*a lot* = a great deal; *too much* = more than is desirable: both in affirmative sentences)
– *I didn't pay **very much/a lot/too much** for this car.*
(*very much* mainly in negative sentences)

toothache

– *I have/I've got **a toothache**. I've got **toothache**.* (Not **I have my tooth.**)
– *I had **(a) toothache** last night.*
(Not **did/made (a) toothache**)

toothpaste • a tube of toothpaste

– *I bought **a tube of toothpaste/two tubes of toothpaste**.*
(Not **a toothpaste* *two toothpastes**)
(*toothpaste* is uncountable)

topical • local

– *Shortage of water is a national problem, not a **local** problem.* (Not **topical**)

- *Acid rain is a **topical** issue at the moment.*
  (*local* refers to a particular place; *topical* refers to present time)

torch

lightbulb

lamp

torch • lamp • light bulb
- *It isn't easy to read for a long time by the light of a **lamp**.*
  (= a device for producing light by burning gas or oil; compare *a table lamp, a bedside lamp*, etc., which are powered by electricity)
- *I'm going to have to change this **light bulb**.*
- *I keep a **torch** (AmE **flashlight**) in my car for emergencies.* (Not **lamp**)

total • whole
- *The **whole bill/the whole sum** came to $894.* (Not **The whole came to**)
- *The **total/The total bill/The total sum** came to $894.*
  (when referring to figures added together, we can use *total* as a noun or as an adjective, but *whole* only as an adjective)
- *You can't give an opinion unless you've read **the whole book**.* (Not **the total book**)

track • trace • sign
- *The robbers have disappeared without **trace**.* (Not **track* *sign**)
  (= any mark to show their presence)
- *Is there any **sign** of improvement in the weather?* (Not **trace* *track**)
  (= something that gives information)
- *We followed the fresh **tracks** as far as the river.* (Not **traces* *signs**)
  (= continuous marks, e.g. footprints, made by a person, animal, etc.)

tranquil • quiet
- *Please be **quiet**.* (Not **tranquil**)
  (= e.g. don't make a noise; don't say anything; also note *Don't worry!*, not **Be/Rest tranquil!**)
- *I prefer a **quiet/tranquil** life in the country to the stresses of town life.*
  (= peaceful)

translated by/from/into
- *Shakespeare's works were **translated into German by** Schlegel.* (Not **translated to German* *translated in German**)

(*translated by* a person, *from* one language *into* another)

travel
- *I often **travel** to Brussels.* (Not **go on a travel* *make/do a travel* *have a travel**)
  (we use *travel* mainly as a verb in English)

traveller • passenger
- ***Passengers** should remain seated till the plane comes to a stop.* (Not **Travellers**)
  (*passengers* are people who are carried on buses, planes and trains and driven in cars)
- *There are problems for **travellers/ passengers** today at all the main airports.*
  (*travellers* are people who travel, whether they are *passengers* or not)

treat • deal with • use • handle
- *I'm not sure how I should **deal with/handle** this difficult situation.* (Not **treat* *use**)
  (= manage)
- *You don't like me. You're just **using** me.*
  (= taking advantage of)
- *Do your students **make use of** the library? - Some do, but they don't **make much use of** it/**make the best use of** it.*
- *Some companies have a reputation for **treating** their employees very well.*
  (= behaving towards them; *using* in this sense is old-fashioned)
- *Every single day a manager has to **deal with** any number of problems.*
  (Not **treat* *use** and preferable to *handle*, which is personal, informal)
  (= take effective action, cope with)
- *We've been **dealing with** the same firm of office stationers for years.*
  (Not **handling* *using* *treating**)
  (= doing business with)

treatment • use • handling
- *The **use** of pesticides in farming should be restricted.* (Not **treatment* *handling**)
- *Countries are often judged by their **treatment** of prisoners of war.*
  (= behaviour towards)
- *In some countries, the **handling** of drugs is punishable by death.*
  (= dealing in, buying and selling)

trial: on trial • approval: on approval
- *We've received these goods by mail order **on approval**.* (Not **on trial**)
  (i.e. we can return them if we're not satisfied with them)

- *The whole gang is going **on trial** for drug smuggling next month.*
  (i.e. they will be tried in a court of law)

trouble • problems

- *Some people seem to be born to **make/cause trouble/problems**.* (Not *do trouble*)
  (*trouble* is frequently uncountable; the plural form *troubles* often refers to personal problems: *You don't want to hear about all my **troubles**.*)
- *That employee **made/caused a lot of trouble for you**.*
  (Not *made/did you a lot of trouble*)
- *My car has been **giving/causing** (me) a lot of **trouble** lately.* (Not *making/doing*)
- *I'm **having a lot of trouble** with my car.*
  (Not *a lot of troubles*)
  (= difficulty)
- *I've got **a lot of troubles** at the moment.*
  (Not *trouble*)
  (= things that are worrying me)

trousers • pantaloons

- *How much is this **pair of trousers**?*
  (Not *pair of pantaloons*)
- *How much **are these trousers**?*
  (Not *is this trouser* *is this pantaloon*)
  (*pantaloons* = tight-fitting trousers worn by men is archaic)
- *The dog sank its teeth into my **trouser-leg**.*
  (plural form only except in compounds)

true • truth

- *The **truth** is, I don't know the answer to your question.* (Not *true*)
- *Is it **true**?* (Not *truth*)
  (*truth* is the noun; *true* is the adjective)
- *Always **tell the truth**.* (Not *say*)

try

- *You really must **try to overcome** your shyness.* (Not *try overcoming*)
  (*try + to* = 'make an effort')
- ***Try holding** your breath to stop sneezing.*
  (Not *Try to hold*)
  (*try + -ing* = 'experiment')
- *I can't get this cap off. - Let me **have a try**.*
  (Not *do a try*)
  (= let me try)

turn

- *You **did me a very good turn**, so I'll do one for you.* (Not *made* ... *to you*)
  (= you were helpful)

turn back • return

- *Jane now lives in America and says she'll never **return**.*

(Not *return back* *turn back*)
(= go back after having been somewhere; the idea of *back* is in the prefix *re-*, so we don't need to say *back* as well)
- *I had to **turn back** halfway to the airport because I had forgotten my passport.*
  (= go back while on the way to a place; *return* can also be used in this sense; we say *return home*, but *return to your country*, not *return your country*)

TV/telly/television

- *I saw it **on TV**.* (Not *in TV* *on the TV*)
  (*on TV* is the usual informal abbreviation; *on (the) television* is the normal non-abbreviated form; *on (the) telly* is very informal)

twice/two times

- *I can't ring her again. I've rung her **twice/two times** already today.*
  (*twice* is more common than *two times*)

type • character • fellow/chap

- *Who's that **fellow/chap** you were with last night?* (Not *type* *character*)
  (*fellow* and *chap* are informal ways of referring to a man; even more informal are *guy* and (BrE only) *bloke*)
- *I've never met her/him, but I hear she's/he's a bit of a **character**.* (Not *type*)
  (= a man or woman whose personality draws attention to itself; usually qualified with *quite a/a bit of a/something of a*, etc.)
- *I'm sure you'll like him/her. He's/She's a cheerful **type/character**.*
  (= a particular kind of man or woman)
- *Some **character** walked off with my coat.*
  (*character* = person, after e.g. *this*, *that* or *some*, expresses strong disapproval)

typist • typewriter

- *You can use this machine as a **typewriter** or a word processor.* (Not *typist* *typing machine* *typewriting machine*)
  (= a machine used for *typing*)
- *Everyone needs to become a competent **typist** these days.* (Not *typewriter*)
  (= a person who can *type*)

typical • formal • customary • official

- *It's **customary** to stand up when you hear the national anthem.* (Not *typical*)
  (= a matter of custom, tradition)
- *'Yours faithfully' is a very **formal** way of ending a letter.* (Not *typical*)
- *As an ambassador, Gerald has a lot of **formal/official** engagements.*
  (*formal* = following strict rules;

official = which go with position and responsibility)
- *This is **typical** of the kind of food that is prepared in this region.* (Not **tipical**)
(= true to type; compare *typically*)

U

unable • impossible
- ***It will be impossible** to see you on Friday.* (Not **It will be unable**)
- ***I'll be unable** to see you on Friday.* (Not **I'll be impossible**)
(*It* + *impossible*; human subject + *unable*)

underground/subway
- *We travelled on the **underground** (BrE)/ **subway** (AmE).* (= the underground railway system; informally *tube* in London, *metro* in Paris)
- *We went there **by underground/subway**.* (Not **with the underground/subway**)
- *Cross the road by the **subway**.* (= a path running under a road or railway)

understand
- ***Do you understand** what I'm telling you?* (Not **Are you understanding**) (stative use only)
- *I **understand his/him refusing** our offer.* (Not **understand him to refuse**)

undertaker • entrepreneur
- *The Channel Tunnel was financed by a group of **entrepreneurs**.* (Not **undertakers**) (= businessmen who take on financial risk)
- *The **undertakers** carried the coffin to a big black limousine.* (= people who take charge of dead bodies and arrange funerals)

underwear
- *I like to wear clean **underwear** every day.* (Not **underwears**) (*underwear* is uncountable)

unknown
- *It was a journey into **the unknown**.* (Not **the unknowns**) (= that thing or those things which are not known)
- ***The unknown is** always to be feared.* (*the unknown* + singular verb)

unless • if ... not
- *She'd be nicer **if she didn't complain** so much.* (Not **unless she complained**)
- ***If you don't co-operate/Unless you co-operate**, I won't be able to help you.*

(*unless* and *if ... not* are interchangeable only when they mean 'except on the condition that')

unsympathetic • disagreeable
- *That shop assistant is extremely **disagreeable**.* (Not **unsympathetic**) (= not nice/friendly, not likeable)
- *The police are rightly **unsympathetic** towards people who drink and drive.* (i.e. they don't show understanding)

until/till • by
- *She will arrive **by** 5.* (Not **until**) (= any time before and not later than; *by* combines with affirmative 'point of time verbs' like *arrive, finish, leave*)
- *She won't arrive **by** 5. She'll arrive **at** 6.*
- *She won't arrive **until/till** 6.* (= any time before and not later than; *by* or *until/till* with negative verbs, but with different meanings; note the spelling *until*, not **untill**)
- *I'll wait here **until/till** 5.* (Not **by**) (*until/till*, not **by**, with 'continuity verbs' like *lie, live, sit, stay, wait, work*)
- *Children have to stay at school **until/till** they are 16.* (Not **by**; preferable to *until/till the time*)
- *Most babies can walk **by the time** they are two years old.* (Not **until/till**)
- *Wait here **until/till** he arrives.* (Not **until/ till he will arrive** **until that he arrives**) (*until/till* as a conjunction + present tense)

up • over
- *We want a roof **over** our heads.* (Not **up**) (= covering, often not touching)
- *The manager's office is **up** the stairs.* (= in that direction)

urbane • urban
- *I don't like **urban** life.* (Not **urbane**) (= of the city)
- *An **urbane** manner is a great social asset.* (Not **urban**) (= relaxed and confident)

use
- *What is the **use** of this gadget?* (noun: pronounced /juːs/)
- *How do you **use** this gadget?* (verb: pronounced /juːz/)
- *The car belongs to my father, but I **make use** of it occasionally.* (Not **do use**) (= I use it)
- ***It's no use crying** over spilt milk.* (Not **It's no use to cry**)

191

– I **get up** at 7. (Not *use to get up*)
(simple present for habitual actions: *used to*
is a past form only)

used to: didn't use to

– You **didn't use to** smoke.
(*usedn't to/used not to* are low-frequency
alternative forms; *didn't used to* is unlikely
because the grammatical forms of the
negative and the question *(Did you use to?)*
require *use*. We often avoid the problem
with *never*: You **never used to** smoke.)

used to • be used to • accustomed to

– I **used to get up** early when I worked as a
baker, but I don't have to get up early in my
present job. (Not *I was used to get up* *I
used to getting up*)
(past habit)
– I **am used to getting up** early.
(Not *am used to get up* *I use to get up*)
– I **am accustomed to getting up** early.
(Not *am accustomed to get up*)
(*be accustomed to* is more formal than *be
used to* but has the same meaning to refer to
present habit)
– When I started working as a baker, I didn't
like getting up early, but I soon **got used to
it/became accustomed to** it.
(Not *I used to it*)
– I soon **got/became accustomed to/got used
to getting up** early when I started working
as a baker. (Not *I got used to get up*)

usually • usual

– I don't feel well and I'm not as hungry **as
usual/as I usually am**. (Not *as usually*)
– I **usually** have one large meal a day.
(adverb of frequency)

V

vacancy • holiday/vacation

– I'm on **holiday/vacation**. (Not *vacancy*)
(*holiday* is the general word in BrE and
vacation is the general word in AmE)
– Most children enjoy their summer **holidays**.
(Not *vacations*)
(we often use the plural *holidays* to refer to
long periods off work or school)
– Ask the hotel if it has **a vacancy/any
vacancies** next weekend.
(= unfilled room(s))
– I need a holiday job. I wonder if the hotel
has a **vacancy/any vacancies**.
(= unfilled position(s))

values • valuables

– Guests are advised to leave all their
valuables at the desk.
(Not *values* *valuable*)
(= things, especially jewellery, that are worth
a lot of money)
– Traditional **values** are constantly being
challenged. (Not *valuables*)
(= principles)

vapour • steam

– The kettle's boiling and the kitchen is full of
steam. (Not *steams* *vapour* *vapours*)
(*steam*, uncountable, is *water vapour*)
– Heat the test tube till a brown **vapour** is
given off. (Not *steam*)
(*vapour*, countable or uncountable = gas that
is produced when liquid is heated)

veal • calf

– One of our cows had a **calf**/twin **calves** last
night. (Not *veal/veals*)
(*calf*, plural *calves*, is the name of the live
animal: a young cow or bullock)
– **Veal** is very expensive meat.
(*veal* is meat from a *calf/calves*; but note
calf-liver, calves' liver)

venison • deer

– The park is full of **deer**.
(Not *deers* *venison* *venisons*)
(*deer* - singular and plural form - is the name
of the live animal)
– **Venison** is lean meat.
(*venison* is meat from *deer*)

very • distant

– Stonehenge was built in the **distant** past, but
no one knows exactly when. (Not *very*)
– We sat through the film to the **very** end.
(*very*, as an adjective meaning 'true',
'precise', has limited uses: *the very
beginning, the very book I want*, etc.)

very • very much

– Your flat is **very much larger** than ours.
(Not *very larger*)
– I **like** your painting **very much**. (Not *I like
your painting very*; I **really like** your
painting is a colloquial alternative)
– I **very much like** your painting.
(Not *I very like*)
– I felt **very much alone**. (Not *very alone*)
(*very much* with comparatives, verbs, and
adjectives beginning with *a-*, like *alone*)
– Tom's **very clever**. (Not *very much clever*)

- *This train's going very **slowly**.*
  (Not **very much slowly**)
  (*very* as an intensifier + adjective/adverb)

via • by
- *Shall I send this **by air**?* (Not **via air**)
  (*by air, by land, by sea*)
- *I couldn't fly to Beijing direct and had to go **via Frankfurt**.*
  (i.e. through one place on the way to another)

vicar • curate • pastor • priest
- *Have you met our new **vicar**?*
  (*a vicar* is the priest in charge of a local Anglican church)
- *The Bishop began his career as a young **curate** in our parish church.*
  (a *curate* is a priest who is junior to the vicar of an Anglican church)
- *Have you met the new **pastor**?*
  (*pastor* = 'priest' in Protestant churches)
- *Father O'Reilly has been a **priest** for more than 20 years.*
  (*priest* is the general term for an appointed/ordained officer of a Christian church; terms like *vicar, curate* and *pastor* are not used to refer to Roman Catholic *priests*)

villager • peasant
- *The **villagers** are opposed to any plans to put a motorway close to the village.*
  (*peasants* is unlikely in ordinary contexts)
  (= the people who live in the village)
- *In this part of the country, the **peasants** still work the land in traditional ways.*
  (= people who live by growing food in traditional ways)

visage • face
- *She's got such a sad **face**.* (Not **visage**)
- *He turned to the child, his grim **visage** softening in a sudden smile.*
  (= facial appearance: old-fashioned/literary)

vis-à-vis • face to face • facing • in front of
- *We moved the chairs so that we sat **face to face/facing** each other.* (Not **vis-à-vis**)
- *Can you remember the name of that hotel **in front of/facing** the station?*
  (*in front of* refers to position in space, not the direction someone/something is *facing*)
- *How do you feel **vis-à-vis** these changes?*
  (formal = with regard to, concerning)

visual • optic(al)
- *You may have damaged the **optic** nerve.*
  (*optic(al)* = of the eye, is technical)
- *Advertising exploits to the full the power of **visual** images.* (Not **optical**)

vital • vivid • lively • alive
- *Professor Flynn's **lively** lectures attract large audiences.* (Not **vital* *alive**)
  (= full of life)
- *The explorer gave us a **vivid** account of life in the Antarctic.* (Not **vital**)
  (i.e. it brought the place to life)
- *If he's to get the job, your recommendation is **vital**.* (Not **lively**)
  (= very necessary; but note that the nouns *vitality* and *liveliness* mean 'the condition of being full of life')
- *Is your grandfather **alive**?* (Not **lively**)
  (= having life; not dead)
- *Even at 90, Grandpa is so **lively**.*
  (= full of life)

vitro: in vitro • crystal • window/shop window • window display
- *Look at this wonderful **window/shop window/window display**.* (Not **vitro**)
- *I want a bag like the one in the **window**/in the **shop window**/in the **window display**.* (Not **in (the) vitro**)
- *It's so hot in here - let's open the **window**.*
- *Someone threw a brick at our **shop window** and broke it.* (Not **crystal**)
  (a *shop window* is made of plate glass, not crystal)
- *Wine tastes better out of a **crystal** glass.*
  (*(lead) crystal* = high quality glass, made with lead)
- *The egg was fertilized **in vitro**.*
  (= 'in glass', outside the body)

W

wage • wages • salary
- *My **salary** is paid on the 28th of the month.* (Not **wage* *wages**)
  (a *salary* is paid monthly)
- *Women often get paid a low **wage**/low **wages**, especially for part-time work.*
  (a *wage* or *wages* are paid daily or weekly)
- *When I worked as a waitress, the **wages** were low, but the tips were good.*
  (preferable to *the wage was low*; we generally use *wages* in front of a verb)

wagon • carriage • car • compartment • cart • sleeper/sleeping car
- *Which **carriage/compartment** are we in?* (Not **wagon* *cart**)
  (a *(railway) carriage* (AmE *car*) is a section of a train which is divided into *compartments* to carry people)

- *We're travelling by **car**.* (Not **wagon**)
  (BrE *motorcar*, AmE *automobile*: formal)
- *The goods have already been loaded onto
  railway **wagons**.*
  (Not **carts** **carriages** **compartments**)
  (a *wagon* is a section of a train, sometimes
  with an open top, for carrying goods)
- *If you're going to travel overnight, you
  should go **by sleeper/sleeping car**.*
  (Not **by sleeping**; preferable to *wagon-lit*)
  (= a railway carriage with beds for
  passengers)
- *People were fleeing from the fighting, on
  carts/wagons piled high with their
  possessions.* (Not **cars**)
  (= vehicles with two or four wheels, drawn
  by horses or pulled by hand)

wait for • expect • look forward to • await
- *I'm **expecting** the bus to arrive in the next
  ten minutes.* (Not **waiting**)
  (i.e. I believe that it will; *expecting* is a
  mental process)
- *My wife's **expecting a baby**.*
  (Not **waiting a baby** **waiting for a baby**)
  (*expecting* is a physical process here)
- *I'm **waiting for** the next bus.*
  (Not **waiting the next bus** **expecting for**)
  (= staying here until the bus comes; *waiting*
  is a physical state)
- *We're (very much) **looking forward to** your
  visit.* (Not **waiting (for)** **expecting**
  we're looking very forward to)
  (= expecting with pleasure; we often end e.g.
  a letter with a polite phrase using *look
  forward to*, not **wait** **expect**; compare *I
  hope to see* you which expresses uncertainty)
- *Outside Parliament, the crowds **wait
  for/await** the arrival of the procession.*
  (Not **await for**)
  (*wait for* and *await* - without *for* - mean the
  same, but *await* is very formal)

wake up/awake • waken
- *It was late when I **woke up/awoke**.*
  (Not **awoke up**)
  (we have to say either *I woke up*, or *I awoke*,
  but we cannot say **I awoke up**; *I awoke* is
  literary and should be avoided in everyday
  speech. The parts are: *wake - woke - woken*;
  awake - awoke - awoken)
- *I was **woken (up)/wakened** by a car alarm.*
  (Not **awoken**)

walk • ride • drive • flight
- *Let's **go for/go on** a **ride**.* (Not **do/make**)

- *I've **had a ride** on my bike.*
  (Not **walk** **made/done a ride**)
- *Let's **go for/go on**/Let's **have a drive** (in the
  car).* (Not **walk** **do/make a drive**)
- *Let's **go for a ride**.*
  (i.e. on horseback)
- *It's a long **flight** to Delhi.* (Not **ride**)
  (i.e. in a plane)
- ***Have a good flight!*** (Not **Make/Do**)
- *We've **had a** very good **walk**.*
  (Not **made/done a walk** **taken**)
- *I think I'll **have a walk**.* (Not **make/do**)
- *I think I'll **go for a walk**.*
  (Not **go for walk** **go walk**)
  (i.e. on foot; *take a walk* also has limited
  uses: *Let's **take a walk** round the garden.*)

want
- *I **want** some water.* (Not **I'm wanting**)
  (stative use)
- *I don't want any tea. Do you? - Yes, I **want**
  some** please.* (Not **I want please.**)
- *Have you ever been to Spain? - No, but **I
  want to**.* (Not **I want.**)
- *Are you coming with us? - No, **I don't want
  to**.* (Not **I don't want.**)
- *I **want to tell you** the truth.*
  (Not **I want tell you** **I want to you tell**)
- *I **want you to tell** me the truth.*
  (Not **want you tell** **want that you tell**)

want • need • demand (nouns)
- *There's a very great **need** for money to help
  the flood victims.* (Not **want** **demand**)
- *I'm ill for **want** of sleep.*
  (Not **need** **demand**)
  (= lack, shortage of)
- *There's very little money left after we've met
  the **wants and needs** of our children.*
  (*wants and needs* is a fixed phrase)
- *There's a big **demand for** umbrellas in wet
  weather.*
  (i.e. a lot of people want to buy them)

war
- ***Make** love, not **war**.* (Not **Do war**)
  *Why does the world **have** so many **wars**?*
  (Not **make/do wars**)

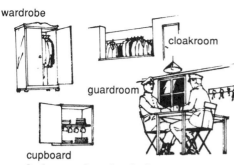

wardrobe

cloakroom

guardroom

cupboard

wardrobe • cupboard • cloakroom • guardroom

- *Put these plates in the **cupboard**.*
  (Not **wardrobe**)
  (a *cupboard* is for general storage)
- *Hang your suit in the **wardrobe**.*
  (Not usually *cupboard*)
  (a *wardrobe* is a cupboard, especially for storing clothes; also 'a collection of clothes' as in *She has a large **wardrobe**.*)
- *Leave your coat in the **cloakroom**.*
  (Not **guardroom**)
  (= the place in a theatre, etc., where you can leave coat, hats, etc. AmE also *checkroom*; there is no word **guardrobe** in English; a *guardroom* is a building for military guards)

warehouse • storeroom • department store

- *There's a large **storeroom** at the back of the shop.* (Not usually *warehouse*)
  (= a room where goods are kept till needed)
- *The new Spring fashions will arrive from our **warehouse** soon.* (Not **storehouse**)
  (= a large separate building where goods are kept on a large scale)
- *You can buy almost anything in a big **department store**.* (Not **warehouse**)
  (= a large shop with different departments)

warn • advise

- *We always **advise/warn** our children to be very careful when crossing the road.*
- *She **warned me of** the danger.* (Not **for**)
- *I **warned** you that you'd be punished if you did that again.* (Not **advised**)
  (*advise* = suggest; *warn* = bring attention to possible danger)

was • were

- *If **you were** me, you'd go.* (Not **you was**)
  (*I/he/she/it was*; *you/we/they were*: not e.g. **You told me you was ill.**)
- *What would he do **if he were/he was** in my position?*
  (*were* can be used in all persons after *if* and expresses greater doubt than *was*)

wash • get washed • wash myself

- *I must get up and **wash/get washed**.*
  (it would not be 'wrong' to say *wash myself*, but it would be unusual)
- ***Have a wash**.* (Not **Wash yourself.**)
- *Polly can almost **wash herself** now.*
  (the reflexive use often refers to children, invalids, etc., to show conscious effort)
- *I think I'll **have a wash**.* (Not **make/do**)
  (= wash myself)
- *I think I'll **do a wash**.* (Not **make a wash**)
  (= wash some clothes: i.e. *do* a task)

washing • washing-up

- *I've **done the washing**.* (Not **made**)
- *I've **done the washing-up**.* (Not **made**)
  (*do the washing* refers to clothes; *do the washing-up* refers to dishes and pans)

waste • waist

- *Let me measure your **waist**.* (Not **waste**)
  (= the middle part of the human body)
- *Consumer societies produce a lot of **waste**.*
  (Not **waist**)
  (= rubbish)

water • a glass of water

- *I've just drunk **a glass of water/two glasses of water**.* (Not **a water** **two waters**)
- *I drink **a lot of water**.* (Not **many waters**)
  (*water* is uncountable)

wax • candle • polish

- *I keep a **candle** by my bed in case of a power cut.* (Not **a wax**)
- *My shoes need a bit of **polish**.* (Not **wax**)
- *All the figures in Madame Tussaud's are made of **wax**.*
  (= the substance from which *candles* are made and which is often used as *polish*)

way

- *It was hard to **make our way** through the crowd.* (Not **do our way**)
- ***In no way can I agree** to these terms.*
  (Not **In no way I can agree ...**)
  (inversion after negative adverbs; formal. Compare normal word order with a negative verb: *I **can't agree** in any way.*)

way • process

- *We're **in the process of** reorganizing our office.* (Not **on/in the way of**)
  (i.e. we are doing this)
- *We've been through a bad economic period, but recovery is now **on the way**.*
  (i.e. it has begun)

ways • manners
- *John may not be very clever, but he has excellent **manners**.* (Not **ways**)
  (= acceptable ways of behaving socially)
- *After I got married, it took me a long time to get used to him and his funny little **ways**.*
  (= behaviour, sometimes eccentric)

weak • weaken • get/become weak
- *Martha **got/became** very **weak** during her illness.* (Not **weaked* *weakened**)
  (= became thin, lost weight and strength)
- *Lack of exercise really **weakens** the muscles.*
  (= makes them weak)
- *I'm afraid I **weakened** at lunchtime and ate a chocolate.* (Not **got weak**)
  (= gave in, lost my determination)

wealth • riches
- *You should see the Crown jewels. It's hard to imagine **so much wealth**.*
  (Not **so many wealths/riches**)
- *The pursuit of **wealth/riches** is the basis of capitalism.*
  (*wealth* is uncountable; *riches* is literary and descriptive)

weather • whether
- *I don't know **whether** you've heard the news.*
  (Not **weather**)
- *What's **the weather** like today?*

wed • marry
- *We're going to **marry/get married** in May.*
  (preferably not *wed, get wed(ded)*)
  (*marry/get married* are the normal words; *wed, be wed* and *get wed(ded)* are old-fashioned)

week
- *I'll go **next week**.* (Not **the other week**)
- *I saw him **last week**.* (Not **the past week**)
- *I've been home late every night in/during **the past/last week**.*
  (= the week that has gone by)

week • weak
- *I feel **weak** with hunger.* (Not **week**)
- *I'll see you in **a week**.* (Not **a weak**)

weekly/once a week • by the week
- *I visit my parents **weekly/once a week**.*
  (Not **by week**)
- *How do you charge - by the day, or **by the week**?* (Not **with the week* *weekly**)

weigh
- *I **weigh** 65 kilos.* (Not **I'm weighing**)
  (stative use)

- *What are you doing? - **I'm weighing** myself.*
  (dynamic use)

welcome (to)
- ***Welcome** home!*
  (spelling: not **Wellcome* *Well come**)
- ***Welcome to** Egypt!* (Not **Welcome in**)
- ***You are welcome!*** (Not **Be welcome!**)
- *Thank you for going to so much trouble. - **You're welcome!***
  (= Don't mention it, etc.)

wet • get wet • wet oneself
- *It's **wet** today.* (Not **It has/It makes wet**)
  (= it's rainy)
- *I got very **wet** walking home without an umbrella.* (Not **I wet* *I wet myself**)
  (= became wet)
- *I **wet/wetted** the car well before I started washing it.*
  (= made it wet; *wet* can be regular or irregular)
- *I think the baby has just **wet himself** again.*
  (= urinated)

What (a)! • How!
- ***How tall** you've grown!* (Not **What tall**)
- ***How difficult** it is!* (Not **What difficult**)
- ***What a tall boy** you are!*
  (Not **How tall boy* *What tall boy**)
- ***What a surprise!*** (Not **What surprise!**)
  (*What + a/an* for countable nouns)
- ***What dreadful weather** we had!*
  (Not **How dreadful weather* *What a dreadful weather**)
  (*What + uncountable noun: no a/an*)

What + noun • Which + noun
- ***What book/books** did you buy?*
- ***What soap** do you use?*
  (*What + noun* makes a general inquiry)
- ***Which book/books** did you buy?*
- ***Which soap** do you use?*
  (*Which + noun* refers to a limited choice)
- ***Which boy** wants/**Which boys** want to come with us?*
- ***What boy** wants/**What boys** want to come with us?*
  (*What + noun* to ask about people is possible, but less common than *Which*)

what for • why
- ***What** did you do that **for**?*
  (Not **For what?**)
- ***Why** did you do that?*
  (Not **Why ... for?* *For why?**)

when • if
- *I'll call for you at 8 tomorrow morning **if** that isn't too early.* (Not **when**)
  (*if* for conditional sentences, not *when*)
- *Come straight home **when** the party's over.* (= at the time when, as soon as)
- ***When/If** it rains heavily, our river floods.* (*if* and *when* are used interchangeably to mean 'on those occasions when')

Who • How
- ***How** wonderful!* (Not **Who**)
- ***Who** is he?*
  (= inquiring about identity)
- ***How** is he?*
  (= inquiring about health)

who • whom
question-words
- ***Who** paid the waiter?* - ***John** did.*
- ***Who(m)** did John pay?* - ***The waiter**.*
- ***Who(m)** did you give it to/buy it for?* - ***John**.*
  (technically, the question-word *Who* asks for the subject and *Whom* asks for the object; in practice, *Who ... ?* is accepted in place of *Whom ... ?* in everyday style)
relative pronouns
- *He's the man **who** rang me.* (Not **whom**)
  (*who* refers to the subject)
- *He's the man **who(m)** I met on holiday.*
  (*whom* refers to the object but is commonly reduced to *who* in everyday speech)
- *The person **to whom** I complained is the manager.* (Not **who** after a preposition)
  (very formal and usually avoided)
- *The person **who(m)** I complained **to** is the manager.*
  (possible, but generally avoided)
- *The person **(-)** I complained **to** is the manager.*
  (normal omission of *whom*)

whoever • whomever
- *Invite **whoever** you like to your party.*
  (preferably not *whomever*)
  (the object form *whomever* is extremely rare and its occasional use is affected; it is commonly quite wrong as a relative after a preposition: *I want to know the name **of whoever** was responsible*, not **whomever**)
- ***Whoever** told you that?* (Not **Whomever**)
  (emphatic form of *Who?*)

whose • his • her
- *He's **the man whose car** was stolen.* (Not **the man his car** **the man whose his car**)

- *She's **the woman whose car** was stolen.*
  (Not **the woman her car** **the woman whose her car**)
- *He's **the man** I told you about. **His car** was stolen.*
- *She's **the woman** I told you about. **Her car** was stolen.*

whose • who's
- ***Who's** coming with us?* (Not **Whose**)
  (= Who is?)
- ***Who's** borrowed my pen?* (Not **Whose**)
  (= Who has?)
- ***Whose** is this car?* (Not **Who's**)
  (= To whom does it belong?)

why: that's why • why ... should
- *We've got high inflation. **That's why** prices keep going up.* (Not **For this** **For that**)
  (= that's the reason)
- *We wanted to know **why we should wait**.*
  (Not **why to wait**)
  (*why* is the only question-word that cannot be followed by a *to*-infinitive in reported questions; compare: *I asked **what I should do/what to do**.*)

why • because
- ***Why** did you leave early?* - ***Because** I had to go to a meeting.* (Not **Why ... ? - Why ...**)
  (*Why* in questions; *Because* in answers)

why don't you/why not
- *If you don't like the wallpaper in this room, **why don't you change it/why not change** it?*
  (Not **why not to change it?**)
- *I think I'll change my mind.* - ***Fine./Go ahead./By all means**.* (Not **Why not?**)
  (*Why not,* suggesting 'there's no objection to it', is not an appropriate rejoinder after an affirmative statement)

wide/width
- ***How wide/What width is** this room?*
  (Not **How much wide is** **How much width has**)
- *This room **is three and a half metres (wide)**.*
  (Not **has width three and a half metres**)

wide • widely
- *He kicked the ball, but it **went wide** of the goalposts.* (Not **went widely**)
  (*wide* is an adjective and gives *go* the sense of *be*)
- *It is **widely** believed that the universe started with a big bang.* (Not **wide**)
  (adverbial use as an intensifier = to a high degree or to a great extent)

widen • let out

- *I think you should **let** the skirt **out** at the waist.* (Not **widen**)
  (*let out* for making clothes wider; the opposite is *take in*)
- *The traffic won't get back to normal till they finish **widening** the road.*
  (= making it wider)

wild • game

- *There's a lot of opposition to hunting **game** these days.* (Not **wild**)
  (= wild animals hunted for food, especially as a sport)
- *There's a lot of opposition to hunting **wild animals**.* (Not **wild* *wilds**)
  (*wild* is an adjective)

wild • savage

- *How could you protect yourself if you were attacked by a **savage/wild** animal?*
  (*savage* = fierce and out of control; *wild* = in a state of nature, and not necessarily *savage*)
- *The ancient Greeks thought that people who lived outside their world were **savages** and barbarians.*
  (= wild people; old-fashioned and now offensive)

will/would

- *He said he **will/would arrive** at 6.* (Not **will/would to arrive**)
- *If you hear a car, that **will** be Roland.*
  (i.e. it's very possible; *would* in past sequences is more uncertain than *will*)
- ***Will/Would you open** the window please?*
  (*Would* is more polite than *Will* in requests)
- *Now he's old, **he will sit** in the sun for hours.*
- *When he was old, **he would sit** in the sun for hours.*
  (*will* for present habit; *would* for past habit)
- *Friday **will be fine/would be** fine.* (*will* and *would* in place of the present: tentative)
- *He **told** me he **would** be late.*
  (past may follow past, especially in indirect speech)

will/won't • shall/shan't

- ***He will/won't** be here at 6.* (Not **shan't**)
- ***We will/won't/We shall/shan't** be here at 6.*
  (*will/won't* in all persons for prediction; *shall/shan't* is a possible alternative only after *I* and *we*; the usual abbreviation is *'ll*, so the *shall/will* distinction is lost; *won't* is the abbreviation of *will not*; *shan't* is the abbreviation of *shall not*; we sometimes use *shall/shan't* after *he, you*, etc., when

granting/refusing permission: *You **shall/shan't** be allowed out.*)

will • want to

- *I **want to have** an early night.*
  (Not **will to have**)
  (Not **will** for *want to*)
- *I think I **will (I'll) have** an early night.*
  (= I intend to)

wish (for)

- *I **wish** I knew the answer to your question.*
  (Not **I'm wishing**)
  (stative use)
- *We often **wish for things** we can never have.*
  (Not **wish things**)
  (*wish for* = desire to have)
- *I **wish things were** better.*
  (Not **wish for things to be**)
  (*wish + (that)* clause)
- *I **wish it was/were** Friday.*
  (Not **I wish it is**)
  (*were* can be used in all persons after *wish* and is more tentative than *was*)
- *I **wish I could/we could** be with you.*
  (Not **I wish I would/I wish we would**)
- *I **wish they could** be with us.*
  (Not **I wish they would**)
- *I **wish he would** do as he's told.*
  (Not **I wish he could**)
  (*could* expresses ability: present or future reference; *would* = be willing to)
- *I **wish to apply** for a visa.*
  (Not **wish that I apply**)
- *I **wish you to know** that I'll be retiring soon.*
  (Not **wish that you know**)

with • and

- *John **and** his brother built up this business.*
  (Not **with**)
- *John built up this business **with** his brother.*

with • in

- *Who's the woman **in** the red dress?*
  (= wearing)
- *Who's the man **with** the stick?* (Not **in**)
  (= carrying)
- *Who's the woman **with** the little boy?*
  (= accompanied by)
- *Who's the man **with** the beard?* (Not **in**)
  (= 'having': physical characteristics; *in a beard* would mean the beard was false)
- *Say it **in** a loud voice.* (Not **with**)
  (*in* + voice quality)

with no • without any

- *I can't manage **without any** help/**with no** help.* (Not **without no help**)

(the preposition *without* contains the negative, so we use *any* after it)

without
- *They tried to leave the restaurant **without** **paying**.* (Not **without to pay**)

wonder • wander
- *I love **wandering** /'wɒndəriŋ/ around second-hand bookshops.* (Not **wondering**) (= walking about without purpose)
- *I **wonder**/I'**m wondering** /'wʌndəriŋ/ if we've made a mistake here.* (Not **wander/wandering**) (stative or dynamic depending on the emphasis you want = would like to know)

wood • wooden
- *Use a **wooden** spoon/a spoon made of **wood** with non-stick pans.* (*wood* is the noun, *wooden* the adjective)
- *Put **some wood** on the fire.* (Not **woods**) (*wood* is uncountable when it refers to the material)

wool • woollen
- *A **woollen** dress is expensive, as is anything made of pure **wool**.*
- *Take a **woollen**/some **woollens** with you.* (abbreviated reference to *a woollen garment, woollen garments*: i.e. cardigans, sweaters) (*wool* is the noun, *woollen* the adjective; *wool* is sometimes used in compound nouns, as in a *wool shop* = a shop for wool; note the spellings *woollen*, BrE; *woolen*, AmE)

words: in other words
- ***In other words**, the answer's No.* (Not **With other words**)

work
- *I must **do** some **work**.* (Not **make ... work**)
- *Are you **in work** at the moment?* (i.e. Do you have a job?; the opposite is *out of work* = unemployed)
- *Don't disturb her. She's **hard at work/ working hard**.* (= actually working)
- *I'm not feeling well and I'm **off work** today.* (= taking time out from work)
- *I expect the children **make a lot of work** for you.* (Not **do ... work**) (i.e. give you extra tasks)

work • job
- *I'd like **a job** in TV. Are there **any jobs** in TV?* (Not **a work* *any works**)
- *I'm looking for **work** as a journalist. Is there **any work** in journalism?* (Not **job* *a*

work* *any works*; *Is there **any job** in journalism?* = any kind of job) (*a job/jobs* is countable; *work* is uncountable)
- *What's your **job**? - I work at the reception desk and I take incoming phone calls.*
- *What's your **work**? - I work as a receptionist.* (*a job/jobs* is specific; *work* is general)
- *'Hamlet' is a wonderful **work**.* (Not **job**) (*a work*, countable, is a piece of writing, a painting, etc.)
- *You've done a wonderful **job** on this report.* (= a piece of work)

works
- *I see you have all Shakespeare's **works**.* (i.e. his entire creative output)
- *If you want to speak to the foreman, you'll find him down at the **works**.* (= the factory)
- *We all pay for **public works** like road maintenance through taxes.* (= road building, etc.)

workshop • laboratory
- *They're sending the sample off to a **laboratory** for analysis.* (Not **workshop**) (= a workplace where scientific tests and analyses are carried out)
- *We repair TV sets in our own **workshop**.* (= a workplace, usually attached to a business, where machines are repaired)

worried (about) • worrying
- *My father's been ill for some time and I'm very **worried about** him.* (Not **worried for**; *I'm worrying* is a verb form)
- *Her symptoms are **worrying**.* (Not **worried**) (= a cause of worry)
- *Sibyl's parents **got** really **worried** when she phoned to say she'd missed the last train.* (preferable to *they worried* which is 'long term' rather than 'instantaneous')

worse • worst
- *This winter is **worse than** the last one.* (Not **worst than* *more bad than**)
- *It's **the worst** winter we've had since records began.* (Not **the worse**) (= worst of all)
- *How is she today? - She's **worse**.* (Not **worst**) (= less well than she was yesterday; opposite: *better*) (*worse* is the irregular comparative form of *bad*, for comparisons between one thing and another; *worst* is the superlative form for

comparing one thing with more than one other in the same group)

worsen • get worse
- *The road **gets worse/worsens** a bit further on.* (Not **gets worser**)
- *Martha hasn't been very well, and **she's worsening/getting worse**.*
  (Not **she's getting worser**)
  (= declining in health)

would • had: ('d)
- *I wish **you'd** tell us what you want.*
  (*you would* abbreviated to *you'd*)
- *I wish **you'd** told me earlier.*
  (*you had* abbreviated to *you'd*)

would • used to
- *I **used to** collect stamps.* (Not **would**)
- *When I worked on a farm, I **would** always/I always **used to** get up at 5 a.m.*
  (*would* in place of *used to* needs a time reference and occurs in narrative, especially when we are reminiscing)

wound
- *The clock went for ten days after I **wound** it.*
  (*wound* /waʊnd/ is the irregular past of *wind* /waɪnd/: *wind - wound - have wound*)
- *Careful with that gun. You could **wound** someone.*
  (*wound* /wuːnd/ is the infinitive form of the regular verb: *wound - wounded - have wounded*)

wound • injure • hurt
- *The train left the rails, but fortunately no one was **injured/hurt**.* (Not **wounded**)
  (*be injured/hurt* = suffer, *injure/hurt* = inflict any kind of physical or emotional damage; the noun is *an injury/injuries*; *hurt* and *hurts* as nouns refer to 'hurt feelings')
- *The battle didn't last long, but a lot of men were **wounded**.* (Not **injured**; *hurt* is possible, but not as precise as *wounded*)
  (*wound/be wounded* = give/receive, e.g. a hole in the skin or flesh, especially with a weapon; the noun is *a wound/wounds*)

wreck • ruin
- *After the fire, the museum was reduced to a **ruin**.* (Not **wreck**)
  (i.e. it was destroyed; note the plural *ruins* for ancient temples, etc.: *Let's visit the **ruins**,* not **wrecks**)
  (a *ruin* is a building that has lost its roof, windows, doors, etc.)

- *Let's swim out to the **wreck**.*
  (Not **ruin/ruins**)
  (= the remains of a ship)
- *I splashed my beautiful silk tie with soup and completely **ruined** it.* (Not **wrecked**)
  (*ruin* clothes, a carpet, decorations, etc.)
- *I drove my car into a wall and **wrecked** it.*
  (Not **ruined**)
  (*wreck* = break up e.g. a vehicle)
- *This **wrecked/ruined** our plans.*
  (occasionally interchangeable: something is *ruined* when it can no longer be used; something is *wrecked* when it is really smashed to pieces)

writing • writings
- *I enjoy Conrad's **writing/writings**.*
  (*writing* = the way he writes; *writings* = the things he has written; note spelling: not **writting**)
- *I can't read your **writing**!* (Not **writings**)
  (= handwriting, uncountable)

wrong (about/for)/mistaken
- ***You're wrong**! All the museums are shut on Mondays.* (Not **You have wrong!**)
- *You were **wrong about** the increase in rail fares.* (Not **wrong for**)
  (*wrong* can be replaced by *mistaken* in the above examples; compare: *You're mistaken,* i.e. in general and *You've made a mistake,* i.e. on this occasion)
- *The question is: is this job **wrong for** you?*
  (Not **mistaken for**)
  (= not suitable for)
- *You **did wrong** to spread these rumours.*
  (Not **made wrong**)
  (= acted improperly; did something bad: not to be confused with *made a mistake*)

wrong • wrongly
- *All our plans **went wrong**.* (Not **wrongly**)
  (*wrong* is an adjective and gives *go* the sense of *become*)
- *You've **spelt** it **wrong/wrongly**.*
  (we can use *wrong*, rather than *wrongly*, in phrases that mean 'make a mistake': *spell it wrong(ly), pronounce it wrong(ly), do it wrong(ly)*; after *get*, only *wrong* is possible: *get it wrong* = make a mistake/an error)
- *Some of the objects in this museum have been **wrongly** dated.* (Not **wrong**)
  (only *-ly* in front of a past participle)
- *You've connected the printer cable **wrongly**.*
  (Not **wrong**)
  (adverb = in the wrong way)

Y

yard • court • courtyard

- *Who introduced Rasputin to the **court** of Czar Nicholas II?* (Not *yard* *courtyard*)
  (= royal household)
- *The children are playing in the **yard** at the back of the house.* (Not *court*)
  (= an open space surrounded by a wall or fence, often paved in BrE; AmE *yard* = 'patch of garden')
- *The building is in the shape of a square and looks on to a lovely **courtyard**.*
  (= an open space enclosed by buildings, e.g. in government offices or universities)

year

- *We're going to visit Australia **next year**.*
  (Not *the other year*)
- *We had a holiday in Australia **last year**.*
  (Not *the past year*)
- *I've had five colds in **the past/last year**.*
  (= the year that has gone by)
- *They celebrated their diamond wedding anniversary **the other year**.*
  (i.e. within the last few years - I can't remember when)
- *He was born **in the year** 1943.*
  (Not *in the 1943 year*)

yellow • go/turn yellow

- *The leaves **have gone yellow/have turned yellow** already.* (preferable to *yellowed*)
- *Paper always **yellows/goes yellow/turns yellow** with age.*

yesterday

- *I got back from New York **yesterday at noon**.*
  (Not *yesterday the noon*)
- *I got back from New York **yesterday morning/yesterday evening/last night**.*
  (Not *yesterday the morning*, etc., *on/in yesterday morning*, etc.)

you • one • someone/anyone

- ***English spoken**.* (Not *One speaks English.* *Man speaks English.*)
- ***One** can speak English/**You** can speak English when travelling in the Far East because so many other people do.*
  (*one* = everyone, formal; *you* = everyone, informal)
- *Is there **someone/anyone** here who can speak Urdu?* (Not *one*)
  (= a particular person)

youngest • latest • newest

- *What's her **latest** book?*
  (Not *youngest* *newest*)
  (= most recent)
- *John is our **youngest/newest** employee.*
  (Not *latest*)
  (*youngest* in years; *newest* = most recently recruited)
- *These are our **newest/latest** CDs.*
  (Not *youngest*)
  (*newest/latest* = most recently acquired)

your • you're

- ***You're** late!* (Not *Your*)
  (*you're* = you are)
- *Here's **your** key.* (Not *you're*)
  (possessive adjective)

youth

- *Tony is **an** awkward **youth**.*
- *Jim and Tony are awkward **youths**.*
  (*young man/young men* are generally preferred)
- ***Youth** is the time for action; **age** is the time for repose.* (Not *the youth ... the age*)
  (general statement with uncountable abstract nouns: no articles)
- ***The youth of today** is/are better off than we used to be.*
  (Not *The youth is/are* *The youngs are*)
  (*the youth* = all the young people, needs to be qualified: *the youth of today*, or we could say *the young* without any modification)

Z

zero • nil/love • nought • 'oh'

- *My telephone code is 0426.* (*oh* four two six)
- *Picasso painted his first modern picture in 1908.* (nineteen eight, or nineteen *oh* eight)
- *The train leaves at 13.04.*
  (thirteen four or thirteen *oh* four)
  (*oh* when giving telephone numbers, years or referring to the 24 hour clock)
- *It's -20°C.* ('It's twenty degrees below *zero*', or 'It's minus twenty')
  (*zero* when talking scientifically: e.g. giving temperatures)
- *Leeds 4, Hull 0.* (Leeds four, Hull *nil*)
  (*nil* when giving scores in team games)
- *Gonzales leads 40-0.* (forty *love*)
  (*love* when giving tennis scores)
- *The percentage difference is 0.7.*
  (*nought* point seven)
- *I scored 0 out of 10.* (*nought* out of ten)
  (*nought* BrE, or *zero* AmE, in mathematics and grades)

Test Yourself

Exercises: 1-41: all levels up to Intermediate

Exercises 42-96: Upper Intermediate to Advanced

1 Social exchanges

Supply the best word or words.

1 You're late for an appointment, so you say, '.*Sorry*...... I'm late.'
   a) Sorry/I'm sorry   b) Excuse me,   c) Forgive me,   d) Pardon me,

2 You fail to hear what someone says to you, so you say, '*PARDON ME* ?'
   a) Excuse me   b) Pardon   c) Forgive me   d) Pardon me

3 A passenger on a bus complains you're standing on his foot; you say, '*Excuse me* !'
   a) Sorry   b) Forgive me   c) Excuse me   d) Pardon me

4 Here's your apology for bad behaviour: '.................... for my awful behaviour last night.'
   a) Please pardon me   b) Please forgive me   c) I beg your pardon

5 You answer the phone and you might say, '.................... !'
   a) Speak   b) Hullo   c) Enter   d) Say

6 You are introduced to a stranger, so you say, '.................... ?'
   a) How are you   b) How do you do   c) What do you do

7 You're leaving, so you say, '.................... !'
   a) Adieu   b) Goodbye

8 You're refusing food that is offered; you say, '.................... .'
   a) Thank you   b) No, thank you   c) Thanks

9 You thank me for holding the door open and my reponse might be, '.................... .'
   a) It's nothing   b) -   c) Please   d) Nothing

10 You meet a friend at the airport on arrival and you might say, '.................... London.'
   a) Welcome to   b) Be welcome to   c) Welcome in   d) Well come to

11 Someone asks you how you are and you answer, '.................... thanks.'
   a) Good   b) Very good   c) Fine   d) Very fine

12 Your friend is waiting for you to finish what you're doing and you say, '.................... .'
   a) One moment   b) A moment   c) One minute   d) Just a minute

13 You're attending an interview and the interviewer says, '.................... .'
   a) Sit yourself   b) Take a seat   c) Sit   d) Sit you

14 The class stands up as you enter the room and you say, '.................... .'
   a) Sit yourselves   b) Take a seat   c) Sit down   d) Sit   e) Sit you

15 This is what you say to a friend on January 1st: '.................... New Year!'
   a) Lucky   b) Happy   c) Merry   d) Good

2 Cars and driving

Read the story. Refer to the list below and fill in the blanks with the best word or words. The first one has been done for you.

I'm what is known as a (0) *learner* driver. I'm learning to (1) .... a car. So far, I've learnt how to (2) .... the (3) .... of my car and I know how to (4) .... I can even (5) .... quite long distances.

Twice a week, my instructor sits in the (6) .... beside me and (7) .... me a lesson. First, we look at the (8) .... and decide on the best (9) .... Then we go for a (10) .... round the town.

My instructor gives me advice like 'Don't (11) ....', or 'Stop before you get to the next (12) ....', or 'We can't go down there. The road is (13) ....', or 'You can't turn right. It says (14) ....', or 'Always stop to allow pedestrians to (15) .... at the zebra.'

Sometimes we stop at a (16) .... and my instructor says, 'You must never fill up when your engine is (17) .... Your engine must be (18) .... before you put any (19) .... in the car.'

There are two things I hate about driving. One is looking for a (20) .... and the other is being held up in a (21) .... of traffic. Yesterday, I sat in a traffic jam for a whole hour and all I could see was the (22) .... of the big truck in front of me!

0 a) teacher b) learner	1 a) conduct b) lead c) drive d) guide	2 a) start b) begin	3 a) engine b) machine c) machinery
4 a) turn it off b) close it c) shut it	5 a) steer b) pilot c) guide d) drive	6 a) seat b) chair	7 a) makes b) does c) gives
8 a) chart b) map c) cart	9 a) road b) route c) way	10 a) drive b) walk c) ride	11 a) run b) go too fast
12 a) corner b) angle c) curve	13 a) shut b) barred c) closed	14 a) No Entry b) No Entrance	15 a) pass b) cross
16 a) filling station b) service station	17 a) on b) open c) alight	18 a) off b) out c) closed d) shut	19 a) essence b) petrol c) benzine
20 a) parking space b) parking	21 a) tail b) row c) queue	22 a) plaque b) plate c) record d) number plate	

3 Adjectives: opposites

Supply the right opposites.

1 *dry* paint   .....WET..... paint
2 *weak* tea   ...STRONG.... tea
3 *tender* meat   ......HARD...... meat
4 a *full* glass   an ...EMPTY..... glass
5 a *solid* cylinder   a .... cylinder
6 an *old* man   a ...YOUNG....... man
7 an *old* suitcase   a ...NEW......... suitcase
8 *salt* water   .... water
9 a *cool* day   a ..(HOT) WARM..day
10 a *cold* day   a ....HOT....... day
11 a *single* person   a ...DOUBLE..... person
12 a *living* person   a ....DEAD....person
13 a *tall* person   a (small short. person
14 a *long* time   a ...SHORT....... time
15 an *open* door   a ...CLOSE.. door
16 a *right* answer   a ..WRONG.. answer
17 a *high* wall   a ...SMALL........ wall
18 a *sick* person   a ....WELL........ person
19 a *loud* sound   a .... sound
20 a *loud* voice   a .... voice
21 a *thin* ruler   a ...THICK...... ruler
22 a *large* suitcase   a ..SMALL........ suitcase

4 Adjectives and noun modifiers

Supply the best words.

1 ..GLASS.......... table tops mark easily. (Glass, Glassy)
2 She fixed me with a ..GLASSY..... stare. (glass, glassy)
3 How much would you have to pay for a ..GOLDEN..... watch? (gold, golden)
4 Silence is ...GOLD.......... . (gold, golden)
5 We danced by the light of the..SILVERY........ moon. (silver, silvery)
6 My mother has a lovely old ...SILVER.... teapot. (silver, silvery)
7 There's an old ...STONE........ wall at the end of the garden. (stone, stony)
8 It's impossible to cultivate such ...STONY........ soil. (stone, stony)
9 ...STEEL.......... cutlery is very practical. (Steel, Steely)
10 Dr Mangold has such terrifying ...STEELY........ blue eyes. (steel, steely)
11 I wouldn't drink water that flows through ...LEAD..........pipes. (lead, leaden)
12 Under a grey sky, the sea looked heavy and ..LEADEN... . (lead, leaden)
13 Take a ...WOOL....... cardigan with you in case it gets cold. (wool, woollen)
14 You might find one in a ...WOOLLEN.. shop. (wool, woollen)
15 They specialize in ....WOOLLEN.......... goods. (wool, woollen)
16 Use a ...WOODEN..... spoon if you want to stir the soup. (wood, wooden)

5 Asking, requesting, commanding

What would you say in these situations? Supply the best word or words.

1   You are calling your dog. You say, ' .... !'
    a) Approach   b) Come here   c) Go near

2   You have finished a meal at a restaurant. You say, 'Let's .... the bill.'
    a) ask for   b) ask   c) ask about   d) demand

3   You repeat a prohibition. You say, 'I asked you .... touch my computer.'
    a) to not   b) not to   c) to don't   d) no to

4   You want some tea. You say, '.................... a cup of tea, please.'
    a) I like   b) I love   c) I'd like   d) I may like

5   You want your friend to wait a moment. You say, ' .... !'
    a) Just a moment   b) A moment   c) One moment   d) The moment

6   Someone offers you some food which you don't want. You say, ' ....'
    a) Please   b) Thank you   c) Thanks   d) No, thank you

7   Do you drink tea? - I do, but I don't .... now, thank you.
    a) want   b) want any   c) want some   d) want it   e) want to

6 Telephoning

Supply the best word or words.

1   You can't get through on the phone because the number you want is ....
    a) busy   b) occupied   c) in use   d) engaged

2   You can make a telephone call from a public ....
    a) phone box   b) cabin   c) cubicle

3   Someone calls your number by mistake, so you say, 'Sorry! .... !'
    a) Wrong number   b) Mistake   c) You've made a mistake   d) Error

4   You want to use the phone. You ask, 'Can I make a .... please?'
    a) ring   b) phone   c) telephone   d) call

5   Someone answers the phone and you say, 'Can I .... Elsa please?'
    a) speak to   b) talk to   c) say to   d) tell

6   How do you pronounce the first figure in this number: 071 499 3725? ....
    a) oh   b) nil   c) love   d) nought

7 Appearance, etc., of people and things

Supply the most suitable words from the list on the right.

1 I'd like one ....*thick*........ loaf and two small ones.
2 Just one fish is a .....*little*....... amount for four people.
3 Tommy is still too ...*(little) short* for an adult-size bicycle.
4 The bride looked very ...*pretty*...... in her wedding dress.
5 You've ...*grown up*... so tall!
6 People with ....*fair*....... skin get sunburnt easily.
7 The bridegroom looked very ..*handsome* in his grey suit.
8 They had a ...*grand*..... wedding reception at a big hotel.
9 I'm so ....*skinny*..... , you can see my ribs.
10 I'm not ......*tall*.......... enough to reach that shelf.
11 I'm too ....*fat*.......... to get into these trousers.
12 I take a lot of exercise so I can stay .....*lean*........ and fit.
13 The snow is four inches ...*high*....... already!
14 Sixteen is very ...*young*...... to get married.
15 No one doubts that Einstein was a ...*great*..... scientist.
16 Berlin was once divided by a ....*meagre*..... wall.
17 Coffee was served in pretty ...*large*....... cups.
18 She's a natural ..*blonde*...... with big blue eyes.
19 I may be a bit fat, but I'm not ....*gross*........ .
20 She may be only 14, but she looks very ..*grown up*.. .

a) blonde
b) fair
c) fat
d) grand
e) great
f) gross
g) grown
h) grown up
i) handsome
j) high
k) large
l) lean
m) little
n) meagre
o) pretty
p) short
q) skinny
r) tall
s) thick
t) young

8 Descriptions, etc.

Supply the best words.

1 She entertained us with a lot of ..*amusing*...... stories.
   a) amusing   b) amused
2 I can't think of the .....*exact*....... word to describe him.
   a) just   b) exact
3 My granny cooks a really ...*tasty*........ meat pie.
   a) tasty   b) tasteful
4 Please be ...*polite*........ to the customers.
   a) polite   b) gentle
5 You have to be ....*tough*....... to survive the army.
   a) hard   b) tough
6 You'll get on well with her. She's really ..*likeable*. .
   a) sympathetic   b) likeable
7 He got a medal for being so ....*brave*...... .
   a) brave   b) nice
8 Michiyo is really ...*fussy*........ about fresh food.
   a) difficult   b) fussy
9 Have you ever taught really ...*vital*........ children?
   a) lively   b) vital
10 Long skirts are the ......*latest*..... fashion.
   a) newest   b) latest
11 They've no money. They're terribly ..*miserable*... .
   a) poor   b) miserable
12 He's not very clever; in fact, he's a bit ...*dull*......... .
   a) dull   b) dim
13 The hours are long and the food is ...*bad*..... .
   a) bad   b) evil
14 She's very ...*generous*...... with her money.
   a) large   b) generous
15 I think it was ....*a fair*.... decision.
   a) a fair   b) an exact
16 Tina is a very ...*pretty*...... woman.
   a) pretty   b) tasty
17 They had a very ....*happy*..... life together.
   a) glad   b) happy
18 I'm really ...*pleased*..... with your results.
   a) content   b) pleased

9 Containers

Choose the best words from the list below. Write them in beside the numbers under the pictures.

1 *parcel*

2 *wallet*

3 *jar*

4 *tube*

5 *bowl*

6 *portfolio*

7 ....

8 *sack*

9 ....

10 *schoolbag*

11 *suitcase*

12 *purse*

bowl	cover	lid	purse
bundle	cup	nylon	sack
cap	glass	parcel	schoolbag
carrier bag	handbag	portfolio	suitcase
coffer	jar	pot	tube
			wallet

10 Countable and uncountable nouns

Supply the best word or words.

1 We drove round for half an hour looking for ....
   a) a parking   b) some parking   c) a parking space

2 I'm afraid I haven't .... on me.
   a) a money   b) any moneys   c) some moneys   d) some money   e) any money

3 I suddenly heard .... from the room next door.
   a) a loud laughter   b) a loud laugh   c) loud laugh

4 Could I have some more .... please?
   a) macaroni   b) macaronis

5 Haven't we done .... !
   a) a lot of shoppings   b) a lot of shopping   c) a shopping   d) some shopping

6 Here's .... that will interest you.
   a) a new   b) a piece of news   c) a news

7 What .... !
   a) beautiful countryside   b) a beautiful countryside   c) beautiful country

8 A lot of people don't eat ....
   a) pig   b) pork   c) hog

9 I receive ....
   a) all kinds of letters   b) all kind of letters   c) all kinds of letter

10 We sell ....
   a) all kinds of cloth   b) all kind of cloth   c) all kind of cloths

11 While you're at the greengrocer's, please get a ....
   a) greens   b) salad   c) lettuce

12 We've had .... lately.
   a) very good time   b) very good weather   c) a very good weather   d) good climate

13 Do you need .... ?
   a) a help   b) any help   c) any helps   d) helps

14 Could I try .... please?
   a) one of this chocolate   b) one of these chocolates

15 I've never seen anyone eat .... as quickly as you do!
   a) a bar of chocolate   b) some chocolate

210

11 Time and frequency

Supply the best word or words in Parts A and B.

Part A

1	I'll see you .... ten minutes.	a)	in	b)	after
2	I arrived first and Tom arrived	a)	after	b)	later
3	We're expecting her .... afternoon.	a)	this	b)	today
4	She invited us, so we must invite her	a)	again	b)	back
5	He hasn't phoned	a)	still	b)	yet
6	I learnt to ride a bike .... I was a boy.	a)	as	b)	when
7	I'll see you .... March.	a)	at	b)	in
8	I'll see you .... Monday.	a)	at	b)	on
9	'Liz - you're wanted on the phone!' - ' .... !'	a)	Coming	b)	At once
10	I met him three years	a)	ago	b)	before
11	Knock before .... enter.	a)	you	b)	to
12	I was a chauffeur then. .... I was a waiter.	a)	Before that	b)	Before
13	I've been a waiter .... three years.	a)	during	b)	for
14	Don't worry. She'll learn to spell very	a)	early	b)	soon
15	What happened .... the end of the story?	a)	in	b)	at
16	We missed the train and .... we got a taxi.	a)	in the end	b)	at last
17	Everything was stolen - .... our clothes.	a)	still	b)	even
18	I'll call on you this .... between 6 and 7 p.m.	a)	afternoon	b)	evening
19	That was his .... wish before he died.	a)	eventual	b)	final
20	I have .... trusted him.	a)	ever	b)	never

Part B

1	The experience wasn't so bad	a)	finally	b)	after all
2	I couldn't understand English at all	a)	firstly	b)	at first
3	It's .... first time I've driven a car on my own.	a)	the	b)	my
4	.... first time I met Harry, he was in the army.	a)	In the	b)	The
5	What .... should we meet?	a)	hour	b)	time
6	I'll see you tomorrow at 10	a)	hour	b)	o'clock
7	Can I borrow your car? - How long .... ?	a)	ago	b)	for
8	Please wait	a)	a moment	b)	an instant
9	Who phoned .... ?	a)	just	b)	just now
10	I can't wait to get to the .... chapter!	a)	last	b)	latest
11	She phoned me .... Monday.	a)	last	b)	the last
12	My name comes .... in the list.	a)	last	b)	lastly
13	We haven't seen much of you	a)	late	b)	lately
14	She'll call some time .... the evening.	a)	long	b)	during
15	I'm afraid I can't stay.................. .	a)	long	b)	much
16	I'll be with you in .... moment.	a)	-	b)	a
17	It .... an hour to get to the airport.	a)	needs	b)	takes
18	We travelled .... night.	a)	at	b)	the
19	She's not free to see us till .... week.	a)	the other	b)	next
20	I only ever met her	a)	once	b)	one time

12 Health

Correct the mistakes, which have been underlined for you. Suggest a suitable alternative for each one. The first one has been done for you.

Yesterday, I decided to visit my (0) <u>medicine</u>. 0 *doctor*
I've been having (1) <u>aches</u> in the chest. 1 *pain*
I (2) <u>heat</u> all the time, and 2 ....
then I suddenly (3) <u>cold</u>. 3 ....
I (4) <u>don't have hunger</u> at all 4 ....
and I think I'm (5) <u>thinning</u>. 5 ....
I (6) <u>tire myself</u> easily, as well. 6 ....
Last week I developed a (7) <u>sore neck</u> and could 7 ....
hardly speak. I hoped it would (8) <u>better</u>, 8 ....
but in fact it got (9) <u>worst</u>. 9 ....
The doctor (10) <u>interrogated</u> me 10 ....
and gave me a (11) <u>recipe</u>. 11 ....
'You can get this medicine at the (12) <u>pharmacist's</u>,' 12 ....
he said. 'Don't worry. You'll soon be (13) <u>alright</u>.' 13 ....
I (14) <u>pleased</u> the doctor to give me 14 ....
some (15) <u>advices</u>. 15 ....
'When you feel better, (16) <u>make</u> plenty of exercise, 16 ....
and you need plenty of (17) <u>open</u> air. 17 ....
You'll be (18) <u>good</u> in no time.' 18 ....
I thanked the doctor as the (19) <u>nanny</u> showed me out 19 ....
before leading in the next (20) <u>customer</u>. 20 ....

13 Holidays

Supply the best words.

		a)	b)
1	Guesthouses with .... are often hard to find.	a) vacations	b) vacancies
2	I looked for a sign which said Rooms	a) To Let	b) To Rent
3	I like a room with its own	a) toilet	b) cabinet
4	or at least with a .... where I can shave	a) washbasin	b) sink
5	and I prefer it to be on the ground	a) stage	b) floor
6	A .... with a view	a) camera	b) room
7	of the surrounding .... is what I like best.	a) countryside	b) land
8	A holiday hotel should have a friendly	a) manager	b) director
9	who welcomes the .... at all times.	a) guests	b) clients
10	Unfortunately, the best hotels are always	a) full	b) filled
11	I like hotels where the lifts aren't	a) out of order	b) broken
12	and which don't cost too	a) much	b) many
13	A big .... at the end always	a) bill	b) addition
14	spoils a good	a) vacancy	b) holiday
15	and makes you wish you had	a) rested	b) stayed
16	at a cheaper	a) place	b) space

14 'Be', 'get', 'go', 'make', etc.

Supply the best word or words.

1 You don't have to .... every time I ask you a question.
   a) annoy   b) get annoyed

2 I avoid eating cakes and biscuits because I don't want to ....
   a) get fat   b) fatten

3 How much .... ?
   a) does it make   b) is it   c) does it   d) has it

4 Take an umbrella with you. You don't want to ....
   a) wetten   b) get wet   c) wet yourself

5 These apples have .... and they're not very nice.
   a) softened   b) gone soft   c) made soft

6 I .... playing tennis.
   a) heated   b) hotted   c) got hot   d) got heat

7 This nice hand cream will .... your hands soft.
   a) do   b) make   c) get

8 I .... waiting for the bus.
   a) cold   b) colded   c) got cold   d) made cold

9 She was weak and thin after two months' illness, but we soon ....
   a) fattened her up   b) got her fat   c) made her fat

10 English is easy when you begin learning but it soon ....
    a) gets difficult   b) does difficult   c) difficults   d) makes difficult

11 This egg smells awful. It's ....
    a) baddened   b) gone bad   c) got bad

12 I .... wandering about all day without any food.
    a) got hungry   b) hungered   c) made hungry

13 Your children have .... since I last saw them!
    a) talled so much   b) got so tall   c) been so tall

14 I don't mean to .... with so many questions!
    a) get you tired   b) tire you   c) tire yourself

15 Why didn't you .... this morning?
    a) shave you   b) shave   c) get shaved yourself

15 Work and jobs

Supply the most suitable words from the list on the right.

1   .... is hard to find at the moment.
2   The quality of the food in a restaurant depends on its ....c........ .
3   I work in a garage as a car .....k............ .
4   Nancy has started a new ......i.......... .
5   Mrs Wilks is the ....j........ of this shop, not the owner.
6   If you want to know the way, ask a ....o.......... .
7   Who's the ....f.......... of the Boston Symphony Orchestra?
8   Brenda Mittens was a university .....p........... at the age of 26.
9   He has a car with a uniformed .....b............ .
10 His .....q.......... at school has given him a good report.
11 What's the name of the ....a........ of your company?
12 An ....h.......... designs bridges or roads.
13 The ....m........ of our shop is putting up the rent.
14 There had been a burglary, so we called the ....n.......... .
15 I went into business after I left ....t.......... .
16 I can't use a .....s............ , never mind a word processor!
17 Gordon is a ....g......... at the local hospital.
18 Has the nurse given you your .....l............ ?
19 Smithers is a ....d....... of mine at the office.
20 It's useful to be a good .....r............ if you use a computer.

a) boss
b) chauffeur
c) chef
d) colleague
e) college
f) conductor
g) doctor
h) engineer
i) job
j) manager
k) mechanic
l) medicine
m) owner
n) police
o) policeman
p) professor
q) teacher
r) typist
s) typewriter
t) work

16 Buildings and parts of buildings

Supply the best words.

1   Is there a .... that sells papers near here?
2   I can't find the .... to the building.
3   We employ 900 workers in this ....
4   You can buy anything in a large ....
5   It's a long way up to the tenth ....
6   Don't stand in the .... !
7   We have all our meals in the ....
8   Our .... is the best room in the house.
9   Have you ever seen the .... at Cologne?
10 Let's have our meal on the ....
11 What does it cost to rent a small .... ?
12 That cupboard takes up too much ....
13 How much is that shirt in the .... ?
14 There's an .... staircase leading to the roof.
15 The .... floor is one up from the basement.
16 Where's mother? - She's ....
17 There's an Anglican .... in Athens.
18 It's up the .... and on the first floor.

1   a) magazine   b) shop
2   a) entry   b) entrance
3   a) factory   b) fabric
4   a) boutique   b) store
5   a) storey   b) story
6   a) doorway   b) door
7   a) kitchen   b) cuisine
8   a) living room   b) saloon
9   a) dome   b) cathedral
10 a) roof   b) terrace
11 a) room   b) camera
12 a) place   b) room
13 a) vitro   b) window
14 a) outside   b) exterior
15 a) first   b) ground
16 a) downstairs   b) down
17 a) church   b) temple
18 a) ladder   b) stairs

17 Verbs/verb phrases with and without prepositions

Supply suitable prepositions *only where necessary* in Parts A and B.

Part A

 1 I completely agree .... you!
 2 A stranger approached .... me in the street and asked me for money.
 3 I'll have to go .... home soon.
 4 I didn't do it. Don't shout .... me!
 5 How long will it take us to reach .... London?
 6 Everyone stood up when the President entered .... the room.
 7 I'll be thinking .... you when you're having your interview.
 8 I told .... my wife I'd be late home this evening.
 9 Why don't you answer .... me when I ask you a question?
10 Shall I ask .... the bill, so we can pay and leave?
11 The car left the road and went .... a tree.
12 What time did you leave .... home?
13 Are you going to attend .... the funeral service?
14 It doesn't matter what her mother says, she never obeys .... her.
15 John married .... the girl next door.
16 I've been married .... John for five years.
17 How long have you been waiting .... the bus?
18 They've replied .... our letter of February 15th.
19 What can I say .... them that they haven't heard before?
20 I think they'll agree .... the terms of our contract.

Part B

 1 I'd like to speak .... the manager please.
 2 Please listen carefully .... what I have to say.
 3 We've entered .... an agreement and we can't change our minds now.
 4 What time did you finish .... work?
 5 They didn't hear you. You'll have to shout .... them again.
 6 I'll be passing .... a letterbox, so I can post this for you.
 7 It's the first time I've ever played chess .... anyone who is as good as you.
 8 Children find it hard to pay attention .... their teachers all day long.
 9 You can't regard a degree .... a passport to a job.
10 I seem to spend most of my time dreaming .... you.
11 Today we hope to visit .... two museums.
12 It's no good raising your voice; he can't hear .... you.
13 We're looking forward .... seeing you again soon.
14 It's taken them a month to respond .... our letter!
15 Smile .... the camera.
16 You shouldn't ask .... people personal questions.
17 I want to spend the afternoon watching .... football on TV.
18 No one ever died .... hard work.
19 We expect to arrive .... London before the shops shut.
20 What do you know .... the care of indoor plants?

18 Occupations, etc.

Supply the best word or words.

1 The person in charge of a business is informally known as the ....
   a) chef   b) chief   c) boss

2 The person who is in charge of a car is the ....
   a) guide   b) leader   c) motorist   d) driver   e) conductor

3 A person who prepares food is a ....
   a) cook   b) cooker

4 A person who works in an office is an ....
   a) officer   b) office worker

5 A person who takes photographs is a ....
   a) photograph   b) photographer   c) photography

6 A person who knows how to use a keyboard is a ....
   a) typewriter   b) typist   c) typing machine writer

7 A woman who looks after other people's children is a ....
   a) nanny   b) nurse

8 The person you work with is your ....
   a) college   b) colleague   c) collaborator

9 The person who is in charge of a restaurant is the ....
   a) patron   b) manager

10 The person who would service your car is ....
    a) a mechanic   b) an engineer   c) a technician

11 A person who studies the origins of the universe is a ....
    a) physician   b) physicist   c) physics

12 Another word for 'a doctor' is a ....
    a) physician   b) physicist   c) medicine

13 The person who teaches you or taught you at school is a ....
    a) teacher   b) professor

14 If you are one of the people waiting to be served in a shop you are a ....
    a) client   b) customer   c) patient   d) guest

15 If you serve people who come into a shop, you are ....
    a) an official   b) a shop assistant   c) an attendant   d) a bank clerk

19 Words easily confused, misspelt, etc.

Supply the best words in Parts A and B.

Part A

1	Have you finished your breakfast .... ?	a) already	b) all ready
2	Don't worry about me. I'll be	a) all right	b) alright
3	I'll expect you to ring me tomorrow. -	a) All right	b) Alright
4	She's .... complaining about something.	a) always	b) all ways
5	.... of those dates will be suitable.	a) Anyone	b) Any one
6	I'm going to the beach for a	a) swim	b) bath
7	.... the wound in warm water.	a) Bath	b) Bathe
8	Keep your foot on the	a) break	b) brake
9	Businessmen usually wear	a) costumes	b) suits
10	Most of my family are	a) died	b) dead
11	My old aunt is	a) dead	b) death
12	They crossed the Sahara .... by camel.	a) desert	b) dessert
13	Most people are afraid of	a) dieing	b) dying
14	I ring my mother	a) everyday	b) every day
15	There are .... people in our office.	a) fiveteen	b) fifteen
16	The river has .... this way for centuries.	a) flown	b) flowed
17	Look! I .... this coin in the garden.	a) found	b) founded
18	How do you write ' .... '?	a) forty-four	b) fourty-four
19	They say .... mad.	a) his	b) he's
20	Have you given the cat .... milk?	a) it's	b) its

Part B

1	Our hen's just .... an egg.	a) lain	b) laid
2	Let's .... on the grass.	a) lie	b) lay
3	How long have you been .... there?	a) lying	b) laying
4	I'd like to .... in the country.	a) live	b) life
5	Don't .... your ticket!	a) loose	b) lose
6	What time did you .... home?	a) live	b) leave
7	Did you hear that .... sound?	a) aloud	b) loud
8	Don't talk so .... !	a) loud	b) aloud
9	.... they're out.	a) Maybe	b) May be
10	Have you .... her yet?	a) meet	b) met
11	Take .... your coat.	a) of	b) off
12	It's just .... the post office.	a) past	b) passed
13	You've .... too much for that bike.	a) payed	b) paid
14	Have you .... the flowers?	a) paid for	b) paid
15	The teacher asked the class to be	a) quite	b) quiet
16	She's still too small to .... the table.	a) rich	b) reach
17	Do you ever see them? -	a) Some times	b) Sometimes
18	.... all mine!	a) There	b) They're
19	I can't find .... coats.	a) there	b) their
20	John will be arriving here .... 7.	a) till	b) by

217

20 Prepositional phrases

Supply *at, by, in, on, to, with* or (-) where necessary.

1 Did you come all this way ......*by*...... foot?
2 I didn't walk. I came here .... the bus.
3 Where's Harry? - I think he's gone .... bed.
4 Aren't the children .... bed yet?
5 What time did you go .... home last night?
6 You may work hard all week, but you do nothing when you're .... home.
7 I don't think it's that much cheaper to go .... bus.
8 Your cheque is ...., the post.
9 Who's that woman .... the black handbag?
10 What time do the children go .... school in the mornings?
11 I don't mind being alone .... the house.
12 I only manage to get the shopping done when the children are .... school.
13 You can't speak to him now. He's .... class.
14 Many young people expect to go .... university after they leave school.
15 Where did you hear about this? - I saw it .... TV.

21 Only one negative

Write these sentences again in the negative using different words from those in italics. Make any other changes. The first one has been done for you.

0 I *haven't ever* been late for work.   *I have never been late for work.*
1 There *are no* people at the bus stop.   ....
2 It *wasn't a* surprise to get your letter.   ....
3 I've done *nothing* all afternoon.   ....
4 I *haven't* seen *anyone* all day.   ....
5 Peg got dressed *without any* help from me.   ....
6 I *haven't* been *anywhere* today.   ....
7 It's *nobody* you know.   ....
8 I left home *with no* money in my pocket.   ....
9 You *can't* trust *anybody* these days.   ....

22 -ed/-ing

Supply the best words.

1 I found the film very ....   a) boring   b) bored
2 I got so .... waiting for you to arrive.   a) boring   b) bored
3 John is the most .... man I've ever met.   a) boring   b) bored
4 Don't look so .... !   a) surprising   b) surprised
5 Mother looks very ....   a) worrying   b) worried
6 The rise in crime is very ....   a) worrying   b) worried
7 Don't you find shopping .... ?   a) tiring   b) tired
8 Don't you find John rather ....?   a) tiring   b) tired

23 Addressing people

What would you do or say in these situations? Supply the best word or words.

1 You want to address an envelope to a whole family. You write: ....
   a) Mr and Mrs Wilson and family   b) Family Wilson   c) Family Mr & Mrs Wilson

2 You want to begin a letter to a woman you have never met. You write: ....
   a) Dear Mrs Grey   b) Dear Miss Grey   c) Dear Ms Grey   d) Dear Mz Grey

3 A pupil is answering a male teacher. The pupil says: ' ....'
   a) Yes, Sir   b) Yes, Mr   c) Yes, Sir Teacher   d) Yes, Mr Teacher

4 A pupil is answering a female teacher. The pupil says: ' ....'
   a) Yes, Madam   b) Yes, Lady   c) Yes, Mrs/Miss Bloggs   d) Yes, Mrs Teacher

5 You stop a man in the street to ask the way. You say: ' ....'
   a) Excuse me, Mr   b) Excuse me   c) Sir

6 You stop a woman in the street to ask the way. You say: ' ....'
   a) Excuse me, Mrs   b) Excuse me   c) Madam   d) Excuse me, Lady

7 You want to address an envelope formally to a young boy. You write: ....
   a) Master John Brown   b) Mister John Brown   c) Mr John Brown

8 You are answering a university professor. You say: ' ....'
   a) Yes, Professor Hawkins   b) Yes, Mr Professor   c) Yes, Professor

9 A shopkeeper might say this to a man: 'Can I help you, ... ?'
   a) Mr   b) Sir   c) Master

10 A shopkeeper might say this to a woman: 'Can I help you, ... ?'
   a) Mrs   b) Miss   c) Madam   d) Lady

24 Names of places

Supply the best word or words.

1 You want some meat so you go to the ....
   a) butcher   b) butcher's   c) butchers   d) butchers'

2 You would buy a tin of sardines at a ....
   a) shop   b) magazine   c) store   d) boutique

3 You want to borrow a book from the local ....
   a) bookshop   b) bookcase   c) library

25 Doing things for people

Correct the mistakes, which have been underlined for you. Suggest a suitable alternative for each one. The first one has been done for you.

I've never done any baby-sitting before, but
tonight I'm going to (0) <u>look</u> Mrs Watkins' little
boy. Mrs Watkins (1) <u>gave to me</u> some advice.
She (2) <u>explained me</u> what I had to do.
I (3) <u>took care of</u> what Mrs Watkins said.
'Timmy goes (4) <u>in bed</u> at 7.30,' she said.
'You don't have to (5) <u>pass</u> a lot of time with him.
You can (6) <u>read to him</u> a story if you want to.
He might ask you to (7) <u>carry</u> him a glass of water.
Do this, then (8) <u>tell</u> goodnight to him.'
Later, Mrs Watkins thanked me. 'You have (9) <u>guarded</u>
Timmy very well,' she said.

0 *look after*
1 ....
2 ....
3 ....
4 ....
5 ....
6 ....
7 ....
8 ....
9 ....

26 Movement to and from

Supply the best word or words.

1 The children were stuck up our apple tree and they couldn't ....
   a) descend   b) get down   c) get off   d) get out

2 I knocked timidly at the door and heard someone shout ' .... !'
   a) Enter   b) Come in

3 Everyone turned round and looked at me as I .... the room.
   a) entered into   b) entered   c) got into

4 The blind man .... carefully to the other side of the road.
   a) crossed   b) passed   c) past

5 What time did you .... London Airport?
   a) reach to   b) arrive to   c) arrive at

6 My son .... at university for the last two years.
   a) has gone   b) has been   c) went

7 What time did you .... London?
   a) leave from   b) live   c) live from   d) leave

8 I was locked out and I had to .... through the window.
   a) enter   b) get in   c) get into   d) enter in

9 Let's go .... in Oxford Street.
   a) for shop   b) shopping   c) to shop   d) shop

27 The human body

Choose the best words from the list below. Write them in beside the numbers under the pictures.

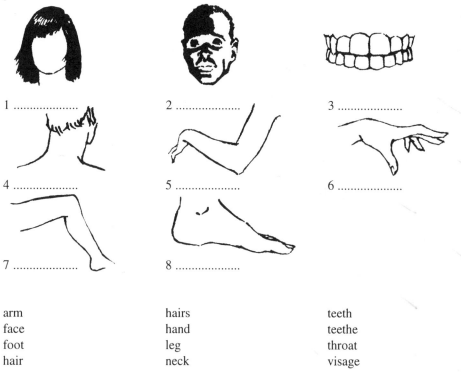

1 ....
2 ....
3 ....
4 ....
5 ....
6 ....
7 ....
8 ....

arm	hairs	teeth
face	hand	teethe
foot	leg	throat
hair	neck	visage

28 Furniture

Choose the best words from the list on the right. Write them in beside the numbers in the picture.

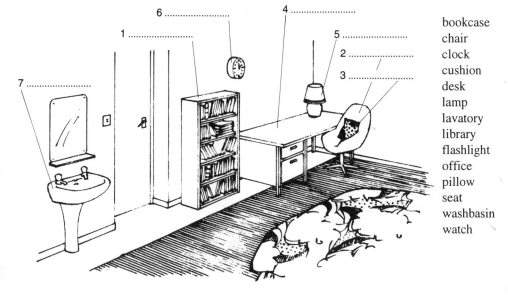

6 ....
1 ....
4 ....
5 ....
2 ....
3 ....
7 ....

bookcase
chair
clock
cushion
desk
lamp
lavatory
library
flashlight
office
pillow
seat
washbasin
watch

29 Money

Supply the best word or words.

1 Money you are paid for your work is money you ....
   a) earn   b) win   c) gain   d) profit   e) benefit

2 You want to make a phone call but only have a note. You need some ....
   a) small money   b) little money   c) (small) change   d) exchange

3 You want to know the price of something, so you say, ' .... ?'
   a) How much is it   b) How many is it   c) How much the price   d) What it costs

4 When you finish a meal at a restaurant, you ask for the ....
   a) bill   b) addition   c) account   d) reckoning

5 If you visit a doctor privately, he will certainly charge a ....
   a) tariff   b) fee   c) tax

6 How much did you .... the plumber before he left?
   a) pay   b) pay for

7 How much did you .... that dress?
   a) pay   b) pay for

8 A professional person's bill is often referred to as ....
   a) a reckoning   b) a tariff   c) a charge   d) an account

9 You might want to have a camping holiday because it is relatively ....
   a) economic   b) cheap

10 You want one of the oranges on display, so you ask how much they are ....
   a) each   b) the one   c) the piece

11 When buying something by weight, you may like to know how much it is ....
   a) a kilo   b) per the kilo   c) for the kilo

12 Someone's selling a car and you want to know how much they're ....
   a) asking   b) demanding   c) charging

13 You pass an empty house and see a notice outside it which reads ....
   a) To sell   b) On sale   c) For sale

14 Nobody likes to pay .... prices.
   a) high   b) tall   c) big   d) great

15 .... should pay more taxes.
   a) Rich   b) The rich   c) The riches

30 Adverbs

Read this text. If you find a mistake in a line, cross it out and suggest an alternative. If there is no mistake, put a tick (✓). The first two have been done for you.

I love travelling on any vehicle that goes ~~fastly~~.	0	*fast*
The Bullet Train in Japan is very fast indeed!	0	✓
It is so smooth, you hardly notice its speed.	1	....
It is extremely punctual, but if it arrives lately,	2	....
you can get your money back. You can see very good	3	....
out of the train windows and admire Mount Fujiyama.	4	....
Some people take it easy and enjoy the trip,	5	....
eating a meal slow, while the train moves	6	....
quick across the country. Others like to work	7	....
hard before they get to the office.	8	....
The train is highly regarded throughout the world.	9	....
A ride on the Bullet Train really is an experience.	10	....

31 Comparatives and superlatives

Supply the best word or words.

1 You can write English better .... anyone in the class.
   a) as   b) than   c) else

2 Red is my .... colour.
   a) best   b) favourite   c) beloved   d) dearest

3 .... people I know are worried about the environment.
   a) Most   b) The most   c) Much

4 Which is the .... building in this town?
   a) eldest   b) most old   c) oldest

5 My brother is .... than I am.
   a) elder   b) older

6 At the present time, ... people can afford to travel abroad for their holidays.
   a) less   b) lesser   c) fewer   d) smaller

7 Your car is .... than mine.
   a) very larger   b) very much larger   c) a lot more larger   d) more larger

8 The Lockerbie crash was one of the .... disasters in aviation history.
   a) worse   b) worst   c) most bad   d) baddest

9 This novel is so exciting, I can hardly wait to get to the .... chapter!
   a) last   b) latest   c) newest   d) youngest

32 Four topics

Read these texts. If you find a mistake in a line, cross it out and suggest an alternative. If there is no mistake, put a tick (✓). The first two have been done for you.

1 The weather

We're having a very ~~heavy~~ winter.	0	*hard*
The temperature often falls to zero.	0	✓
Today it makes cold	1	....
and there's a lot of air.	2	....
You expect bad climate in winter.	3	....
You expect to cold when you go out.	4	....
Even so, I really enjoy winter weather	5	....
and I don't mind if it darkens early.	6	....

2 The news

What I enjoy most on television	1	....
is the actualities.	2	....
You can see actual events as they occur.	3	....
You can see famous people being examined	4	....
and giving their opinions on world events.	5	....
I enjoy reading daily journals as well.	6	....
There are not only plenty of news,	7	....
but interesting histories about ordinary people as well.	8	....
Life would be boring without all the	9	....
entertainment and informations you get	10	....
in newspapers and on television.	11	....

3 Luck and misfortune

I had a bad incident the other day.	1	....
I was carrying a tray across the garden	2	....
when a wasp pricked me on the nose.	3	....
It dropped the tray on the grass,	4	....
but by luck nothing was broken.	5	....
I had such a shock, I fell into a table	6	....
and ended up with a headache as well as a sting!	7	....

4 Keeping clean

Every morning when I awake up	1	....
I have a bathe	2	....
before getting dressed.	3	....
Sometimes I have a douse instead,	4	....
but if I've got up late	5	....
I just have time for a wash myself.	6	....
I like to do a shampooing	7	....
every day as well.	8	....
Washing up frequently	9	....
and keeping clear is	10	....
one of the pleasures of the life.	11	....

33 Questions and exclamations

Supply the best word or words.

1 I haven't met our new secretary yet. .... ?
   a) What's she like   b) How is she   c) How is she like

2 I don't know the English word for this. ....?
   a) What do you call it   b) How do you name it   c) What do you name it

3 I don't know your friend's name. ....?
   a) How's she called   b) What's she named   c) What's she called

4 .... paid the waiter? - Jane did.
   a) Whom   b) How   c) Who   d) Whose

5 .... borrowed my pen?
   a) Whose   b) Who's   c) How's

6 I hear you've been ill. .... now?
   a) How do you do   b) How are you   c) What do you do

7 .... for a living? - I'm an engineer.
   a) What are you doing   b) How do you do   c) What do you do

8 There are two coats here. .... is yours?
   a) Which   b) What   c) What one

9 I've never met your son. ....?
   a) How old is he   b) What age has he

10 .... 's the weather like today?
    a) What   b) Who   c) How

11 I've never heard of John Nashe. .... is he?
    a) Who   b) What   c) How

12 .... tall you've grown!
    a) What   b) How   c) How much

13 .... you are!
    a) What a tall girl   b) How tall girl   c) What tall girl

14 It's so nice to see you. .... !
    a) What surprise   b) What a surprise

15 .... we've been having!
    a) What a dreadful weather   b) What dreadful weather   c) How dreadful weather

34 Quantities and amounts

Supply the best word or words in Parts A and B.

Part A

1	Have you got .... pen on you?	a) one	b) a
2	I'd like .... water please.	a) some	b) one
3	Please .... the room carefully.	a) count	b) measure
4	I'll be needing .... of those plates.	a) ten	b) a decade
5	.... house round here has a TV aerial.	a) Each	b) Every
6	You must tell me .... truth.	a) all the	b) the whole
7	I've lost .... hair.	a) all my	b) my whole
8	Would you like some .... ?	a) else	b) more
9	Serve the soup in .... amounts.	a) equal	b) even
10	My family have lived here for .... years.	a) fourty	b) forty
11	They're visiting us next week. - How long .... ?	a) ago	b) for
12	How .... names are on the list?	a) much	b) many
13	I've got .... things to do!	a) 100 and one	b) 100 one
14	How many letters did you get? - Two	a) hundreds	b) hundred
15	Two .... workers have been employed.	a) hundreds of	b) hundred
16	How many times did you phone me? -	a) Twice	b) Two times
17	They beat us four -	a) nil	b) nought
18	There's not .... enough food for everybody.	a) almost	b) nearly
19	There are a large .... of students this year.	a) amount	b) number
20	Give me .... cup please.	a) an other	b) another

Part B

1	The .... of them get on well together.	a) two	b) both
2	Is there .... food for everyone?	a) enough of	b) enough
3	I'd like to ask .... questions.	a) few	b) a few
4	I'd like .... more time.	a) little	b) a little
5	I'd like .... kilo of coffee please.	a) a half	b) half a
6	I think he's got .... money.	a) a lot of	b) much
7	They've cut down .... trees.	a) a lot of	b) many
8	.... people like ice cream.	a) Most	b) The most
9	You're asking for .... money than I have.	a) much more	b) very much
10	There are .... messages for you.	a) none	b) no
11	Was there much rain last winter? - .... much.	a) No	b) Not
12	What did you say? -	a) Not anything	b) Nothing
13	They're $2	a) the piece	b) each
14	.... money has been wasted.	a) Several	b) A lot of
15	I'd like .... room for the night.	a) an only	b) a single
16	Is there any coffee? - Yes, would you like .... ?	a) some	b) one
17	Are there any eggs? -Yes, would you like .... ?	a) one	b) it
18	Give him a spoonful .... medicine.	a) of	b) -
19	I'd like coffee with .... sugar.	a) no	b) any
20	I'd like coffee without .... sugar.	a) no	b) any

35 Travelling by train

Read the story. Refer to the list below and fill in the blanks with the best word or words. The first one has been done for you.

There are so many things you have to do when you (0) *travel.* Always make sure your (1) .... has (2) .... on it!

If you're going (3) .... train, the (4) .... you have to do is buy yourself (5) .... You usually have to stand in a (6) .... and it's easy to (7) .... your train and then waste hours (8) .... the next one!

You buy (9) .... or return ticket, and then look for a (10) .... where you hope you will find a free (11) ....

At last, you can (12) .... the train and settle down to enjoy the (13) .... If you're lucky, the train (14) .... the station (15) ....

Sometimes (16) .... comes round to (17) .... your ticket, but usually you travel without interruption and can enjoy the (18) .... You can relax till (19) .... time for you to (20) .... when you arrive at your (21) ....

0 a) journey b) travel	1 a) luggage b) valise c) coffer	2 a) a cartel b) a card c) a label d) an etiquette	3 a) with b) by c) via
4 a) first b) first thing	5 a) a billet b) a ticket c) a card d) an etiquette	6 a) queue b) line c) row d) tail	7 a) miss b) lose c) loose
8 a) waiting b) expecting c) waiting for	9 a) a single b) an ordinary	10 a) wagon b) carriage c) car	11 a) seat b) place c) chair d) space
12 a) get into b) enter into c) enter d) go in	13 a) travel b) voyage c) journey d) travels	14 a) leaves for b) leaves from c) leaves d) lives	15 a) on time b) in time c) to time
16 a) a conductor b) a driver c) an inspector d) a guide	17 a) examine b) interrogate c) question d) look	18 a) ride b) drive c) flight d) walk	19 a) it's b) its c) it has
20 a) get off b) go down c) get down d) descend	21 a) term b) terminal c) station d) terminus		

36 Outside

Supply the best word or words.

1   The line you cross to go from one country to another is called the ....
    a) frontier   b) boundary

2   It's wide and large and it's often lined with trees. It's ....
    a) an avenue   b) an alley   c) a street

3   Climb to the top of a hill so that you can admire the ....
    a) country   b) land   c) countryside

4   You have to drive very carefully if a road is full of ....
    a) angles   b) bends   c) corners

5   If you want to put up a tent, you'll have to look for a nice flat piece of ....
    a) ground   b) soil   c) earth

6   There are quite a few islands off the west .... of Scotland.
    a) shore   b) cost   c) coast   d) beach   e) seaside

7   It can be very cold at night in the ....
    a) dessert   b) desert

8   How many people are there in the .... ?
    a) cosmos   b) earth   c) world

9   An open place in a city, town or village where people like to sit.
    It's called ....
    a) a square   b) a circus   c) a place

10 You'd expect to be able to buy fresh fruit and vegetables in ....
    a) a market   b) a bazaar

11 Where you were born is your .... of origin.
    a) countryside   b) country   c) nation

12 If we ask 'How long will you be in this country?', we are referring to ....
    a) the country we are in   b) some other country

13 Look up and you will see ....
    a) the sky   b) heaven   c) the heaven

14 It's often made of iron and can lead into a garden. It's ....
    a) a port   b) a door   c) a gate   d) a doorway

15 I think Mauritius is my favourite .... on earth.
    a) place   b) part   c) space   d) room

37 'Do', 'make' and 'have'

Supply the correct forms of *do, make* or *have* in Parts A and B.

Part A

1   Have you .... your English exam?
2   I must congratulate you. You've .... a very good job.
3   When are you going to .... your bath?
4   We'll be .... a big party next Saturday.
5   Excuse me. I've got to .... a phone call.
6   I wish you wouldn't .... so much noise!
7   You've .... dirty marks on the wall!
8   Did you hear that Mrs Simpson has .... a baby boy?
9   I .... a pain in the stomach after eating too many figs.
10 I'll join you in a minute, after I've .... a shower.
11 She doesn't say very much. It's difficult to .... conversation with her.
12 Try not to .... too many mistakes!
13 I'd like to know how he has .... so much money.
14 We've got a lot to do, so it's time we .... a start.
15 Did you .... English at school?
16 I didn't finish my exam paper. I couldn't .... all the questions.
17 .... something! Don't just stand there watching me!
18 I won't be free at 11. I'm going to .... a driving lesson.
19 Let me .... a try!
20 The world has .... so many wars!

Part B

1   Let's hope European nations will never again .... war on each other.
2   I hope you .... a nice sleep!
3   You'll have to .... what you think is right.
4   A long walk in the fresh air will .... you a lot of good.
5   I've .... my suitcase lighter by removing a couple of books.
6   Don't blame me. I didn't .... anything!
7   John's a wonderful cook. He can .... anything out of a few ingredients.
8   It .... no difference whether you believe me nor not!
9   Everyone will .... fun of you if you go to school dressed like that!
10 I'm sure you'll have a lovely evening and I hope you'll .... a lot of fun.
11 I've .... an appointment to see my dentist on Wednesday.
12 I can't see you at 11. I .... an appointment with my dentist.
13 I .... a headache, so I took an aspirin.
14 It looks as though those two cats have been .... a fight.
15 Did you .... a good game?
16 I don't want to .... trouble for you.
17 If it's fine tomorrow, we can go for a long walk and .... a picnic.
18 .... a good trip!
19 I don't like being criticized after I've .... my best.
20 You can watch TV after you've .... your homework.

38 Dressing and clothes

Supply the best word or words.

1 How long does it take you to .... in the morning?
   a) get dressed   b) dress up   c) dress yourself

2 You can't go to the interview .... jeans and an old jacket!
   a) dressed with   b) dressed in   c) dressed up

3 Just a minute! I must have a shower and .... before we go out.
   a) change   b) exchange

4 You'd better .... your coat before you go out into the cold.
   a) wear   b) dress in   c) have on   d) put on

5 .... that blue dress to see if it suits you.
   a) Test   b) Prove   c) Try on   d) Probe

6 I can't go out in this shirt. I've .... all day.
   a) dressed in it   b) had it on   c) got dressed in it

7 The doctor asked me to .... my shirt.
   a) put off   b) take off   c) take out   d) put out

8 We got John a new .... for his job interview.
   a) dress   b) costume   c) suit   d) suite

9 How much would you expect to pay for a pair of men's .... ?
   a) socks   b) stockings   c) tights

10 They won't let you into the restaurant without a ....
   a) cravat   b) tie

11 These are the .... I work in.
   a) clothing   b) clothe   c) clothes   d) cloth

12 Your collar looks very tight. Why don't you .... your tie?
   a) loose   b) lose   c) loosen

13 Ticket inspectors usually wear a blue suit and a ....
   a) peaked cap   b) casket

14 It was so early in the morning that she answered the door in a ....
   a) dressing gown   b) robe   c) dress

15 How much .... in the window?
   a) is that trouser   b) are those trousers   c) are those pantaloons

230

39 Food and drink

Read the story. Refer to the list below and fill in the blanks with the best word or words. The first one has been done for you.

(0) '*I'm not very hungry*. I think I'll skip the first (1) .... I'll order just one (2) .... I don't want the (3) .... , but I might have (4) .... , (5) .... , (6) .... or (7) ....'

'You eat (8) .... ,' Anita said to me. 'It isn't good for you to have so much (9) .... I'm going to have (10) ....'

'I'll have a (11) .... ,' I said. 'I hope it will be (12) ....'

'I'll start with (13) .... and (14) .... ,' Anita said. 'This is a wonderful (15) .... ,' she added, looking round. 'The (16) .... very good here.'

My meat was very (17) .... , but a bit (18) .... 'I should have chosen (19) .... beef,' I said. 'I really prefer meat done in the (20) ....'

Anyway, we enjoyed the meal and finished with (21) .... sorbet and (22) .... , followed by (23) .... which was rather (24) ....

'The (25) .... was quite reasonable,' I said, as we were leaving. 'We should come here more often.'

Anita didn't agree. 'From tomorrow,' she said, 'we'll both be back on a (26) .... !'

0 a) I haven't much hunger b) I'm not very hungry	1 a) course b) dish c) plate	2 a) plate b) dish	3 a) menu b) cart c) dish of the day
4 a) fowl b) chicken c) poultry d) hen	5 a) sheep b) lamb	6 a) beef b) bullock c) ox	7 a) hog b) pig c) pork
8 a) too many meats b) too much meat	9 a) flesh b) meat	10 a) fish b) fishes	11 a) beef b) steak
12 a) tender b) soft	13 a) bouillon b) soup	14 a) a bread b) a roll	15 a) canteen b) restaurant
16 a) foods are b) food is c) kitchen is	17 a) tasty b) tasteful	18 a) hard b) tough	19 a) roasted b) roast c) toasted
20 a) furnace b) oven	21 a) citron b) lemon	22 a) fruits b) fruit	23 a) café b) coffee
24 a) strong b) stark	25 a) addition b) reckoning c) bill	26 a) diet b) system c) regime	

40 Countable and uncountable nouns

Supply the best word or words.

1 We do .... business in Latin America.
   a) a   b) a lot of

2 Our daughter has done very well. She runs .... very profitable business.
   a) a   b) a lot of   c) -

3 We can hardly say .... business is booming at the moment.
   a) a   b) -   c) some

4 How .... are you checking in?
   a) many pieces of luggage   b) many luggages   c) many baggages

5 We'll be lucky to find .... at this time of the night.
   a) a camping   b) a camping site   c) camping   d) any camping

6 What does a .... like that cost?
   a) clothing   b) clothes   c) garment   d) clothe

7 The .... looks pretty full.
   a) dance   b) dance hall   c) dancing

8 Would you like .... ?
   a) a fruit   b) some fruits   c) some fruit   d) fruits

9 I can't imagine where we can put such ....
   a) a large piece of furniture   b) a large furniture   c) large furnitures

10 It's time I had my .... cut!
   a) hair   b) hairs   c) a hair

11 There are only three of us. Why have you ordered .... ?
   a) so many foods   b) so much food

12 Can you give me .... help with these accounts?
   a) a   b) some   c) -

13 I'm sure Tourist .... will be able to recommend a cheap hotel.
   a) Informations   b) Information

14 How .... do you want?
   a) many toasts   b) much toast

15 While you're out, could you please buy a couple of .... ?
   a) soaps   b) bars of soap   c) soap

41 Education

Supply the best words in Parts A and B.

Part A

1	A nursery school is a school for	a) babies	b) infants
2	Who is the .... of your grammar school?	a) head	b) director
3	My favourite .... at school is Mr Watkins.	a) professor	b) teacher
4	This book is for .... at university.	a) students	b) pupils
5	Our teacher always sets us a lot of	a) housework	b) homework
6	What will you be doing in the summer .... ?	a) vacation	b) vacancy
7	Children often have to carry heavy	a) schoolbags	b) sacks
8	Class 2 are waiting for me in the	a) classroom	b) lesson
9	We have a very good school	a) canteen	b) restaurant
10	What year did you leave .... ?	a) college	b) colleague
11	I want to be a .... when I leave school.	a) teacher	b) learner
12	When did you .... your exam?	a) take	b) give
13	There are 15 students in our English	a) class	b) grade
14	I'm .... English classes.	a) attending	b) following
15	Please write .... ink.	a) in	b) with
16	Teachers use a lot of	a) crayon	b) chalk
17	She's in the headmaster's	a) bureau	b) study
18	Our teacher is sitting behind her	a) desk	b) office
19	Sit .... your desk and get on with your work.	a) on	b) at
20	I made too many .... in my essay.	a) faults	b) mistakes

Part B

1	.... as much as you can about Antarctica.	a) Find	b) Find out
2	I can't .... you with your homework.	a) help	b) aid
3	Everyone needs a good English	a) dictionary	b) lexicon
4	You .... too many lessons last term.	a) missed	b) lost
5	Explain .... why you are late.	a) to me	b) me
6	Children soon learn .... do what they're told.	a) how to	b) to
7	You will each need a .... paper for this.	a) sheet of	b) -
8	Do you know .... spell 'cough'?	a) to	b) how to
9	.... your knowledge!	a) Try	b) Test
10	You'll have to .... it's true.	a) test	b) prove
11	What did you get out of ten in the test? - .... !	a) Nought	b) Nil
12	How many .... do you speak?	a) languages	b) tongues
13	.... is my favourite subject.	a) Story	b) History
14	How are you enjoying your English .... ?	a) course	b) coarse
15	Maths .... easy for everybody.	a) aren't	b) isn't
16	I'm afraid you .... wrong.	a) are	b) have
17	I'm not good .... sports.	a) in	b) at
18	Children know it isn't .... to betray a friend.	a) correct	b) right
19	I've started learning	a) German	b) german
20	I'm doing a course in	a) cookery	b) cuisine

42 Greetings, conventional social utterances and exchanges

Write what you would say in each of these situations. The first one has been done for you.

0 Express your pleasure to a friend who has just passed a driving test.
Congratulations on passing your driving test!

1 Use a phrase with *time* to express the wish that your friends will enjoy themselves.
....

2 You want to get past someone. Use a suitable two-word phrase.
....

3 Someone says *Shall I open the door for you?* Use a polite phrase with *Yes, if* ... in reply.
....

4 Use a phrase with *matter* to tell someone it isn't important they forgot to do something.
....

5 Use a phrase with *moment* to tell someone to wait.
....

6 A friend is going on a journey. Use a well-wishing phrase with *trip*.
....

7 Use a suitable two-word phrase to tell a friend not to be anxious.
....

8 You want to know what a young child is called. How do you ask the child?
....

9 You're a shop assistant and you ask if a customer is receiving attention. Use *served*.
....

10 You meet in the street a married woman (Jane Smith) whom you don't know very well. Say good morning to her.
....

11 You're a shop assistant and you're about to serve a female customer. What do you say?
....

12 You're a shop assistant and you're about to serve a male customer. What do you say?
....

13 Use a not-very-polite phrase with *business* to tell someone not to interfere with things that don't concern that person.
....

14 You didn't hear what someone said. Ask them to repeat it using a single word.
....

15 Use a phrase with *indeed* to express your special thanks.
....

43 Comparing and contrasting

Supply the best word or words.

1 Two things are very alike, so you say they are the .... each other.
   a) same with   b) same as   c) same like

2 You like chocolate, ...
   a) and me too   b) and I too   c) and so do I   d) and also I

3 .... a doctor, I must advise you to give up smoking.
   a) Like   b) Else   c) As

4 She said it .... she meant it.
   a) as   b) like   c) like as if   d) as if

5 You play tennis .... I do.
   a) better than   b) more good than   c) more good as   d) better as   e) more well

6 .... a lot of other people, we managed to survive the recession.
   a) Contrary to   b) In contrast to   c) On the contrary with

7 If you .... me, just say so.
   a) disagree with   b) differ from   c) differ with   d) differ by

8 If you don't like this one, try something ....
   a) other   b) more   c) else   d) another

9 There's little to choose between them. They're ....
   a) equally nice   b) equally as nice

10 The two models are exactly the same ....
   a) in all cases   b) in all respects   c) in any event

11 How are you feeling today? - .... better, thank you.
   a) More   b) Much   c) Very   d) Many

12 I've got a place at college! - .... !
   a) So I have   b) So have I   c) And I

13 Do it ....
   a) like this   b) like so   c) so   d) like this way

14 You're not the only one who didn't hear the news. I didn't ....
   a) neither   b) also   c) too   d) either

15 How do you like London? - ....
   a) I very much like   b) I like very much   c) I like it very much

44 Socializing, entertainment, etc.

Supply the most suitable words from the list on the right.

1 You look for this if you want to leave a cinema: ....
2 In Britain, it's polite to open a present when you .... it.
3 This is where you leave your coat at a theatre: ....
4 Your theatre ticket might say ' .... One'.
5 People who enjoy the company of others are ....
6 Express your enthusiasm by shouting: ....
7 To be present: ....
8 A special day on the religious calendar: ....
9 A mixture of drinks, often alcoholic: ....
10 What you do when you say 'yes' to an invitation: ....
11 If someone needed help, you might .... them.
12 A popular person often has a busy .... life.
13 At a .... you are served alcoholic drinks and food.
14 You do this when you want to decline an invitation: ....
15 The cost of entry to a cinema, for example: ....
16 They put 'No' in front of this when you can't go in: ....
17 You do this to people who have never met: ....
18 You can't sit at a restaurant table if it says this: ....
19 Someone is sitting in that seat. That seat is ....
20 What you need if you've been overworking: ....
21 A collection of clothes for all occasions: ....
22 A large number of people leaving a place: ....
23 Show your appreciation by clapping your hands: ....
24 Permit someone to do something: ....
25 Someone wants you to .... a good hotel.
26 You don't know about something. You .... all knowledge.

a) accept
b) admission
c) admit
d) admittance
e) allow
f) applaud
g) assist
h) attend
i) cheer
j) cloakroom
k) cocktail
l) cocktail party
m) deny
n) exit
o) exodus
p) festival
q) holiday
r) introduce
s) occupied
t) receive
u) recommend
v) refuse
w) reserved
x) sociable
y) social
z) wardrobe

45 What goes with what?

Suggest the words that go together. The first one has been done for you.

0 This verb goes in front of *presents* or *guests*.
1 This adjective goes in front of *room*, *parts*, or *time*.
2 You can .... *flowers* or *a meeting*.
3 Two things you can do with *money* and *time*.
4 This noun comes after words like *dinner* or *cocktail*.
5 A .... of *applause*.
6 You .... a *puzzle* or a *problem*.
7 You play a game .... the *rules*.
8 You can .... *a game* or *a trick*.
9 You .... *flowers* or *fruit*.
10 You go for a walk to .... your *legs*.
11 What you do to a photo to make it bigger: .... it.
12 Many people .... things like *stamps*.

0 *receive*
1 ....
2 ....
3 ....
4 ....
5 ....
6 ....
7 ....
8 ....
9 ....
10 ....
11 ....
12 ....

46 Phrasal verbs

Match the underlined verbs and phrases with the phrasal verbs on the right. Some of these phrasal verbs are more 'natural' than the verbs they replace.

1 She <u>was wearing</u> a beautiful new dress. ....
2 I'm up this ladder and can't <u>descend.</u> ....
3 We're <u>eagerly expecting</u> your arrival. ....
4 I knocked and a voice said, '<u>Enter</u>!' ....
5 How did you <u>discover</u> my address? ....
6 Now they are <u>adults</u>, they can decide for themselves. ....
7 The Wests have <u>reared</u> a large family on very little. ....
8 <u>Select</u> the one you want. ....
9 What time shall I <u>collect you</u>? ....
10 John didn't <u>arrive</u> till after midnight. ....
11 <u>Identify</u> your mother in this photograph. ....
12 <u>Show me</u> the spot on the map with your finger. ....
13 <u>Remove</u> your jacket please. ....
14 I'd like to <u>participate in</u> the wedding preparations. ....
15 It's too late to <u>return</u> to the house now. ....
16 I don't know how you can <u>endure</u> these conditions! ....
17 What <u>delayed you</u>? ....
18 The bomb <u>exploded</u> without warning. ....
19 You don't have to <u>make me look silly</u> in public. ....
20 Try to <u>reduce</u> the number of cigarettes you smoke. ....
21 The baby got so upset we couldn't <u>pacify</u> her. ....
22 We have <u>assumed control of</u> the company. ....
23 Shall I <u>make it into a parcel</u> for you? ....
24 We've <u>postponed</u> the meeting till next week. ....
25 <u>Extinguish</u> the lights before you go to bed. ....
26 The earthquake <u>caused</u> the collapse of the building. ....

a) blew up
b) brought about
c) brought up
d) calm her down
e) come in
f) cut down on
g) find out
h) get down
i) grown up
j) had on
k) held you up
l) looking forward to
m) pick out
n) pick you up
o) point out
p) point to/at
q) put off
r) put off/out
s) put up with
t) show me up
u) show up
v) take off
w) take part in
x) taken over
y) turn back
z) wrap it up

47 Adjective + preposition

Supply suitable prepositions.

1 Make sure the label is properly attached .... your suitcase.
2 John's ashamed .... his bad spelling.
3 Margot looks stunning dressed .... black.
4 I'm getting pretty fed up .... my present job.
5 This computer is similar .... the one we have in our office.
6 George became interested .... antiques at a very early age.
7 Tanya expects to be successful .... anything she does.
8 My name is Wills, but I'm not related .... the Wills you know.
9 You must be very proud .... your son.
10 I've never been very keen .... flying.
11 Anyone would feel nervous .... having an operation.
12 Our daughter's shy .... meeting strangers.

48 Verb + 'to' or verb + '-ing'?

Fifteen of these verbs can be followed by (object) + *to* + verb and fifteen by verb + *-ing*. Add *to* or *-ing* against each verb in the list, then supply the right forms of the verbs in brackets in the sentences below. The first two sentences have been done for you.

0	advise + *to*	9	enjoy	19	miss
1	agree	10	face	20	order
2	allow	11	fail	21	prevent
3	ask	12	fancy	22	promise
0	avoid + *-ing*	13	forbid	23	resist
4	dare	14	imagine	24	risk
5	delay	15	keep	25	suggest
6	deny	16	learn	26	want
7	direct	17	manage	27	warn
8	dislike	18	mind	28	wish

0 My doctor has advised me *to take* (take) more exercise.
0 You should avoid *travelling* (travel) during rush hour.

1 We have all agreed .... (take) a pay cut so that our company will survive.
2 For the time being, the police won't allow anyone .... (leave) the building.
3 We've been asked .... (contribute) towards the new school gymnasium.
4 Personally, I wouldn't dare .... (criticize) my boss.
5 We've delayed .... (fix) the date of the wedding to please everybody.
6 The accused deny .... (be) anywhere near the bank during the robbery.
7 Visitors have been directed .... (not carry) cameras into the museum.
8 Most men dislike .... (wear) the same shirt two days running.
9 I can't imagine that anyone enjoys .... (wait) in a queue.
10 I can't face .... (go) to work on an empty stomach.
11 Surely you just can't fail .... (notice) the constant rise in the cost of living.
12 I don't fancy .... (be) responsible for a party of schoolchildren for a week.
13 No one can forbid you .... (use) a public footpath.
14 It's hard to imagine .... (live) without electricity.
15 I keep .... (leave) my glasses all over the place.
16 Didn't you learn .... (do) long division when you were at school?
17 I've never managed .... (get) to the end of 'War and Peace'.
18 Most people don't mind .... (work) overtime occasionally.
19 We miss .... (see) all our old friends now we've left the district.
20 There's been a chemical leak and we've been ordered .... (stay) indoors.
21 You can't prevent a disabled driver .... (park) near a crossroads.
22 We've promised .... (not discuss) company business with strangers.
23 It's impossible to resist .... (accept) such an attractive offer.
24 You risk .... (lose) everything you have if you become self-employed.
25 I suggest .... (take) a taxi if it will save us a bit of time.
26 It's hard to imagine that anyone actually wants .... (work) down a mine.
27 Employees have been warned .... (expect) a number of redundancies.
28 If we wish .... (visit) Canada before we're old, we'd better start saving.

49 Approval and disapproval

Supply the words asked for in the clues. The first one has been done for you.

0 What verb + preposition beginning with A means you
have a favourable opinion of someone or something?   0   *approve of*

1 A 9-letter adjective beginning with F and ending with -IC
that describes your feelings about something wonderful.   1   ....

2 What verb beginning with B means saying who is
responsible for doing something bad? (5 letters)   2   ....

3 A plural noun of 15 letters beginning with C that you use
to express your pleasure at someone's success.   3   ....

4 What verb beginning with A means to clap your hands
together to show approval? (7 letters)   4   ....

5 What adjective beginning with D describes someone
or something unpleasant, or 'not agreeable'? (12 letters)   5   ....

6 A 4-letter adjective beginning with K meaning 'enthusiastic'.   6   ....

7 What adjective beginning with S means 'giving
satisfaction'? (10 letters)   7   ....

8 What adjective beginning with I and ending with T means
'lacking knowledge'? (8 letters)   8   ....

9 A verb of 6 letters beginning with O and ending with E
which means 'act against' someone or something.   9   ....

10 An adjective of 6 letters beginning with B and ending
with L meaning 'very cruel'.   10   ....

11 The past participle of a verb beginning with E which
tells us someone is admired and respected. (8 letters)   11   ....

12 A 10-letter adjective beginning with I which you use
to describe something that has impressed you.   12   ....

13 What verb beginning with D and ending with T means
'dislike very much'? (6 letters)   13   ....

14 When people go to a church they do something beginning
with W. (7 letters)   14   ....

15 What 10-letter adjective beginning with C would you use
to describe an arrangement that suits you?   15   ....

16 What adjective beginning with P means 'too valuable
to be measured' or 'beyond price'? (9 letters)   16   ....

17 A verb beginning with C is what you do when you
express feelings of dissatisfaction. (8 letters)   17   ....

18 An 8-letter adjective beginning with A for someone
or something that is irritating.   18   ....

19 This three-word noun beginning with 'So' is used in
place of a swear word to decribe someone unpleasant.   19   ....

20 What adjective beginning with A means that someone
or something has great appeal? (10 letters)   20   ....

21 What 5-letter adjective beginning with W means 'mistaken'?   21   ....

22 What adjective beginning with C and ending with N means
'rough' or 'socially unacceptable'? (6 letters)   22   ....

50 Red tape

Choose the best explanation in each case.

1 A *diploma* is
a) a qualification you obtain after a course of study at university.
b) often awarded for a practical skill rather than academic achievement.
c) given to you when you pass your driving test.

2 One meaning of the word *literature* describes
a) explanatory material you might get at a travel agency.
b) all the papers you need to obtain a passport, for example.

3 *Domicile*
a) is the legal word which describes where you live and pay tax.
b) describes a period of stay in a foreign country.
c) can be used easily in place of *address*.

4 The word *duplicate* might describe
a) a person who looks exactly like someone else.
b) an exact copy of a document.

5 We would use the word *published*
a) to describe a work that is printed, distributed and sold.
b) to describe something that is widely known.

6 *Protocol* is
a) the first sheet of paper in a book.
b) the rules of correct diplomatic procedure.
c) an official application to a government ministry.
d) a sheet of examination paper.

7 You get a *reference*
a) to show you have passed an exam.
b) from a former employer or person in authority who knows you well.
c) at the end of a term's or a year's study at school or university.

8 You would expect to find a *register*
a) showing names in a hotel.
b) listing contents at the back of a book.
c) showing stock market prices in a newspaper.
d) showing the names and addresses of individuals in a little book.

9 *Permission*
a) describes consent you give to others or others give to you.
b) is the word used for 'holidays', especially in the armed forces.
c) describes the document you need to drive a car or own a dog.
d) describes the document you need to work in a foreign country.

51 Character and reputation

Supply the best word or words.

1 People who are generally too concerned with their own thoughts to notice what is happening round them can be described as ....
a) abstracted   b) absent-minded   c) distracted

2 A person whom other people admire has ....
a) great fame   b) an excellent reputation   c) good rumour   d) character

3 A person who works seriously and with care ....
a) is conscious   b) is conscientious   c) has conscience   d) has consciousness

4 A person who is well-known and has a good reputation is ....
a) notorious   b) famous   c) infamous

5 People who think only of themselves are ....
a) egoist   b) selfish   c) egotist

6 A person who is not distinguished in any way is ....
a) vulgar   b) common   c) ordinary

7 A person who reads and thinks a lot is ....
a) intellectual   b) spiritual   c) witty

8 A person who is easily annoyed or often in a bad mood is ....
a) nervous   b) tense   c) irritable

9 People who apply themselves seriously to their work are ....
a) hardworking   b) laborious

10 People who are 'full of life' have a lot of ....
a) liveliness   b) temperament

11 People who have had a lot of practice at doing something are ....
a) practical   b) practicable   c) practised

12 A person who is not very nice or friendly is ....
a) disagreeable   b) unsympathetic

13 A person who has good sense and judgement is ....
a) sensible   b) sensitive   c) conscious

14 We can describe someone who is fond of sport as ....
a) sporting   b) sportive   c) sporty

15 Beethoven was ....
a) a genie   b) a genius   c) genial

52 Everybody, Somebody, Anybody, Nobody

Give the best explanations you possibly can, either in English or in your own language, of the
words in bold type in this story. The first one has been done for you.

This is a story about four people named
Everybody, Somebody, Anybody and Nobody.
There was an important job to be done and

0	**Everybody** was asked to do it.	0	*All the (four) people*
1	**Everybody** was sure	1	....
2	**Somebody** would do it.	2	....
3	**Anybody** could have done it,	3	....
4	but **Nobody** did it.	4	....
5	**Somebody** got angry about that because it was	5	....
6	**Everybody's** job.	6	....
7	**Everybody** thought	7	....
8	**Anybody** could do it, but	8	....
9	**Nobody** realized that	9	....
10	**Everybody** wouldn't do it.	10	....
11	It ended up that **Everybody**	11	....
12	blamed **Somebody**	12	....
13	when **Nobody** did what	13	....
14	**Anybody** could have done!	14	....

53 Regular and irregular verbs which are easily confused

Choose the right verb and/or supply the right form.

0	It was our policy to deal with problems as they (arise/rise).	0	*arose*
1	You shouldn't walk on a field that's just been (sew/sow).	1	....
2	Rock bands have (rise/raise/rouse) millions for charity.	2	....
3	All the mistakes in my essay have been (ring).	3	....
4	The motor (spring) into life at the touch of a button!	4	....
5	I don't know how we'll ever cure her of (lay/lie).	5	....
6	It looks as though the terrorists had been (lay/lie) in wait.	6	....
7	You don't have to go round (lay/lie) down the law!	7	....
8	We've all (lay/lie) bets on the favourite.	8	....
9	I've lost count of the number of times she's (lay/lie) to me.	9	....
10	Why have they (lie/lay) quiet for so long?	10	....
11	How long is it since you (wind/wound) this clock?	11	....
12	How many soldiers were (wind/wound) in the gun battle?	12	....
13	How many metres down is the (sink) ship?	13	....
14	We'll have to wait till the sun has (rise/raise/rouse).	14	....
15	Wait till everyone has (wake up/awake).	15	....
16	The business was (find/found) in 1842.	16	....
17	Flood water (fly/flow) right through our house!	17	....
18	How many trees have you (fall/fell) today?	18	....
19	The traitors have been (hang).	19	....
20	Meat needs to be (hang) for a few days to become tender.	20	....

54 Animals, birds and plants

Associate a clue in column **A** with a word in column **B**. The first one has been done for you:
A0 a large furry animal → **B0** bear

A		**B**	
0 a large furry animal	*B0*	0	bear
1 footprints left by animals	....	1	bite
2 a cat could do this to you with its claws	....	2	breed
		3	calf
3 fire comes out of its nose	....	4	chick
4 a male duck	....	5	dragon
5 birds do this when they're eating	....	6	drake
6 an animal uses its teeth to do this	....	7	flock
7 fruit becomes this in the sun	....	8	game
8 wild animals, hunted for food, are referred to as	....	9	hen
		10	herd
9 the inside part of a nut	....	11	hide
10 men, women and children are	....	12	human
11 a large area of leather	....	13	kernel
12 meat from deer	....	14	peck
13 a wasp could do this to you	....	15	peel
14 small grapes become this when they have dried	....	16	pips
		17	plague
15 a ... of locusts	....	18	prune
16 we refer to the whole of humanity as 'the human ...'	....	19	race
		20	raisins
17 a chihuahua is an unusual ... of dog	....	21	rind
		22	ripe
18 a lot of cows together	....	23	scratch
19 a lot of sheep together	....	24	shell
20 you do this to an orange before you eat it	....	25	species
		26	sting
21 it's called this when it's just come out of an egg	....	27	stone
		28	tracks
22 a baby cow or bull	....	29	veal
23 meat from a baby bull	....	30	venison
24 it lays eggs	....		
25 a dry plum	....		
26 the inside part of an apple contains these	....		
27 you might grate this to flavour food	....		
28 the outside body of a crab	....		
29 you'd find one inside a peach	....		
30 animals or plants which are all alike are referred to as this	....		

55 Shopping

Supply the best word or words.

1 You'd like some spicy sausage. You might try a ....
   a) delicacy   b) delicatessen

2 You're standing in front of a shop window and admiring the ....
   a) exhibition   b) show   c) display   d) exposition

3 A large shop that sells all kinds of goods is called a ....
   a) warehouse   b) storeroom   c) department   d) department store

4 What .... of toothpaste do you use?
   a) mark   b) brand   c) marque

5 When you're on holiday you might buy a .... to take home with you.
   a) souvenir   b) memento   c) memory   d) remembrance

6 A shop may sell things cheaply when it is having a ....
   a) liquidation   b) clearance sale

7 Personally, I do all my shopping locally and prefer to deal with local ....
   a) traders   b) tradesmen   c) merchants   d) dealers

8 Something you buy at a good price can be described as ....
   a) a bargain   b) an occasion   c) an opportunity   d) second-hand

9 A business has to pay a lot for .... on TV.
   a) advertising   b) propaganda   c) publicity

10 Spain is a fertile country and exports a lot of its ....
    a) product   b) products   c) produce   d) production

11 When you buy something, make sure you don't throw away your ....
    a) prescription   b) receipt   c) recipe

12 You'll have to .... if you want to buy an oriental carpet.
    a) make a bazaar   b) bazaar   c) bargain   d) do a bazaar

13 You can have these goods .... for up to a month.
    a) on trial   b) on approval

14 You'll find the prices of our goods in our published ....
    a) tariff   b) charges   c) price-list

15 We've been .... with the same company for years.
    a) treating   b) dealing   c) using   d) handling

56 Counting and measuring

Choose the best explanation in each case.

1 *Estimate* is what you do when you want
a) a general idea about price, size, amount, etc.
b) an accurate measure of money, size, amount, etc.
c) to describe the respect you have for someone.

2 *Control*
a) is what an official might do to your passport or driving licence.
b) is what you might do to your tyres to check their pressures.
c) is what you might do to set your watch to the exact time.
d) can mean 'limit something' (e.g. the spread of disease).

3 A *decade* describes
a) a period of ten years.
b) ten people or things, etc.
c) a set of ten things that match like cups or plates.

4 *Net*
a) means clean and tidy.
b) describes a road that is free of traffic.
c) can combine with words like *weight* or *tax* to mean 'actual'.

5 A *series* refers to
a) any collection of items that forms a related whole.
b) things arranged in a particular order.
c) several collections of items arranged in order.

6 If you say that accounts are being *audited*, this means that
a) they are being looked at again.
b) they are being officially checked.
c) changes are being made to them.
d) they are being put right after mistakes have been found.

7 You could use the word *paces* to describe
a) a rough measurement of length.
b) the sound of someone walking behind you.
c) where you put your feet when you are learning a particular dance.

8 You might use the word *index*
a) when you are talking about the cost of living.
b) to point to something.
c) to refer to something which shows the weather is changing.

9 *Equal* describes something that is
a) the same measurement or value.
b) a surface that is smooth and flat.

57 Verbs with and without prepositions

Fourteen of the verbs in the box on the left can be matched with a preposition in the box on the right. Choose the most suitable preposition to go with each verb in the context of the sentences below. Some verbs require no preposition. The first two sentences have been done for you.

~~answer~~ approach approve argue begin borrow comply defend demand differentiate discuss divide divorce enjoy enter face match object promise reach regard rely resemble ~~stare~~ succeed wait	as about against ~~at~~ between by for from in into of on to with

0 Children should be taught never to *stare at* strangers.
0 Please *answer* my question. (*no preposition needed*)

1 We could .... the room .... two parts with a curtain.
2 I'm afraid you have to .... these new regulations.
3 I've heard that Molly is going to .... her husband.
4 When do you think this letter will .... its destination?
5 I don't know how I'll find a colour that will .... these curtains.
6 You always want to .... politics, so we end up shouting at each other.
7 I wonder if I could .... this matter in private with you.
8 Don't let her .... any money .... you because she'll never repay it.
9 I wonder if I could .... asking you a few questions.
10 I don't think your mother would .... such bad language.
11 Don't make eye contact with people who .... you in the street.
12 I've noticed how heads turn when you .... a crowded room.
13 These days, a lot of people .... smoking in public places.
14 It isn't surprising that I should .... my twin sister in so many ways!
15 I'm afraid the bank is going to .... repayment of the money.
16 They're so alike, it's sometimes impossible to .... them.
17 Thank goodness I can always .... my colleagues!
18 Life will change completely for me if I .... passing my driving test.
19 Learn judo and you'll be able to .... yourself .... attack.
20 You must .... me faithfully you will never do that again.
21 We're preparing to .... the biggest challenge of our lives.
22 I can hardly .... him .... a serious competitor.
23 I know we'll .... your company if we all go on holiday together.
24 Don't worry if you're a bit late. I'll .... you.

58 Household equipment, power, etc.

Supply the best word or words.

1 The device used on top of buildings to pick up a TV signal is called an ....
   a) aerial   b) antenna

2 The usual modern word for a 'WC' is ....
   a) cabinet   b) closet   c) toilet

3 We would say that a well-equipped house has every ....
   a) convenience   b) facility   c) commodity   d) ease

4 The term 'white goods' refers to things like ....
   a) sheets   b) bathrooms   c) refrigerators

5 If you put your fingers into a power point you would get an .... shock.
   a) electronic   b) electrical   c) electric

6 Wire that carries electrical power has to be very well ....
   a) insulated   b) isolated

7 Your water supply is provided through ....
   a) pipes   b) tubes   c) inner tubes

8 An electrically-charged wire is described as being ....
   a) alive   b) live   c) living

9 What kind of system would you fit to guard against burglars? - A(n) .... system.
   a) safety   b) security   c) insurance

10 The thing you use to turn electrical power on and off is called ....
   a) an interrupter   b) a switch

11 The container that holds water behind a lavatory is called a ....
   a) cistern   b) tank   c) washbasin   d) reservoir

12 Which of these items are you likely to find on the wall? ....
   a) a carpet   b) a tapestry   c) moquette

13 We describe material used to make clothes, etc., as ....
   a) stuff   b) fabric   c) matter   d) substance

14 A device used to keep a room at a comfortable temperature is an ....
   a) air-conditioner   b) air-conditioning   c) air-condition

15 An electric toaster is an electrical ....
   a) sort   b) kind   c) appliance   d) goods

59 Expressing feelings of approval

Read this letter of thanks. Refer to the list below and fill in the blanks with the best word or words. The first one has been done for you.

Dear Harry,

I am (0) *writing* to thank you for a (1) .... evening. I really must (2) .... you on your (3) .... as a host! You made us all very (4) .... in the warm and (5) .... atmosphere of your home, and (6) .... us enormously with your funny (7) .... They really made us (8) .... I liked all your impressions (9) .... famous (10) .... from (11) .... , though my (12) .... was the one (13) .... Winston Churchill. Congratulations (14) .... your performance! Now I know why you have such a great (15) .... as a (16) .... It was a (17) .... evening. All your (18) .... (19) .... it and had a lot of (20) ....

I look forward to (21) .... you soon.

Yours,

Fred

0	a) writting	1	a) delightful	2	a) complement	3	a) skill
	b) writing		b) delighted		b) compliment		b) craft
			c) delighting				c) technique
							d) technology

4	a) welcome	5	a) sympathetic	6	a) enjoyed	7	a) stories
	b) wellcome		b) friendly		b) pleased		b) histories
	c) well come		c) likeable		c) amused		

8	a) laugh	9	a) of	10	a) types	11	a) history
	b) to laugh		b) for		b) characters		b) story
			c) about		c) chaps		
					d) fellows		

12	a) favourite	13	a) of	14	a) on	15	a) character
	b) beloved		b) for		b) for		b) fame
	c) dearest		c) about		c) to		c) reputation
	d) best						

16	a) mime	17	a) terrific	18	a) guests	19	a) enjoyed
	b) mimic		b) formidable		b) customers		b) entertained
			c) terrible		c) clients		c) amused
					d) hosts		

20	a) enjoyment	21	a) see
	b) pleasure		b) seeing
	c) fun		

60 Writing, literature, language

Supply the best word or words.

1 A book about imaginary people and events is a ....
a) fiction b) novel c) roman d) romance e) soap opera

2 People who can read and write can be described as ....
a) literati b) literate

3 Politicians often write their .... at the end of their careers.
a) memories b) memoirs c) remembrances d) souvenirs e) mementos

4 If you enjoy reading poetry and fiction, you enjoy ....
a) literature b) philology

5 A book you are obliged to study in detail for an examination is a ....
a) novel b) short story c) set book

6 A poem is often divided into ....
a) strophes b) verses

7 The people in a play are usually referred to as the ....
a) people b) persons c) characters d) types

8 T. S. Eliot, the poet and critic, might be described as a ....
a) scientist b) man of letters c) literati

9 Only three examples of Shakespeare's .... have survived.
a) firm b) trademark c) signature

10 You would look up a word in a dictionary if you didn't know what it ....
a) signified b) meant

11 A work of fiction which is shorter than a novel is a ....
a) short story b) history c) romance

12 An observant writer might carry a .... to make notes.
a) block b) pad

13 Observant writers would probably .... their observations.
a) mark b) note down c) signify

14 Someone who briefly assesses a play or book in the press writes a ....
a) critic b) criticism c) critique d) review

15 Make sure you end each sentence with a ....
a) dot b) point c) comma d) full stop

61 Items of clothing, etc.

Choose the best words from the list below. Write them in beside the numbers under the pictures.

 1 .....overalls.....

 2 ....trouser.....

 3 ...pantaloons...

 4 ..Bath robe..

 5 ...Necklace...

6 ....Collar....

 7 ....tie....

 8 ...Sailor...

 9 ...suit...

10 ...Underwear...

 11 ..petticoat..

12 ....

 13 ...scarf...

 14 ...shawl...

bathrobe	combination	form	robe	suit
brace	costume	necklace	scarf	tie
braces	cravat	overalls	shawl	trousers
collar	dinner jacket	pantaloons	smoking	underwear
collier	flannel	petticoat	socks	veil
			stockings	vest

62 Nouns ending in 's'

To be correct noun forms, twenty-one of these words should end in 's'. Add 's' only to those items that need it. Number 8 has been done for you.

1	acoustic	12	earning	23	mump
2	athletic	13	economic	24	phenomenon
3	barrack	14	ethic	25	scaffolding
4	belonging	15	good	26	physic
5	billiard	16	gymnastic	27	politic
6	cattle	17	linguistic	28	serie
7	clothe	18	literati	29	specie
8	~~congratulations~~	19	mathematic	30	sud
9	criterion	20	measle	31	tooth
10	data	21	media	32	veal
11	deer	22	medium	33	venison

Write sentences using any of the nouns to which you've added 's' in the above list. Take particular care that a noun subject 'agrees' with the verb that follows.

0 *I hear you passed your driving test. Congratulations!*

1 ....

2 ....

3 ....

4 ....

5 ....

6 ....

7 ....

8 ....

9 ....

10 ....

11 ....

12 ....

13 ....

63 Food

Supply the best words in Parts A and B.

Part A

1	Tomatoes are very nice *stuffed*.	a) filled	b) stuffed
2	A *sideboard* is a piece of furniture in a dining room.	a) sideboard	b) buffet
3	A light meal. *a snack*	a) a collation	b) a snack
4	We can speak of the con .... of food.	a) summation	b) sumption
5	The first course is	a) an entrée	b) a starter
6	A large meal for important guests.	a) a feast	b) a banquet
7	Weigh it on the kitchen	a) scales	b) balance
8	Boil the milk in this small	a) saucepan	b) casserole
9	Food becomes this in a deep freeze.	a) congealed	b) frozen
10	*Melt* .... a little butter in a pan.	a) Dissolve	b) Melt
11	The salad has been dressed *with* .... oil.	a) in	b) with
12	Vegetables should be stored in a *cool* .... place.	a) fresh	b) cool
13	I love *smoked* salmon.	a) smoked	b) fumed
14	I have a very good *recipe* for onion soup.	a) receipt	b) recipe
15	Please *squeeze* a couple of lemons for me.	a) squeeze	b) press
16	I must consult the .... for the food mixer.	a) directions	b) instructions
17	*Reserve* some of that pie for me, won't you?	a) Reserve	b) Save
18	What shall I do with the *leftovers* ?	a) remainders	b) leftovers
19	Do you want your food *with sauce* or not?	a) with sauce	b) saucy
20	The toast has been	a) scalded	b) burnt

Part B

1	.... two egg whites until they're stiff.	a) Hit	b) Beat
2	.... some butter on your toast while it's hot.	a) Spread	b) Stretch
3	You can't stop .... coming out of a kettle!	a) steam	b) vapour
4	Here's a packet of .... biscuits.	a) assorted	b) matching
5	These apples have	a) gone bad	b) decayed
6	These peaches are the finest. They're	a) extra	b) best quality
7	That fruit salad smells	a) delicate	b) delicious
8	You should avoid all .... foods.	a) processed	b) artificial
9	These peaches need a couple of days to	a) mature	b) ripen
10	Get me some .... steak from the butcher's.	a) lean	b) meagre
11	Don't pour .... sauce over everything.	a) hot	b) piquant
12	I prefer .... grilled fish without sauce.	a) plain	b) simple
13	This milk has	a) gone sour	b) soured
14	You can't live .... a diet of nuts.	a) with	b) on
15	We felt quite .... after a good meal.	a) rejuvenated	b) restored
16	You'll rot your teeth .... sweets!	a) licking	b) sucking
17	An excellent meal! My compliments to the	a) chief	b) chef
18	Shall we .... a pudding?	a) order	b) command
19	.... the dish first before you comment.	a) Taste	b) Probe
20	.... the dish first before you comment.	a) Try	b) Try on

64 Health

Supply the words asked for in the clues. The first one has been done for you.

0 What verb beginning with B means 'take air into the
lungs and put out again'? (7 letters)   0 *breathe*

1 What noun beginning with C and ending -TION describes
the way the blood travels round the body? (11 letters)   1 ....

2 A noun beginning with P and ending with E that describes
a substance that forms on the teeth. (6 letters)   2 ....

3 What verb beginning with S (5 letters) describes what boiling
water does to you if it comes in contact with your skin?   3 ....

4 A noun beginning with P (6 letters) that describes an infectious
disease borne by rats and common in the Middle Ages.   4 ....

5 What noun beginning with M describes having a baby
too early so that it doesn't survive? (11 letters)   5 ....

6 What 6-letter adjective beginning with P means 'unwell'?   6 ....

7 A 9-letter verb beginning with S and ending -IZE describes
what a dentist does to his instruments to make them germ-free.   7 ....

8 What verb beginning with DIS describes what a nurse
does to a wound to make it germ-free? (9 letters)   8 ....

9 A 10-letter noun beginning with S that describes a medically
qualified person with detailed knowledge about a subject.   9 ....

10 What noun beginning with I describes a tool used
for scientific and technical purposes? (10 letters)   10 ....

11 What adjective beginning with IM and ending -ILE
means 'completely without movement'? (8 letters)   11 ....

12 What 12-letter noun beginning with P describes an order
for medicine made by a doctor and supplied by a chemist?   12 ....

13 A noun beginning with D that has two meanings: a
medicine or a narcotic. (4 letters)   13 ....

14 What noun beginning with S is the name of a doctor's
consulting room? (7 letters)   14 ....

15 What two-word noun beginning O and T describes
the special room where a surgeon does his/her work?   15 ....

16 A technical, medical noun beginning with PRO that refers
to a medicine or injection that prevents disease. (12 letters)   16 ....

17 What noun beginning with S describes emotional and
physical stress that might follow a car accident? (5 letters)   17 ....

18 What 11-letter adjective beginning with H describes a
person who suffers from a physical or mental disadvantage?   18 ....

19 A two-word adjective beginning L-S that describes
a person who can see things well at a distance.   19 ....

20 What adjective beginning with I often goes in front
of 'pain' to mean 'acute'? (7 letters)   20 ....

21 What adjective beginning with G means 'very serious'
when we use it to describe an illness? (5 letters)   21 ....

65 Behaviour

Choose the best explanation in each case.

1   If you call a person an *ass*,
a) you might be saying that he or she is a silly fool.
b) you are being extremely offensive and insulting.
c) you are saying that the person has terrible manners.

2   If you say that a person is *extravagant*, you might be suggesting that he or she
a) spends too much money.
b) is rather peculiar.
c) is always extremely wasteful.

3   If you were to use *womanly* to refer to a woman, you would be
a) referring to sexual attractiveness.
b) distinguishing her as female, compared with male.
c) referring to her qualities as a woman.

4   If we refer to a person's *temperament*, we are
a) referring to his or her basic nature or character.
b) suggesting that he or she is normally lively.
c) saying the person is 'full of spirit'.

5   A *far-sighted* person is one who
a) is often absent-minded.
b) needs glasses.
c) is capable of imagining the future.

6   A *sensible* person is one who
a) is quick to feel pain.
b) has good sense and judgement.
c) quickly reacts to heat or cold.

7   A *delicate* person is one who
a) gets ill easily.
b) has good manners.
c) has fine looks.

8   If we refer to a person's *high spirits*, we are suggesting he or she
a) has a lot of determination.
b) has drunk too much alcohol.
c) is in a very cheerful mood.

9   If you say that a person *has a temper*, you are
a) suggesting he or she is capable of getting very angry.
b) suggesting he or she often gets depressed.
c) referring to his or her state of mind which may be good or bad.

66 Two topics

Read these sentences. If you find a mistake in a line, cross it out and suggest an alternative. If there is no mistake, put a tick (✓). The first two have been done for you.

1 War and peace

0	The object of war is to ~~do~~ peace.	0	*make*
0	The soldier sprang to attention.	0	✓
1	The terrorists planned to burst the bridge.	1	....
2	After the war, many enemy collaborators were arrested.	2	....
3	The Romans carried out the total destroy of Carthage.	3	....
4	How will the escaped prisoners get past the guardians?	4	....
5	The military have surrounded the building.	5	....
6	Members of the Special Services are highly trained.	6	....
7	Members of the Special Services are highly drilled.	7	....
8	The soldiers are drilled every morning on the parade ground.	8	....
9	Good war pensions should be paid to all the invalids.	9	....
10	Did Alexander the Great set out to defeat the world?	10	....
11	Who commanded the soldiers to fire?	11	....
12	A great power should have a large marine.	12	....
13	Every village has its own War Memorial.	13	....
14	The losing side always has to pay reparations.	14	....
15	I'm not a member of the armed powers.	15	....
16	When were you discharged from the army?	16	....
17	Few people oppose the execution of traitors.	17	....
18	The army have put a cord round the city.	18	....
19	It is defended for anyone to go out after dark.	19	....

2 Geography, natural phenomena

1	The whole mountainside is full of caves.	1	....
2	An earthquake is a physical event.	2	....
3	Melted lava flows down the slopes.	3	....
4	What's the next frontier in exterior space?	4	....
5	Which explorer discovered the source of the Nile?	5	....
6	Can you imagine a journey to the centre of the earth?	6	....
7	Anything will grow in this dark rich soil.	7	....
8	The Kalahari covers a very large district.	8	....
9	There's a lot of shipping in the English Canal.	9	....
10	They're showing the film on a different canal.	10	....
11	Britain has an enormous cost line.	11	....
12	In Kuwait, sweet water is more precious than oil.	12	....
13	Titanium is a rare substance.	13	....
14	How many states are there in America?	14	....
15	Urbane development needs to be controlled.	15	....
16	You can't calculate the amount of matter in the universe.	16	....
17	An eclipse is a wonderful phenomena.	17	....
18	They had to blast through solid rock to build this road.	18	....
19	The Amazon is fed by interior rivers.	19	....
20	The Sahara has a very harsh weather.	20	....

67 Adjectives and -*ly* adverbs

Sometimes only one word will fit; sometimes two. Circle the right word or words.

Part A

1 Our landlady greeted us bright/brightly in French.
2 The moon was shining so bright/brightly, we decided to go out.
3 Industrial goods are often produced cheap/cheaply in developing countries.
4 You can buy fresh vegetables cheap/cheaply at the market.
5 They broke the window, stole what was on display and got clean/cleanly away.
6 With one stroke, he cut the log clean/cleanly down the middle.
7 He's in a bad mood and I'm going to stay clear/clearly of him for a while.
8 Write your name and address clear/clearly at the bottom of the form.
9 We cancelled our insurance policy and that cost us dear/dearly.
10 We really paid dear/dearly for our mistake.
11 She didn't mean to hurt you and deep/deeply regrets what she said.
12 If anyone phones while I'm out, tell them I'll be back direct/directly.
13 Is it possible to fly direct/directly to Tahiti?
14 I dislike playing chess with Janet. She never plays fair/fairly.
15 I'm sure the shop will treat you fair/fairly if you ask for a refund.
16 Four o'clock will suit me fine/finely.
17 Our whole project is balanced fine/finely between success and failure.
18 If she offers you less than £1,000, you must firm/firmly refuse.
19 We're standing firm/firmly against any changes in policy.
20 If your name begins with an A, you often come first/firstly in a list.

Part B

1 First/Firstly you press the eject button, then you load the tape.
2 I was so exhausted, I could only lie flat/flatly on my back.
3 She flat/flatly denies he has anything to do with this business.
4 We full/fully appreciate your support during this difficult period.
5 He had a fight at school and was punched full/fully in the face.
6 Planes coming in to land have to fly low/lowly over buildings.
7 He began life as a low/lowly bank clerk and rose to the position of chairman.
8 I suppose you expect me to smile pretty/prettily at the camera.
9 With a job and that salary, you're sitting pretty/prettily.
10 You did right/rightly in refusing payment for giving them advice.
11 I did what I was asked to do, but I'll never know if I acted right/rightly.
12 He was sent off the rugby field for playing rough/roughly.
13 I only caught a glimpse of her so I can only describe her rough/roughly.
14 You should never speak rough/roughly to young children.
15 You don't have to answer so sharp/sharply if I ask you a simple question.
16 Turn sharp/sharply left at the corner and you'll be in Brick Street.
17 We'll let you know short/shortly whether your application has been successful.
18 We'll have to leave soon because we're running short/shortly of time.
19 She's been ill for some time, but she's beginning to feel strong/strongly again.
20 I know how strong/strongly you feel about law and order.

68 Communicating

Supply the best word or words.

1 Business people might arrange a meeting in order to have ....
   a) a discussion   b) a conversation   c) an argument   d) a dialogue

2 If you've disagreed very strongly with someone, you've probably been ....
   a) conversing   b) disputing   c) quarrelling   d) discussing

3 If you make a remark, you are probably .... something.
   a) noticing   b) regarding   c) observing   d) saying

4 You might pin this on a notice board. ....
   a) a notice   b) a placard   c) a sign   d) a cartel

5 If you nodded, you would probably be ....
   a) agreeing   b) disagreeing   c) accepting

6 You see someone you know across the street, so you .... them.
   a) salute   b) wave to   c) welcome

7 You probably think carefully before deciding how to .... a business letter.
   a) respond to   b) respond   c) reply   d) answer to

8 You are driving and want to turn left, so you ....
   a) do a sign   b) sign   c) signal   d) signify

9 You and your friend spent the afternoon talking. You had a nice ....
   a) speech   b) chat   c) speak

10 Someone asks you for a favour and you .... to do it.
   a) accept   b) agree

11 I'm not opposed to what you're saying. .... , I completely agree with you.
   a) Contrary   b) The contrary   c) In contrast   d) On the contrary

12 You never feel comfortable until you have .... an argument.
   a) sorted   b) settled   c) arranged

13 In normal circumstances when you are asked if it's hot outside, you say,' .... !'
   a) Of course   b) Naturally   c) Yes, it is   d) Indeed

14 If a discussion or argument becomes intense, we may describe it as ....
   a) hot   b) warm   c) heat   d) heated   e) hotted

15 If we have the same point of view, we are ....
   a) agreeable   b) in agreement

69 Reflexive pronouns after verbs

Supply reflexive pronouns (*myself*, etc.) *only where strictly necessary* in Parts A and B.

Part A

1   I hope you all enjoy .... !
2   It's always a problem adjusting .... to a new time zone after a long flight.
3   You need to relax .... after a long period of intensive work.
4   I have to assure .... that I've made the best possible decision.
5   It looks as though the plane-crash victims suffocated ....
6   No one will ever know whether she intentionally drowned ....
7   I hope you will all amuse .... constructively while I'm out.
8   If ever we go jogging together, John quickly tires ....
9   Take care you don't overdo it and tire ....
10 You can't prevent babies from wetting .... !
11 Hamlet revenged .... on his father's murderer.
12 I got confused .... about the date of our meeting.
13 Frequent washing .... is just a matter of habit.
14 Go and wash .... before you come to the table.
15 Have you heard? Debbie's engaged .... to Tristan.
16 You can't have a shower without wetting .... all over!
17 I don't know where to hide ....
18 I thought she conducted .... with great dignity.
19 We should never resign .... to a breakdown in law and order.
20 Have you shaved .... yet?

Part B

1   Mind you don't burn .... on that hot pan!
2   I feel .... cold.
3   She's named .... Jennifer, isn't she?
4   I suggest you rest .... before dinner.
5   Hamlet avenged .... his father's murder.
6   It's time those boys learnt how to behave .... !
7   Don't worry about me. I know how to occupy ....
8   You'd better check .... that our hotel booking is OK.
9   Count up to ten if you feel .... getting angry!
10 Do you ever wonder .... how top people's children get top jobs?
11 I washed this shirt in cold water, but it has still shrunk .... !
12 It's always wise to insure .... before you travel abroad.
13 Take it or leave it. Please .... !
14 I nearly choked .... on that fish bone!
15 The bath water was too hot and I nearly scalded ....
16 He was called .... Podge when he was a schoolboy.
17 Mind you don't get dirty .... !
18 I wish you wouldn't keep repeating ....
19 It's impossible to excuse .... such bad behaviour.
20 I feel I have to excuse .... for my bad behaviour last night.

70 Food and drink

The clues in **A** have answers in **B**. Find and match them. Here's the first one:
A0 an apparatus for cooking food, especially meat, over an open fire → **B**0 barbecue

A

0 an apparatus for cooking food,
   especially meat, over an open fire   *B*0

1 strong wine from Jerez, Spain   ....
2 sweet spiced mixture of raisins
   and candied fruit   ....
3 potatoes that have been boiled
   then crushed to make them soft   ....
4 fruit boiled with sugar   ....
5 sardines come in one of these   ....
6 a cake with fresh cream filling   ....
7 any type of macaroni   ....
8 you'd put this on a salad   ....
9 the word in British English for thin
   fried slices of potato in packets   ....
10 these are often roasted in winter   ....
11 a substance added to food to
    prevent it from going bad   ....
12 a general word for birds reared
    for food   ....
13 the hard outside of a nut   ....
14 large dried grapes   ....
15 a dried plum   ....
16 pieces of meat grilled on a skewer   ....
17 a general word for butter,
    margarine, seed oil, etc.   ....
18 caviare would be considered to
    be this   ....
19 you would use the juice from
    roast meat to make this   ....
20 Christmas ... is a sweet dish   ....
21 if you crushed fruit to feed to a
    baby you would turn it into this   ....
22 you might do this to a tin before
    using it to bake cakes or biscuits
    in the oven   ....
23 a metal shelf on which food,
    especially meat, is cooked from
    above or below   ....
24 distilled drinks like gin or whisky
    can be called this   ....

B

0	barbecue		
1	alcohols	31	kernel
2	biscuit	32	maroon
3	cherry	33	mash
4	chestnuts	34	mincemeat
5	chicken	35	minced beef
6	chips	36	pasta
7	compost	37	pastry
8	conserve	38	peel
9	cream cake	39	pip
10	crisps	40	poultry
11	currants	41	preservative
12	damask	42	preserve
13	damson	43	prune
14	delicacy	44	pudding
15	delicatessen	45	puree
16	desert	46	raisins
17	dessert	47	sauce
18	dressing	48	shell
19	fat	49	sherry
20	flan	50	skewer
21	fowl	51	skin
22	french fries	52	spirit
23	gateaux	53	spirits
24	grapes	54	spit
25	gravy	55	sponge cake
26	grease	56	stewed fruit
27	grill	57	stone
28	hen	58	sultanas
29	juice	59	tart
30	kebab	60	tin

71 Two topics

Read these sentences. If you find a mistake in a line, cross it out and suggest an alternative. If there is no mistake, put a tick (✓). The first two have been done for you.

1 Entertainment, leisure

0	Who's the greatest ~~live~~ conductor?	0	*living*
0	I love listening to live music.	0	✓
1	What are your favourite pieces of classic music?	1	....
2	Charlie Chaplin was a wonderful comedian.	2	....
3	The play has a complicated intrigue.	3	....
4	I hardly ever use my pick-up any more.	4	....
5	You're really a gifted mimic.	5	....
6	It's a play with very few persons.	6	....
7	Charlie Chaplin was a master of slapstick.	7	....
8	Jim's always playing farces on people.	8	....
9	I'll never learn the footsteps of this dance.	9	....
10	They're doing a repeat of the play tomorrow on TV.	10	....
11	How long have you been rehearsing this play?	11	....
12	The sales of long-playing plaques have fallen dramatically.	12	....
13	The film was extremely well doubled.	13	....
14	It isn't easy to write good dialogue.	14	....
15	Who's directing the orchestra this evening?	15	....
16	Monica is a wonderful dancing partner.	16	....
17	The spectators applauded the orchestra.	17	....
18	The audience applauded the orchestra.	18	....
19	The scenery in the play is quite magical.	19	....

2 Games, sports, outdoor activities

1	Billiards are my favourite indoor game.	1	....
2	I defy you to a game of chess.	2	....
3	You have to train hard to build up a physique like that.	3	....
4	What's the latest tennis score? - Three games to zero.	4	....
5	The new Olympic Stage holds 100,000 people.	5	....
6	She plunged straight into the pool.	6	....
7	How much time do you spend in the gymnasium?	7	....
8	Chelsea won Liverpool.	8	....
9	Liverpool were conquered.	9	....
10	They're building a big basin at the back of their house.	10	....
11	Children shouldn't be allowed to waste time playing flipper.	11	....
12	Who won the 100 metre race?	12	....
13	Anyone can enter the concurrence.	13	....
14	Don't blame me. I didn't do the rules!	14	....
15	There were at least 10,000 spectators at the match.	15	....
16	Shall we play a volleyball?	16	....
17	Whose side are you on?	17	....
18	Chasing has been described as the sport of kings.	18	....
19	They've bought a lot of new equipments for our gym.	19	....
20	In this school, athletics is compulsory.	20	....

72 What comes after the verb?

Supply the best word or words.

1 Listen! I can hear someone .... at the door.
   a) to knock   b) knocking   c) knock

2 Do you want to come for a walk with us next Sunday? - Yes, I want ....
   a) it   b) to   c) -

3 The whole class rose .... when the head came into the classroom.
   a) -   b) their hands

4 I've explained .... as patiently as I know how.
   a) to you the situation   b) the situation to you   c) you the situation

5 I suggest .... for them to answer before getting in touch with them again.
   a) you wait   b) you to wait   c) to wait

6 John and Emily always buy .... for her birthday.
   a) for their daughter something nice   b) their daughter something nice

7 Did you have a good time on holiday? - Yes, we enjoyed .... a lot.
   a) -   b) it

8 Would you please .... this case into the boot of the car?
   a) help to lift   b) help me lifting   c) help lift

9 My solicitor has advised .... take legal action.
   a) me to not   b) me not to   c) to me not to   d) me against to

10 I hope your father gets better soon. - Yes, I hope ....
   a) -   b) to   c) it   d) so

11 So you begin university next term. - Yes, I hope ....
   a) -   b) to   c) it

12 One of these days there'll be a terrible accident on this corner. - I .... !
   a) don't hope it   b) don't hope so   c) hope not   d) hope no

13 Our teacher makes us .... very hard!
   a) to work   b) work   c) working

14 Pupils are made .... very hard at this school.
   a) work   b) to work   c) working

15 You have to let your children .... their own way in the end.
   a) to go   b) going   c) go

73 Newspapers, broadcasting, publishing

Choose the best explanation in each case.

1   We use the word *actual* to
a) say that something is 'in the news'.
b) mean 'up to date'.
c) mean 'the thing we are concerned with', as in *the actual day it happened.*

2   An *announcement* in the press is
a) an event like an engagement or a wedding that is made known.
b) a large advertisement of a product which aims to inform and sell.
c) a small advertisement placed by people who are buying and selling things.

3   A *broadcast* is
a) what is put out or transmitted on radio or TV.
b) another word for 'radio waves'.
c) an announcement in the press.

4   If we say that a book has been *edited*, we mean it
a) has been printed, distributed and sold.
b) hasn't been accepted for publication.
c) has been prepared for publication.

5   A *critic* is
a) a person who might write a review of a book or a film in a newspaper.
b) an account of a book or a film that might appear in a newspaper.
c) unfavourable comment on a book or a film that might appear in a newspaper.

6   If you received a *copy* of a book, you would be receiving
a) an example of the kind of publication that is being prepared.
b) a free sample so that you can see what it's like.
c) one book of many that have been published.

7   *Publicity* is the word we use for
a) bringing something to the attention of the public.
b) information that interests the public.
c) propaganda, which is usually political, and often false.

8   A *journal* is
a) a newspaper that comes out on weekdays and/or Sundays.
b) a serious magazine that comes out weekly, monthly, quarterly or yearly.
c) a diary in which you keep a record of day-to-day appointments.

9   The word *bureau* can be used to refer to
a) a room for academic or domestic reading and writing.
b) a room which is devoted to business.
c) an office for collecting and distributing information.

74 'Do', 'make', 'have' and 'take'

Supply the correct forms of *do, make, have* or *take* in Parts A and B.

Part A

1 If you pay in cash, we can .... you a small discount.
2 .... a step towards me.
3 I think you should .... it easy for a while.
4 Please let me know if you have any criticisms to ....
5 Tying a knot in my handkerchief .... me remember what I have to do.
6 Your explanation simply doesn't .... sense.
7 I'm just learning how to .... the steps of the tango.
8 Pesticides .... immense damage to the environment.
9 Overwork finally caused her to .... a nervous breakdown.
10 I can't join you for coffee. I .... a lecture in ten minutes.
11 They .... a row yesterday and aren't on speaking terms.
12 When do the new regulations .... effect?
13 You never .... my side in any argument.
14 Teachers .... a lot of influence on the young.
15 We all spent the evening together and really .... a laugh.
16 I wonder if you could .... me a small favour?
17 First our teacher gives us an explanation, then we .... an exercise.
18 You've .... me a very good turn and I won't forget it.
19 You .... a nerve coming to me for advice!
20 We .... a lot of fog in this part of the country.

Part B

1 I wonder who .... the gardening.
2 Your mother will .... a fit when she sees what you've done to your room!
3 I've applied for a teaching job and I .... an interview tomorrow.
4 How many will be .... part in this play?
5 It's time for me to .... my medicine.
6 She still hasn't got over .... that miscarriage.
7 I can't do it. Why don't you .... a try?
8 I'm .... problems with my car at the moment.
9 The baker got into debt and was .... bankrupt.
10 Silly questions really .... me angry.
11 I've never had to .... such a difficult choice.
12 I .... a small profit on the sale of my car.
13 Matthew .... a degree in engineering two years ago.
14 You should .... advantage of this opportunity.
15 I'm very glad I .... your advice.
16 It's time for us to .... a move.
17 I think I'll .... a short nap.
18 .... a look at this, will you?
19 Something I've eaten has .... a very bad effect on me.
20 Delia .... excellent taste.

75 Education

Supply the best words in Parts A and B.

Part A

			a)		b)	
1	A _schedule_ lists the times of classes, etc.		a)	timetable	b)	schedule
2	When schools close, the children are on ..._holiday_..		a)	leave	b)	holiday
3	Children who live in a school are called _boarders_.		a)	pensioners	b)	boarders
4	The head of a school could be called the ..._principal_..		a)	principal	b)	principle
5	A school for the very young is a ..._nursery_..		a)	kindergarten	b)	nursery
6	The function of a school is to ..._educate_.. children.		a)	educate	b)	bring up
7	You can remove mistakes with a		a)	gum	b)	rubber
8	A .... describes the activities of a school.		a)	prospectus	b)	prospect
9	Have you seen the new ..._programme_..for the exams?		a)	programme	b)	syllabus
10	A student might win one of these. ..._prize_..		a)	a premium	b)	a prize
11	You would do an _experiment_ in a laboratory.		a)	experience	b)	experiment
12	Alexander Fleming _invented_ penicillin.		a)	discovered	b)	invented
13	Some students learn languages with _convenience_.		a)	convenience	b)	ease
14	We're building a car in our ..._laboratory_..		a)	laboratory	b)	workshop
15	After ..._gymnasium_..you can attend university.		a)	gymnasium	b)	grammar school
16	The children sat on ..._benches_.. to watch the match.		a)	benches	b)	banks
17	We're .... for the football match.		a)	training	b)	drilling
18	Write your answers on this ..._sheet_.. .		a)	protocol	b)	sheet
19	You might receive _a report_ at the end of each term.		a)	a reference	b)	a report
20	Universities can only ..._admit_.. a few students.		a)	admit	b)	receive

Part B

			a)		b)	
1	I need to pass my Cambridge First		a)	Certificate	b)	Diploma
2	She's got a .... to do French at Oxford.		a)	position	b)	place
3	Teachers .... so many exercise books!		a)	note	b)	mark
4	Our course provides you with .... experience.		a)	practicable	b)	practical
5	You do this before you take an exam.		a)	revision	b)	repetition
6	High .... requires capital investment.		a)	technique	b)	technology
7	Different .... have edited Shakespeare.		a)	scholars	b)	students
8	What .... did you get for the spelling test?		a)	mark	b)	degree
9	Sh! I want to listen to the		a)	conference	b)	lecture
10	.... lessons are very expensive.		a)	Particular	b)	Private
11	I .... down what the teacher said.		a)	marked	b)	noted
12	My essay was illustrated with a		a)	diagram	b)	scheme
13	Few people add to the sum of human		a)	science	b)	knowledge
14	No one likes to .... an exam.		a)	fail	b)	lose
15	History is my favourite .... at school.		a)	topic	b)	subject
16	.... is treated like any other school subject.		a)	Gymnastics	b)	Exercise
17	.... is the most difficult of all subjects.		a)	Physic	b)	Physics
18	Discipline is the best		a)	politics	b)	policy
19	I don't know how mistakes like this can		a)	rise	b)	arise
20	It's hard to .... into university.		a)	get	b)	enter

76 Buildings, parts of buildings, surroundings

The clues in **A** have answers in **B**. Find and match them. Here's the first one:
A0 a platform on the outside of a building where you can sit → **B**0 balcony

A

0   a platform on the outside of a
    building where you can sit   *B0*

1   a rough place to live in   ....
2   buildings to house the military/
    soldiers   ....
3   You might want to visit the ...
    of the Unknown Soldier   ....
4   builders can't repair a roof without
    this   ....
5   an open-air space in a building   ....
6   nuns live in this kind of building ....
7   you would associate this structure
    with petroleum   ....
8   it's man-made, often decorative,
    and water comes out of it   ....
9   children play in this   ....
10 fine buildings are often built from
    this   ....
11 a place where whisky might be
    made, for example   ....
12 the rear part of a building could be
    referred to as 'the ...'   ....
13 an ancient building like the
    Colosseum may be one of these   ....
14 the modern term for this might be
    'a psychiatric hospital'   ....
15 everyone enjoys a room with
    a ...   .
16 a scientist might conduct
    experiments in this   ....
17 once a year there's a ceremony
    at the War ...   .
18 another word for 'build'   ....
19 a small family hotel   ....
20 a pub where you could also rent
    a room for the night is a ...   .
21 this can be applied to the outside
    surface of a building   ....
22 often a very expensive flat at the
    top of a building   ....

B

0	balcony		
1	asylum	26	pension
2	at the side	27	penthouse
3	back	28	playground
4	backside	29	pub
5	barracks	30	refinery
6	behind	31	relief
7	boarding house	32	rendering
8	construct	33	rock
9	construe	34	roof
10	convent	35	ruin
11	courtyard	36	scaffold
12	direction	37	scaffolding
13	distillery	38	scene
14	fountain	39	scenery
15	grave	40	shack
16	guesthouse	41	shed
17	headquarters	42	sideways
18	home for the old	43	source
19	house	44	spring
20	inn	45	stone
21	laboratory	46	tomb
22	management	47	view
23	memorial	48	workshop
24	monastery	49	wreck
25	monument	50	yard

77 Countable and uncountable nouns

All the nouns in the list below are normally uncountable. For example:

> *We eat a lot of fruit.* (Not *fruits*)

However, thirteen of the nouns have countable uses, sometimes with a change of meaning, especially when we use them in the plural:

> *Exotic **fruits** are easily available these days.* (= different varieties)

Tick the remaining twelve nouns that have countable uses.

advice	jewellery	rock
business	knowledge	rubbish
capital	laughter	scaffolding
china	lightning	scenery
cloth	machinery	thunder
crime	mud	time
equipment	noise	trouble
experience	patience	underwear
~~fruit~~ ✓	poetry	veal
fuel	pollution	wealth
gossip	progress	youth

Write twelve sentences using the plural forms of the nouns you have ticked.

0   *Exotic fruits are easily available these days.*

1   ....

2   ....

3   ....

4   ....

5   ....

6   ....

7   ....

8   ....

9   ....

10 ....

11 ....

12 ....

78 Fear, worry, embarrassment, etc.

Supply the best word or words.

1 Jean gets very .... if her daughter doesn't ring her once a week.
   a) moved   b) agitated   c) shaken

2 I was in a state of .... waiting for my exam results.
   a) agony   b) anxiety

3 Pilots always .... the passengers when there is air turbulence.
   a) alarm   b) alert

4 We're going to have an early night and we don't want to be ....
   a) deranged   b) molested   c) perturbed   d) disturbed   e) deranged

5 He's suffered from poor health all his life and that has made him ....
   a) nervous   b) irritable

6 You came in without knocking and made me jump. You really .... me!
   a) frightened   b) scared   c) startled

7 You can't communicate with her at the moment. She's in a real ....
   a) situation   b) state   c) position   d) condition

8 I got really .... when I didn't hear from you.
   a) preoccupied   b) worried

9 Thank you for waking me up. I was .... a nightmare!
   a) doing   b) making   c) seeing   d) having   e) dreaming

10 I'm glad you've phoned. I've been very .... you.
   a) concerned about   b) concerned with   c) concerning with   d) concerning about

11 My advice is: don't panic; stay ....
   a) calm   b) tranquil   c) peaceful   d) quiet

12 I could see the house had been burgled, but I .... when I went inside.
   a) shocked   b) shocked myself   c) had a shock

13 I wasn't properly dressed for the party and felt .... my appearance.
   a) ashamed for   b) shy of   c) embarrassed about   d) ashamed of

14 I always feel .... if I hear footsteps behind me in a dark and empty street.
   a) shy   b) timid   c) fearful

15 She always .... if you mention a subject that embarrasses her.
   a) reddens   b) goes red   c) reds

79 Crime and punishment

The mistakes in these sentences have been underlined for you. Suggest a correct or better alternative for each mistake in Parts A and B. The first one has been done for you.

Part A

0	The <u>affair</u> remains unsolved.	0	*case*
1	<u>Stealing</u> banks is on the increase.	1	....
2	We must be sure he receives a fair <u>process</u>.	2	....
3	They found the <u>corps</u> in the garden.	3	....
4	Many people have bought <u>false</u> Dali paintings.	4	....
5	The police <u>examined</u> the suspect for ten hours.	5	....
6	There are <u>austere</u> penalties for dangerous driving.	6	....
7	The little boy was able to <u>make</u> us a good description.	7	....
8	The most <u>famous</u> criminals used to be held on Alcatraz.	8	....
9	Everyone agrees the judge's decision was <u>exact</u>.	9	....
10	How can you <u>test</u> this man is guilty?	10	....
11	Can you <u>acknowledge</u> the person in this photo?	11	....
12	His strange behaviour <u>raised</u> my suspicions.	12	....
13	She <u>refuses</u> all knowledge of what happened.	13	....
14	The police <u>searched</u> the missing boy for ten days.	14	....
15	Will this <u>proof</u> stand up in court?	15	....
16	Some young people disappear without <u>track</u>.	16	....
17	The police have been <u>remarking</u> his movements.	17	....
18	He has <u>evaded</u> from prison several times.	18	....
19	The <u>sentence</u> was 'Not Guilty'.	19	....
20	Murderers aren't often <u>hung</u> these days.	20	....

Part B

1	The gang specialized in <u>robbing</u> bikes and selling them.	1	....
2	I dialled a <u>false</u> number.	2	....
3	I saw a <u>suspected</u> person outside the shop.	3	....
4	You can't <u>do</u> an accusation without proof.	4	....
5	It will be two weeks before the <u>injury</u> heals.	5	....
6	She received a life <u>verdict</u> for murder.	6	....
7	I'm going to conduct my own <u>apology</u>.	7	....
8	She was <u>held</u> stealing goods at a department store.	8	....
9	The murderer <u>choked</u> his victim with a stocking.	9	....
10	There's a big police <u>chase</u> for the criminals.	10	....
11	He was <u>convicted</u> to death.	11	....
12	I was sued and had to pay <u>damage</u> of £500.	12	....
13	We have a list of missing <u>peoples</u>.	13	....
14	These new credit cards are easy to <u>imitate</u>.	14	....
15	A lie is intended to <u>cheat</u> someone.	15	....
16	When does the murder <u>try</u> begin?	16	....
17	Laws are <u>done</u> to be broken.	17	....
18	The <u>innocents</u> were punished along with the guilty.	18	....
19	Someone has <u>roused</u> the alarm.	19	....

80 Clothes, materials, etc.

Supply the best words in Parts A and B.

Part A

1	You often find these on shoes.	a) shoelaces	b) cordons
2	A monk might wear a	a) costume	b) habit
3	A man's three-piece suit includes a	a) waistcoat	b) vest
4	A .... is a bit of thin material covering the face.	a) veil	b) shawl
5	36 .... is a woman's chest measurement.	a) bust	b) breast
6	Items of clothing that go together are	a) assorted	b) matching
7	You're having a suit made, so you have a	a) fitting	b) fit
8	If it's the right size for you, it .... you.	a) fits	b) suits
9	If something looks good on you, it .... you.	a) matches	b) suits
10	Up-to-date clothes are this.	a) fashionable	b) chick
11	Clothes you feel easy in are this.	a) comfortable	b) convenient
12	Jackets are often .... with satin.	a) lined	b) doubled
13	Costume jewellery is	a) imitation	b) forged
14	A new skirt might be .... from bits and pieces.	a) made up	b) formed
15	A silk blouse is made .... silk.	a) of	b) with
16	If everyone's wearing it, it must be in	a) mode	b) fashion
17	Shoes are usually made of	a) skin	b) leather
18	A stylish piece of clothing may be	a) snob	b) elegant
19	You often make curtains out of heavy	a) stuff	b) material
20	I think that dress is quite .... for you.	a) wrong	b) mistaken

Part B

1	A woman might wear a .... in her hair.	a) ribbon	b) tape
2	Damaged clothing needs to be	a) corrected	b) repaired
3	When we wear clothes, they	a) get dirty	b) dirty
4	Clothes often .... in the wash.	a) enlarge	b) stretch
5	You can make a dress from a paper	a) patron	b) pattern
6	You might use a .... on a baby's nappy.	a) safety pin	b) pin
7	It's easy to drop a .... when you're knitting.	a) stitch	b) point
8	I've .... that button on for you.	a) sown	b) sewn
9	A thing becomes smaller in the wash; it	a) gathers	b) shrinks
10	Boys and girls are taught how to .... sewing.	a) make	b) do
11	Just look at the .... of your clothes!	a) situation	b) state
12	How did you get that .... on your tie?	a) spot	b) speck
13	Let me .... your jacket.	a) sweep	b) brush
14	.... coming out of the washing machine!	a) Sud is	b) Suds are
15	I'll have to .... my skirt at the waist.	a) widen	b) let out
16	It only takes a spot of oil to .... a tie.	a) ruin	b) wreck
17	It's often very hard to .... what you want.	a) choose	b) elect
18	You can .... a costume for the party.	a) hire	b) rent
19	I can't .... which one I want.	a) decide	b) determine
20	I'll try it on in the	a) cabin	b) cubicle

81 Are you a hypochondriac?

Supply the best word or words.

1 Hypochondriacs are healthy people who imagine they are .... serious illnesses.
    a) suffering from   b) enduring

2 Do you often visit the doctor's .... ?
    a) surgery   b) office

3 Do you often imagine you will be killed in a .... accident?
    a) mortal   b) fatal

4 Have you ever experienced .... pain?
    a) intensive   b) intense

5 Do you think you might suddenly drop dead from a heart .... ?
    a) insult   b) attack

6 Do you think you need to see .... ?
    a) an expert   b) a specialist

7 Do you sometimes feel you have a mysterious .... in the chest?
    a) ache   b) pain

8 Do you ever find it difficult to .... ?
    a) breath   b) breathe

9 Do you often .... of mysterious headaches?
    a) protest   b) complain

10 Are you losing your ....?
    a) remembrance   b) memory

11 Do you constantly feel .... ?
    a) exhausted   b) exhausting

12 When you get up in the morning, do you usually feel .... ?
    a) poorly   b) sickly

13 Do even the smallest things .... ?
    a) get on your nerves   b) enervate you

14 If you have a cough, are you convinced you have a bad case of .... ?
    a) grippe   b) flu

15 Do you imagine you have .... ?
    a) temperature   b) a fever

16 If you are in a crowd, are you afraid you will .... a cold?
    a) pick   b) pick up

17 Do you wash your hands all the time because you are afraid of .... ?
    a) microbes   b) germs

18 Do you only eat things that are .... for you?
    a) hygienic   b) good

19 Do you think that lack of sleep will .... you?
    a) harm   b) hurt

20 Do you have bad .... ?
    a) flesh   b) skin

21 Do you worry about .... on your face?
    a) spots   b) specks

22 Are you convinced that life is a fatal .... ?
    a) disease   b) decease

82 Housework, gardening, maintenance

Supply the words asked for in the clues. The first one has been done for you.

0 What 4-letter verb beginning with T means 'put things in order'?   0   *tidy*

1 What adjective beginning with G and ending in Y
means 'covered with cold solid fat'? (6 letters)   1   ....

2 What adjective beginning with H and ending in -IC describes
conditions in a kitchen, etc., which are germ-free? (8 letters)   2   ....

3 What noun beginning with P and ending in -CE refers to
items such as fruit and vegetables grown as food? (7 letters)   3   ....

4 What noun (4 letters) beginning with T describes an
object like a hammer, used for general handiwork?   4   ....

5 What 12-letter noun beginning with C and ending in -TION
describes steam turning into water on a cold surface?   5   ....

6 What verb beginning with R means to fix something
that is broken? (6 letters)   6   ....

7 What adjective beginning with D describes the condition
of, say, clothes which are slightly wet? (4 letters)   7   ....

8 What noun (9 letters) beginning REND- describes
a paint with a cement base used on outside walls?   8   ....

9 What verb beginning FUMI- describes the act of treating
with chemical smoke to kill germs, insects, etc.? (8 letters)   9   ....

10 What 3-letter verb beginning with F means the same as
'repair'?   10   ....

11 What noun (5 letters) beginning with D and ending with R
describes the style and appearance of a room, for example?   11   ....

12 What noun P - - D describes a man-made area of water you
might find in a garden?   12   ....

13 What noun beginning with M and ending in -URE would
you use to describe water held in soil? (8 letters)   13   ....

14 What verb (4 letters) beginning with P would you use to
describe the act of taking flowers that are growing?   14   ....

15 What verb S - - - P means to use a broom?   15   ....

16 What noun M - - S describes conditions
that are dirty and untidy in, say, a kitchen?   16   ....

17 What noun T - - - - - MAN describes a person who
lives by buying and selling, e.g. in a shop?   17   ....

18 What 4-letter noun, plural in form, beginning with S
describes the foam made by soap in a washing machine?   18   ....

19 What 5-letter verb beginning with C describes the
noise floorboards might make when you walk on them?   19   ....

20 What verb beginning with A and ending -GE describes
the way you put flowers into a vase artistically? (7 letters)   20   ....

21 What noun L - C - - ER describes paint or varnish
that dries to a hard shiny surface?   21   ....

22 What verb S - - - PE describes what you might
do to the bottom of a pan to remove burnt-on food?   22   ....

83 Degree and intensifying

These words will fit into the spaces below. Choose the right word or words for each sentence.

> at all deeply extra far fully greatly honestly highly indeed largely most
> mostly not much real so specially strongly such a true very much widely

1 These shelves have been .... designed to fit into this space.
2 They claim it's Diana's .... story.
3 I'm m.................... at home in the evenings.
4 Health care in our district has been g.................... improved.
5 The government is .... responsible for the present state of the nation.
6 It's your birthday, so I've prepared something .... special for dinner.
7 I've received a final demand even though the bill has been .... paid.
8 Finding hotel accommodation in the high season can be a .... nightmare.
9 Air fares are .... less expensive if you fly mid-week.
10 The plane was .... crowded, there wasn't a single empty seat.
11 The musical was .... disaster it only ran for a week.
12 I've been having treatment for a week, but I'm .... better.
13 Can anyone .... believe the earth is flat?
14 You shouldn't worry about it. It doesn't matter ....
15 We're m.................... grateful for your help.
16 Thank you very much .... for taking care of our house while we were away.
17 David Bellamy is .... known as an environmentalist.
18 Mrs Grey has been .... alone since her daughter went away.
19 We .... support the Green Party.
20 We .... regret the inconvenience you have been caused.
21 Truffles are hard to find and .... prized.

84 -ic/-ical

These words will fit into the spaces below. Choose the right word for each sentence.

> art artistic classic classical dramatic electric electrical electronic historic
> historical magic magical tragic

1 'Between you and I' is a .... mistake in grammar.
2 .... accidents occur daily on our motorways.
3 Sally can paint, but I have no .... talents at all.
4 Many people believe the fire was caused by an .... fault.
5 This photograph of Churchill, Roosevelt and Stalin captures a .... moment.
6 .... music is appreciated by a very wide audience.
7 You can control the whole system with this .... button.
8 The .... records of that pre-war period are now available to the public.
9 You can't keep warm with a small .... fire.
10 Many of the .... treasures stolen during the war have never been recovered.
11 They use lights to create .... effects on the stage.
12 It was a .... win in the last two minutes' of play.
13 You can play amazing music on an .... keyboard.

85 Inversion after negative adverbs

Re-write these sentences using the words provided and making necessary changes.

1　We can't offer a discount for our services on any account.
　On no account ....
2　We had hardly left the house when we had to go back for our passports.
　Hardly ....
3　John little realizes just what it's going to be like working in a restaurant kitchen.
　Little ....
4　There have never been so many beggars on the streets.
　Never ....
5　We not only missed our plane, we had to spend a night at the airport as well.
　Not only ....
6　I had no sooner complained than the parcel arrived.
　No sooner ....
7　You seldom see so many people trying to get tickets.
　Seldom ....
8　You will understand what true responsibility is only when you become a parent.
　Only when ....
9　They mustn't be allowed to come in on any condition.
　On no condition ....
10　I have no idea what happened to him, and I don't care, either.
　I have no idea what happened to him and neither ....
11　We realized, only then, what a mess we had got ourselves into.
　Only then ....
12　You rarely see this variety of butterfly any more.
　Rarely ....
13　You shouldn't reply to this letter in any circumstances.
　In no circumstances ....

86 Adjective + preposition

Supply suitable prepositions.

1　It's time she ceased to be so dependent .... her parents.
2　You don't want to get involved .... that kind of business.
3　He now has an excellent job and is independent .... his parents.
4　He was convicted .... burglary and sentenced to three years in prison.
5　We're really indebted .... you for all the help you've given us.
6　The concert hall was filled .... music students.
7　I don't think I'm very susceptible .... advertising.
8　He's incapable .... even driving a nail in straight.
9　We were all surprised .... their sudden decision to leave the district.
10　How long has she been married .... him?
11　I'm afraid Kirsty is jealous .... her younger sister.
12　The committee is composed mainly .... local tradesmen.
13　It's immaterial .... me whether our neighbours approve or not.
14　He denies he's guilty .... spreading rumours.

87 Words easily confused, misspelt, etc.

Supply the best words in Parts A and B.

Part A

1	We'd like .... bills please.	a) seperate	b) separate
2	When were you .... ?	a) borne	b) born
3	Open the window. I can't .... !	a) breathe	b) breath
4	Have you ever visited the British .... ?	a) Council	b) Counsel
5	The greatest problems are poverty and	a) disease	b) decease
6	Which ones have you .... ?	a) choosen	b) chosen
7	We're not .... on anybody.	a) dependant	b) dependent
8	Wipe up the mess with this	a) cloth	b) clothe
9	There are very strong .... in the Pacific.	a) currents	b) currants
10	She looks rather .... in her new outfit.	a) chick	b) chic
11	I seem to have .... a cough.	a) developped	b) developed
12	I might have .... a company director by now.	a) being	b) been
13	We've got some nice .... cakes.	a) housemade	b) homemade
14	How can we improve the .... condition?	a) human	b) humane
15	It's a question of	a) principle	b) principal
16	I .... up early every morning.	a) get	b) use to get
17	She certainly has plenty of	a) stile	b) style
18	Those who agree, please .... their hands.	a) raise	b) rise
19	What a small .... you have.	a) waist	b) waste
20	I .... what the time is.	a) wonder	b) wander

Part B

1	What would you .... ?	a) advise	b) advice
2	You can be banned from driving for being	a) drunken	b) drunk
3	Pay no attention if he .... at you.	a) gets mad	b) maddens
4	Goodnight. I'm going upstairs to	a) bed	b) sleep
5	Sh! .... now.	a) Go to sleep	b) Go asleep
6	I've had a lovely .... and I feel quite fresh.	a) relax	b) rest
7	Tell me the .... !	a) true	b) truth
8	It was only a mild	a) flirtation	b) flirt
9	This is our new recreation centre for the	a) young	b) youngs
10	Don't be so .... with your money!	a) miser	b) mean
11	Men often get bald in their middle	a) ages	b) years
12	I was .... fright.	a) sick with	b) sick of
13	Joan .... when she was quite young.	a) greyed	b) went grey
14	Don't be so .... !	a) foolish	b) fool
15	.... your belt.	a) Get tight	b) Tighten
16	I was overcome by a sense of	a) loneliness	b) lonely
17	What can prevent the .... of the rain forests?	a) destruction	b) destroy
18	English is different .... German.	a) than	b) from
19	Are you afraid .... the dark?	a) -	b) of
20	He published a magazine called 'The .... '.	a) Selfish	b) Egoist

88 Experiences, perception, thought

Supply the best word or words.

1 If you overhear someone, you ....
   a) hear something by accident   b) understand something wrongly   c) fail to hear

2 If you sympathize with someone, you ....
   a) like them very much   b) love them   c) share their emotions

3 If you're conscientious, you ....
   a) are awake   b) know right from wrong   c) do things seriously and with care

4 Remarking has to do with ....
   a) seeing   b) saying   c) thinking

5 A sentimental person ....
   a) has strong feelings   b) arouses strong feelings   c) has feelings that aren't deep

6 You are in love, so you have ....
   a) strong sentiments   b) strong feelings   c) deep senses

7 You had to survive without food and water for several days, so you had ....
   a) a terrible adventure   b) a terrible experience   c) a terrible experiment

8 If you recognize someone, you ....
   a) see who they are   b) say who they are   c) see them differently

9 You can see someone in your mind's eye. You have an .... of them.
   a) icon   b) image

10 You're very anxious. You have .... of anxiety.
   a) a sense   b) an impression

11 If you're gazing at something you're looking at it ....
   a) steadily   b) with your mouth open   c) in a way that causes offence

12 Which of these words warns you of danger? ....
   a) Care!   b) Attention!   c) Caution!

13 If something is curious to you, it seems ....
   a) unusual   b) foreign   c) exceptional

14 If you are curious about something, you are ....
   a) peculiar   b) foreign   c) eager to know about it   d) anxious

15 If you perceive something, you .... it.
   a) imagine   b) notice   c) think about   d) have ideas about

89 What sort of person are you?

Tick (✓) a) or b) on the right of each exercise.

1 A sensitive person is one who
....
a) is very aware of other people's feelings
b) has good sense and judgement

2 If you fantasize about things, you
....
a) daydream about the impossible
b) often dream when you sleep

3 You're a reasonable person, so you're
....
a) logical
b) just and fair

4 You have a lot of curiosity, so you
....
a) are a very strange person
b) like to know about everything

5 You revise your opinions. You
....
a) change them
b) look at them again

6 You recall things that happen, so you
have ....
a) a lot of souvenirs
b) a good memory

7 If you make sense of things, you
....
a) know they are sensible
b) can understand things easily

8 You always calculate what things
cost, so you ....
a) work things out accurately
b) make a good guess.

9 You're easily moved, so you
....
a) like to go from place to place
b) are emotional

10 You're a mature person, so you're
....
a) grown up
b) ripe

11 You're capable of affection, so you
....
a) like to impress others
b) have feelings of love for people

12 You're frank, so you ....
a) like to tell the truth
b) don't steal, cheat or lie

13 You don't like people who are
vulgar because ....
a) they behave badly
b) they are ordinary

14 You have a genial nature, so you
are ....
a) very talented
b) cheerful and friendly

90 Politics and government

The mistakes in these sentences have been underlined for you. Suggest a correct or better alternative for each mistake in Parts A and B. The first one has been done for you.

Part A

0	The new law <u>effects</u> today.	0	*comes into effect*
1	The paper is running <u>an action</u> against the new privacy laws.	1	....
2	Are you interested in British <u>civilization</u>?	2	....
3	The Minister was the victim of a <u>combine</u> against him.	3	....
4	We're electing a new party <u>conductor</u>.	4	....
5	We must <u>join ourselves</u> to win the next election.	5	....
6	Are you a member of the <u>Preservative</u> Party?	6	....
7	They'll have to <u>control</u> your passport before they let you in.	7	....
8	<u>Conversations</u> about trade agreements are continuing.	8	....
9	They've set up centres to <u>council</u> the unemployed.	9	....
10	Has he got the necessary qualities to <u>direct</u> the country?	10	....
11	The government was <u>chosen</u> with a small majority.	11	....
12	She's one of the greatest <u>faces</u> in modern politics.	12	....
13	Are you a member of the Labour <u>Faction</u>?	13	....
14	The <u>folk</u> will be voting on May 14th.	14	....
15	Dictators have a lot of <u>craft</u>.	15	....
16	What is the basis of political <u>force</u>?	16	....
17	A dictator rules by <u>strength</u>.	17	....
18	Do you know all the words of our National <u>Hymn</u>?	18	....
19	The great <u>forces</u> decide the destiny of smaller nations.	19	....
20	We pay <u>imposition</u> on everything.	20	....

Part B

1	An <u>industrious</u> nation needs a lot of capital investment.	1	....
2	Civil service departments are full of <u>plot</u>.	2	....
3	Paris was <u>discharged</u> in 1945 by the allied forces.	3	....
4	The <u>most</u> of people are in favour of a change in the law.	4	....
5	There's been a peaceful <u>manifestation</u> against motorways.	5	....
6	What is the date of the annual party <u>lecture</u>?	6	....
7	You have to tackle <u>misery</u> before you tackle crime.	7	....
8	The German <u>country</u> is a formidable force in Europe.	8	....
9	She's been <u>named</u> to lead the party into the next election.	9	....
10	Whose <u>part</u> are you on?	10	....
11	I'm enjoying <u>peasant</u> life now I've moved out of London.	11	....
12	It's government by the <u>peoples</u> for the <u>peoples</u>.	12	....
13	What's your political <u>conviction</u>?	13	....
14	<u>Politic</u> is central to the study of history.	14	....
15	A government must <u>reign</u> or resign.	15	....
16	Britain has a <u>republican</u> government.	16	....
17	The way we are governed affects the whole of <u>community</u>.	17	....
18	Britain is a small country which is divided into <u>lands</u>.	18	....
19	Trade <u>Syndicates</u> defend workers' interests.	19	....

91 Stative and dynamic uses of certain verbs

All the verbs in the list below are often used in simple tenses. For example:

John *sees* very well without glasses. (Not *is seeing*)

However, thirteen of the verbs can be used quite easily in the progressive, sometimes with a change of meaning:

John **is seeing** his dentist on Wednesday. (= has an appointment with)

Tick the remaining twelve verbs that can be used in the progressive.

admire	desire	imagine
appear	detest	matter
believe	differ	measure
belong	disagree	need
concern	disbelieve	own
consider	dislike	possess
consist	envy	say
contain	excel	see ✓
correspond with	fear	think
cost	feel	want
deserve	hope	weigh

Write twelve sentences using the present progressive with the verbs you have ticked.

0 *John is seeing his dentist on Wednesday.*

1 ....

2 ....

3 ....

4 ....

5 ....

6 ....

7 ....

8 ....

9 ....

10 ....

11 ....

12 ....

92 Travelling

Supply the words asked for in the clues. The first one has been done for you.

0 What adjective beginning with S describes a vehicle that isn't moving? (10 letters)

0 *stationary*

1 What 5-letter verb beginning with P means to 'drive' a plane?

1 ....

2 What 6-letter noun beginning with F and ending with L is found on a ship and often has smoke coming out of it?

2 ....

3 What verb B - - - D describes what we do when we get on a plane?

3 ....

4 What noun B - - - - T is the name of a shop on a train where you can buy food over the counter?

4 ....

5 What verb E - - - - - - E describes what people do when they leave their country to live in another country?

5 ....

6 What noun beginning with S goes in front of *belt* to describe what you have to wear on a car journey?

6 ....

7 What noun (6 letters) beginning with A goes after *travel* to describe an office which provides travel services?

7 ....

8 What noun beginning with C and ending in H is the name of a bus for long-distance travelling? (5 letters)

8 ....

9 What adverb beginning with A is the general word which means 'outside this country'? (6 letters)

9 ....

10 What noun beginning with S is the name of a special compartment in a train in which you can sleep?

10 ....

11 What noun beginning with P and ending in N describes a person getting around on foot? (10 letters)

11 ....

12 What adjective P - N - - - - L describes the arrival or departure of someone or something that is on time?

12 ....

13 What 4-letter adjective beginning with S describes what you feel when you are suffering from nausea?

13 ....

14 What 5-letter adjective beginning with V and ending in D describes a passport or a ticket that can be legally used?

14 ....

15 What 6-letter verb beginning with E and ending in K means to begin a journey on a ship?

15 ....

16 What 4-letter verb beginning with M describes failure to be on time for the departure of a train, bus, etc.?

16 ....

17 What verb beginning with C describes what an official does when he or she looks at your passport?

17 ....

18 A sea-journey = V - - - - - .

18 ....

19 What 5-letter noun beginning with C describes the sleeping accommodation you get on a ship?

19 ....

20 What noun beginning with F and ending in R describes the line that separates one country from another? (8 letters)

20 ....

21 What verb I - - - - - - - E describes entering a country which is not your own in order to live there?

21 ....

22 England is separated from France by a stretch of water called the English C - - - - - - .

22 ....

93 Prepositional phrases

Supply the missing prepositions in Parts A and B.

Part A

1 No one enjoys being .... debt.
2 There's so much .... offer, you hardly know what to choose.
3 She twisted her ankle and was .... terrible pain.
4 The Wentworths have sold their business .... a huge profit.
5 .... average there are more than a hundred fatal accidents each year.
6 Do you mind if I pay .... cheque?
7 I never worry when I have to be in the house .... my own.
8 Apparently, you have to apply for a visa .... person.
9 We haven't dealt with your application yet, but it is .... hand.
10 The police will have to get into the building .... force if necessary.
11 My car's .... your disposal any time you'd like to use it.
12 Has there been much news .... the time we've been away?
13 We didn't realize what was happening .... first.
14 There's a dramatic scene .... the beginning of the film.
15 You have to write an account of the accident .... detail.
16 Never overtake when .... doubt.
17 We couldn't get past because there was a broken-down truck .... our way.
18 We had to ask for directions several times .... our way here.
19 You're allowed to have these goods .... approval for ten days.
20 How long have you been .... this diet?

Part B

1 You should play according .... the rules.
2 They're rarely seen .... public these days.
3 We're .... a loss to know what to do next.
4 Let me tell you the news .... brief.
5 I think I've dialled the wrong number .... mistake.
6 It's really .... her credit that her children have done so well.
7 Please write out your name .... full.
8 Please try not to be late .... future.
9 There's no place .... earth that isn't affected by pollution.
10 It's his aim .... life to be a millionaire by the time he's 21.
11 I'll be visiting the USA .... the very first time.
12 Are these books arranged .... any kind of order?
13 You can be sure I didn't knock the teapot over .... purpose!
14 I'm afraid you can't speak to her now. She's .... conference.
15 He's .... leave at the moment but will be returning to his regiment next week.
16 They're throwing a party .... our honour!
17 What's the biggest dam .... the world?
18 Don't answer the phone .... any account.
19 We'd like to present you with this watch .... behalf of the company.
20 Mrs Willis is away .... business at the moment.

94 Cars, driving, maintenance, traffic

Supply the best words in Parts A and B.

Part A

1 You buy a car from a	a) merchant	b) dealer
2 You can't drive without a	a) licence	b) diploma
3 You pay a lot for a .... model.	a) luxurious	b) luxury
4 Fasten your .... belts.	a) security	b) safety
5 .... costs a lot of money.	a) Assurance	b) Insurance
6 What .... is your car?	a) mark	b) make
7 Where do you keep your .... ?	a) spare tyre	b) reserve
8 How many litres does your .... hold?	a) tank	b) reservoir
9 How loud is your .... ?	a) horn	b) corn
10 You need a parking .... to park here.	a) permission	b) permit
11 I always carry a .... key.	a) double	b) duplicate
12 Take good care of your	a) tyres	b) rubbers
13 I was .... by roadworks on a motorway.	a) blocked	b) held up
14 The .... today is very heavy.	a) circulation	b) traffic
15 You need real .... to drive a vehicle.	a) art	b) skill
16 Be careful when you're .... !	a) taking over	b) overtaking
17 There's so much .... on modern roads!	a) traffic	b) motion
18 I've lost my way. Can you give me .... please?	a) instructions	b) directions
19 Turn left, then follow the	a) placards	b) signs
20 We go this way. It says, 'All Other .... '.	a) Routes	b) Directions

Part B

1 What's the speed .... ?	a) limitation	b) limit
2 There's a .... vehicle in front of us.	a) stationary	b) stationery
3 What's the quickest .... to the town centre?	a) road	b) route
4 It isn't easy to .... a big car into a small space.	a) pilot	b) steer
5 Look first, then .... !	a) sign	b) signal
6 We can only go fast if the roads are	a) clear	b) clean
7 .... your tyres frequently.	a) Control	b) Check
8 I lost control and hit the	a) kerb	b) edge
9 What do you do if a tyre .... ?	a) blows up	b) bursts
10 Most taxis have .... engines.	a) benzine	b) diesel
11 I drove into a wall and .... the car.	a) ruined	b) wrecked
12 My car has a big	a) machine	b) engine
13 Turn off the lights or you'll .... your battery.	a) discharge	b) unload
14 The cost of .... is frightening.	a) reparations	b) repairs
15 Does your car .... on diesel?	a) run	b) function
16 .... you've got enough fuel.	a) Assure	b) Make sure
17 I can't shake hands. I'm covered in	a) grass	b) grease
18 We'll have to .... the engine.	a) overhaul	b) revise
19 There's a .... in the system somewhere.	a) mistake	b) fault
20 My tank's nearly	a) empty	b) vacant

95 Referring to facts, the truth

Choose the best explanation in each case.

1   If you say that a person is *disinterested*, you mean he or she
a)   has lost interest in something.
b)   is not interested in something.
c)   has no personal bias when making a decision.

2   *Evidence* is
a)   information that might be produced in court to support a case.
b)   a statement in court which does not require any proof.
c)   something that is extremely obvious to everybody.

3   We would use the word *effectively*
a)   to say that a person really did something.
b)   to describe an activity that produced good results.
c)   like *indeed*, to add emphasis to what we say.

4   If you *verify* something, you
a)   confirm or show that it is true.
b)   examine it closely.
c)   consider it carefully.

5   *Curiosity* refers to
a)   the quality of wanting to know about people and things.
b)   the strangeness of people and things.
c)   a quality of being peculiar or exotic.

6   *Fantasy* refers to
a)   dreams that can't be realized.
b)   the power to make the imagined seem real.
c)   creations that are quite original.

7   You could use the word *logical* to describe, for example,
a)   a just or fair request for a rise in salary.
b)   a sensible investment of money.
c)   a well-argued case.

8   A person who is *interrogated* is probably someone who
a)   has been arrested by the police.
b)   is applying for a job.
c)   is being examined by a doctor.

9   A *rumour* refers to
a)   information that is passed around which may or may not be true.
b)   the reputation of a person who is known to a lot of people.
c)   the qualities that make up a person's character.

96 A campaign against litter

Read this text. If you find a mistake in a line, cross it out and suggest an alternative. If there is no mistake, put a tick (✓). The first two have been done for you.

Our local council is conducting ~~an action~~	0	*a campaign*
to reduce the amount of litter in our streets.	0	✓
We are all being encouraged to pick	1	....
any rubbish we see laying in the street	2	....
and fetch it to the nearest litter bin.	3	....
If we see anyone drop litter in the street,	4	....
we're supposed to tell them to collect it.	5	....
Council workers regularly brush the streets	6	....
and collect rubbish from big green bins.	7	....
There are large posters everywhere which say:	8	....
'Do a good act today! Keep our streets	9	....
clear! Don't be a litterbug!'	10	....
Of course, it isn't easy to tell people	11	....
what to do. A lot of people object to be	12	....
told to pick up their rubbishes.	13	....
The problem is extremely bad out of	14	....
fast food restaurants. Though these restaurants kindly	15	....
supply large bins, a lot of people	16	....
neglect them and leave their litter in the street.	17	....
The consumption of food at these places is	18	....
very great, so it is difficult to control	19	....
garbage disposition. Girl guides	20	....
and boy scouts have volunteered to make an example	21	....
to others. If these girls and boys see	22	....
anyone letting something to drop	23	....
they directly pick it up and then they speak	24	....
very politely to the person who dropped it.	25	....
'I think this belongs to you,' they say, handing it back.	26	....
Even the biggest litterbugs feel shy of themselves.	27	....
They usually redden and accept the litter.	28	....
They also accept to dispose of it properly	29	....
and immediately search the nearest rubbish bin.	30	....
The other day I saw a young mother with her little boy.	31	....
The boy picked up a dirty ice-cream carton and	32	....
his mother said, 'That's dirty! Throw it!'	33	....
A boy scout who was following them said,	34	....
'No. Give it to me. I'll put it in a bin for you.'	35	....
The young mother angered. 'I can do that myself,'	36	....
she said and she took the carton from the scout.	37	....
Then she decided to give a good example to her son.	38	....
'We must take place in this campaign, too!' she said.	39	....
She thanked the scout for being so genteel	40	....
and he thanked her, too. There's not doubt	41	....
the counsel's campaign is going to be a great success.	42	....

Answer Key

1 Social exchanges
1a 2b (a AmE) 3a 4b 5b 6b
7b 8b 9b 10a 11c 12d 13b
14c 15b

2 Cars and driving
1c 2a 3a 4a 5d 6a 7c 8b 9b
10a 11b 12a 13c 14a 15b 16a
17a 18a 19b 20a 21c 22d

3 Adjectives: opposites
1 wet 2 strong 3 tough 4 empty
5 hollow 6 young 7 new 8 fresh
9 warm 10 hot 11 married
12 dead 13 short 14 short
15 closed 16 wrong 17 low
18 healthy 19 soft/quiet
20 quiet/soft 21 thick 22 small

4 Adjectives and noun modifiers
1 Glass 2 glassy 3 gold 4 golden
5 silvery 6 silver 7 stone 8 stony
9 Steel 10 steely 11 lead
12 leaden 13 woollen (woolen AmE)
14 wool 15 woollen (woolen AmE)
16 wooden

5 Asking, requesting, commanding
1b 2a 3b 4c 5a 6d 7b

6 Telephoning
1d 2a 3a 4d 5a 6a

7 Appearance, etc., of people and things
1k 2n 3p 4o 5g 6b 7i 8d 9q
10r 11c 12l 13s 14t 15e 16j
17m 18a 19f 20h

8 Descriptions, etc.
1a 2b 3a 4a 5b 6b 7a 8b 9a
10b 11a 12b 13a 14b 15a 16a
17b 18b

9 Containers
1 parcel 2 wallet 3 jar 4 tube
5 bowl 6 cap 7 carrier bag 8 sack
9 coffer 10 schoolbag 11 suitcase
12 purse

10 Countable and uncountable nouns
1c 2e 3b 4a 5b 6b 7a 8b 9a
10a 11c 12b 13b 14b 15a

11 Time and frequency
Part A
1a 2b 3a 4b 5b 6b 7b 8b 9a
10a 11a 12a 13b 14b 15b 16a
17b 18b 19b 20b
Part B
1b 2b 3a 4b 5b 6b 7b 8a 9b
10a 11a 12a 13b 14b 15a 16b
17b 18a 19b 20a

12 Health
1 pains 2 get hot 3 get cold 4 am
not hungry 5 getting thin(ner) 6 get
tired 7 sore throat 8 get better
9 worse 10 examined
11 prescription 12 chemist's 13 all
right (preferably) 14 asked
15 advice 16 take 17 fresh
18 well 19 nurse 20 patient

13 Holidays
1b 2a 3a 4a 5b 6b 7a 8a 9a
10a 11a 12a 13a 14b 15b 16a

14 'Be', 'get', 'go', 'make', etc.
1b 2a 3b 4b 5b 6c 7b 8c 9a
10a 11b 12a 13b 14b 15b

15 Work and jobs
1t 2c 3k 4i 5j 6o 7f 8p 9b
10q 11a 12h 13m 14n 15e 16s
17g 18l 19d 20r

16 Buildings and parts of buildings
1b 2b 3a 4b 5a (b AmE) 6a 7a
8a 9b 10b 11a 12b 13b 14a
15b (a AmE) 16a 17a 18b

17 Verbs/verb phrases with and without prepositions
Part A
1 with 2 - 3 - 4 at 5 - 6 -
7 of/about 8 - 9 - 10 for 11 into
12 - 13 - 14 - 15 - 16 to 17 for
18 to 19 to 20 to
Part B
1 to 2 to 3 into 4 - 5 to 6 -
7 against/with 8 to 9 as
10 of/about 11 - 12 - 13 to 14 to
15 at 16 - 17 - 18 of 19 in
20 about

18 Occupations, etc.
1c 2d 3a 4b 5b 6b 7a 8b 9b
10a 11b 12a 13a 14b 15b

19 Words easily confused, misspelt, etc.
Part A
1a 2a 3a 4a 5b 6a 7b 8b 9b
10b 11a 12a 13b 14b 15b 16b
17a 18a 19b 20b
Part B
1b 2a 3a 4a 5b 6b 7b 8a 9a
10b 11b 12a 13b 14a 15b 16b
17b 18b 19b 20b

20 Prepositional phrases
1 on 2 on/in 3 to 4 in 5 - 6 at
7 by 8 in 9 with 10 to 11 in
12 at 13 in 14 to 15 on

21 Only one negative
1 There *aren't any* people ... 2 It *was
no* surprise ... 3 I *haven't* done
anything ... 4 I *have* seen *no one* ...
5 ... *with no* help ... 6 I *have* been
nowhere ... 7 It *isn't/It's* not
anybody ... 8 *without any* money ...
9 You *can* trust *nobody* ...

22 -ed/-ing
1a 2b 3a 4b 5b 6a 7a 8a

23 Addressing people
1a 2c 3a 4c 5b 6b 7a 8a 9b
10c

24 Names of places
1b 2a (c AmE) 3c

25 Doing things for people
1 gave me 2 explained to me 3 paid
attention to/listened to 4 to bed
5 spend 6 read him 7 bring/fetch
8 say 9 looked after

26 Movement to and from
1b 2b 3b 4a 5c 6b 7d 8b 9b

27 The human body
1 hair 2 face 3 teeth 4 neck
5 arm 6 hand 7 leg 8 foot

28 Furniture
1 bookcase 2 chair 3 cushion
4 desk 5 lamp 6 clock
7 washbasin

29 Money
1a 2c 3a 4a 5b 6a 7b 8d 9b
10a 11a 12a 13c 14a 15b

30 Adverbs

1 ✓ 2 ~~lately~~/late 3 ~~good~~/well 4 ✓
5 ✓ 6 ~~slow~~/slowly 7 ~~quick~~/quickly
8 ✓ 9 ✓ 10 ✓

31 Comparatives and superlatives

1b 2b 3a 4c 5b 6c 7b 8b 9a

32 Four topics

Text 1: The weather

1 ~~makes~~/is 2 ~~air~~/wind 3 ~~climate~~/
weather 4 ~~cold~~/get cold/feel cold
5 ✓ 6 ~~darkens~~/gets or turns/grows
dark

Text 2: The news

1 ✓ 2 ~~actualities~~/news 3 ✓
4 ~~examined~~/interviewed 5 ✓
6 ~~journals~~/(news)papers 7 ~~are~~/is
8 ~~histories~~/stories 9 ✓
10 ~~informations~~/information 11 ✓

Text 3: Luck and misfortune

1 ~~incident~~/accident 2 ✓
3 ~~pricked~~/stung 4 ~~It dropped the
tray~~/The tray fell/I dropped the tray
5 ~~by luck~~/luckily 6 ~~fell~~/bumped 7✓

Text 4: Keeping clean

1 ~~awake~~/wake 2 ~~bathe~~/bath 3 ✓
4 ~~douse~~/shower 5 ✓ 6 ~~myself~~/ -
7 ~~do a shampooing~~/wash my hair
8 ✓ 9 ~~up~~/ - 10 ~~clear~~/clean
11 ~~the life~~/life

33 Questions and exclamations

1a 2a 3c 4c 5b 6b 7c 8a 9a
10a 11a 12b 13a 14b 15b

34 Quantities and amounts

Part A

1b 2a 3b 4a 5b 6b 7a 8b 9a
10b 11b 12b 13a 14b 15b 16a
17a 18b 19b 20b

Part B

1a 2b 3b 4b 5b 6a 7a 8a 9a
10b 11b 12b 13b 14b 15b 16a
17a 18a 19a 20b

35 Travelling by train

1a 2c 3b 4b 5b 6a 7a 8c 9a
10b 11a 12a 13c 14c 15a 16c
17a 18a 19a 20a 21c

36 Outside

1a 2a 3c 4b 5a 6c 7b 8c 9a
10a 11b 12a 13a 14c 15a

37 'Do', 'make' and 'have'

Part A

1 done/had 2 done 3 have
4 having 5 make 6 make 7 made
8 had 9 had 10 had 11 make

12 make 13 made 14 made 15 do
16 do 17 Do 18 have 19 have
20 had

Part B

1 make 2 had/have 3 do 4 do
5 made 6 do 7 make 8 makes
9 make 10 have 11 made 12 have
13 had 14 having 15 have
16 make 17 have 18 Have
19 done 20 done

38 Dressing and clothes

1a 2b 3a 4d 5c 6b 7b 8c 9a
10b 11c 12c 13a 14a (b AmE)
15b

39 Food and drink

1a 2b 3c 4b 5b 6a 7c 8b 9b
10a 11b 12a 13b 14b 15b 16b
17a 18b 19b 20b 21b 22b 23b
24a 25c 26a

40 Countable and uncountable nouns

1b 2a 3b 4a 5b 6c 7b 8c 9a
10a 11b 12b 13b 14b 15b

41 Education

Part A

1b 2a 3b 4a 5b 6a 7a 8a 9a
10a 11a 12a 13a 14a 15a 16b
17b 18a 19b 20b

Part B

1b 2a 3a 4a 5a 6b 7a 8b 9b
10b 11a 12a 13b 14a 15b 16a
17b 18b 19a 20a

42 Greetings, conventional social utterances and exchanges

Possible answers

1 Have a good time! 2 Excuse me.
3 Yes, if you will/would. 4 It doesn't
matter. 5 Just a moment. 6 Have a
good trip! 7 Don't worry! 8 What's
your name? 9 Are you being served?
10 Good morning, Mrs Smith. 11
Can I help you, madam? 12 Can I
help you, sir? 13 Mind your own
business! 14 Sorry?/Pardon? 15
Thank you very much indeed.

43 Comparing and contrasting

1b 2c 3c 4d 5a 6b 7a 8c 9a
10b 11b 12b 13a 14d 15c

44 Socializing, entertainment, etc.

1n 2t 3j 4c 5x 6i 7h 8p 9k
10a 11g 12y 13l 14v 15b 16d
17r 18w 19s 20q 21z 22o 23f
24e 25u 26m

45 What goes with what?

1 spare 2 arrange 3 spend, save
4 party 5 round 6 solve
7 according to 8 play 9 pick
10 stretch 11 enlarge 12 collect

46 Phrasal verbs

1j 2h 3l 4e 5g 6i 7c 8m 9n
10u 11o 12p 13v 14w 15y
16s 17k 18a 19t 20f 21d 22x
23z 24q 25r 26b

47 Adjective + preposition

1 to 2 of 3 in 4 with 5 to 6 in
7 in 8 to 9 of 10 on 11 of/about
12 of

48 Verb + 'to' or verb + '-ing'?

1 agree + to: agreed to take; 2 allow
+ to: allow anyone to leave; 3 ask +
to: asked to contribute; 4 dare + to:
dare to criticize; 5 delay + -ing:
delayed fixing; 6 deny + -ing: deny
being/having been; 7 direct + to:
directed not to carry; 8 dislike + -ing:
dislike wearing; 9 enjoy + -ing:
enjoys waiting; 10 face + -ing: can't
face going; 11 fail + to: can't fail to
notice; 12 fancy + -ing: fancy being;
13 forbid + to: can forbid you to use;
14 imagine + -ing: imagine living;
15 keep + -ing: keep leaving; 16 learn
+ to: learn to do; 17 manage + to:
managed to get; 18 mind + -ing: don't
mind working; 19 miss + -ing: miss
seeing; 20 order + to: ordered to stay;
21 prevent + -ing: prevent a disabled
driver parking; 22 promise + to:
promised not to discuss; 23 resist +
-ing: resist accepting; 24 risk + -ing:
risk losing; 25 suggest + -ing: suggest
taking; 26 want + to: wants to work;
27 warn + to: warned to expect; 28
wish + to: wish to visit

49 Approval and disapproval

1 fantastic 2 blame
3 Congratulations! 4 applaud
5 disagreeable 6 keen 7 satisfying
8 ignorant 9 oppose 10 brutal
11 esteemed 12 impressive
13 detest 14 worship 15 convenient
16 priceless 17 complain
18 annoying 19 so-and-so
20 attractive 21 wrong 22 common

50 Red tape

1b 2a 3a 4b 5a 6b 7b 8a 9a

51 Character and reputation

1b 2b 3b 4b 5b 6c 7a 8c 9a
10a 11c 12a 13a 14c 15b

52 Everybody, Somebody, Anybody, Nobody

Possible answers

1 Each of the (four) people. 2 One of them: it's not important which. 3 'Any person', in general. 4 None of the (four) people. 5 One of the (four) people (not named). 6 (a job) belonging to/to be done by all of them. 7 Each of the (four) people. 8 Any of the (four) people, or anyone in general. 9 None of the (four) people. 10 All the (four) people. 11 Each of them. 12 One of the others. 13 None of them. 14 Any of them/anyone in general.

53 Regular and irregular verbs which are easily confused

1 sown 2 raised 3 ringed 4 sprang 5 lying 6 lying 7 laying 8 laid 9 lied 10 lain 11 wound 12 wounded 13 sunken 14 risen 15 woken up 16 founded 17 flowed 18 felled 19 hanged 20 hung

54 Animals, birds and plants

A1/B28 A2/B23 A3/B5 A4/B6 A5/B14 A6/B1 A7/B22 A8/B8 A9/B13 A10/B12 A11/B11 A12/B30 A13/B26 A14/B20 A15/B17 A16/B19 A17/B2 A18/B10 A19/B7 A20/B15 A21/B4 A22/B3 A23/B29 A24/B9 A25/B18 A26/B16 A27/B21 A28/B24 A29/B27 A30/B25

55 Shopping

1b 2c 3d 4b 5a 6b 7b 8a 9a
10c 11b 12c 13b 14c 15b

56 Counting and measuring

1a 2d 3a 4c 5a 6b 7a 8a 9a

57 Verbs with and without prepositions

1 divide ... into 2 comply with 3 divorce (no preposition) 4 reach (no preposition) 5 match (no preposition) 6 argue about 7 discuss (no preposition) 8 borrow ... from 9 begin by 10 approve of 11 approach (no preposition) 12 enter (no preposition) 13 object to 14 resemble (no preposition)

15 demand (no preposition) 16 differentiate between 17 rely on 18 succeed in 19 defend ... against 20 promise (no preposition) 21 face (no preposition) 22 regard ... as 23 enjoy (no preposition) 24 wait for

58 Household equipment, power, etc.

1a (b AmE) 2c 3a 4c 5c 6a 7a 8b 9b 10b 11a 12b 13b 14a 15c

59 Expressing feelings of approval

1a 2b 3a 4a 5b 6c 7a 8a 9a 10b 11a 12a 13a 14a 15c 16b 17a 18a 19a 20c 21b

60 Writing, literature, language

1b 2b 3b 4a 5c 6b 7c 8b 9c 10b 11a 12b 13b 14d 15d

61 Items of clothing, etc.

1 overalls 2 braces 3 trousers 4 bathrobe (robe: AmE) 5 necklace 6 collar 7 tie 8 socks 9 dinner jacket 10 vest 11 petticoat 12 costume 13 scarf 14 shawl

62 Nouns ending in 's'

1 acoustics 2 athletics 3 barracks 4 belongings 5 billiards 6 - 7 clothes 8 (congratulations) 9 - 10 - 11 - 12 earnings 13 economics 14 ethics 15 goods 16 gymnastics 17 linguistics 18 - 19 mathematics 20 measles 21 - 22 - 23 mumps 24 - 25 - 26 physics 27 politics 28 series 29 species 30 suds 31 - 32 - 33 -
Possible sentences
1 The *acoustics* in this hall *are* excellent. 2 *Athletics is* one of the most popular sports in schools. 3 *This barracks was* (or *These barracks were*) built in 1807. 4 All our *belongings were* lost when the ship sank. 5 *Billiards is* not played so often as snooker these days. 6 All my *clothes need* washing and mending. 7 Our average *earnings are* lower than the average in Germany. 8 *Economics is* my least favourite subject. 9 The *ethics* of tax avoidance *are* hard to explain. 10 *Goods* such as alcohol and tobacco *are* heavily taxed. 11 *Measles is* an illness that you can only have once. 12 *Is physics* a compulsory subject at your school?

13 *Suds* from the washing machine *were* all over the floor.

63 Food

Part A

1b 2a 3b 4b 5b 6b 7a 8a 9b 10b 11b 12b 13a 14b 15a 16b 17b 18b 19a 20b

Part B

1b 2a 3a 4a 5a 6b 7b 8a 9b 10a 11a 12a 13a 14b 15b 16b 17b 18a 19a 20a

64 Health

1 circulation 2 plaque 3 scald 4 plague 5 miscarriage 6 poorly 7 sterilize 8 disinfect 9 specialist 10 instrument 11 immobile 12 prescription 13 drug 14 surgery 15 operating theatre 16 prophylactic 17 shock 18 handicapped 19 long-sighted 20 intense 21 grave

65 Behaviour

1a 2a 3c 4a 5c 6b 7a 8c 9a

66 Two topics

1 War and peace

1 ~~burst~~/blow up 2 ✓ 3 ~~destroy~~/destruction 4 ~~guardians~~/guards 5 ✓ 6 ✓ 7 ~~drilled~~/trained 8 ✓ 9 ~~invalids~~/war-wounded 10 ~~defeat~~/conquer 11 ~~commanded~~/ordered 12 ~~marine~~/navy 13 ✓ 14 ✓ 15 ~~powers~~/forces 16 ✓ 17 ✓ 18 ~~cord~~/cordon 19 ~~defended~~/forbidden

2 Geography, natural phenomena

1 ✓ 2 ~~physical~~/natural 3 ~~Melted~~/Molten 4 ~~exterior~~/outer 5 ✓ 6 ✓ 7 ✓ 8 ~~district~~/area 9 ~~Canal~~/Channel 10 ~~canal~~/channel 11 ~~cost~~/coast 12 ~~sweet~~/fresh 13 ✓ 14 ✓ 15 ~~Urbane~~/Urban 16 ✓ 17 ~~phenomena~~/phenomenon 18 ✓ 19 ~~interior~~/inland 20 ~~weather~~/climate

67 Adjectives and -ly adverbs

Part A

1 brightly 2 bright/brightly 3 cheaply 4 cheap/cheaply 5 clean 6 clean/cleanly 7 clear 8 clearly 9 dear 10 dear/dearly 11 deeply 12 directly 13 direct/directly 14 fair/fairly 15 fairly 16 fine 17 finely 18 firmly 19 firm 20 first

67 Adjectives and -ly adverbs
Part B
1 First 2 flat 3 flatly 4 fully 5 full
6 low 7 lowly 8 prettily 9 pretty
10 right 11 right/rightly 12 rough/
roughly 13 roughly 14 roughly
15 sharply 16 sharp 17 shortly
18 short 19 strong 20 strongly

68 Communicating
1a 2c 3d 4a 5a 6b 7a 8c 9b
10b 11d 12b 13c 14d 15b

69 Reflexive pronouns after verbs
Part A
1 yourselves 2 - 3 - 4 myself
5 - 6 herself 7 yourselves 8 -
9 yourself 10 themselves
11 himself 12 - 13 - 14 - 15 -
16 yourself 17 - 18 herself
19 ourselves 20 -
Part B
1 yourself 2 - 3 - 4 - 5 - 6 -
7 myself 8 - 9 yourself 10 - 11 -
12 yourself 13 yourself 14 -
15 myself 16 - 17 - 18 yourself
19 - 20 myself

70 Food and drink
A1/B49 A2/B34 A3/B33 A4/B56
A5/B60 A6/B9 A7/B36 A8/B18
A9/B10 A10/B4 A11/B41
A12/B40 A13/B48 A14/B46 or 58
A15/B43 A16/B30 A17/B19
A18/B14 A19/B25 A20/B44
A21/B45 A22/B26 A23/B27
A24/B53

71 Two topics
1 Entertainment, leisure
1 classic/classical 2 ✓
3 intrigue/plot 4 pick-up/record-
player 5 ✓ 6 persons/characters
7 ✓ 8 farces/(practical) jokes or
tricks 9 footsteps/steps 10 ✓
11 ✓ 12 plaques/records
13 doubled/dubbed 14 ✓
15 directing/conducting 16 ✓
17 spectators/audience 18 ✓ 19 ✓
2 Games, sports, outdoor activities
1 are/is 2 defy/challenge 3 ✓
4 zero/love 5 Stage/Stadium 6 ✓
7 ✓ 8 won/beat
9 conquered/beaten
10 basin/(swimming) pool
11 flipper/pinball 12 ✓
13 concurrence/competition or race
14 do/make 15 ✓ 16 a/- 17 ✓
18 Chasing/Hunting
19 equipments/equipment 20 ✓

72 What comes after the verb?
1b 2b 3a 4b 5a 6b 7b 8c 9b
10d 11b 12c 13b 14b 15c

73 Newspapers, broadcasting, publishing
1c 2a 3a 4c 5a 6c 7a 8b 9c

74 'Do', 'make', 'have' and 'take'
Part A
1 do 2 Take 3 take 4 make
5 makes 6 make 7 do 8 do
9 have 10 have 11 had 12 take
13 take 14 have 15 had 16 do
17 do 18 done 19 have 20 have
Part B
1 does 2 have 3 have 4 taking
5 take 6 having 7 have 8 having
9 made 10 make 11 make
12 made 13 took or did 14 take
15 took 16 make 17 take or have
18 Take or Have 19 had 20 has

75 Education
Part A
1a 2b 3b 4a 5a 6a 7b 8a 9b
10b 11b 12a 13b 14b 15b 16a
17a 18b 19b 20a
Part B
1a 2b 3b 4b 5a 6b 7a 8a 9b
10b 11b 12a 13b 14a 15b 16a
17b 18b 19b 20a

76 Buildings, parts of buildings, surroundings
A1/B40 A2/B5 A3/B46 A4/B37
A5/B11 A6/B10 A7/B30 A8/B14
A9/B28 A10/B45 A11/B13
A12/B3 A13/B25 or 35 A14/B1
A15/B47 A16/B21 A17/B23
A18/B8 A19/B16 A20/B20
A21/B32 A22/B27

77 Countable and uncountable nouns
Ticks for:
1 business 2 capital 3 cloth 4 crime
5 experience 6 fuel 7 gossip 8 noise
9 rock 10 time 11 trouble 12 youth
Possible answers
1 I've got two *businesses,* one in
Rome and the other in Turin. 2 He
knows the names of all the state
capitals in the US. 3 Where do you
keep your *cloths* for cleaning?
4 *Crimes* like robbery have been
increasing. 5 We had a few hair-
raising *experiences* on the motorway.
6 Fossil *fuels* like coal harm the
ozone layer. 7 You shouldn't believe

what a couple of old *gossips* tell you.
8 What's making those strange *noises*
in the garden? 9 His boat was
wrecked on the *rocks* near Jersey.
10 I've tried to ring the passport office
eight *times.* 11 Are our *troubles* ever
going to end? 12 Five *youths* were
lounging around outside the pub.

78 Fear, worry, embarrassment, etc.
1b 2b 3b 4d 5b 6c 7b 8b 9d
10a 11a 12c 13c 14c 15b

79 Crime and punishment
Part A
1 Robbing 2 trial 3 corpse/(dead)
body 4 fake 5 questioned/
interrogated 6 strict/severe/heavy
7 give 8 notorious/infamous
9 just/fair 10 prove 11 recognize/
identify 12 aroused 13 denies
14 searched for/sought 15 evidence
16 trace 17 observing 18 escaped
19 verdict 20 hanged
Part B
1 stealing 2 wrong 3 suspicious-
looking 4 make 5 wound
6 sentence 7 defence 8 caught
9 strangled 10 hunt 11 condemned/
sentenced 12 damages 13 persons/
people 14 forge/fake 15 deceive
16 trial 17 made 18 innocent
19 raised

80 Clothes, materials, etc.
Part A
1a 2b 3a (b AmE) 4a 5a 6b 7a
8a 9b 10a 11a 12a 13a 14a
15a 16b 17b 18b 19b 20a
Part B
1a 2b 3a 4b 5b 6a 7a 8b 9b
10b 11b 12a 13b 14b 15b 16a
17a 18a (b AmE) 19a 20b

81 Are you a hypochondriac?
1a 2a 3b 4b 5b 6b 7b 8b 9b
10b 11a 12a 13a 14b 15b 16b
17b 18b 19a 20b 21a 22a

82 Housework, gardening, maintenance
1 greasy 2 hygienic 3 produce
4 tool 5 condensation 6 repair
7 damp 8 rendering 9 fumigate
10 fix 11 decor 12 pond
13 moisture 14 pick 15 sweep
16 mess 17 tradesman 18 suds
19 creak 20 arrange 21 lacquer
22 scrape

83 Degree and intensifying

1 specially 2 true 3 mostly
4 greatly 5 largely 6 extra 7 fully
8 real 9 far 10 so 11 such a
12 not much 13 honestly 14 at all
15 most 16 indeed 17 widely
18 very much 19 strongly
20 deeply 21 highly

84 -ic/-ical

1 classic 2 Tragic 3 artistic
4 electrical 5 historic 6 Classical
7 magic 8 historical 9 electric
10 art 11 magical 12 dramatic
13 electronic

85 Inversion after negative adverbs

1 On no account *can we offer ...*
2 Hardly *had we left ...* 3 Little *does
John realize ...* 4 Never *have there
been ...* 5 Not only *did we miss ...*
6 No sooner *had I complained ...*
7 Seldom *do you see ...* 8 Only when
you become a parent *will you
understand ...* 9 On no condition *must
they be allowed ...* 10 ... and neither
do I care 11 Only then *did we
realize ...* 12 Rarely *do you see ...*
13 In no circumstances *should you
reply ...*

86 Adjective + preposition

1 on 2 in 3 of 4 of 5 to 6 with
7 to 8 of 9 at/by 10 to 11 of
12 of 13 to 14 of

87 Words easily confused, misspelt, etc.
Part A
1b 2b 3a 4a 5a 6b 7b 8a 9a
10b 11b 12b 13b 14a 15a 16a
17b 18a 19a 20a
Part B
1a 2b 3a 4a 5a 6b 7b 8a 9a
10b 11b 12a 13b 14a 15b 16a
17a 18b 19b 20b

88 Experiences, perception, thought
1a 2c 3c 4b 5c 6b 7b 8a 9b
10a 11a 12c 13a 14c 15b

89 What sort of person are you?
Ticks for:
1a 2a 3b 4b 5a 6b 7b 8a 9b
10a 11b 12a 13a 14b

90 Politics and government
Part A
1 a campaign 2 life and institutions
3 conspiracy 4 leader 5 unite

6 Conservative 7 check
8 Discussions 9 counsel 10 lead
11 elected 12 figures 13 Party
14 people 15 power 16 power/
strength 17 force 18 Anthem
19 powers 20 tax(es)
Part B
1 industrial 2 intrigue 3 liberated
4 majority 5 demonstration
6 conference 7 poverty 8 nation
9 nominated 10 side 11 country
12 people ... people 13 persuasion
14 Politics 15 govern
16 democratic 17 society
18 counties 19 Unions

91 Stative and dynamic uses of certain verbs
Ticks for:
1 admire 2 appear 3 consider
4 correspond with 5 cost 6 feel
7 hope 8 imagine 9 measure
10 say 11 think 12 weigh
Possible answers
1 I *am* just *admiring* your paintings.
2 Which group *is appearing* at the
Odeon this week? 3 We're
considering selling our car. 4 I'm
corresponding with a pen-friend in
Thailand. 5 This holiday *is costing*
us a fortune. 6 I'm *feeling* the
temperature of the water. 7 We're
hoping to have a holiday in the
autumn. 8 *Am* I *imagining* it, or did I
hear the doorbell? 9 Keep still while
I'm *measuring* your waist! 10 The
band's so loud I can't hear what you're
saying. 11 Don't interrupt the
professor while he's *thinking*. 12
Our baby always screams when
they're *weighing* her.

92 Travelling
1 pilot 2 funnel 3 board 4 buffet
5 emigrate 6 safety/seat 7 agency
8 coach 9 abroad 10 sleeper/
sleeping car 11 pedestrian
12 punctual 13 sick 14 valid
15 embark 16 miss 17 check
18 voyage 19 cabin 20 frontier
21 immigrate 22 Channel

93 Prepositional phrases
Part A
1 in 2 on 3 in 4 at 5 On 6 by
7 on 8 in 9 in 10 by 11 at
12 during 13 at 14 at 15 in 16 in
17 in 18 on 19 on 20 on

Part B
1 to 2 in 3 at 4 in 5 by 6 to
7 in 8 in 9 on 10 in 11 for 12 in
13 on 14 in 15 on 16 in 17 in
18 on 19 on 20 on

94 Cars, driving, maintenance, traffic
Part A
1b 2a 3b 4b 5b 6b 7a 8a 9a
10b 11b 12a 13b 14b 15b 16b
17a 18b 19b 20a
Part B
1b 2a 3b 4b 5b 6a 7b 8a 9b
10b 11b 12b 13a 14b 15a 16b
17b 18a 19b 20a

95 Referring to facts, the truth
1c 2a 3b 4a 5a 6a 7c 8a 9a

96 A campaign against litter
1 ~~pick~~/pick up 2 ~~laying~~/lying
3 ~~fetch~~/take 4 ✓ 5 ~~collect it~~/pick it
up 6 ~~brush~~/sweep 7 ✓ 8 ✓
9 ~~act~~/deed 10 ~~clear~~/clean 11 ✓
12 ~~be~~/being 13 ~~rubbishes~~/rubbish
14 ~~out of~~/outside 15 ✓ 16 *supply* is
just possible, but *provide* is
preferable 17 ~~neglect~~/ignore 18 ✓
19 ✓ 20 ~~disposition~~/disposal
21 ~~make~~/set 22 ✓ 23 ~~to drop~~/drop
24 ~~directly~~/immediately 25 ✓
26 ✓ 27 ~~shy~~/ashamed
28 ~~redden~~/go/turn red 29 ~~accept~~/
agree 30 ~~search~~/look for/search for
31 ✓ 32 ✓ 33 ~~Throw it~~/Throw it
away/Drop it 34 ✓ 35 ✓
36 ~~angered~~/got angry 37 ✓
38 ~~give~~/set 39 ~~place~~/part
40 ~~genteel~~/polite 41 ~~not~~/no
42 ~~counsel's~~/ council's

Technical terms

abstract noun: a noun that refers to a quality or a concept, e.g. *security*.

active: the form of the verb where the subject is a person or thing doing the action: *John **made** some coffee.*

adjective: a word that describes a person, thing or event: *a **tall** man, a **big** room.*

adverb: a word or phrase that tells us how, when, where, etc., something happens: *He walked **slowly** towards me.*

adverb of degree: words like *altogether* and *enough* that answer the question *To what extent?*: *The film was **quite** good.*

adverb of duration: a word or phrase that refers to a period of time: ***since July**.*

adverb of frequency: a word or phrase like *always*, *every day* that answers the question *How often?*

adverb of manner: words often ending in *-ly* like *carefully* that answer the question *How?*

affirmative: not negative: *John **lives** here.*

AmE: American English.

apostrophe: a mark (') used to show a contraction (*haven't*) or possession (*Tim's*).

article: the words *a/an*, which are indefinite: *a book, an envelope*; or *the*, which is definite: *It's on **the** shelf.*

BrE: British English.

causative: forms with *have* or *get* which show that we 'cause' someone else to do a service for us: *I had my car **serviced**.*

clause: a group of words, often part of a sentence, containing a subject and a verb: ***While she was at college**, she wrote a novel.*

collective noun: a noun that refers to a group: *a **flock** of sheep, an **audience**.*

colloquial: very informal language of everyday speech: *loo* for *lavatory*.

common noun: a noun that is not the name of a particular person, place or thing: *a book, clothing, courage.*

comparative: adjectives or adverbs formed with *-er*: *bigger, faster*.

compound noun: a noun with two parts: *drinking water, a car key.*

concrete noun: a noun that refers to people or things that have physical existence: *a girl, a desk, an army.*

conditional: a clause, often introduced by *if*: ***If you miss the bus**, take a taxi.*

conjunction: *conjunctions* are 'joining words' like *and, but, since, when*.

consonant: any letter (*b, c, d*) in the alphabet except the vowels *a, e, i, o, u*.

continuity verb: verbs like *lie, live, rain*, which naturally express continuity: *I **live/I'm living** in London.*

countable noun: a noun we use with *a/an* (*a book*) and which has a plural (*books*).

direct object: what comes immediately after a transitive verb: *He annoys **me**.*

double genitive: the use of *'s* in a phrase with *of*: *a friend **of my father's**.*

dynamic verb: a verb which can be used in progressive tenses: ***I'm reading**.*

-ed form: the form of a verb or adjective that ends in *-(e)d*: *annoyed, surprised*.

empty subject: usually, the pronoun *it*, which doesn't refer to something in particular: ***It's** hot today.*

figurative: referring to an abstract rather than literal meaning: *She **can't stomach** him.* (= has a strong feeling of dislike for)

formal style: speech or writing which is careful, correct and polite.

full stop: a mark (.) which is used to end a sentence or show an abbreviation: ***etc.***

gender: the way nouns or pronouns may be classified to show whether they are masculine, feminine or neuter: *he* is masculine; *she* is feminine.

gerund: a noun, formed from a verb, which ends in *-ing*: *I'm tired of **waiting**.*

gradable: usually applied to adjectives which can be used with *very/too* and can have *-er/-est* forms: *very big; bigger*.

idiom: a phrase which does not have a literal meaning: *He **hit the ceiling**.* (= became angry)

imperative: the form of a verb we use for commands, warnings, etc.: ***Stand up!***

indefinite pronoun: pronouns like *anyone, everyone, someone* which don't refer to anyone in particular.

indirect question: one that follows a reporting verb like *ask*: *He asked (me) **if I was ready**.*

indirect speech: the act of reporting what someone else says: *The boss **told me/said he was busy**.*

infinitive: the basic form of a verb which may be with or without *to*: *to go, go*.

informal style: speech or writing used among friends.

-ing form: any word ending in *-ing*, which may be part of a verb (*I'm **reading**.*), a noun or gerund (***Reading** is taught early.*) or an adjective (*He told me a **frightening** story.*).

intensifier: an adverb which stengthens (or 'intensifies') another word: ***very** slowly, I **entirely** agree.*

intransitive: this refers to a verb not followed by an object: *My head **aches**.*

inversion: changing round the normal word order: *Seldom **have** we received so many complaints.*

irregular: often applied to a plural noun (*children*) or verb (*go - went*) which doesn't follow the usual pattern.

jargon: referring to words and/or phrases used in special or technical ways.

main verb: the verb in the most important clause in a sentence. *You always ring when I'm out.*

modal verb: *modals* are verbs like *can* or *may* which we use for giving or receiving advice, permission, etc.

negative: the opposite of affirmative: anything that says or means 'no'.

negative adverb: adverbs like *never, seldom, rarely, hardly ever.*

negative imperative: the imperative with *Don't*: *Don't forget what I told you.*

negative question: a question beginning with a negative form like *Can't* or *Don't*: *Can't you wait a moment?*

noun: a word that tells us what someone or something is called (*a doctor, a book, fear, water*); also the name of a person (*John*) or a place (*London*).

noun modifier: the first of two nouns in a compound noun: *car key, kitchen table.*

noun phrase: a combination of words that includes a noun: *the man next door.*

object: usually a noun or pronoun that comes after a verb: *Ask a question.*

participle: the present *-ing* form of a verb (*waiting*) or the past *-ed* form (*seated*): *While waiting for a bus ...*; *Seated in the back of a taxi, ...*

passive: the form of the verb where the action is done to the subject: *Our house has been decorated.*

past participle: the third part of a verb: *act - acted -acted*; *be - was - been.*

person(s): grammatical persons: 1st: *I/we*; 2nd: *you*; 3rd: *he, she, it, they.*

plural: more than one; plural noun: *cats*; plural form of verb: *they have.*

point of time: exact time reference in the past: *yesterday, this morning*, etc.

possessive adjective: *my, your, his*, etc.

possessive case: possession shown by *'s/s'*: *a boy's jacket; a girls' school.*

possessive pronoun: *mine, yours, his*, etc.

prefix: *un-, in-, over-*, etc., added to an adjective: *uninterested, overdone.*

preposition: words like *across, at, in*, used in front of nouns, etc., to show relationships: *across the road.*

prepositional phrase: a phrase introduced by a preposition: *in doubt, on time.*

present perfect tense: *have been, have done, have eaten*, etc.

present tense: simple present (*I eat*); present progressive (*I'm eating*).

progressive: a tense which shows that an action is or was in progress: *He is eating. He was eating.*

pronoun: a word like *he* or *she* that can be used in place of a noun or noun phrase.

proper noun: the name of a person or place, spelt with a capital letter: *John, London.*

quantifier: a word or phrase like *any, some, (a) few* which describes how many things or how much of something.

question-word: *How?*, or a word beginning with *Wh-*: *When?, Why?*, etc.

reflexive pronoun: words like *myself, yourself, himself, herself.*

reflexive verb: a verb which can be followed by a reflexive pronoun: *enjoy yourself.*

regular: anything that follows the same pattern as most other words in the same class: regular plural: *boys.*

relative pronoun: words that refer to people (*who, whom, that*) or things (*which, that*).

reporting verb: a verb like *say* or *tell (me)* which introduces indirect speech.

sentence: a complete unit of meaning, which in writing begins with a capital letter and ends with a full stop.

short response: a short answer e.g. to a question: *Is he here? - Yes, he is.*

singular: the grammatical form that describes one person or thing: *a pen.*

slang: very informal language which is not used in serious speech or writing.

stative: a verb that is not normally used in the progressive: *It belongs to me.*

subject: usually a noun or pronoun that goes before a verb: *Joe works, I work.*

superlative: an adjective or adverb formed with *-est*: *the quickest*, or with *most*: *the most interesting.*

tag: a short question after a statement: *He's gone, hasn't he?* or a short 'Yes/No' answer: *Yes, he has.*

(that)-clause: a clause introduced by *(that)* used after a reporting verb: *He said (that) he would be home late.*

transitive: this refers to a verb that is always followed by an object: *I like it, I enjoyed the film.*

uncountable noun: a noun which we don't normally use after *a/an* and which doesn't normally have a plural: *sugar.*

verb: a word (*love*) or phrase (*look at*) which describes a state or an action.

verb of perception: a stative verb that refers to the senses: *see, hear*, etc.

vowel: *a, e, i, o, u.*

word order: this refers to the order of words in a normal English sentence: subject/verb/object/manner/place/time.

Index

Major items are listed in **bold**; incidental items are listed in *italics*. All page number references are followed by **a** or **b** (= **column a** or **column b** in the reference section).

User's Notes